JONATH[illegible]
CAINER[illegible]

GUIDE TO THE ZODIAC

Also by Jonathan Cainer

Cosmic Ordering: How to make your dreams come true

and

Complete Book of the Zodiac

JONATHAN CAINER'S GUIDE TO THE ZODIAC

PIATKUS

First published in Great Britain in 1997 by Piatkus Books
Reprinted 2000
Revised and updated edition published in 2006 by Piatkus Books
Reprinted in 2007
This paperback edition published in 2009 by Piatkus Books

A CIP catalogue record for this book
is available from the British Library

ISBN 978-0-7499-3978-6

Text design by Richard Mason
'Wheel design' originally by Dick Vine
Reproduced for this edition by Rodney Paull

Typeset by Phoenix Photosetting, Chatham, Kent
www.phoenixphotosetting.co.uk
Printed and bound in Great Britain by Clays Ltd, St Ives plc

Papers used by Piatkus are natural, renewable and recyclable products made from wood grown in sustainable forests and certified in accordance with the rules of the Forest Stewardship Council.

Piatkus Books
An imprint of
Little, Brown Book Group
100 Victoria Embankment
London EC4Y 0DY

An Hachette Livre UK Company
www.hachettelivre.co.uk

www.piatkus.co.uk

To M, with love

CONTENTS

INTRODUCTION

If life is a journey, where is the map? Why, when we come into this world, is there no instruction manual tied in a little polythene bag to our left foot and containing valuable tips and hints about how to get the most out of our time here? What stops some people from discovering their full potential? When will we ever truly discover what we are here for and what we are capable of?

There is a map. There is an instruction book. Every human being is officially issued with a detailed outline plan of their life at the very moment that they draw their first breath. It is called a horoscope; a chart of the planets as they stood in the sky at the exact moment when you were born. Every human being who has ever lived on the face of this earth has been blessed with their own version of this personal guide. But only a few have had it revealed to them. To see the invisible map you must either consult an astrologer – or learn the art of astrology yourself.

The information in this book is designed to help you to begin the magical process of lifting this veil. Gradually, as you read it, you will discover what really makes you tick and what wonders you could achieve if you really set your mind to the task. You will also uncover similar secrets about your friends and loved ones. As you compare their charts to yours you will even be able to see how closely their needs and aspirations truly match your own and thus establish how compatible with each other you truly are.

Just one word of warning. Exploring astrology, though deeply rewarding, is a bit like wandering through a jungle.

There are lions and tigers out there – in the shape of 'false assumptions' and 'dangerous but popular misconceptions'. There are also some creatures that look pretty scary but are actually so tame that they will eat out of your hand. The tables at the back of this book fall into that category. They look big, dense and deeply off-putting. But they are, I promise you, simplicity itself to use. You'll be just fine as long as you join the tour at the beginning and stick with me, step by step, chapter by chapter.

We're going to begin with your Sun sign – the zodiac sign you've always 'related to' and the one that you read about every time you open a magazine or newspaper. Next, we'll explore your Moon sign … and investigate the hidden side of your personality that this powerful cosmic symbol reveals. After which … well, I won't give you a blow-by-blow account of what's in store!

In the first chapter you can do a little bit of skipping: you don't have to read about every single sign unless you want to. Simply find your own zodiac sign and then join me again, on page 119, for an explanation about how to go a big stage further in Chapter 2, The Magic of Your Moon Sign.

Jonathan Cainer

Chapter 1

THE SECRETS OF YOUR SUN SIGN

THE SECRETS OF YOUR SUN SIGN

Before you go racing ahead to read what I've got to say about your Sun sign, let me ask you two questions:

- Do you know what a Sun sign actually is?
- Are you 100 per cent sure that you know what *your* Sun sign is?

We all read Sun sign predictions every day in the newspaper – they have become an integral part of our popular culture. It doesn't necessarily follow, though, that we all know what they are or what they mean. The dates, for example, that appear underneath the name of each sign are only approximate. They can vary, in a most baffling way, from one publication to another – as any poor soul whose birthday falls close to such a date will tell you. Or perhaps you've heard one of the following statements:

- 'Scorpios are sex mad.'
- 'Geminis will sell their own grandmother if they think there's a profit in it.'

- 'Leos can't let five minutes pass without looking in a mirror.'

I'm sorry to say that a lot of what passes for 'common astrological knowledge' is actually just myth, superstition, invention or embroidery.

As we work our way through this book, you'll gradually begin to see how these outrageous myths have come about. You'll also come across a full explanation of what a Sun sign is and how it differs from a Moon sign, a rising sign or, come to that, a 'Please-don't-walk-on-the-grass' sign. You'll discover that in many ways you are definitely *not* typical of your sign – and you'll begin to understand why.

Please feel free now to turn to your zodiac sign – unless you're not completely happy that you can give me a straight answer to my second question. In which case, read on.

HAVE YOU BEEN TOLD THAT YOU WERE BORN 'ON THE CUSP'?

The following does not apply to anyone born nicely in the middle of any zodiac sign, but it's an all-too-painful problem for anyone born near the end of one sign and the start of another. If you fall into this category, I'm delighted to inform you that you were not born 'on the cusp'. Nobody ever has been – or will be! The 'cusp', at least in this sense of the word, is an artificial invention, created to cover up the fact that the zodiac signs don't conveniently click over at midnight on a particular date. Everyone belongs to one zodiac sign and one sign only; nobody is 'a little bit of both'. It's just that the actual start and end dates of each sign can vary by up to quite a few hours – backwards or forwards – from year to year.

The only way to find out for sure which sign you were born under is to look up your date of birth in a special table such as the one on page 352. I know you're keen to get started and probably don't much fancy taking a detour, but I promise you it's worth the effort and you won't find the process difficult. So please turn now to page 352 – and I'll wait here till you get back.

OK. Now you know your Sun sign for certain. If your little trip to page 352 just confirmed what you already thought you knew, there's no problem. But what if it has thrown you into the midst of a major identity crisis? You always thought you were an X and it now turns out that you are a Y. Please don't panic. First, read what I've got to say about your new sign. You may find that a lot suddenly begins to make a great deal of sense to you. Still not satisfied? Well, there could be another reason why you've always identified closely with your 'old sign', even though it now turns out that you don't technically belong to it. It may yet turn out to be your Moon sign – or your Venus sign. Just keep reading the book!

ARIES

21 MARCH – 20 APRIL

NO ARIES-BORN PERSON WILL EVER LET A PROBLEM GET THE BETTER OF THEM FOR LONG. NO MATTER HOW DAUNTING THE TASK, AN ARIES WILL RISE TO IT WITH ENTHUSIASM, COURAGE AND COMMITMENT. THE ARIES HEART IS AS WARM AS A SUMMER'S DAY. THE ARIES MIND IS AS BRIGHT AS A BEACON. AN ARIES WILL NEVER LET A FRIEND SUFFER OR AN INJUSTICE GO UNAVENGED.

Arians don't beat about the bush. Whether or not you like what they have to say, at least they always say it clearly. Energetic, impulsive Arians reach conclusions swiftly; they are quick-witted and grasp many facts in a short time.

If you want to know what it's like to be an Arian, imagine owning a Ferrari sports car. Your vehicle is a waste of power and potential if it's not being pushed to the limit. The temptation is to speed dangerously and brake sharply, even on city streets. That's why Arians are often considered impatient. It's also why they are accused of using sledgehammers to crack nuts. But when there's a long distance to travel in a hurry, that Ferrari comes into its own. And when there's an important task to tackle, Arians are unbeatable! Put Arians under pressure and they'll show inspiring efficiency. If you need to move a mountain, ask an Arian.

Arians love to be kept busy and like their friends to understand this. An Arian is a powerhouse of restless energy which must be channelled constructively if it isn't to become self-destructive. If you are planning a party for your Arian, make sure it's based on an event. And if you're expecting an Arian to meet you at a certain time, give an urgent reason why they must be there. Or, better still, a dare! If you give an Arian a chance to take the initiative, you'll never regret it.

HOME

An Arian's home can be cosy but never quiet. Even in the depths of domesticity an Aries person needs to scale the heights of challenge and stimulation.

Outside your own four walls, you may just be able to take orders or compromise. Inside them, however, you loathe having to play second fiddle. You need space in which to let off steam, and a place where you can be in command. What's important is not where your home is or what it looks like, but who you share it with and how much respect they give you. If that's to your satisfaction, a portacabin in Penge will bring you as much pleasure as any palace in Persia.

Your ideal house number is 10… as in Downing Street!

CLOTHES

ARIANS DRESS AS THEY ACT – QUICKLY! USUALLY, THEY WEAR WHATEVER IS NEAREST TO THEM IN THE MORNING. WHEN THEY DRESS UP, THEY PICK CLOTHES WHICH HAVE INSTANT IMPACT.

Though you have enough confidence and elegance to shine in almost anything you wear, you don't much care for fancy, ornate items of jewellery or clothing. When you pick things that are plain, simple, strident and strong, they look absolutely great on you. Many people, for example, look uncomfortable in a big hat … or unconvincing when dressed in the colour red. You don't. You can take red as bright as it comes – and hats as big as they make 'em. Should the effect be too overwhelming you can always tone yourself down or add a touch of softness just by wearing a small floral scarf, hat or belt.

CARS

As a lively, energetic, go-ahead Arian, you naturally want to live life in the fast lane. This is fine if you happen to live near Le Mans but a little frustrating if your normal circuit is the local ring road. Your driving technique is further influenced by a tendency to treat the accelerator as if it were a wasp. All you want to do is stamp on it and grind it into the floor. For some reason, this makes your passengers nervous – or it would, if it weren't for the fact that you rarely carry any. They all seem to prefer the bus. In theory, you're the ideal Porsche or Lamborghini driver. In practice, you don't need such extravagant engines. You're the only person on the planet capable of hitting warp factor 5 in a milk float!

FOOD

IF AN ARMY MARCHES ON ITS STOMACH, SO MUST AN ARIAN. ARMIES AND ARIES ARE BOTH RULED BY MARS, THE POWER PLANET. WHEN YOU'RE HUNGRY, YOU JUST CAN'T OPERATE EFFICIENTLY!

Mars, which rules your sign, has an affinity with all things hot and spicy. In theory you're a curry-lover, able to take vindaloo as hot as it comes and always happy to experiment with Mexican, Thai or Indonesian restaurants. If you don't have an asbestos tongue, you probably show your most typically Arian food traits at breakfast time. You prefer instant to filter coffee, soft boiled eggs to hard, and packet orange juice to frozen or fresh. Why? Because you can't be bothered to wait those extra few minutes. Unless someone else is doing the cooking, it's a case of the quicker it is to prepare, the better!

MONEY

'BANKING ESTABLISHMENTS ARE MORE DANGEROUS THAN STANDING ARMIES.'

'MONEY CAN'T BUY YOU FRIENDS BUT YOU CAN GET A BETTER CLASS OF ENEMY.'

Although these remarks were made two hundred years apart, it's not easy to tell that the former comes from US founding father Thomas Jefferson, the latter from humorist and ecology campaigner Spike Milligan. Both are pithy, incisive and somewhat cynical. Both reveal a great deal about the Aries attitude to wealth. You are under no illusions about matters material. The idea of being wealthy may attract one part of your personality, but it sets alarm bells ringing elsewhere in your psyche. You *can* make progress – but only if you really set your mind to it. You have to create your own openings through working hard and, just as importantly, by putting in *consistent* effort. This isn't always as easy as you might imagine, because you find yourself continually tempted to change horses in midstream or make a series of wild, spontaneous decisions to enter new territory. You often conclude that you'd rather sacrifice security and wealth for the sake of adventure, creative challenge and/or job satisfaction. Such choices will leave you poorer in economic terms but richer in spirit. How far you feel able to take them depends on how strong your need is for a more regular, conventional source of income.

JUST THE JOB?

Adventurer, brain surgeon, campaign manager, chimneysweep, dermatologist, diamond cutter, fireman/woman, hairdresser, impresario, ironworker, knife sharpener, optician, physiotherapist, political climber, racing driver, satellite dish installer, self-publicist, shepherd, sportsperson, surgeon.

Five ways to cash in

- Put £1 in a jar whenever you lose your temper.
- Look in more than one shop for your purchases.
- Persuade yourself that Richard Branson has upset you and you must teach him a lesson by earning more than him.
- Find a fast food store and open up next door offering even faster food.

- Form a partnership with a Virgo (this will drive you insane as well as make you rich, but then who says life is fair?).

Four ways to branch out

- Get a job as a test driver of sports cars for Ferrari.
- Sail round the world single handed.
- Get sponsored in a fast and furious sport by a stopwatch company.
- Run the marathon.

LOVE

Arians may get misty-eyed over love, but they're normally very down-to-earth about sex. They are demonstrative and passionate. Arians, despite their forceful nature, are incurable romantics at heart. They can be amazingly soft, tender or soppy.

Because your sign traditionally symbolises 'new beginnings', in your relationships you tend to be forever seeking the excitement of a fresh start. You love that magical feeling which comes into your heart when you are first getting to know someone special – and if you're not careful, you'll allow this addiction to spoil your chances of attaining long-term security. Permanence in your love life can only be attained by learning to develop a mature outlook. You have to overcome your inner restlessness, your tendency to imagine that the grass grows greener on the other side of the fence, and your personal boredom threshold. One sure way to do this is deliberately to keep an edge of tension in your closest relationships. Up to a point at least, you actually like not knowing where you stand with your partner. If nothing else, it keeps you on your toes. Consequently, even if your spouse is naturally loyal and steadfast, you subconsciously seek ways to push them to the limits of their patience. You stir up trouble and then act surprised when the sparks fly.

For this reason, you are probably best suited to someone with an equally strong need for a sparring partner. As long as your loved one equally enjoys the occasional battle, power struggle or confrontation, you can rest comparatively comfortably in a tense arrangement that would have most people desperate for a way out. But if your beloved is not of this disposition, you have to find a way to become more placid and predictable without fearing that your love life has grown stagnant. Almost certainly the best way involves building or creating some kind of shared challenge. United against a common enemy, you and your loved one can have all the joy of a relationship which contains the necessary tension without the unnecessary heartache.

A SIDEWAYS LOOK AT YOUR SIGN

- 'Aries people are impulsive, rash, hot-headed, excitable, overbearing bullies who never forget who their enemies are, who hate to compromise and who refuse to take orders.'
- 'Arians are wise, efficient, quick-witted, dynamic, affable people who can get along with anyone. These open-hearted, gregarious, spontaneous people rarely feel the need to hold a grudge.'

The two statements nicely sum up the glaring difference between the 'popular myth' about your zodiac sign and the stark truth. So … which is which?

I'm sure you already know the answer to that question – but to help me illustrate the point, let me tell you about two rather typical Arians I know. Their names are Robbie and Jane, they have different lives and personalities, but I think you'll soon see what they have in common with each other – and with you.

Robbie is a builder, in his thirties. He actually has a degree in philosophy – but says that having stretched his mind in his youth, he now feels it important to stretch his body. He is good-humoured, with bright brown eyes above a smiling, generous mouth. His favourite phrase is 'No problem!' The good looks are typically Arian: most people born under this sign have striking features. The talent for building is also quite typical. Not all Arians build, but they all prefer jobs which give them power over their environment. But that magic phrase clinches it. Arians simply hate to be negative.

Jane is a high-flyer in the world of publishing. She's larger than life, with an instantly attractive face that radiates compassion, determination and mischief. You wouldn't know to look at her that she's one of the most widely respected people in her field, but when you see her at work you realise why she has managed to work her way up from the very bottom to the absolute top. She is irrepressible and uses up more energy in a day than many people do in a week.

Jane and Robbie are two of the kindest people I know, and they'll bend over backwards to help anyone. Neither of them minces their words and both have a deep belief in making the world a better place by working hard and playing fair. Like all Arians, they are almost belligerently optimistic. They don't just look on the bright side, they walk around with portable sun lamps in their pockets. Whenever they come across doom or gloom they plug those lamps into the nearest socket and let the light shine down mercilessly until the darkness has scurried away. This usually makes them popular. Just occasionally, though, this zest for life puts backs up. Nobody likes to be made to look like a stick in the mud, so sometimes people get annoyed when an Arian comes bounding along with an instant answer to a question they have been fretting over for so long that they've begun to treat it like a pet. They forget they are being done a favour and start to think they are being robbed!

Arians, however, are not easily put off. They know they are right to trust their instincts and resent being told to forget them. They just roll up their sleeves, ignore the objections and dive straight in. Nine times out of ten, once they've started to prove their point the other person will follow (which is why Arians are natural leaders). On the tenth occasion, the other person will start jealously nitpicking. It's then that the Arian gets upset and says something impolite. 'Aha,' says the person whom the Arian is trying to help, 'aren't you an irritable so-and-so!'

And that's how the bad press comes about. So now you know the truth.

TAURUS

21 APRIL – 21 MAY

A TAUREAN'S GREATEST GIFT IS HIS OR HER EMPATHY WITH THE NATURAL WORLD. TAUREANS CANNOT HELP BUT APPRECIATE THE MAJESTY AND MAGNIFICENCE OF CREATION AND SO THEY STRIVE, IN ALL THEY DO, TO EMULATE THE BEAUTY AND STRENGTH THAT THEY SEE IN NATURE. TAUREANS ARE LOYAL, CONSISTENT AND BLESSED WITH A POWERFUL ABILITY TO INSPIRE OTHERS TO REACH NEW HEIGHTS.

Taureans are tenacious. They know what they want and don't stop till they get it. Tenacity without capacity is, of course, pointless – but fortunately Taureans are also diligent and discriminating. While your Taurean friend probably prefers efficiency to excitement, it doesn't mean that he or she is dull. Nothing but the best will do for Taureans. They have insatiable appetites – not just for food but for everything fine and refined. Elegant eccentricity is a Taurean trademark.

It's not easy to explain why Taureans are so acquisitive and earthy, yet so creative and ethereal. But it's easy for

Taureans to be this way. They don't see it as a problem, and nor should you. If there's a drawback to being a bull, it's moodiness. When Taureans aren't plodding slowly but surely towards a goal, they can be melancholic or morose. These patient people always need to feel they are getting somewhere.

Taureans gain a vital sense of identity and security from their possessions, so if you want to give your Taurean friend a real thrill give him or her something to complete or complement a collection. Taureans also collect 'experiences'. Your ideal gift could well be a thoughtfully arranged party or outing – or perhaps a rare chance to experience a very special luxury.

HOME

Even a Taurean with a humble abode will manage to furnish it and decorate it more grandly than a palace. They not only love luxury, they insist on it.

The key question, when you're choosing a home, is not so much 'Will it house my family?' as 'Will it house the paraphernalia I've been gathering over all these years?' You collect nick-nacks faster than any carpenter could ever hope to put up shelves. It's a shame because, if you could only pare down your possessions, you might fit nicely into a rustic cottage. It wouldn't need roses round the door (with your horticultural skill, you could soon grow these) but it would need to have a big garden and a capacious kitchen (see Food).

Your ideal house number is 50 (this always gets top marks in the bull's eye!).

CLOTHES

ALTHOUGH TAUREANS KNOW HOW TO DRESS IMMACULATELY, THEY DON'T NORMALLY LIKE TO BE TOO BRIGHT OR BOLD. THEY PREFER TASTEFULLY SMART BUT MUTED CLOTHES.

On special occasions some people wear silk, velvet and lace – materials which tend to make most of us look vulnerable and sensitive. When you wear them, however, you usually look affluent, creative and confident – especially when you pick them in deep, rich colours. Your ideal accessory ought to be a necklace, cravat or choker. Taurus rules the throat – and though you may not realise this, your neck has the potential to be one of your most strikingly impressive assets. You also often need to pick clothes that flatter your figure (see Food).

CARS

As a sensual, refined Taurean, you like a car with style and elegance. Ideally, you would drive a restored masterpiece from a bygone era: perhaps an early Jaguar or an Austin Cambridge. Only two drawbacks put you off this idea: mpg and the gpm (garage hours per month). In consequence, natural pragmatism steers you reluctantly towards the more reliable and economical if rather boringly similar range of modern euro-cars. With these, your choice is likely to be chiefly based on driver comfort – the softness of the seats, the visual line of the interior design and the amount of room in the driver's door for king-sized bags of sweeties (see Food). Big engines don't particularly entice you, for you drive as you live – sedately, gracefully and, just occasionally when heavy traffic demands it, creatively.

FOOD

GOURMET FOODS NATURALLY SUIT THE TAUREAN PALATE. YOU LIKE TO SAVOUR YOUR MEALS AND HAVE AN INSATIABLE APPETITE FOR THE FINEST CUISINE.

Taurus is traditionally the sign of the gourmet. Some might argue it is also the sign of the gannet but, in fairness, though you love to tickle your tastebuds, you can usually stop while your waistline still sees the funny side. Your favourite foods tend to be exotic. Given a chance, you'd live on a diet of asparagus, caviar, blueberries, mangoes and quails' eggs. Every night, you'd eat at a different upmarket restaurant – and you'd wash it all down with the kind of wine you need to take out a mortgage for. And for dessert? It has to be chocolate. For all your refinement, you have a terrible sweet tooth.

MONEY

THE SUCCESSFUL CONDUCT OF AN INDUSTRIAL ENTERPRISE REQUIRES TWO DISTINCT QUALIFICATIONS: FIDELITY AND ZEAL.

These wise words come from your fellow Taurean John Stuart Mill, one of the leading economists of the nineteenth century. I quote them partly to illustrate your sign's long history of shrewd financial thinking – and partly because the quote includes two key words which encapsulate the essence of a Taurean's innate ability to make money. Whether or not he realised it, when J.S. Mill chose those words 'fidelity' and 'zeal' he was naming the strongest qualities of your sign.

When you believe in something, you stick at it and continue to persevere long after more weak-willed individuals might have given up the ghost. Although this occasionally puts you at a temporary disadvantage (you are not always able or inclined to drop your commitments and pursue a sudden special offer), in the long term it is a sure-fire formula. You have the potential, as part of a strong, successful team, to generate a lot of wealth, to rise in status, to become more secure and to see difficult projects through to successful conclusions. Your capacity to fulfil this potential, however, tends to hinge almost entirely on your ability to sacrifice, temporarily at least, the desire for greater independence and freedom.

JUST THE JOB?

Actor, architect, antique dealer, artist, art collector, auctioneer, banker, baker, blacksmith, carpenter, carpet designer, cattle breeder, chef, confectioner, dancer, farmer, financier, gardener, jeweller, loan shark, musician, nurse, pianist, sculptor, singer, throat specialist, treasurer, vocal coach, yodeller.

Five ways to cash in

- Stop working to pay for your all-consuming hobby.
- Start making your all-consuming hobby pay its way.
- Stop undervaluing your natural talent.
- Start charging for the advice you dish out so readily – particularly to people who don't deserve it.
- Stop feeling so responsible for improving the lot of others.

Five ways to branch out

- Become a restaurant reviewer.
- Become a valuer for Christie's the auctioneers.
- Become the conductor of the London Philharmonic Orchestra.
- Become the conductor of the number nine bus (you like collecting money).
- Become famous for your natural sex appeal – it's your best asset.

LOVE

TAUREANS, IT MUST BE SAID, ARE RATHER POSSESSIVE. THEY CHERISH THE THINGS THEY OWN, BUT SOMETIMES THEY CAN MISTAKENLY THINK THEY OWN A CERTAIN PERSON.

The biggest single obstacle to ongoing harmony in your love life is, ironically, your innate and powerful desire for stability. Because you are so anxious to keep magic alive, you tend to resent anything that seems, even vaguely, to threaten the emotional status quo. For you, it's a case of better the devil you know than the one you don't and, often, better the reliable hatchback than the trouble-prone sports car.

Why should this pose a problem? Because the only thing we can all be sure of in this uncertain world is that every situation, every person and, yes, even every partnership will eventually change. As a Taurean, you are first and foremost a consolidator. Your instinct is to preserve and protect, to keep and collect. If your partner is of a more adventurous or experimental disposition, it's likely to render you perpetually nervous. And yet, if they are equally conservative in their outlook, you run the risk of winding up bored, listless and unfulfilled in a superficially sublime but secretly stagnant situation.

In order to rescue a relationship which has begun to slide down this slippery slope, you simply need to conquer your fear of the great unknown. All too often, we cause our greatest fears to come true simply by working so very hard to keep them at bay. If you can recognise this, you may be able to see the wisdom in becoming just a little less determined to hang on to all that you so earnestly want to remain the same. Let it go. Tell yourself you hardly even care whether your partner leaves you, rejects you or simply grows apart from you.

For anyone else, this might be a recipe for disaster. For you, however, it's a sure formula for success. Your natural caution will never let you take the policy too far. When the danger signals start flashing red, you'll see them. And then, if you respond, you'll be all the better equipped to take the right sort of remedial action because you haven't used up all your energy panicking as soon as they started to flicker on amber.

Taureans are terribly sensual. They throw themselves into all forms of physical experience and can't get enough of a good thing! Some people think they're greedy!

A SIDEWAYS LOOK AT YOUR SIGN

To understand the nature of your sign fully, you need to think of it as a place rather than a personality trait. So come with me to the island of Taurus. Hop into my plane, fasten your safety belt and prepare to visit a land of unrivalled beauty...

On arrival, you'll be invited to remove your shoes. It's a local custom in honour of Taureans, who like to feel the earth beneath their feet. Speaking of local customs, our first stop must be immigration control. The Taurean official will want to know whether you intend to fit in with the island routine, and whether you've brought with you something nice to eat – or look at!

Having cleared customs, we can now proceed to our hotel. Taurean hospitality is legendary. As you lie on the softest yet most supportive bed you've ever seen, look at the items provided for your comfort. Notice the gold taps in the bathroom: one for hot water, one for cold and one for 'just the temperature you like best'. That painting on the wall of your room is an original and yes, the carpet is indeed a hand-woven masterpiece. You've come to the home of all luxury, where, within the confines of a reasonable budget at least, no expense has been spared.

Don't get too settled, though – we're going first of all to the famous Taurean beaches, where the sand is white as snow, the sun hot and the sea as blue and creamy as a piece of willow-pattern china. You'll see some real fine china later on, when we get to the museum. If that surprises you, it's because you're thinking of Taurus the bull as a bull in a china shop. Clumsiness, however, is most definitely not a Taurean trait.

Next we'll go to the craft market – and here, if you wish, you can sample the local goods. You'll find everything from sculpture to scarves and from hand-woven baskets to home-made bread. Notice that the air is full of lilting music and that thousands of tantalising perfumes keep wafting into your nose. But I must issue a word of warning before I let you go shopping alone. Please don't hurry. Taureans hate it when people try to do things too quickly: it confuses them and makes them angry. And when you ask the price of any item, please don't haggle. Taureans always mean what they say – especially when talking about money! When you've finished admiring the treasures, we can proceed to the high spot of our trip – to see things so precious that they are not for sale at any price. These are the items in the Taurean museum. Taureans are the world's greatest collectors: some collect books, records, film memorabilia, stamps and paintings, while others collect things like ideas, recipes or techniques for healing.

Since we arrived, the sky has been calm, the climate warm and the wind light. Now a Taurean storm is brewing. It won't last long, but like the storms which occasionally flash over the temperaments of calm Taurean people, it will be ferocious and sudden. Let's get safely back to the hotel. I know from experience that a bitter wind will soon blow down hailstones the size of golfballs. It's the only drawback to life on the otherwise idyllic paradise of Taurus – just as those occasional dark moods are the only drawback to life with (or as) a Taurean.

After the storm, why not join me for dinner? Whatever your favourite food, you can be sure they know how to cook it to perfection. Taureans all love to eat well – and these are not the only sensual pleasures they like to indulge in!

GEMINI

22 MAY – 22 JUNE

EVERY GEMINI IS A DREAMER OF DREAMS AND A WEAVER OF VISIONS. GEMINIS ARE THE ZODIAC'S PERPETUAL CHILDREN – REFUSING, EVEN IN OLD AGE, TO BETRAY THEIR INNOCENT FAITH IN THE POSSIBILITY OF A HAPPIER WORLD FOR ALL. IT IS THIS DEEP INNER WELL OF SIMPLE, TRUSTING ENTHUSIASM WHICH MAKES EVERY GEMINI SUCH A POTENTIALLY POWERFUL PERSON.

Never, if you value your sanity, try to argue with a Gemini – at least not unless you can handle a conversation that sweeps wildly from one subject to another, speeding up, slowing down, twisting and turning like a sort of intellectual roller-coaster. Geminis love a good debate, caring more for the process of persuasion than for the final outcome. They love to ask questions and they're never afraid to probe people on subjects which others would diplomatically avoid.

Geminis suffer from intermittent dark moods when they don't want to talk to anyone about anything. These, happily, don't last long and they're soon ready to communicate again. You can say things to a Gemini which most other people would consider crazy – and find yourself being taken seriously. Likewise, you can expect to hear the oddest thoughts and ideas being earnestly expressed by your Gemini friend.

Geminis can be exasperating because they prefer thoughts to feelings. They try to rationalise things which can't be rationalised, like love, affection, sorrow or desire. This sometimes leads to brilliant, original insights, but it can just lead to trouble or misunderstanding.

If you want to ensure that a Gemini has a good birthday, forget the cake and the candles. Give them something or take them somewhere that inspires plenty of rambling, excited and fulfilling conversation!

HOME

A Gemini's home needn't be palatial but it must have plenty of interesting things to look at and fiddle with. Geminis can't stand sitting around being bored.

Your perfect home is probably a wigwam in Wisconsin. A lifestyle in the heart of the Native American community would suit you to a teepee – especially if the tribe were to acknowledge your interest in communication by putting you in charge of smoke signals! Failing that, a terraced house in an old-fashioned 'Coronation Street' environment would let you keep up to date with local news. Wherever you live and whatever sort of abode you have, your favourite room is the front hall. The heart of a home, for every Gemini, is the letterbox!

Your ideal house number might be 192 (or 411)

because you always like to feel that you have got everybody's number.

CLOTHES

NO MATTER HOW SMARTLY A GEMINI TRIES TO DRESS, THERE'S ALWAYS SOMETHING IN THEIR OUTFIT WHICH IS OUT OF PLACE OR OVER THE TOP. SUBTLETY IS NOT A GEMINI STRONG POINT!

Nobody knows quite like a Gemini how to dress to kill. Your wardrobe is not so much a treasure trove as an armoury. Each outfit is picked to make a statement and, as a changeable (dare we even say contrary) Gemini, there are many statements you want to make. Your favourite items are those which can adjust to your mood. You go wild when you find a shop that sells reversible jackets or dresses with detachable sleeves. You're also a believer in accessories. You have a special liking for large, chunky pieces of jewellery and a tendency to wear, as earrings, items which most people would be more inclined to display on their mantelpiece!

CARS

As you are an adaptable, versatile, spur-of-the-moment Gemini, your dream vehicle has to be something nippy. In moments of fantasy you fancy a luxury limo, but common sense soon puts paid to that. Where would you park it? How would you protect it? And, most crucially, how would you steer it into those enticing little gaps in the traffic that you're so fond of claiming? What you really want is the best of all worlds – an enviable status symbol with a slim body and endless energy. But never mind your ideal partner, we're supposed to be describing your ideal vehicle! This has to be a customised two-seater sports car, with an ejector seat for tiresome passengers and a device for shooting nails into the tyres of anyone who has the temerity to tailgate you!

FOOD

VARIETY IS THE SPICE OF LIFE FOR EVERY GEMINI, AND THIS IS ESPECIALLY TRUE WHEN IT COMES TO FOOD.

If you're a truly typical Gemini, for you food is rarely a big deal. You'll happily eat whatever happens to be lying around in the fridge, as long as it's quick to cook and easy to digest. What it actually tastes like hardly seems to matter. The only time your mouth really starts to water is when there's a tremendous variety of new and unusual food on offer. Your naturally irrepressible Gemini curiosity can't resist trying a tiny little bit of absolutely everything. Smorgasbords, for example, really get you going – and some Geminis have been known to travel miles for the chance to try a new delicacy.

MONEY

'IT IS ENTERPRISE WHICH BUILDS AND IMPROVES THE WORLD'S POSSESSIONS ... IF ENTERPRISE IS AFOOT, WEALTH ACCUMULATES WHATEVER MAY BE HAPPENING TO THRIFT; AND IF ENTERPRISE IS ASLEEP, WEALTH DECAYS, WHATEVER THRIFT MAY BE DOING.'

It will, I'm sure, come as no surprise to you to learn that the words above were written by a Gemini. You may be even more gratified to learn that they come from the famous economist John Maynard Keynes. If only you (or he) were in charge of the country's finances, our economic progress would always be a success story to inspire the world. But of course if you were in charge of the national debt you wouldn't have time to pursue all those other exciting financial possibilities that you're now so keen on. And this of course is part of your trouble. You want to have your cake and eat it too. You try to keep as many fingers in as many pies as you can. To extend the culinary analogy still further, you pile far more on to your plate than you can ever hope to digest. It's a sense of insecurity that prevents you putting all your eggs in one basket, and it's got to be overcome. It doesn't matter whether you pick the safe route or the more adventurous one. You'll enjoy a great deal of success and enough economic progress to keep the wolf from the door whatever you do, as long as you don't try to be all things to all people or spread your resources too thinly over too many plans and projects. Specialise, and you'll thrive.

JUST THE JOB?

Advertising agent, bicycle-maker, book-keeper, bookseller, broadcaster, broker, bus driver, canvasser, editor, engineer, journalist, lecturer, linguist, mechanic, messenger, nerve specialist, porter, post office worker, press baron, telephone salesman, traffic manager, typist, weather forecaster, writer.

Five ways to cash in

- Charge for any information you ever have to offer.
- Sell a product you really have faith in.

- Stop showing off your knowledge in front of your bosses. It makes them insecure and is costing you a pay rise.
- Let someone else get the better of you deliberately so that you can lull them into a false sense of security.
- Spend less time on the phone!

Five ways to branch out

- Become a sex symbol. (What do you mean, 'What do I mean, *become?*')
- Launch a website to rival ebay.
- Become a technology guru.
- Write speeches for politicians.
- Become a champion of consumer rights.

LOVE

Romance, in the classic sense, does not appeal to most Geminis. They simply want someone to talk to and, more importantly, someone who'll listen to them! There's a very low boredom threshold in every Gemini. That's why they tend to chop and change so much – they hate the thought of being stuck in a rut.

There are some who believe that it is not possible for Geminis to go through the whole of their life with just one romantic partner. They argue that people born under your sign can no more manage monogamy than a disc jockey can cope with silence. The theory is that you simply have to have variety, excitement, distraction, entertainment… and a certain amount of danger in your world.

Up to a point it's true. You certainly can't stick with the

wrong partner. Unlike some who, having made an error or miscalculation, might be inclined to learn to live with it and suffer the consequences stoically for years, you value your freedom and your happiness far too highly. But this doesn't mean that you are destined to limp from one unsatisfactory relationship to the next until you grow too old even to contemplate trying any more. It simply means that, instead of constantly changing partners, you need to think about picking one partner who will keep changing to meet the different requirements of a new day.

As a many-sided personality, you need, naturally enough, a multi-faceted companion. You need somebody who will at least accept and adapt to your moods – at best actually relish them. Almost certainly this will involve their being a little eccentric and exceptional – but as this ought to be a bonus, the only real difficulty here is that your ideal mate may well turn out to be every bit as volatile and mercurial as you are! It might be you who has to do the running to keep up while he or she forges ahead. But this is still far preferable to being stuck in a relationship where the same old arguments keep being trotted out day after day and the same old bones of contention keep being squabbled over.

So don't let anybody tell you that true love is not attainable or that permanency is impossible. It's merely a matter of thinking about what you're entering into before you enter into it next time… or of thinking now about how you might encourage your existing soulmate to explore ways in which he or she can 'grow together' with you.

A SIDEWAYS LOOK AT YOUR SIGN

Geminis are supposed to be terribly talkative, but this, of course, is not always true. There are silent Geminis just as there are shy Leos and pessimistic Pisceans. There aren't many, but they do exist. Even the quiet ones, however, have some noisy thoughts. There's no such thing as a Gemini without a strong opinion.

Normally that opinion is well informed, because all Geminis are insatiably inquisitive. They devour newspapers, magazines, TV programmes and books like hungry wolves. What's more they aren't fussy about what they learn because they feel it all comes in useful. Sometimes, though, the Gemini opinion can be very tenuous – and deliberately so, for Geminis can see real links between the most unlikely, unrelated things. That's what drives them to keep asking questions, and it's also what drives anyone who wants a straight answer to despair!

You see, Gemini is ruled by Mercury, who was in legend the messenger of the gods. If you've ever seen a motorbike messenger weave and dodge through rush-hour traffic, you'll understand why Geminis, firmly under the influence of Mercury, can be so hard to pin down.

The one thing of which every Gemini is convinced from birth is that no point of view is immune to compromise. In fact, it's probably the only thing a Gemini is ever convinced of, because Geminis can always see at least two sides to every story – and often more.

If that last sentence has caused you to raise an eyebrow, perhaps it's because I told you a little earlier that all Geminis have strong opinions. Well done! You've spotted the first of many contradictions in the Gemini mental make-up. You either love them or hate them for it – but if you want to get on well with a Gemini you have to understand that they change their minds more often than some people change their socks. They do have strong opinions – but they treat them as starting points, not finishing lines. After every sentence you hear a Gemini utter, no matter how emphatic it is, feel free to add the words 'unless, of course, you can persuade me of a better idea'. These words are not always spoken, but they are always implied.

Some people say this proves that Geminis are unprincipled, unreliable or just plain awkward. Geminis insist it proves that they are open-minded and able to adapt. At the risk of delivering a Gemini-style judgement, I must say that both points of view have a bit of truth in them. Geminis spring to life when there's a good dispute or debate going on. They hate to battle but they love to barter, and they'll often play devil's advocate just to see what can be learned from pushing a point too far. All this, of course, gives every Gemini a natural market-stall holder's mentality. Not all Geminis wheel and deal for a living, but every Gemini has an eye for a bargain, an endless obsession with the fast buck and a terrific talent for making people offers they can't refuse.

By now you're probably feeling a little hurt. I've painted a rather mercenary picture and have told you little about the wonderful, soulful, sensitive qualities of this sign. I won't apologise, because what you've just read is fair as far as it goes, but I will stress that Geminis are also kind, amenable, considerate and creative people. They are wise and yet adventurous, fun-loving and yet thoughtful. They're very definitely not stubborn, proud, pessimistic or cold-hearted.

CANCER

23 JUNE – 23 JULY

CANCERIANS ARE THE ZODIAC'S MOST SENSITIVE SOULS. THEY CANNOT HELP BUT EMPATHISE WITH, AND FEEL CONCERN FOR, THEIR FELLOW HUMANS. THEY ARE NEVER HAPPIER THAN WHEN MAKING SOMEONE ELSE HAPPY, NEVER SADDER THAN WHEN THEY FEAR THEY HAVE INADVERTENTLY CAUSED HURT. ANYONE WHO HAS A CANCERIAN FOR A FRIEND HAS LITTLE NEED OF ANYTHING ELSE IN LIFE.

Cancerians like to play it safe. They would be dull, unadventurous people were it not for one thing: powerful emotions. When a Cancerian feels a strong attraction to someone or something, all caution flies out of the window. It doesn't happen often, but when it does it's dramatic. Consequently, Cancerians spend their lives trying to restabilise between the last big upheaval and the next one.

In the attempt to be steady and settled, Cancerians can put up with amazing inconvenience and let people take them for granted. But when one of those strong inner urges surfaces, they'll overthrow everything they've worked so hard to build and take breathtaking risks and liberties. They justify it with the hope that their action will lead to equal stability under better circumstances. Usually it does.

It's no use encouraging Cancerians to widen their horizons while they're putting down roots. And it's no use trying to speak to them about common sense when they're in the throes of passion. Either way, they'd have to ignore you. For, while Cancerians are good at looking after others, they hate to be told what to do!

There is one thing that you can always give Cancerians: reassurance. They suffer from guilt and need to be told that it's all OK. The right word at the right time will always mean more to a Cancerian than any expensive gift.

HOME

You can recognise a Cancerian home as soon as you walk into it. It's soft, homely and womb-like. Once your visitors get settled in, they never want to leave.

Although Cancer is the sign of the crab, you have no inclination to carry your home on your back. The very idea of living without a fixed abode is enough to make you retreat into your shell! To you, home is the most important place in the whole world, and it has to be made cosy at all costs. You delight in creating a safe haven – a secure, warm, welcoming, comfortable and friendly place. As long as you know you have a space where you can do this, you don't really care if it's a mansion or a humble hut. Your ideal house number is 69 (no, nothing to do with that! It's just that it happens to be the zodiac symbol for Cancer.)

CLOTHES

CANCERIANS LIKE CLOTHES THAT MAKE THEM FEEL SAFE. EVEN THOSE WHO DRESS GLAMOROUSLY WILL HAVE ONE REGULAR ITEM WHICH THEY FEEL NAKED WITHOUT.

Some people choose clothes that will help show off their personality. Cancerians tend to prefer clothes that will mask it. This doesn't mean you pick dowdy items – indeed, you probably have a wardrobe bursting with enviably elegant gowns and outfits. It's just that all of these are designed to disguise the sensitive, slightly vulnerable person you tend to feel you are. Your greatest asset is your eyes. These, even without a trace of make-up, are bursting with more character and colour than you realise. If you dress to complement the colour and shape of the top half of your face, you'll always look a million dollars.

CARS

To some people, a car is a sex symbol; to others it's a status symbol. To a Cancerian it's a sort of mobile cupboard-under-the-stairs. Never mind the size of the engine, you want to know about the size of the glove compartment. Will it hold all your CDs, cosmetics, slippers, sandwiches and maps? For the maps, frankly, you could use a trailer. The idea of being lost in a strange city terrifies you so much that you don't only carry an *A–Z* but an atlas, just in case you should take a wrong turn and end up on a ferry without noticing. Which brings us to the thorny question of what you do notice when driving. Not the maker's marque, that's for sure. For you, any car will always be just another car until they invent one with a periscope to give a better view of what the people are up to in the vehicle in front!

FOOD

THE STOMACH IS RULED BY CANCER, WHICH IS WHY CANCERIANS FIND A SENSE OF SECURITY IN EATING THEIR FAVOURITE FOODS. THIS, THOUGH, MAKES IT HARD FOR THEM TO FOLLOW A DIET!

Cancerians are ruled by the Moon, which in turn governs dairy produce. In theory you're keen on milk, cream, butter, cheese, yoghurt and eggs. You're also supposed to have an affinity with melons, mushrooms and marrows. Whether or not this is true I bet, if you are a truly typical Cancerian, you'd far rather have a proper sit-down meal than eat on your feet. Oddly enough, though you can resist the temptation of instant snacks, you are almost perpetually hungry. Like J.R.R. Tolkien's famous Bilbo the Hobbit, you've always got room for a 'little something' to fill up the corners.

MONEY

'THE GROWTH OF A LARGE BUSINESS IS MERELY A SURVIVAL OF THE FITTEST...'

'THE AMERICAN BEAUTY ROSE CAN BE PRODUCED IN THE SPLENDOUR AND FRAGRANCE WHICH BRING CHEER TO ITS BEHOLDER ONLY BY SACRIFICING THE EARLY BUDS WHICH GROW UP AROUND IT.'

J.D. Rockefeller, who made these remarks, was a Cancerian and an exceedingly rich one at that. His words sum up a dilemma which all born under your sign must face from time to time. On the one hand, you are aware of your natural ability to make ruthless business and financial decisions. On the other, you resent having to compromise the more sentimental side of your nature in the process. Rather than be constantly torn in this way, many Cancerians back away from their chances to make big money. Others compensate by giving free rein to their mercenary instincts for a while, then generously redistribute the proceeds. Rockefeller was a case in point.

I'm not promising you will ever grow as wealthy as he was, but you will always be able to do pretty well for yourself provided you have a clear idea about what you want to do with your future. Cancerians often find it hard to believe that an old idea or project has now run its course – they keep wanting to pour time, energy and hope into an investment even if it continually fails to live up to its promise. You'll always be able to make more of your potential provided you can overcome your ingrained resistance to the notion of a radical change of direction.

JUST THE JOB?

Baker, builder, caretaker, caterer, cook, dairymaid, fishmonger, glassblower, gynaecologist, home economist, kindergarten teacher, hotelier, inn-keeper, jacuzzi maker, laundry person, mushroom grower, mammologist, market gardener, nurse, nutritionist, plumber, sailor, shopkeeper, welfare worker.

Five ways to cash in

- Respond only to every other charity appeal you get, instead of to all of them.

- Get a flat above your local branch of Habitat and save the bus fare.
- Entertain a little less lavishly.
- Start charging wear and tear on your shoulder to those who keep crying on it.
- Stop being frightened of grown-ups or people whom you see as being in authority.

Five ways to branch out

- Run a home for waifs and strays in a depressed inner city area.
- Run for Parliament and eventually become Home Secretary.
- Run a healing centre which people will rush to enter.
- Run a pub and become known as the happy host.
- Run away to sea, make your fortune, buy a boat and open up a floating supermarket.

LOVE

Sensuality is a key word for Cancerians. They have a keen appreciation of touch, taste and smell – especially in love. In partnerships, Cancerians will go to great lengths to keep the union alive, even if it's unhappy. But if their patience snaps, that's the end.

To be in partnership with a Cancerian is to live on the edge of an emotional volcano, forever waiting for a sign that the dormant beast is about to erupt. It's just as well that most of the time you are sensitive, compassionate, caring and sharing. If all your lover had to look forward to were those angry outbursts, they'd have packed their bags and headed for the safety of sleepier shores long ago.

If you want to make your relationship withstand the test of time you must learn how to control those intermittent explosions. It's no use being a delightfully charming Dr Jekyll if this is merely causing each rare appearance of Mr Hyde to be more devastating than the previous one. And it's unfair to expect anyone – including your worst enemy, let alone the person you love more than anyone else in the world – to put up with the kind of anger you are capable of bottling up for ages before letting it manifest with all the devastating potency of a nuclear weapon.

So we have to ask what it is within you that puts the fear of God into others – even though most of the time you seem to live in total terror of everyone else. The answer to a question is often contained within it, and in the situation we have just identified it's clear that the cause of the former is the latter! Your 'trouble' is that you swing between too many extremes. You forgive and forget petty transgression after petty transgression. You let the matter of the top of the toothpaste tube ride. You leave the issue of who does the washing up totally undiscussed. You give the false impression that you are happy to be taken for granted, left to carry the can and treated as a simple appendage… and then you hit the roof over a matter so trivial as to make all the aforementioned seem like issues worth debating in Parliament!

I hate to say it, but your every relationship is in essence a power struggle. You hate to be contradicted, can't stand being criticised, and live in terror of being undermined. You don't want things to be equal – you want to dominate like a dictator. And your poor old partner is supposed to put up with this! So what can you do to make things better? You can find other outlets for your need to be in control. Instead of putting all your energy into the relationship you should put as little as possible into it, on the grounds that your idea of 'less' is inevitably going to be most other people's idea of far more than is really necessary.

A SIDEWAYS LOOK AT YOUR SIGN

Anyone who really wants to know about the zodiac sign Cancer needs to think long and hard about a particular four-letter word. To each of us, this word means something different but important. It's a terribly emotive word. In a moment, when I tell you what it is, notice how you react: whether you say 'ooh', 'aah' or 'ho hum', you'll reveal a secret about yourself. And that, as much as the word itself, says a lot about the kind of people that Cancerians really are.

You see, in the great zodiac scheme of life Cancerians are guardians of a fundamental value, and as such they are like mirrors, absorbing and reflecting other people's feelings about that value. This makes Cancerians both powerful and vulnerable. But before I say any more, I'd better tell you the word. It is… *home.*

But I don't mean that all Cancerians are domesticated, house-proud, cosy creatures. Some are – but most embody the spirit of home in a much broader sense. Home is (or should be) a place where everything is right, where you come from and to which you return. Home is security, home is safety, home is strength and, most of all, home is something that goes beyond words and clever arguments.

When you really come home, you don't need to think

about where you are. You just sink into the comfort and familiarity of your environment, turn off your defences and open up your heart. To you home is not a place, it's a feeling, a state of mind, a state of perfection and a state of grace. So the thing that all Cancerians seek is a feeling of being 'at home', and the thing that all Cancerians have to offer is a way of making others feel they have arrived at a perfect place.

No matter who you are, where you are or what you're doing, if you've got a Cancerian nearby the part of the world you're in will feel just like home. Cancerians can do this for you just by being themselves. They don't always do it as soon as you meet them. But never doubt that they are able to, and don't assume that they will foist their idea of home on you, rather than your idea. Cancerians, as I've said, are like mirrors: they are really sensitive and can tune into the very deepest part of your soul and understand exactly what you need.

Why then, if all that is true, can Cancerians sometimes be so crusty, so difficult to get along with, and so tough? Well, there are two reasons for this, both linked to the fact that Cancer is the sign of the crab. Reason one is that, just as a crab has a hard shell but a soft underbelly, Cancerians protect themselves from their own sensitivity by pretending to be harsh. Only when they feel safe enough to come out of their shell will you discover how sweet they are underneath. Reason two is that crabs live by the sea. They only come out when the tide is out, and the thing that makes the tide go in and out is the Moon. The lives of crabs (and Cancerians) are ruled by the Moon and, like the Moon, they go through phases. That's why Cancerians sometimes seem to be moody!

LEO

24 JULY – 23 AUGUST

A LEO'S GREATEST GIFT IS HIS OR HER NATURAL BUOYANCY. NO MATTER WHAT MISFORTUNE MAY BEFALL THEM, LEOS ALWAYS MAINTAIN FAITH IN HUMANITY AND TRUST IN LIFE'S HIDDEN MAGIC. BY BURNING THESE TWO INNER FLAMES, LEOS CANNOT HELP BUT BRING LIGHT AND WARMTH TO THE LIVES OF OTHERS.

Leos love to be admired. They can't help it – they're just built that way. The trouble is that they are also headstrong, highly strung and able to put people's backs up without meaning to. So while they can easily attract the attention they want, they don't always attract the respect which ought to come with it. This is not helped by the fact that Leos can be strong about wanting their own way and difficult when they don't get it! Other people are like this too but Leos don't manage to hide their feelings so well. It's the chief Leo failing, but the best Leo asset.

Leos may not be able to mask their less acceptable emotions, but they're equally unable to disguise their nicer ones. A happy Leo radiates enough warmth to defrost an icebox! With such a sunny disposition there's normally much contagious enthusiasm to be enjoyed in a Leo's company. Sadly, though, some people find the Leo equilibrium upsetting. They mistake the self-contained smile for insensitivity. However, Leos feel deeply and care passionately. They know that once they let go of their cheery veneer, they'll unleash an avalanche of uncontrollable emotion. You'll see the truth in this when a Leo gives you a present – for Leos never hold back (feelings or cheque books) if there's a chance to give. And, when giving to a Leo, neither should you.

HOME

THE FINEST THINGS IN LIFE ALWAYS, SOMEHOW, FIND THEIR WAY INTO A LEO'S LIFESTYLE. BUT LEOS LOVE TO SHARE THE BEST OF EVERYTHING WITH THOSE THEY CARE FOR.

Leos are famed for their generosity but also for their sense of self-importance. What could suit you better then, than a country manor complete with antiques, tennis courts and a covered swimming pool? It's just the thing to go with your chauffeur (see Cars) and, of course, to entertain your friends in impressive style. Delusions of grandeur? Absolutely! Every healthy Leo needs plenty of those. Your current abode may not fit the bill exactly, but I'd like to bet it's the swankiest place on the street or, more relevantly, that you *think* it is! Leos, basically, see themselves as the Joneses with whom everyone else needs to keep up.

CLOTHES

LEOS, WITHOUT EXCEPTION, DRESS AS IF THEY ARE PLAYING A PART IN A PLAY. MOST LIKE TO BE BRIGHT AND GLAMOROUS; ALL THINK ABOUT THEIR APPEARANCE.

Do you have a glorious mane of hair that flows in ringlets right down your back? If not, why not? Are you ashamed of your link to the biggest cat in the jungle? Are you trying to cultivate a more reserved image? A typical Leo's hair is their crowning glory. Its shape, texture and colour should dictate the nature of every single item of clothing and accessory in their wardrobe. Leos who for any reason wear their hair short have a harder job selecting clothes that feel right. They need to pick deliberately ostentatious outfits in order to project their proper power, whereas those with the locks can just let the rest of the look fall into place.

CARS

If you're a truly typical Leo, you're not particularly interested in the question of what kind of car you ought to be driving. The real debate centres around what kind of cap your chauffeur ought to wear. There might also be some concern as to whether your limo needs a fully stocked bar or just a jacuzzi, but otherwise it's simple. You were born to cruise the streets of Hollywood, issuing orders like 'Just stop here for an hour or three, James.' If you haven't yet reached this desirable position in life, don't worry – there's still time. Meanwhile you can carry on driving, in your typically imperious Leonine fashion, as if you have a divine right of way and a licence to ignore everything else on the road!

FOOD

Food, for a Leo, should be spicy, colourful and expensive. Leos aren't greedy but they can't resist a tasty delicacy, even if they aren't hungry!

As a Leo, ruled by the Sun, you have a natural affinity with citrus fruit, pomegranates, olives… indeed, pretty much anything that needs a hot climate in which to grow. You're fond of heat in your food, too; not necessarily curry or chilli, but the sharp, aromatic tang of ginger, peppermint, cinnamon, nutmeg and mustard. You tend to be more of a nibbler than a muncher not least because, as a figure-conscious calorie-watcher, you don't like to pile too much on your plate. Instead, you secretly graze on snacks throughout the day, then burn them all off with your amazing, hyper-active nervous energy.

MONEY

'Time… is the centre of the chief difficulty of almost every economic problem.'

These words from the classical economist Alfred Marshall sum up all too well the astrological pressure that you, as a Leo, so often seem to face. The fact that their author was born under your sign gives them extra poignancy. Was he, I wonder, writing purely from a professional standpoint? We astrologers often discuss the irony of Leonine finances. We notice that, far too frequently for comfort, you either get an opportunity that there is no time to take, or time on your hands but no facility to do anything constructive with it. You often have to struggle to introduce a new idea into your world or to bring about a long-desired change in circumstances. Next time the going becomes rough and variable you may like to take comfort from another statement by the same erudite Leo financial expert. 'A new discovery is seldom fully effective for practical purposes till many minor improvements and subsidiary discoveries have gathered themselves around it.'

It's the most natural thing in the world for Leos to find their domestic and personal expenses prone to spiral upwards at the slightest provocation. Unexpected repair bills or travel requirements combine with your desire to maintain rather indulgent habits and leave you worryingly short of cash. Usually the syndrome unfolds as follows. You are just about to sell your home or pawn your heirlooms, when you have an inspiring revelation: you're worth far more than your current lifestyle is enabling you to earn. You will either get a substantial rise, be offered more lucrative employment elsewhere or be shown a better, more reliable source of income. The funny thing is often as not, the above turns out to be true.

JUST THE JOB?

Actor, athlete, banker, brewer, broker, bookmaker, dancer, entertainer, film star, film director, forester, gambler, goldsmith, heart specialist, jeweller, leisure consultant, mayor, matchmaker, monarch, moneylender, mountaineer, novelty goods salesperson, pop singer, circus ringmaster or mistress, theatre owner, usher.

Five ways to cash in

- Offer advice to God.
- Claim your divine reward.

- Send it back, telling God that no-one takes payment in camels anymore.
- In fact, blow that, tell God to move over and that you're taking charge.
- Be merciful on the rest of us.

Five ways to branch out

- Lead a revolution in a foreign country and become the new ruler.
- Persuade a television company to let you host your own chat show.
- Start a fashion trend – and watch everyone follow your lead.
- Star in a movie.
- Make a hit record. It doesn't matter if you can't sing – just pose.

LOVE

LEOS LIKE TO HAVE ADMIRERS, BUT THEY AREN'T ATTRACTED TO PEOPLE WHO FAWN ON THEM. TO WIN A LEO'S LOVE YOU MUST FIRST WIN HIS OR HER RESPECT. THERE'S NOT A PERSON ON THE PLANET WHO IS IMPERVIOUS TO LEO CHARM, THOUGH SOME FIGHT HARDER THAN OTHERS TO RESIST IT.

As a Leo you are by nature proud and independent. This, all on its own, poses an intriguing question about the kind of partner you ought to be aiming to live your life with. Should they be (a) someone supportive and admiring who will give you the freedom you need? (b) someone equally independent and strong who will provide the stimulating challenge you seek? (c) someone special who somehow

combines both the above qualities? or (d) none of the above – indeed, nobody at all, because ultimately there is no such thing as an ideal match for a Leo? Though you may be inclined to imagine, in your darker moments of disillusionment, that (d) is indeed the answer, I can assure you that this is completely untrue – as the bright spark of hope in your heart knows only too well.

The key to comfort and long-lasting success in your love life simply involves learning to recognise that romance, in the classic, heart-stopping, nerve-tingling, pulse-racing sense, is simply not a sustainable phenomenon. Real relationships not only have their ups and downs, their strains and stresses and their moments of complete and total communication breakdown – they have something potentially far more devastating. They have their periods of emptiness, of shallowness and of frustrating vagueness. It's at times like these that both partners tend to be most attracted to the idea of separation, divorce or extra-marital dalliance, but it's also at times like these that there is the greatest chance to find depth and empathy. Nobody is ever happy to have their partner push them into talking when they don't want to talk, sharing when they don't want to share or loving when they feel they have nothing to give… but there's not a person in the world who cannot be coaxed or tempted into feeling better if their partner is truly prepared to show them enough sympathy, support and non-judgemental understanding.

The trouble is that, understandably, you tend to feel you want to receive all this rather than be obliged to give it. So don't feel obliged to give it – feel inspired. Try a little harder and let that ferocious Leo love of independence be what encourages you to persevere when others might give up, rather than stalk off into the jungle in search of a more superficially appealing mate.

A SIDEWAYS LOOK AT YOUR SIGN

Leos are warm, generous, lively, sweet-natured people with hearts of gold and nerves of steel. They are full of fun, soft as butter, sweet as honey and sharp as lemons. Leos can take anything the world throws at them – anything, that is, except perhaps advice. Offering advice to a Leo is like offering a cigarette to a fish finger. It's just totally pointless.

Leos, you see, hate to admit that they have got something wrong or that they can't cope. They like to walk tall and show the world that they have endless confidence in themselves. Because of this they often give the impression of being head-over-heels in love with their own self-image. It's really not fair, though, to call them arrogant or vain. A better, more accurate word would be 'proud'. A Leo is as lost without dignity as a dentist is without a drill. In fact, if it wasn't for their pride and, perhaps, their stubborness, Leos would be perfect.

Get on the right side of a Leo and you'll have a firm friend for life. Leos are loving and lovable, humorous and human, excitable and exciting. Get on the wrong side of a Leo, however, and you'll live to regret it. Leos, when crossed, are more than just stubborn – in the same way that, for example, superglue is more than just glue.

A Leo with a point to prove is rock solid – a living example of determination, willpower and sheer bloody-mindedness. These characteristic qualities are, of course, every bit as good as they are bad. When you need someone to stand up for you, when it's necessary to be steadfast and resolute, or when there's plain speaking to be done, a Leo on your team is the most valuable asset you can have. Leos are loyal, Leos are larger than life – and Leos are also, I'm afraid it must be said, occasionally a little lazy!

Just like the lion in the jungle who sleeps as much as twenty hours out of every twenty-four, the lion in the zodiac likes to go at a gentle pace. When the lion wakes up and emits a ferocious roar everyone stands to attention. But when the lion is quietly snoozing, everyone just defiantly (if cautiously) ignores him. So Leos can be stubborn, Leos can be lazy and, most of all, Leos can be proud. It's no accident that the collective noun for a group of lions is a 'pride'.

But, when all is said and done, despite these faults Leos are still wonderful people. Leo is ruled by the brightest star in the sky, the Sun. And potentially, every Leo is a shining star here on earth. There's something very attractive and pleasurable about basking in sunlight, or basking in the warmth of a Leo's company – which pretty much amounts to the same thing. Leos have sunny dispositions and they carry all the qualities of their personality up-front. They don't bother to hide their character defects, and they don't muck around hiding their light under a bushel. As a result, they shine. And because of that, others are quickly drawn to them. That's why most social circles have a Leo at the centre, why so many Leos find themselves surrounded by fans and admirers, and why such an extraordinarily large number of showbiz celebrities are born under the sign of Leo. It's true that Leos have outrageous tempers which flare up suddenly and burn with terrifying ferocity, but these always die down just as quickly. They are never used to express vindictiveness – only spontaneous justified anger.

VIRGO

24 AUGUST – 23 SEPTEMBER

EVERY VIRGO HAS A MISSION TO INFORM AND EDUCATE. THEY RARELY LECTURE OTHERS OR INSIST ON LOUDLY PUTTING THEIR POINT ACROSS, PREFERRING TO LISTEN, UNDERSTAND AND THEN TEACH BY GENTLE EXAMPLE. THE VIRGO SPIRIT IS ESSENTIALLY A HEALING SPIRIT. VIRGOS WANT NOTHING MORE (OR LESS) THAN TRUE PHYSICAL AND EMOTIONAL WELLBEING FOR ALL THEIR FELLOW HUMANS.

Virgos have tremendous timing and impeccable insight. Fortunately for the rest of us, they also have searing self-doubts. These inhibit them from abusing their talents and make them very reasonable people. Neither passive nor aggressive, Virgos are simply sensible yet sensual. They want to enjoy life to the full but they know that there are dangers attached to such hungers. They form elaborate contingency plans and see the potential repercussions of every move. This may sound staid, but in Virgoan hands common sense is not a restrictive force. Unlike those who shoot first and ask questions later, Virgos ask first and only fire if they know they've aimed the right weapon at the right target.

Virgos don't see their own lives from such a confident viewpoint – they couldn't be so well organised if they did. Virgos, on the inside, feel intimidated by their own ambitions, but at the same time frustrated by their reticence. It's a dichotomy which can't ever (and should never) be resolved. It's also the reason why Virgos are attracted to other Virgos. Knowingly or unknowingly, they seek each other out.

Virgos are sociable, amenable and helpful people, no matter who they are with. They are forgiving, patient and thoughtful. When they give presents they choose them carefully, and when you give to them you should do the same.

HOME

DESPITE ALL THAT YOU HAVE READ ELSEWHERE, VIRGOS ARE NOT OBSESSIVELY TIDY – THEY JUST LIKE TO ARRANGE THINGS IN AN ORGANISED FASHION, WHICH IS NOT THE SAME THING.

Virgos are supposed to be tidy-minded. Up to a point it's true, but it doesn't follow that your home is a show house. Your personality is far too warm for the stark, cold lines of an immaculate room, and you have better things to do with your time than be forever putting things in drawers. Instead, you plump for organised chaos. Despite your billions of possessions (you hate to throw anything away) you have a place for absolutely everything. The piles, stacks and bundles, however, make sense only to you. It all adds to your air of genial eccentricity – as, indeed, does your quirky, inventive but effective approach to interior design.

Your ideal house number is 60 or 65 (to suit your retiring disposition).

CLOTHES

VIRGOS NEVER WEAR ANY CLOTHES BY ACCIDENT. EVEN SCRUFFY VIRGOS WILL HAVE CAREFULLY CHOSEN EACH ITEM THEY WEAR FOR MAXIMUM 'SCRUFFY EFFECT'!

Anyone who thinks that Virgo is the sign of purity, and that you therefore ought to dress in white, clearly knows little about astrology and even less about the price of washing powder. Yours is the fecund sign of the harvest goddess, not the prudish sign of the eternal spinster. If you want to show off your best qualities, choose 'earth colours': dark greens, russet browns and clay reds. Pick smartly cut, cleverly designed clothes which give an air of authority, keep accessories simple and watch your shoes. For some reason you're prone to looking good from your head to your ankles, after which it all tends to go to pot!

CARS

V is for Virgo… and Volvo. You may not actually drive one, but something about the unassuming, safety-conscious image of this particular make suits you perfectly, right down to its traditional link with country life. Another reason why you need a tank of a car is because your critical faculties go into overdrive when you get out on the road. Maybe it's the intoxicating aroma of air freshener mixed with carbon monoxide or the nerve-jangling noise of a grinding gear-stick but, oddly, for such a usually reserved person you can't drive far without muttering things like: 'What an idiot!', 'Who let him out without a minder?' or 'Get out of the way you ****!' In a less adequately sound-proofed vehicle, there is a horrible chance that other motorists might hear you!

FOOD

VIRGOS ARE VERY FUSSY ABOUT FOOD. WHAT THEY WANT TO EAT DEPENDS ON THE MOOD THEY'RE IN; OFTEN THEY'LL GO TO GREAT LENGTHS TO GET WHAT THEY FANCY.

How do you fancy a starter of fennel, walnut and parsley salad, followed by carrot, celery and bean stew flavoured with dill and caraway? You could eat it with hazelnut pâté on oatcakes and follow up with treacle tart. Mouth-watering? It ought to be, for every single one of these ingredients is traditionally governed by Mercury, the ruler of your sign. Even the absence of meat on the list is apt because, though not every Virgo turns vegetarian, yours is the sign of dietary discrimination. You take great pleasure in keeping yourself intelligently nourished.

MONEY

'NOTHING WILL EVER BE ATTEMPTED IF ALL POSSIBLE OBJECTIONS MUST BE FIRST OVERCOME.'

As the esteemed Dr Johnson, the author of these words, was born under your sign, I'm sure you'll understand just what lay behind that remark. Virgos have a magnificent ability to overcome their fears and problems by subjecting them to close analysis. They dissect and probe them so carefully and cleverly as to render them totally impotent. Sadly, they sometimes put their opportunities through the same process – with less encouraging results. You could be a far wealthier person if only you could train yourself to apply just a little less cautious forethought from time to time.

You may well want to dwell on this idea at your leisure. You have long suspected that your skills are being undervalued and your talents underexploited. You may decide that the way to attain greater wealth is to gain specialised knowledge in a vital subject: to study, research or train.

Or you may discover that you don't need to learn so much as to teach – to delegate some of the mundane tasks on your plate while you profit from your more specific expertise. One thing's for sure: if you want to make the most of your prospects, you definitely need to overcome your natural reticence and your false assumption that others are better qualified than yourself to be successful in commerce. As Dr Johnson once so pithily observed: 'Trade could not be managed by those who managed it if it had much difficulty.'

JUST THE JOB?

Accountant, administrator, animal trainer, book-keeper, butler, charity worker, chemist, chicken-breeder, civil servant, clothier, dentist, dietician, doctor, editor, grocer, governess, librarian, microbiologist, naturopath, nurse, osteopath, photographer, piano tuner, sanitation inspector, teacher, vet.

Five ways to cash in

- Team up with someone who is far less logical than yourself.

- Next time someone asks if you happen to have noticed where they put something, charge them for the answer.
- Only agree to play Scrabble if it is for cash stakes.
- Become a rent collector – and accept bribes to make you go away.
- Sell some of those juicy secrets you are keeping.

Five ways to branch out

- Take a job editing the *Encyclopedia Britannica* – that will certainly challenge your talent.
- Offer your services to proofread telephone directories.
- Take a course in computers and set yourself up as a programmer.
- Open up a lost property office.
- Visit Italy, having set yourself the task of straightening out the Leaning Tower of Pisa.

LOVE

VIRGOS ARE IMPERVIOUS TO FLATTERY. TRY TO PULL THE WOOL OVER THEIR EYES AND THEY MAY STRING YOU ALONG FOR AMUSEMENT, BUT THEY'LL NEVER FALL FOR IT. VIRGO IS REALLY AN 'INTROVERTED' SIGN. EVEN EXTROVERT VIRGOS TEND TO HIDE BEHIND A FAÇADE, A SOCIAL ROLE OR STAGED PRETENCE OF ONE SORT OR ANOTHER.

Virgos, so we are led to believe, are about as romantic as a cold bath, as sensitive as a lump of concrete and as vulnerable as a crocodile. If only it were true. You could leave passion to those who possessed the stomach for its punishing after-effects, and withdraw to the safety of your ivory tower to be alone and untouchable for evermore. The idea, I'm sure, is appealing. But you and I both know that in truth you yearn to be held, to be touched, to be tenderly kissed – and to be lovingly adored. It may all sound gruesomely Mills and Boon, but though the cynic in your mind groans at the very notion, the poet in your soul simply shudders with desire. All this, naturally enough, makes you a bit of a tough person to partner. How is your beloved supposed to tell when you want to be shown respect for your intellect and when you want to be swept off your feet? How can they know whether to whisper sweet nothings in your ear or put complicated diagrams in front of your eyes? How indeed? And how are you supposed to know whether you want to spend the rest of your life with a lover who looks good but lacks brainpower or with a sophisticated genius who happens to have the dress sense of a down-and-out?

The answer, in a nutshell, is that you want, need, deserve and are capable of getting (if you have not got already) an intuitive expert – a genuine soulmate, an emotional partner who can read you like a book. The only remaining question is: how are you going to find this emotional miracle? The answer to that one is that you're going to create it. You're going to stop fantasising about that perfect stranger you vaguely imagine you may one day meet, and start working with the material that's already to hand.

Almost certainly it's your existing partner – unless they have absolutely definitely proved themselves to be beyond all hope. If so, or if you have no partner, possibly it's a friend or acquaintance with whom you have always felt a certain rapport. With this individual you're going to explore new horizons of inter-personal understanding. You're going to take courses in communication, if necessary. But you're going to build, and keep building, until you have a bond of understanding that lasts not just till death do you part but beyond. For every Virgo, this is not just a dream but a perfectly attainable proposition. All you have to do, besides recognise that you want it, is work on it.

A SIDEWAYS LOOK AT YOUR SIGN

Virgos are difficult to write about and even harder to predict for, because they are so erratic. If you find this surprising, I'm not surprised! Most Virgos present a very stable, sensible face to the world. They like others to think they're completely controlled and consistent. To a degree it's true. Virgos are undoubtedly loyal, dependable, exceptionally intelligent, good-humoured, generous and compassionate. But if you probe a little deeper, you'll quickly come across the factor that makes every Virgo so impossible, impenetrable and infuriating. What is this characteristic? Oh, how I wish there was a word in the English language that could sum it up!

When I read about how Virgos are rather dull, neat and tidy folk who detest controversy and make perfect librarians, I laugh! That kind of description may fit some of the Virgo behaviour patterns, but it says nothing about the true Virgo spirit. The true spirit makes Madonna look positively prim. It's a wild, chaotic, sensual spirit hidden behind a cool, calm, careful façade.

This, though, is still only half the story about the 'dark side' of Virgo. Here's the other half. Every Virgo is, somehow, in some way a martyr. Martyrs are people who put up with all sorts of pain, deprive themselves of all sorts of pleasure and deny themselves all sorts of freedom, just for the satisfaction of feeling that they are 'doing the right thing'. Virgos are people who do all the above because they're afraid that if they did what they really wanted to do, they might end up 'doing the wrong thing'. So how do Virgos reconcile this 'Florence Nightingale' syndrome with the self-indulgent qualities I've just mentioned? They don't. They can't. And that's why they are so impenetrable.

If Virgos were extrovert, it might not matter so much. They could display one side in public, the other in private. But most Virgos find little pleasure in showing off. Even those who are prepared to stand in the spotlight never let it shine on their true character. As introverts, Virgos are analytical, perceptive and thoughtful. They're highly aware of the inconsistencies in their own nature and, to make matters worse, they're normally highly self-critical about them. So they keep their mouths shut and suffer in silence. And what they mainly suffer from is an endless inner battle between the desire to serve others and the desire to serve their passions.

I want to make a confession. I really like Virgos. Many of the people I love most have been born under this sign. I've nothing but admiration and respect for them. The things I like best of all about my Virgo friends are, usually, the things they like least of all about themselves. I like their eccentricities and idiosyncrasies. I like their passions.

But the things I dislike about Virgos are the things they normally think are their finest social assets. I dislike the way they let other people take the credit, the way they humbly accept unjust blame or criticism. However, Virgos have X-ray vision. There is no pretence that a Virgo cannot see through, no social grace that a Virgo will be impressed by. Within seconds of meeting you, a Virgo will have decided exactly what makes you tick. That judgement will be absolutely accurate and potentially devastating. Virgos know that they have the potential to reduce other people to a quivering mass of embarrassment just by expressing a few of their observations – and that makes them feel burdened. If you've ever been 'seen through' by a Virgo you'll know that it hurts! The truth does.

The irony of all this is that Virgos, if they weren't so cripplingly self-critical, would be the most powerful people on earth. Their infallible perceptions could make them an unstoppable force. The only reason why Virgos don't rule the world is that they're so harsh on themselves.

LIBRA

24 SEPTEMBER – 23 OCTOBER

AS THE ZODIAC'S APPOINTED GUARDIAN OF JUSTICE, A LIBRAN'S TASK IS PERHAPS THE MOST THANKLESS OF ALL: TO WEIGH INTELLECT AGAINST INTUITION AND THE NEED TO BE FAIR AGAINST THE NEED TO BE FIRM. IN SO DOING, LIBRANS ARE OFTEN OBLIGED TO MAKE CHOICES FEW PEOPLE CAN UNDERSTAND. THIS COSMIC BURDEN THEY BEAR WITH ETERNAL GRACE AND GOOD HUMOUR.

Librans, like chameleons, can fit in almost anywhere with almost anyone. That's why they are accused of being indecisive. They are sensitive to social undercurrents and want to do what's expected of them. This stems from a great need to be accepted. Yet it conflicts with another Libran need – to make a strong impression on their social and physical environment. In a Libran mind, that conflict is reconciled like this: if you want your own way, it's better to inspire cooperation than confrontation.

As a philosophy it's admirable, but in practice… Libra is the sign of the scales. Often Librans swing from one extreme to another in an attempt to find a perfect balance. One day they'll bend over backwards to accept someone else's viewpoint; next day they'll charge forward in a furious effort to impose their own. It's a pattern which is consistently inconsistent. Whether trying to be helpful or trying to take control, Librans are affable and charming. It's impossible to know if they are taking care of you, or advantage of you! But Librans don't see it that way. They always believe that what they are doing is for the greater good.

Librans can make even strangers feel special, but, ironically, if your Libran friend is a true friend he or she won't feel the need to turn on that charm with you. So if you want to charm a Libran, do something for them that lets them know it's OK, that you love them just the way they are!

HOME

LIBRANS, BEING SOCIABLE, GREGARIOUS CHARACTERS, USUALLY LOVE TO ENTERTAIN PEOPLE IN THEIR HOMES. THEIR HOMES CAN BE HUMBLE BUT THEY ARE ALWAYS GRACEFUL.

Librans are friendly and fair about most things, but tend to have highly discriminating artistic tastes. You would far prefer a hovel with the right blend of colour to a gaudily painted mansion. You like to live in partnership, but when it comes to decor you must have the final say. Especially important to you is the look of your bedroom. If it doesn't reflect your aesthetic aspirations, it won't inspire you to sleep – or to do anything else!

Your ideal house number is 2 (as in 'Tea For').

CLOTHES

Librans have excellent taste in almost every area of life, but they sometimes fail to apply the same discriminating eye to their own appearance. Often, to be on the safe side, they will find one successful fashion formula and stick to it like superglue.

Being born under the sign of the balance gives you a natural understanding of the need to wear simple outfits with complex accessories – and vice versa. It also allows you enough artistic flair to know when you can get away with breaking fashion ground rules, and take courageous risks which pay off. If you're looking for clothes and colours which show off more of your magical, endearing personality, try light touches – a Dennis the Menace badge on the lapel of a straight-cut business two-piece, or an arty beret worn at a jaunty angle with simple jeans and jumper. It's in the art of clever combination that the well-dressed Libran excels.

CARS

What's the ideal car for a Libran? The answer, as with so many questions involving the sign of the balance, is: it depends. On Mondays you want a traffic-beating bicycle, on Tuesdays a status-conferring sedan. The antidote to a dull Wednesday must be a quirky VW Beetle while a busy Thursday usually requires a roomy estate. As Friday is pay-day and there's never enough in the packet, an economical diesel becomes desirable. And for those 'anything-could-happen' weekends the ideal vehicle is probably a Land Rover. In the absence of a car for each day of the week, you tend to drive whatever you've got according to your rapidly changing mood. And this, of course, explains your tendency to misjudge those parking spaces!

FOOD

LIBRANS ARE FUSSY ABOUT DECOR. IN A RESTAURANT THEY NOTICE THE TABLECLOTH MORE THAN WHAT'S ON THE MENU!

Voluptuous Venus, the ruler of your sign, gives you a healthy appetite for life's most sensual pleasures. It also gives you an affinity with fruit – which possibly explains why, though you yearn to be part of a 'pear', you drive your close friends bananas and often end up playing gooseberry. Joking apart, you do find yourself keen on sweet and juicy fruits but you also have a terrible weakness for rich and fattening delicacies, especially confectionery. To balance this, you are forever embarking on intense, demanding, disciplined diets which you stick to rigidly, come hell or high water… for all of twenty-five minutes.

MONEY

'WEALTH IS NOT WITHOUT ITS ADVANTAGES AND THE CASE TO THE CONTRARY, ALTHOUGH IT HAS OFTEN BEEN MADE, HAS NEVER PROVED WIDELY PERSUASIVE.'

This carefully worded, tongue-in-cheek remark comes from one of the twentieth century's most widely read (and readable) economists, J. K. Galbraith. Impressive though his many qualifications are, I'm sure you'll feel even more endeared towards the great professor if I tell you he was born under the sign of Libra. So he must know what he is talking about, mustn't he? Actually, that's a trick question. Before you answer it, I suggest you read another of his famous maxims: 'One of the best ways of avoiding necessary and even urgent tasks is to seem busily employed on things that are already done.'

Does this ring any bells? Various astrological factors suggest that it ought to. Librans detest being given orders. This is partly why you aspire so profoundly to running your own business – or at least your own department of somebody else's business, without anything more than cursory interference from a benign boss or respectful client. The trouble is that life's never like this for any Libran, no matter how successful he or she becomes. You will always be able to earn good money, make solid career progress and even, up to a point, express your creative ingenuity – but only by accepting that every so often, regrettable though it may be, we all have to become a small cog in a greater machine. Temporarily it will be necessary to subjugate your desire for autonomy, repress your resentment of bureaucracy, control your urge to defy authority and generally bite a series of bullets. Learn to play your part with as much good grace as you can muster, then bide your time. Eventually, the shots will be yours to call.

JUST THE JOB?

Artist, beautician, bedroom designer, civil rights campaigner, cosmeticist, decorator, diplomat, dramatist, dressmaker, fashion designer, florist, golfer, judge, juggler, lawyer, milliner, musician, pianist, poet, politician, public relations consultant, receptionist, salesperson, solicitor, tailor, union leader, wigmaker, woodsman.

Five ways to cash in

- Charm the socks off your bank or building society manager.
- Put your money where your mouth is.
- Stop siding with the underdog.
- Get a job as a Kissogram.
- Put a penny in a jar each time you change your mind – or maybe 10p, but then again, perhaps 1p…

Five ways to branch out

- Become a colour therapist and redesign rainbows.
- Balance feathers on the end of a pin.
- Repaint the ceiling of the Sistine Chapel with a modern design.
- Save the world.
- Which came first, the chicken or the egg? Establish the definitive answer.

LOVE

SOME PEOPLE SHOW THEIR TEMPER UNDER STRESS; LIBRANS SIMPLY TURN ON THE CHARM. A LIBRAN SMILE CAN MELT THE ICIEST HEART AND SOFTEN THE HARDEST ADVERSARY.

If, as a British Prime Minister once said, 'A week is a long time in politics', it's a veritable eternity in a Libran's love life! Odd though it may sound, your only chance of getting from here to the end of your life with your current partner, no matter how wonderful (or otherwise) they may be, is to forget the idea. Give up. Concentrate instead on just getting from here to the end of the week. And then the next one. As a Libran, you are simply not equipped to plan far into the future. The very thought of what you might be doing twenty years from now is enough to give you a simultaneous attack of the collywobbles, the screaming habdabs and the dull ache of depression.

All this is mainly because you consider yourself a highly changeable, reactive individual who at any moment is likely to go off and do something radically different. Maybe you will. But you'll come back to what you went off from… as sure as eggs are eggs and Librans are Librans. You are far less unpredictable than you imagine. If something or someone means something to you now, they will continue to mean as much, if not more, to you in the far-flung future – even if you have oscillated and wobbled about the matter all the way from here to there. So if you want to make your love last forever, just relax and stop worrying about it all.

A SIDEWAYS LOOK AT YOUR SIGN

Librans are supposed to be placid, well-balanced, easy-going people. But whenever I read that I either end up in tears of laughter or tears of frustration. Who writes such rubbish? Haven't they seen a Libran in action? I can only say if Librans are wishy-washy, what about Margaret Thatcher? If Librans are unexciting, what about Will Smith? If Librans have unimposing personalities, what about Jesse Jackson?

I'll agree you have to look a little harder through the list of famous Libran males before you come across equally strong characters – but you'd hardly say that John Lennon was an uncontroversial character. And I don't think Oscar Wilde was exactly keen to promote social harmony. No –

as far as I can see, there's a strong desire in every Libran to create a world which is fair and peaceful; but there's also a very argumentative side to the Libran character which normally lies closer to the surface of their personalities. Librans are, in fact, magnificently cussed, courageous and contemptuous of compromise; they simply disguise it behind a façade of congeniality and charm. Librans instinctively know how to put you at ease and off your guard. They know how to smile and nod, how to lull others into a false sense of security – and how to act as if all they really need, in order to be happy, is for you to be happy.

It's the ability to play devil's advocate which bestows every Libran with a special kind of creative genius – and yet this is also the thing which gives every Libran a very heavy cross to bear. You see, although we're forever being told that the cosmic scales represent intellect at its most powerful, justice at its most benign and equality at its most fair, the spirit of Libra is the spirit of the balancing process itself, not of the things that may be weighed in that balance. Libra is the only sign of the zodiac to be symbolised by a machine. Consequently, there's a certain something at the heart of the Libran personality which is a little cold or mechanical. I'm not saying they don't have deep, passionate emotions or that they don't care, cry, laugh, love and live to the full; they most undoubtedly do. But no matter what they are going through, whether it's happy or sad, Librans always follow their thoughts rather than their feelings.

The true spirit of Libra is about as far removed as you can get from basic, earthy, primitive human nature. It's the spirit of intellect's triumph over instinct, logic over emotion. And this is why we get the old chestnut about Librans being indecisive. Decisions are what Librans' lives are all about, but no Libran ever makes any decision lightly. They analyse, weigh up all arguments carefully and, while they're in the process of making a decision, swing wildly from one extreme point of view to the other, expressing the virtues and vices of each with great force and enthusiasm. Some decisions take them seconds, others take years – but once they're made, they're made for good.

Sometimes the decision-making process can tire a Libran. Sometimes they'll deliberately 'let' certain things happen so as to avoid having to make a decision about them. Often they'll prefer to be in a position where they have no option, rather than be given a choice between one thing or another. Perhaps it's from this that the 'easy-going, placid' description has really come. But in my experience, even when a Libran decides to let a decision be made for them, it's only because they have decided that that's the best decision. And one thing I know for sure: woe betide anyone who ever tries to persuade a Libran to rethink anything once their mind is made up!

SCORPIO

24 OCTOBER – 22 NOVEMBER

BECAUSE THIS SIGN GOVERNS SEX, DEATH AND 'BODILY FUNCTION', SOME PEOPLE ASSUME THAT SCORPIOS MUST BE PERMANENTLY PREOCCUPIED BY THESE TOPICS. YET SCORPIO ULTIMATELY, SYMBOLISES SIMPLY 'THE INTEGRITY OF HONESTY'. LONG AGO, THE SYMBOL FOR THIS PART OF THE SKY WAS AN EAGLE. IN HONOUR OF THIS TRADITION – AND AS A COUNTER MEASURE TO THE MODERN POPULAR IMAGE OF THIS SIGN, I MAKE A POINT, IN ALL MY WORK, OF PORTRAYING THE NOBLE BIRD, NOT THE STINGING INSECT.

Scorpios are determined and direct. They normally get what they want – or at least what they think they want at the time. The trouble is that at the heart of every Scorpio there's an insatiable hunger for an impossible dream. Enough is never enough, and you had better get used to this if you want to get on with your Scorpio friend. Happily, that restlessness is the hardest thing to handle in a Scorpio, unless you hate straight talking. Scorpios aren't afraid of taboos: they find it amazing (or amusing) that people are squeamish about things like sex, death, toilets or overdrafts.

Scorpios know that their honesty can be controversial, which is why they are careful about who they allow to get close to them. This, in turn, is why Scorpios are sometimes considered unapproachable or secretive. It's also, partly, why they are accused of having an obsession with sex. Scorpios are passionate and they throw themselves body and soul into every experience. But it's not just sexual intensity they enjoy. They want the most out of life and take their pleasures as seriously as their commitments. This is another reason why they can be guarded in company. Scorpios are in awe of their own powerful desires and hate to be criticised for them.

You won't win a Scorpio's trust by giving a present; only time and sincerity will allow you to do that. But you might win a smile if you give your Scorpio friend something which shows you accept and approve of them.

HOME

SCORPIOS ARE VERY PARTICULAR ABOUT THE ATMOSPHERE OF THEIR HOMES AND CANNOT ABIDE AN ABRASIVE ABODE.

Plenty of people have household security systems these days, but only Scorpios have burglar alarms to protect their burglar alarms! It's easier to get into Fort Knox than to get into your home, yet despite all those triple-lock doors, chains, spyholes and 'Beware of the Dog' signs, you still tend to wonder if you ought not to go the whole hog and put a moat and drawbridge round your property. Some people suspect this is not to protect your possessions at all but to guard the secret of what you get up to in the privacy of your own four walls.

CLOTHES

SCORPIOS KNOW HOW TO DRESS TO KILL, BUT THEY LIKE TO WEAR OUTFITS WITH A SUBTLE RATHER THAN A DRAMATIC EFFECT.

If all they say about Scorpio is true, where are your split skirts, stilettos and fishnet stockings? Or your gold medallions, tight trousers and open-necked shirts? Actually, some Scorpios do sometimes wear a toned-down, more elegant version of this attire, but they do so for reasons entirely the opposite of the obvious – not to be seductive, but to hide their natural shyness. Most Scorpios, however, are content to wear deliberately quiet, smart, sober clothes which let them fade into the background so that they can emerge from it at a moment of their own choosing.

CARS

Though Ford make a car named after your sign, it's not necessarily the one you want to drive. For one thing, you rarely like to do the obvious. For another, as a lover of privacy and mystery you really don't want such a revealing announcement permanently plastered on your rear end! Ideally, indeed, your sleek and stylish vehicle should have a two-way mirror for a windscreen so that you can see out but nobody else can see in! As for *how* you drive… well, oddly enough, despite your Scorpionic reputation for passion and drama in other areas, on the road you tend to be as highly reserved as a ticket for Wimbledon, until that is, somebody cuts you up.

FOOD

GENERALLY, SCORPIOS LIKE FOOD WITH SHARP, DISTINCTIVE FLAVOURS. THEY TEND TO PREFER SAVOURY DISHES TO SWEET AND HAVE DISCRIMINATING PALATES.

The test of a true Scorpio is not their taste in clothes but their taste for cloves … of garlic. If, for example, you like the stuff but think of it as a potent, pungent flavouring, you are only slightly Scorpionic. To fully epitomise your sign, you need to see garlic not as a seasoning but as a vegetable – to be eaten cooked, like cabbage or, better still, raw like fruit! Other sure signs of a typically Scorpionic palate include a liking for sharp, sour or bitter foods such as horseradish, capers, pickled onions, watercress, radicchio and rhubarb.

MONEY

'MONEY IS COINED LIBERTY, AND SO IT IS TEN TIMES DEARER TO A MAN WHO IS DEPRIVED OF FREEDOM. IF MONEY IS JINGLING IN HIS POCKET, HE IS HALF CONSOLED, EVEN THOUGH HE CANNOT SPEND IT.'

The author of these words, the nineteenth-century Russian novelist Fyodor Dostoevsky, was a Scorpio. They say a lot about your sign's bitter-sweet relationship with money. You may have a talent for making it and an even more highly developed talent for spending it, but you have long since learned that what it does to you outweighs what it can do for you. Money, or rather worry about money, robs you of precious peace of mind and distracts you from deeper, more important issues. It doesn't necessarily follow that extra cash solves the problem – nor does the answer lie in living the life of an economic renunciate. You simply need a way to enjoy the freedom it brings whilst avoiding the trouble.

To do this, you need not a trust fund but a fund of trust in a higher power. Be neither greedy nor careless, but diligent and sensitive, and your finances will always sort themselves out more than adequately. If you ever want to make a little extra money, resolve to bring out the masterpiece you always knew you had within you. The novel, symphony, sculpture or movie you produce will ensure a tidy nest egg for your old age, provided you give yourself wholeheartedly to such a project. It may be, however, that for practical reasons you are not free to lock yourself in a garret for the necessary time. If these reasons are purely financial, transcend them. If, however, other commitments prevent you from a fully fledged frenzy of artistic indulgence, just do what you can to employ your imagination profitably in more mundane areas of life.

JUST THE JOB?

Aircraft designer, acupuncturist, dentist, detective, environmentalist, healer, journalist, loss adjuster, lumberjack, market gardener, pathologist, pest controller, pharmacist, psychiatrist, radiotherapist, researcher, satirist, snake charmer, sex therapist, spy, surgeon, tanner, taxation specialist, undertaker.

Five ways to cash in

- Pretend your cash belongs to someone else and treat it accordingly.
- Refuse to pay any more of the bills which are constantly landing on your doormat.

- Stop allowing money to intimidate you.
- Take the advice that you are always so free to give to others.
- Offer your services to the CIA – at a price, of course.

Five ways to branch out

- Become a personal trainer.
- Study psychotherapy.
- Find the lost city of Atlantis.
- Form your own religion.
- Invent your own reality TV show.

LOVE

Scorpios are not really sex maniacs. They're just very honest and demonstrative about their urges and feelings. It takes a long time before a Scorpio will put his or her trust in another person. But once that trust is given, it soon becomes unshakeable loyalty.

If you have difficulty with the idea of making your current love last forever, I put it to you that this is mainly because you feel that you already have an old love, the magic and the pain of which you suspect, in your heart of hearts, is going to last forever no matter what you try to do about it. Scorpios are, as you know only too well, the most sensitive people in the zodiac. And sensitive people tend to get their hearts broken very early in life. Once broken, sensitive people's hearts never seem to mend fully. Their hearts harden around the places where the scars lie, and it becomes very difficult for the owners of these hearts to let anyone, no matter how deserving and potentially wonderful, get near enough to let them run the risk of being hurt again.

You may consider yourself to be carrying a torch or nursing a wound or – perhaps more likely, considering Scorpios' tendency to deny what they don't like to think about – simply feeling rather numb for reasons you don't care to examine further. But whatever it is, it's certainly not very fair on the person you are now with or would like to be with one day – or even on yourself. One way or another, you've got to lay the ghost of your past, get what happened when you were so much younger out of your system, and give your future the chance it deserves. And if you can do that, bearing in mind all you have learned in the meantime about how to be realistic rather than hopelessly idealistic in love, the chances of your finding that genuine happy-ever-after are a lot greater than you might imagine.

A SIDEWAYS LOOK AT YOUR SIGN

Some star signs I look forward to writing about, while others are more difficult. But there's just one that I dread and will do anything to avoid.

Not that there's anything wrong with Scorpios, you understand – it's just that everyone already thinks that they know all there is to be said about people born under this sign, and most of it isn't good. Explaining the truth even to a Scorpio is a major battle. I suppose I should get to the point, but I warn you – the following contains explicit reference to matters of a sexual nature. If you find such frankness offensive, please don't read on.

Scorpios are hot-blooded, sensual people with an endless appetite for physical pleasure. They cannot keep their passions under control and are for ever surging with primal lust which must be fulfilled, no matter what the cost. They're jealous, mean, broody characters who never trust anyone. Woe betide you if you ever poke fun at a Scorpio. They'll bear the grudge with deep malice, plotting revenge and scheming your downfall. Most mass murderers are Scorpios. So are most child beaters, torturers, prostitutes, drug dealers… and estate agents!

Aha! Just checking that you were awake. That was a powerful paragraph. But just how far through did you get before you realised I was joking? If you did believe that summary of the many slanderous lies which are frequently told about those who were born under this noble sign, don't feel too bad. Millions of people all over the world believe it – including a large number of Scorpios themselves.

This probably explains the other great myth about Scorpios – the idea that they are 'secretive'. Many Scorpios feel so ashamed of their sign that they refuse to confess their date of birth in public. It's not surprising, but it's sad, because Scorpios truly have a lot to be proud of. There is, you see, a very big difference between a zodiac sign and a person born under that zodiac sign.

Scorpio (the sign) actually does represent sex, penetration, reproduction, the elimination of bodily waste, death by unnatural causes and pretty much everything that's unmentionable in polite society. Scorpio (the person), however, does not – just as Aries rules pimples but not all Arians are spotty, and Pisces rules the feet but that doesn't give them more than ten toes!

So what's the difference between 'the sign' and 'the person'? Well, what's the difference between Britain the country and Britons the people? While you're chewing that one over, let me ask you two more questions.

First, have you ever seen a full horoscope based on someone's date of birth – the year, time and place? If so, you'll know that all twelve signs of the zodiac are in everybody's chart. Astrology works on the principle that, no matter what sign we are, we all have the potential to display Leonine pride, Cancerian compassion, Geminian wit and so on. Secondly, why were you so excited when you read that little warning earlier on? Go on, admit it! You thought you were going to read something spicy, racy and rude, and you could hardly wait! Well, that's because, no matter what sign you are, that warning struck a chord with the Scorpio side of your nature.

So what is that Scorpio factor? Is it really a lust for titillation? No! Think harder about what the warning implied. It did not mention perversion or even passion. All it contained, in fact, was a promise of honesty. If you found it exciting, it was only because it suggested I might tell you some raw truths about life. And these, in our polite society, are fascinatingly rare.

SAGITTARIUS

23 NOVEMBER – 21 DECEMBER

The Sagittarian quest is for spiritual enlightenment. In all their travels, adventures, escapades and fascinations, Sagittarians are seeking only one thing – the elusive bridge of wisdom which links the world of the finite to the world of the infinite. Though many choose to wear the jester's cap, it rests on the head of the zodiac's deepest philosopher.

If you're free and easy, a Sagittarian is your ideal companion. They're game for anything, full of wild ideas and normally bold as brass. If you're cautious, though, you can rely on a Sagittarian to unnerve you! Sagittarians are as deep and sensitive below the surface as they're happy-go-lucky above it. They hate convention and prefer to express feelings when they really feel them. A Sagittarian, for example, may shower you with gifts one day out of the blue but totally forget your actual birthday. They won't hold it against you if you do the same. In fact they'd rather you did that than give some dull or predictable token.

Sagittarians love the spur of the moment and can feel badly trapped by a standing commitment. Their enthusiasm lasts only while there's challenge or novelty. This doesn't make them unreliable for they will always honour an obligation, but they don't really enjoy being dutiful and are at their happiest when anything can happen.

Sagittarians also have great difficulty saying the word 'no'. It's an endearing quality based on irrepressible optimism. The closest they'll normally come to a refusal is a sort of hesitant 'maybe', which might easily be mistaken for a guarded 'yes'. If you can learn to read the signs and tell which is which, your life will be easier and their relationship with you will be much happier.

HOME

SAGITTARIANS WILL HAPPILY LIVE IN THE STRANGEST PLACES OR FAILING THIS THEY WILL TRY HARD TO MAKE AN ORDINARY HOME AS ODD AS POSSIBLE.

Your home may not be sumptuous but it is always welcoming – or it would be if only your visitors could ever find a chair to sit on. These, and the tables, tend to be piled high with items you've been meaning to get around to putting away. Fortunately, your friends make allowances for your lack of domesticity. They know you thrive on adventure and would rather spend your cash on plane tickets than roof repairs. They might, however, appreciate it if you could, one day, invest just a little money in a sweeping brush or a hoover that actually worked!

A Sagittarian's ideal house number is probably 2001, because they never have enough space and they are always longing for an odyssey!

CLOTHES

SAGITTARIANS ARE NOTORIOUS FOR WEARING ANYTHING THEY FIND TO HAND, BUT IF THERE'S AN OCCASION WORTH DRESSING UP FOR THEY CAN OUTSHINE EVERYONE!

You're as likely to find a vegetarian at an abattoir as a Sagittarian at a fashion show. You're hopelessly out of touch with current trends and totally unapologetic about it. This might be fine if you were a timelessly tasteful dresser. But are you? Not a bit of it. Not only do you spurn modernity, you snub tradition. You think you have a perfect right to wear denim with tweed, army boots with silks, bright red tops with vivid green skirts and so on. Worse still, you have the downright temerity to look good in these bizarre combinations – most of the time, at least.

CARS

You ought to drive a Pony, a Mustang or a Cavalier. Why? Because yours is the sign of the centaur – half human, half horse. You don't so much buckle into the driving seat as strap yourself into the saddle, and when you set off you want plenty of horsepower. Wealthy Sagittarians express this preference, along with a tendency towards incorrigible optimism, by choosing cars capable of speeds which could get a 747 airborne. Poorer ones just wistfully wonder whether they could get a V8 engine by pouring Campbell's vegetable juice into the tank! For these, and other reasons too numerous and embarrassing to mention, Sagittarian-driven cars tend to end up at the breaker's yard earlier than most.

FOOD

SAGITTARIANS ARE ALWAYS HUNGRY. LUCKILY THEY BURN UP LOTS OF CALORIES WITH THEIR NERVOUS ENERGY. THEY ALSO TEND TO EAT THEIR FOOD VERY QUICKLY.

How tempted are you by leek and asparagus soup followed by chickpeas in spicy tomato sauce, on a bed of wild rice with a side dish of roast parsnip? And, for dessert, apricot and almond tart spiced with cinnamon and cloves. Each of the above ingredients is governed by Jupiter, ruler of your sign, so if you're a typical Sagittarian you don't just fancy that menu, you're already halfway into the kitchen to cook it. If cooking is not a thing you do much of, you're either not a typical Sagittarian or you're a frustrated one. Yours is potentially the sign of the brilliant chef and the great entertainer.

MONEY

'IF YOU CAN ACTUALLY COUNT YOUR MONEY THEN YOU ARE NOT A REALLY RICH MAN.'

Thus spake Sagittarian millionaire John Paul Getty earlier this century. Though he used the word 'man' I'm sure he meant 'person', and I hope this little linguistic lapse won't stop Sagittarian females from identifying with the spirit of his statement. For those born under the sign of the centaur, there really is no such thing as 'enough'. Your motto might as well be: 'If a thing's worth doing, it's worth doing to wild excess and then a few times more for good measure.'

It's not that you're greedy – just that you're endowed with a hearty appetite. It's not that you're unaware of the need for financial restraint – just that you're helplessly extravagant. It's not even, come to think of it, that you're ambitious in the traditional sense. It's just that you have an insatiable curiosity to see how far you can push your luck. As a Sagittarian you tend, sadly, to spend with all the prudence of a drunken lottery winner – even when your financial picture ought to be giving rise to far more sobering thoughts.

Occasionally you will nobly attempt to discipline yourself in one area, only to spoil matters soon afterwards by blowing wildly all you have saved elsewhere. This is one reason why your bank balance keeps going up and down like a yo-yo. Another is your propensity to eschew steady sources of income in favour of speculative ventures and dubious get-rich-quick schemes. Happily, your ruling planet, Jupiter, has an avuncular disposition and usually steps in to instil common sense when your own proves sorely lacking.

JUST THE JOB?

Air hostess/steward, announcer, barrister, broadcaster, clergyman, court officer, engineer, explorer, film director, foreign correspondent, humorist, importer, inventor, jockey, judge, philanthropist, philosopher, preacher, publicist, safari leader, sportsman/woman, travel agent, tour guide, university professor, writer.

Five ways to cash in

- Forget about get-rich-quick schemes.
- In fact, forget about getting rich in general.
- Go off and do something self-sacrificing instead.
- Make sure you are given plenty of publicity in the media for your noble endeavour.
- And there you have it – the best way for you to get rich quick.

Five ways to branch out

- Learn to levitate.
- Negotiate an end to Jihad.
- Create the 'calorie-free' cream cake.
- Open an exclusive holiday camp – on the moon.
- Save the dodo.

LOVE

When Sagittarians fall in love, the fulfilment and expression of that love becomes of paramount importance. They find it impossible to play it cool. Loyalty means everything to Sagittarians. They give their whole hearts to people they trust, and expect similar dedication in return.

If you are having difficulty now, or have had trouble in the past, with making a relationship stand the test of time, it is almost certainly because you have tried too hard. As a Sagittarian, you cannot help but feel overwhelming optimism about everything you ever attempt or dream of. You either don't care at all, or you care so passionately that it drives you barmy. And when, as so often, you do care deeply, you find it impossible to turn your emotions on and off like the proverbial tap. All this makes you incorrigible and irrepressible; potentially very successful at getting what you want, but sadly, just occasionally, a mite difficult to live with.

People who are prone to a little more self-doubt, emotional insecurity or just general pessimism find your faith inspiring but overwhelming. It has even been known for them to need a break from your Sagittarian smile simply to find out how to manifest one of their own. The trouble here is that you find it hard to let them go. Swinging in classic centaurian fashion from one extreme to the other, you change from having every confidence in the fact that your relationship can eventually be made to work to having none whatsoever.

Making a partnership last a lifetime is thus, for every Sagittarian, ultimately a matter of learning how to make due allowance for the slower speed at which their companion probably needs to operate… or for the greater depth in which they feel they need to analyse their feelings. And it may also involve learning how to stand back a little when the occasion demands it, without actually going so far as to storm out of the door in a huff!

A SIDEWAYS LOOK AT YOUR SIGN

Before I begin to tell you about the sign of Sagittarius I must confess a complete lack of objectivity. While it's the sign I know most about, it's also the sign that puzzles me more than any other. And the reason I must be so courageously, self-defeatingly honest is that I am as much a fearlessly frank Sagittarian as you are!

We Saggies, you see, simply can't resist being up-front, outspoken and a little outrageous. And while that has a lot to do with what being a Sagittarian is all about, it often leads us into hot water. We end up getting accused of being tactless, effusive and offensive. We just don't know where to draw the line – or rather we do, but sometimes we just don't care!

Fortunately, despite our many alleged faults and character defects, most people seem to agree that we are wonderfully enthusiastic. They sometimes think that we can be unbearably optimistic, intolerably hopeful and nauseatingly bright and breezy, but at least they concede that our zest for life rarely fails us and we're never down for very long.

When I was a kid, I used to have a blow-up Yogi Bear with a weight at the bottom. It was as big as I was and, no matter how hard you hit it, it would just wobble a bit and then bounce right back to an upright position, ready for more punishment. That, in a nutshell, is the Sagittarian spirit – and it's probably also true that, at a physical level, most Sagittarians have similarly extraordinary recuperative powers.

Contrary to popular belief, however, Sagittarians don't all like sport and horse riding. What most of them do like is challenge. If you want to get a Sagittarian to do something, tell them it's impossible or, better still, dare them to do it! We Sagittarians like the thrill of pitting our wits (and bodies) against adverse conditions and emerging triumphantly. If we really think we can't do it, we won't try. But by and large the only things that frighten us are rules, regulations, bureaucracies, routines and people who believe that the point of living is to keep your head down, act normal and do what the world expects.

Having said all this, though, I mustn't leave you with the impression that Sagittarians are one-dimensional beings who have a good sense of humour and a love of travel and adventure but not much else. I would *like* to leave you with that impression, of course, because it's the picture I want the world to have of me and the image that I suspect you, too, would probably prefer to project. But the reason why we try so hard to come across as unflappable and light-hearted is that inside we are sensitive and thoughtful. We care so much about our fellow humans that it sometimes hurts. We feel deeply, we empathise strongly and we want to do our best for others. But it can't always be done. Occasionally, pain is a necessary part of human growth. That's the fact that we find hardest to face, and when times are tough or we and those we care for are suffering, it's only our unshakeable faith in a happier future that keeps us going despite the problems. We are optimistic and positive because we feel we have to be. We see it as our duty to be court jesters, and the worse the world gets, the broader our painted smiles will be.

We Sagittarians somehow instinctively know that faith creates hope, hope creates inspiration and inspiration creates magic. And when we apply these principles, they work.

CAPRICORN

22 DECEMBER – 20 JANUARY

CAPRICORNS ARE THE KEEPERS OF THE COSMIC CLOCK. THE CAPRICORN QUEST IS TO TREASURE THE HISTORY AND MEASURE THE MYSTERY OF THE PASSING HOURS. A CAPRICORN, HOWEVER, DOESN'T SO MUCH SEEK TO TAKE TIME AS TO GIVE IT. TO CREATE OPPORTUNITY FOR OTHERS BY HELPING THEM MAKE MORE OF LIFE'S MOST PRECIOUS YET LIMITED RESOURCE IS EVERY CAPRICORN'S NOBLE WISH.

If you need to get something done, contact a Capricorn. These down-to-earth people tackle every task one step at a time and rarely let anything or anyone intimidate them. Even when they're under extreme pressure, you'll rarely see a Capricorn crumble. On the surface, at least, they're steady and stable, inspiring others to entrust them with responsibility and authority. Beneath the Capricorn crust, however, is a very soft centre. Capricorns seethe with hidden hopes and intense emotions. They usually repress these, using them as a driving force to propel them towards ambition. Even so, those emotions are still potentially dangerous. Imagine someone who keeps explosives in a safe deposit box, buried in the bowels of a bank. Sooner or later, something will detonate the lot. Capricorns know this, but still hate to admit their feelings.

You must understand this if you are to be a true friend to a Capricorn. It's easy to get along with them at a superficial level because they're so full of useful information and practical ideas. They've always got something interesting to say, and they're good listeners too. But at a deeper level, there's another story to be told. Gain a Capricorn's confidence and they'll gradually share their secret, volatile fears. The very act of admission defuses them. So while your Capricorn might appreciate a handy gadget as a birthday present, what you really should give is a chance to bare their soul.

HOME

CAPRICORNS LIKE THEIR HOMES TO BE A PLACE OF SAFETY, IN EVERY SENSE OF THE WORD.

Some people's homes look like palaces, but are full of items you dare not touch or sofas which look lovely but turn out to be as hard as nails. Yours is low on gloss and glamour but high on comfort and practicality. You'd rather have double glazing than stained glass, you'd rather have one sturdy grandfather clock than a shelf full of bijou china ornaments, and you'd rather hang your clothes on the back of the chair than spend a fortune on fitted bedroom furniture that nobody's ever going to see. Your house is usually the last in the street to have the latest decor, but it's always the first place people head for when they want to relax.

Your ideal house number is 40, to remind you of when life begins for a Capricorn!

CLOTHES

CAPRICORNS DRESS AS THEY SPEAK. THEY LIKE FUNCTIONAL, PRACTICAL CLOTHES AND HAVE LITTLE INTEREST IN FRILLS OR FINERY UNLESS IT'S NECESSARY FOR A ROLE THEY WANT TO PLAY.

In the mythology of the zodiac, Capricorn rules the past. Though you're quite capable of carrying off an up-to-the-minute outfit, you feel far more comfortable in something classic, timeless and universally smart. If it happens to be something your mother might once have worn, so much the better. Indeed, better still if it would have suited your grandmother or even grandfather! I'm not suggesting you ought to wander round town in a bustle or a crinoline, but you might well look splendid in culottes and hacking jackets, plus-fours and gilets and similar garb from the turn of the century onwards.

CARS

You won't thank me for saying this – and nor, come to think of it, will your bank manager. None the less, your ideal car is probably a BMW, a Mercedes, a Rolls or a Jaguar. As a Capricorn, you place a lot of importance on precision, efficiency and reliability. You're also, frankly, not immune to a little bit of status-seeking. If you're not already the proud owner of one of the above, it's probably because you feel you can't afford to be. Next time you change cars, however, you might consider an upmarket OAP in preference to a younger model of less repute.

Such vehicles, like Capricorns themselves, tend to mature beautifully if well maintained. They also drive, just as you do, comfortably, satisfyingly… and safely.

FOOD

CAPRICORNS TEND TO PREFER PLAIN, WHOLESOME HOME COOKING. THEY HAVE COSMOPOLITAN TASTES BUT ARE UNIMPRESSED BY FANCY CUISINE OR EXPENSIVELY PRESENTED FOOD.

Some might call you unadventurous when it comes to your eating habits. You prefer to see yourself as unpretentious. Wholesome, simple 'foods of the earth' are the typically preferred fare of a Capricorn. Let the food faddists keep their complicated cuisines – you'll settle for plain, basic, good old bangers and mash, bacon and eggs, lentil and barley soup, buttered turnips and boiled beetroot. Prunes and custard to follow? Why not! Your attitude towards food – as towards so much in life – boils down to: if you've got a successful formula, why change it?

MONEY

'IT IS IN EXCHANGING THE GIFTS OF THE EARTH THAT YOU SHALL FIND ABUNDANCE AND BE SATISFIED. YET, UNLESS THE EXCHANGE BE IN LOVE AND KINDLY JUSTICE IT WILL LEAD BUT SOME TO GREED AND OTHERS TO HUNGER.'

If you have just skimmed over the quote above in a hurry to get to the 'meat' of your analysis, please read it again. It is the meat. The words were written by a Capricorn, the poet Kahlil Gibran. They come from his beautiful book *The Prophet* and sum up all there is to say about your relationship with money. Forget all thought of get-rich-quick schemes or your opportunities to make a fast buck in an ethically debatable venture. All you ever need in order to keep the wolf from the door is to start doing more of what you're best at, what you know makes sense – and what you know is fundamentally fair and wholesome.

As a Capricorn you are capable of turning your hand to many things. You are efficient, incisive, organised and diligent. You are also capable of manifesting great authority. Other people sit up and take notice when you make an emphatic statement. Really, though, you need apply none of the above qualities to your financial enterprises. If you do, you will almost certainly end up in a situation where you may have wealth but you have little by way of satisfaction to show for it. The great secret of success, in the true sense of that word, for every Capricorn is to apply dedication to a project or plan that truly means the world to you. When you're engaged in such an honourable undertaking, money finds its way to you like a salmon finds its way home through the ocean.

JUST THE JOB?

Architect, builder, businessperson, chiropractor, clock-maker, economist, excavator, furniture restorer, gardener, government official, leather worker, manicurist, mining engineer, osteopath, plasterer, prison officer, property developer, restoration worker, sculptor, transport controller, vocational counsellor.

Five ways to cash in

- Next time someone makes you a promise, be certain to get it confirmed in writing.
- Stick to what you're good at and let the rest look after itself.
- Stop worrying about everything going wrong. It might never happen.
- Charge more, apologise less.
- Eat at cheaper restaurants and bring your own wine.

Five ways to branch out

- Go to work for a government department and get it to run efficiently.
- Convert your car to run on solar power and used teabags.
- Star in a steamy XXX-rated movie (but don't tell your friends).
- Get the last word in a conversation with Ruby Wax.
- Write how-to-do-it manuals.

LOVE

Capricorns have no time for the flowery trappings of romance. But if they really care for you, they'll show it in a genuine, endearing way. If you're not convinced that Capricorns are more sensually responsive and better able to give pleasure than any other sign, take a straw poll amongst your friends!

For you, as a Capricorn, the question is not so much how can you make your love last forever as how can you make your feelings for another person come to life in the first place? Unless you're highly atypical of your sign or are in the company of someone who has a tremendously natural, almost chemical, rapport with you, you tend to hold back a great deal of your heart – and even your head. You can play the game of love as well as, if not better than, anyone. You can say all the right words, make all the right gestures, do all the right things. But can you really feel sure that you are doing more than going through the motions? More relevantly, can your partner?

You can be certain that if your partner is truly the right person for you they will have noticed, much earlier in the relationship than you might ever have imagined, just what a difficult nut to crack you can be. They may have discreetly avoided mentioning it. Or they may, perhaps, have commented, realised there was little they could do about it, and decided to make the most of whatever they could get. But they will have sensed your reticence and they will (naturally enough) have put up barriers of their own in order to protect themselves. These barriers are probably the only things that stand between you and your partner making it through from here to the day when time stands still. To dismantle them, you do not suddenly have to turn into a gushing fountain of soppiness. But you do have to acknowledge their existence, communicate your concern about them, and consciously work on ways to ensure that your relationship is based on more than just a routine, a lifestyle, a habit… and a fear of change!

A SIDEWAYS LOOK AT YOUR SIGN

When Capricorns aren't busy calling a spade a spade, the chances are they're using that spade to dig deep and prepare strong foundations for whatever project they happen to be involved in. They don't waste time waiting for things to be perfect before rolling up their sleeves and getting to work. They cope with whatever happens to be in front of them, compensating for what's missing, adapting to what's needed and inventing new ways to use what they've actually got.

Unlike some 'bodgers' in the zodiac, Capricorn 'bodgers' normally hold up quite well. If they're putting up a shelf with the wrong-size screws, they'll pop in a couple of extra ones at strategic points of weakness in the wall. If they're advertising an event with a limited budget, they'll pick their words carefully to ensure that those who see the publicity feel obliged to attend – and bring their friends! Capricorns are masters or mistresses of the 'authority game'. Even when they're shaking with terror, anxiety or despair on the inside, you wouldn't know it to look at them. They have magnificent composure and incredible self-restraint.

So far I've been describing an asset, a characteristic that explains why so many Capricorns rise to positions of great responsibility and power. People sense that they're trustworthy, so they delegate authority to them. This is fine – apart from one thing. Capricorns are actually sensitive human beings who suffer from base emotions like fear, jealousy or insecurity just as much as the rest of us. So sometimes, just sometimes, the things they do or say are unwise, unfair or unjust. This is an accusation that could be accurately levelled at anyone of any sign, but the trouble with Capricorns is that everything they say comes out sounding sensible and reasonable, even when it's complete and utter rubbish.

This wouldn't be quite so bad if all it meant was that Capricorns occasionally abuse their position of respect by misleading other people; you could say it's not their fault – it's up to others to see through the façade. However, Capricorns are inscrutable not only to others but also to themselves. They have great difficulty separating what they really feel from what they think they ought to be feeling. They try hard always to do the right thing no matter what the circumstances, and they judge themselves harshly when they discover they've been wrong. Despite the fact that Capricorns are rarely wrong, when they do make an error they make it in style. They make it with their heart and soul – convinced, at the time of making it, that it can't possibly be an error at all. They find it almost impossible to forgive themselves for their mistakes and, even worse, they have elephantine memories.

Many people find it easy to treat the past as a mysterious world which belongs to someone else; Capricorns are the zodiac's natural historians. To a Capricorn, yesterday is the unalterable foundation upon which every tomorrow is built. They take the past and themselves very, very seriously. A Capricorn who loses self-confidence finds it very hard to regain it – which is why some people born under the sign fail to reach their deserved position in the order of things. What's more, a disillusioned Capricorn can soon become convinced that he or she 'deserves to suffer'. When that happens, as it often does, they can spend large chunks of their lives turning down opportunities. Fortunately this doesn't last forever. Eventually, their confidence comes back and the essential qualities of strength, stamina and leadership re-emerge.

AQUARIUS

21 JANUARY – 19 FEBRUARY

AQUARIUS MAY BE THE SIGN OF THE WATER-BEARER, BUT AQUARIUS IS NO WATER SIGN. AQUARIUS BELONGS TO AIR AND THUS TO THOUGHT, PHILOSOPHY AND INTELLECT. AQUARIANS HAVE PLENTY OF SENSITIVITY AND PASSION BUT BELIEVE EMOTION SHOULD BE THE SERVANT, NOT THE MASTER, OF THE HEART. AQUARIANS THUS SEEK TO HELP US ALL TREASURE AND CHERISH THE GIFT OF OBJECTIVITY.

If you need expert advice, ask an Aquarian. No matter what the subject, you can be sure your Aquarian friend will venture a definitive answer. Nine times out of ten, that answer will be informed and accurate – it's the tenth time you must watch for! Then, though the comments may be delivered with equal confidence, they'll be perilously wrong. How can you tell? You can't. Aquarians don't consider themselves capable of error, so they give no clues. Only if you try to follow the advice will you find it fallible. If you then go back and confront your Aquarian with the evidence, you may get a humble apology but you're more likely to get a pompous excuse. So, if you are to get along well with them, you need to have a good sense of humour and a slightly sceptical nature. Aquarians are what they are. They can't be changed, so you must learn to love them for it. It's worth doing, because Aquarian assets far outnumber Aquarian defects.

Aloof, know-it-all and self-important they may be, but they are also generous, considerate and extraordinary. There's nothing dull or predictable about an Aquarian. They're far-sighted idealists, humanitarian philosophers and open-minded thinkers. Once you've got used to their odd ways, you'll find their friendship irresistible and their company addictive.

If you want to give an Aquarian a special treat, remember that they're attracted to unusual ideas, eccentric people and innovative objects. Show them you recognise their special powers of discrimination. They'll love you for it.

HOME

AQUARIANS FEEL MOST COMFORTABLE IN A HOME WITH A NICE GARDEN.

Aquarians are quirky, quarrelsome and querulous. You hate queues, detest crowds and love to assert your individuality. You wouldn't want to live anywhere run-of-the-mill – unless, of course, it was an old, abandoned watermill! That, or a converted railway carriage, would suit you fine. Even if circumstances (financial or otherwise) don't allow this, your home still tends to be a museum of self-expression. It's certainly a tribute to the art of experimentation, for there is something that almost (but doesn't quite) work in every room!

Your ideal house number is probably 999 (for the state of emergency they so often live in!).

CLOTHES

THE POLITEST WORDS TO DESCRIBE THE AQUARIAN COLOUR SENSE WOULD BE 'CREATIVELY INDIVIDUALISTIC'.

Although you can be outrageous in many ways, you're surprisingly conventional when it comes to clothes. I would even go so far as to say 'restrained', but then, financially at least, that's not quite so true. You have expensive taste and a keen eye for quality. You would far rather own a few excellently made suits than an entire wardrobe of cut-price clothes. On high days and holidays, you'll parade with panache in fashionable, even futuristic outfits – but for everyday wear you prefer to find one basic formula and stick to it. For many Aquarians, this will involve knitwear. You're fond of natural materials like cotton and leather, but have a special preference for wool.

CARS

The following dialogue sums up the Aquarian approach to motoring.

Judge: 'You are accused of going the wrong way up a one-way street. What do you say?'

Aquarian: 'I was only going one way.'

Judge: 'But didn't you see the arrows?'

Aquarian: 'Arrows? I didn't even see the Indians!'

Your copy of the highway code contains little footnotes which the printers carelessly omitted to place in the other copies. For example; 'Never enter a box junction unless your exit is clear'* (*unless you feel like it), or

'Don't overtake on the inside'* (*unless you're in a hurry). Only one thing is more idiosyncratic than your driving – your choice of car. It *must* be a make that nobody else has heard of and a model that no garage can get parts for because (a) you're fussy and (b) more than anything, you love to be exclusive!

FOOD

AQUARIANS LOVE TO EXPERIMENT WITH NEW RECIPES AND DISHES. HOW THESE ACTUALLY TASTE IS OF SECONDARY IMPORTANCE TO THEIR POTENTIAL VALUE AS A TALKING POINT.

If you're a truly typical Aquarian, you adore eating out: Indian one night, Chinese the next, Italian the night after – and French the night after that. The more obscure and eclectic the cuisine the better – for, arguably, you enjoy the discovery of new tastes and textures more than the actual process of eating. Unlike some people, you rarely eat for succour and emotional comfort. Indeed, being terribly fussy, you'd almost rather deliberately go hungry than settle down to eat a tediously boring meal.

MONEY

'MONEY IS LIKE A SIXTH SENSE WITHOUT WHICH YOU CANNOT MAKE A COMPLETE USE OF THE OTHER FIVE.'

The writer Somerset Maugham, who made the memorable remark above, was an Aquarian, and to me his statement reveals a lot about a very specific Aquarian tendency. Few and far between are the people born under your sign who pursue money for its own sake. As an

Aquarian you may be shrewd, you may be successful and you may even have expensive tastes, but you are not, unless I am very much mistaken, avaricious. To you, money is indeed a sixth sense. Just as you do not actively seek to develop your intuition, you simply expect it to be there when you need to call on it, so you tend to take financial gain for granted. It comes naturally when you're doing the right thing – just as an inspired idea or a smart hunch might do. Your instincts, of course, are pretty good, and so are your potential money-making abilities. Both, however, work best when you're not really trying – in other words when they come to the fore as a side-effect of trying to accomplish another goal altogether.

You must beware, however, of a tendency to let your generosity and compassion get the better of you. These laudable qualities can sometimes place an enormous burden on your resources. Should this prove to be an ongoing problem, change the nature of your charitable activities. See them not as a sideline but as integral to your overall gameplan. Explore the possibility of doing professionally an aspect of what you are already doing voluntarily. You'll find an opportunity opens up almost as soon as you're in a frame of mind to see it. You'll also find the general economic trend becomes extremely positive.

JUST THE JOB?

Actor, art dealer, aviator, broadcaster, civil rights campaigner, computer consultant, cooperative organiser, counsellor, electrician, faith healer, furniture designer, inventor, laser technician, lighting specialist, mechanic, navigator, MP, psychotherapist, recording studio engineer, social worker, telecommunications worker.

Five ways to cash in

- Stop trying to 'do it yourself' to save cash. You will only end up having less time on your hands to do the things that matter.
- Swallow your pride and accept other people's suggestions.
- Make friends with a wealthy person who likes helping you.
- Stop trying so hard to keep up with the Joneses.
- Don't throw good money after bad.

Five ways to branch out

- Invent a 'better mousetrap'.
- Teach your skills to others.
- Open a charm school.
- Become a movie critic.
- Become a top-level, high-ranking government adviser.

LOVE

Aquarians can be charming and seductive when romance first blossoms. They know how to use any trick in the book to capture your heart. Aquarians are traditionally reputed to be aloof, detached and unemotional. If only it were true!

Although Aquarians tend to be supremely confident about what they know, what they believe and what they want to accomplish, many people born under your sign find this natural sense of certainty tends to desert them when asked to quantify what they actually feel. Because they don't like having to confess to doubt at any level, under any circumstance, they will go to great lengths to disguise their confusion. They will make either make unconvincingly emphatic statements or else deliberately appear as non-committal as possible in the hope that they can fob off requests for emotional reassurance with the excuse that they never talk about things like that.

You may notice that so far I have deliberately been depersonalising my suggestions about how to make your love last forever. I have given you the option of assuming that I am describing other people born under your sign, but not you. Ultimately, it's a question of 'if the cap fits'. But while you decide whether it does, may I make another potentially confrontational comment in the softest possible terms? The great psychologist Carl Jung was a firm believer in the idea that, when one person finds another irritating or difficult to be with, it's because the second person's faults remind the first person of the things they most dislike about themselves. And now we really must depart from the realm of the theoretical and impersonal. What I am trying to tell you – gently and discreetly because I know that as an Aquarian you loathe and detest the very notion of being offered advice – is this. If you want to get on better with the person you are now with, or ever find yourself with in the future, you must look at what it is about them that you cannot abide. And you must ask yourself, not how they might possibly change in time, but how you might. And that's how you'll become able to make your love last forever.

A SIDEWAYS LOOK AT YOUR SIGN

Aquarius is the eleventh sign of the zodiac, and lies opposite Leo in the celestial circle. Many people labour under the misapprehension that Aquarius is a water sign, this is largely because the symbol of Aquarius is a water bearer; an elegant male or female figure who carries an earthenware vessel. The confusion is compounded by the fact that sometimes artists illustrate Aquarius with a simple picture of water being poured from a jug. That's a shame, because central to the symbol of the sign is the figure of a human who has travelled to the fountain of eternal wisdom and is now carrying a precious burden of knowledge and understanding. It is the person, not the jug, which is the focal point of the sign. The content of the jug may be liquid, but because it represents a high lofty concept it more properly belongs to the element 'air'. Hence the reason that Aquarius (like Libra and Gemini) is an 'air' sign. People born under all these analytical, intellectual air signs tend to 'think' their way through life – and they often place more importance on big ideas than on feeling and actions. Aquarius is also a 'fixed' sign. There are four fixed signs in the zodiac – the other three are Leo, Scorpio and Taurus. Although these signs are very different, people born under them tend to be set in their ways. The 'fixed air' sign, Aquarius, therefore tends to produce people who use their intelligence at all times but who find it hard to change their minds about anything.

Astrologers believe that every object or idea can be catalogued under one zodiac sign. Here is a list of things ruled by Aquarius: altruism, ankles, aviation, batteries, blood circulation, broadcasting, clubs, colleagues, cooperatives, Cyprus, electricity, exploration, frankincense, friends, gas, hope, humanitarianism, inventions, Iran, January, kinetic energy, legislation, modernisation, motors, novelty, opals, organisations, paradoxes, parliaments, pilots, progress, radar, reform, revolution, Russia, salt, sapphires, science, shins, society, spasms, stereos, technology, television, wireless, wishful thinking, X-rays.

Aquarians hope for a chance to make themselves useful, especially to others; a world in which everyone is happy and healthy; a glamorous and exciting social life; and a place in history as the person who made a brilliant, unique and unforgettable contribution to their environment. Aquarians fear public embarrassment, private conflict, emotional blackmail, boredom, repetition, mundanity, social ostracisation, family gatherings, compromises and financial failure. Aquarians like to be one step ahead, to be different, to argue over fine points, to show people how to do things, to be given an intellectual challenge, and to be generous.

Aquarians are simple souls at heart – though most of them will never admit it. They like to give you the impression that they are complex, mysterious and confident. That's partly why they are misunderstood – and they don't really mind, because it means that the only people who get close to them are those perceptive enough to penetrate the veil.

If you want to learn how to spot an Aquarian on first meeting, look out for someone who lets slip a strong, probably controversial opinion shortly after the conversation begins. It won't be delivered in a challenging way – just in a sort of off-hand but very knowledgeable manner. If you want to disarm Aquarians, ask them to explain something to you and look interested while they go through all the endless details. If you want to annoy an Aquarian, ask how they feel. And if you want to know what all Aquarians have in common, the answer is nothing except a keen desire to be individual, which is why many Aquarians dislike astrology. They hate being lumped together with other Aquarians!

PISCES

20 FEBRUARY – 20 MARCH

PISCEANS ARE THE ZODIAC'S MAGICIANS. THEY MAY NOT PULL RABBITS FROM HATS BUT THEY NONE THE LESS PERFORM ACTS OF AMAZING TRANSFORMATION EVERY DAY. THE PISCEAN'S GREATEST GIFT IS THE ABILITY TO TURN DESPAIR INTO HOPE AND FEAR INTO FAITH. PISCEANS SPECIALISE IN HELPING US TO FIND THE HIDDEN WONDER IN THAT WHICH WE MIGHT BE TEMPTED TO DISMISS AS ORDINARY.

Pisceans don't miss much. They have a special inner radar which lets them tune into hidden messages, and somehow they always know what's really going on in people's hearts. You'll rarely find a Piscean abusing this gift, though, because Pisceans are as sensitive as they are sympathetic. It's just as well. If their ambitions were as ruthless as their instincts were keen, there'd be no stopping a Piscean, ever.

Happily, nature has made most Pisceans content to value human warmth above material gain. There are, of course, exceptions to any rule, but even the occasional avaricious Piscean is prone to the same basic handicap as his or her less competitive cousin – an over-active imagination.

Pisceans are full of visionary enthusiasm. They day-dream in Technicolor. Creativity comes as naturally to a Piscean as strength to an athlete. It's the sort of creativity which every poet, artist, musician, storyteller or inventor needs. It's inspirational energy, but, while it's wonderful to have on tap, it's hard to control. Pisceans who don't have a creative job or hobby often find themselves over-whelmed by ideas which they can't put to use or emotions which they can't understand.

The best thing you can give your Piscean friends is an outlet for this imagination. Join them in their reveries, encourage their idealism and, most important of all, help them see which of their fantasies should be followed and which should be ignored.

HOME

THERE'S A CHAMELEON-LIKE QUALITY TO PISCEANS. THEY USUALLY MANAGE TO BLEND IN WITH THEIR SURROUNDINGS NO MATTER HOW MUCH OR HOW QUICKLY THESE CHANGE.

Your Piscean home is, I'm sure, comfortable and cleverly furnished, but I'd like to bet it's also forever full of friends and neighbours in various states of severe distress. Who *are* these people who sit on your sofa, pouring their hearts out from morning till night – and then just pull out the cushions, turn it into a bed, snore loudly and wake up to start sobbing on your shoulder all over again the next day? Where do they come from? And why do you encourage them? Their perpetual presence means your house is never quiet, dull or empty, but it also means you never have time to live the domestic idyll you once intended.

You ideal house number is 1… to remind you of who you should be looking out for.

CLOTHES

PISCEANS LIKE TO WEAR CLOTHES WHICH EMPHASISE THEIR ROMANTIC OR IDEALISTIC ASPIRATIONS. THEY CAN GET AWAY WITH VERY FLAMBOYANT, PROVOCATIVE OUTFITS.

Pisces is a mysterious, exotic sign, so Pisceans ought to wear mysterious, exotic clothes. You were born to swan around in kaftans and kimonos, saris and sarongs, pelerines and ponchos. Though you don't always wear such adventurous attire, you don't fool anyone when you dress more conventionally. Your faraway eyes still look as if they're longing to be set off by clothes from faraway places, so if you want to do yourself a real favour let loose the poet in your soul. Find the courage to wear those long flowing robes and intricately patterned prints you're forever being tempted by.

CARS

For you a car is a sort of elaborate mounting for your stereo speakers. You're so bothered about your sound system that, even when you break down, you're more inclined to change the tape than the wheel. Other useful things in your car include a selection of mirrors in which to check your appearance. You suspect they have another purpose – but, off-hand, you can't quite recall what it is. Such vagueness does, however, have its advantages. Salesmen give up aghast when they ask what kind of vehicle you want, only to be told: 'A nice blue one, please.' Sadly, this makes you a liability on the road. You are, for example, supposed to indicate just prior to turning – not because you want to point out, to the motorist behind, a particularly pretty rose bush over there on the right!

FOOD

THE IDEAL PISCEAN MEAL WOULD PROBABLY TAKE THE FORM OF A BUFFET TABLE BULGING WITH MANY COLOURFUL, EXOTIC DISHES ON WHICH TO NIBBLE SLOWLY.

Pisceans are particularly fond of food that looks like it's going to taste of one thing but turns out to be entirely different. Rice that's been subtly flavoured with coconut or lemon, white sauce that's been cleverly seasoned with cumin or coriander, cheese that has been matured with beer or onions would all be Piscean favourites. It's all to do with being born under the influence of Neptune, the great celestial illusionist. You like your meals to be masterpieces and, to accompany them, you like wines full of character, wit and subtlety. Your Piscean palate is tremendously sensitive and you simply love having it stimulated.

MONEY

'THE HARDEST THING IN THE WORLD TO UNDERSTAND IS THE INCOME TAX.'

This quote comes from Albert Einstein, who was not just a genius but a Piscean genius. I have chosen it to begin your forecast partly because it's amusing to think of the person who gave the world $E = mc^2$ having trouble working out his tax return, and partly because I haven't been able to find an eminent Piscean economist to quote. I'm not too surprised, mind you. Yours is a creative sign. Creative people don't always do well in areas where people are expected to be dry, logical and matter of fact. Einstein managed to get away with being a creative scientist, but even he couldn't bring himself to wrap his brilliant mind around such a dull matter as money. Creative people rarely can. When they do, it gets them into trouble. Creative economists are mistrusted, creative accountants frowned on and creative financiers very often put into prison!

If you work in any of these fields, please don't take offence. I'm sure you're very good at following the rules all day as long as you get to do something more inspiring by night. Even so, I maintain that if, as a Piscean, you really wish to *make* money, your best bet is to do something… well, creative! Long ago you had a keen interest in a subject that circumstances eventually obliged you to move away from. Rediscover your old hobby, area of interest or big idea. With a few modifications it can become an important, profitable part of your future. You'll find yourself saying something like 'I never realised what a goldmine I was sitting on', or 'Who would have thought that my interest in X would eventually lead to Y?' It should all result in a great deal of pleasure and satisfaction.

JUST THE JOB?

Anaesthetist, artist, bartender, cartoonist, charity worker, chemist, clairvoyant, cobbler, dancer, distiller, drug rehabilitation worker, escapologist, film director, fisherman, hydraulics engineer, impressionist, oceanographer, petrochemical worker, photographer, plumber, poet, private eye, sailor, spy.

Five ways to cash in

- Write your life story (in the third person, with the names changed) as a best-selling romantic novel.
- Cut back a little on that naughty and expensive habit.
- Sell some of the shoes you no longer wear.
- Pay as much attention to your bank manager as you normally do to your conscience.
- Become a chiropodist… or a reflexologist.

Five ways to branch out

- Build your own multi-national corporation from scratch.
- Write beautiful, heart-warming poetry.
- Breed exotic tropical fish in your own aquarium.
- Take underwater photographs around gloriously exotic coral reefs.
- Become a dream therapist.

LOVE

When a Piscean falls in love, the whole world turns rosy. Piscean fantasies can make a romantic novel look like a textbook on economics! In long-term relationships, boredom is rarely a problem for Pisceans. They can somehow make every day with their loved one seem new and exciting.

No Piscean is capable of giving their love exclusively and continuously to one person for their whole life. This doesn't mean you cannot successfully maintain a joyous, monogamous relationship from now until the day you die or even (bearing in mind that you are a mystical Piscean) beyond. But is does mean that you have to recognise the limits of what any partnership, no matter how well starred, can be expected to bring to you.

Because you're imaginative, idealistic and, to a degree at least, susceptible to the mythology with which we were all brought up, you cannot help but half believe in the notion that two people can, if they try hard enough, become as one. It's a lovely idea, with a particular attraction to the poetic Piscean personality. But it's not necessarily quite so simple in reality.

Very often the most successful partnerships are those in which both participants have wide-ranging and very separate interests and commitments outside the relationship. To work successfully as a couple, they do not have to agree on every issue or area of interest. They do not even, indeed, have to tell each other every last detail of what they have been up to in their time apart. They do have to be honest and they do have to have a bond of trust, but they also have to have enough commitment to and faith in one another not to feel obliged to weave a web of pretence. They do not have to (and should not try to) feign fascination in each others' hobbies or even jobs. Nor should they feel their relationship is only valid or worthwhile if they never argue, disagree or differ.

Almost certainly you already know all this, in which case you are presumably well on the way to making your love last forever. But if it's lately begun to look as if this is something that can or will never happen, maybe it's time to look again at ways to separate, in your mind, the theoretical ideal from the pragmatic reality.

A SIDEWAYS LOOK AT YOUR SIGN

Pisceans are not just good fun to be with – it's never long before their amusing idiosyncrasies bubble to the surface. They're deeply sensitive and make loyal companions. Pisces is the twelfth sign of the zodiac, lying opposite Virgo in the celestial circle.

Pisces is a 'water sign', like Cancer and Scorpio. People born under the water signs tend to rely on their emotions rather than their intellects. They can be very brainy or academic, but deep down inside they trust their feelings more than they trust their thoughts. Pisces is also a 'mutable sign', like Sagittarius, Gemini and Virgo. People born under the water signs tend to be easy-going, flexible and adaptable; they can also be lackadaisical or prone to change horses in midstream. The 'mutable water sign' Pisces produces people who are exceedingly sensitive and open to new ideas, and also people who could benefit from more discipline in their lives.

Pisces is symbolised by a pair of fish swimming away from each other. The idea is that one fish represents the world of material things and the other fish the 'world of the inner spirit'. Pisceans supposedly don't belong to either world, but have one foot (or fish) in each camp. But there's something else in the symbol – water – which represents life itself. Pisceans are born not to struggle with themselves but to help others. Their message is that we must all learn to appreciate both worlds in order to be truly happy.

Pisceans don't just have strong instincts – they have

accurate, long-range radar systems. Because they can rely on their sixth sense to guide them through life, they often act as if they don't know where they're going or what they're doing. Somehow, though, they always end up in the right place at just the right time. In fact, the endearing innocence which Pisceans project is a smoke-screen, which is another reason why people born under this sign are so often successful. They disarm would-be adversaries by appearing to be lucky bumblers.

Because Pisceans are sensitive, sympathetic and sweet-natured, they can sometimes be gullible. They are prone to pangs of guilt, and suckers for a sob story. A Piscean will always let you cry on his or her shoulder and will soak up your sorrow like a sponge. Then they'll walk around, carrying your burden and trying to solve your problems as well as their own. While this is a drawback to being a Piscean, it's also a part of a big advantage. The natural sixth sense protects them from harm, even when they make themselves dangerously responsible for the wrong people. It ensures that, even when they set out to help others, they end up coincidentally helping themselves.

Pisceans fear aggression, conflict, anger, confrontation, criticism, rejection, boredom, limitation, authority, competition, mundanity and being taken advantage of. They like to help other people, be thought of as wise, tell long stories, experiment with new ideas, wear fancy dress, be near the ocean, play at fortune telling, be mysterious and get carried away.

These are just some of the things which are traditionally ruled by Pisces: abstracts, alcohol, ambidexterity, anaesthetics, aquariums, artists, bogs, boots, chaos, charity, cheats, chemistry, chiropody, cisterns, clairvoyance, clouds, confinement, conspiracy, dance, disappointment, dissolution, escape, February, fog, gas, hermits, hospitals, institutions (of all kinds), intoxication, jellyfish, lilies (water), liquids, mediums, navies, nuns, oceans, opium, photography, poetry, poison, retirement, sand, secrets, ships, sleep, suffering, time (power over), unconscious thought, wells, X-rays.

Chapter 2

THE MAGIC OF YOUR MOON SIGN

THE MAGIC OF YOUR MOON SIGN

Have you ever read about your zodiac sign but felt that, while you could identify with some of it, this wasn't enough to explain everything about you? Have you, perhaps, even felt a little insulted to hear an astrologer suggest that you share your personality with one-twelfth of the population? We're now going to look, not at what you have in common with those who share your sign but at what makes you different.

THE REAL YOU

At the moment, all you really know about yourself in astrological terms is what Sun sign you were born under. Your Sun sign is the zodiac sign you turn to every day when you read your forecast in my daily column. It's the sign you share with everyone else who happens to have been born within the same thirty-day period of any year.

You can, if you like, consider your Sun sign to be the nationality under which you were born. Just as American people tend to expect instant service where British people are more conditioned to expect a delay, so Aries and Virgo people tend, on the whole, to have contrasting ideas about what life ought to be offering them. You share, with everyone else born under your sign, certain influences which have shaped your outlook on life. They have given you an accent, an attitude or a set of mannerisms. But you are more than your Sun sign, just as you are more than a product of your birthplace.

Between the 'sunny' façade you put up for the benefit of others and the vulnerable, sincere individual you are in private, there's a gap as big as the difference between night and day. This is where your Moon sign comes in. If the Sun depicts the way you tend to be on the surface, the Moon describes what you are like deep down within. It tells you how you cope with problems, what you cling to for hope, plus when or why your moods are likely to alter. Your Moon sign, in other words, describes the kind of person you really are.

You may be wondering why nobody has ever told you about this before. To do the answer justice, I need to give you a brief history of popular astrology.

A SHORT HISTORY OF ASTROLOGY

Back in the distant past, if you'd asked an astrologer what sign you were, he or she would have told you your Moon sign, not your Sun sign. The Roman Emperor Augustus, for example, had the sign of Capricorn the goat embossed on the reverse of his coinage. But according to our modern way of looking at things, Augustus was actually a Libran born on 23 September 63BC. It just so happens, however, that on the day he was born the Moon was in Capricorn. That was the part of his horoscope which he considered significant enough to show off.

Throughout the next two thousand years or so, nothing much changed. The great and the good all had an astrologer present at their birth. The rest of the population, meanwhile, were lucky if they even knew what year they were born in, let alone what month. When or if they consulted an astrologer, it would be to get a straight answer to a question like 'Who stole my sheep?' or 'Will my son's ship return safely from foreign shores?' Astrologers would often answer these questions with surprising accuracy, but they would not consider the enquirer's date of birth. They simply got their answer from a chart of the sky as it stood at the precise moment of consultation.

This cosmic status quo prevailed throughout British astrology's long, proud history. From the Emperor Hadrian, who cast horoscopes in between building walls, to King Henry VIII, who cast horoscopes in between divorcing wives, to Queen Elizabeth I who had horoscopes cast for her by the court 'mathematician' John Dee, the division remained simple. If you were 'important' you got a full, personal, 'time of birth' horoscope. If you were not so well off, you got a form of cosmic 'rune reading'.

All this changed on 1 July 1837, when the Registration Act came into force and everyone was obliged by law to have a record of their exact date of entry into the world. No longer were personal horoscopes exclusively reserved for the priviliged few. The practice of astrology began to alter almost immediately, but still the Moon sign was seen as the most important factor within a chart.

That situation didn't change until 1930, when the *Sunday Express* began to print the first regular weekly column by a professional astrologer. R. H. Naylor's articles were rather dry to begin with, but he did once imply that the heavens were making air travel inauspicious. When the R101 airship crashed horrifically a few days later, Naylor's reputation was made. And history was made when, one week, Naylor wrote a little piece called 'What the Stars Foretell' for people born at various times of the year. This was an instant hit which had the public clamouring for more. So loudly did they clamour that the face of popular astrology was changed for good. I imagine the conversation between Naylor and Lord Beaverbrook, the proprietor of the *Express*, might have run something like this:

'Can you do more of this sort of thing, please?'

'Yes, indeed. We can work with people's Moon signs. You'll need to publish a few pages of look-up tables so people can see what Moon sign they were born under. And then I can predict what sort of week they are going to have.'

'I can't spare that sort of space. Do you think paper grows on trees? Can't we do anything that requires less to look up?'

'Er . . . [*reluctantly*] well, I suppose you could use Sun signs.'

'Oh, yes? What are they?'

'Well, they're less specific indicators of personality and future, but they do have one distinct advantage. They're based on the movement of the Sun, which follows almost exactly the same pattern from year to year.'

'So?'

'So instead of printing thousands of dates you only need to print twelve, thus saving loads of space.'

'Splendid, old chap. Have a cigar!'

And so a star was born – or rather, twelve star signs were. Within weeks American newspapers were on the bandwagon, and soon Sun sign columns were everywhere. The rest, as they say, is history. Except that it's not necessarily the sort of history about which all serious astrologers feel happy. 'It's like,' they say, 'having a beautiful symphony you could play to people and then proceeding to hammer out a few extracts with one hand on the piano.' As an astrologer who once trained long and hard to learn the art of working with the full celestial orchestra, I have long wanted to be able to offer, if not the complete symphony, at least the left hand piano part. And now, I can! All I need you to do, in order to make the magic happen, is turn to page 359 and discover your Moon sign.

WHAT THE MOON REVEALS

There's just one more point I need to make. The Moon has a lot to do with the irrational, intuitive side of your nature. Unfortunately, just as society's statisticians and scientists feel it is their duty to provide a sensible explanation for everything, so most people have within their psyche a desire to refute the existence of the subconscious. It's the reason why we wake up after a vivid dream and try to shake it off; or why we all try, so often, to deny what we really feel. The Moon, being primarily an entity of the night, is all about dreams and feelings. To appreciate what I have to say about your Moon sign, you need to have a wish to explore your own dreams and feelings in more depth. You can gain a great deal more control over your destiny by understanding the urges that the Moon pulls like tides across your inner ocean. But first you must be brave enough to look objectively and honestly at what these are.

A lot of people don't want to do this. They feel, perhaps, a little afraid that they may harbour a seething mass of emotional needs beneath the calm surface of their inner world. They even fear they may find, if they look, that they are a little crazy – or that others may think so.

I won't deny that there is a link between the Moon and craziness. The Latin word for Moon is *luna*, and it is from this that we get 'lunacy'. But actually we don't get lunacy from looking at the Moon; we get it from denying its influence or trying to pretend that we are 'normal'. It's the constant stress of feeling socially obliged to repress a host of hidden feelings that causes most people to go over the edge. If we lived in a more honest, Moon-celebrating world, our asylums would probably mainly contain the people insensitive enough to imagine that they had no poetry in their soul. The way things stand in our Sun-centred, superficial society, it's often those with vision who cannot take the pace, whilst those without it set it!

'But what,' you may say, 'if I find, when I look at my Moon sign [or 'into my soul' – it amounts to the same thing] that I am not just mildly oddball but dangerously potty? Am I not in danger of opening up a Pandora's Box?'

Maybe. But maybe you're potentially a lot more dangerous to yourself and others if you *don't* want to know what's within, and just allow the steam of your inner pressure cooker to rise till it blows the lid! I promise not to prise off the top of your Pandora's pressure cooker any further than you can immediately slam back down. But I do hope I'll show you something that helps you, even if at first you resent a little of what I have to say. If you *do* strongly object, it could be because the Moon itself is currently at the wrong phase in relation to your Moon sign, making you unreceptive to today's topic. Try rereading it in a few days' time.

YOUR MOON SIGN

Please remember – the following information will make no sense unless you first turn to page 350 and follow the simple instructions you will find there. NB: There is a 1 in 12 chance that when you turn to the tables from page 352 you will discover that your Moon sign is the same as your Sun sign. This simply means that you are, in some respects, extremely typical of your sign!

MOON IN ARIES

'Fools rush in where angels fear to tread.' People with the Moon in Aries, however, cheerfully plunge into situations that even fools would think twice about! 'Rash' is not the right word to describe the emotional side of your character. 'Rash' implies someone who is sometimes just a little too hasty, reckless and lacking in forethought. 'Rash' also implies a malaise that can be 'cured' by removing certain irritants. You, however, are permanently, irrevocably and quite unashamedly impulsive. Your notion of propriety is to keep a few clothes on while dancing drunkenly up to a policeman and inviting him to tango. Your idea of self-restraint means stopping short of actually sawing in half the broken meter that's preventing you from parking your car where you want to. And what's more, you're proud of all this!

If I were to make comments like these to anyone born under any other Moon sign, I'd cause them mortal offence. You, though, I suspect, are sitting there grinning, saying, 'Go on, tell me more!' Well, OK then. You're daft as a brush, mad as a hatter and blind as a bat to anything you do not want to see. You are also, however, as sweet, as kind and as forgiving a soul as the world has ever known. There's hardly an ounce of malice in your personality, and though you can be absolutely outrageous on the spur of the moment you find it impossible to bear a grudge or keep up a feud for longer than half an hour.

Your greatest talent is the ability to think on your feet. You are spontaneous, witty, alert and energetic with a natural air of authority and purpose. Rarely does an opportunity pass you by unnoticed. Your eyes are constantly peeling the horizon for signs of imminent change which you might be able to turn to your advantage. If the horizon happens to be quiet, you simply go out and make what you need to happen, happen.

Your biggest fear is that one day the pace of life might slow down so much that you become obliged to think about where you're going and why. Were you ever to do this, you suspect you might realise that you have become like a driver so keen to cruise in the overtaking lane that you have long since overshot your destination.

Arguably, your worst vice is laziness. Not the physical kind – nobody could accuse you of using energy sparingly. But you tend not to bother about the likely consequences of your actions. 'Let's just give it a whirl and see what happens,' you say to yourself as you hurl yourself into yet another half-baked scheme or ill-advised relationship. 'Whoops!' is usually the comment that follows as you try to make light of the need to extricate yourself from the ensuing sticky situation.

'Whoops', however, is not the word your exasperated loved ones would necessarily apply. Their reactions to your escapades tend to be a little stronger – though they do need to be similarly brief. At the slightest suspicion that you are being given a lecture, you make your eyes look bright and attentive whilst secretly closing your ears to ensure that not a syllable permeates your brain! Your favourite song is 'Anything you can do, I can do better'. Fortunately, what you lack in self-restraint and diplomacy you more than make up for in natural warmth. Friends, family members and partners alike simply can't help admiring your audacity.

Somewhere deep within, you lust for power. You have it within you to be a ruthless conqueror, a shameless despot, a supreme ruler of not just your world but the whole world. When people cross you, your first impulse is usually to send your army to raze their city to the ground. Of course it only lasts a few seconds before you check yourself – usually by remembering that you haven't got an army, they haven't got a city, and anyway it's probably all a bit of an extreme reaction. But it *is* a reaction that you often have. Your temper doesn't just flare, it erupts into a supernova.

Much the same can be said of your passion. When you really want something (or someone) you want it bad. It's why you're such a high achiever. And it's also why you're such a bad person to make an enemy of. You may not hold a grudge or even entertain a wild desire for long, but in the short time that it consumes you you can cause plenty of damage!

The good news, however, is that you're better than you were. As a child you were absolutely impossible. Siblings and schoolfriends probably need counselling to get over the profound impact that your fiery personality made on them as a child! And the exploits you got up to as a teenager are almost certainly not fit to repeat. The adults who were faced with the challenge of bringing you up deserve a medal. But then, so do you, for you have lived and coped with your own impetuous nature surprisingly well. You'll be glad to hear that the worst is over. People with the Moon in Aries always grow a little more mellow with each passing year.

MOON IN ARIES, *SUN IN...*

Aries You're the original human dynamo. Nothing stops you from getting what you want – apart, perhaps, from your occasional lack of foresight or self-restraint.

Taurus Underneath your cool, calm, collected exterior beats an impatient, irascible but highly-motivated and decisive heart.

Gemini Ideas come to your mind so fast that you can sometimes hardly even enunciate them. You're bright, lively, witty and endlessly energetic.

Cancer You're rarely relaxed about anything for long, but you're a very high achiever with great power and ability to do good in the world.

Leo You're warm and wise, charming and confident. But sometimes you can be just a little too sure of the wisdom of your own judgement.

Virgo Though you seem meek and mild-mannered enough on first impression, there's a raging tiger waiting to pounce on those who cross you.

Libra You're about as mellow and easy-going as a hippopotamus on heat! Once an idea is in your head, you'll move mountains to see it through.

Scorpio You take your commitments exceedingly seriously. You passionately believe in fulfilling your promises, whatever this takes.

Sagittarius You're a barrel of laughs and a bundle of fun. Pragmatism? That's a long word for a short day. Why not fill it with adventure instead?

Capricorn You're very sure about where you want to live and who you want to live with. And you'll fight hard to protect the interests of your family.

Aquarius You may have a penchant for fast cars or yearn to learn speed-reading. Something in you can never get from A to B quickly enough.

Pisces Because you're not afraid to put your money where your mouth is, others are often happy (and right) to put their money into your hands.

MOON IN TAURUS

You'll probably want to cut out and keep this explanation of what it means to have the Moon in Taurus. But then, you tend to want to cut out and keep almost everything you see. You're an incorrigible collector. Where others are content to look at things and then let them go, you yearn to own them. Your home contains all the luxurious creature comforts that have ever been invented, plus spares in the cupboard 'just in case'. You're a hopeless hoarder and a salesperson's dream customer. Never mind what it costs, if it's fine, precious, special and exquisite you've got to have it. You're also breathtakingly stubborn. When you come under pressure to do something you don't feel inclined to do, you anchor yourself to the nearest immovable object and defy anyone to budge you.

But enough of your good points! What's wrong with you? Well, I have to point out that you're far too clever a cook, too gifted a gardener or too talented a creative artist for your own good. You're forever having to fend off requests for your time and energy from the many people who stand in awe of your skill. And though there are few to rival you as a bon viveur, there are occasions when your insatiable sensual appetite leads to trouble. You're such a connoisseur of the finest things in life that you cannot bear to have, or give to others, anything less than the best. And, of course, you're sensitive, cautious and clever. Less blessed individuals are sometimes jealous of this.

The Moon in Taurus gives you an overwhelming need to be emotionally and financially secure. You'll put up with a lot of hassle, hardship or aggravation before you feel inclined to rock the boat or leave a devil you know for one you don't. This makes you exasperatingly set in your ways, but heart-warmingly loyal. A loved one has to be proven guilty of not one but a host of heinous crimes before you'll consider relinquishing the relationship. You hate to see any investment go to waste, so you'd rather not make one at all than make one you regret. In consequence, you never give your love quickly or easily. Maybe it's the traditional Taurean association with horticulture that makes you so keen to give a person time to grow on you before you transplant them from the seedbed of fancy to the garden of your heart. Certainly you consider it important to nurture and nourish personal bonds before deciding to prize and protect them. You secretly worry about making the wrong choice or being sold a shallot instead of a daffodil bulb.

Though you actually have a great ability to spot the real gem within a mountain of fakes, you like to inspect the pile carefully. There's always the chance you'll find a rough diamond that you can gradually polish. This desire to get value for money from your every acquisition makes some people shy of you. They may be afraid that they can't afford to share your expensive tastes, or that you want more from them than they can easily give. You are demanding – there's no doubt about it. But since all you ever demand from a person is that they do their very best (for themselves as much as for you), it's just as well if your attitude naturally deters impostors, ne'er-do-wells and fly-by-nights. You need to be saved for those with enough taste to appreciate yours, enough sincerity to match your own and enough energy to fulfil your insatiable appetite for deep, warm, demonstrative communication.

You've been your own worst enemy on several occasions in the past and, though you've recently become more adept at controlling the tendency to want to cut off your nose to spite your face, it's still a fairly constant temptation. It's all down to your reluctance to compromise. You feel that if you can't have exactly what you want, precisely when you want it, you'd rather not have anything at all. Time and again you've turned down openings that could have become opportunities, simply because they weren't gift-wrapped and clearly labelled as such.

You also suffer, aptly enough for someone whose Moon is linked to cattle, from 'foot and mouth' disease. Every so often you open your big mouth and put your foot in it! It's bullish instinct that causes you to do this, in much the same way as it inspires your four-legged namesake to charge relentlessly at strangers who stray into his territory. You sense a potential threat, no matter how small, and you don't wait to give it the benefit of the doubt. Down goes the head, up flare the nostrils, and out of your way (if they have any sense) runs the innocent holder of what you perceive to be a red rag.

This inclination to treat others as guilty till proven innocent has saved your hide once or twice before, but it's also been the reason why, to this day, there are people to whom you dare not speak because you once vented more rage than was reasonable on them. As a child you were probably obedient. As an adolescent you were probably sulky. As an adult, however, you grew those horns and discovered you could use them to great effect. Now, you need to learn to hold them high with pride instead of lowering them in anger so often.

MOON IN TAURUS, *SUN IN...*

Aries You're not as reckless or as hasty as you'd like others to think. You've got enough caution to counter your enthusiasm and to guarantee you success.

Taurus If you aren't a millionaire, you ought to be. You certainly know how to spend money, and you possess more than enough talent to make it.

Gemini You know how to make marvellous investments, not just of money but of time and energy and in your choice of friends.

Cancer Some people call you over-cautious, but you very rarely make mistakes. You can tell a person's or an object's true worth at a glance.

Leo It's useless trying to persuade you of anything once you've made up your mind. But since you're usually right, that's no problem.

Virgo It takes a lot to stir you into action, but when you've got a mission there's no stopping you. And no criticising you, either!

Libra You're so laid back you're positively supine. You can take everything in your stride except, perhaps, too much pressure.

Scorpio You yearn for stability in your love life – to the point where you will often let your partner off a hook they ought to be hoisted by.

Sagittarius You're surprisingly serious for a Sagittarian. You take great care to do your duty diligently and to be a healing influence in this troubled world.

Capricorn You sometimes have a terrible weakness for 'pleasures of the flesh'. It makes you great fun to know. You may be naughty, but you're very nice.

Aquarius It doesn't matter how chaotic the rest of your world is as long as your home is safe, secure and full of people and objects you can 'relate' to.

Pisces You know the value of a sound education. You may not care for academia, but you certainly love to acquire information.

MOON IN GEMINI

I don't hold out much hope that you'll agree with the following description. People with the Moon in Gemini never agree with anything if they can help it. You court controversy and find heated debates as comforting as most folk find heated towel rails. What do you mean, 'Oh no I don't!' You see? You're quarrelling now!

But let's not fall out over this. After all, you never intend your outbursts of devil's advocacy to be taken seriously, and are often upset to find they have thrown more sensitive souls off balance. You're always happy to reach a compromise between two points of view or even to retract your own entirely. It's the scent of an argument that excites you, never the taste of victory.

Some people, noticing this, call you inconsistent. What can they mean? Your habit of changing your mind more often than your socks is as reliable as the rising of the Sun. Or, as we're considering lunar influences here, perhaps we should say Moon. Only the Moon, of course, is not so constant. It has its moods and phases. And so do you. One moment you're as confident as a cuckoo, the next as restless as a wren. Similarly, you can change from being a mischievous magpie to a vulnerable partridge. I make these ornithological references intentionally, for in many respects you are like a bird. You were born to fly free from life's petty restrictions and see the world from a high perspective; and, more than anything else in life, you hate to feel caged.

Having the Moon in Gemini makes you witty and bright, lively and good-humoured, but prone to occasional dark moods. These, oddly enough, are usually triggered by trivia. Life's bigger challenges you can easily cope with, but it's the silly little things that make you despair. By nature you're an explorer, experimenter and innovator, prepared to try almost anything once. Your partner needs to be similarly open-minded if the relationship is to provide the challenge and constant stimulation you seem to require. Your family don't, however, have to try so hard to hold your interest. If there's no excitement or drama on the home front, you'll simply create it for everyone.

You love persuading people to do what you think is good for them, especially if you can do it so subtly as to make them think it was all their own idea. You've been known to lie awake at night thinking, 'If I tell Fred this, point out such-and-such to Mabel and leave Zelda's letter lying around where Cecil can see it, then Cecil will have to confront Mabel. This will oblige her to come clean with Fred – which will worry him enough to ask Zelda for the help he's afraid she'll refuse to give.' Complicated? Not half as much as the actual workings of your inner mind. No wonder your emotional life is such a soap opera.

In fairness, your desire to control situations is not linked to a yearning to turn things to your own advantage. You're just keen to make sure that your loved ones' problems are solved as cleverly as possible. This is why you've always got so many questions to ask your nearest and dearest. If you don't know all the facts about everyone and everything, how can you possibly apply your brain to sorting things out for them?

Some astrologers might argue that, for greater happiness in love, you need to be less calculating and a little more relaxed. There is, however, another way to look at this: maybe you ought to spend more time with people smart enough to appreciate how smart you are!

If you go around telling your friends that you have the Moon in the sign of the twins they will no doubt nod wisely and say, 'That explains a lot.' Indeed it does. Solar Geminis are just a little prone to being different people on different days, but lunar Geminis are veritable Jekyll and Hydes. Well, almost: it's not from nice to nasty that you switch, but from tame to wild. Nor do you alter suddenly and dramatically. None the less, if we rewind the video of your life, then run it fast forward on 'play', we can see the trait powerfully. Your inner twins may take it in turns to dominate on a weekly, monthly or even several-yearly rota, but it's hard to see how your history can be the handiwork of just one entity.

This in itself is not always a problem. The different aspects of your character are not so much at loggerheads as in cahoots, for they are, after all, twins – mutually supportive in their agreement to differ. But twins are famous for getting up to naughty tricks, like swapping places in class to see if the teacher notices. You have, you must confess, found yourself in many situations where you have felt very much like an impostor. And to a degree you have been. It's no use asking the real you to please stand up. You *are* both the wilful, wacky and outrageous one *and* the Goody Two Shoes. But you need to admit this rather than denying that your other half exists.

MOON IN GEMINI, *SUN IN...*

ARIES You're a very bright spark, but you change your mind more often than your socks and fail to see why others can't keep up.

TAURUS You've got good financial acumen and a way of appearing reasonable and fair even when you're determinedly getting your own way!

GEMINI You ought to work in the city. You're a great wheeler and dealer even if you do sometimes tie even yourself up in intellectual knots!

CANCER You're a much tougher cookie than you pretend to be – and you're exceedingly good at talking friends and loved ones round to your viewpoint.

LEO You've got a natural ability to see things from others' point of view... as you gradually and cleverly talk them round to your own.

VIRGO Your trouble is that you think you've got all the answers – in fact, what you're really good at is making others ask all the questions!

Libra Your tendency to ask too many questions and never leave enough time for people to answer them is probably your only major fault.

Scorpio You're fascinated by social taboos. Things that polite people never discuss in public excite your desire to get at the truth.

Sagittarius You want a long and stable relationship, but you're not always sure who with – so you're often tempted to find out by trial and error.

Capricorn You think hard about ways to help others help themselves. You're giving and considerate, if rather too clever for your own good at times.

Aquarius Life may not be one long round of joyous celebration, but it often seems this way when you're around to share a little sunshine.

Pisces Where you really feel at home and inspired is in a place full of bright, friendly people making interesting, intelligent conversation.

MOON IN CANCER

To have the Moon in Cancer is to be as soft as a damp sponge and every bit as soppy! It's to want, more than anything else in the world, to protect and care for the people, items, causes and beliefs that mean most to you. And it is also, oddly enough to have a thick skin. The very fact that you recognise how vulnerable you are, deep inside, makes you determined not to be a sucker for every sob story. You pretend to be like the character in the Paul Simon song who says, 'I am a rock… I am an island.' You often convince others and even yourself of this. But every so often that inner ocean of emotion sends a tidal wave crashing over a shore that's not so sure. Then your no-nonsense, 'don't-mess-with-me' façade cracks to reveal a quivering bundle of concern. You'll do almost anything for anyone when you're in such a state, no matter how counter-productive.

A psychologist might say that all this has something to do with your mother. An astrologer would dispute whether the chicken came before the egg, but they would agree that no male or female with the Moon in Cancer ever has an ambivalent relationship with the woman who gave birth to them. There may be extreme resentment or intense adoration, but there's certainly some tremendously powerful feeling. Which in turn, I suppose, is why you often find yourself needing to fight so hard against a sense of guilt, a constant need to earn approval or an inappropriate desire to mother those around you.

Sensitivity is your middle name. Try though you may to shorten it to 'sense' or to leave it off your signature completely, the tag comes back to haunt you. What other people feel about you counts for so much that you seem to spend the whole of your life erecting and maintaining complex self-defence mechanisms. Sometimes you try being bombastic. You figure if you're extrovert enough, nobody will be able to find the chink in your psychological armour. Sometimes you go to the other extreme and withdraw completely, on the basis that if you don't ever have anything to do with anyone you can't possibly cause offence. None of it works. Where some people have an insatiable appetite for sex, power or money, the Moon in Cancer gives you an unquenchable thirst for reassurance. You even have to be reassured about the fact that it's all right to need reassurance! Unless your closest loved ones are all aspiring saints, they may occasionally tire of giving it to you.

None of this, I hasten to add, makes you a wimp. In a funny way, it might be better if it did. But, almost despite yourself, you are forever making bold statements or embarking on adventurous escapades. This is because the Moon's influence comes and goes in phases. When you're on one of your 'ups', there's no stopping you. You'll take on enemies twice your size and go to outrageous lengths to defend the rights of those you care for. But then you'll suddenly realise what you've done and stop yourself before you go too far (or before you've gone far enough, depending on how you look at it!). Only when your protective instincts are awakened do you feel safe to open the emotional floodgates of your heart. Your partner therefore needs to be weak enough to inspire you to do this, yet strong enough not to be a liability. And as for your family? They just need to be glad they've got such an endlessly giving person in their midst.

I'm sorry to have to ask you this but, if we're going to make sense of your more unfathomable urges and impulses, I need to know how you really feel about your mother. Aha! I thought so. That deep intake of breath you just took was all the confirmation I required. You *have* got the Moon in Cancer. Your emotional outlook on life has been shaped, perhaps more than you care to admit, by the woman who brought you into the world. Maybe you feel devotion to her, and maybe anger. I can only tell which by checking your lunar 'aspects', and we are not going this far into astrology here. But you know that, whatever else it is, the relationship has always been 'intense'. This is normal and natural – to a degree, it is so for all of us.

Freud, Jung and the other great psychologists were mining a rich seam when they began to hypothesise that our behaviour patterns can be traced back to very early childhood. But where most children go through a phase of being unable to separate their own identity from that of their primary parent – followed by a healthy stage of rejection before eventual reconciliation in adulthood – Lunar Cancerians take longer than most to arrive fully at this latter point. You may have travelled to the corners of the earth, or you may have never left home. Geography has nothing to do with this psychological tie – and there's nothing wrong with it unless it happens also to be the cause of a sense of guilt. Many positive celestial developments have already helped you move on a stage, and I predict you will eventually go through a series of experiences and inner-realisation processes that help you go a long way further towards letting yourself off the hook.

MOON IN CANCER, *SUN IN...*

ARIES You are the original hard nut with a soft centre. You are also a born leader – which is just as well, for you hate taking orders.

TAURUS You care passionately and deeply about the people in your world. Your loyalty is unshakeable, your generosity most impressive.

GEMINI You like to pretend that your every decision is totally logical, but actually you're a tremendously intuitive and very successful operator.

CANCER You either wear your heart on your sleeve or never let anyone see it at all. You're very giving, but rarely agree to accept anything from anyone.

LEO Your Moon in the sign of the sensitive crab doesn't need a shell to retreat into. It just lets your tough Leo persona fend off all enemies.

Virgo You try hard not to let others realise you're so soft in case they take advantage of your good nature – but you usually fail to convince them.

Libra You go out of your way to protect those you love from things they don't need to know… such as how worried you often are.

Scorpio You love to learn as much as you can about what life is really all about. You're open-minded and at ease with yourself.

Sagittarius You're a deep philosopher, though you're also wise enough to recognise that none of us lives by theory alone. We have to trust what we feel.

Capricorn You're deeply loyal to those you love, and happy, if not actually to give a partner the upper hand, certainly to let them think they've got it!

Aquarius You worry a great deal about letting other people down. Consequently you're very dedicated and discriminating about what you promise.

Pisces You've got a sunny disposition and a desire to keep life light, happy and simple. It's much appreciated by all around you.

MOON IN LEO

You don't need me to tell you what a wonderful person you are. If you've got the Moon in Leo, you already know it to be true beyond question. Nor is this the only thing about which you feel entitled to consider yourself certain. You know a great deal about a great many subjects and your opinions are invariably right – or so, at least, you passionately believe. Actually, they usually are, but sometimes people resent this – partly because you tend to deliver your opinion in too knowing a tone of voice, and partly because they sense that, while you're very good at making suggestions, you're not so good at taking them. Nobody, but nobody, gets away with giving you advice. Nor do they give you orders!

Your biggest recurring fantasy involves the idea that one day you may get proof that your beloved parents are actually foster parents and you are actually the Queen's love child, secretly born two years before Prince Charles. One day the world will find out and you will claim the throne! Or, at least, your attitude to life suggests that you must think along such grandiose lines. Fortunately, despite your occasionally pompous posture, your smart alec disposition and your tendency to want to be the star of every show, you are also one of the kindest, warmest, most generous and genuine individuals who have ever graced the face of planet earth. And for this you can be forgiven a multitude of sins.

With Shakespeare's assertion that 'all the world's a stage' you can, I'm sure, heartily agree. You're very much a class act and a natural celebrity. You exude warmth, charisma and confidence; it's no pretence. There's something about you that was born to shine.

None the less, it's not quite the whole story. Like many of the greatest media personalities, you secretly suffer stage fright. No matter how many times you step in front of the spotlight to thunderous applause, it's always preceded by a period of nervous pacing round your dressing room. Those who love and live with you soon learn to make allowances for these sudden swings between anxiety and bravado. They have to be able to supply the necessary quota of post-performance 'darling, you were wonderfuls', and they also need some theatrical blood of their own in order to co-star with you in a succession of demanding roles.

Where some people's lives are soap operas and others just border on the farcical, the Moon in Leo is like a celestial agent who keeps booking you into good, old-fashioned melodramas. No problem is ever an ordinary problem, no emotional reaction is ever just a mild sensation. You either feel nothing or you feel as if you are on fire. This is why you give yourself so wholeheartedly to the projects you tackle and the people you care for. It is also, however, why you often go over the top, putting more into a situation or conversation than it actually warrants.

You're an incorrigible perfectionist, not because you have some perverse fascination with detail but because you simply cannot bear the thought of being judged and found wanting. Yet you're always suspicious of being fobbed off with platitudinous praise. This, probably, is the greatest drawback or difficulty you have to overcome on the road to a happy love life. Like Groucho Marx, you can never feel quite comfortable about belonging to any club that would want to have you as a member!

As a child, you were probably precocious. As a teenager, you may well have been 'old before your time' – haughtily aloof from the trivial fascinations of your more immature peers, but also probably extrovert and confident. Who would have thought that, as an adult, you would entertain such intense self-doubts and insecurities about yourself? Probably only an astrologer, familiar with the traits of a Lunar Leo.

Your Moon sign is a blessing in that it gives you a natural air of dignity and authority. It is, however, a curse in so far as it makes you desperately worried that you may one day lose the respect others have for you. Often, you will take refuge in righteousness or stick with tried and tested techniques rather than risk falling on your face as a result of exploring some unfamiliar manoeuvre. The result is that you become too easily set in your ways.

If all these ways were means to a worthwhile end, that would be no problem. But you have habits that could sorely do with being conquered, and tendencies that really do you no favours. You're often so nervous about 'getting it wrong' that you hold yourself back, even when you have a chance to 'get it right'. You're so hungry for approval that you'll court it in areas where, frankly, you'd be better off being condemned for not going. You're so fearful of criticism that you'll refuse to listen even to the most well-informed and sincerely meant advice, for fear it makes you look silly to take it.

No, no. Of *course* you're not like this all the time – just some of it, when the Moon happens to catch you in the wrong phase. But I draw it to your attention so mercilessly because you are able to do something very constructive about your worst emotional worries. Eventually, a career or creative project is going to take off like a rocket. When it does, give it all you've got and you'll soon regain enough pride to allow yourself to be humble.

MOON IN LEO, *SUN IN...*

ARIES You're calm and at ease with yourself – and with most people, most of the time. You exude charm, confidence and ready good humour.

TAURUS You're proud of who you are and what you stand for. Others may see you as stubborn, but you simply cannot settle for less than the best.

GEMINI You often say things for dramatic effect without thinking about their likely consequences. But you have a heart of pure gold.

CANCER You've got a winning way with people, and money too. Somehow, you're never emotionally or financially insecure for very long.

Leo You're magnetically attractive and charismatic, though it has to be said that you fall for your own charms as much as everyone else!

Virgo Yet to be born is the person able to get the better of you in an argument, or talk you into anything you don't want to be talked into.

Libra Because you're so charming, few people realise how cleverly you have talked them into something. It's a good job you have scruples.

Scorpio You're probably very keen to get to the top of the career ladder. Even if you're not, others are keen to put you there. And deservedly so.

Sagittarius You're not a graduate of the university of life – you're a perpetual student and proud of it. Every day's a glorious education.

Capricorn You're very conscious of your responsibility to others. You hate to see money go to waste. And you yearn to explore life's deeper mysteries.

Aquarius To take all you have to give, a partner must be very strong and special. But it's your very dear wish to find (or keep) such a person.

Pisces You take great pride in your work and even more in your ability to recognise what's wrong with someone and how to put it right.

MOON IN VIRGO

You may be a little nervous to read what it means to have the Moon in Virgo. You probably expect to have confirmed what you have long suspected: namely that you are a worthless individual, hopelessly lacking charm or originality. The only reason (you imagine) that you have been lucky enough to do at all well in life so far is because others have been either too blind or too kind to notice this.

I'm so glad you've finally identified your Moon sign, because it gives me the chance to say what you have long needed someone to walk up and shout into your ear. You are a marvellous, magnificent individual. The only thing 'wrong' with you is that you have the Moon in Virgo. And this is not really 'wrong'. It's just that it often makes you doubt your skill, undervalue your contribution and rip yourself to shreds with viciously sharp self-criticism.

Many people like the fact that you are this way inclined. It allows them to exploit you, manipulate you and hire your services for a fraction of their true value. It's only those who truly love you who are baffled and frustrated.

Why are you so self-denigrating when it's clear to them that you are the most intelligent, sexy, sensitive, talented and funny individual they have ever met? All you need do to reassure them (and yourself) is learn to laugh at your inherited astrological tendency to sell yourself short and become the wise, witty and talented star you truly are.

Your Moon in Virgo makes you a very easy person to get along with. You are tolerant, considerate and always willing to see the good in others. Most people, in their turn, find you fair and thoughtful, wise and reasonable, bright and interesting. It's only fools you don't suffer gladly and they, conveniently enough, tend to be similarly dismissive of you. A 'fool', according to your definition at least, is someone who puts quantity before quality, style before substance and money before happiness. As a highly principled person you find such short-sighted, unprincipled behaviour anathema. You consider it essential to keep away from such dangerously disruptive characters.

Unfortunately, in today's world it is not always easy to do this. As a result you frequently find yourself arguing with or being impeded by these noisy, presumptuous beings with their incessant stream of ill-thought-through judgements. You grow tired of dealing with them, and your loved ones sometimes grow tired of dealing with the frustration you find so hard to hide. They often have to remind you not to let yourself be so bothered by what you consider to be waste or stupidity.

The Moon in Virgo makes you yearn to live in a world that 'makes sense', but the sad fact is that few things in life ever really do. An ability to appreciate the bizarre, funny and ironic side of life is the psychological defence mechanism you need to put in place if you want to become more relaxed about your closest relationships. You probably also need to counter a tendency to undervalue what you have to offer others. You seem to swing between feeling that you're not good enough for anyone and (usually by way of psychological over-compensation for this fear) that you're far too good for everyone. Concentrate on giving more and judging less, and you'll find all the emotional fulfilment you so richly deserve.

We've already discussed your tendency to be viciously self-critical and similarly sharp about those you feel are wasting their potential in life. What we haven't discussed is the link between these traits.

Before we do, I must remind you of the many assets the Moon in Virgo bestows. Diligence, wisdom and reliability are the most obvious. You have all three qualities in abundance, plus the ability to be magnificently sensual, creative and compassionate. What you lack is sufficient defiance, arrogance and rebelliousness. More than all that, you find it almost impossible to voice the phrase 'I couldn't care less.' Sometimes, we all need to be able to say this. The trouble with you is that, no matter how trivial the scenario, you 'couldn't care more'. You may have a great sense of humour, but you only find some things funny. By and large, you take life and yourself too seriously. Your overwhelming sense of duty makes you yearn to do your best at every juncture. Because you have such impossibly high standards, you frequently fail to live up to them. Thus you're forever driving yourself harder and further forward. When you see others, who clearly need to do the same, resting on their laurels, it triggers resentment. You ask: 'How come *they* can live with themselves when they have so far to go, while I don't seem able to?' But the solution is simple. You don't need therapy. You just need to relax, relax and then relax some more!

MOON IN VIRGO, *SUN IN...*

Aries You're far from a typical Aries. You notice details and worry about problems *before* they arise. But you're very swift to adapt.

Taurus You're deeply sensual but determinedly pragmatic. Quality counts for everything, and details matter immensely to you.

Gemini You're very clever but can sometimes be too smart for your own good, talking yourself out of ideas that are actually worth pursuing.

Cancer You're careful, cautious, kind and considerate. You're also extremely clever. Few ever manage to pull the wool over your eyes.

Leo You take pride in your ability to make the right decision. You worry more than you need to, for your instincts are rarely misleading.

Virgo You're so marvellously inscrutable that you won't even tell yourself what you really feel. But you're none the less a very powerful person.

Libra You're witty, wise and exceedingly good at understanding what really makes other people tick. Little escapes your notice.

Scorpio You have many friends who admire you for your great integrity and insight, plus your ability to manifest both with even greater modesty.

Sagittarius You've got just enough seriousness to counterbalance your Sagittarian excessiveness without becoming too inflexible. You were born to succeed.

Capricorn You're rather fond of travelling. You like to go to new places and learn new ways of looking at life. And you have deep, strong, natural faith.

Aquarius For a person with two key planets in supposedly 'logical' signs, you're surprisingly compassionate, sensitive and deeply intuitive.

Pisces You're an incorrigible romantic and not really a secret one – no matter how much you may claim to be logical in your choice of partner.

MOON IN LIBRA

With the Moon in Libra, you always know exactly how you feel. Unsure! You always have done, you always will and you have no doubt had to learn, long ago, how to live with constantly fluctuating emotions. The trick, in case you have yet to discover it, is to stop thinking about how you feel or at least to stop thinking you ought to feel the same way from day to day. Other than the fact that you're never quite clear whether you're worried or confident, happy or upset, energetic or apathetic, you're an absolutely A1 human being.

This may sound contradictory, but then aren't *all* humans contradictory? Isn't the only real difference between you and everyone else the fact that you are happy to own up to your own contrariness whereas most other people fight hard to hide theirs? And doesn't this make you more emotionally honest and therefore, in an odd way, more straightforward?

Sorry to ask so many questions, but in doing so I'm only reflecting yet another classic Moon in Libra tendency. You delight in pondering the imponderable. Yet you get along in life pretty well despite it all. Why? Because having the Moon in Libra also makes you charming, affable, seductive, creative, fun to be with and generally fascinating. And because you're so aware of your own faults, you're loath to condemn others for theirs. Which, naturally enough, makes you very popular.

Your biggest problem is that you're so easily able to make yourself absolutely irresistible to others. Not only have you got natural charisma, poise and elegance, you've got something even more potentially devastating – adaptability. You can instinctively sense what a person wants you to be like and effortlessly alter your personality to supply it. Worse still, you actually want to do this. Little gives you greater pleasure than to provide what a loved one is looking for. Willingly and instantly, you will say what they want to hear you say, respond as they want you to respond and, most appealingly of all, put the look into your eyes that they most want to see. How can anyone fail to fall hopelessly for someone who so accurately mirrors their own most deep and secret desire?

It's all fine until they find out that in a different situation, with a different companion, you're a different person entirely! When they turn and ask if the 'real you' will please stand up, you have to reply meekly, 'Er… which real me did you want me to show you?' Well, OK, maybe you're not quite *that* bad. But you do have a tendency to be an emotional chameleon, and it does have to be watched.

Members of your family sometimes grow fed up with your habit of weighing up every pro and con so carefully that, by the time you've found a fair formula, the issue under discussion has become irrelevant. Friends are never quite sure where your loyalties lie. Romantic partners despair of ever getting a straight answer to anything. They'll all forgive you – for you're so good at turning on the charm that, even when you're letting someone down, you can make it seem as though you're offering them an opportunity. But if you want a happier love life you have to become secure in yourself, not to need to find your security by winning everyone's approval all the time.

You'll see that your Moon sign has been depicted as a precariously balanced tightrope walker. Meditate on it for a few minutes and you'll have the benefit of twice as much commentary as I'm giving to every other zodiac sign.

This should please you for, though your Moon may be in the sign of the balance, the desire to be fair to everyone all the time is not your primary concern. You're conscious of how nice it would be if you could – but you're more conscious of what you see as the less than ideal hand that fate has dealt you. A lot of your energy is spent attempting to redress this balance. You want what you haven't got but feel you ought to be entitled to. If there's a chance to get it, you'll go to almost any length. Tightrope? You'll walk along a piece of tightly stretched cotton if that's what's required.

One thing the Moon in Libra has surely provided you with is plenty of courage. If the odds of success are so slim as to deter most people, or the window of opportunity so small that only a contortionist could enter it, you consider yourself to be looking at a challenge that has your name stamped all over it! You have your Moon sign to thank for the occasions in your life when you have pulled off some magnificent coup. You also have it to blame for the rather greater number of times when you have come a cropper. Much of your irrepressibility is, ironically, a reaction to the way you always felt you were being kept down as a child. If you want to learn how to make it work for rather than against you as an adult, you must come to terms with these memories. In the meantime, if you can't be good at least be a little more careful.

MOON IN LIBRA, *SUN IN...*

Aries You have a very strong urge to constantly prove yourself though you aren't always sure how to go about doing so.

Taurus You've got a magnificent aesthetic eye. You appreciate colours, textures and flavours, and probably love to create them too.

Gemini You try so hard to rationalise and analyse everything in your world that your own spontaneous instincts often take you by surprise.

Cancer You go to great lengths to protect the people and principles you believe in. You are generous with both your time and your heart.

Leo Few can resist your silver tongue, your golden smile and your eyes that usually twinkle like diamonds but can also give very cutting looks.

Virgo You sometimes feel sorry for those who try to pin you down, for you know you can run rings round just about anyone.

Libra Rarely, if ever, do you give others reason to take offence, which really infuriates your more impassioned friends and loved ones.

Scorpio You're never quite sure whether you really feel what you feel or just think you feel it. But you're a person of great vision and strength.

Sagittarius Your social diary is never empty. You have more friends than you can keep track of – even though they can't quite keep track of you!

Capricorn You have a lot of charisma, which is no doubt a contributory factor to the reason why you so often seem to make such a success of all you do.

Aquarius If your mind was open any wider, jumbo jets could fly in formation through it. You believe anything is possible, and you may be right.

Pisces You have an endless hunger to discover the true meaning of life and are forever asking deep, searching and highly valuable questions.

MOON IN SCORPIO

I hope, when you checked your date of birth in the Moon sign tables, that you didn't mark the page. You really don't want anyone else to know you've got the Moon in Scorpio. If there's someone looking over your shoulder now, quickly scan an adjacent definition and throw them off the scent. Come back and read the rest when you've made sure the door is locked, the curtains are drawn and there are no hidden cameras.

Am I joking? Not especially. I'm simply trying to illustrate the way that the Moon in Scorpio makes a person very sensitive about things they want nobody ever to find out about. They fear that they are unreasonably and exceptionally jealous, desirous, passionate and competitive. So powerful, indeed, do they consider their inner emotions that they keep a very tight lid on them, often denying to others and even to themselves that they exist. These people pretend to be easy-going, light and breezy, when all the time below the surface they are in a seething sea of angst, insecurity and turmoil.

Recognise the syndrome? I thought you might. So let me tell you something else. You may be mean and moody, possessive and broody, incurably suspicious of other people's true motives and insatiably hungry for emotionally intense encounters. But you're also deeply intuitive, magnificently creative and awe-inspiringly, accurately sensitive to the things that other people think and feel. None of which is anything to be ashamed of.

You can tell whether a person is worthy of respect from one look at their face or one word uttered on the telephone. Your instincts are never wrong and, once a person has passed your instant but stringent 'trust test', nobody, but nobody, is capable of giving them more support and care. Your compassion is deeper than a magician's pocket, your loyalty stronger than a jeweller's safe. It's just a shame that your mind is sharper than a surgeon's knife.

As intense as the emotions you experience in your heart are the thoughts that pass through your head. Where other people have opinions, you have judgements. Where others have ideas, you have brainwaves. And where others have fears, you have nameless dread.

The first two differences are assets. Nobody would dispute this, not even those who sometimes find themselves being outshone by the superior might of your intellect. However, your capacity to conjure up so freely the angel of anxiety, the demon of doubt and the spectre of suspicion rather reduces your ability to let the good times roll.

Your loved ones are more than happy to make allowance for this. They have to be, for they are often more aware of your tendency to worry than you are yourself. This, of course, is because primarily, it's them you worry about. Most of them appreciate being shown so much concern, but sometimes they wish you could take what you feel a little less seriously. Those who are wisest know that the best way to help you do this is to find you a good cause to fight for or a real threat to fend off. And an astrologer can always tell when a person with the Moon in Scorpio has got the right partner. They just look for the person who is smiling because they have managed to convert their lover's emotional energy into energy of an altogether more physical nature.

Before I tell you about the darker side of having the Moon in Scorpio, I need to level with you. I'm trained as an astrologer, not as a psychiatrist. The term I'm about to apply to you is one that I really have no right to bandy about, so you can reject it if you wish. If you choose to accept it, please do so only on the understanding that I'm not using it in a medical sense. It's only what it has come to mean in popular parlance that I wish to convey.

The word is 'paranoid'. Now before I qualify this, I want to level with you some more. I've got the Moon in Scorpio too. So believe me, I'm not just saying this in order to get at you! You can see how nervously sensitive I am by the run-up I took to uttering that dreaded word. And you can also see how self-defeatingly honest the Moon in Scorpio makes me by the fact that I eventually went ahead and said it.

We Moon in Scorpios see far more than is good for us. We cannot deny what our instincts are telling us, no matter how much we would like to for the sake of a quiet life. We frequently find ourselves needing to say things that we know others don't want to hear. Not surprisingly, we live in fear of the reaction we're going to get. Often, when we confront others with the truths we have seen, they deny them. Some even actively try to discredit us in an attempt to defend the pretence they wish to keep up. So we close down, clam up and either become recluses or find a more superficial aspect of our personality to hide behind. Are we really paranoid? No. But the defence mechanisms we are obliged to maintain for our own and others' good sometimes lead us to display all the classic symptoms.

Now, having confided all this, I have great news. Between now and the year 2008 Pluto, the ruler of our Moon sign, will be passing through Sagittarius, the most expansive and optimistic sign of the zodiac. We Lunar Scorpians find with each passing year that we become less inclined to apologise for, or feel afraid of, our sensitivity and more easily able to apply our special brand of insight in a very powerful way.

MOON IN SCORPIO, *SUN IN...*

ARIES Woe betide the person who ever crosses you. Both your Sun and Moon are ruled by Mars, planet of power, strength and victory at all costs!

TAURUS Though you are often a little emotionally restless and eager to assert your will, you are also deeply wise, sensitive and intuitive.

GEMINI Your breezy and bubbly Gemini 'front' is a very convenient mask behind which to hide your deep insight and emotional sensitivity.

Cancer You're far too sensitive for your own good. You take too much to heart – but then you've got an awful lot of heart to take it all!

Leo There's an iron fist behind your velvet glove. It only ever comes out in self-defence, but those who underestimate you should take care.

Virgo If it were not for your devastating ability to be so self-critical you'd probably rule the country, if not the world, by now.

Libra You're good at putting your tremendous insight to practical use. People usually find you wise and money tends to find its way to you.

Scorpio Others can take you or leave you, for you are who you are and there'll never be any changing you. Most, rightly, prefer to take you!

Sagittarius You're always surprised by how deep your emotions run – they sneak up on you sideways. But your intuition is almost invariably right.

Capricorn You are very selective about who you will allow to be your friend but those in your special circle are as close to you as your family.

Aquarius Your Scorpio Moon is very conscious of what others think, so it tones down your Aquarian excesses and causes many people to look up to you.

Pisces You don't really care where you're going as long as you're not forever staying in the same old place or frame of mind.

MOON IN SAGITTARIUS

The astrological textbooks tell us that people with the Moon in Sagittarius are jolly and approachable, open-minded, adventurous, extravagant and generous. In all this they are right – but they are only telling half the story. While you may be the life and soul of every party, and the office clown or family comedian, looking closer, we have to consider the words of that wise philosopher Smokey Robinson: 'It's easy to trace… the tracks of your tears.' Your ebullience is an act, your magnanimity a defence mechanism. You figure that, if you're always merry, nobody will realise how vulnerable you truly feel or how afraid you are of being rejected. Deep within, you're not so much a hotbed of emotion as a veritable inferno of unfulfilled (and arguably unfulfillable) passion.

Every so often, you find yourself unable to keep up the cavalcade of quips a moment longer. The inner volcano simply has to erupt. It doesn't happen often but, when your heart wells up with longing, the 'amplifying' influence of Sagittarius on your Moon causes you to go to extreme lengths to pursue what you yearn for. You take risks that nobody else would even dare to dream of. You make outrageous statements, you chase impossible rainbows and you take it all exceedingly seriously. Luckily, it's never long before your sense of humour returns and your dangerous desires subside.

Sagittarius is an exuberant, energetic, humorous and hearty sign. It is also a kind, compassionate one. The Moon, however, can sometimes feel a little 'lost' here, in the same way that someone from a small village can feel lost in a big city. The Moon is a part of the personality that always wants to know where it stands. Sagittarius is a part of the zodiac that is perpetually changing. The ethos of the sign is 'onwards and upwards', which doesn't always gel with the Moon's inclination to be steady and safe. The result is that a person with the Moon in Sagittarius can often feel restless and insecure, constantly on the look-out for something solid to cling to yet never quite able to settle for what they've got.

Behind your buoyant, good-natured, confident persona there's a competitive edge. Not only are you forever measuring yourself against others, you are frequently trying to improve on your own past record. You frequently pursue unrealistic goals or extravagant ideas which you pick to test your own nerve and courage.

Your loved ones can find it hard to live with such a driven individual. They might be able to understand it if your aim never wavered from one target, but your tendency to chop and change priorities confuses those in your family who are by nature more consistent. Your partner finds you fun to be with, but can't work out why one moment you're sweet, light and bubbling with the desire to respond to the spur of the moment, yet the next you're sharp, serious and flatly insistent on a particular point. Frankly, nor can you. It's the fact that you never really know what you want from your lover that makes it so hard for your lover to provide what you need. All of which is why you get on best with others when there's a challenge to rise to that's big enough to cause all concerned to forget about their feelings and just get on with teaming up to succeed against the odds.

You might find it hard to imagine how a sign as traditionally light, bright, joyous and jolly as Sagittarius can possibly have a dark side. It's like contemplating curry-flavoured cornflakes or a mugging on Sesame Street. There's definitely, however, a danger-loving streak in your Moon sign, albeit not an obvious one. It springs, ironically, from the very fact that you are so keen to do what's right. Sometimes, you can become such a champion of justice as to turn into an angel of revenge. You can forgive almost anyone almost anything and it takes a lot to turn your benevolence to malevolence. But if you really feel someone has done something beyond all excuse, you can be almost as inexcusable in the methods you employ to let them know.

I'm not talking about something that happens often – but it doesn't need to happen often in order to have a profound impact on your outlook. And while you rarely get such a large hornet under your hat, you are forever getting a series of smaller bees in your bonnet. You frequently want to come to the rescue of those you feel are getting a raw deal. In the process, you bite off more than you can chew or, worse, find that the object of your act of heroism turns round and bites the hand that has come to feed it.

A lot of this stems from the desire to emulate a person who was a kind and supportive influence on you in early childhood. You may, however, do their memory more credit by learning to hold back your desire to see justice done and having more faith in the ability to let natural justice prevail. Focus on putting your inner world to rights before you set off with the intention of sorting out the wider one.

MOON IN SAGITTARIUS, *SUN IN...*

ARIES You're a reckless adventurer and a wild, free spirit. You do everything at the last minute and will do almost anything for a laugh.

TAURUS Though you like to play it cool, deep down you are tremendously excitable, enthusiastic and very often lucky.

GEMINI Your trouble is that when you have an idea, no matter how far-fetched, you simply have to act on it. Happily, things usually work out well.

CANCER You'll willingly go out of your way to do someone a favour. You're adaptable, easy-going and very warm-hearted.

Leo Others sometimes feel you lack common sense. But as you are usually so full of fun and appreciation for life, why should you care?

Virgo Little baffles or perplexes you for long. You've got an enquiring mind, an adaptable heart and a healthy sense of the ridiculous.

Libra You're a bright and lively character full of great ideas, but you sometimes let the voice of enthusiasm drown out that of common sense.

Scorpio You've got a rather good relationship with money. You don't worry about it … and it runs after you to see why you're not bothered!

Sagittarius You're the original 'Weeble' toy. No matter what knocks you for six, you may wobble but you simply won't fall down!

Capricorn You like the idea of being part of a large, worthy organisation or institution to which you can safely dedicate your heart.

Aquarius You're exceedingly affable and good-natured. Your Sun and Moon signs are so sociable, it's a wonder you ever get any work done.

Pisces Your exuberance and enthusiasm make you popular, but it's your ability to seize an opportunity that makes you so successful.

MOON IN CAPRICORN

Many of history's highest achievers have been born with the Moon in Capricorn. There's something about the influence of this sign that turns otherwise timid characters into despots, dictators and tyrants. You no doubt recognise that somewhere deep within you too have a hunger for status, a desire to control and a yearning to be treated with respect verging on awe. And you have probably allowed this to influence you in one of two ways. Either you have deliberately climbed to a position of great and unquestionable authority at work, within your social circle or in your family; or you have spent most of your life repressing the urge so successfully as to become the ultimate underdog, allowing everyone to get the better of you rather than release your lust for supreme power.

Either way, you know that, when you really need to, you can manifest motivation that will brook no opposition or release rage that knows no bounds. Luckily, as treasurer of such a valuable inner resource your personality is wise and responsible enough to expend it sparingly. Most of the time, you're the very model of calm, common sense and restraint. Many people admire your level-headedness and ability to keep contentious issues in perspective. But when you've got a mission, a purpose, a justified battle to fight or a mighty wrong to right, woe betide the person or organisation that stands in your way!

Others see you as strong, self-assured, mature, responsible and discriminating. What's most intriguing to an astrologer about the Moon in Capricorn is how it manages to make them think that, while simultaneously causing you to see yourself as weak, insecure, childish, careless and thoughtless. Perhaps it's the very fact that you're so conscious of what you consider to be your many faults that you work so hard to compensate for them. Perhaps this is also why, occasionally, the tendency I have outlined above gets inverted. It's when you try too intently to manifest those positive traits that you end up drawing the negative ones to your loved ones' attention.

You have a strong need to control. Mainly you apply this to yourself, repressing powerful urges and restricting what you consider to be stray emotional weaknesses. At times though, you become determined to act as a restraining influence in the lives of others, and you do so in what could only be called a very passionate fashion. Others are surprised to discover both the extent of your feeling and of your desire to do something about it, the more so because they are not used to the idea that anything ever bothers you. You're usually happy enough to let your partner take charge of day-to-day decisions, but only when (in your mind at least) they're playing the role of ship's captain to your admiral of the fleet.

You are very attracted to individuals who are powerful in their own right. As a 'great commander' you want to be able to delegate with confidence. But tension can arise when a serious situation inspires you to leave your lofty office and take over the helm, obliging you to challenge your partner's notion about who is really in charge. The more confident you can become about how much power you really hold, the less you will ever need to prove the point and the calmer your more tempestuous relationships will become.

It's surprising that you have an interest in astrology. One might have imagined that you were fed up to the back teeth of being told what you were destined to be. From an early age you have been surrounded by people with clear ideas about your future. A certain authority figure, probably male, certainly determined, tried hard when you were but a small child to make an indelible impression on your memory. They left you in no doubt about what they expected of you, yet quite possibly in some considerable doubt about whether you might ever be able to live up to their ideal. If you got as much praise as blame or as much understanding as criticism, you were lucky.

Probably a softer person was also there to intervene on your behalf. But even if there was, you grew up torn between the desire to fulfil the ambition that the dominant character clearly had for you, and the desire to rebel against it. A part of you wanted to prove something to them; another part figured that, as you could probably never be good enough to please your hard taskmaster, you might as well give up. No matter how many years have passed from that day to this, you have still not fully managed to shake off that aspect of your upbringing. Perhaps you never will, and perhaps it doesn't matter.

What *does* matter, however, is that you understand the mark it has all made on you. An aspect of your own psyche now plays that role of chastiser and disapprover. You keep yourself so firmly in line as to hold back a side of yourself that sorely needs to be let out. Of late, the desire to do this has been exceptionally strong. You've made magnificent headway in freeing yourself from redundant inhibitions; but you still have further to go, and far greater freedom than you have ever known before lies ahead for you.

MOON IN CAPRICORN, *SUN IN...*

ARIES You want respect and work hard to reach a position of such power that people have to give it, no matter what they may think.

TAURUS There's never any arguing with you. You find it easy to say no, though you rarely wind up in situations where you need to!

GEMINI You're very good at explaining things to people and persuading them to see your point of view – sometimes, indeed, a little *too* good at it.

CANCER You take your responsibilities exceedingly seriously and never quite feel satisfied till you know all your jobs are done.

Leo You can be very masterful when you want to be, and sometimes even when you don't. Many people are a bit in awe of you.

Virgo You doubt your own judgement more than you need to. It's just as well, or others would never stand a chance against your strong will.

Libra Home and family mean a great deal to you. Perhaps partly to compensate for a chaotic past, you're keen to ensure that all around you are safe.

Scorpio You've got a very strong intellect, capable of absorbing many complicated ideas. And you've got a very strong character to go with it.

Sagittarius You've got a magnificent ability to make far-fetched ideas sound perfectly feasible – and often to turn them into money-makers, too.

Capricorn Your shell is as tough as titanium but underneath it your heart is as soft as jelly. Your personality is even sweeter and more colourful.

Aquarius You tend not to remember the dreams you have when you're asleep, but you never stop working to fulfil your waking ones.

Pisces You take your friends and your friendships very seriously. And others know you're a rock to which they can always cling.

MOON IN AQUARIUS

You may well be one of the most sensual, physically demonstrative and intellectually astute people the world has ever known. But when it comes to emotions, you're as numb as a frozen finger. When you first began to notice that you were surrounded by people who could pour out the contents of their hearts by turning on some inner tap, you began to fear you were less than a whole human being. 'Let out your feelings,' others would say. 'How can I,' you would reply, 'when I don't know what they are?' And so despondent would your lack of sensitivity then make you feel that, privately, you would sob bitter tears of confusion into your pillow. Er … what, pray tell, were those if not an expression of profound inner feeling?

I put it to you that you are not at all the robot you paint yourself as. Far from being shallow, you are so full of sensitivity as to be mortally afraid of admitting the fact for fear of diving into a pool from which you might never emerge. Your Moon in Aquarius makes you not devoid of feeling but devoid (or almost devoid) of stupidity. You cannot help but question the logic of giving vent to passions that have not been fully thought through. But all emotions, are of course, ultimately irrational. So the fact that your feelings well up only intermittently, in response to some rather unlikely stimuli, makes you neither perverse nor cold. It simply makes you normal in the eyes of everyone except yourself.

What others love most about you is your eccentricity. They have no choice other than to adore or abhor it, for it is as integral a part of your personality as your nose is a part of your face. Those whose own emotional predilections naturally incline them towards a more conventional companion rarely get close enough to you to form a deep bond. After all, you hardly go to any great lengths to disguise your idiosyncrasy for the sake of making a good first impression. People have to take you as they find you and, since they rarely find you the same from one day to the next, your world is full of folk who have vastly different ideas about what kind of a person you actually are.

This suits you fine, for variety is not just the spice in your recipe for a happy life, it's the meat. Having friends who not only don't know each other but wouldn't, even if they happened to meet and chat about you, necessarily realise they were talking about the same person, amuses you greatly.

Fortunately, you don't need a partner who can adapt to all the facets of your wide-ranging personality. You're happy just to have someone who sits contentedly in the department marked 'spouse', and who trusts you enough to know that you'll keep coming back once you've gone off and been who you are to everyone else. If you don't currently have such a companion, it shouldn't be hard to find one in time, for, while you may be unusual, you're also unusually vibrant, attractive and fun to be with.

It's more with loved ones of a non-romantic nature, such as other members of your family, that personality clashes can arise. They don't have the freedom to choose when, how or where they get involved with you – nor vice versa. Consequently, they can never be quite sure which of your personalities they are likely to encounter! Some acknowledgement of this on your part could improve these relationships a lot.

To have the Moon in Aquarius is to have two mutually incompatible aspirations battling, your whole life long, for supremacy in your personality. It's by no means a disadvantage: this kind of internal conflict often creates the material from which great characters are carved. However, to become the truly successful and contented person you would dearly love to be, you need to reconcile the difference in your own mind between that which makes you feel successful and that which makes you feel content. Success, to you, implies proving to yourself and the whole world that you are quite unlike any other being who ever walked the face of the earth. You don't care how many people have trodden a path like yours before and what tricks they employed to make it work. You're determined to be different – to do it your way and to do it without compromising a single thing you stand for. You want others to look at you and say 'There goes one of a kind', and say it with a note of awe and admiration in their voice.

All of which is fine except that you also yearn to be accepted, welcomed, loved, trusted and shown a group of people to whom you feel you can fully belong! Nonconformists don't, by definition, find it easy to fit in, even with other avowed eccentrics. As a child, you were equally famous for your stubbornness and your exceptional gifts and talents. As a teenager, you went in search of love everlasting and still nurse the broken heart to which this quest led you. Now, as an adult, you have to accept yourself for who you are and be proud of it, rather than act out a series of roles designed to persuade others that they are safe to embrace you.

MOON IN AQUARIUS, *SUN IN*...

ARIES You really couldn't care less what other people think of you – which is just as well, for most people don't know *what* to think of you!

TAURUS Your home may be full of gadgets, or it may just be with relationships that the new, the daring and the different excite you.

GEMINI You like to consider yourself above the ordinary world and its silly problems. And in a funny sort of way, perhaps you are.

CANCER You never really know whether you are coming or going, and nor do your loved ones. But you're very perceptive about everyone else.

LEO Your somewhat imperious personality disguises (sometimes completely) the soft, warm heart that beats beneath.

Virgo You've got a unique way of looking at life and can always be relied on to come up with the one side of the story that nobody else has seen.

Libra You're an adventurer, an explorer and a bit of a party animal – though you may enjoy debating the night away as much as dancing it.

Scorpio You take pride in looking after the interests of loved ones carefully and cleverly. Only when you really feel at home do you let your feelings show.

Sagittarius You're certainly an original thinker. Few have a mind as cleverly convoluted as yours, and even fewer can actually articulate such thoughts.

Capricorn You're a great innovator with a handy ability to anticipate future needs and be ready for them. It all does your bank balance no harm.

Aquarius After they made you, they broke the mould – assuming there ever was one. You constantly amaze everyone, including yourself.

Pisces Your mind works in mysterious ways – mysterious, at least, to you. Others often seem to know what you feel more clearly than you do.

MOON IN PISCES

Do you yearn for a life on the ocean wave? If so, you are manifesting a typical tendency of people born under the Moon in Pisces. So deep are your needs, so profound are your yearnings, so passionate are your impulses that no relationship, no matter how intense and committed, with any other human being will suffice to fulfil them. You need a relationship with something vaster, more unfathomable and more mysterious – the sea, for example. Your heart constantly wants to sail, swim, surf and dive. If it can't feel safe or able to do that, it prefers to sit patiently doing nothing other than splash pathetically through some shallow puddle.

This is why so many of your loved ones consider you an enigma. You often reveal little or no trace of emotion, yet it is clear that you are far from being heartless or insensitive. And no matter how successful you become at your job, in your lifestyle or in your family life, there's always something about you that seems to be a 'fish out of water'. It may not be the actual ocean that you require in order to find complete satisfaction. It could be a stimulating, demanding role to play in some large organisation or institution that fills the 'gap' you sense in your heart. But it's certainly true that no Piscean is emotionally content unless they're in the process of trying to do the impossible in an environment where 'anything' can happen next – and probably will.

If you read the descriptions of some of the other Moon signs, you will see that most follow a pattern. I begin by describing the assets of having the Moon in a certain sign, go on to discuss the drawbacks, and end with an appraisal of how these may cause problems in a person's love life. I cannot, however, apply such a formula when writing about you.

There is, as far as I am aware, no romantic disadvantage to having been born with the Moon in Pisces. Nor is there some particular attitude to life that can make family relationships stressful. To have the Moon is Pisces is to be everyone's friend, nobody's enemy and some very lucky body's ideal partner.

Well, almost. I'm not trying to say you're perfect. But you're certainly harmless without being insipid, sympathetic without being soppy, wise without being arrogant and good-humoured without being giddy. Your faults, if it's proper to call them these, are all connected with being 'too good to be true'. You can make even the most un-self-critical companion feel unworthy of your love. You can be unreasonably reasonable, so fair that it's unfair and so unresentfully self-sacrificing as to make others resent you!

Many people are simply not psychologically geared up to the challenge of co-existing with someone as nice to know as you are. When they try to probe you for weaknesses or goad you into a heated emotional reaction, you don't even give them the satisfaction of feeling patronised by a refusal to respond. You bravely go through the motions of anger, jealousy or angst in the sincere hope that this will help.

None of this is to say that you're devoid of emotion – far from it. You're tremendously deep, and prone to profound inner feelings that sweep like tidal waves across your heart. It's just that, even when these feelings have more to do with despair than joy, you don't allow them to cause problems to others in your world. You're one of a very extraordinary Moon-in-Pisces kind.

Some people lust for power. Others crave money, love or sensual fulfilment. You may not be entirely immune to such desires but they hardly dominate your life. If they did, one way or another you'd have more of them – for you're not the kind of person to deny yourself anything you crave. What you crave, however, is something that the modern world seems to have in short supply: meaning. Your life must have point and purpose, though the conventional goals and aspirations that others strive for seem somehow petty to you. There has to be a sense of sublime transcendence on offer before you're interested. Painting, poetry, music or other creative activities fulfil this need in some Lunar Pisceans. Others find it through their devotion to a spiritual or charitable cause.

But if all this is beginning to sound like the light side of your Moon, hold on. There's a hunger in your soul for a strong, powerful experience. You simply cannot bear mundanity, so you throw yourself into whatever you feel is most likely to provide you with an escape hatch from the ordinary world. You can all too easily become obsessive about your art, fanatical about your faith or, worse still, convinced that even these are not sufficient to take you as far as you want to go. In the absence of a psychological anchor you can become dangerously cavalier about your wellbeing, taking risks for the sheer thrill of seeing how close to the edge you can go. As a child you were inquisitive, as a teenager argumentative and now, as an adult, you have to learn how to construct a lifestyle that satisfies rather than merely deconstructs the available options.

MOON IN PISCES, *SUN IN*...

Aries Others can't help but respect you for your wisdom and integrity, even if they find you a little too outspoken or pushy at times.

Taurus Though you try not to let the poetic side of your nature run away with you, you're a soppier, more sensitive soul than you care to admit.

Gemini You're never one to let a prior engagement stand in the way of a good spur-of-the-moment idea. Hopefully, your friends are as flexible.

Cancer Most of the time you're at ease with yourself and with life in general. Somehow, your intuition always leads you to the right place.

Leo It's a good job you can put up such a commanding front. If people knew how much fun you really were, they'd never take you seriously.

Virgo Tension in early childhood may have left you too ready to believe that dreams don't come true. Yet yours frequently do, despite this.

Libra You have a pronounced sense of duty. You work hard to keep your wilder impulses under control and at least give an impression of being sensible.

Scorpio You're a light and easy-going character most of the time. Your sense of humour is never far from the surface, no matter what's going on.

Sagittarius Though Sagittarians love to travel, something in you also loves to come home. Ideally, you'd have a home that was capable of travelling!

Capricorn You'd make a great teacher, largely because you're such an enthusiastic student of all that life has to offer. You have a permanent hunger for facts.

Aquarius The combination of a sensitive heart and a logical mind makes you an unbeatable force, as your bank manager will testify – one day, anyway.

Pisces You're impossible! A law unto yourself, a living example of why there's an exception to every rule… and a very wonderful person.

Chapter 3

YOUR UNIQUE WHEEL OF DESTINY

Your Wheel of Destiny

You can use this wheel to plot your own signs

YOUR WHEEL OF DESTINY

Now that you know your Moon sign as well as your Sun sign, I'm sure you're keen to find out as much as possible about how the two factors work with one another. You may, indeed, be wondering why the previous chapter only contained a quick 'one-liner' about each Sun/Moon combination.

I could have said more. I could even, I suppose, have written 144 different chapters – one for each permutation. By keeping my comments brief, I'm really not trying to short change you. It's just that there's a better, more astrologically accurate way to look at this whole business.

Think for a moment about tins of paint – in a range of colours. Why carry a full range of 144 different shades when you can mix to order any shade you want from a handful of 'base' colours?

If you know the secret formula, you can pack an entire decorator's warehouse into a small suitcase. Likewise, if you know how astrology really works, you can dispense with a library full of reference books.

It's my aim in this chapter – and, indeed, throughout the remainder of this book – to teach you the ultimate trick of this trade. I want to free you from the need to keep looking things up in some astrological 'book of rules' by explaining the simple principle on which the rule book itself has been based.

Welcome then, to the wheel of destiny; a diagram of the sky which will reveal the secret of your personality and free your future potential. It's not difficult, nor is it time-consuming, but it is very revealing because the principle I'm about to explain to you is, in essence, a simplified version of a full, traditional personal horoscope.

PLOTTING YOUR PLACE ON THE WHEEL

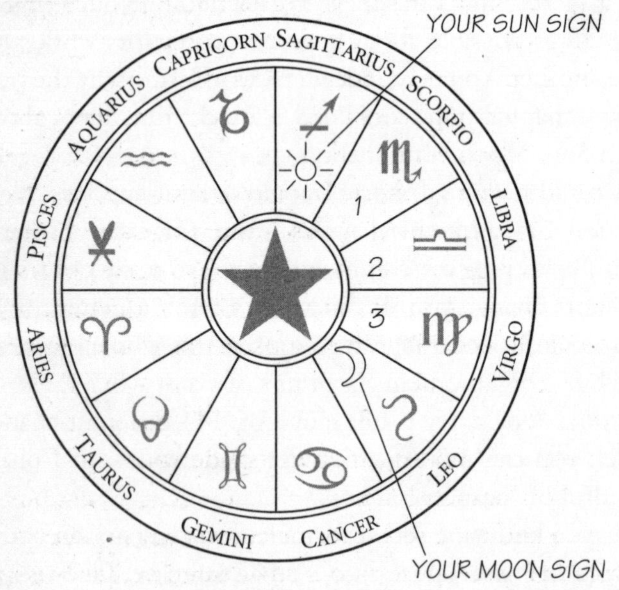

Step 1

This is easy, for it merely involves writing down a piece of information that you already know. Turn to the blank chart wheel on p.190 and find the zodiac sign that you always read when you look for your forecast. Then write the words 'My Sun' in the appropriate space or, if you're feeling artistic and would like to do the job in the same way that we professional stargazers do it, draw in a little Sun symbol.

What you have just done

Congratulations! By entering on to the wheel the approximate position of the Sun on the day you were born, you have taken your first step towards plotting a personal horoscope. Now you are ready for something a little more complicated.

Step 2

Turn once more to the wheel, and this time look for the zodiac sign that corresponds to your Moon sign. Write the word 'My Moon' in the appropriate space, or draw a little Lunar symbol. You may be among the one in twelve readers whose Sun and Moon are both in the same sign. In this case you will have to squeeze them both into the same box.

What you have just done

You have now charted your second reference point on the wheel of destiny and are nearly ready to start putting it to work. You have also, by the way, followed in the footsteps of great scientific astrologers from Claudius Ptolemy through Galileo to Kepler, by plotting a diagrammatic map of the sky according to an ancient, mystical method. You now have only one more step to perform.

Step 3

Turn once more to your now not-so-blank chart wheel and count the number of spaces between your Sun and your Moon. Once you have done this, you are ready to find out what your wheel of destiny has to tell you.

By counting the spaces you will end up discovering that your Sun and Moon are one of the following:

- In the same sign as one another
- In the sign next door to one another
- Two signs apart
- Three signs apart
- Four signs apart
- Five signs apart
- Six signs apart (i.e. opposite one another)
- If they are more than six signs apart, please count around the wheel in the other direction!

The 'what it all means' section that follows will explain what the relationship between your Sun sign and your Moon sign says about you.

WHAT IT ALL MEANS

SUN AND MOON IN THE SAME SIGN

Your childhood influences

Because you were born when both the Sun and the Moon were passing through the same sector of the sky, you tend to oscillate between manifesting the very best and very worst traits of your sign. Being born under the new Moon makes you exceptional in a further way, for traditionally the maternity wards are much busier when the Moon is full. But though there may have been a shortage of light in the sky on the night preceding your birth, there has been no shortage of light in your life.

In many ways you have led a charmed existence, and have been helped to do so both by a succession of kind, supportive individuals and by the naturally even balance of your own temperament. None of this is to say that you are perfect (even though some people accuse you of seeing yourself as so), nor that your entire life has been a bed of roses (even though you have managed to come up smelling of them time after time). But on balance you have somehow been 'celestially protected' from many of the tough scenarios that your peers and contemporaries had to face.

You may or may not have been showered with parental affection, but you certainly spent most of your formative years free from too many challenges to your sense of security. Key factors remained stable, allowing you the luxury of being a child rather than feeling forced into premature maturity. Even when big events and changes did rock the boat of home and family life, you found a way to cope by turning your attention inwards and developing a sense of independence. You may have had an imaginary playmate who seemed very real, or a profound interest from an early age in some highly absorbing hobby.

You certainly developed some strong techniques to keep yourself at an emotional distance from the outside world – a way of protecting yourself from your own immense sensitivity. You feel a great deal more than you care to reveal – a fact which those you are close to know only too well, but which it suits you to keep hidden when you can.

One of your parents had a much stronger influence on you than the other, perhaps even to the point where you were left feeling estranged from the less dominant one. This, too, has had its part to play in creating the self-contained, quietly confident character which others tend to see you as today.

Your approach to relationships

When people are of a mind to criticise you, they usually begin by having a little dig at your tendency to be rather set in your ways. They accuse you of being too keen to stick with tradition or too sure that your way is the right way. Up to a point this may be fair comment, but it doesn't mean you should feel obliged to adjust your personality drastically. Often our quirks and foibles are merely our special gifts and talents, taken a step too far.

We can easily see the truth of this in your case. What is your resistance to change, other than a deep desire to be loyal and consistent? What is your occasional tendency to seem self-righteous, if not a natural sense of faith in what you feel and believe?

If you do need to alter some aspect of your character, it's almost certainly a need to change your tone of voice rather than redefine your actual message. Stressful developments in your key relationships usually come about when you fail to realise what an impact your words are having on others. Your humble requests sometimes end up sounding like demands. Your sincere attempts to offer advice can come across like lectures. Your wise preference for precedent can make you seem like a reactionary.

It's all a little ironic because, deep within, you're an exceedingly soft, small, approachable, even 'cuddly' character. Harm a fly? Why, you'd even be tempted to put a wasp on probation. You're naturally inclined to see the best in everyone and will offer to forgive and forget with a frequency that your less tolerant friends find alarming.

It is, as a matter of fact, your very lack of guile that causes you to be so misunderstood. Because a hidden agenda is the very last thing you look for in others, it's the last thing you imagine others will be looking for when they encounter you. So you say what's on your mind without sufficient regard for what it's going to sound like when it reaches *their* mind. All you ever really want, from a lover, friend or family member, is a little trust and cooperation. You're quite prepared to give as much back in return – so why should there be a problem in asking for it? The answer is, there shouldn't be. And there won't be, once you learn to think a little more carefully about how to ask for it.

SUN OPPOSITE (SIX SIGNS AWAY FROM) MOON

Your childhood influences

Werewolves, witches and vampires all traditionally come out when the Moon is full. Babies born under this astrological configuration don't, you'll be glad to hear, turn into any of the above – but they do have extremely strong, determined personalities and can certainly seem, to their long-suffering parents, like proper little imps! So the first thing we can conclude, from finding a full Moon in your wheel of destiny, is that you were no easy child to bring up. You had a mind of your own from the moment you drew your first breath, and have hardly stopped arguing the toss from that day to this!

It's probably just as well that you were blessed with such a lively, inventive personality, because events in your early life created quite a powerful need for you to pit your wits against something and prove to the world what you were capable of. You found yourself born into what could best be described as a somewhat unconventional family. Your parents lived in very different worlds, even if physically they remained under the same roof. They either agreed to differ (in which case you probably got let off lightly), or they suffered from the strait-laced legacy of their generation and, while putting on a fine front in public, privately conducted a constant war of attrition. This was no doubt intended to go over your head, but in fact a lot of it went straight to your heart. It left you feeling unsure of how to please one without offending the other – or even feeling vaguely responsible for the rift between them.

Your uppity, idiosyncratic character was originally a sort of cosmic compensation for all this. It gave you the strength to blot out impressions that might have rendered you very weak had you been more sensitive by nature. It's served you well and helped you become the highly motivated, wise and thoughtful bright spark that others tend to see you as today.

But deep within, you suffer from a couple of secret hang-ups. You're never quite sure whether you're coming or going, and for all your outward air of confidence you frequently suffer from agonising bursts of profound self-doubt. And you yearn for the perfect partnership, yet try so hard to bring one into being that in the process you sometimes create unnecessary tension between yourself and your partner.

Your approach to relationships

You're a person of extremely strong opinions. Rarely, if ever, do you allow yourself to feel ambivalent about anything or anyone. This might be fine if you really knew why, but you sometimes develop unreasonable prejudices which you then go on to dress up as perfectly justifiable likes and dislikes. We're all entitled to our preferences and there's no law that these must be thoroughly logical, but you're particularly 'naughty'. You tend, almost on point of principle, to develop ideas and beliefs that conflict with those held by your nearest and dearest. Mr and Mrs Jack Sprat may have made a good team with their differing tastes in meat, but your partner probably yearns to hear you say, 'Actually, dear, I do agree with you.'

You say this a lot? Ah, but *do* you? Or do you just think it and then go on, in your next breath, to utter a counter-argument? Could it be that you find it so easy to play devil's advocate that you step into the role without even noticing? Could it also be that loved ones have got so used to feeling challenged that, when they hear you beginning to think through both sides of an issue out loud, they automatically assume you are going to settle on a contrary position to their own?

Could all this be why your social, romantic and family bonds are a tad too full of dynamic tension for comfort? A little variety adds spice to a relationship, but to make someone feel they are part of a perpetual tug of war is to tip a whole tin of curry powder into the pot.

SUN OPPOSITE (FIVE SIGNS AWAY FROM) MOON

So ought you to learn how to compromise? No. You already know perfectly well how to do that (though you might benefit from learning how to do it without complaining quite so much). But really, it's not compromise you need more of in your life, it's confidence.

You're a thoroughly splendid, kind, incisive and deeply giving character who, deep down within, rarely feels completely secure. To compensate, you posture and pretend when you really ought to confide and confess. Approach the other people in your world with a little less self-defensive certainty. You won't just feel a bit more loved, but positively overwhelmed by the amount of affection, gratitude and reciprocated honesty that begins to come your way.

Your childhood influences

On the day you were born, the Sun and Moon were five signs apart. The Moon, therefore, was either nearly but not quite full or just beginning to wane. If you want to know which, go back to the wheel and count again. Start with your Sun and work anti-clockwise till you find your Moon. If, going this way round, it's five spaces away, you were born under a waxing Moon. If it's seven spaces away, your Moon was waning.

This factor doesn't make too much difference, except perhaps in one respect. If anything you read about yourself strikes you as especially true, yet at the same time significantly uncomfortable, you may want to make a conscious effort to alter certain habits. If you were born under a waxing Moon, the best way to do this is to reach a little further and try a little harder for what you feel tends to elude you. If, however, you were born under a waning Moon, your path to greater personal contentment probably has more to do with giving up a little and learning to relax.

And now let's return to what this particular five-sign-wide angle between the Sun and Moon in your wheel tells us about you. Chiefly, it says you're a born worrier – you find it impossible to rest on your laurels, or indeed on anything else! You can hardly ever sit still, leave things be or believe that you are entitled to a life of comparative ease.

All this has something to do with a rather turbulent childhood. Your parents may have got along like a house on fire or lived in a state of burning mistrust – or perhaps their relationship swung between the two extremes. One thing's for sure, though: they had about as much in common as chalk and cheese. Thus you grew up with two highly contrasting role models, and never felt quite sure which you were more at home emulating. While this has made you exceedingly versatile as an adult, it has also left you with a slightly strange fascination. You constantly hunger to reconcile the irreconcilable, resolve the paradoxical or explain the inexplicable. Up to a point, it's an exciting challenge. Sometimes, however, it's a very exhausting tendency.

Your approach to relationships

You're a thoroughly lovely person. About this much, at least, most of the world is in firm agreement. But as to quite why, or what it is that makes you so special, there are as many theories as you have friends.

You're a different person under different circumstances – not in any false fashion, but because you have such an impressive ability to adapt to what you can intuitively sense the person by your side requires. To some, you're a tower of strength and self-sufficiency, to others a soft, vulnerable soul. Between these two extremes are many more acquaintances who have each formed a different idea about what you have to offer and where they fit into your life.

As you also take a delight in spanning widely diverse social circles, it's feasible that if two of your closest companions were to meet on the street and discuss their mutual friend, neither would recognise you from the other's description. What makes this even more remarkable is that if you were then to stroll up and join in the conversation, neither you nor they would feel as though any great game were being given away.

You're not pretentious – you're genuinely versatile. Just occasionally, however, your ability to be casually chameleon-like can leave a loved one feeling flustered or threatened. Possessive characters secretly want to pin you down. When you honestly and innocently respond with, 'Fine… pin this bit of me down if you like, but I'm afraid the other part of me has to go out now,' they feel a little cheated.

If you only ever kept the company of relaxed, easy-going characters, the ensuing tension would not arise. But something within you is drawn like a magnet to those of an intense disposition. You like a little fire and passion, and sometimes it seems easier to huddle round someone else's burning flame than to ignite one of your own. But if you ever feel a need to make some of your key relationships easier, you'll find the best way to take the heat off is to find some passion that's all your own and put it not into a person but into some great mission or vision. Let this be the primary source of warmth in your world and then, as others come to gather round it, they will naturally offer to do things your way rather than expecting you to obey their rules.

SUN TRINE (FOUR SIGNS AWAY FROM) MOON

Your childhood influences

You were born under one of the most harmonious influences known to the world of astrology. Your Sun and Moon are 120 degrees (or one third of the wheel) apart, and occupy mutually supportive signs of the same element. They're in a state of agreement with one another, and so you, by and large, are in a state of agreement with yourself. 'Why?' you may ask. 'What on earth else should I be?' and the answer to this is, 'Nothing – but you're lucky, because a lot of people spend a great deal of time feeling anything but comfortable with who they are and what they have to offer.'

You, however, have had the benefit of a relatively stable childhood during which, even if all was far from perfect in your environment, you never felt too far from one very special adult who treated you with constant love, kindness and respect. Quite feasibly, there would have been more than one. Astrologers often find that people born under your particular cosmic alignment have been fortunate enough to enjoy what in modern times has become an increasingly rare phenomenon – a childhood home in which both parents lived in genuine harmony.

Even those who were brought up in less idyllic circumstances usually have genuinely happy memories of their youth. They recall at least some warm, wise, sympathetic adults who got along well with one another and with their junior charges. They remember being given only gentle discipline and sweet encouragement, rather than being too harshly pushed and pulled. As a result, they now have less of an axe to grind in their day-to-day adult life. They naturally tend to look on the bright side and to trust that all in life will work out well in the end.

If you can identify with this it may be why you are so popular, so easy to get along with and so often entrusted with other people's secrets. It may also, however, be part of the reason why you don't always fight certain battles quite as determinedly as you could – or perhaps, even, as you should. Unless there are other extenuating factors in your personal chart, you probably feel more inclined to compromise than to court conflict. Just sometimes, however, you need a slightly harder, more ambitious edge in order to get on in life. And so, just sometimes, you tend to feel your own easy-going nature is working against you.

Your approach to relationships

If a manufacturer of beauty products could only capture the essence of what you've got, they might bottle it and sell it for a fortune. To be born with your Sun and Moon positions so well balanced within the cosmic circle is to have oodles of what some call charisma and others, less delicately, refer to as sex appeal.

You weren't aware of possessing any such natural advantage? Come, come, surely you're being modest. You mean to say you've never noticed the impact you make on certain people from time to time? What did you think was causing all those wobbly knees and glazed eyes? Flu? Oh well, perhaps you did. Perhaps Mother Nature, in her endless struggle to strike an even balance, imbued you with drop-dead good looks with one hand while rendering you totally unconscious of their potential with the other. But if she did she didn't manage to be fair to the rest of us, for this only gave you a meltingly innocent demeanour to go alongside your air of subtly inviting promise.

Even more annoyingly to those who would willingly give their eye teeth for a small fraction of the magnetism you exude with every step, you probably still aren't particularly interested in exploiting it, even now you've had it pointed out to you. A part of you would far rather stay within the bosom of your family, tending to the needy or carrying out some other noble duty, than be swept away by a tide of wild and exciting offers. Even if you do crave a life of adventure, you'd far rather have one that depended on something a little less nebulous than this 'X factor'.

Does all this ensure that in relationships, romantic and otherwise, your life will always be sweet and successful? Sadly not. Among members of your own sex you have a tendency to evoke jealousy, no matter how hard you try to play down your assets. Among members of the opposite sex, there's always a slight doubt about whether you're being appreciated for your mind or your body. And can any spouse ever feel completely comfortable with a partner who turns more heads than a cranial osteopath? Unless, of course, they were to be similarly celestially well endowed? But then would you, with all your natural preference for a quiet life, really want to get involved with such potential trouble?

SUN SQUARE (THREE SIGNS AWAY FROM) MOON

Your childhood influences

On the day you were born, the Sun and Moon were forming a 90 degree angle to one another. Unfortunately, as far as astrologers are concerned this is anything but a 'right' angle. It's primarily an angle of tension, challenge, inner disquiet and (often) external discord to boot. This is precisely why it's so often found in the horoscopes of the world's high achievers, from pop stars to politicians and from big business financiers to big-time celebrities.

If you think about it, it's obvious. To get ahead in life you've got to have an 'edge' to your personality. If you're naturally contented and relaxed, you're not going to have any motivation to prove yourself. You need a little psychological stimulus in your birth chart in order to become a major success. What's questionable, however, is whether you also need the constant disruption that tends to come with it.

You have never really known a quiet life. As a child you were constantly pushing your luck and testing adults to see how much they meant the word 'no'. Not surprisingly, this led you into a strained relationship with at least one of your parents. You looked for examples of their hypocrisy with which to justify your defiance, and because, like all human beings, they were less than perfect you found it. You also looked, indeed hunted like a hawk, for topics on which grown-ups disagreed. When they inevitably did, you slipped through as many of those disciplinary loopholes as you could.

Whether the authority figures in your formative years could have set a better example in the way they related to you (and to one another) is a moot point, but what's certainly clear is that you *felt* they could. All this left you with a healthy disrespect for petty rules but also, perhaps, an unhealthy tendency to challenge life's less trivial restrictions. So keen are you now not to take orders that you will sometimes baulk against doing today what you decided to do yesterday. This doesn't make you the easiest person in the world to get along with – which is ironic, because deep down what you long for more than anything else is a life full of harmonious relationships.

Your approach to relationships

Most ancient mythologies saw the Moon as female and the Sun as male. Modern astrologers overwhelmingly agree with this view. You, however, may not be so willing to accept this notion, or indeed any other. Because you were born with the Sun and Moon approximately 90 degrees apart, you are not the kind of person to take anything at face value. You always want to know 'Why?', you always want to know 'What else?', and you often take special pleasure in supporting unconventional minority beliefs.

In deference to your desire to differ, I'll concede that certain historical civilisations perceived the Sun as a mother figure and the Moon as a patriarch. What's certain beyond question, though, is that no culture since the dawn of time has considered the Sun and Moon to be of the same sex. So any way you look at it, the key cosmic symbols of male and female energy are, in your wheel of fortune, aligned in mutually challenging positions.

This explains why you tend to be so restlessly argumentative, not just when dealing with others but when trying to make up your own mind. You're forever trying to reconcile distinctly incompatible inner yearnings; on the one hand an urge to be sensible and assertive, on the other a quest to be intuitive and adaptable.

The down-side of all this you already know. You're notorious among your friends, colleagues and family for being an awkward so-and-so. They see you as erratic, unpredictable and almost impossible to persuade. They may love and respect you regardless, but they don't find you easy. Your key relationships are thus best described as 'dynamic'. They involve plenty of lively debate and tend to go through phases – periods of quiet, contented co-existence followed by conflict and upheaval.

The way to improve your relationships is, by happy

coincidence, also the way to make your Sun/Moon configuration help carve you out a brighter career. It is to harness the immense creativity, inventive talent and imagination that your wheel of destiny bestows. It is to learn to wrestle with concepts rather than people, to argue with artistic or scientific tradition rather than with mundane routine. When you're busily asking pertinent, provocative questions on behalf of humanity as a whole, you're doing us all a favour and, into the bargain, using up excess emotional fighting energy that's far too potentially powerful to be squandered on some trivial personal battleground.

SUN SEXTILE (TWO SIGNS AWAY FROM) MOON

Your childhood influences

On the day you were born, the Sun and Moon were in zodiac signs approximately 60 degrees apart from one another. Astrologers call this particular angular relationship a sextile because it spans a sixth of the zodiac circle. It has long been regarded as a constructive influence – indeed, the ancient astrologers used to believe that a person with such a link between their Sun and Moon was automatically destined for a life of good health and fortune.

Much though I hate to throw a spanner in the works, I have to point out that this may not be quite so automatic in all cases today. We are working with slightly imprecise measurements and therefore your sextile may be what we call a 'weak aspect' (that is, one you have to reach for consciously rather than one that life has handed to you on some silver platter). But I can confirm that to have your Sun and Moon in the signs next door but one to each other is indeed to have a special celestial advantage operating in your life.

It suggests that you were probably blessed with a widely supportive family environment in your formative years, and as a youngster you were certainly much loved and protected by one very special parental figure. Even if not all in your childhood garden was rosy, someone went to great lengths to keep you safe from as much as they could. You will never forget the influence that this adult's sweet, generous nature had upon you. It's both the inspiration you draw on whenever you encounter conflict in your life today, and the source of your motivation to help others, in your turn, wherever you can.

You're well known and much admired for your even temper, sincerity, consistency and creativity. You have a naturally philosophical way of coping with the slings and arrows of ignoble fortune and of cutting your coat to suit your cloth without ever compromising your principles in the process. Even though you sometimes encounter misplaced jealousy from those who think you're a little too perfect to be true, you rarely rise to an emotionally baited hook. You prefer to find some way to understand what lies behind an individual's anger or bad behaviour and thus to reach out to the better nature that you remain absolutely convinced can always be found in everyone, if only one looks hard enough for it.

Your approach to relationships

By and large you're an easy-going, affable character. You can snap and crackle rather fiercely sometimes, but it takes a lot to pop the bubble of goodwill that surrounds you. You're benign, trusting, sincere and self-assured. You take pleasure in helping others and are even wise enough to recognise that this can't be done unless some effort is made to reach their level. So you work hard to be a good listener and a fair, open-minded friend. In theory all this ought to make you everyone's ideal choice for marriage, employment or just social company. In practice? Well, it can… but there are drawbacks associated with your generous spirit. You have a tendency to mother or father people; you can rarely resist the urge to protect, nurture, guide and console. It's a lovely trait, but it means that weak, unsettled characters are drawn towards you like moths to a flame. You've got one shoulder which is perpetually damp from the number of people who seem to think they have some right to cry on it, and another that constantly aches from the burdens it's ended up carrying.

All this you normally accept without complaint, though it's arguable whether sometimes you don't give certain people a little more support than they deserve, thus depriving them of a chance to learn their own lessons the hard way. But what really causes conflict in your world is another syndrome stemming from the same source.

Parental figures aren't always appreciated and honoured: often they're resented and rebelled against. Some of the 'lost souls' that seem to surround you take the unresolved issues that they have with their actual mothers or fathers and project these on to their relationship with you. They test your trust, tax your patience or, worse, secretly complain about you to others. When you realise this is happening, you're left wondering what you've done wrong.

The answer is nothing, other perhaps than that you've cared a little more than you ought to have done. All you need, in order to develop a more settled, satisfactory personal life is to be a little more selective about who you extend your protective wing to, and perhaps in future to make a deliberate point of forging relationships on a distinctly adult-to-adult basis, where each person takes ultimate responsibility for their own problems.

SUN SEMI-SEXTILE (IN SIGN NEXT DOOR TO) MOON

Your childhood influences

You were born either just before or just after a new Moon. Before we go any further we ought to establish which, for it makes a slight difference to the rest of this reading. You can easily find this out by going back to your wheel of destiny for a moment and finding the segment containing your Sun. If your Moon is in the next sign reading clockwise, it had just begun to wax. If you have to look anti-clockwise to find it, your Moon was still on the wane.

As a rule of thumb, people with waning Moons tend to hide the way in which they are being led through life by their emotions, feeling perhaps a little afraid of seeming silly. People with waxing Moons on the other hand, are less inhibited about announcing that they are running on instinct. This is an important distinction to make in your case because, whether you were born while the Moon was waxing or waning, you were certainly born with a powerful sense of intuition. That's your blessing.

Your curse, if that's not too strong a word to use, is that the feelings which move you so strongly never seem to fit very logically into the lifestyle you lead on the outside. You either end up like the top accountant who secretly wants to be an artist (if your Moon is waning), or (if your Moon is waxing) like the great artist who proudly proclaims that a bohemian lifestyle is a thing of the past and the avant-garde is to be found through double-entry book-keeping. One way, you seem odd to yourself; the other, odd to others.

Either way you're definitely an odd mixture – and indeed you've been so ever since you were born. Your parents were probably something of an odd couple, and your early lifestyle was probably an eccentric one. You've somehow been exposed to a series of logical non sequiturs all through life and have rather come to relish them. The way you lead your life may not make very much sense to you or anyone else, but it's fun for all that and surprisingly successful too. Furthermore, in your perpetual quest to find a compromise between wildly different impulses, you often manage to bring together the most unlikely ideas or people and make them work wonderfully well together.

Your approach to relationships

People can never be quite sure which side of your character they are going to see. Sometimes you can be tremendously down to earth, almost business-like in your dealings with others. But every so often you will reveal a very different, much deeper and more emotionally vulnerable side of your character, even to those it might be considered inappropriate to show it to. Consequently, while you probably have some colleagues who feel safe to confide great personal secrets to you because you in turn have been open with them, there are some members of your immediate family who feel unsure about approaching you on any topic more emotionally loaded than the colour of their new sofa.

Even though you don't deliberately set out to make things go this way, a part of you may quite like the arrangement. For you're never quite sure how closely you want to get involved with anyone. Powerful inner feelings fascinate you in one way and worry you in another. You like life to be straightforward; complex emotions are usually anything but. Which is not to say that you deny their existence, either in yourself or in others – more that you prefer to play a game of peek-a-boo with profound and intense matters, acknowledging their vast importance one moment but carrying on as if you have seen nothing to remark upon the next.

It's all tied up with the way that your Sun and Moon, respectively representing the primary conscious and unconscious forces in your psyche, are aligned a little too closely for comfort. You find it hard to get a perspective on what's going on deep in your heart, for much the same reason that an overtaking motorist cannot always be sure when it's safe to re-enter the slow lane. Too much seems to take place in your psychological blind spot. This, in turn, is why you often find yourself surprised to hear that others have been upset by something you have said or done (or failed to say or do).

Your equivalent of an extra mirror needs to be a policy of asking your nearest and dearest to honk their horns when they feel you're in imminent danger of accidentally squeezing them off the road. And then they'll somehow be more able to accept and love your erratic behaviour for what it actually is – the hallmark of a harmless, eccentric genius at work!

Chapter 4

VENUS – THE LOVE PLANET

VENUS – THE LOVE PLANET

For the purposes of this chapter, please forget all you know about the zodiac sign you normally consider you belong to. To discover what kind of lover you are, what kind of lover you really want, and what kind of love you may one day be able to enjoy in your life, I must ask you once more to look up your date of birth. This time do it in the Venus tables on p.460. These will tell you what sign Venus was in on the day you were born. It won't take you more than a moment to consult them, but the information they lead you to may change the way you see yourself forever!

THE NATURE OF VENUS AND THE VENUS SIGN

We're going to find out why some people cannot stand you yet others feel so powerfully attracted to you that they simply cannot resist your charm. And, as Venus rules art and music as much as she rules romance, we're going to explore your instinctive aesthetic preferences. We're going to look at both the shapes and colours that strike your fancy, plus the figures and faces that fill your fantasies.

Venus is a planet for romantics. Her very name conjures up an image of mystery and sensuality, but she was a seductive symbol long before the Romans coined this name for her. The Babylonians called her Ishtar, Goddess of Fertility. The Sumerians knew her as Inanna, Queen of Thunder. To the Egyptians she was Isis the Enchantress, and to the Greeks Aphrodite, ultimate icon of feminine charm and the mother of Cupid.

If you are a typical male, your Venus sign represents your ideal woman. Aphrodite wears many disguises. Today, you will see which she dons when she wants to capture your heart. If you are a woman, your Venus sign governs the kind of person you turn into when you exploit your feminine charm. I have to confess, though, that when reading romantic preference in a horoscope, all astrologers find female psychology more complicated.

Aphrodite was the ultimate free woman. She belonged to no man yet she awakened a deep and profound spirit of desire in the heart of every man she encountered. She had passionate and fruitful romantic involvements with gods as diverse as the witty, intellectual Hermes, the silent, muscular Adonis and the pompous, powerful Zeus. Throughout all this she also had a tolerant husband: aloof and irritable Hephaestus, the wounded craftsman. Forget for a moment any judgement you might feel inclined to make about her character. We are dealing here with a symbolic goddess, not a real human being and we must view her in her proper context: as an icon of femininity. One day, I hope to write an entire book about her. For our purposes here, though, all we need to understand is that we are dealing with the image of a woman who is attractive to every type of man. A man's Venus sign tells us whether

he is more likely to try and appeal to Aphrodite by acting like a Hermes, an Adonis, a Zeus or a Hephaestus. A woman's Venus sign, however, does not tell us which of these four symbolic gods she is most likely to be drawn to. There is an image of an ideal man inside the mind of every woman, but to identify this using astrology we have to look at a woman's Mars sign, not her Venus sign. That comes later in this book.

For now, while we're looking at the Venus sign, we simply need to remember that every woman has the spirit of Aphrodite somewhere within her and that her spirit is forever a free spirit. It reserves the right to pick and choose between all four types according to the mood of the moment.

In a man's horoscope, the Venus sign represents his ideal female fantasy figure: the guise in which he is most likely to perceive Aphrodite when he thinks of her and the way in which he would most like to relate to her. In a woman's horoscope, the Venus sign represents the way of being which is most likely to make her feel relaxed, at ease, sensual, confident, charming and appealing. It tells us what kind of role in life is most likely to make her feel supremely free and feminine.

'Are two people with the same Venus sign compatible?' The short answer is, sometimes, yes… but please don't be misled, especially where you notice that the female description of a Venus sign appears to be a direct match for the male fantasy outlined below it. It's more a point in favour of the partnership's potential than a cast-iron guarantee.

Your Venus sign reveals a lot about your attitude to love but it also speaks volumes about the way you relate to Mother Nature.

Mother Nature is a powerful entity. To some, she appears in an impersonal, scientific disguise. To others, she is very much a living individual with tastes and preferences, habits and hobbies. But to all, she is a source of inspiration and support. Without the environment that she so carefully creates we would have no air to breathe, no water to drink, no sunshine to bathe in nor, indeed, no world within which to pursue the love of one another.

We may not understand all that nature does, but we cannot help but appreciate how vast, powerful and influential her activities are. Whether we take her for granted, live in awestruck appreciation of her strength or actively seek a logical explanation of why she does what she does, we are bound to have a relationship with her. It is the particular quality of this constant relationship that your Venus sign describes.

Do you see yourself as needing to compensate for what nature has seemingly failed to endow you with? Or as overwhelmed by the generous gifts that she has bestowed? Do you see nature as an abundant force, constantly offering to supply whatever you need? Or as a weak, easily corrupted character, in need of sensitive protection? How you feel about the wider world you inhabit speaks volumes about your attitude to other people. If you're naturally inclined to trust nature, you'll trust loved ones. If you're always suspicious that the elements are about to play some nasty trick, you'll be similarly guarded about giving too much to those close by. In these and a thousand other ways, the links between you and nature are as revealing as any session on a relationship counsellor's couch.

Venus is the second planet from the Sun and the

nearest to our own. She is roughly the same size as Earth but, as the planet is covered in clouds of sulphuric acid and has a surface temperature of 460°C, it is hardly the place you would want to go to for a holiday. Yet even astronomers have to concede that Venus has a bright, compelling beauty that makes you want to run to her. She may be a planet, but she twinkles like a star. She may have no gravitational effect on the human body, but she never fails to pull the heart-strings of any soul whose gaze wanders skyward. Venus's days may be four months long, but she is the ultimate symbol of nocturnal promise.

Those who are only prepared to see Venus as some distant ball of gas and rock can hardly be expected to recognise her power to influence events on Earth. There is, as yet, no satisfactory scientific explanation why Venus or any other planet should do this. But then love itself is not a scientifically provable phenomenon. To experience it, you have to stop asking what it is and just give yourself over to something you feel to be true. If you're going to say that Venus is only a planet, you may as well say that a rainbow is nothing more than an intriguing phenomenon involving the refraction of light. Or that a kiss is only an expression of some primal urge to reproduce the species. Romance defies logical explanation – and so, to some degree, does astrology. But that doesn't make either of them any less real.

Now, if you have not already done so, please turn to the tables on p. 460 and look up your Venus sign before you read on. Bear in mind that it is quite possible for your Venus sign to turn out the same as your Sun sign.

VENUS IN ARIES

YOU AND NATURE

To have Venus in Aries is to have an admiration for earthquakes, an interest in infernos, a taste for tornadoes and a respect for raging waters. You have no desire to live near nature at its most violent, but you can certainly empathise with the sheer energy it's capable of manifesting. You too yearn to move the immovable, inflame the impervious, whip up an enormous storm or make waves that no one can resist.

To deny this is not just to suppress the fire in your soul but to risk unconsciously aligning yourself with others who will set the cat amongst pigeons you dare not disturb. If there's ever tension in your world, it's usually got a power struggle at its heart. You were born to lead rampaging armies, conduct exciting campaigns, fight furious battles and shake awake a sleepy world. You have to find some way, in this tame, restrained modern society, to pit your wits against the elements or put yourself at the head of some worthwhile, challenging enterprise.

If you can't or won't, you'll find your excess energy gets absorbed controlling the actions of some partner who both attracts you (by daring to do what you'd half like to) but horrifies you (by doing it clumsily or thoughtlessly). For as long as you feel you need to assert, over an individual, the kind of power you ought more properly to be asserting over an environment, any companion will be in danger of becoming an adversary. But when you've got your work wisely cut out, you're too busy fulfilling a universal calling to contemplate personal conflict. As none can resist the magnetic appeal of a Venus in Aries person ploughing ahead in a direction that truly makes sense, this is all you have to do if you want to surround yourself with love.

YOU AND YOUR CREATIVITY

Your greatest skills lie in starting things from scratch. Unlike some people, whose talents lie in refining or improving an existing idea, you're best at conjuring up the new from next to nothing. It's probably for this reason that you're drawn to primary colours, clearly defined textures or strong, striking tastes. Life's more subtle nuances certainly don't escape you, but as far as you're concerned they're icing on the cake or paint on the wall. First, the cake has to be baked and the wall has to be built. Others can have the joy of decorating them. They can even, if they wish, have the pleasure of beating the eggs or piling up the bricks. For you, the chief joy is in making a space in which magic can happen. It's in hunting down the ingredients, ordering up the materials, and then setting the creative process in motion. Just put you in charge of setting the ball rolling and you'll rapidly sketch out brilliant blueprint after brilliant blueprint, which others can turn into reality at their leisure.

YOU AND ROMANCE

To have Venus in Aries is to be a powerhouse of passion. You've probably never spent a day wistfully yearning in your life. The only thing to do with a dream, as far as you're concerned, is to get out there in the world and do whatever it takes to turn it into a reality. If others think your plan is too risky, you merely try all the harder for the added joy of proving them wrong. You're competitive about all your conquests: romantic, creative and financial. You need to perceive yourself as a winner (which is fine), but you're constantly comparing yourself to others and wondering why you haven't yet got what they've got (which is not quite so fine!).

Your most attractive quality is your nerve. No matter how timid you may appear on the surface, you're rarely too shy to speak your mind or make a bold proposition. You're spontaneous, strong and charismatic though rather too prone to do things in haste that you regret at leisure. Your eyes may sometimes flash with fire, but generally they sparkle with a kind of infectious enthusiasm that can melt the iciest heart. People tend to admire your confidence and resent your arrogance.

As you spend most of your life treading a paper-thin line between the two, this makes for relationships that tend to be full of drama. You're one of those people who simply 'won't be told'. Not only will you rush in where angels fear to tread, you'll rush right back in there again even after someone has gone to a lot of trouble to get you out of trouble! As a lover you're adventurous, energetic and deeply demonstrative, though your tendency to blow hot and cold can confuse those of a more stable disposition.

THE WAY YOU MANIFEST YOUR FEMININITY

Female

The day you flutter your eyelids helplessly and pretend that only a big strong man can help solve your problem is the day the coyote captures the road runner. You're not a weedy Wendy, a lacy Tracey or a flimsy Fiona but a capable Caroline, a passionate Penelope and an independent Eileen. You're strong, self-contained and sensual, but you're a real woman and not one of those pre-packaged plastic Barbie dolls. Macho men don't impress you. You want someone who will treat you as an equal, respect your territory and join you in a serious campaign to right the world's wrongs. If he's a little on the quiet side, that's fine as long as there's plenty of personality below the surface. The up-front performance you can manage by yourself, if not all the better without some noisy, insensitive male constantly mishandling the conversational ball.

YOUR IDEAL WOMAN

Male

Your ideal woman has to be lively, powerful and self-motivated. She must be quick on the uptake and quicker still on the trigger of the gun you envisage her holding at the end of her leather-clad arm – a sort of Annie Oakley with overtones of Mae West in her wit and refusal to let anyone get the better of her. You have a secret desire, if not to be dominated, certainly to be given a jolly good run for your money. You don't want her to play hard to get, you want her to *be* hard to get. And ultimately, when you've run out of all possible ways to catch up with her, you want her to turn around and fetch you! You're quite happy to play second fiddle to her first violin – but only if she's an absolute virtuoso. You'd rather be not quite secure with the wildest woman in the west than waited on hand and foot by some gorgeous geisha.

VENUS IN TAURUS

YOU AND NATURE

Venus in Taurus means you ought to be a planter of acorns, a builder of windmills, a designer of reservoirs or a mender of engines. You are in your element in any element, as long as you are patiently investing time, care and skill in some enterprise to improve the quality of life. To seize efficiently the power of the earth (to grow trees), air (to harness power), rain (to irrigate) or fire (to propel) is to express perfectly the delicate, respectful relationship you have with nature – that of mutual servants, each providing what their partner most requires. A similarly purposeful balance is all you aspire to in love. The problem is, we live in a modern world. Unless you're lucky, you have little chance to interact with natural forces. You're more likely to be a consumer or end user than a person who can make what they need from start to finish. Even if you work with natural elements, you may feel more like a cog in the machine than someone with freedom to respond to the needs of their environment.

Domestically, too, similar artificial pressures may be creating tension and dissatisfaction. Neither you nor your partner may be free to live the lifestyles you might choose. It can all make you feel resentful, thus unwilling to let the love in your heart guide your life. The key to change lies in some means of self-expression (be it gardening, painting, sculpting or basket-weaving) that puts you in command of an entire natural process of transformation. Through filling at least your leisure time with this activity, you can respond to the yearning of your Venus in Taurus for a joint creative venture with creation itself. If you can share the task with a soulmate, you really can lead a life abundant in joyous give and take.

YOU AND YOUR CREATIVITY

In this modern world of 'make it fast, pile it high, sell it cheap' you're a genuine rarity: a person who believes in the old-fashioned ethos of care and craftsmanship. You'd far prefer to spend your life creating one outstanding novel, symphony, painting, sculpture or garden than churn out endless works of just-above-average quality. If you can't be sure you've got the time and resources to get something perfect, you'd rather not even try.

Subtle shades and textures make all the difference as far as you're concerned. No way can you stain pine dark and call it oak, or pass off polyester for silk. Nor can you feel relaxed about entrusting responsibility to others. Unless you've got a promising apprentice you've personally trained, you'd far prefer to do your own dirty work and know you've done it to the highest standard. You're similarly discriminating when it comes to spending the money you've worked so hard to earn. One item of real quality is worth a house full of junk. But better still would be a collection of excellence. You're an exceedingly wise investor of time, skill… and money.

YOU AND ROMANCE

To have Venus in Taurus is to be almost breathtakingly responsive to physical stimuli. Where some people have photographic memories, you have full sensual recollection. You only have to touch, feel, taste or hear something once to remember it forever. This is why the quality of your environment is so important to you. Just as an ecological campaigner hates the thought of some chimney polluting the atmosphere, you cannot stand the idea of a substandard item or possession lowering the tone of your life. Everything has to be of the highest possible quality.

If you're selective about what you sit on, eat off, sleep under or listen to, you're even more choosy about who you allow to awaken your deepest, most passionate urges. A lover who pays only lip service to your needs cannot be tolerated simply because they happen to be good company in other respects. When you give yourself to anything or anyone, you do so completely. Whether pursuing the enjoyment of art, music, literature, natural beauty or romantic expression, you want to feel interest awaken slowly in the tips of your toes, rise gradually to the top of your head, and cause your whole body to writhe with endlessly powerful waves of involvement.

None of this is necessarily obvious to the casual observer. You rather like the idea of being a dark horse with a misleadingly bland persona. You're interested in what others do, not what they say – so you tend to appeal only to people who share an instinctive desire to put experience before philosophy. Those who cannot resist you recognise your capacity to meet them at a private and immensely deep level. Those who find your company hard going resent your refusal to act out false roles or put on social airs and graces.

THE WAY YOU MANIFEST YOUR FEMININITY

Female

Some women go to great lengths to maximise their assets: for a date or special occasion they will dress up to the nines in an attempt to look appealing. But you find yourself needing to tone down your appearance in order not to radiate more sultry, sensual magic than already flows naturally out of your every pore. You're not so much glamorous (for that word implies a superficial glitz) as sumptuous, in so far as the ability to manifest deep feminine strength comes as a standard feature on your psychological operating system. You no more need a man to make you feel like a complete woman than a Rolls-Royce needs a go-faster stripe to make it seem like a proper car. Consequently, you can pick and choose your partner from a wide range of willing applicants. The show-offs, the smart alecs and the wise guys don't get past the first hurdle. You're only interested in someone deep, sensual and sincere.

YOUR IDEAL WOMAN

Male

Your vision of loveliness wears a long gown with a wide hood. She's an angel of mercy, a figure of mystery, a radiant-eyed bestower of warmth and kindness. Quite how she's supposed to manage to juggle the nine kids that she's anxious to bear for you without a murmur of complaint whilst simultaneously tending to the needy and the sick who queue for her healing touch, plus (of course) fulfilling your every physical whim and fancy, is a puzzle – but somehow she'll do it all… and more besides. She'll cook, clean and make a comfortable home while selling the prize orchids she's grown on the back lawn for such high sums that you never need to work again. A difficult fantasy for any flesh-and-blood female to live up to? Indeed, but the one who comes (or appears to come) closest will always be the one who wins your heart.

VENUS IN GEMINI

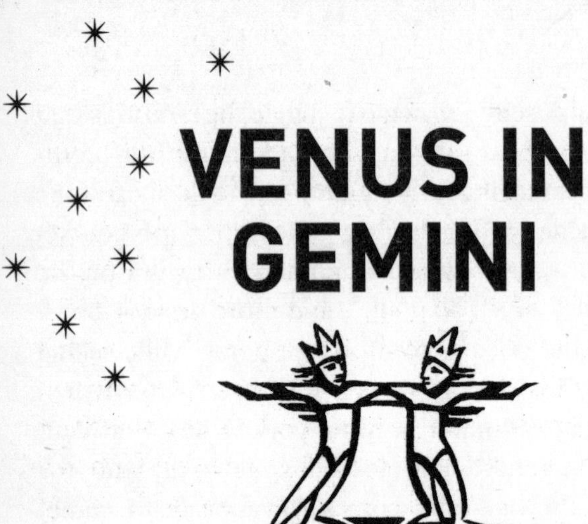

YOU AND NATURE

To have Venus in Gemini is to be a connoisseur of variety and ingenuity. It is to appreciate, in people, plants and animals alike, the subtle distinguishing features that make up the detail in life's rich tapestry. It is to be keen to communicate all you can see, to share your knowledge with others and absorb from them any additional information they may be able to supply. It is also, however, to risk becoming a critic rather than a commentator, a disenchanted pundit rather than an enthusiastic observer.

For when something captivates your heart, you want to know every little thing about it. So you tend to play about with it: to see how it responds under condition X or environment Y, or whether it will benefit from this change or that adjustment. Sometimes, you discover you can work minor miracles with your experiments, vastly improving the efficiency of a machine, the emotive impact of a piece of music, the taste of a recipe or the sales potential of a product. And sometimes, like the child who dismembers an insect just to see what will happen, you tinker too much with your toy, disabling it beyond repair.

There is a very human (but none the less misplaced) tendency at such times to blame the failure on the fiddle rather than the fiddler. At which point you become cynical: 'Oh, I know all about such-and-such. It's useless.' If this means you sometimes give up in an area of endeavour where you might have persevered to great success, that's a shame. If it's also the reason why you sometimes abandon faith in a relationship, it's a tragedy! To fill your life with loving acceptance, you simply have to overcome the tendency to fill your mind with negative dismissal. For while you have one, you simply have nowhere to put the other.

YOU AND YOUR CREATIVITY

You ought to consider becoming a writer, for you have a real way with words. You might also make a promising cartographer, for you can always find a clever way to get from from A to B. Then again, a career in meteorology might suit, for you're certainly fascinated by changing climates and conditions.

Yet for all your intelligence, wit and fascination with detail, you're sometimes more inclined to help others display their genius than use your own. You can find yourself interested in assisting absent-minded professor types who have a lot to teach you and hopefully a lot to learn from your somewhat more substantial grasp of reality. Often, though, they end up talking you out of the common sense you're trying to talk into them. Venus in Gemini makes you willing to listen (which is good) but a little too easily persuaded (which is problematic).

For much the same reason, you have to take care in business matters. You have great ideas and a real talent for making ordinary things look special. But you're sometimes afraid to ask for what a thing is worth, or a little too quick to agree to a deal that benefits the other participant more than it suits you.

YOU AND ROMANCE

Venus in Gemini makes you witty, perceptive, inventive and vivacious. Given a straight, non-negotiable choice between a partner with devastating looks but a dull personality or one with, shall we say, an unusual appearance but a brilliant mind, you'd have no hesitation in opting for the intelligence. Ultimately, the quality of pillow talk matters far more to you than the quality of anything else that can happen in a bedroom.

This is not to say you're ambivalent about the physical side of romance, nor that you've no appreciation of a fine face and figure. It's just that, to you, love is about good communication or it's about nothing at all. In an ideal world, you'd have a lover with brains *and* beauty – or, dare I say it, you'd have one of each type. You can just about cope with the concept of monogamy, but only if the word never becomes confused with monotony, for you thrive on variety and change. Your partner, therefore, has to be lively and interesting enough to hold your interest and self-contained enough not to see your flirtatious personality as a threat.

It's the nature of Venus in Gemini never to be satisfied with anything, always to be looking out for something new, often to be questioning conventional ideas and expectations. People similarly stimulated by the desire to push back life's boundaries find you devastatingly attractive. You make them think, you make them fight and, most of all, you make them laugh. People whose primary desire is to conform for the sake of a quiet life find you more likely to make them cry. Here you have to be careful for, despite your general preference for thought over feeling, you are a soft and sensitive soul and a sucker for a sob story.

THE WAY YOU MANIFEST YOUR FEMININITY

Female

There may be a sexier woman on earth but you've yet to meet her. Once or twice you've come across someone superficially similar, but on closer inspection she's proved a little too dull, dreary or desperate. It's a shame, really, because you could do with some competition if only to enliven those tediously long days of fending off admirers. There's certainly not a man alive who can withstand your charm when you lay it on thickly enough for – with your sharp wit and infallible insight – you can turn yourself, like a chameleon, into whoever you suspect your quarry most happens to be dreaming of. But as you really want to be loved for who you are, your ideal man has to be smart enough to see through you without being quite smart enough to see past you. He also has to be good-looking (so others will envy you), but not so cute as to make you constantly nervous that he'll be stolen (not that he could be, of course, but it's as well not to run the risk).

YOUR IDEAL WOMAN

Male

The siren of your secret dreams probably wears a mortar board, a black academic gown… and precious little else. Before agreeing to respond to your amorous advances, she wants you to name the capital of Assyria, calculate π to ten decimal places and list the Roman emperors in chronological order. Should you fail in any of these tasks she will have to help you find some novel way to tease the answer into your memory.

It's debatable whether you really yearn for a seductress or an instructress – though, as the latter has overtones of punishment, we'd better add immediately that Venus in Gemini gives you no taste for stern discipline. The woman of your dreams needs to be light-hearted and good-humoured about her role as educator and debater of topical issues. She simply has to be as bright as she is bubbly, as soft as she is sharp… and as attractively formed as she is impressively informed.

VENUS IN CANCER

YOU AND NATURE

To have Venus in Cancer is to be in love with the Moon. It is to be moved by its beauty, pulled by its gravity and influenced by its phases. And it is to have an affinity with all in nature that is traditionally governed by this queen of the tides. In particular, it is to admire the oceans, lakes and rivers; not just for their charm but for their historical claim to be the mother of all earthly life.

Our earliest ancestors were amphibians who gradually moved from the sea to the land. Some species (such as frogs, newts and crabs, who symbolise your Venus sign) still need to keep in contact with their place of origin. Others pay only lip service to the relationship in the enjoyment of liquid refreshment or the occasional pleasure they take from a brief immersion. However, rather like the conscientious member of a large family who takes on the duty of ringing round to remind everyone that it's nearly Mum's birthday, people with Venus in Cancer are somehow cosmically required to remember, on behalf of the entire human race, what debt we owe to H_2O. This is why, silly though it may sound, you need plenty of water in your world if you want plenty of love in your life. The more you float, bathe, swim or sail, the more you will be in your element. And the more you share these activities with others, the more interpersonal tensions will somehow just be washed away.

YOU AND YOUR CREATIVITY

Venus the artist brings to Cancer the home lover the ability to turn a humble abode into a glorious palace. But then Cancer (the unpretentious) brings to Venus (the great pretender) a determination to put comfort before style. So, while your chosen environment definitely conjures up a mood, it creates a real atmosphere, not an idealised, artificial but superficially impressive one.

Much the same balancing process takes place wherever you seek to express creative skills. You are a creature, first and foremost, of honesty, integrity and intuition. You'd far rather take a chance on the truth than have a safe bet on a piece of deceit. So the cheap success that certain other people seem to get in life rarely comes your way. Your artistic, horticultural, healing and people-management skills either get recognised for the valuable rarities they truly are – or taken for granted. Which it is matters little to you. Your interest is in doing what's right to the best of your ability, and letting that satisfaction be its own reward.

It is only when pursuing success on behalf of others or in connection with some heartfelt cause that you feel inspired to be pushy. You cannot bear to stand by and watch others being ill treated, so, when you see someone getting a raw deal, you seek ways to champion their cause, relieve their suffering or rescue them from their predicament. In aid of some official charity or as part of some private campaign to help a friend you will perform feats of creative genius that no amount of financial incentive alone could ever spur you on to.

All of this is admirable and worthy, except that sometimes you will deny yourself an opportunity to which you are fully entitled simply because you don't feel that you should have it while others are suffering. Next time this syndrome crops up, think about how much more you might be able to do for others if you were in a position of greater power.

YOU AND ROMANCE

To have Venus in Cancer is to have an insatiable appetite for reassurance. You yearn to be loved, wanted, even needed. This may sound like a description of someone suffering from inner weakness, but it is actually the reason for your phenomenal strength. So anxious are you not to feel rejected that you think very carefully before ever putting your heart in a vulnerable position. Someone else with similar reservations might be destined to spend their life hiding behind a barrier of non-communication.

Venus in Cancer, however, compensates for its tendency to make you defensive by imbuing you with a vast capacity to give. Just as a wealthy person may donate £500 to charity without denting their bank balance while a poor one may only give £5 but will have to go without something in consequence, you are rich in compassion and can afford to give generously. But while a poor person is always aware of their limits, a rich one can more easily assume they have endless reserves. If they make a mistake and draw too heavily on funds they cannot truly spare, they have much further to fall!

Your apparent emotional affluence coupled with your desire to be of real use to others naturally makes you a beacon in the night of this modern world. Fluttering round your attractive flame come all creatures seeking guidance or warmth. Moved by an equally strong urge to stay away, however, are not just those who prefer to be where it's cold and dark but sometimes those who want to create their own light rather than just take from yours. That's a shame, for it's among such people that you're most likely to find a lover worth letting past the psychological no entry signs in the back room of your heart.

THE WAY YOU MANIFEST YOUR FEMININITY

Female

The idea of being a siren, seducer, vamp or even a Venus appeals to you about as much as a holiday in hospital. In fact ward 10 seems a better idea all round. There you could tend to the needy, protect the vulnerable and fulfil the urge of your warm, caring heart to help others. While the idea of cynically exploiting your sexuality strikes you as ridiculous, the notion of clutching some woe-begone soul to your bosom strikes straight to the core of your sincere psyche. This, of course, is precisely why certain people find you so desirable. Your honesty and integrity are as intoxicating to some men as fishnet stockings are to others. The only down-side to this seemingly ideal arrangement is that, though the weak and weary beat a path to your door in droves, strong, self-sufficient types (who awaken less noble yearnings within you) tend to keep away lest they end up tied to your apron strings.

YOUR IDEAL WOMAN

Male

Venus in Cancer makes you deeply sensual and responsive to physical stimuli. But while most men dream of drowning in the mysterious haze of some exotically perfumed lover, you drool over the aroma of home-baked apple pie. The woman of your secret fantasy serves hot chocolate on cold nights before a roaring log fire. She takes a genuine interest in your work, sympathises with your problems and even acts fascinated when you talk sport. Heaven is no higher or more distant than a giant train set in the loft, the points of which are being lovingly tended by your smiling soulmate, eagerly clutching a can of engine oil. For all you may make yourself out to be macho, you're a purring, domesticated pussy cat. Only one thing turns you on more than the idea of a woman who's happy when you're happy – and that's a chance to prove that you understand the precise technique for making her very happy indeed!

VENUS IN LEO

YOU AND NATURE

Next time you get a chance to scan the cable or satellite channels, see if there's a station showing *Bewitched.* This sixties' TV series features, as you may recall, a modern witch called Samantha. All she has to do is twitch her nose and whatever she wants to happen, happens. Her husband, however, has made her promise to accomplish everything by conventional means. So she struggles, as best she can, to do the hard way what she could do, if she chose, in an instant.

Does this description remind you of anyone? Males and females with Venus in Leo seem similarly bound by restrictions that they could easily defy if only they dared. How often have you found yourself tempted to take certain short-cuts for the sake of a little more 'jam today'? And how often have you denied yourself the opportunity, reflecting that it would be somehow wrong to use the power at your disposal?

You're laudably conscientious, but sometimes just a little too quick to see self-restraint as a virtue in its own right. There are occasions when you're fully entitled to go down the easy road. To refuse to contemplate those valid chances, just because you might then go on to take naughty ones, is as drastic as to ban toothpaste from your bathroom just in case the kids decide to eat it.

You may not have unearthly powers, but you certainly have impressive ones. There's very little on the material plane that you cannot achieve if you set your mind to it. There are very few people whose hearts will not succumb to your persuasive charm if you set out to melt them. In holding yourself back from what you could be capable of, you're also holding back some of the love that could be flooding into your world.

YOU AND YOUR CREATIVITY

The notion of a career in front of the cameras might (or might not) horrify you, but it would certainly suit you. You're terribly good at projecting a convincing, reassuring, capable, calm and controlled image. If you could convince yourself that the viewers were not going to see the real you but only the act you were putting on, you'd take to the idea like a duck to water. This provision, however, is all-important, for you're dreadfully keen not to make a fool of yourself in public.

This isn't to say that you can't or won't act the fool, but when you crack a joke you aim it with all the precision of an expert archer at the funnybone of a carefully targeted audience. You're never afraid to take risks, but only if you're quite sure they're fully calculated. Whether dancing or designing, cooking or composing, innovating or restoring, your aim is to manifest grace and elegance, flair and finesse. Thus you want to test the type of ground you're intending to tread on and ascertain how much weight it will take before you go leaping on to it with both feet.

You're keen to exercise a similar degree of precise control over every project you undertake. You don't just like to consider yourself an expert in your chosen field, you insist on making yourself one. You hold your every effort up to intense critical scrutiny, dismiss creations that others would consider minor masterpieces – and, when commissioned to do a job or perform a task, take the clearest, straightest, most simply effective route to success. It very rarely fails. And nor do you.

YOU AND ROMANCE

Venus in Leo makes you a popular person. People from all walks of life are drawn towards you by some inexplicable, magnetic impulse. Strangers feel inspired to tell you their life stories, friends feel safe to confide secrets they have been hiding even from themselves. It's almost as if your very presence has a hypnotic influence, yet this is not due to any conscious effort on your part. You often feel slightly estranged from society – happy enough to link up with friends if they want to make the running, but equally at ease with your own company.

You come across as endearingly ambivalent, yet it's not true to say that you are without desires. The Lion in your birth chart is a lusty creature with a powerful urge to reign supreme in its chosen territory. Confident, however, of its own strength, it rarely needs to manifest aggression. Since none but a fool would risk challenging a Lion, you have little cause to feel the motivation of fear; nor do you always feel inclined to challenge yourself just for the sake of it. With Venus in Leo you can sometimes be a little too much like a furry, sleepy, sensual pussy cat!

When it comes to choosing a partner, you have another potential celestial disadvantage to conquer. Lions easily draw admirers. Their equals, though, are usually clever enough to keep a distance. And what betters could they possibly have? So when it comes to romance, who is going to offer the Lion a worthwhile challenge? Again none but a fool would risk it. So all hangs on you finding the right kind of fool. Does the right type really exist? Most definitely.

THE WAY YOU MANIFEST YOUR FEMININITY

Female

Men flutter round you like moths round a flame. If they get their wings burned, are you to blame? It depends whether you're deliberately waving the lamp. Unlike some women who must spend hours in and out of the wardrobe before they dare step out of the door, you can throw on any old rags and still attract admiring glances. It's something about the way you move. You carry yourself like a princess, even an empress. There's no deliberate effort. It just happens naturally – as does the inevitable reaction.

This is fine except that, if you're hot stuff when you're not even trying, you become an incendiary bomb when you are! Every so often, you decide there's a man worth making an effort to attract. The lioness within you is a skilled huntress who rarely misses her quarry. But whether she still likes him once she's caught him is another matter. A greater part of you would rather be tamed than tempted.

YOUR IDEAL WOMAN

Male

You've got a bit of a thing about prima donnas. When a woman starts stamping her foot, laying down the law and telling you what she will or won't stand for, you find it both amusing and exciting. It shows she has spirit, it makes her a challenge and it obliges you either to comply with her wishes or risk her wrath. Which you do depends on what else is in your horoscope. But the fact that such a fiery female fuels your fantasy is a point that no other cosmic condition can counteract. Your dream goddess is wilful, powerful, charismatic and aristocratic. She's also stroppy, sultry and self-centred. But she's so hypnotically attractive that you can forgive or forget her faults and foibles. All you know is that, when she finally does get round to needing you, she envelops you in such a passionate embrace as to squeeze out every last drop of the love you have to express.

VENUS IN VIRGO

YOU AND NATURE

To have Venus in Virgo is to have not so much an empathy with nature as an encyclopedic understanding of it. It is to be able to see similarities between vastly different scenarios such as how a rising tide submerging an island mirrors a fire slowly suffusing a piece of coal. It is to be an observational scientist by disposition if not by profession; a careful analyst of both nature and human nature.

Just as you watch creation with a sense of awe and wonder, rarely wanting to do anything more drastic than discuss your latest impressions, so you rarely seek to interfere in the activities of those you love. As long as they're doing fine, that's fine by you. Even when they seem to be making mistakes, you would rather wait until they asked for help than volunteer it prematurely. When pushed for your theory about what law a natural phenomenon is following, you'll give it – and research will usually prove you right. Likewise, when someone does want to know what they've been doing wrong, you'll tell them, gently and diplomatically but usually with uncanny accuracy.

Ironically, for all your natural wisdom you're afraid – afraid of speaking out of turn, afraid of rocking boats, afraid, perhaps, of being right but being resented for it. Yet you also fear being approached for an answer and failing to have one ready. So your life is often spent preparing for events that never happen and feeling resentful that though you took your harp to the party, nobody asked you to play. You deserve more, in career and love alike. If you want clients for your services and takers for the love you have to give, abandon your reservations or concerns about rejection, and advertise.

YOU AND YOUR CREATIVITY

You have magnificent organisational skills, which is precisely why your world often seems a little chaotic. It's people with less than full confidence in their ability to cope who need to have everything marked up, written down, checked over and filed away. You know what you've got and roughly where you've put it, so your time is better spent getting on with some new project than triple-checking the old one.

This explains why you're prolific as well as proficient. You design neither with a bullish broad brush nor with a nervously narrow nib, but with the happy medium of an implement which can, under the hand of a deft decorator, accomplish either stroke.

Having Venus in Virgo allows you to marry the charm of sensual Aphrodite with the wit and flexibility of business-like Mercury. It also entitles you to claim the legacy of Chiron the cosmic Healer. Hence your desire to be expedient and practical when expressing your creative urges. You see little point doing things the hard way just for the experience. If it's a tried and tested technique, why not use it? If it's not broken, why fix it? And if it's clearly popular with many people, why knock it? You'd far prefer to praise what's good in someone else's work than rip what's bad to shreds. You're far more inclined to repair and renew than to knock something down and begin again from scratch.

A genuine willingness to adapt the way you impart your art without compromising its integrity is the reason you find your creative skills frequently complimented by everyone from the connoisseur to the inexperienced consumer. You are equally capable, in potential at least, of success in any field. Whether you paint, pot, cook, garden, weave, knit, sing, dance, act, write, heal, mend, massage, measure, research, advise or entertain, you do it with humble sincerity and dedication and it does you proud.

YOU AND ROMANCE

To have Venus in Virgo is to possess not so much an eye for detail as an entire sensory system. It is the ability to hear the difference between a Bechstein and a Steinway, taste one between a King Edward and a Cara, feel one between silk and satin... even to smell the difference between a rat and a politician. To others, you can come across as a bit of a fusspot. Those who dislike you usually cite such a reason. Fortunately, these insensitive individuals are vastly outnumbered by the many who admire your discrimination, even if they don't share it.

While, however, your talent to apply subtle scrutiny stands you in excellent stead in the creative and aesthetic departments of life, it is not the primary reason for your popularity. Your fans and fanciers chiefly appreciate another talent that Venus in Virgo invariably bestows: the ability to defy the ageing process. You may not be aware that anyone has ever given you the secret of eternal youth, but you undoubtedly know it instinctively. This is why you draw admiring glances from people half your age – and presumably why you still insist on thinking, if not dressing, like a teenager. Your contemporaries get wrinkles but you get laughter lines. Your peers get weighed down by worldly cares but you get buoyed up by giddy ideas. You have no more intention of growing old gracefully than you have of being fobbed off with Coke when you specifically ordered Diet Coke.

To be with you is to be with someone who is always fun, always fresh and always full of enthusiasm for some new plan or project. It is also to be with someone who is deeply sensual, demonstrative and emotionally attentive. The only thing it's not is dull!

THE WAY YOU MANIFEST YOUR FEMININITY

Female

Some women carry cosmetics in their handbags. You may have one or two aids to beauty but they're vastly outnumbered by other kinds of lotion and potion. A veritable dispensary of stomach settlers, headache dispellers, corn plasters, lip salves, antiseptics and insect repellents cause you to rattle like a football fan as you walk down the road. And that's to say nothing of the other useful items you constantly carry. It's not that you're neurotic: none of them are there for your personal use. It's in case you come across a hurt or sick body. You see yourself, not so much as a Florence Nightingale as a female Dr Dolittle. You want to heal *all* creatures, great and small, because it's when you feel you're in a position to help someone that the waves of radiant womanhood emanate from you. Your ideal man is a patient physician's assistant. Yet all too often he just turns out to be another one of your physician's patients in need of assistance.

YOUR IDEAL WOMAN

Male

The lady of your dreams has strict protocols to observe before she's prepared to embrace you. First aphrodisiac sweetmeats must be washed down with honeyed mead. Then she must bathe in ox milk and anoint herself in flower essence while candles are lit to summon spirits of passion. Next she must don robes and consult a crystal ball for proof of an auspicious moment. Only then can the magical mating ritual be properly performed. If, later, she climbs on a broomstick and flies to some hilltop meeting of her sisterhood, you're just happy to await the return of your mysterious medicine woman. Possibly her love potions contain no more black magic than Cadbury's and her mead is merely Martini. Perchance her ox milk is Badedas, her flower essence Chanel, her light ceremony a deft flick of the dimmer switch. But even if her session with a glass oracle is a check that there's nothing good on TV, her broomstick a hatchback and her coven no more than a girl's night out, in essence it's the same. Your dream figure is a mistress of the environmental elements with an electric sense of timing.

VENUS IN LIBRA

YOU AND NATURE

The question for you, with Venus in Libra, is not how to surround yourself with love but how to make more of the love that already constantly surrounds you. When you complain that you feel unwanted, rejected or uncared for, it has much the same ring as an actress stepping back from the stage after her fourth standing ovation of the evening, in tears because one newspaper has savaged the show. But you can choose to hear genuine applause and ignore nit-picking criticism, partly through employing physical or psychological techniques and partly by simply allowing your ultimate asset, the will to survive, to guide you through life.

In nature, it's always persistence that most inspires you. When grass forces a crack in a concrete paving stone, when fresh buds appear on the stump of a blasted oak, or when you sense the Sun waiting patiently for a chance to appear fleetingly through a gap in the cloud, your spirits rise. In love, in partnership and in creativity, you simply have to apply the same refusal to be beaten. For almost invariably what defeats you will not be some unconquerable problem but the fear of defeat itself. Conquer that, and the love that perpetually surrounds you will never take long to step forward and make its presence felt.

YOU AND YOUR CREATIVITY

You turn out to be good at everything you turn your hand to, so you never know whether you ought to be doing this on the one hand or that on the other. Not only are you ambidextrous when it comes to creativity, you're double-jointed. Thus you are able to give yourself that most physically demanding of accolades, the pat on the back. Blessed as you also are with a fertile imagination, you can envisage, before you even lift a finger, the thumbs up that your work is likely to get. So you finish before you start, deciding that, as you've already triumphed in your mind, you may as well turn your hand to some other challenge.

If you were bereft of true talent, this capacity to be your own worst enemy might be your best friend. But as Venus in Libra is one of the most precious planetary gifts that a person can be handed, it's a shame. Others accomplish far more with less. Your talents could be winning you a big hand from an admiring audience, plus earning you cash in hand and causing you to win the game of life hands down. But first you have to put your hands up and admit that a bit more self-discipline would come in handy.

Probably the best way to attain this is to form some kind of creative partnership. If you can work hand in glove with someone who is a dab hand at a complementary skill to your own, you will probably feel much more inspired to knuckle down.

YOU AND ROMANCE

To have Venus in Libra is to be wickedly sensual and wildly indulgent at every opportunity. It goes without saying that you're hot stuff between the sheets. What's more remarkable is how you manage to fill the rest of the time obtaining paroxysms of pleasure from seemingly innocuous activity. Where some people might, for example, make themselves a quick sandwich when they feel peckish, you will disappear into the kitchen and come back with a gourmet creation. Where some might sink into a hot bath after a hard day, you will submerge yourself in an exotic cocktail of oils and essences. Where others will give their appearance a quick once-over in the mirror, you will preen yourself to perfection, departing the bathroom reluctantly with the sad thought that you won't see anyone quite so lovely till the next time you look in the glass!

You think a lot of yourself, and that's precisely why others think such a lot of you. You're a living refutation of the theory that self-praise is no recommendation. To the contrary, you believe there's no point keeping a sundial in the shade! You shamelessly flaunt your assets and rudely ignore your own bad points – and most people absolutely adore you for it. They like you even more because you are similarly uncritical about them in return, assuming (reasonably enough) that anyone who appreciates you must be worth liking in return! There are, of course, a few who remain singularly unimpressed by what they consider your lack of modesty, but, as these rather snooty characters tend to go out of their way to keep out of your way, you rarely have to be reminded of their existence. Nor need you be. With Venus in its home sign of

Libra it's a safe bet that you really are every bit as wonderful as you think.

THE WAY YOU MANIFEST YOUR FEMININITY

Female

You are a creator of illusions, a weaver of dreams, a tilter at windmills and an architect of castles in the air. The rainbows you chase, however, you usually catch – for your Venus position is a heavenly gift and not a cosmic curse. You can make ordinary things look fantastically special. You can turn mundane rooms into electric pleasure domes. And you can make yourself look a million dollars, not necessarily by dressing cleverly but by summoning a certain sparkle to your eyes and subtly adjusting the way you walk or even talk. Men take one look at you and decide you're full of promise.

You may be – but whether that promise comes true depends on whether those men are buying into your image or tuning into your true personality. Your dream is of a partner who is strong, true and straightforward. Somehow, though, if you're not careful, you end up with complicated characters who mistake your ability to reflect their hopes for an ability to fulfil them.

YOUR IDEAL WOMAN

Male

They say it's a woman's prerogative to change her mind. You find that appealing, but you'd prefer to go one better and get one who frequently changes her entire personality. You want her one moment to be a free spirit, beckoning you towards the hayloft with a wild and seductive gaze of passion, but the next to be a studious companion, looking up knowingly from a textbook on law, engineering or quantum mechanics. She needs to be as likely to cook your dinner, light your pipe, pour you a drink and fetch your slippers one evening as she is to drag you the next to a series of nightclubs where you'll dance non-stop till dawn. The only thing you expect her to be consistently is radiantly graceful. It's a tall order for any true-life partner to live up to.

But if you want anyone to come close, you could try looking at your own behaviour and deciding to make it light-hearted and flexible enough to inspire an existing partner to be at her best.

VENUS IN SCORPIO

YOU AND NATURE

Impressed though you may be by many aspects of nature, few sights inspire you more than the feat of wizardry displayed each time a caterpillar creates a cocoon from which to emerge as a butterfly; or the sight of some bare winter tree becoming a cascade of growth and life in the warmth of spring. Change excites and inspires you, especially when it's change that happens over time rather than distance. Those who adapt as they travel may be clever but those who can stay in the same situation yet become something totally different are surely brilliant beyond praise.

Venus in Scorpio makes you something of an alchemist, bestowing the desire to find the psychological equivalent of the philosopher's stone. Gold from lead you may not be able to produce, but this was only ever meant to be a metaphor. Transformation you most certainly can achieve, and frequently do. You aspire to it in yourself, and hope to find the tendency towards it in those you love. Hence the keen enthusiasm for sex of many people born with Venus in Scorpio. It transforms, albeit briefly, the body and mind.

To a degree, though, sex is a substitute for a far less base Venus-in-Scorpio aspiration: the desire to create a magical awakening of human potential. You merely want to bring forth what is most vibrant in everyone around you. Your efforts to do so, however, sometimes meet with objections. Some consider you too severe, demanding or intense. To surround yourself with more love, you merely need to refine the technique of explaining to others why you really want them to go further, try harder and reach deeper for life's truths. Perhaps, also, you need to be a little less unforgiving of what you sometimes feel to be failings within yourself.

YOU AND YOUR CREATIVITY

You really don't believe in wasting energy. If a job can be accomplished with the merest wave of a hand, why on earth get into a flap about it? Only if it cannot be done any other way than through sheer hard work, intense dedication and near superhuman sacrifice will you muster all these qualities without a moment's reticence. It's because you know what incredible concentration you're capable of giving that you're extremely careful about what you agree to give yourself to. Once you allow a project, plan or enterprise to matter, you surrender your life to it. You will leave absolutely no stone unturned, no angle uninvestigated, no obstacle in your path – or you'll keel over in the attempt.

People with Venus in Scorpio make especially good doctors, scientists and company directors. But then they make equally good artists, writers and musicians. For what they have is a burning desire, not to be the best but to *do* the best. Venus in Scorpio means you refuse to be fobbed off with phrases like 'but it's not cost-efficient' or 'nobody will ever notice if you cut a corner here'. You may find some clever way to reach a certain standard by subterfuge if there's no more direct alternative, but you certainly won't ever abandon your commitment to quality. You're a zealous perfectionist with a burning belief that, if a point's worth making at all, it's worth giving everything to. You may be enough of a realist to see the need for compromise, but you're not enough of a coward to see the need for giving up – ever!

YOU AND ROMANCE

You don't have to be a stargazer to know that Venus is a symbol of seduction. If you have even a passing familiarity with the zodiac you will know what three-letter word the sign of Scorpio is synonymous with. So you don't have to be a genius to work out what the key fascination is likely to become when you mix these potent symbols. I shall leave you to digest this heavy hint while I tell you that, to an astrologer, Venus in Scorpio means much the same as toddler in sweetshop, pop star in fan club concert or drinker in distillery. Venus is *not* in its element in Scorpio. The toddler needs to be at nursery, the pop star needs the challenge of a new audience, the drinker needs to be where alcohol flows less freely. In all cases, there's a tempting opportunity for over-indulgence combined with a possibility that things could go too far.

So do you have something to worry about? Probably not. By this point in your life you have, I'm sure, learned either to restrain yourself or to live with the consequences of not doing so! But if you do feel the above strikes a painful chord, you may like to know that Venus is a symbol of creativity as well as procreativity, while Scorpio can govern a quest for spiritual, as much as physical, fulfilment. The way out of any predicament you ever get into is to channel excess energy into art, music or poetry.

Whichever route you take to self-expression, however, you'll never be short of admirers. One thing that Venus in Scorpio inevitably imbues is the ability to render others awe-struck by your power to trigger feelings within them that other signs cannot reach!

THE WAY YOU MANIFEST YOUR FEMININITY

Female

You are a very, naughty girl. No matter how prim and proper you may choose to appear on the surface, there's mischief in your soul. You usually know what people are feeling and you always know what men are thinking. You can manipulate this to your advantage so deftly as to make the other person totally unaware that they have been steered. It's true that you don't do this half as often as you could, but you still do it twice as often as you should.

You're potentially an extremely sexy person, but the sexiest part of your anatomy is your little finger. Around this, you effortlessly wrap the men in your life. Yet you yearn for a partner who won't fall for the trick. You want one who knows his own mind well enough to know yours too. That's why you often fall for the rare character you cannot read like a book. Sometimes, though, you do so without checking whether this is because they are cleverly composed or just lacking substantive content!

YOUR IDEAL WOMAN

Male

Some men dream of women who will dazzle their eyes with beauty, melt their hearts with compassionate understanding or baffle their brains with sheer intelligence, Venus in Scorpio leads you to hope for one who will, not to put too fine a point on it, overwhelm you with an appetite for physical passion. You want her to have wicked ideas and make outrageous invitations on a daily (no, make that hourly) basis! Many adolescents entertain such vivid fantasies for a year or two at the height of their hormonal change. Venus in Scorpio seems to have you destined for a lifetime dreaming of very rude ladies.

Not true? Of course not. Sorry, silly me. I forgot. Venus in Scorpio also makes you exceedingly keen to protect your privacy. The last thing you want is to see your X certificate imagination revealed in a national newspaper. So, er, it's all a joke, OK? Actually, you like women who are good at knitting.

VENUS IN SAGITTARIUS

YOU AND NATURE

To have Venus in Sagittarius is to feel somewhat cheated by nature, for she has given you the spirit of a free, strong bird within a frail, earthbound body. You can compensate by travelling as far as possible as much as possible and, unless extenuating circumstances forbid it, you probably do. But short of owning your own plane and having limitless funds to fly it, you're always going to have a sense of wanderlust. You can identify with migrating creatures from salmon to buffaloes or even with weather systems that have the flexibility to sweep across the globe in hours.

For your love, like life, needs to be a journey. You need to feel that a partnership is going somewhere, leading to something, growing in some way – and you want to feel much the same way about all plans, activities or involvements. What's the point in standing still, preserving the status quo, keeping to the same old paths, habits and routines? None for you, perhaps. But if you want to surround yourself with love, you have to take into account the needs of some of your more pedestrian companions. You make certain people nervous. You represent a maverick force; a disruptive influence, a threat, even, to the stability and consistency they have worked so hard to achieve in their lives.

You cannot stop wanting to explore the new, the different and the daring, but you can stop insisting that others are failing somehow if they don't follow you. Become more tolerant of what you consider to be your loved ones' great mistakes, and they in turn will become both less defensive and less inclined to point out yours. Anyway, how free can a free spirit truly be if they won't grant themselves the freedom to stay in the same place for a while?

YOU AND YOUR CREATIVITY

Whatever you do, you do with gusto! Rather like Tigger in *Winnie the Pooh*, you're full of irrepressible enthusiasm and energy even if a little unsure of what it is you truly like best. Where Tigger's tastebuds variously tried Piglet's haycorns, Eeyore's thistles and Pooh's honey before they settled on the unlikely flavour of Roo's strengthening medicine, your tastes variously try the patience of those with less eclectic preferences. Today it's jazz-rap, tomorrow it's Bach. Today it's Gauguin, but yesterday it was Constable. Next week it may be hot baths, but this week you confidently prescribe cold showers to anyone with an ache or pain to cure. I exaggerate to make my point – but then again, sometimes, so do you!

People with Venus in Sagittarius are not exactly jacks of

all trades, but they are certainly Renaissance men and women. Your Venus position makes you diligent and determined to reach high standards in every endeavour, but it sometimes makes it hard for you to know what you want your next endeavour to be. You never rest on your laurels or fall into a creative rut. Onwards and upwards is your motto. And very often, it's also an apt description of your career path.

YOU AND ROMANCE

To have Venus in Sagittarius is to have an insatiable appetite for adventure. It's to live for the thrill of the different and the daring, the bold and the brave, the wild and the free. Beyond all else, it's to be an absolute law unto yourself. You're a leader, not a follower; a prime subscriber to the motto 'Do as I say, not as I do.' Others either love you or hate you. You don't much care which, but you cannot help notice that the members of both groups have something intriguing in common: a tendency to stand with their mouths agape as they watch you sail close to the wind time and time again – and seemingly get clean away with it! On the few occasions when you do come a cropper, it's usually in some spectacularly silly way. You'll perform a death-defying leap, emerge without a scratch and then put your back out bending to pick up a flower thrown by some admirer in the crowd. Or you'll make a promise you can't possibly keep, back-pedal in a rare moment of common sense and discover that, had you persevered, you would have been the beneficiary of a lucky coincidence.

You may not be wealthy (though you could be if you really chose) but you've got a brilliant knack of turning up in the right place at the right time, time and time again. Lovers seeking a stable, predictable partner are better off plighting their troth to a tornado. Those who have enough sense of fun to appreciate a source of constant challenge and entertainment, however, will run for any chance to get near to you – even though they know they'll have to run even harder if they want to stay there.

THE WAY YOU MANIFEST YOUR FEMININITY

Female

Braver, more adventurous women may exist, but where they're hiding you'd love to know. You could do with a girlfriend who might egg you on rather than run nervously behind, alternately marvelling at your bottle and being terrified of it.

If your ability to be independent, fearless and frank leaves most females flabbergasted, it has an even more devastating effect on men. In theory you're the intelligent, fun-loving, uninhibited lass every red-blooded male dreams of. In practice? He can find your potential to be his equal intimidating. He may prefer to score cheap victories over wimpish women, seeing you only from the safety of a fantasy. If you're not careful, you wind up either with a devoted servant or an arrogant oaf who can't recognise your true worth. If you are careful, however, you can get the lover you need and deserve: a fellow traveller on the road that leads, via various dragons to be conquered and prisoners to be freed, to life's court of supreme justice.

YOUR IDEAL WOMAN

Male

Your dream woman has not a shred of uncertainty in her personality. What turns you on is a woman who knows what she wants, where she's going and how she's going to get there. She has plenty of heart and soul, compassion and sensitivity, emotion and spirit, but she doesn't believe in wasting time feeling sorry for herself, crying over spilt milk or worrying about things that might possibly go wrong one day. She tosses her head, summons a smile and carries on bravely and determinedly with the difficult task she has set herself. Your role in her life is to be not just a supporter from the sidelines but an equal partner in the great adventure. You expect to argue with her occasionally – indeed you get something of a thrill out of hearing her put her case with conviction. And once in a blue moon or so, you hope to be able to draw her attention to some key point she's missed. But mainly you just like the idea of some wonder woman, taking you by the hand and neither leading nor following, just sharing with you one great adventure after another.

VENUS IN CAPRICORN

YOU AND NATURE

Venus in Capricorn gives you tremendous respect for nature, but it doesn't necessarily give you limitless faith in human nature. This is partly because you're keenly conscious of some of creation's less savoury facets: the law of the jungle, the bias towards survival of the fittest, the tendency for certain beings to devour their mates or eat their young. You're not quite a cynic, but you're certainly a realist.

Not everything in the world's garden is rosy. Indeed, even the roses have sharp thorns. A cautious streak thus runs through your attitude to life and love. You don't feel able to trust that everything is always going to be all right. Experience has taught you that sometimes it just isn't. So contingency plans need to be prepared and undesirable developments guarded against. All of which is wise as long as it's in perspective. But when you start looking at gorgeous rolling hills and wondering what they reveal about the tectonic fault line below, or noticing some bright, beautiful star and wondering how long we have before our own sun goes into Supernova, it's time to check yourself. Similarly, when someone tells you they love you madly and forever, it's a bit rich to envisage, in response, some day in the future when they'll be saying the same thing to someone else.

As all astrologers will testify, there's a phenomenon called self-fulfilling prophecy that has to be watched. Put simply: research has proved that people who expect good things to happen are more likely to find that they do, while those who are on the look-out for disaster normally find it. Venus in Capricorn makes you lovable, trustworthy and worthwhile to be with. But until you start to believe this, how can you expect others to?

YOU AND YOUR CREATIVITY

Architectural and engineering skills are often found among people of both sexes with your Venus position. You tend to be fascinated by how things work and keen to construct durable items of practical use. This doesn't prevent you from being an impulsive artist or a free, creative spirit, but it certainly implies that, even if you are this way inclined, you won't allow your work to be bought cheap and sold on at a high profit margin by some fancy agent. You have a keen understanding of the value of money, based not on greed but on precisely the same natural desire you feel to understand the mechanics of any medium you ever happen to work with. If you paint, you like to know how the pigment is made up. If you throw pots, you like to experiment with firing temperatures. If you play music, you like to know a little about sound waves. By the same token, you have an intelligent, enquiring, half scientific/half creative approach to many mundane occupations. The preparation of Sunday lunch becomes an exercise in attaining perfect roasting times. You can even turn getting the washing up done just right into a fine art!

YOU AND ROMANCE

People with Venus in Capricorn are tremendously loyal. They'll quietly put up with dreadful conditions and terrible treatment as long as they feel they're fulfilling a worthwhile commitment. Their primary desire is to make themselves useful to others and, often because they feel guilty about the idea of putting themselves first, they will let people walk all over them before they finally declare that enough is enough.

Do you recognise a little something of yourself in the above? It is, I hope, only a little something, for there are bound to be other factors in your chart that prevent you from manifesting your full potential to become a martyr. None the less it's a tendency to watch, as is the tendency to draw towards you people with a need to dominate. It's not that you're weak; far from it. Your strength is enviable. But it's a carthorse's strength, not a bucking bronco's. All you ask is to be given a task you can perform with honour and integrity, yet we live in a world full of people seeking short-term solutions. Some of these take one look at you and see an eager willingness which they can turn to their advantage.

The great irony is that you could, if you choose, be a leader rather than a follower. You have all the right qualifications, except perhaps for a reticence to throw your weight about. At a creative level, Venus in Capricorn makes you a genuine craftsperson. You are as painstaking as you are perceptive, as discriminating as you are dedicated. But just as you often find that others profit from your work more than you do, you sometimes find yourself getting a raw deal in love, emotionally or physically. The worst (or best?) thing about you is that you're so big-hearted that you hardly mind.

THE WAY YOU MANIFEST YOUR FEMININITY

Female

Many women feel a great need to protect their dignity and composure. Because you have Venus in Capricorn, you can afford to play the giddy kipper and present yourself to the world as a wild, wacky, even slightly 'dangerous' character. It's a bit of an act, but it's one you feel safe to play for much the same reason that a child feels safe to stick out his tongue at the school bully while holding his parent's hand. Knowing that, ultimately, you have vast reserves of common sense, you can push yourself to the limits of what's socially, morally or emotionally acceptable. You know you'll never go over the brink!

Because you're in such rare control of yourself, you can afford the luxury of a partner whose grasp of reality is, shall we say, a little more tenuous. You may even deliberately over-accentuate your more bizarre qualities precisely to attract such a poet. And even if this means that you end up linked to a bit of an unworldly no-hoper, you're capable of turning him round and causing him to become a success in spite of himself. Indeed, you rather fancy the challenge.

YOUR IDEAL WOMAN

Male

Dithery, vacuous, silly-little-girly types hold no romantic fascination. Give you, if not a significantly older woman every time, at least a girl with a mature outlook and a no-nonsense look in her eyes. If she lays down certain rules and generally has a slightly stern demeanour, you're more likely to find this amusingly attractive than off-putting. Indeed, there are some males with Venus in Capricorn who find the idea of exceedingly strict women in positions of very direct control a definite turn-on. Quite how far down this road your fantasies take you depends what else is in your horoscope. But even if you're not quite inclined to see Anne Robinson in much the same light as others see Beyonce, you're certainly far more inclined to prefer a woman who wears her common sense on the surface and hides her uncommon sensuality deep below. Strength and self-sufficiency appeal far more to you than any amount of airy, fairy, hopeless, helpless 'femininity'.

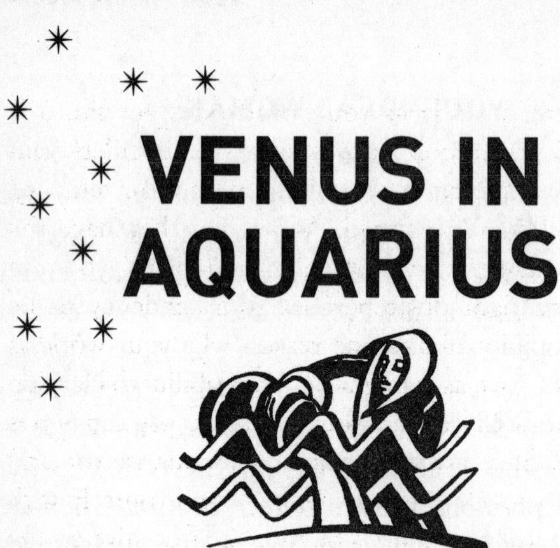

VENUS IN AQUARIUS

YOU AND NATURE

In some households, the cats and dogs never fight. They eat from the same bowl and snuggle in the same basket. In some countries there is hardly enough annual rainfall to fill a teacup, but by ingenious methods of irrigation or sea reclamation life is supported. There are some birds that can't fly, yet some fish that can. And in some jungles, tiny carnivorous beasts live alongside enormous vegetarian elephants.

To you, with Venus in Aquarius it's the anomalies, eccentricities and downright oddities of nature which appeal most of all. When someone tells you a thing cannot be done, your question is 'Why not?' If the reply is 'There's no precedent', you'll find one or, better still, set one. Little amuses you more than a chance to challenge convention, tradition or even nature itself. And if you see the patterns within creation as frameworks to build on rather than boundaries never to cross, you see the structures within human relationships as starting points, not finishing lines.

This is fine so long as your loved ones are similarly attracted to the notion of pushing back frontiers. But when they want to remain within more familiar territory, you can feel a little trapped. And when they have the temerity to argue with your ideas and plans, you can become downright obstreperous. Your tendency to be assertively opinionated is one reason why your world is not so full of love as it might be. Your ability to clam up and refuse to hold a debate you're not sure you can win is another. Yet there are many people who admire you and would like to get close to you. To surround yourself with love, all you really need do is be more appreciative of the possible and less keen always to pursue the impossible.

YOU AND YOUR CREATIVITY

You like to be at the cutting edge of fashion, thought, art and/or technology. You want to feel you're doing today what the rest of the world will be doing in five years. Usually, five years later, once you've defended yourself against the doubters and experienced the stress of being a guinea pig, it turns out that this is precisely what you *were* doing. But by then you're busy being innovative in some other field.

Being innovative, mind you, doesn't always mean being futuristic. Your sensitive, creative antennae are often among the first to pick up the imminent revival of some old trend. It does mean, though, that if you're ever going to turn your best ideas into money you're going to need the courage of your convictions and enough enthusiasm to convince others to take a risk. Those who don't understand you may question your need to lead such an eccentric lifestyle, to communicate with so many odd characters or to spend your money on such unconventional items. But as Venus in Aquarius gives you an impressive ability to communicate cleverly when you want, you can normally bring others round to accepting, if not quite believing, your unique point of view.

YOU AND ROMANCE

Venus in Aquarius makes you about as perverse a person as it is possible to be. Please don't misunderstand: I'm casting no aspersions here upon your nocturnal preferences. It's quite possible (though not, I concede, usual) for people with your Venus sign to have perfectly unremarkable love lives. But regardless of what you may or may not get up to in areas beyond the scope of this family publication, you're certainly unconventional in your choice of friends and partners. You like to be surrounded by oddballs, eccentrics, innovators and outcasts. It's almost as if you get a real sense of satisfaction when you hear a staid acquaintance saying, 'Honestly. I really can't understand *what* you see in so-and-so.' Then a part of you knows you've made the right choice, and will do all it can to cement the relationship. 'All it can' often has to be quite a lot, for if there's one thing you like more than a peculiar person, it's an elusive or unattainable companion.

When it comes to love, it seems you'd far rather have half a tatty swallow, hovering precariously just above the bush, than any number of fine feathered friends in your hand. You have a similar attitude to creativity. You don't just feel you want to be good at what you do, you feel you want to be doing something that nobody else would ever dream of doing. One of your favourite tricks is to abandon a promising project just when it's starting to take off, because you'd like to have a bash at something that it's even harder to make a success of. Happily, you are talented and charming enough to do well in life and love, despite the tendency to be your own worst enemy.

THE WAY YOU MANIFEST YOUR FEMININITY

Female

You're a highly principled, confident character but also a little contrary. Whilst, for example, being very sure of who you actually are, you get a kick out of pretending to be who you aren't. Venus in Aquarius gives you natural acting talent. You can if it suits you, for example, manifest the kind of 'come hither' look that would melt any red-blooded male, yet you can play the part of a sober, inscrutable businesswoman with equal conviction. Those who accuse you of blowing hot and cold tend to be types who like a lukewarm life. You simply have very specific tastes: in art, in music, in environment… and in men. You're either moved to the core or deeply ambivalent. Your eyes light up or glaze over accordingly unless (and this is what causes the confusion) you can see some fun to be had in feigning enthusiasm. The men who see you as deeply vibrant and sexy (and there are many of these) are not your ideal mates. It's the few who see beyond the façade and understand what you're really up to who fire your genuine passion.

YOUR IDEAL WOMAN

Male

It's not especially easy to define your ideal woman, for what you appreciate most in a female is her ability to surprise you. How can you ever be surprised if you know exactly what you're expecting? It's for this reason that you often find yourself drawn to rather crazy mixed up types, or women with something of a reputation for being difficult. You like the interesting challenge of a partner you can never quite be sure of. She needs to have either some very erratic, even inconsistent, behaviour patterns or some deep mysterious secret in her past – or both. You think you want to understand her and you certainly go to some impressive lengths to try, but ultimately you want to be hypnotised by her strong personality and even slightly in awe of it. Your relationships often appear to the outside observer a little volatile. It *looks* as if you're at loggerheads with your loved one, but in fact you thrive on a little creative tension and so too, most definitely, does the siren of your secret dreams.

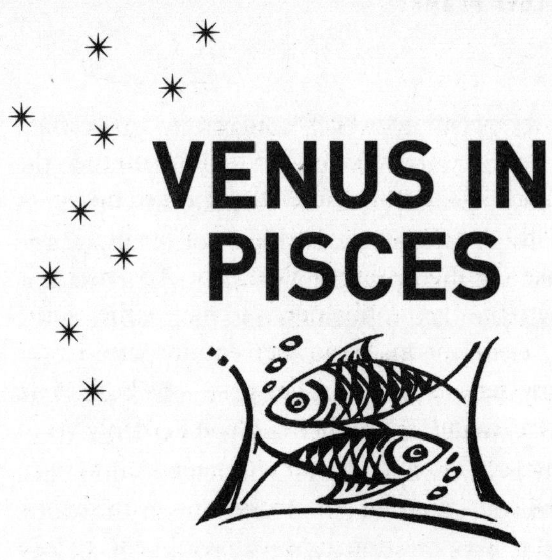

VENUS IN PISCES

YOU AND NATURE

For all our scientific knowledge and understanding, there are many things we understand no more nor less than our cave-dwelling ancestors. Quite why, for example, we need to spend a third of our lives asleep, oblivious and unconscious is still not fully explained. Nor, for all our carefully charted territory, do we know very much about the vast majority of our planet which happens to lie under water. Venus in Pisces naturally draws you towards the aspects of nature which are shrouded in the most mystery. Why do some salmon swim so far upstream to spawn? Why do some creatures apparently choose to make their lives unduly difficult? And why, by contrast, do people seek their happiness in such shallow, unlikely places? How can humans expect to find true contentment in pursuits that cannot possibly ever bring more than momentary distraction? How can they put their faith in such pretentious philosophies, empty dreams, artificial aspirations? How, for that matter, can they prefer plastic to wood, concrete to grass, fizzy cola to pure, clear water? Where in us humans, are the deep, instinctive, primeval urges? Where, in this over-sanitised, civilised, officialised world of social taboos and market forces, are the opportunities to celebrate nature, express spontaneity, laugh from the toe-tips, cry from the soul and love from the heart?

If anyone knows, you do – or you intend to find out. To surround yourself with even more love than there surely already is in your world, all you have to do is discover the greatest secret of all. The fountain of youth, the reservoir of happiness, the ultimate source of all love and appreciation for life, lies not in some ideal policy, process, way of being or relationship. It lies deep within you! Seek it, tap it and let the good times roll.

YOU AND YOUR CREATIVITY

People with Venus in Pisces fall into two categories: those who are immensely musical and know it – and those who are just as talented but don't. As members of the first group hardly need to be told about their skill, I will address the second here. Even in the unlikely event of your having cloth ears or even, for that matter, being stone deaf, there's still a vast amount of rhythm, harmony and poetry in your soul. Deafness never stopped Beethoven. And as for cloth ears – well, how many modern pop stars would you like me to cite?

Music is not just a matter of technical precision. Indeed, when that's all it involves, it becomes a branch of mathematics (see Bach). Music is feeling, emotion, artistry, spontaneity and the ability to create infectious, attractively subtle patterns in your environment. There's far more music in a finely tuned engine than in a poorly tuned guitar; more harmony in a well-chosen outfit than in any singer's ill-tailored arrangement; and more rhythm in a well-conducted car sale than in any badly conducted orchestra. You may never have touched a musical instrument in your life and may never feel the desire to, but in your ability to recognise life's most subtle sequences, turn random ideas into beautifully organised plans and hear how a piece of material is crying out to be used, you are very much in touch with the ever-unfolding, silent symphony of the universe. Respond to this call and you'll never be short of notes.

YOU AND ROMANCE

To have Venus in Pisces is to have the planet of romance in the sign of pure poetry. It's to be about as soft and soppy as a person can possibly get, yet simultaneously to be as perceptive, intuitive and ingeniously creative. Only one thing in your life knows fewer bounds than your imagination, and that's your generosity. You'll bend over backwards to please others; and while that, plus your generally warm, physically demonstrative disposition may account for some of your popularity in the sphere of romance, it's nothing compared with how far you'll go to accommodate other people's creative, emotional or spiritual needs. These you rarely need to have pointed out to you. A sixth sense guides you, like an infallible inner radar system, straight to the heart of what another individual is thinking or feeling. A seventh sense then shows you, in a flash of inspiration, precisely what you can do to help their dearest dream come true.

You're not especially good at getting what you want for

yourself in life, nor even at achieving consistently average success. But given someone else's trust in you and someone else's problem to solve, you turn instantly into a fairy godmother. (Male Pisceans, awkward about this image, can, if they prefer, see themselves as grinning leprechauns with three special wishes to grant.) Sometimes you do more for people than you ought to and sometimes you do more for them than they need, depriving them of a chance to find out the hard way which of their own ideas are good and which are bad. But always your motives are sincere, your results are impressive and your admirers manifold. The only people who don't like you very much are the grumps and pessimists who feel shamed and confronted by your open, friendly manner.

THE WAY YOU MANIFEST YOUR FEMININITY

Female

Years ago, the Zombies had a hit with 'She's Not There'. It was about an exceptionally elusive, ethereal woman. The singer could watch her in awe but never quite pin her down. Was she just a dream? Did she really exist? Or did she just have Venus in Pisces? You could be her or indeed, the mysterious, head-turning 'Girl from Ipanema'. It's got nothing to do with what you look like, what you wear or any conscious effort you may make to be a certain way. It's to do with an unaffected but engaging air of mystique you cannot help but exude. You're Sarstedt's Marie Claire, Lennon's Lucy in the Sky, Dylan's Lady of the Lowlands and Donovan's Jennifer Juniper all rolled into one. But while others may envy you the ability to inspire a thousand poets without even trying, a part of you wants to be treated like a real woman, not some goddess on a pedestal. Which perhaps explains why you sometimes go for the men who will do anything *but* worship you.

YOUR IDEAL WOMAN

Male

Your Venus comes rising out of watery Pisces like some mythical sea nymph. She's captivating and soft, yet dangerous and exciting in her role as emissary of some other world beyond comprehension. Abandon all to join her, and you may merge with some ocean of deep emotion from which you can never return. Ignore her, and you may spend your whole life yearning for another chance to glimpse her again. When you allow your fantasy to get as far as co-existence with this dream goddess, the communication is definitely 'non-verbal' but still more psychic than physical. Intense telepathic waves of empathy bridge, at least temporarily, the gulf between your different worlds. Together you can act to rid the universe of its pain, or cleanse it of its selfishness. Does sex enter into this equation? Perhaps. But not sex as most people know it. The ecstasy of worldly transcendence is both the golden reward and enormous sacrifice that a man must make when he falls in love with a mermaid.

Chapter 5

ZODIAC ROMANCE AND ASTRO-COMPATIBILITY

ZODIAC ROMANCE AND ASTRO-COMPATIBILTY

Is your most important relationship based mainly on physical attraction? Is it primarily platonic? Do you have a true bond of trust or a classic love-hate relationship? And what, if your partnership is less than ideal, can you do to improve it?

The fascinating answers to all these questions are revealed by your horoscope. To find them, however, we have to forget all about those twelve zodiac signs we have all come to know and love. We must explore, instead, the angular relationships between the planets in our own chart and the planets in our partner's chart. If this sounds complicated, don't worry. Angular relationships, otherwise known as 'aspects', are precisely what we've been charting in our wheels of destiny so far. To proper astrologers, they're by far the most revealing factor in any birth chart. Having used them to reveal a little about your own personality, I now want to show you how to 'marry' any two horoscopes, so that you can see precisely what kind of marriage the owners of those two horoscopes are likely to have!

To get right to the heart of what's in your heart, you'll need nothing more demanding than a pencil and a little patience. Just be aware that the techniques you are about to learn will place you in great demand. Many of your friends will want to know what the planets have to say about their relationships – so it may be wise to photocopy a few extra wheels before you fill them all up.

We are going to begin by looking at what the two of you have in common on, or just below, the surface. By comparing your Sun and Moon positions, we shall see whether you are two of a kind or something of an odd couple. This will no doubt amuse you but, as all who have ever delved into the realm of the heart know full well, it's no indication of your prospects for lasting harmony. Superficially perfect unions have been known to crumble just as often as strange combinations have withstood the test of time.

That's why we shall then go one step deeper and explore the creative connections plus the sensual preferences that are essential to a comfortable co-existence. Last but by no means least, we'll assess the all-important animal magnetism between you and your loved one. Some of the tests we are about to perform involve Venus, some the Moon and some the Sun. Take care not to plot the wrong planets on your wheel, or you'll get very misleading results!

ROMANTIC RAPPORT

✱✱✱✱✱✱✱✱✱✱✱✱✱ **TEST 1** ✱✱✱✱✱✱✱✱✱✱✱✱✱

TWO OF A KIND

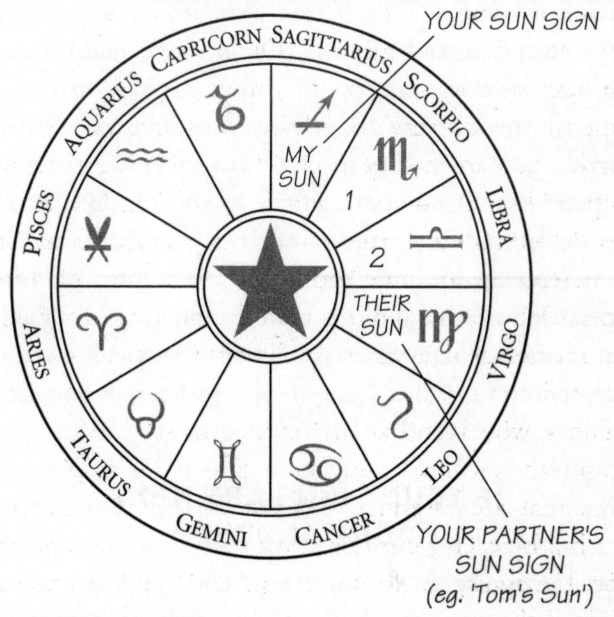

We shall begin our look at romantic rapport in the place where most other astrological features leave off – by comparing your Sun signs. Look at the wheel, find the empty space next to your zodiac sign and write your initials in it. Next, look for the empty space next to your partner's sign and write their initials in that. Now just

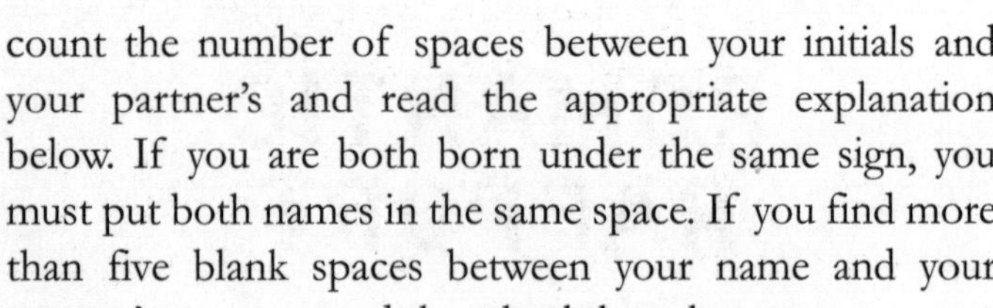

count the number of spaces between your initials and your partner's and read the appropriate explanation below. If you are both born under the same sign, you must put both names in the same space. If you find more than five blank spaces between your name and your partner's, count round the wheel the other way.

IF YOU SHARE A SUN SIGN

Having a partner who shares your zodiac sign can be very much a mixed blessing. On the one hand it gives you a lot in common; on the other it tends to remove some of the mystery about how your loved one's mind works. You can end up so close as to feel like sister and brother, so mutually competitive as to fight like cat and dog, or most interesting of all you polarise, rather like twins tend to do. Little differences turn into big differences. One of you ends up manifesting all of your sign's best characteristics, while the other displays all the most excessive traits. On a scale of one to ten, sharing a Sun sign gives you a five.

IF YOUR SIGNS ARE NEXT TO ONE ANOTHER

Does the phrase 'chalk and cheese' mean anything to you? While it is quite possible that we shall uncover secret cosmic links between you and your partner which point to a magical, meaningful bond, on the basis of this factor alone you are about as likely to understand one another as a Swiss scientist and a South American samba dancer. Only if your minds are very open and your hearts are very mutually responsive do you stand a chance. Otherwise, on a scale of one to ten you get a cautious three.

IF YOUR SIGNS ARE ONE BLANK SPACE APART

Most of the time, you enjoy a bright, lively rapport. As characters you complement one another, even if you do not always compliment each other. In a way, though, the fact that you do feel able gently to rib or criticise your companion is an indication of the ease and comfort of your rapport. You are like-minded enough to have plenty to say to one another, yet different enough not to end every conversation in a dull nod of agreement. If superficial compatibility were the only measure of success within a relationship, you would be a perfect pair. Whether you actually are, however, depends on how deep the other cosmic connections go. On a scale of one to ten, this aspect of your relationship warrants a hopeful seven.

IF YOUR SIGNS ARE TWO BLANK SPACES APART

Whether you are merely looking at this relationship as a possibility, or striving to understand it because it is one to which you are committed, the very fact that you are entertaining a romantic interest in a person whose Sun sign forms a right angle to your own proves that you are a brave individual who thrives on challenge. People whose primary concern is a quiet life do not even contemplate relationships like this.

None of this is to be taken as an indication that the union does not or cannot work. It is potentially a healthy, dynamic sparring partnership that can bring out the very best in both parties. Rarely do you agree or even agree to differ, but if you both respect one another you can have endless fun attempting to bring each other round to a very different point of view – as long as neither of you ever expects to win. On a scale of one to ten, this liaison deserves a suggestive six.

IF YOUR SIGNS ARE THREE BLANK SPACES APART

There's a delightful rapport between you and your loved one. You were born under signs of the same element, so you share a natural inclination to enjoy similar environments, experiences and challenges. But this alone is no guarantee of a successful relationship. Indeed, it can be a problem in so far as it gives you a potentially false sense of security about one another. Your superficial similarities can disguise a host of deeper differences so well that it may be months or even years before either of you realises how many cracks you have managed to paper over with a few glib exchanges. In conjunction with other, more important celestial links, however, to have your Sun signs in trine can be a tremendous asset. On a scale of one to ten, this partnership must be given the benefit of the doubt and awarded a generous nine.

IF YOUR SIGNS ARE FOUR BLANK SPACES APART

No matter how close you may be as lovers or partners, as friends you will always be less than fully in sympathy. You will never feel you really know or understand your other half, and may forever find yourself wishing that you could be at ease with them as naturally as you are with so many other companions.

This alone, however, is no reason to write the relationship off. If you are both well-adjusted individuals with reasonable expectations of what a relationship needs to be (that is, if you don't want to live permanently in one another's pocket), and if other links between your horoscopes offer the right potential for deeper communication, this superficial level of incompatibility can be a source of mutual amusement or a drawback easily overcome. On its own, however, it warrants on the scale of one to ten no higher than a two.

IF YOUR SIGNS ARE FIVE BLANK SPACES APART

You are born under opposite signs. Like magnets, you either attract each other so strongly as to make an astrologer's opinion irrelevant, or you repel each other with equal force. Unless, of course, you are like a pair of electromagnets between whom the current keeps alternating, so that one moment you are best buddies and the next mortal enemies! If so, you probably need a mutual common enemy to bind you together. Couples born under opposite signs often thrive together when times are tense and circumstances demanding, but grow apart when they have no special reason to join forces. To make this relationship work, it is essential for both parties to be characters who like to live life close to the edge. On a scale of one to ten, this cosmic link scores a debatable four.

************* TEST 2 *************

WHAT DO YOU SECRETLY WANT?

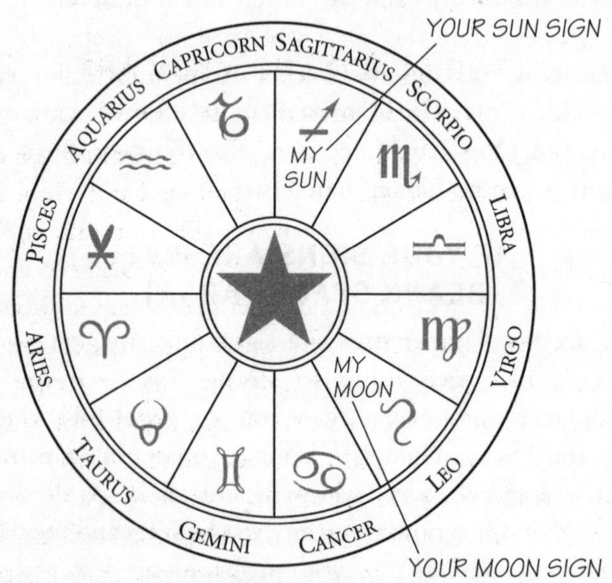

One good way to work out how well any two people are likely to get along is to consider them as individuals and decide what, deep down, they each expect a relationship to be like. This exercise is effectively a repetition of the trick we tried out back in Chapter 3. This time, though, we're going to compare your Sun and Moon with the specific purpose of clarifying your own definition of a 'dream team'. Then we're going to give it an interesting twist to see how closely your definition compares to that of your partner.

Into the wheel above place your Sun sign, just as you did in the previous exercise, only this time write the words 'My Sun'. Now put your Moon sign into the appropriate space by writing the words 'My Moon'. Then simply count the number of spaces between your Sun and Moon … and read on.

IF YOUR SUN AND MOON ARE IN THE SAME SIGN

Your idea of an ideal relationship is one in which the two partners are so close as to be almost joined at the hip! You want your partner to know you inside out, and to feel equally sure that you know all there is to know about them. You feel it's important that you both agree about as much as possible, and that you share as many experiences as you can. Some might consider this a recipe for boredom, but you don't worry about the risk of such a relationship growing stale. You believe that if your loved one is really the right person for you to be with, you'll always be able to stride through life together, side by side, in a state of constant close communication, enjoying each other's company every minute of every day.

IF YOUR SUN AND MOON ARE IN ADJACENT SIGNS

It doesn't matter much to you if your loved one lives in a different world. In some ways, you far prefer this to the notion of having a partner who is forever in your pocket. You can easily identify with Kahlil Gibran's famous suggestion that a couple should 'Stand together yet not too near together: for the pillars of the temple stand apart and the Oak tree and the Cypress grow not in each other's shadow.' For you, a degree of distance is healthy. You feel it's important to maintain a sense of being two distinctly separate people, each with a right to their own opinions and tastes. You have plenty of deep, sincere, consistent loving to give, but you don't feel that, to share it successfully, you or your partner have to keep proving the commitment to one another. Though you may have powerful passions, you feel trapped in any relationship that doesn't give you room to be yourself.

IF YOUR SUN AND MOON ARE ONE BLANK SPACE APART

You are fundamentally an easy-going soul who finds it simple enough to get along with most people. This may be why you don't always notice straightaway when a relationship is running into trouble – you somehow expect everything to be OK as long as it seems OK on the surface.

You can act as a stable foil to someone who thrives on tension or loves to argue, but you can also sometimes feel drained or unfairly picked on if you spend too much time in the company of such a soul. You certainly don't feel any need to be in a state of permanent semi-warfare in order to feel as though you have an exciting relationship. Often you find that you are the one who is doing all the compromising, the 'propping up' or the smoothing over of rough edges.

IF YOUR SUN AND MOON ARE TWO BLANK SPACES APART

You have a tendency to feel strongly attracted to people with whom you have little or nothing in common. If they happen to be erratic, changeable and prone to unreasonable, bad-tempered outbursts, this only makes you more fascinated. It's almost as if you secretly feel that a

relationship has to be painful to be real. In consequence you can, if you're not careful, either fall for very difficult characters or find yourself constantly goading a more mild-mannered partner into a display of stroppiness! If you understand this inner predilection you can work to get it under control, and thus improve your chances of finding harmony within your love life. It's worth the effort, for your heart is full of strong passion and you have plenty that's special to share and give, if only you can overcome your mistrust of everything that seems safe.

IF YOUR SUN AND MOON ARE THREE BLANK SPACES APART

Although you are a very loving, giving, sweet and stable soul, your relationships don't always contain quite as much fire as you might like them to have. This is in part, ironically, because you don't suffer so many pangs of desperate longing to be loved as most people do. By and large you tend to be a contented, self-contained and (some might even say) slightly self-satisfied character. You're not one to make a drama out of a crisis (which is good), but then there are times when an element of exaggeration can work wonders for a relationship that has become slightly too safe or set in its ways. If you were occasionally to allow yourself to worry or over-react more, you might avoid the tendency to make your partner wonder whether or not you truly need them!

IF YOUR SUN AND MOON ARE FOUR BLANK SPACES APART

You are either the most hopeless romantic ever to have walked on the face of the Earth, or the most incurable cynic. Either way, you have a tendency to spoil potentially great relationships either by being far too non-committal or, worse, by swinging to the other extreme and being far too demanding.

This isn't much helped by your tendency to subscribe to the Groucho Marx philosophy of being deeply mistrustful of any society that would want to have you as a member. If someone likes you, you wonder what's wrong with them. It doesn't necessarily follow that you prefer to be treated like dirt, but your friends do often wonder why you take it upon yourself to pick partners with whom you can hardly expect life to be anything other than a constant struggle to find a single point in common.

IF YOUR SUN AND MOON ARE FIVE BLANK SPACES APART

Your craving for a soulmate is one of the strongest forces in your personality. Either it keeps you constantly on the look-out for a better relationship than the one you currently have, or it makes you determined to stick with your existing partner no matter how stressful or awkward the partnership is becoming. For a partner to be ideal for you they may need a hundred special qualifications, but the one thing they are going to need most of all is an ability to be philosophical about your permanent sense of insecurity. When you're not worrying about being left, you're worrying about letting your loved one down. Ironically, the only thing likely to turn either of those remote possiblities into a reality is your tendency to worry so much about the idea that your partner needs to be a saint that you start behaving in ways likely to test a saint's patience!

************* **TEST 3** *************

WHAT DOES YOUR PARTNER REALLY WANT?

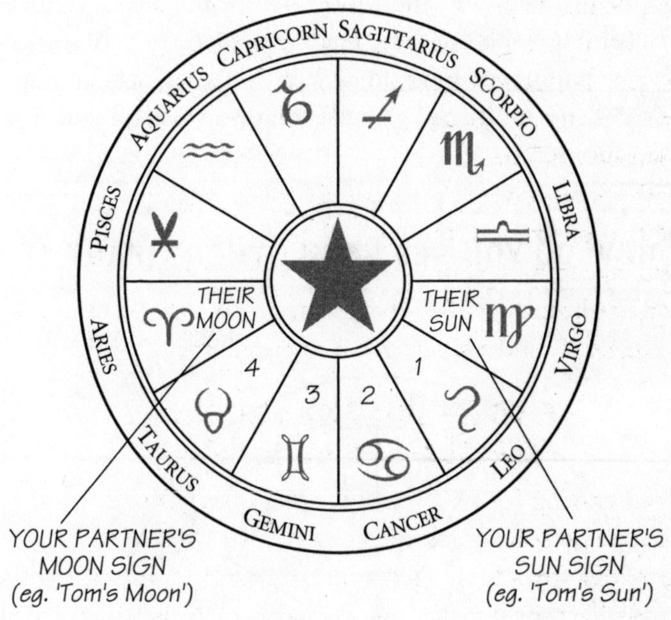

Now that you've read about the link between the Sun and Moon in your own horoscope, you need to see how they line up in your partner's chart wheel. Do precisely what you did for your own date of birth, only this time put your partner's Sun sign into the appropriate space in the wheel by writing their name, followed by the word 'Sun'. Then place their Moon sign in the appropriate space by writing their name, followed by the word 'Moon'. Now count the spaces between their Sun and Moon, remembering that, if you find more than five blank spaces, you need to count again the other way round the wheel. Now go back and reread the relevant section in the previous set of interpretations.

There's a possibility that, even if your partner has a totally different Sun and Moon sign from your own, they may end up with the same reading that you got. If so, see this as an encouraging omen but don't get carried away. It's not necessarily a promise that you were made for one another!

************* TEST 4 *************

HOW DO YOU SEE EACH OTHER? (PART 1)

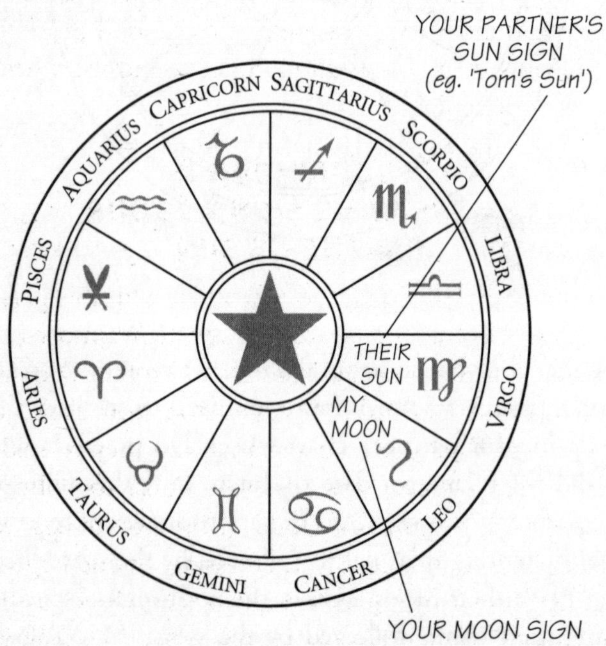

In the last test we looked at how you and your partner each tend to treat relationships in general. It's now time to look at how you both respond to *this* relationship in particular. As each of you is likely to see the relationship from a different perspective, we'll begin by looking at how you tend to think of your partner and then go on to see what your partner secretly tends to think about you.

Begin by putting your Moon sign into the appropriate empty space in the wheel by writing the words 'My Moon'. Then put your partner's Sun sign in the appropriate empty space by writing their name, followed by the word 'Sun'. Now just count the number of blank spaces between your Moon and their Sun, and read the relevant interpretation below. (Remember, if you find more than five blank spaces, you need to count round the wheel in the other direction!)

IF YOUR MOON IS IN THE SAME SIGN AS YOUR PARTNER'S SUN

You find it extremely easy to empathise with this person. Sometimes, indeed, you seem to know them almost a little too well. At times you feel more like brother and sister than husband and wife. At times, too, you can't quite believe that they don't understand why they've said or done a certain thing, when to you it's all too obvious. Although you sometimes find the petty things your partner does more than a little annoying, by and large you feel very proud of them and extremely relaxed in their company. There's an almost telepathic link between you. You can often instinctively tell how they're feeling, even when you're miles apart.

Together you can withstand a lot of worldly pressure –

indeed, you feel very enthusiastic about the marvellous team you make when it's the two of you against the rest of the world. When it's the two of you against each other, however, you're not so comfortable. Thankfully, you rarely fall out, for on the few occasions when you do it seems you never quite understand why. All you know is that you don't just mildly disagree, you deeply (and occasionally bitterly) differ.

IF YOUR MOON IS IN THE ADJACENT SIGN TO YOUR PARTNER'S SUN

No matter how many years you pass in this person's company, there'll always be a sense of mystery in so far as there's something about your loved one that you simply cannot fathom.

You also suspect (unless there are other powerful links between your two horoscopes) that you too are often sorely misunderstood. Yet, though your partner doesn't always appreciate what makes you tick, they certainly know how to wind you up!

The relationship is often what some astrologers call 'challenging' and most other people call 'exasperating'. None the less, it has its distinct advantages. You feel sure you're in no danger of ever settling into a dull, predictable routine – if only because you can never be quite sure what your partner is going to do or say next! What you can't cope with, your partner usually can – and vice versa!

IF YOUR MOON IS ONE BLANK SPACE FROM YOUR PARTNER'S SUN

No matter how well or badly you may get along at some levels, your relationship is helped greatly by the fact that you cannot help but see many qualities in your partner that you deeply admire. You feel a constant sense of warmth towards (and appreciation of) their general demeanour, which probably explains why you let them get away with so much more than they probably deserve to! Your loved one has an instinctive way of putting you at your ease, defusing your anger and encouraging you to see the funny side of whatever's worrying you.

Does this, then, make you a perfect pair? Not on its own. It depends how well the celestial synastry (compatibility) between you both is working elsewhere in the horoscope. Your tendency to want to forgive and tolerate this person can just as easily be the spoonful of sugar which makes an otherwise unpalatable dish seem edible or the natural sweetness of a truly fruitful bond.

IF YOUR MOON IS TWO BLANK SPACES FROM YOUR PARTNER'S SUN

You more often see your loved one as an adversary than as an ally. For as long as you feel happy that you are both only play-fighting, this can be a source of much amusement. The trouble comes when, instead of having a jovial joust with your spouse you find yourself bitterly battling. After a while, their tendency to disagree with you on principle, to engage in perpetual point-scoring or one-upmanship, or to disapprove of so many of your friends, can become a little wearing. There's also a tendency for you both to lapse into role play, with one of you acting stern parent to the other's naughty child.

That said, many people with this cosmic link find it an inconvenience that's well worth putting up with. As long as effort is made on both sides to keep the relationship on an equal footing between two mature adults who can forgive each other for (and even laugh about) their respective differences, there's the potential for an almost never-ending source of mutual inspiration, motivation and stimulation.

IF YOUR MOON IS THREE BLANK SPACES FROM YOUR PARTNER'S SUN

It's one thing to perceive your partner as bright, warm and sunny, but quite another to imagine that the Sun actually shines out of their posterior. Watch out for your tendency to hang on to your loved one's every word or follow them trustingly wherever they lead, regardless of how debatable their judgement. Though you may be steadfastly independent in all other circumstances, when the romantic mood sweeps over you you can be putty in the hands of this particular person. You're not entirely blinkered to their faults, but you're certainly in the habit of acknowledging them through the rosiest of tinted spectacles.

It's lovely that you have so much respect, affection for and pride in your beloved, and lovelier still if the beloved in question happens to deserve all this; but it's possibly wise to seek a second, more objective opinion if you want to be sure whether they do. Might you be projecting on to the screen of your partner's personality a magnificence that might be more aptly and properly recognised in yourself?

IF YOUR MOON IS FOUR BLANK SPACES FROM YOUR PARTNER'S SUN

Your loved one is an enigma, both fascinatingly mysterious and irritatingly difficult to understand. You cannot decide quite how you feel about this person, for you're never quite sure whether you know them well enough to be a fair judge of their character. This isn't likely to change, whether you're with them for forty minutes or forty years. Nor, even if you've been with them for forty years already, are you ever likely to feel sure whether you have forty more years or minutes left in the relationship – your partner doesn't exactly make you feel secure.

There may, though, be other reasons why you're happy to put up with (or even thrive on) this perpetual sense of uncertainty. In this particular person's company you get constant excitement and interest: they take you (or drive you) to do and feel things that you might otherwise never experience. A rare, precious and highly constructive creative spark can be ignited by living your life with someone you can never quite bring yourself to believe you are actually living your life with!

IF YOUR MOON IS FIVE BLANK SPACES FROM YOUR PARTNER'S SUN

The success or failure of this relationship has a great deal to do with the success or failure of, firstly, your relationship with your parents and, secondly, the nature of your partner's relationship with their own mother and father. There's a tendency for you both to play out the roles you saw enacted between the adults in your life when you were little, exacerbated by a tendency for you both to play out parent/child relationships in your partnership. You tend, no matter which sex you are, to mother your loved one by being over-protective or concerned for their well-being. Your partner, in turn, tends to father you by encouraging you to conquer challenges you might otherwise shy away from.

As long as this is just one facet of a multi-dimensional relationship, this can be magnificently healthy for you both. It's when it becomes the dominant, or even seemingly sole, behaviour pattern that you can begin to yearn for someone with whom there's less friction. Two well-adjusted adults can enjoy a deeply fulfilling, mutually stimulating relationship with this Moon/Sun opposition between them. Two less well-adjusted adults will either find it difficult or will soon have to take steps to learn how to become more mature in their approach to one another.

* * * * * * * * * * * * * **TEST 5** * * * * * * * * * * * * *

HOW DO YOU SEE EACH OTHER? (PART 2)

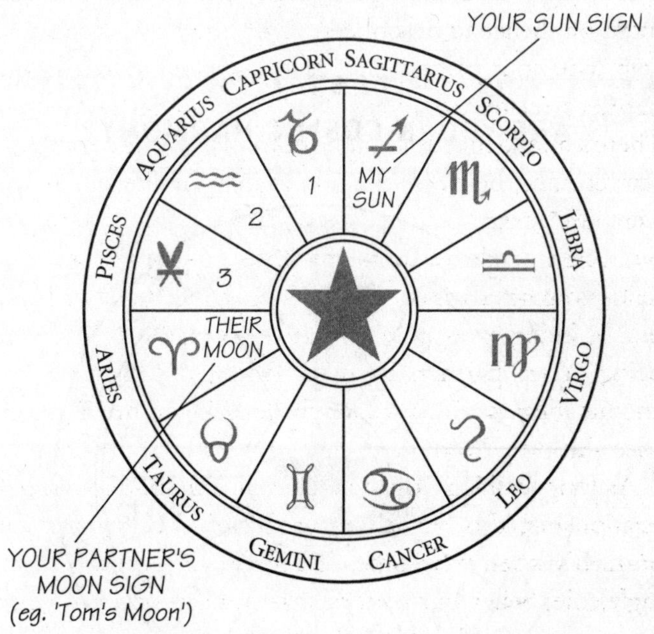

Having looked at how you see your partner, you now need to see how your partner sees you. On the wheel above, place their Moon in the appropriate space by writing their name followed by the word 'Moon', and then write 'my Sun' in the space next to your Sun sign. Count the spaces once more, remembering to go the other way round the wheel if you find more than five blank spaces.

Now go back and reread the relevant section in the previous set of interpretations. It's entirely possible (though somewhat unusual) for your partner's Moon to have the same angular relationship to your Sun as your Moon enjoys to their Sun. If you do find yourself led to the same interpretation that you've just read, see it as neither a good sign nor a bad sign – merely as a strong reinforcement of the trend described.

************* TEST 6 *************

ARE YOU IN COSMIC HARMONY?

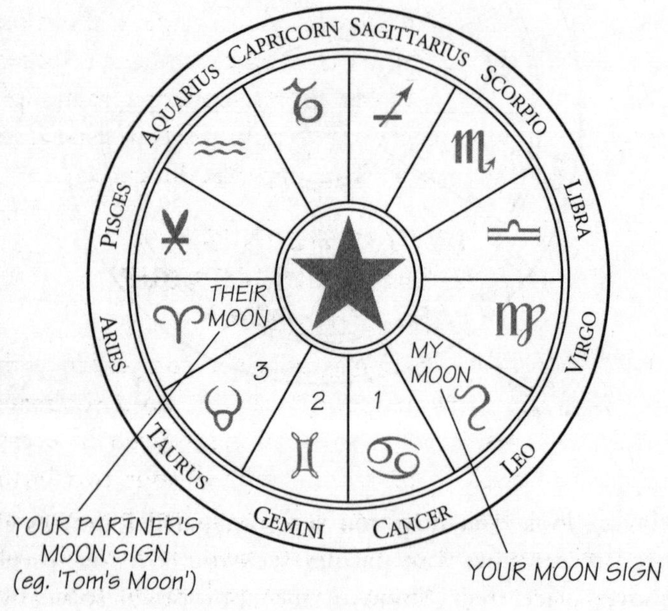

Although you've now learned a lot about the way in which you and your partner get along, you're about to perform an exercise which counts for more than all the previous tests put together. The ultimate test of any couple's compatibility has to be a comparison between their Moon signs. Once we've performed this psychological health check, all that remains is to see how you match up at the more earthly, physical level. Animal magnetism without emotional empathy is, however, not much good for anything other than a very brief, shallow encounter. So draw a deep breath and be brave as we ask the sky for an honest answer to the question: 'Are you in cosmic harmony?'

Plot your Moon sign in the appropriate space on the wheel in the usual way, then put your partner's Moon on the wheel. Now, as before, count the number of spaces between your Moon and theirs, remembering, as always, that if you find more than five blank spaces you need to count around the wheel in the opposite direction.

IF YOUR MOON IS IN THE SAME SIGN AS YOUR PARTNER'S MOON

You are in many ways magnificently compatible with this particular person. I don't use the word soulmate lightly, but this is an exceptional case. Even if every other astrological comparison between your two birth charts spells bad news, you have sufficient potential in this one positive link to overcome it if you feel so inclined. Almost certainly, you do feel so inclined. You can't help instinctively liking your partner, and they can't help thinking the world of you. Both of you, deep down, want the relationship to work so intently and sincerely as to turn a blind eye to a host of superficial incompatibilities.

The only serious down-side to this combination is a tendency to be too close for comfort. When one of you is feeling low, the other is likely to be similarly despondent. You won't always enjoy quite the same ability to cheer one another up that some other couples have.

You may also have a problem if either of you, by nature, thrives on a degree of friction and tension. You may differ and disagree on the surface, but you should always be able to empathise deeply with your other half, and they with you. Soulmates, it must be remembered, sometimes make better friends than lovers.

IF YOUR MOON IS IN THE ADJACENT SIGN TO YOUR PARTNER'S MOON

You each have a dramatically different way of looking at life, and of responding to emotional challenges. What one of you feels just fine about is often likely to be a source of great concern to the other. What one of you sees as an appropriate emotional response is likely to leave the other flabbergasted.

Your relationship may well have the potential to succeed, and to do so pretty happily too; but, if so, it must be because you both meet at some other level than the purely heartfelt. It could be an intellectual approach that you share, or a powerful physical attraction, or both. What it isn't going to provide naturally is a true sense of psychological belonging.

As such, the relationship may be vulnerable to the possibility of one or both partners eventually meeting someone with whom they click more instantly at an emotional level. This can be avoided or kept under control by a pact of honesty or a firm, frequently renewed promise of commitment. With determination on both sides it can be made to work, but it's important to understand that this is a fire that needs to be constantly stoked with fresh fuel if it is not to burn out.

IF YOUR MOON IS ONE BLANK SPACE FROM YOUR YOUR PARTNER'S MOON

You understand one another remarkably well. You may be far from a pair of bookends, but you certainly go together like a knife and fork or a table and chair! You naturally complement one another's personalities and are able, too, to prop each other up at times of stress or tension. There's not only an inspiring bond of empathy between you but a vibrant line of mutual attraction. You make each other feel at ease, most of the time at least, because neither of you feels much need to keep scoring points or establishing who's boss. Without trying too hard, you can share your deepest feelings and your most pressing responsibilities too, trusting that each will respect and appreciate what the other considers truly important.

Does it all sound too good to be true? Perhaps it is. Perhaps other factors in the astrological relationship are not so helpful by a long chalk. It may be that you don't click mentally as well as you get along when all the words have run out. Or it may be that, overall, your partnership is more platonic than physical. Whatever the answer, you undoubtedly have the makings of a low-maintenance liaison with a high satisfaction quotient.

IF YOUR MOON IS TWO BLANK SPACES FROM YOUR YOUR PARTNER'S MOON

If yours is a marriage made in heaven, heaven must be a pretty competitive place! There's undoubtedly an exciting spark between you and your other half, but it's just as likely to ignite a flame of fury as to light a torch of undying affection. You empathise exceedingly well at some levels, but on the occasions when you disagree you each fight hard to bring the other round to your own point of view. And neither of you takes easily to the notion of defeat. On the positive side, this ensures that the relationship is never dull. You won't become one of those couples who have so much in common that they run out of things to say to one another.

The other face of this coin, however, suggests that you both have to keep your tempers under control when you are together. If you're united in a common cause, or if you're both well-adjusted individuals who don't feel a perpetual need to prove points to one another in anything other than the lightest, most good-humoured way, this relationship can be a source of constant mutual stimulation and excitement. If, however, one or both of you are prone to feel a constant hunger for emotional reassurance, you will have to find some way to learn to live with the fact that you may not always find it within this partnership.

IF YOUR MOON IS THREE BLANK SPACES FROM YOUR YOUR PARTNER'S MOON

No matter what you've read so far, you can rest assured that, in one key area of life at least, you and your partner are gloriously compatible. Your Moon signs are linked in such a way as to give you a deep and lasting empathy. For this reason you are cosmically suited, no matter how different your superficial personalities may be. You have a natural, easy rapport, and an instinctive desire to treat one another with genuine respect.

If there *is* a potential problem with this planetary pairing, it lies in the possibility that your relationship can at times be a little too easy. You can both feel so safe together, or as if you have so little to prove, that there's a danger you may start taking each other for granted. You can also, if you're not careful, become a very insular couple. Because you gain so much contentment from being in one another's company, you may not always bother to keep up your outside interests and friendships. This can leave the relationship growing peacefully stale or cause you to seem like a rather uninteresting pair. It's a slight danger, but frankly not one worth worrying too much about.

Technically and officially, you need to check that other important connections between your two horoscopes are aligning as they should before you can be absolutely sure that you have done very well in choosing your other half. In fact, though, you knew before you even read this that you had something special going for you. And, indeed, you have.

IF YOUR MOON IS FOUR BLANK SPACES FROM YOUR YOUR PARTNER'S MOON

From an emotional point of view, you have about as much in common with one another as a kipper and a bicycle. You are magnificently mismatched – and there's nothing much you can do about this other than to learn to see the funny side. Never, if you both try with all your might from now till the day that Oprah Winfrey takes a vow of silence, will either of you fully understand what makes the other tick! You will perpetually baffle, astound and amaze your other half – and in turn, be flabbergasted, staggered and surprised by them. Two peas in a pod this may not make you – but then who seriously wants to live with a carbon copy?

Your relationship has plenty of potential for happiness, fulfilment and success, provided both you and your loved one are prepared to celebrate all that's good within it while remaining philosophical about what it can never be. If you're both willing to find other, platonic friends with whom to share your deeper fears and feelings you can fulfil the yearning for a confidant in another way, and decide to let your partner be the person with whom you perform an ever intriguing dance of disagreement. By constantly questioning their attitude (as you are prone to do) and by accepting that your own deepest instincts will always be subject to healthy scrutiny in return (as they are undoubtedly bound to be) you can turn a possible problem into a unique advantage. What you have, if you can only see it from this angle, is a recipe for mutual growth within a partnership of two very different people who are none the less prepared to treat each other as equals.

IF YOUR MOON IS FIVE BLANK SPACES FROM YOUR YOUR PARTNER'S MOON

There's a very powerful emotional link between your horoscope and your partner's birth chart. This has the

potential to make you an inseparable couple who constantly finish one another's sentences, read one another's minds and feel very much like two halves of one whole. It also, however, has just as much potential to turn you into a pair who fight like cat and dog.

It's the very fact that you *are* in some ways so similar that can make you both feel inclined on occasions to dwell on the little differences and turn them into big ones. But it's a way, if you can only see it as such, of protecting your own sense of identity. Twins do something similar when they decide, early in life, to separate into the dominant one and the passive one. By polarising their personalities, they can each take the character traits they share to opposite extremes and thus turn two potentially similar lifestyles into dramatically different experiences.

The trouble is that you and your partner may never quite so easily agree about which one of you is going to lead and which one is going to be happy to follow. Your emotional make-up is so much the opposite of your partner's as to make the two of you feel like a mirror image of one another. When they're up, you're down. When they're all for it you are totally against it.

You have, as I began by saying, a great deal in common. If you're both willing to accept this rather than fight against it, you can become delightfully close and remain so forever. But for as long as one of you insists on refusing to budge an inch, the other will feel inclined to be equally stubborn!

PHYSICAL ATTRACTION

Now we're going to take a look at the physical side of romance. I have left this till last in deference to the proprieties of courtship itself! While you don't have to be an astrologer to recognise that men and women often want very different things, this fact is certainly writ large in the laws of horoscope interpretation. Hence our need now to consider the position of a new planet previously unmentioned in this book. We're going to look at Mars, the god of war and the ultimate symbol of male energy.

Mars in a woman's birth chart symbolises something very different from Mars in the chart of a man. Similarly, as we discovered in Chapter 4, Venus has a double meaning. To understand what's going on in a relationship it's essential to view each horoscope from both a male and female point of view. This, plus the fact that there are so many planetary factors to consider, makes the astrology of sex almost as complicated as the biology of it – reasonably enough, considering that what we're really trying to define is an elusive form of chemistry.

************* TEST 7 *************

WHAT KIND OF LOVER DO YOU SEEK?

You now need to look up your Mars sign in the tables on p. 465. If you're a woman, your Mars sign tells you what kind of a man you secretly want as a lover. If you're a man, your Mars sign describes the aspect of your personality that most women are likely to find most attractive.

Mars in Aries

FEMALE The notion of a soft, soppy new man awakens little passion in you. You prefer to be swept off your feet by a tough, rugged, no-nonsense individual who isn't afraid of a fight, or at least manifests an air of assertive authority when he needs to.

MALE Women like your nerve, cheek and ability to act on impulse.

Mars in Taurus

FEMALE You fancy a man who is cool as a cucumber, solid as a rock and strong as an ox. He must, of course, have a softer side, and preferably an artistic or musical streak too. But he needs to be sure of himself if he is to be sure of you!

MALE You score when you show your strength, especially when you also suggest that it stems from sensitivity rather than swagger.

Mars in Gemini

FEMALE It's not what he looks like that you care about; it's how he talks and what he has to say. He needs to be witty, amusing, inventive and knowledgeable. He also needs to be an adaptable, interesting character – you can't stand stick-in-the-muds.

MALE Women love your enquiring mind and your ability to address them as equals.

Mars in Cancer

FEMALE For you, the notion of the 'new man' holds a distinct appeal. You don't want him to be tied to the kitchen sink, but you do want compassion, tenderness and sensitivity in a lover – far more than you want a hunk, a hulk or a hard man.

MALE It's your loyalty, integrity and obvious sincerity that women appreciate most of all.

Mars in Leo

FEMALE You want a man who knows what he wants. You like the idea of a lover who sees himself as a king – partly because he will then treat you like a queen, but mainly because you find a great deal of satisfaction in being with someone who has supreme confidence.

MALE You are sexiest when you simply relax and show others how charming you can be just by being yourself.

Mars in Virgo

FEMALE Men who are all talk and no action do nothing for you. You like a man who can express himself physically – who can build machines or work with the earth, or show, even if he does do something more cerebral, that his hands are as sensitive as his heart!

MALE Women like the way you can be so deep, patient, dependable and diligent.

Mars in Libra

FEMALE You generally go for the artistic type or for men who clearly appreciate the finer things in life. Your ideal man will take you into his confidence, involve you in his work, share with you his secrets, plus, most crucially of all, seek and take your advice.

MALE Your innate willingness to share is seen by most women as a sexier asset than all your other social skills.

Mars in Scorpio

FEMALE You seek a hard-working, go-getting man of substance who will brook no opposition when he believes he is right. When you see him dedicating himself to a subject with passion, you feel reassured that he will give himself to you with equal commitment.

MALE It's your refusal to compromise that, oddly enough, makes most women want to compromise themselves for you!

Mars in Sagittarius

FEMALE Your fantasy lover is a sort of Indiana Jones. He's probably a very physical, sporty type. He certainly doesn't shy away from a challenge. He's probably also very well travelled and experienced in the ways of the world. Your dream is to journey by his side.

MALE Women are most drawn to your devil-may-care determination to explore all that life has to offer.

Mars in Capricorn

FEMALE You like a man who is business-like, masterful and, not to put too fine a point on it, preferably wealthy! This isn't because you want his money but because, if he's proved himself a success in the world, he'll have what it takes to conquer your reservations successfully.

MALE You're most attractive to women when you show that you're not afraid to carry a heavy responsibility with dignity.

Mars in Aquarius

FEMALE Your dream lover is someone who defies all attempts at categorisation. You like idiosyncratic, even controversial types who can constantly surprise you and fulfil your desire to experience aspects of love and life that few but the boldest ever get to taste.

MALE It's your ability to stand out from the crowd that most makes women want to give their hearts to you.

Mars in Pisces

FEMALE If he's to stand a chance of winning your heart, he has to have the soul of a poet. You couldn't care less about his worldly achievements. You want someone who has a vivid imagination, a sensitive personality and a deep, inspiring vision to share with you.

MALE It's your child-like enthusiasm for life, and your deep faith in the dream of making the world more magical, that women cannot resist.

************** **TEST 8** **************

WHAT KIND OF LOVER DOES YOUR PARTNER SEEK?

Now return to Test 7 and look up your partner's Mars sign. If you share the same Mars sign it's probably a good omen. But we have more to explore before we can be sure.

************** **TEST 9** **************

DO YOU WANT DRAMA OR DEVOTION? (PART 1)

We must ask a crucial question before we directly compare the positions of your Venus and Mars to those of your partner. What kind of spark do you need to make a physical relationship come alive? Just as crucially, what kind of spark does your partner require? Two people are not necessarily well matched because their planets align harmoniously. If one or both of you secretly thrive on a sense of conflict, you may be more attracted to a lover whose planets inflame rather than soothe you!

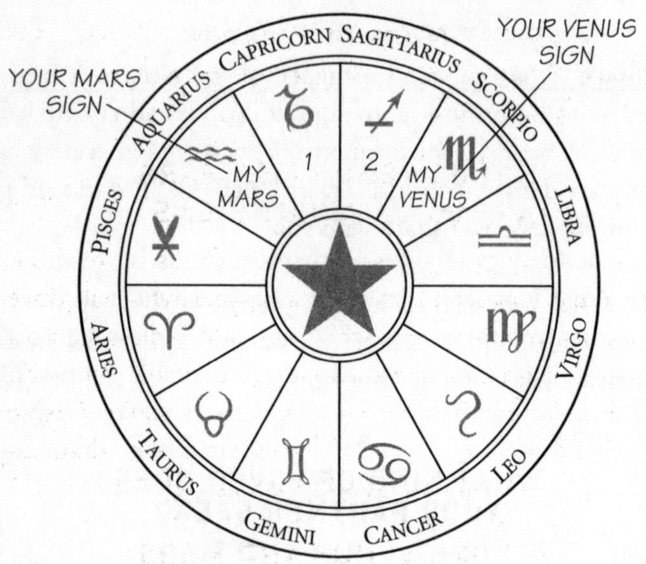

To find this out, we need to plot on the wheel the relationship between your Mars and your Venus. You should by now have taken all the information you need from the tables. For wheel one just write 'Mars' in the space next to the appropriate sign, and then do the same for your Venus. Now count the number of blank spaces between these two planets. (Remember, if you find more than five blank spaces you need to count round the wheel in the opposite direction!)

IF YOUR VENUS AND MARS ARE IN THE SAME SIGN

You're exceedingly selective about the kind of lover you want. Only a very particular type of person will do, and they'd better have plenty to give because shallow relationships have no appeal. You'll put up with a lot of tension but only because you're a stable character. You certainly don't need anger to spark your flame of passion. Trust is what you yearn for.

IF YOUR VENUS AND MARS ARE IN ADJACENT SIGNS

You can adapt yourself well to most kinds of relationship. What you seek is neither a partner who will drive you into a frenzy nor one who'll provide endless support and succour, but simply a sensitive, adaptable soul who will understand that much of the time you're unsure about what you need – and that this can change dramatically depending on mood and situation.

IF YOUR VENUS AND MARS ARE ONE BLANK SPACE APART

Without a doubt, you prefer a cuddle to a battle. If your partner's Venus and/or Mars turn out to be forming antagonistic links to your own, you're far more likely to perceive this as a disadvantage to be overcome with good grace than as a stimulating aphrodisiac.

IF YOUR VENUS AND MARS ARE TWO BLANK SPACES APART

You thrive on tension. If you can't successfully (and sometimes dramatically) argue with your partner, you feel you can't get quite as close to them as you would like. This doesn't necessarily mean you are destined to a life of romantic conflict, but it does mean there has to be a healthy degree of combat or competition in your most important relationship.

IF YOUR VENUS AND MARS ARE THREE BLANK SPACES APART

Though you probably prefer a partner who will whisper sweet nothings in your ear to one who will goad you with sharp comments, you can handle either at a pinch. Indeed, you can handle most things in life very well. You don't feel you need a partner to make you complete. This can make you easy to live with, and on the other hand it can make your loved one wonder why they bother!

IF YOUR VENUS AND MARS ARE FOUR BLANK SPACES APART

Where most people want a lover to make them feel complete, you seem to want a lover in order to feel happily baffled. You don't much care for open conflict, yet you don't feel very comfortable about close harmony either. You like it when you're just not quite sure where you stand. You had better have a partner who similarly thrives on uncertainty and spontaneity.

IF YOUR VENUS AND MARS ARE FIVE BLANK SPACES APART

You're emotionally well balanced, but more like a seesaw than a pair of scales. You feel uneasy when everything is still. You can accept a partner whose planets harmonise with your own, but you're probably better off with someone who appreciates the constant challenge in a game of love where the goalposts are constantly shifting – albeit within certain extreme parameters.

************ TEST 10 ************

DO YOU WANT DRAMA OR DEVOTION? (PART 2)

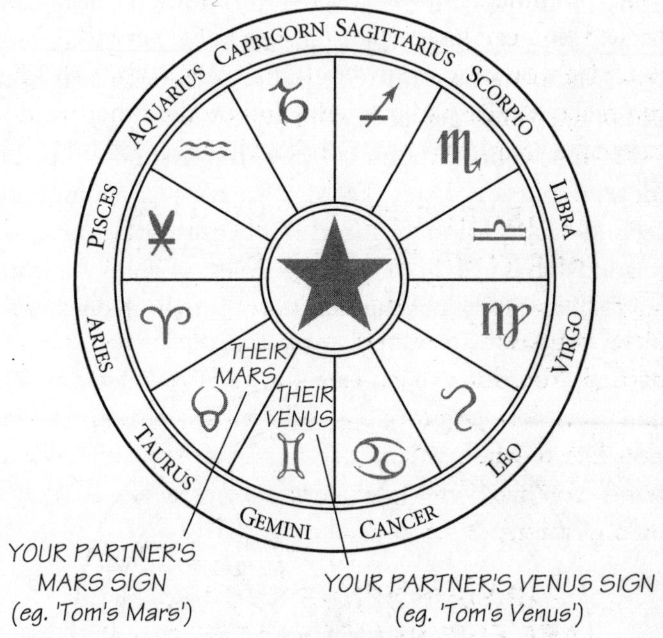

Now you've read about yourself, plot your partner's Mars and Venus on the second wheel and count the spaces between them. Now go back to the preceding text to see, if you dare, what kind of dynamic your partner prefers!

*********** *** **TEST 11** ************

SEXUAL COMPATIBILITY (PART 1)

We've used our wheels to answer many interesting questions about the nature of your relationship. It's now time to ask the two most telling questions of all. How does your Mars line up with your partner's Venus? And how does their Venus get along with your Mars?

From a woman's point of view, the first is by far the more important issue. From a man's standpoint, the second counts for much more. But because, of course, no relationship is ever going to work unless it works for both parties, we simply must have the answer to both questions.

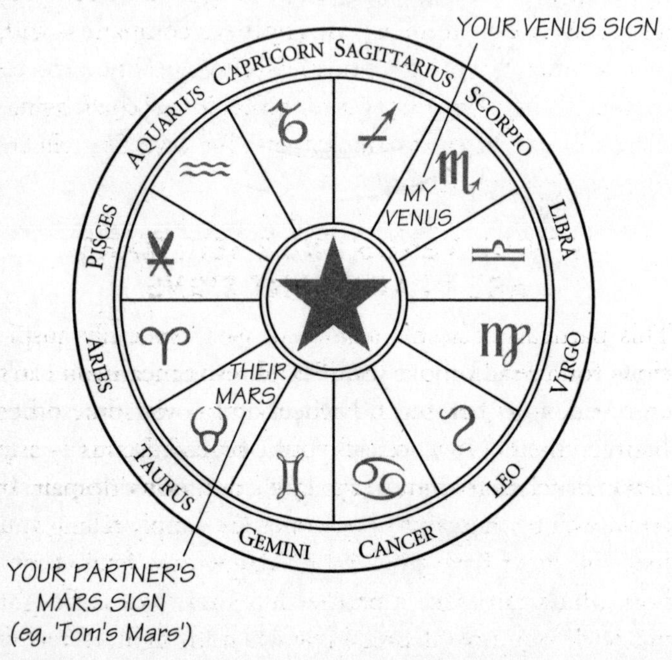

Use the wheel to plot your Venus and then your partner's Mars. Now count the number of blank spaces between these two planets. (Remember, if you find more than five blank spaces you need to count round the wheel in the opposite direction.)

IF YOUR VENUS AND THEIR MARS ARE IN THE SAME SIGN

You undoubtedly have a strong rapport. Each of you can instinctively supply a great deal of what the other is looking for. The physical attraction between you is powerful and not especially likely to diminish over time, regardless of whether that time is spent together or apart. No matter what other differences may lie between you, it's relatively easy to be in one another's company – and, unless either of you has a deep psychological need to be partnered by someone more difficult or challenging, there's every reason to think that your love life will be forever pleasing together.

IF YOUR VENUS AND THEIR MARS ARE IN ADJACENT SIGNS

This particular celestial alignment isn't especially auspicious for a red-hot love life. That doesn't mean you can't enjoy one together, but it needs to come via some other cosmic link. Look to see if your partner's Venus is any better matched to your Mars. If it's not, don't despair. It could well be that your horoscopes are simply telling you that you don't have the kind of dangerous 'fatal attraction' which can make a partnership sizzle by candlelight but fizzle out most depressingly when the light of reality finally dawns.

IF YOUR VENUS AND THEIR MARS ARE ONE BLANK SPACE APART

A most encouraging bond of empathy exists between you, which certainly makes you excellently matched for all creative undertakings. Whether it's similarly encouraging with regard to procreative activity depends on the answers you derived from Test 2. If this has told you that there's a hunger within either party for a more tense dynamic, you must hope that elsewhere in the synastry between your respective horoscopes there exists a nice, meaty bone of contention! Here, your problem (if you want to call it that) is simply that, when the two of you get close, everything is very sweet and tender. If sweetness and tenderness mean more to you than raw expressions of fierce passion, you don't have a problem at all!

IF YOUR VENUS AND THEIR MARS ARE TWO BLANK SPACES APART

You and your partner have the ability to drive each other to a state of absolute frenzy. Those who like their personal love stories to reflect Jane Austen more than Jilly Cooper may find the heat, in this particular kitchen, a little too intense. It isn't, of course, the kitchen that we are interested in here so much as another room, usually found upstairs. None the less, a point well worth remembering is that the force which creates such a steamy scenario in one area of life is highly likely to raise the temperature in other, not so enjoyable ways. The probable price you pay for having such an electric love life is a tendency for you both to short-circuit one another in areas of life where you might prefer to encounter less resistance.

IF YOUR VENUS AND THEIR MARS ARE THREE BLANK SPACES APART

Your relationship is like a fire grate, covered in crumpled up newspapers, above which a stack of kindling has been carefully built up. By the side of the hearth, an endless supply of fuel has been placed. All that's missing is the vital spark to set it off. If this can be supplied by any other factor, no matter how otherwise insignificant, in the various cosmic connections between your two horoscopes, you will have a roaring flame that never dies out. You are almost too well suited. You respect and admire each other almost too much. Even if you are a pair of folk who both like a quiet love life, you need just a little friction to set the necessary chemical reaction in motion. Find that, and you've found an ideal partner.

IF YOUR VENUS AND THEIR MARS ARE FOUR BLANK SPACES APART

From a purely physical, totally animal point of view you're not ideally suited. All this really means is that, where some people merely have to glance at one another in order to start a smouldering volcano erupting, you each have to work a little harder at learning how to supply what the other needs. Rather than feel disappointed by this less than glowing celestial report on your romantic potential, think about wine, or olives, or garlic. Acquired tastes are invariably more satisfying in the long run than those which come naturally to us – assuming, of course, that you're both willing to make enough effort to acquire the taste for one another.

IF YOUR VENUS AND THEIR MARS ARE FIVE BLANK SPACES APART

The electric currents that race between you and your partner carry an extremely high voltage. Assuming the connections are made correctly, you can transfer a great deal of energy and end up with a tremendously exciting, mutually fulfilling partnership that never loses its power to make you both light up. If, however, the links are loose, the wires are crossed or the lines are subject to adverse environmental conditions, the relationship can become dangerously volatile. It's even possible that, if you and your partner enjoy life close to the edge – as you will both have to do if you are to make this work – innocent bystanders could end up getting an accidental shock if they unwittingly step into the middle of the highly charged field that the two of you create. All this has to be watched for – and yet it may be that you're always so busy watching each other with awe, fascination and hunger that you never feel inclined to worry about it.

************ TEST 12 ************

SEXUAL COMPATIBILITY (PART 2)

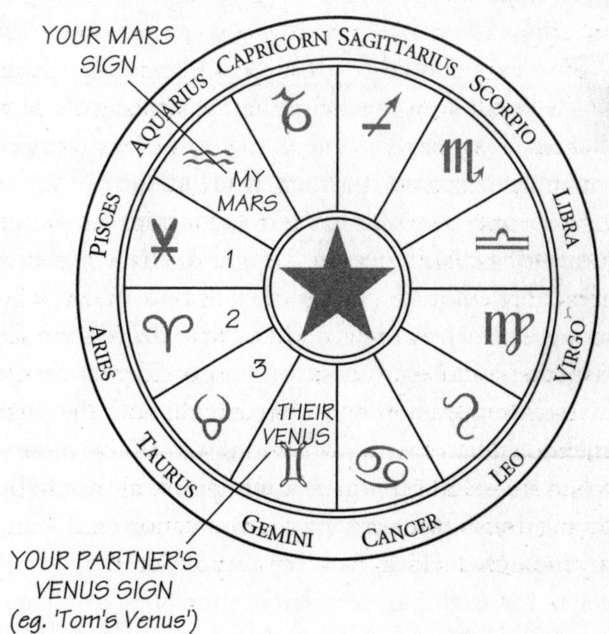

Here, on this wheel, we need to plot your Mars and your partner's Venus. Count round the wheel in the usual way, read the relevant explanation from earlier in the chapter and then read the conclusion, below.

CONCLUSION

You now know a great deal about the synastry between your horoscope and your partner's. If you feel reasonably content that you're astrologically compatible with your partner, read no further. If anything you've read so far has left you worried about your future with a certain person, I ought to stress that there's a great deal more to discover. For one thing, we are working with whole signs and not with degrees of signs, as a professional astrologer would do. For another, the planets Saturn, Jupiter and Mercury can alter the picture tremendously and without printing tables for these, we can only guess. But if you *do* want to look more closely at your relationship, there's plenty more you can do even with the information you've already been given. We haven't, for example, compared your Sun or Moon to your partner's Mars and Venus. Nor have we looked at the link between your Mars and their Mars or their Venus and your Venus. By using further copies of the wheel, you can perform all these tests.

All you need to know is that, as a rule of thumb, it's an easy, encouraging link if the planets are in the same sign, one blank space apart or three blank spaces apart. It's a challenging link if they are two or five blank spaces apart (but remember that some challenges can be healthy). And it's probably a bit of a non-starter if the two planets turn out to be in adjacent signs or four blank spaces apart. Good luck!

Chapter 6

PREDICTING THE FUTURE

PREDICTING THE FUTURE

They say you should always save the best till last. Here, then, is the trick that I expect you've been waiting for me to show you since you first opened the book all that time ago. Thank you for your patience. And, if by chance, you haven't been patient at all and have just cheekily skipped straight to this section – go away – read the rest of the book in sequential order and don't you dare come back till you've performed every single exercise!

Honestly. Some people!

OK. Now that I'm hopefully addressing only the diligent reader, let's get down to the business of predicting the future

You may think that all we've been doing so far is entering a couple of details on to a pretty little circle and counting the spaces between them. Actually, we've been plotting angular relationships between the positions occupied by key celestial bodies on the exact day of your birth. In other words, we've been following precisely the same principles employed by famous stargazers from the Emperor Hadrian through to Nostradamus.

We are not going to use the Sun for our predictions,

because that's what all newspaper astrologers do all the time. There is no other option. When I'm writing about what your future holds in my newspaper column, I can only discuss the Sun – it's the only factor I know about you. But here, however, we now have the wonderful luxury of being able to compare the positions of some much more personal planets (such as the Moon and Venus) to the heavyweight outer planets that tend to have such a profound, long-term influence over so many people's lives.

In these forecasts, we're going to paint an outline picture of the challenges you're likely to face between September 2007 and October 2009. If that seems like a long way into the future to be looking, don't worry – it will come round soon enough. But if that seems to you like a very reasonable period to be covering because it's the time you are currently living through, thank you. You've just proved my point about how fast the future becomes the present!

MOON AND SATURN

We're going to compare the position of the Moon on your day of birth (that is, your Moon sign) with the position that Saturn is due to occupy in the sky. Saturn enters the sign of Virgo in September 2007 and remains there until the end of October 2009.

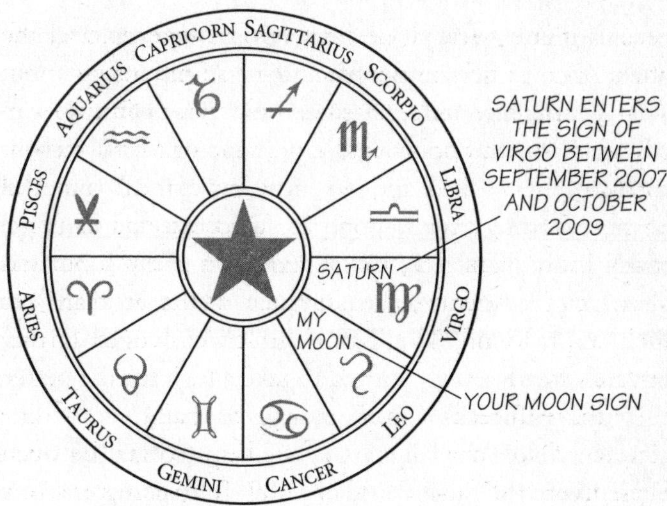

Find the segment labelled Virgo in the wheel. In it, write the word 'Saturn'. Now, simply write the word 'Moon' into the segment appropriate to your Moon sign. If your Moon sign is Virgo, squeeze the word 'Moon' into the same segment into which you've already placed Saturn and go straight on to read 'Saturn and Moon in the same sign', below. Otherwise, find your Saturn and count, anti-clockwise, the number of blank spaces between it and your Moon. If you find there are more than six spaces, go back to Saturn and count clockwise.

SATURN PASSING THROUGH YOUR MOON SIGN

Life for you at the moment is anything but frivolous. You've been going, for some while, through what could most politely be called a challenging phase and might less deferentially be referred to as a seemingly endless series of frustrations. You've felt hurt, ignored or even, at times, abandoned by certain people and organisations.

The cumulative effect has been to render you emotionally numb to the point where perhaps you now feel the world can go ahead and do its worst, for all you care, because you've already gone so far down you can't get much lower. You have my genuine sympathy – but you also have my genuine reassurance that things are not going to carry on like this for very much longer. If they haven't already slowly started to take a turn for the better, they will within a few more months.

Meanwhile, you will start to see what so far has often eluded you: the positive side of this debilitating era. You may be down but you are not out – not by a long chalk. Nor, no matter how deprived or ripped off you feel, have you really been cheated. It's more that you've been given something whose true value you have yet to appreciate.

Hard though this may sound to believe, there will come a day when you look back on all that's currently taking place and see it in a very different light. You'll realise that, though this was a time during which you had to face certain harsh realities and learn several difficult lessons, you also found a new and much more reliable source of inner strength. It was a time when you reached an emotional turning point and stopped looking to others for something that, all along, you knew you really ought to be supplying for yourself. And thus it was a time in which you grew far more mature, made an essential series of long overdue decisions and resolved to set off on the next stage of your journey through life in a very different direction.

It may be a year or so before this perspective is granted you but, once it comes, I promise that you will feel glad of all you went through. For only one thing ever follows a period during which Saturn represses the energy of a person's Moon: a time during which hope is reborn, enthusiasm is regained and the joy of success is rediscovered.

SATURN OPPOSING (FIVE BLANK SPACES FROM) YOUR MOON

A certain person currently seems to be doing everything within their power to make your life difficult. You can hardly believe you've allowed yourself to get so involved with someone so unyielding, unsympathetic and dominating. Just possibly it's not an individual but an organisation of some kind, yet the effect is much the same. You keep feeling crushed, squashed and stifled, and it seems to be going on week after week.

What have you done to deserve this? What great error of judgement have you made? What possible way is there to alter the situation?

The answer to this last question depends on the answer you feel most inclined to give to the first two. For as long as you feel that somehow it's all your fault, you'll continue to lack the confidence you require to make things better. And in a funny sort of way it's your sense of guilt, regret or responsibility which is most directly contributing to this oppressive character's ability to hem you in.

Even if you're normally a person of great strength and independence, you've recently started to behave much more like the kid at school who always got picked on by the class bully. You've had such a draining sense of helplessness that you've virtually invited others to exert their will over your own. The more they've done so, the more the cycle has perpetuated itself. You've become ever more passive and accepting, while they've grown ever more outrageously assertive.

What's even more ironic, if you stop to think about it, is that this feeling of being small originally stemmed from your own, seemingly failed, attempt to be big. You sorely wanted to alter a certain person's plan or control a particular sequence of events. It didn't work out as you wished. Thus the downward spiral began.

The good news is that unlike some celestial influences, which, like antibiotics, have to be allowed to work their natural course, Saturn/Moon oppositions can be conquered and their energy turned around. All you have to do is confront, not the person you feel so flummoxed by, as the part of yourself that won't take yes for an answer. Force yourself to regain faith and confidence, little by little, day by day. Refuse to be daunted by the occasional setback. Just ensure that each step forward is as big as you dare make it. There will come a point, sooner than you think, when you are able to stand up tall and proud to anyone or anything. At which point, the constant sense of being hopelessly opposed will crumble quicker than a thug before a magistrate.

SATURN INCONJUNCT (FOUR BLANK SPACES FROM) YOUR MOON

Issues relating to 'health and wellbeing' often crop up when Saturn is forming this kind of an alignment to a person's Moon. Note please, that I use the word issues, not problems. I know that you won't jump to the wrong conclusion but there are some types of people who may. Astrologers soon learn by experience that even a casual mention of the word 'health' can be sufficient to make a person's eyes glaze over with panic. 'Why,' they wonder, 'is my cosmic advisor talking to me about the state of my body? Do the stars foretell some dreadful illness?' Paranoia, rather like flu, is easy to catch and hard to shake off. I therefore want to precede your prediction with a clear promise that there's no reason in the world why anything should go wrong with you, physically and mentally, in the period during which Saturn and the Moon are in this angle to one another. Is that understood? Completely? OK then. Now I can explain. There's no reason to expect a problem but there is a reason to expect increased sensitivity to the factors which might, one day, possibly cause a problem if they are not addressed. You may, for example, realise that you've got a habit which is doing you no favours. You may discover that certain foods don't agree with one part of your body, even though your tongue likes the taste. You could recognise the need to do more exercise, to get more sleep or to supplement your diet with minerals or vitamins. It could also be that the development which brings you to this conclusion is a temporary state of malaise. This could manifest in more than one way, on more than one occasion. Hopefully though, now you're on the lookout for it, you'll spot more quickly the message that your body has for you... and without becoming neurotic about it, you'll take sensible, reasonable steps to improve the level of care you take of yourself.

I must now address an alternative manifestation of the same astrological influence. Maybe you'll have no such warning symptoms... but the wellbeing of a loved one could give you cause for concern. Maybe you'll want to 'mother' this person and maybe the stress of feeling so responsible for them will sap a little of your own strength. I repeat my insistence that we're talking here about being alerted to something minor in plenty of time to take successful, positive action. I also remind you that if you are dealing with someone else's health, no matter how young or old they may be, you must not mollycoddle them to the point where your own health begins to suffer. And now, after all that serious talk, here is something brighter to look forward to. You will discover during this phase that you grow stronger, more able to discipline yourself, more able to see what you truly need and less inclined to worry unduly about irrelevant fears; all of which will work wonders for your confidence, your ability to succeed, your capacity to make wise choices... and your potential to enjoy life.

SATURN TRINE MOON (THREE BLANK SPACES APART)

The current link between your ruler and Saturn is what we astrologers consider to be an especially harmonious one. In theory, you're going through a strengthening process, a period of consolidation – and a time of comparative emotional stability. In practice? Well, that's probably still a pretty fair overall assessment, even if it does rather glibly gloss over a lot of intense daily ups and downs that are also taking place. These, however, are ripples on the surface of a pond that, deep down below the surface, is surprisingly still. You know where you're going, you know why you're going there and you rightly believe you have a good chance of making it all the way through to your destination. All you really need is consistency of approach, steady effort and a refusal to be sidetracked by passing dramas. In this regard you are definitely being helped by a constructive sky and, quite probably, by a constructive person too.

You're lucky enough, at the moment, to have at least one person in your world who is solid as a rock and sensible with it. Their advice and support are invaluable. You may feel a little concerned about how you'd manage if they were suddenly withdrawn for any reason, but really you might as well worry about what you'd do if the Sun were to stop rising each morning. For as long as you really require assistance with your current, most worthwhile endeavours, you're going to find you get it, somehow, somewhere, from someone. And though you may have no need or call directly to repay those who now seem to be giving you so much emotional back-up, you're also at the moment in a nice position to pass the favour on – to other, less centered or less confident characters who, in their turn also require a spot of propping up.

You're currently being very kind to a particular 'wobbly' individual and this sensitivity is much appreciated, even if the gratitude isn't always being very clearly demonstrated. As long as you continue to tread that delicately fine line between caring about and actually taking control of their problem, you will eventually have the satisfaction of seeing them find their feet once more – and gaining their rightful status as a stalwart citizen. It may sometimes be necessary to apply a little bit of 'tough love' by refusing to wipe away every single tear or bail them out every time they make a mistake – but as long as you balance this with a lot of positive encouragement for their better decisions, all will come right in the end.

SATURN SQUARE MOON (TWO BLANK SPACES APART)

Are you beginning to wonder if your guardian angel has taken an extended vacation and left you in the care of some bumbling apprentice? Do you seem to keep bumping into unforeseen obstacles and stumbling headlong into emotional quagmires, no matter how hard you try to tread a cautious path? Even if the situation has been carrying on for some while, it's not a permanent problem – nor have you been abandoned by any protective force. You're just caught in the cosmic crossfire between two celestial influences with different agendas.

The Moon in your personal chart represents your desire to sail sweetly through life on an ocean of emotion. It's the bit of you that wants to go wherever the warmest wind is blowing, following no other chart than your heart. But Saturn is a force that restricts without remorse, and it favours only those who are prepared to accept direction and discipline. Currently, it's forming a tense right angle to your Moon, creating the internal equivalent of storms to port, icebergs to starboard. Suddenly, there's a sense of danger and a growing need to check carefully your internal navigation equipment. The dynamic tension between these heavenly hotshots is making more waves than you can surf without getting seasick. Your luxury cruise on a hot yacht is beginning to feel more like a rough ride on some dingy dinghy.

For now, you have little option other than to seek shelter. But this is not as easy as it sounds for you are being pulled by a strong current that seems to be leading to anything but a safe harbour. You simply cannot, for the next few weeks, allow your intuition to be stronger than your intellect. If you are not to grow so tired of mounting a constant vigil that you end up being swept overboard by the conflict all around, you must sacrifice a little freedom for the sake of pragmatism.

If this involves swallowing sufficient pride to send out a mayday signal or even suffering the ignominy of being towed back to the nearest port, it's still wiser than trying to pretend you can go it alone. Especially as, once you do let go of whatever goal you feel so reluctant to relinquish, you'll discover that, far from having lost anything you need to keep, you have dropped only a burden you should never have been carrying in the first place. Once free from this misplaced sense of responsibility, you can set out on a new journey – this time with a far more pleasant course to follow and the help of a supportive crew.

SATURN SEXTILE MOON (ONE BLANK SPACE APART)

Many things in your world may be far from perfect, but at least you're not feeling desperately idealistic about your ideals. Instead of looking at life through rose-tinted spectacles, you're wearing your common-sense glasses. You feel able to accept what you're sure you cannot alter, yet not so passive as to put up with what you know can be improved. Your current plan for progress involves a series of stepping stones. First you'll do this, then (opportunity allowing) you'll do that. All of which, in time, should lead to a chance to do something else. Unless, of course, when you reach the next decision point, you see other options. In which case, you will consider them on their merits, trusting that one will prove just the ticket.

All this is why, though there may be big questions that you wouldn't mind having answered about your long-term future, you don't feel too concerned. Something within has already decided it's going to be pretty much OK. It's that, as much as anything else, which is going to be your guarantee that this prophecy comes true.

In the light of this, I'd be reluctant to go into too much more detail, even if I had more to say. I wouldn't want to leave you with the impression that too much of what's to come is predestined at a time in your life when it's clear that the power to shape tomorrow rests very much in your own hands. So all I shall add is that you are due, soon, to see some encouraging developments on the domestic front. A key emotional relationship is going to deepen and strengthen. A sense of belonging is going to grow. A feeling that you are surrounded by stable, helpful, wise and supportive characters is likely to increase significantly.

All this is going to help you find the courage to turn your relationship with a particularly oppressive, dominant force or figure into a more adult arrangement. Instead of feeling afraid to speak your mind, confront authority or question an unfair code of practice, you're going to become something of a champion of the underdog. As you shake off your fear of being undermined or overlooked and discover what you want to stand up for and why, in these next few months you're going to turn into a quietly confident force to be reckoned with. As fast as you do, the niggling fears and insecurities that now occasionally cut across your mood of calm like stray waves of radio interference spoiling a pleasant broadcast will die down to an unobtrusive minimum.

SATURN SEMI-SEXTILE MOON (IN THE SIGN NEXT DOOR)

Do you really know the extent of your own strength? Are you fully aware of your greatest weakness? Don't be so sure. During the period in which Saturn forms a semi sextile to your Moon, you may find that you have to seriously reappraise your own view of yourself. It would seem that you have been propping yourself up by indulging in a certain habit – or by fostering a particular attitude. This attitude or habit pattern is one that you are very fond of. It provides you with much psychological support and reassurance. It may not be at all unhealthy. It may even involve an adherence to high standards. Even so, there is something just a little awkward about the extent to which you use it as a crutch. It's like having a magic potion that you can take any time the world seems as if it is trying to threaten or destabilise you. One sip from the bottle and you are right as rain again. What's wrong with that? Nothing except that, if you want to be a free, fully grown, wise, conscious individual, you can't afford to rely too heavily on anything. Not even something 'good'. You have to be able to learn to live without it – so that if it is ever taken away from you – or if you ever find yourself in a situation where it is appropriate to act differently, you are capable of adapting. You don't like the sound of this do you? You can't see why you *need* to give something up. Especially not something that you are keen on and which doesn't really seem to be doing you any harm. That's understandable. But the cosmos has your best interests at heart. *It* wants you to be a free, fully grown, wise, conscious individual, even if *you* don't want to be!

It can't, of course, force you to become one. But it can at least put you in a situation where the opportunity exists. And that's what it is doing now. And it is what it will continue to do for most of the period during which Saturn is forming this 30 degree angle to your Moon. In the process, it will cause you to take a look at your biggest fear. What really winds you up? What is it that you cannot bear the thought of? What kind of event, scenario or situation do you tend to have an unreasonable, disproportionately bad reaction to? And *why*?

You are being asked, by the cosmos, to investigate this tendency within yourself. Because it is *this* tendency that you tend to compensate for by leaning so heavily on your favourite, strength-giving attitude or behaviour pattern. In order to free yourself from over-dependence on that 'bottle of magic potion' you have to find out why you are so inclined to drink from it sometimes…and *then* you can conquer the need.

Your life can continue much as normal, in most ways, if you want it to during this period. Or it can change dramatically. That's down to you – and how willing you are to learn something about yourself and about your relationship to the world at large. You are going to find yourself periodically encountering issues, situations and people that you don't much care for. You are going to want to alter your circumstances in order to escape this. Or you are going to want to draw even more deeply on that reassuring 'psychological bottle'. Do either of these things and you may end up feeling forced to instigate major change in your environment. But if, instead, you just decide to work out *what* it is you are so prone to be upset by and why – and if you then decide to develop a way of turning this into something that really doesn't phase or bother you any more...you can take full advantage of this astrological aspect. You can use it in order to liberate an aspect of your personal potential that goes on to help you achieve spectacular levels of spiritual and material progress in the future.

CONCLUSION

This is the end of the book. If you have arrived here at this page because you have now read everything else – congratulations and thank you. In a moment, I shall explain how to take your new found expertise in astrology a stage further.

First though, I must address a word to anyone who is reading this merely because they happen to be having an idle flick through the pages.

If you're standing in a bookshop wondering whether to buy this… stop dithering and get your credit card out. It's a purchase you won't regret.

If you're thumbing through someone else's copy, wondering whether or not you want to borrow this book, don't! You'll only want to keep it forever – and it's not worth spoiling a good friendship for. Buy your own copy instead!

OK. Now, as I'm sure you're aware there's still an awful lot more to astrology than we've had a chance to cover in this book. You can dedicate a lifetime to studying the art and still only skim the surface. There are some good books by other authors that may well prove worth investing in and you should also look out for a more advanced book by me called *How to Interpret a Horoscope*.

Oh – just one more thing. In the world of astrology there's absolutely no substitute for experience. If you really want to know what makes one horoscope different from another – and avoid the embarrassing mistake of looking at a chart and saying 'aha!' only to realise, later, that you have gone and got excited about some celestial alignment that almost everybody gets born with, you need to draw up and look at lots and lots of horoscopes. Work with your friends' dates of birth. Do your family. Look up your favourite famous people's birth details and cast a horoscope for them. Then do the people you loathe and detest – you may learn what it is they all really have in common!

And DO remember to have fun. That's what it's all about.

THE ZODIAC CHARTS

The charts that follow may look terrifyingly complex but they are simplicity itself to use.

1. Find your year of birth.
2. Now find the period that encompasses your date of birth. If you don't see your date of birth listed, go to the nearest date *before* the day when you were born. You've now found your Sun sign, Moon sign, Venus sign or Mars sign – depending on which chart you are looking at.
3. Look to the right of that date and you will see the name of the sign of the zodiac. For example, if you were born on 10 May 1952, these tables show that the Sun was in Taurus from 20 April (at 03.37) until 21 May (at 03.04).

WHY HAVE THESE TABLES GOT TIMES OF DAY ON THEM?

You need only worry about the times given on these tables if your actual date of birth appears on the list. The dates and times given show the precise moment when the celestial body in question entered each zodiac sign. If you were born one minute earlier the zodiac sign you need is the previous zodiac sign.

If you were born outside the UK, you will need to convert to GMT.

Simply locate your birthplace on a map showing world-wide time zones. If it is left of the central GMT line add the corresponding number of hours to your time of birth. If it is right of the GMT line, subtract the number of hours difference. For example, if you were born in Perth, Australia at 10:45pm you would subtract 8 hours (because Perth is 8 hours ahead of GMT), which would make your time of birth 2.45pm GMT.

Once you have converted your birth time to GMT you need to decide whether it is necessary to deduct a further hour for 'summertime' or 'daylight saving' time. In many countries, the clock goes forward one hour during the summer months. This is not important unless, when you look at the charts, you find that an hour would make a difference. If so, you will need to ascertain whether the clocks were forward on the day you were born.

There are inconsistencies in this system from one country to another and from one year to another. Professional astrologers possess a list of such changes, so try asking an astrologer in your area or contacting a local astrological study group or organisation. Failing that, contact me free of charge via my website *www.cainer.com.*

If you were born in the UK you will also need to check whether you were born in 'summertime'. Should you require free help with this please contact me via the above website address.

SUN CHARTS

1925

20 Jan	01:20 pm	Aq
19 Feb	03:43 am	Pi
21 Mar	03:12 am	Ar
20 Apr	02:51 pm	Ta
21 May	02:33 pm	Ge
21 Jun	10:50 pm	Ca
23 Jul	09:45 am	Le
23 Aug	04:33 pm	Vi
23 Sep	01:43 pm	Li
23 Oct	10:31 pm	Sc
22 Nov	07:35 pm	Sa
22 Dec	08:37 am	Cp

1926

20 Jan	07:12 pm	Aq
19 Feb	09:35 am	Pi
21 Mar	09:01 am	Ar
20 Apr	08:36 pm	Ta
21 May	08:14 pm	Ge
22 Jun	04:30 am	Ca
23 Jul	03:25 pm	Le
23 Aug	10:14 pm	Vi
23 Sep	07:27 pm	Li
24 Oct	04:18 am	Sc
23 Nov	01:28 am	Sa
22 Dec	02:33 pm	Cp

1927

21 Jan	01:12 am	Aq
19 Feb	03:34 pm	Pi
21 Mar	02:59 pm	Ar
21 Apr	02:32 am	Ta
22 May	02:08 am	Ge
22 Jun	10:22 am	Ca
23 Jul	09:17 pm	Le
24 Aug	04:05 am	Vi
24 Sep	01:17 am	Li
24 Oct	10:07 am	Sc
23 Nov	07:14 am	Sa
22 Dec	08:18 pm	Cp

1928

21 Jan	06:57 am	Aq
19 Feb	09:19 pm	Pi
20 Mar	08:44 pm	Ar
20 Apr	08:17 am	Ta
21 May	07:52 am	Ge
21 Jun	04:06 pm	Ca
23 Jul	03:02 am	Le
23 Aug	09:53 am	Vi
23 Sep	07:05 am	Li
23 Oct	03:54 pm	Sc
22 Nov	01:00 pm	Sa
22 Dec	02:04 am	Cp

1929

20 Jan	12:42 pm	Aq
19 Feb	03:07 am	Pi
21 Mar	02:35 am	Ar
20 Apr	02:10 pm	Ta
21 May	01:48 pm	Ge
21 Jun	10:01 pm	Ca
23 Jul	08:53 am	Le
23 Aug	03:41 pm	Vi
23 Sep	12:52 pm	Li
23 Oct	09:41 pm	Sc
22 Nov	06:48 pm	Sa
22 Dec	07:53 am	Cp

1930

20 Jan	06:33 pm	Aq
19 Feb	09:00 am	Pi
21 Mar	08:30 am	Ar
20 Apr	08:06 pm	Ta
21 May	07:42 pm	Ge
22 Jun	03:53 am	Ca
23 Jul	02:42 pm	Le
23 Aug	09:26 pm	Vi
23 Sep	06:36 pm	Li
24 Oct	03:26 am	Sc
23 Nov	12:34 am	Sa
22 Dec	01:39 pm	Cp

1931

21 Jan	12:17 am	Aq
19 Feb	02:40 pm	Pi
21 Mar	02:06 pm	Ar
21 Apr	01:40 am	Ta
22 May	01:15 am	Ge
22 Jun	09:28 am	Ca
23 Jul	08:21 pm	Le
24 Aug	03:10 am	Vi
24 Sep	12:23 am	Li
24 Oct	09:15 am	Sc
23 Nov	06:25 am	Sa
22 Dec	07:30 pm	Cp

1932

21 Jan	06:07 am	Aq
19 Feb	08:28 pm	Pi
20 Mar	07:53 pm	Ar
20 Apr	07:28 am	Ta
21 May	07:07 am	Ge
21 Jun	03:23 pm	Ca
23 Jul	02:18 am	Le
23 Aug	09:06 am	Vi
23 Sep	06:16 am	Li
23 Oct	03:04 pm	Sc
22 Nov	12:10 pm	Sa
22 Dec	01:14 am	Cp

1933

20 Jan	11:53 am	Aq
19 Feb	02:16 am	Pi
21 Mar	01:43 am	Ar
20 Apr	01:18 pm	Ta
21 May	12:57 pm	Ge
21 Jun	09:12 pm	Ca
23 Jul	08:05 am	Le
23 Aug	02:52 pm	Vi
23 Sep	12:01 pm	Li
23 Oct	08:48 pm	Sc
22 Nov	05:53 pm	Sa
22 Dec	06:57 am	Cp

1934

20 Jan	05:37 pm	Aq
19 Feb	08:02 am	Pi
21 Mar	07:28 am	Ar
20 Apr	07:00 pm	Ta
21 May	06:35 pm	Ge
22 Jun	02:48 am	Ca
23 Jul	01:42 pm	Le
23 Aug	08:32 pm	Vi
23 Sep	05:45 pm	Li
24 Oct	02:36 am	Sc
22 Nov	11:44 pm	Sa
22 Dec	12:49 pm	Cp

1935

20 Jan	11:28 pm	Aq
19 Feb	01:52 pm	Pi
21 Mar	01:18 pm	Ar
21 Apr	12:50 am	Ta
22 May	12:25 am	Ge
22 Jun	08:38 am	Ca
23 Jul	07:33 pm	Le
24 Aug	02:24 am	Vi
23 Sep	11:38 pm	Li
24 Oct	08:29 am	Sc
23 Nov	05:35 am	Sa
22 Dec	06:37 pm	Cp

1936

21 Jan	05:12 am	Aq
19 Feb	07:33 pm	Pi
20 Mar	06:58 pm	Ar
20 Apr	06:31 am	Ta
21 May	06:07 am	Ge
21 Jun	02:22 pm	Ca
23 Jul	01:18 am	Le
23 Aug	08:10 am	Vi
23 Sep	05:26 am	Li
23 Oct	02:18 pm	Sc
22 Nov	11:25 am	Sa
22 Dec	12:27 am	Cp

1937

20 Jan	11:01 am	Aq
19 Feb	01:21 am	Pi
21 Mar	12:45 am	Ar
20 Apr	12:19 pm	Ta
21 May	11:57 am	Ge
21 Jun	08:12 pm	Ca
23 Jul	07:07 am	Le
23 Aug	01:58 pm	Vi
23 Sep	11:13 am	Li
23 Oct	08:06 pm	Sc
22 Nov	05:16 pm	Sa
22 Dec	06:22 am	Cp

1938

20 Jan	04:59 pm	Aq
19 Feb	07:20 am	Pi
21 Mar	06:43 am	Ar
20 Apr	06:15 pm	Ta
21 May	05:50 pm	Ge
22 Jun	02:04 am	Ca
23 Jul	12:57 pm	Le
23 Aug	07:46 pm	Vi
23 Sep	04:59 pm	Li
24 Oct	01:54 am	Sc
22 Nov	11:06 pm	Sa
22 Dec	12:13 pm	Cp

1939

20 Jan	10:51 pm	Aq
19 Feb	01:09 pm	Pi
21 Mar	12:28 pm	Ar
20 Apr	11:55 pm	Ta
21 May	11:27 pm	Ge
22 Jun	07:39 am	Ca
23 Jul	06:37 pm	Le
24 Aug	01:31 am	Vi
23 Sep	10:49 pm	Li
24 Oct	07:46 am	Sc
23 Nov	04:58 am	Sa
22 Dec	06:06 pm	Cp

1940		
21 Jan	04:44 am	Aq
19 Feb	07:04 pm	Pi
20 Mar	06:24 pm	Ar
20 Apr	05:51 am	Ta
21 May	05:23 am	Ge
21 Jun	01:36 pm	Ca
23 Jul	12:34 am	Le
23 Aug	07:28 am	Vi
23 Sep	04:45 am	Li
23 Oct	01:39 pm	Sc
22 Nov	10:49 am	Sa
21 Dec	11:55 pm	Cp

1941		
20 Jan	10:34 am	Aq
19 Feb	12:56 am	Pi
21 Mar	12:20 am	Ar
20 Apr	11:50 am	Ta
21 May	11:23 am	Ge
21 Jun	07:33 pm	Ca
23 Jul	06:26 am	Le
23 Aug	01:17 pm	Vi
23 Sep	10:33 am	Li
23 Oct	07:27 pm	Sc
22 Nov	04:38 pm	Sa
22 Dec	05:44 am	Cp

1942		
20 Jan	04:23 pm	Aq
19 Feb	06:47 am	Pi
21 Mar	06:11 am	Ar
20 Apr	05:39 pm	Ta
21 May	05:09 pm	Ge
22 Jun	01:16 am	Ca
23 Jul	12:07 pm	Le
23 Aug	06:58 pm	Vi
23 Sep	04:16 pm	Li
24 Oct	01:15 am	Sc
22 Nov	10:30 pm	Sa
22 Dec	11:40 am	Cp

1943		
20 Jan	10:19 pm	Aq
19 Feb	12:40 pm	Pi
21 Mar	12:03 pm	Ar
20 Apr	11:31 pm	Ta
21 May	11:03 pm	Ge
22 Jun	07:12 am	Ca
23 Jul	06:04 pm	Le
24 Aug	12:55 am	Vi
23 Sep	10:12 pm	Li
24 Oct	07:08 am	Sc
23 Nov	04:21 am	Sa
22 Dec	05:29 pm	Cp

1944		
21 Jan	04:07 am	Aq
19 Feb	06:27 pm	Pi
20 Mar	05:49 pm	Ar
20 Apr	05:18 am	Ta
21 May	04:51 am	Ge
21 Jun	01:02 pm	Ca
22 Jul	11:56 pm	Le
23 Aug	06:46 am	Vi
23 Sep	04:02 am	Li
23 Oct	12:56 pm	Sc
22 Nov	10:08 am	Sa
21 Dec	11:15 pm	Cp

1945		
20 Jan	09:54 am	Aq
19 Feb	12:15 am	Pi
20 Mar	11:37 pm	Ar
20 Apr	11:07 am	Ta
21 May	10:40 am	Ge
21 Jun	06:52 pm	Ca
23 Jul	05:45 am	Le
23 Aug	12:35 pm	Vi
23 Sep	09:50 am	Li
23 Oct	06:44 pm	Sc
22 Nov	03:55 pm	Sa
22 Dec	05:04 am	Cp

1946		
20 Jan	03:45 pm	Aq
19 Feb	06:09 am	Pi
21 Mar	05:33 am	Ar
20 Apr	05:02 pm	Ta
21 May	04:34 pm	Ge
22 Jun	12:44 am	Ca
23 Jul	11:37 am	Le
23 Aug	06:26 pm	Vi
23 Sep	03:41 pm	Li
24 Oct	12:35 am	Sc
22 Nov	09:46 pm	Sa
22 Dec	10:53 am	Cp

1947		
20 Jan	09:32 pm	Aq
19 Feb	11:52 am	Pi
21 Mar	11:13 am	Ar
20 Apr	10:39 pm	Ta
21 May	10:09 pm	Ge
22 Jun	06:19 am	Ca
23 Jul	05:14 pm	Le
24 Aug	12:09 am	Vi
23 Sep	09:29 pm	Li
24 Oct	06:26 am	Sc
23 Nov	03:38 am	Sa
22 Dec	04:43 pm	Cp

1948		
21 Jan	03:18 am	Aq
19 Feb	05:37 pm	Pi
20 Mar	04:57 pm	Ar
20 Apr	04:25 am	Ta
21 May	03:58 am	Ge
21 Jun	12:11 pm	Ca
22 Jul	11:08 pm	Le
23 Aug	06:03 am	Vi
23 Sep	03:22 am	Li
23 Oct	12:18 pm	Sc
22 Nov	09:29 am	Sa
21 Dec	10:33 pm	Cp

1949		
20 Jan	09:09 am	Aq
18 Feb	11:27 pm	Pi
20 Mar	10:48 pm	Ar
20 Apr	10:17 am	Ta
21 May	09:51 am	Ge
21 Jun	06:03 pm	Ca
23 Jul	04:57 am	Le
23 Aug	11:48 am	Vi
23 Sep	09:06 am	Li
23 Oct	06:03 pm	Sc
22 Nov	03:16 pm	Sa
22 Dec	04:23 am	Cp

1950		
20 Jan	03:00 pm	Aq
19 Feb	05:18 am	Pi
21 Mar	04:35 am	Ar
20 Apr	03:59 pm	Ta
21 May	03:27 pm	Ge
21 Jun	11:36 pm	Ca
23 Jul	10:30 am	Le
23 Aug	05:23 pm	Vi
23 Sep	02:44 pm	Li
23 Oct	11:45 pm	Sc
22 Nov	09:03 pm	Sa
22 Dec	10:13 am	Cp

1951		
20 Jan	08:52 pm	Aq
19 Feb	11:10 am	Pi
21 Mar	10:26 am	Ar
20 Apr	09:48 pm	Ta
21 May	09:15 pm	Ge
22 Jun	05:25 am	Ca
23 Jul	04:21 pm	Le
23 Aug	11:16 pm	Vi
23 Sep	08:37 pm	Li
24 Oct	05:36 am	Sc
23 Nov	02:51 am	Sa
22 Dec	04:00 pm	Cp

1952		
21 Jan	02:38 am	Aq
19 Feb	04:57 pm	Pi
20 Mar	04:14 pm	Ar
20 Apr	03:37 am	Ta
21 May	03:04 am	Ge
21 Jun	11:13 am	Ca
22 Jul	10:07 pm	Le
23 Aug	05:03 am	Vi
23 Sep	02:24 am	Li
23 Oct	11:22 am	Sc
22 Nov	08:36 am	Sa
21 Dec	09:43 pm	Cp

1953		
20 Jan	08:21 am	Aq
18 Feb	10:41 pm	Pi
20 Mar	10:01 pm	Ar
20 Apr	09:25 am	Ta
21 May	08:53 am	Ge
21 Jun	05:00 pm	Ca
23 Jul	03:52 am	Le
23 Aug	10:45 am	Vi
23 Sep	08:06 am	Li
23 Oct	05:06 pm	Sc
22 Nov	02:22 pm	Sa
22 Dec	03:31 am	Cp

1954		
20 Jan	02:11 pm	Aq
19 Feb	04:32 am	Pi
21 Mar	03:53 am	Ar
20 Apr	03:20 pm	Ta
21 May	02:47 pm	Ge
21 Jun	10:54 pm	Ca
23 Jul	09:45 am	Le
23 Aug	04:36 pm	Vi
23 Sep	01:55 pm	Li
23 Oct	10:56 pm	Sc
22 Nov	08:14 pm	Sa
22 Dec	09:24 am	Cp

1955

20 Jan	08:02 pm	Aq
19 Feb	10:19 am	Pi
21 Mar	09:35 am	Ar
20 Apr	08:58 pm	Ta
21 May	08:24 pm	Ge
22 Jun	04:31 am	Ca
23 Jul	03:25 pm	Le
23 Aug	10:19 pm	Vi
23 Sep	07:41 pm	Li
24 Oct	04:43 am	Sc
23 Nov	02:01 am	Sa
22 Dec	03:11 pm	Cp

1956

21 Jan	01:48 am	Aq
19 Feb	04:05 pm	Pi
20 Mar	03:20 pm	Ar
20 Apr	02:44 am	Ta
21 May	02:13 am	Ge
21 Jun	10:24 am	Ca
22 Jul	09:20 pm	Le
23 Aug	04:15 am	Vi
23 Sep	01:35 am	Li
23 Oct	10:34 am	Sc
22 Nov	07:50 am	Sa
21 Dec	09:00 pm	Cp

1957

20 Jan	07:39 am	Aq
18 Feb	09:58 pm	Pi
20 Mar	09:17 pm	Ar
20 Apr	08:41 am	Ta
21 May	08:10 am	Ge
21 Jun	04:21 pm	Ca
23 Jul	03:15 am	Le
23 Aug	10:08 am	Vi
23 Sep	07:26 am	Li
23 Oct	04:24 pm	Sc
22 Nov	01:39 pm	Sa
22 Dec	02:49 am	Cp

1958

20 Jan	01:29 pm	Aq
19 Feb	03:49 am	Pi
21 Mar	03:06 am	Ar
20 Apr	02:27 pm	Ta
21 May	01:51 pm	Ge
21 Jun	09:57 pm	Ca
23 Jul	08:51 am	Le
23 Aug	03:46 pm	Vi
23 Sep	01:09 pm	Li
23 Oct	10:11 pm	Sc
22 Nov	07:29 pm	Sa
22 Dec	08:40 am	Cp

1959

20 Jan	07:19 pm	Aq
19 Feb	09:38 am	Pi
21 Mar	08:55 am	Ar
20 Apr	08:17 pm	Ta
21 May	07:42 pm	Ge
22 Jun	03:50 am	Ca
23 Jul	02:46 pm	Le
23 Aug	09:44 pm	Vi
23 Sep	07:08 pm	Li
24 Oct	04:11 am	Sc
23 Nov	01:27 am	Sa
22 Dec	02:34 pm	Cp

1960

21 Jan	01:10 am	Aq
19 Feb	03:26 pm	Pi
20 Mar	02:43 pm	Ar
20 Apr	02:06 am	Ta
21 May	01:34 am	Ge
21 Jun	09:42 am	Ca
22 Jul	08:38 pm	Le
23 Aug	03:34 am	Vi
23 Sep	12:59 am	Li
23 Oct	10:02 am	Sc
22 Nov	07:18 am	Sa
21 Dec	08:26 pm	Cp

1961

20 Jan	07:01 am	Aq
18 Feb	09:17 pm	Pi
20 Mar	08:32 pm	Ar
20 Apr	07:55 am	Ta
21 May	07:22 am	Ge
21 Jun	03:30 pm	Ca
23 Jul	02:24 am	Le
23 Aug	09:19 am	Vi
23 Sep	06:43 am	Li
23 Oct	03:47 pm	Sc
22 Nov	01:08 pm	Sa
22 Dec	02:20 am	Cp

1962

20 Jan	12:58 pm	Aq
19 Feb	03:15 am	Pi
21 Mar	02:30 am	Ar
20 Apr	01:51 pm	Ta
21 May	01:17 pm	Ge
21 Jun	09:24 pm	Ca
23 Jul	08:18 am	Le
23 Aug	03:13 pm	Vi
23 Sep	12:35 pm	Li
23 Oct	09:40 pm	Sc
22 Nov	07:02 pm	Sa
22 Dec	08:15 am	Cp

1963

20 Jan	06:54 pm	Aq
19 Feb	09:09 am	Pi
21 Mar	08:20 am	Ar
20 Apr	07:36 pm	Ta
21 May	06:58 pm	Ge
22 Jun	03:04 am	Ca
23 Jul	01:59 pm	Le
23 Aug	08:58 pm	Vi
23 Sep	06:24 pm	Li
24 Oct	03:29 am	Sc
23 Nov	12:49 am	Sa
22 Dec	02:02 pm	Cp

1964

21 Jan	12:41 am	Aq
19 Feb	02:57 pm	Pi
20 Mar	02:10 pm	Ar
20 Apr	01:27 am	Ta
21 May	12:50 am	Ge
21 Jun	08:57 am	Ca
22 Jul	07:53 pm	Le
23 Aug	02:51 am	Vi
23 Sep	12:17 am	Li
23 Oct	09:21 am	Sc
22 Nov	06:39 am	Sa
21 Dec	07:50 pm	Cp

1965

20 Jan	06:29 am	Aq
18 Feb	08:48 pm	Pi
20 Mar	08:05 pm	Ar
20 Apr	07:26 am	Ta
21 May	06:50 am	Ge
21 Jun	02:56 pm	Ca
23 Jul	01:48 am	Le
23 Aug	08:43 am	Vi
23 Sep	06:06 am	Li
23 Oct	03:10 pm	Sc
22 Nov	12:29 pm	Sa
22 Dec	01:41 am	Cp

1966

20 Jan	12:20 pm	Aq
19 Feb	02:38 am	Pi
21 Mar	01:53 am	Ar
20 Apr	01:12 pm	Ta
21 May	12:32 pm	Ge
21 Jun	08:34 pm	Ca
23 Jul	07:23 am	Le
23 Aug	02:18 pm	Vi
23 Sep	11:43 am	Li
23 Oct	08:51 pm	Sc
22 Nov	06:14 pm	Sa
22 Dec	07:28 am	Cp

1967

20 Jan	06:08 pm	Aq
19 Feb	08:24 am	Pi
21 Mar	07:37 am	Ar
20 Apr	06:55 pm	Ta
21 May	06:18 pm	Ge
22 Jun	02:23 am	Ca
23 Jul	01:16 pm	Le
23 Aug	08:13 pm	Vi
23 Sep	05:38 pm	Li
24 Oct	02:44 am	Sc
23 Nov	12:05 am	Sa
22 Dec	01:16 pm	Cp

1968

20 Jan	11:54 pm	Aq
19 Feb	02:09 pm	Pi
20 Mar	01:22 pm	Ar
20 Apr	12:41 am	Ta
21 May	12:06 am	Ge
21 Jun	08:13 am	Ca
22 Jul	07:08 pm	Le
23 Aug	02:03 am	Vi
22 Sep	11:26 pm	Li
23 Oct	08:30 am	Sc
22 Nov	05:49 am	Sa
21 Dec	07:00 pm	Cp

1969

20 Jan	05:38 am	Aq
18 Feb	07:55 pm	Pi
20 Mar	07:08 pm	Ar
20 Apr	06:27 am	Ta
21 May	05:50 am	Ge
21 Jun	01:55 pm	Ca
23 Jul	12:48 am	Le
23 Aug	07:44 am	Vi
23 Sep	05:07 am	Li
23 Oct	02:11 pm	Sc
22 Nov	11:31 am	Sa
22 Dec	12:44 am	Cp

1970
20 Jan 11:24 am Aq
19 Feb 01:42 am Pi
21 Mar 12:57 am Ar
20 Apr 12:15 pm Ta
21 May 11:38 am Ge
21 Jun 07:43 pm Ca
23 Jul 06:37 am Le
23 Aug 01:34 pm Vi
23 Sep 10:59 am Li
23 Oct 08:04 pm Sc
22 Nov 05:25 pm Sa
22 Dec 06:36 am Cp

1971
20 Jan 05:13 pm Aq
19 Feb 07:27 am Pi
21 Mar 06:38 am Ar
20 Apr 05:54 pm Ta
21 May 05:15 pm Ge
22 Jun 01:20 am Ca
23 Jul 12:15 pm Le
23 Aug 07:15 pm Vi
23 Sep 04:45 pm Li
24 Oct 01:53 am Sc
22 Nov 11:14 pm Sa
22 Dec 12:24 pm Cp

1972
20 Jan 10:59 pm Aq
19 Feb 01:12 pm Pi
20 Mar 12:22 pm Ar
19 Apr 11:38 pm Ta
20 May 11:00 pm Ge
21 Jun 07:06 am Ca
22 Jul 06:03 pm Le
23 Aug 01:03 am Vi
22 Sep 10:33 pm Li
23 Oct 07:42 am Sc
22 Nov 05:03 am Sa
21 Dec 06:13 pm Cp

1973
20 Jan 04:48 am Aq
18 Feb 07:01 pm Pi
20 Mar 06:13 pm Ar
20 Apr 05:31 am Ta
21 May 04:54 am Ge
21 Jun 01:01 pm Ca
22 Jul 11:56 pm Le
23 Aug 06:54 am Vi
23 Sep 04:21 am Li
23 Oct 01:30 pm Sc
22 Nov 10:54 am Sa
22 Dec 12:08 am Cp

1974
20 Jan 10:46 am Aq
19 Feb 12:59 am Pi
21 Mar 12:07 am Ar
20 Apr 11:19 am Ta
21 May 10:36 am Ge
21 Jun 06:38 pm Ca
23 Jul 05:30 am Le
23 Aug 12:29 pm Vi
23 Sep 09:59 am Li
23 Oct 07:11 pm Sc
22 Nov 04:39 pm Sa
22 Dec 05:56 am Cp

1975
20 Jan 04:37 pm Aq
19 Feb 06:50 am Pi
21 Mar 05:57 am Ar
20 Apr 05:08 pm Ta
21 May 04:24 pm Ge
22 Jun 12:27 am Ca
23 Jul 11:22 am Le
23 Aug 06:24 pm Vi
23 Sep 03:55 pm Li
24 Oct 01:06 am Sc
22 Nov 10:31 pm Sa
22 Dec 11:46 am Cp

1976
20 Jan 10:25 pm Aq
19 Feb 12:40 pm Pi
20 Mar 11:50 am Ar
19 Apr 11:03 pm Ta
20 May 10:21 pm Ge
21 Jun 06:25 am Ca
22 Jul 05:19 pm Le
23 Aug 12:19 am Vi
22 Sep 09:48 pm Li
23 Oct 06:58 am Sc
22 Nov 04:22 am Sa
21 Dec 05:35 pm Cp

1977
20 Jan 04:15 am Aq
18 Feb 06:31 pm Pi
20 Mar 05:43 pm Ar
20 Apr 04:58 am Ta
21 May 04:15 am Ge
21 Jun 12:14 pm Ca
22 Jul 11:04 pm Le
23 Aug 06:01 am Vi
23 Sep 03:30 am Li
23 Oct 12:41 pm Sc
22 Nov 10:07 am Sa
21 Dec 11:23 pm Cp

1978
20 Jan 10:04 am Aq
19 Feb 12:21 am Pi
20 Mar 11:34 pm Ar
20 Apr 10:50 am Ta
21 May 10:09 am Ge
21 Jun 06:10 pm Ca
23 Jul 05:01 am Le
23 Aug 11:57 am Vi
23 Sep 09:26 am Li
23 Oct 06:37 pm Sc
22 Nov 04:05 pm Sa
22 Dec 05:21 am Cp

1979
20 Jan 04:00 pm Aq
19 Feb 06:14 am Pi
21 Mar 05:22 am Ar
20 Apr 04:36 pm Ta
21 May 03:54 pm Ge
21 Jun 11:57 pm Ca
23 Jul 10:49 am Le
23 Aug 05:47 pm Vi
23 Sep 03:17 pm Li
24 Oct 12:28 am Sc
22 Nov 09:54 pm Sa
22 Dec 11:10 am Cp

1980
20 Jan 09:49 pm Aq
19 Feb 12:02 pm Pi
20 Mar 11:10 am Ar
19 Apr 10:23 pm Ta
20 May 09:42 pm Ge
21 Jun 05:47 am Ca
22 Jul 04:42 pm Le
22 Aug 11:41 pm Vi
22 Sep 09:09 pm Li
23 Oct 06:18 am Sc
22 Nov 03:42 am Sa
21 Dec 04:56 pm Cp

1981
20 Jan 03:36 am Aq
18 Feb 05:52 pm Pi
20 Mar 05:03 pm Ar
20 Apr 04:19 am Ta
21 May 03:40 am Ge
21 Jun 11:45 am Ca
22 Jul 10:40 pm Le
23 Aug 05:39 am Vi
23 Sep 03:06 am Li
23 Oct 12:13 pm Sc
22 Nov 09:36 am Sa
21 Dec 10:51 pm Cp

1982
20 Jan 09:31 am Aq
18 Feb 11:47 pm Pi
20 Mar 10:56 pm Ar
20 Apr 10:08 am Ta
21 May 09:23 am Ge
21 Jun 05:23 pm Ca
23 Jul 04:16 am Le
23 Aug 11:16 am Vi
23 Sep 08:47 am Li
23 Oct 05:58 pm Sc
22 Nov 03:24 pm Sa
22 Dec 04:39 am Cp

1983
20 Jan 03:17 pm Aq
19 Feb 05:31 am Pi
21 Mar 04:39 am Ar
20 Apr 03:51 pm Ta
21 May 03:07 pm Ge
21 Jun 11:09 pm Ca
23 Jul 10:05 am Le
23 Aug 05:08 pm Vi
23 Sep 02:42 pm Li
23 Oct 11:55 pm Sc
22 Nov 09:19 pm Sa
22 Dec 10:30 am Cp

1984
20 Jan 09:05 pm Aq
19 Feb 11:17 am Pi
20 Mar 10:25 am Ar
19 Apr 09:39 pm Ta
20 May 08:58 pm Ge
21 Jun 05:03 am Ca
22 Jul 03:59 pm Le
22 Aug 11:01 pm Vi
22 Sep 08:33 pm Li
23 Oct 05:46 am Sc
22 Nov 03:11 am Sa
21 Dec 04:23 pm Cp

1985		
20 Jan	02:58 am	Aq
18 Feb	05:08 pm	Pi
20 Mar	04:14 pm	Ar
20 Apr	03:26 am	Ta
21 May	02:43 am	Ge
21 Jun	10:45 am	Ca
22 Jul	09:37 pm	Le
23 Aug	04:36 am	Vi
23 Sep	02:08 am	Li
23 Oct	11:22 am	Sc
22 Nov	08:51 am	Sa
21 Dec	10:08 pm	Cp

1986		
20 Jan	08:47 am	Aq
18 Feb	10:58 pm	Pi
20 Mar	10:03 pm	Ar
20 Apr	09:13 am	Ta
21 May	08:28 am	Ge
21 Jun	04:30 pm	Ca
23 Jul	03:25 am	Le
23 Aug	10:26 am	Vi
23 Sep	07:59 am	Li
23 Oct	05:15 pm	Sc
22 Nov	02:45 pm	Sa
22 Dec	04:03 am	Cp

1987		
20 Jan	02:41 pm	Aq
19 Feb	04:50 am	Pi
21 Mar	03:52 am	Ar
20 Apr	02:58 pm	Ta
21 May	02:10 pm	Ge
21 Jun	10:11 pm	Ca
23 Jul	09:06 am	Le
23 Aug	04:10 pm	Vi
23 Sep	01:46 pm	Li
23 Oct	11:01 pm	Sc
22 Nov	08:30 pm	Sa
22 Dec	09:46 am	Cp

1988		
20 Jan	08:25 pm	Aq
19 Feb	10:36 am	Pi
20 Mar	09:39 am	Ar
19 Apr	08:45 pm	Ta
20 May	07:57 pm	Ge
21 Jun	03:57 am	Ca
22 Jul	02:52 pm	Le
22 Aug	09:54 pm	Vi
22 Sep	07:29 pm	Li
23 Oct	04:45 am	Sc
22 Nov	02:12 am	Sa
21 Dec	03:28 pm	Cp

1989		
20 Jan	02:07 am	Aq
18 Feb	04:21 pm	Pi
20 Mar	03:29 pm	Ar
20 Apr	02:39 am	Ta
21 May	01:54 am	Ge
21 Jun	09:53 am	Ca
22 Jul	08:46 pm	Le
23 Aug	03:47 am	Vi
23 Sep	01:20 am	Li
23 Oct	10:36 am	Sc
22 Nov	08:05 am	Sa
21 Dec	09:22 pm	Cp

1990		
20 Jan	08:02 am	Aq
18 Feb	10:15 pm	Pi
20 Mar	09:20 pm	Ar
20 Apr	08:27 am	Ta
21 May	07:38 am	Ge
21 Jun	03:33 pm	Ca
23 Jul	02:22 am	Le
23 Aug	09:21 am	Vi
23 Sep	06:56 am	Li
23 Oct	04:14 pm	Sc
22 Nov	01:47 pm	Sa
22 Dec	03:07 am	Cp

1991		
20 Jan	01:48 pm	Aq
19 Feb	03:59 am	Pi
21 Mar	03:02 am	Ar
20 Apr	02:09 pm	Ta
21 May	01:21 pm	Ge
21 Jun	09:19 pm	Ca
23 Jul	08:12 am	Le
23 Aug	03:13 pm	Vi
23 Sep	12:49 pm	Li
23 Oct	10:06 pm	Sc
22 Nov	07:36 pm	Sa
22 Dec	08:54 am	Cp

1992		
20 Jan	07:33 pm	Aq
19 Feb	09:44 am	Pi
20 Mar	08:49 am	Ar
19 Apr	07:57 pm	Ta
20 May	07:13 pm	Ge
21 Jun	03:15 am	Ca
22 Jul	02:09 pm	Le
22 Aug	09:11 pm	Vi
22 Sep	06:43 pm	Li
23 Oct	03:58 am	Sc
22 Nov	01:26 am	Sa
21 Dec	02:44 pm	Cp

1993		
20 Jan	01:23 am	Aq
18 Feb	03:36 pm	Pi
20 Mar	02:41 pm	Ar
20 Apr	01:49 am	Ta
21 May	01:02 am	Ge
21 Jun	09:00 am	Ca
22 Jul	07:51 pm	Le
23 Aug	02:51 am	Vi
23 Sep	12:23 am	Li
23 Oct	09:38 am	Sc
22 Nov	07:07 am	Sa
21 Dec	08:26 pm	Cp

1994		
20 Jan	07:08 am	Aq
18 Feb	09:22 pm	Pi
20 Mar	08:29 pm	Ar
20 Apr	07:37 am	Ta
21 May	06:49 am	Ge
21 Jun	02:48 pm	Ca
23 Jul	01:41 am	Le
23 Aug	08:44 am	Vi
23 Sep	06:20 am	Li
23 Oct	03:37 pm	Sc
22 Nov	01:07 pm	Sa
22 Dec	02:23 am	Cp

1995		
20 Jan	01:01 pm	Aq
19 Feb	03:11 am	Pi
21 Mar	02:15 am	Ar
20 Apr	01:22 pm	Ta
21 May	12:35 pm	Ge
21 Jun	08:35 pm	Ca
23 Jul	07:30 am	Le
23 Aug	02:35 pm	Vi
23 Sep	12:14 pm	Li
23 Oct	09:32 pm	Sc
22 Nov	07:02 pm	Sa
22 Dec	08:17 am	Cp

1996		
20 Jan	06:53 pm	Aq
19 Feb	09:01 am	Pi
20 Mar	08:04 am	Ar
19 Apr	07:10 pm	Ta
20 May	06:24 pm	Ge
21 Jun	02:24 am	Ca
22 Jul	01:19 pm	Le
22 Aug	08:23 pm	Vi
22 Sep	06:01 pm	Li
23 Oct	03:19 am	Sc
22 Nov	12:50 am	Sa
21 Dec	02:06 pm	Cp

1997		
20 Jan	12:43 am	Aq
18 Feb	02:52 pm	Pi
20 Mar	01:55 pm	Ar
20 Apr	01:03 am	Ta
21 May	12:18 am	Ge
21 Jun	08:20 am	Ca
22 Jul	07:16 pm	Le
23 Aug	02:20 am	Vi
22 Sep	11:56 pm	Li
23 Oct	09:15 am	Sc
22 Nov	06:48 am	Sa
21 Dec	08:08 pm	Cp

1998		
20 Jan	06:47 am	Aq
18 Feb	08:55 pm	Pi
20 Mar	07:55 pm	Ar
20 Apr	06:57 am	Ta
21 May	06:06 am	Ge
21 Jun	02:03 pm	Ca
23 Jul	12:56 am	Le
23 Aug	07:59 am	Vi
23 Sep	05:38 am	Li
23 Oct	02:59 pm	Sc
22 Nov	12:35 pm	Sa
22 Dec	01:57 am	Cp

1999		
20 Jan	12:38 pm	Aq
19 Feb	02:47 am	Pi
21 Mar	01:46 am	Ar
20 Apr	12:47 pm	Ta
21 May	11:53 am	Ge
21 Jun	07:50 pm	Ca
23 Jul	06:45 am	Le
23 Aug	01:52 pm	Vi
23 Sep	11:32 am	Li
23 Oct	08:53 pm	Sc
22 Nov	06:25 pm	Sa
22 Dec	07:44 am	Cp

2000		
20 Jan	06:24 pm	Aq
19 Feb	08:34 am	Pi
20 Mar	07:36 am	Ar
19 Apr	06:40 pm	Ta
20 May	05:50 pm	Ge
21 Jun	01:48 am	Ca
22 Jul	12:43 pm	Le
22 Aug	07:49 pm	Vi
22 Sep	05:28 pm	Li
23 Oct	02:48 am	Sc
22 Nov	12:20 am	Sa
21 Dec	01:38 pm	Cp

2001		
20 Jan	12:17 am	Aq
18 Feb	02:28 pm	Pi
20 Mar	01:31 pm	Ar
20 Apr	12:36 am	Ta
20 May	11:45 pm	Ge
21 Jun	07:38 am	Ca
22 Jul	06:27 pm	Le
23 Aug	01:28 am	Vi
22 Sep	11:05 pm	Li
23 Oct	08:26 am	Sc
22 Nov	06:01 am	Sa
21 Dec	07:22 pm	Cp

2002		
20 Jan	06:03 am	Aq
18 Feb	08:14 pm	Pi
20 Mar	07:17 pm	Ar
20 Apr	06:21 am	Ta
21 May	05:30 am	Ge
21 Jun	01:25 pm	Ca
23 Jul	12:15 am	Le
23 Aug	07:18 am	Vi
23 Sep	04:56 am	Li
23 Oct	02:18 pm	Sc
22 Nov	11:54 am	Sa
22 Dec	01:15 am	Cp

2003		
20 Jan	11:53 am	Aq
19 Feb	02:01 am	Pi
21 Mar	01:00 am	Ar
20 Apr	12:03 pm	Ta
21 May	11:13 am	Ge
21 Jun	07:11 pm	Ca
23 Jul	06:05 am	Le
23 Aug	01:09 pm	Vi
23 Sep	10:47 am	Li
23 Oct	08:09 pm	Sc
22 Nov	05:44 pm	Sa
22 Dec	07:04 am	Cp

2004		
20 Jan	05:43 pm	Aq
19 Feb	07:51 am	Pi
20 Mar	06:49 am	Ar
19 Apr	05:51 pm	Ta
20 May	05:00 pm	Ge
21 Jun	12:57 am	Ca
22 Jul	11:51 am	Le
22 Aug	06:54 pm	Vi
22 Sep	04:30 pm	Li
23 Oct	01:49 am	Sc
21 Nov	11:22 pm	Sa
21 Dec	12:42 pm	Cp

2005		
19 Jan	11:22 pm	Aq
18 Feb	01:33 pm	Pi
20 Mar	12:34 pm	Ar
19 Apr	11:38 pm	Ta
20 May	10:48 pm	Ge
21 Jun	06:47 am	Ca
22 Jul	05:41 pm	Le
23 Aug	12:46 am	Vi
22 Sep	10:24 pm	Li
23 Oct	07:43 am	Sc
22 Nov	05:16 am	Sa
21 Dec	06:36 pm	Cp

2006		
20 Jan	05:16 am	Aq
18 Feb	07:26 pm	Pi
20 Mar	06:26 pm	Ar
20 Apr	05:27 am	Ta
21 May	04:32 am	Ge
21 Jun	12:26 pm	Ca
22 Jul	11:18 pm	Le
23 Aug	06:23 am	Vi
23 Sep	04:04 am	Li
23 Oct	01:27 pm	Sc
22 Nov	11:02 am	Sa
22 Dec	12:23 am	Cp

2007		
20 Jan	11:01 am	Aq
19 Feb	01:10 am	Pi
21 Mar	12:08 am	Ar
20 Apr	11:08 am	Ta
21 May	10:13 am	Ge
21 Jun	06:07 pm	Ca
23 Jul	05:01 am	Le
23 Aug	12:09 pm	Vi
23 Sep	09:52 am	Li
23 Oct	07:16 pm	Sc
22 Nov	04:50 pm	Sa
22 Dec	06:08 am	Cp

2008		
20 Jan	04:44 pm	Aq
19 Feb	06:50 am	Pi
20 Mar	05:49 am	Ar
19 Apr	04:52 pm	Ta
20 May	04:01 pm	Ge
21 Jun	12:00 am	Ca
22 Jul	10:55 am	Le
22 Aug	06:03 pm	Vi
22 Sep	03:45 pm	Li
23 Oct	01:09 am	Sc
21 Nov	10:45 pm	Sa
21 Dec	12:04 pm	Cp

2009		
19 Jan	10:41 pm	Aq
18 Feb	12:47 pm	Pi
20 Mar	11:44 am	Ar
19 Apr	10:45 pm	Ta
20 May	09:52 pm	Ge
21 Jun	05:46 am	Ca
22 Jul	04:36 pm	Le
22 Aug	11:39 pm	Vi
22 Sep	09:19 pm	Li
23 Oct	06:44 am	Sc
22 Nov	04:23 am	Sa
21 Dec	05:47 pm	Cp

2010		
20 Jan	04:28 am	Aq
18 Feb	06:36 pm	Pi
20 Mar	05:33 pm	Ar
20 Apr	04:30 am	Ta
21 May	03:34 am	Ge
21 Jun	11:29 am	Ca
22 Jul	10:22 pm	Le
23 Aug	05:28 am	Vi
23 Sep	03:10 am	Li
23 Oct	12:36 pm	Sc
22 Nov	10:15 am	Sa
21 Dec	11:39 pm	Cp

2011		
20 Jan	10:19 am	Aq
19 Feb	12:26 am	Pi
20 Mar	11:21 pm	Ar
20 Apr	10:18 am	Ta
21 May	09:22 am	Ge
21 Jun	05:17 pm	Ca
23 Jul	04:12 am	Le
23 Aug	11:21 am	Vi
23 Sep	09:05 am	Li
23 Oct	06:31 pm	Sc
22 Nov	04:08 pm	Sa
22 Dec	05:31 am	Cp

2012		
20 Jan	04:10 pm	Aq
19 Feb	06:18 am	Pi
20 Mar	05:15 am	Ar
19 Apr	04:13 pm	Ta
20 May	03:16 pm	Ge
20 Jun	11:09 pm	Ca
22 Jul	10:01 am	Le
22 Aug	05:07 pm	Vi
22 Sep	02:50 pm	Li
23 Oct	12:14 am	Sc
21 Nov	09:51 pm	Sa
21 Dec	11:12 am	Cp

2013		
19 Jan	09:52 pm	Aq
18 Feb	12:02 pm	Pi
20 Mar	11:03 am	Ar
19 Apr	10:04 pm	Ta
20 May	09:10 pm	Ge
21 Jun	05:05 am	Ca
22 Jul	03:57 pm	Le
22 Aug	11:02 pm	Vi
22 Sep	08:45 pm	Li
23 Oct	06:10 am	Sc
22 Nov	03:49 am	Sa
21 Dec	05:12 pm	Cp

2014		
20 Jan	03:52 am	Aq
18 Feb	06:00 pm	Pi
20 Mar	04:58 pm	Ar
20 Apr	03:56 am	Ta
21 May	03:00 am	Ge
21 Jun	10:52 am	Ca
22 Jul	09:42 pm	Le
23 Aug	04:47 am	Vi
23 Sep	02:30 am	Li
23 Oct	11:58 am	Sc
22 Nov	09:39 am	Sa
21 Dec	11:04 pm	Cp

2015

20 Jan	09:44 am	Aq
18 Feb	11:50 pm	Pi
20 Mar	10:46 pm	Ar
20 Apr	09:42 am	Ta
21 May	08:45 am	Ge
21 Jun	04:39 pm	Ca
23 Jul	03:31 am	Le
23 Aug	10:38 am	Vi
23 Sep	08:21 am	Li
23 Oct	05:47 pm	Sc
22 Nov	03:26 pm	Sa
22 Dec	04:49 am	Cp

2016

20 Jan	03:28 pm	Aq
19 Feb	05:34 am	Pi
20 Mar	04:31 am	Ar
19 Apr	03:30 pm	Ta
20 May	02:37 pm	Ge
20 Jun	10:35 pm	Ca
22 Jul	09:31 am	Le
22 Aug	04:39 pm	Vi
22 Sep	02:22 pm	Li
22 Oct	11:46 pm	Sc
21 Nov	09:23 pm	Sa
21 Dec	10:45 am	Cp

2017

19 Jan	09:24 pm	Aq
18 Feb	11:32 am	Pi
20 Mar	10:29 am	Ar
19 Apr	09:28 pm	Ta
20 May	08:32 pm	Ge
21 Jun	04:25 am	Ca
22 Jul	03:16 pm	Le
22 Aug	10:21 pm	Vi
22 Sep	08:02 pm	Li
23 Oct	05:27 am	Sc
22 Nov	03:05 am	Sa
21 Dec	04:29 pm	Cp

2018

20 Jan	03:10 am	Aq
18 Feb	05:19 pm	Pi
20 Mar	04:16 pm	Ar
20 Apr	03:13 am	Ta
21 May	02:15 am	Ge
21 Jun	10:08 am	Ca
22 Jul	09:01 pm	Le
23 Aug	04:09 am	Vi
23 Sep	01:55 am	Li
23 Oct	11:23 am	Sc
22 Nov	09:02 am	Sa
21 Dec	10:23 pm	Cp

2019

20 Jan	09:00 am	Aq
18 Feb	11:05 pm	Pi
20 Mar	09:59 pm	Ar
20 Apr	08:56 am	Ta
21 May	08:00 am	Ge
21 Jun	03:55 pm	Ca
23 Jul	02:51 am	Le
23 Aug	10:03 am	Vi
23 Sep	07:51 am	Li
23 Oct	05:20 pm	Sc
22 Nov	03:00 pm	Sa
22 Dec	04:20 am	Cp

2020

20 Jan	02:55 pm	Aq
19 Feb	04:58 am	Pi
20 Mar	03:50 am	Ar
19 Apr	02:46 pm	Ta
20 May	01:50 pm	Ge
20 Jun	09:44 pm	Ca
22 Jul	08:38 am	Le
22 Aug	03:46 pm	Vi
22 Sep	01:31 pm	Li
22 Oct	11:00 pm	Sc
21 Nov	08:40 pm	Sa
21 Dec	10:03 am	Cp

2021

19 Jan	08:40 pm	Aq
18 Feb	10:45 am	Pi
20 Mar	09:38 am	Ar
19 Apr	08:34 pm	Ta
20 May	07:38 pm	Ge
21 Jun	03:33 am	Ca
22 Jul	02:27 pm	Le
22 Aug	09:36 pm	Vi
22 Sep	07:22 pm	Li
23 Oct	04:52 am	Sc
22 Nov	02:34 am	Sa
21 Dec	04:00 pm	Cp

2022

20 Jan	02:40 am	Aq
18 Feb	04:44 pm	Pi
20 Mar	03:34 pm	Ar
20 Apr	02:25 am	Ta
21 May	01:23 am	Ge
21 Jun	09:14 am	Ca
22 Jul	08:08 pm	Le
23 Aug	03:17 am	Vi
23 Sep	01:04 am	Li
23 Oct	10:36 am	Sc
22 Nov	08:21 am	Sa
21 Dec	09:49 pm	Cp

2023

20 Jan	08:30 am	Aq
18 Feb	10:35 pm	Pi
20 Mar	09:25 pm	Ar
20 Apr	08:14 am	Ta
21 May	07:10 am	Ge
21 Jun	02:58 pm	Ca
23 Jul	01:51 am	Le
23 Aug	09:02 am	Vi
23 Sep	06:51 am	Li
23 Oct	04:21 pm	Sc
22 Nov	02:03 pm	Sa
22 Dec	03:28 am	Cp

2024

20 Jan	02:08 pm	Aq
19 Feb	04:14 am	Pi
20 Mar	03:07 am	Ar
19 Apr	02:00 pm	Ta
20 May	01:00 pm	Ge
20 Jun	08:52 pm	Ca
22 Jul	07:45 am	Le
22 Aug	02:56 pm	Vi
22 Sep	12:44 pm	Li
22 Oct	10:15 pm	Sc
21 Nov	07:57 pm	Sa
21 Dec	09:21 am	Cp

2025

19 Jan	08:01 pm	Aq
18 Feb	10:07 am	Pi
20 Mar	09:02 am	Ar
19 Apr	07:57 pm	Ta
20 May	06:55 pm	Ge
21 Jun	02:43 am	Ca
22 Jul	01:30 pm	Le
22 Aug	08:34 pm	Vi
22 Sep	06:20 pm	Li
23 Oct	03:52 am	Sc
22 Nov	01:36 am	Sa
21 Dec	03:04 pm	Cp

MOON CHARTS

January 1925

1st	02:57 am	Aries
3rd	11:31 am	Taurus
5th	10:52 pm	Gemini
8th	11:32 am	Cancer
11th	12:14 am	Leo
13th	11:54 am	Virgo
15th	09:32 pm	Libra
18th	04:11 am	Scorpio
20th	07:34 am	Sagittarius
22nd	08:22 am	Capricorn
24th	08:09 am	Aquarius
26th	08:45 am	Pisces
28th	11:59 am	Aries
30th	06:58 pm	Taurus

February 1925

2nd	05:32 am	Gemini
4th	06:10 pm	Cancer
7th	06:49 am	Leo
9th	06:01 pm	Virgo
12th	03:06 am	Libra
14th	09:54 am	Scorpio
16th	02:27 pm	Sagittarius
18th	05:02 pm	Capricorn
20th	06:21 pm	Aquarius
22nd	07:36 pm	Pisces
24th	10:21 pm	Aries
27th	04:03 am	Taurus

March 1925

1st	01:26 pm	Gemini
4th	01:38 am	Cancer
6th	02:22 pm	Leo
9th	01:24 am	Virgo
11th	09:44 am	Libra
13th	03:37 pm	Scorpio
15th	07:51 pm	Sagittarius
17th	11:07 pm	Capricorn
20th	01:51 am	Aquarius
22nd	04:33 am	Pisces
24th	08:04 am	Aries
26th	01:34 pm	Taurus
28th	10:07 pm	Gemini
31st	09:42 am	Cancer

April 1925

2nd	10:32 pm	Leo
5th	09:55 am	Virgo
7th	06:04 pm	Libra
9th	11:04 pm	Scorpio
12th	02:05 am	Sagittarius
14th	04:32 am	Capricorn
16th	07:23 am	Aquarius
18th	11:02 am	Pisces
20th	03:45 pm	Aries
22nd	09:59 pm	Taurus
25th	06:33 am	Gemini
27th	05:45 pm	Cancer
30th	06:36 am	Leo

May 1925

2nd	06:38 pm	Virgo
5th	03:26 am	Libra
7th	08:22 am	Scorpio
9th	10:27 am	Sagittarius
11th	11:30 am	Capricorn
13th	01:08 pm	Aquarius
15th	04:23 pm	Pisces
17th	09:34 pm	Aries
20th	04:41 am	Taurus
22nd	01:50 pm	Gemini
25th	01:07 am	Cancer
27th	01:59 pm	Leo
30th	02:35 am	Virgo

June 1925

1st	12:30 pm	Libra
3rd	06:21 pm	Scorpio
5th	08:33 pm	Sagittarius
7th	08:45 pm	Capricorn
9th	08:54 pm	Aquarius
11th	10:40 pm	Pisces
14th	03:03 am	Aries
16th	10:15 am	Taurus
18th	07:57 pm	Gemini
21st	07:36 am	Cancer
23rd	08:30 pm	Leo
26th	09:21 am	Virgo
28th	08:15 pm	Libra

July 1925

1st	03:32 am	Scorpio
3rd	06:55 am	Sagittarius
5th	07:24 am	Capricorn
7th	06:49 am	Aquarius
9th	07:06 am	Pisces
11th	09:53 am	Aries
13th	04:05 pm	Taurus
16th	01:37 am	Gemini
18th	01:33 pm	Cancer
21st	02:32 am	Leo
23rd	03:17 pm	Virgo
26th	02:30 am	Libra
28th	10:56 am	Scorpio
30th	03:56 pm	Sagittarius

August 1925

1st	05:46 pm	Capricorn
3rd	05:40 pm	Aquarius
5th	05:23 pm	Pisces
7th	06:46 pm	Aries
9th	11:24 pm	Taurus
12th	07:57 am	Gemini
14th	07:39 pm	Cancer
17th	08:41 am	Leo
19th	09:13 pm	Virgo
22nd	08:05 am	Libra
24th	04:44 pm	Scorpio
26th	10:49 pm	Sagittarius
29th	02:19 am	Capricorn
31st	03:41 am	Aquarius

September 1925

2nd	04:02 am	Pisces
4th	05:02 am	Aries
6th	08:27 am	Taurus
8th	03:39 pm	Gemini
11th	02:35 am	Cancer
13th	03:30 pm	Leo
16th	03:56 am	Virgo
18th	02:18 pm	Libra
20th	10:18 pm	Scorpio
23rd	04:17 am	Sagittarius
25th	08:37 am	Capricorn
27th	11:29 am	Aquarius
29th	01:19 pm	Pisces

October 1925

1st	03:06 pm	Aries
3rd	06:20 pm	Taurus
6th	12:35 am	Gemini
8th	10:33 am	Cancer
10th	11:09 pm	Leo
13th	11:43 am	Virgo
15th	09:57 pm	Libra
18th	05:12 am	Scorpio
20th	10:11 am	Sagittarius
22nd	01:57 pm	Capricorn
24th	05:12 pm	Aquarius
26th	08:14 pm	Pisces
28th	11:23 pm	Aries
31st	03:29 am	Taurus

November 1925

2nd	09:44 am	Gemini
4th	07:06 pm	Cancer
7th	07:16 am	Leo
9th	08:07 pm	Virgo
12th	06:52 am	Libra
14th	02:05 pm	Scorpio
16th	06:12 pm	Sagittarius
18th	08:38 pm	Capricorn
20th	10:48 pm	Aquarius
23rd	01:37 am	Pisces
25th	05:31 am	Aries
27th	10:46 am	Taurus
29th	05:50 pm	Gemini

December 1925

2nd	03:19 am	Cancer
4th	03:13 pm	Leo
7th	04:13 am	Virgo
9th	03:52 pm	Libra
12th	12:03 am	Scorpio
14th	04:23 am	Sagittarius
16th	05:59 am	Capricorn
18th	06:35 am	Aquarius
20th	07:51 am	Pisces
22nd	10:57 am	Aries
24th	04:25 pm	Taurus
27th	12:18 am	Gemini
29th	10:26 am	Cancer
31st	10:26 pm	Leo

January 1926

3rd	11:26 am	Virgo
5th	11:44 pm	Libra
8th	09:19 am	Scorpio
10th	03:01 pm	Sagittarius
12th	05:09 pm	Capricorn
14th	05:07 pm	Aquarius
16th	04:48 pm	Pisces
18th	06:03 pm	Aries
20th	10:15 pm	Taurus
23rd	05:55 am	Gemini
25th	04:30 pm	Cancer
28th	04:52 am	Leo
30th	05:49 pm	Virgo

February 1926

2nd	06:10 am	Libra
4th	04:39 pm	Scorpio
7th	12:02 am	Sagittarius
9th	03:49 am	Capricorn
11th	04:37 am	Aquarius
13th	03:57 am	Pisces
15th	03:47 am	Aries
17th	06:08 am	Taurus
19th	12:22 pm	Gemini
21st	10:28 pm	Cancer
24th	11:00 am	Leo
26th	11:59 pm	Virgo

March 1926

1st	12:03 pm	Libra
3rd	10:28 pm	Scorpio
6th	06:40 am	Sagittarius
8th	12:06 pm	Capricorn
10th	02:40 pm	Aquarius
12th	03:03 pm	Pisces
14th	02:51 pm	Aries
16th	04:06 pm	Taurus
18th	08:41 pm	Gemini
21st	05:30 am	Cancer
23rd	05:35 pm	Leo
26th	06:36 am	Virgo
28th	06:27 pm	Libra
31st	04:17 am	Scorpio

April 1926

2nd	12:08 pm	Sagittarius
4th	06:04 pm	Capricorn
6th	10:00 pm	Aquarius
9th	12:03 am	Pisces
11th	01:02 am	Aries
13th	02:31 am	Taurus
15th	06:20 am	Gemini
17th	01:54 pm	Cancer
20th	01:07 am	Leo
22nd	01:59 pm	Virgo
25th	01:52 am	Libra
27th	11:18 am	Scorpio
29th	06:19 pm	Sagittarius

May 1926

1st	11:32 pm	Capricorn
4th	03:31 am	Aquarius
6th	06:32 am	Pisces
8th	08:55 am	Aries
10th	11:33 am	Taurus
12th	03:46 pm	Gemini
14th	10:53 pm	Cancer
17th	09:20 am	Leo
19th	09:54 pm	Virgo
22nd	10:04 am	Libra
24th	07:41 pm	Scorpio
27th	02:14 am	Sagittarius
29th	06:24 am	Capricorn
31st	09:19 am	Aquarius

June 1926

2nd	11:53 am	Pisces
4th	02:45 pm	Aries
6th	06:28 pm	Taurus
8th	11:43 pm	Gemini
11th	07:14 am	Cancer
13th	05:29 pm	Leo
16th	05:48 am	Virgo
18th	06:18 pm	Libra
21st	04:40 am	Scorpio
23rd	11:35 am	Sagittarius
25th	03:18 pm	Capricorn
27th	05:01 pm	Aquarius
29th	06:13 pm	Pisces

July 1926

1st	08:14 pm	Aries
3rd	11:59 pm	Taurus
6th	05:57 am	Gemini
8th	02:16 pm	Cancer
11th	12:50 am	Leo
13th	01:07 pm	Virgo
16th	01:52 am	Libra
18th	01:07 pm	Scorpio
20th	09:10 pm	Sagittarius
23rd	01:28 am	Capricorn
25th	02:48 am	Aquarius
27th	02:46 am	Pisces
29th	03:13 am	Aries
31st	05:46 am	Taurus

August 1926

2nd	11:24 am	Gemini
4th	08:08 pm	Cancer
7th	07:12 am	Leo
9th	07:39 pm	Virgo
12th	08:26 am	Libra
14th	08:17 pm	Scorpio
17th	05:39 am	Sagittarius
19th	11:23 am	Capricorn
21st	01:31 pm	Aquarius
23rd	01:14 pm	Pisces
25th	12:30 pm	Aries
27th	01:24 pm	Taurus
29th	05:39 pm	Gemini

September 1926

1st	01:48 am	Cancer
3rd	01:01 pm	Leo
6th	01:40 am	Virgo
8th	02:23 pm	Libra
11th	02:15 am	Scorpio
13th	12:21 pm	Sagittarius
15th	07:37 pm	Capricorn
17th	11:23 pm	Aquarius
20th	12:06 am	Pisces
21st	11:20 pm	Aries
23rd	11:12 pm	Taurus
26th	01:50 am	Gemini
28th	08:35 am	Cancer
30th	07:10 pm	Leo

October 1926

3rd	07:49 am	Virgo
5th	08:28 pm	Libra
8th	07:59 am	Scorpio
10th	05:54 pm	Sagittarius
13th	01:47 am	Capricorn
15th	07:02 am	Aquarius
17th	09:29 am	Pisces
19th	09:56 am	Aries
21st	10:01 am	Taurus
23rd	11:50 am	Gemini
25th	05:08 pm	Cancer
28th	02:30 am	Leo
30th	02:43 pm	Virgo

November 1926

2nd	03:22 am	Libra
4th	02:37 pm	Scorpio
6th	11:51 pm	Sagittarius
9th	07:11 am	Capricorn
11th	12:41 pm	Aquarius
13th	04:22 pm	Pisces
15th	06:28 pm	Aries
17th	07:54 pm	Taurus
19th	10:10 pm	Gemini
22nd	02:54 am	Cancer
24th	11:10 am	Leo
26th	10:36 pm	Virgo
29th	11:13 am	Libra

December 1926

1st	10:39 pm	Scorpio
4th	07:32 am	Sagittarius
6th	01:52 pm	Capricorn
8th	06:21 pm	Aquarius
10th	09:43 pm	Pisces
13th	12:33 am	Aries
15th	03:23 am	Taurus
17th	06:59 am	Gemini
19th	12:20 pm	Cancer
21st	08:16 pm	Leo
24th	07:02 am	Virgo
26th	07:31 pm	Libra
29th	07:28 am	Scorpio
31st	04:50 pm	Sagittarius

January 1927

2nd	10:51 pm	Capricorn
5th	02:10 am	Aquarius
7th	04:05 am	Pisces
9th	05:59 am	Aries
11th	08:56 am	Taurus
13th	01:30 pm	Gemini
15th	07:59 pm	Cancer
18th	04:31 am	Leo
20th	03:10 pm	Virgo
23rd	03:27 am	Libra
25th	03:54 pm	Scorpio
28th	02:21 am	Sagittarius
30th	09:12 am	Capricorn

February 1927

1st	12:22 pm	Aquarius
3rd	01:06 pm	Pisces
5th	01:19 pm	Aries
7th	02:50 pm	Taurus
9th	06:54 pm	Gemini
12th	01:51 am	Cancer
14th	11:11 am	Leo
16th	10:15 pm	Virgo
19th	10:31 am	Libra
21st	11:08 pm	Scorpio
24th	10:34 am	Sagittarius
26th	06:56 pm	Capricorn
28th	11:14 pm	Aquarius

March 1927

3rd	12:05 am	Pisces
4th	11:19 pm	Aries
6th	11:07 pm	Taurus
9th	01:29 am	Gemini
11th	07:29 am	Cancer
13th	04:51 pm	Leo
16th	04:22 am	Virgo
18th	04:48 pm	Libra
21st	05:21 am	Scorpio
23rd	05:06 pm	Sagittarius
26th	02:39 am	Capricorn
28th	08:39 am	Aquarius
30th	10:52 am	Pisces

April 1927

1st	10:30 am	Aries
3rd	09:36 am	Taurus
5th	10:25 am	Gemini
7th	02:42 pm	Cancer
9th	11:00 pm	Leo
12th	10:19 am	Virgo
14th	10:53 pm	Libra
17th	11:20 am	Scorpio
19th	10:49 pm	Sagittarius
22nd	08:35 am	Capricorn
24th	03:43 pm	Aquarius
26th	07:37 pm	Pisces
28th	08:43 pm	Aries
30th	08:28 pm	Taurus

May 1927

2nd	08:52 pm	Gemini
4th	11:51 pm	Cancer
7th	06:39 am	Leo
9th	05:03 pm	Virgo
12th	05:27 am	Libra
14th	05:52 pm	Scorpio
17th	04:57 am	Sagittarius
19th	02:11 pm	Capricorn
21st	09:16 pm	Aquarius
24th	02:01 am	Pisces
26th	04:37 am	Aries
28th	05:50 am	Taurus
30th	07:02 am	Gemini

June 1927

1st	09:50 am	Cancer
3rd	03:37 pm	Leo
6th	12:55 am	Virgo
8th	12:49 pm	Libra
11th	01:16 am	Scorpio
13th	12:16 pm	Sagittarius
15th	08:51 pm	Capricorn
18th	03:04 am	Aquarius
20th	07:25 am	Pisces
22nd	10:29 am	Aries
24th	12:54 pm	Taurus
26th	03:26 pm	Gemini
28th	07:03 pm	Cancer

July 1927

1st	12:48 am	Leo
3rd	09:27 am	Virgo
5th	08:47 pm	Libra
8th	09:17 am	Scorpio
10th	08:37 pm	Sagittarius
13th	05:06 am	Capricorn
15th	10:31 am	Aquarius
17th	01:43 pm	Pisces
19th	03:58 pm	Aries
21st	06:24 pm	Taurus
23rd	09:46 pm	Gemini
26th	02:31 am	Cancer
28th	09:00 am	Leo
30th	05:41 pm	Virgo

August 1927

2nd	04:44 am	Libra
4th	05:16 pm	Scorpio
7th	05:14 am	Sagittarius
9th	02:23 pm	Capricorn
11th	07:46 pm	Aquarius
13th	10:04 pm	Pisces
15th	10:57 pm	Aries
18th	12:12 am	Taurus
20th	03:08 am	Gemini
22nd	08:19 am	Cancer
24th	03:39 pm	Leo
27th	12:55 am	Virgo
29th	12:02 pm	Libra

September 1927

1st	12:36 am	Scorpio
3rd	01:10 pm	Sagittarius
5th	11:28 pm	Capricorn
8th	05:50 am	Aquarius
10th	08:16 am	Pisces
12th	08:18 am	Aries
14th	08:02 am	Taurus
16th	09:28 am	Gemini
18th	01:49 pm	Cancer
20th	09:13 pm	Leo
23rd	07:01 am	Virgo
25th	06:30 pm	Libra
28th	07:05 am	Scorpio
30th	07:54 pm	Sagittarius

October 1927

3rd	07:13 am	Capricorn
5th	03:07 pm	Aquarius
7th	06:50 pm	Pisces
9th	07:14 pm	Aries
11th	06:17 pm	Taurus
13th	06:12 pm	Gemini
15th	08:50 pm	Cancer
18th	03:07 am	Leo
20th	12:43 pm	Virgo
23rd	12:27 am	Libra
25th	01:08 pm	Scorpio
28th	01:48 am	Sagittarius
30th	01:22 pm	Capricorn

November 1927

1st	10:26 pm	Aquarius
4th	03:55 am	Pisces
6th	05:53 am	Aries
8th	05:37 am	Taurus
10th	05:03 am	Gemini
12th	06:15 am	Cancer
14th	10:48 am	Leo
16th	07:13 pm	Virgo
19th	06:41 am	Libra
21st	07:26 pm	Scorpio
24th	07:53 am	Sagittarius
26th	07:01 pm	Capricorn
29th	04:06 am	Aquarius

December 1927

1st	10:37 am	Pisces
3rd	02:20 pm	Aries
5th	03:47 pm	Taurus
7th	04:10 pm	Gemini
9th	05:11 pm	Cancer
11th	08:31 pm	Leo
14th	03:25 am	Virgo
16th	01:55 pm	Libra
19th	02:31 am	Scorpio
21st	02:59 pm	Sagittarius
24th	01:37 am	Capricorn
26th	09:54 am	Aquarius
28th	04:00 pm	Pisces
30th	08:19 pm	Aries

January 1928

1st	11:14 pm	Taurus
4th	01:20 am	Gemini
6th	03:28 am	Cancer
8th	06:52 am	Leo
10th	12:53 pm	Virgo
12th	10:18 pm	Libra
15th	10:26 am	Scorpio
17th	11:06 pm	Sagittarius
20th	09:49 am	Capricorn
22nd	05:27 pm	Aquarius
24th	10:24 pm	Pisces
27th	01:48 am	Aries
29th	04:42 am	Taurus
31st	07:47 am	Gemini

February 1928

2nd	11:21 am	Cancer
4th	03:53 pm	Leo
6th	10:09 pm	Virgo
9th	07:03 am	Libra
11th	06:41 pm	Scorpio
14th	07:32 am	Sagittarius
16th	06:54 pm	Capricorn
19th	02:47 am	Aquarius
21st	07:05 am	Pisces
23rd	09:09 am	Aries
25th	10:42 am	Taurus
27th	01:07 pm	Gemini
29th	05:04 pm	Cancer

March 1928

2nd	10:38 pm	Leo
5th	05:51 am	Virgo
7th	03:04 pm	Libra
10th	02:31 am	Scorpio
12th	03:24 pm	Sagittarius
15th	03:33 am	Capricorn
17th	12:31 pm	Aquarius
19th	05:20 pm	Pisces
21st	06:54 pm	Aries
23rd	07:06 pm	Taurus
25th	07:53 pm	Gemini
27th	10:41 pm	Cancer
30th	04:04 am	Leo

April 1928

1st	11:53 am	Virgo
3rd	09:47 pm	Libra
6th	09:27 am	Scorpio
8th	10:20 pm	Sagittarius
11th	10:56 am	Capricorn
13th	09:07 pm	Aquarius
16th	03:19 am	Pisces
18th	05:40 am	Aries
20th	05:36 am	Taurus
22nd	05:09 am	Gemini
24th	06:14 am	Cancer
26th	10:11 am	Leo
28th	05:28 pm	Virgo

May 1928

1st	03:36 am	Libra
3rd	03:38 pm	Scorpio
6th	04:32 am	Sagittarius
8th	05:09 pm	Capricorn
11th	03:57 am	Aquarius
13th	11:35 am	Pisces
15th	03:30 pm	Aries
17th	04:25 pm	Taurus
19th	03:56 pm	Gemini
21st	03:57 pm	Cancer
23rd	06:16 pm	Leo
26th	12:07 am	Virgo
28th	09:36 am	Libra
30th	09:40 pm	Scorpio

June 1928

2nd	10:38 am	Sagittarius
4th	11:00 pm	Capricorn
7th	09:41 am	Aquarius
9th	05:54 pm	Pisces
11th	11:13 pm	Aries
14th	01:46 am	Taurus
16th	02:24 am	Gemini
18th	02:34 am	Cancer
20th	04:02 am	Leo
22nd	08:27 am	Virgo
24th	04:42 pm	Libra
27th	04:17 am	Scorpio
29th	05:13 pm	Sagittarius

July 1928

2nd	05:23 am	Capricorn
4th	03:32 pm	Aquarius
6th	11:22 pm	Pisces
9th	05:04 am	Aries
11th	08:49 am	Taurus
13th	10:59 am	Gemini
15th	12:20 pm	Cancer
17th	02:06 pm	Leo
19th	05:52 pm	Virgo
22nd	01:02 am	Libra
24th	11:47 am	Scorpio
27th	12:34 am	Sagittarius
29th	12:47 pm	Capricorn
31st	10:33 pm	Aquarius

August 1928

3rd	05:34 am	Pisces
5th	10:33 am	Aries
7th	02:18 pm	Taurus
9th	05:22 pm	Gemini
11th	08:03 pm	Cancer
13th	10:57 pm	Leo
16th	03:07 am	Virgo
18th	09:53 am	Libra
20th	07:57 pm	Scorpio
23rd	08:29 am	Sagittarius
25th	08:59 pm	Capricorn
28th	06:57 am	Aquarius
30th	01:30 pm	Pisces

September 1928

1st	05:26 pm	Aries
3rd	08:07 pm	Taurus
5th	10:43 pm	Gemini
8th	01:51 am	Cancer
10th	05:49 am	Leo
12th	11:01 am	Virgo
14th	06:12 pm	Libra
17th	04:04 am	Scorpio
19th	04:23 pm	Sagittarius
22nd	05:16 am	Capricorn
24th	04:01 pm	Aquarius
26th	11:01 pm	Pisces
29th	02:31 am	Aries

October 1928

1st	03:59 am	Taurus
3rd	05:09 am	Gemini
5th	07:21 am	Cancer
7th	11:18 am	Leo
9th	05:13 pm	Virgo
12th	01:14 am	Libra
14th	11:28 am	Scorpio
16th	11:44 pm	Sagittarius
19th	12:50 pm	Capricorn
22nd	12:33 am	Aquarius
24th	08:50 am	Pisces
26th	01:04 pm	Aries
28th	02:16 pm	Taurus
30th	02:11 pm	Gemini

November 1928

1st	02:40 pm	Cancer
3rd	05:14 pm	Leo
5th	10:41 pm	Virgo
8th	07:05 am	Libra
10th	05:53 pm	Scorpio
13th	06:20 am	Sagittarius
15th	07:25 pm	Capricorn
18th	07:40 am	Aquarius
20th	05:19 pm	Pisces
22nd	11:14 pm	Aries
25th	01:30 am	Taurus
27th	01:23 am	Gemini
29th	12:43 am	Cancer

December 1928

1st	01:28 am	Leo
3rd	05:16 am	Virgo
5th	12:52 pm	Libra
7th	11:46 pm	Scorpio
10th	12:29 pm	Sagittarius
13th	01:29 am	Capricorn
15th	01:35 pm	Aquarius
17th	11:49 pm	Pisces
20th	07:15 am	Aries
22nd	11:25 am	Taurus
24th	12:40 pm	Gemini
26th	12:16 pm	Cancer
28th	12:06 pm	Leo
30th	02:12 pm	Virgo

January 1929

1st	08:08 pm	Libra
4th	06:10 am	Scorpio
6th	06:50 pm	Sagittarius
9th	07:50 am	Capricorn
11th	07:33 pm	Aquarius
14th	05:21 am	Pisces
16th	01:07 pm	Aries
18th	06:37 pm	Taurus
20th	09:43 pm	Gemini
22nd	10:52 pm	Cancer
24th	11:16 pm	Leo
27th	12:47 am	Virgo
29th	05:19 am	Libra
31st	01:57 pm	Scorpio

February 1929

3rd	01:59 am	Sagittarius
5th	03:00 pm	Capricorn
8th	02:34 am	Aquarius
10th	11:42 am	Pisces
12th	06:41 pm	Aries
15th	12:02 am	Taurus
17th	04:01 am	Gemini
19th	06:45 am	Cancer
21st	08:41 am	Leo
23rd	10:58 am	Virgo
25th	03:15 pm	Libra
27th	10:54 pm	Scorpio

March 1929

2nd	10:03 am	Sagittarius
4th	10:55 pm	Capricorn
7th	10:44 am	Aquarius
9th	07:44 pm	Pisces
12th	01:51 am	Aries
14th	06:04 am	Taurus
16th	09:23 am	Gemini
18th	12:23 pm	Cancer
20th	03:27 pm	Leo
22nd	07:05 pm	Virgo
25th	12:11 am	Libra
27th	07:49 am	Scorpio
29th	06:26 pm	Sagittarius

April 1929

1st	07:02 am	Capricorn
3rd	07:18 pm	Aquarius
6th	04:52 am	Pisces
8th	10:57 am	Aries
10th	02:17 pm	Taurus
12th	04:12 pm	Gemini
14th	06:04 pm	Cancer
16th	08:50 pm	Leo
19th	01:05 am	Virgo
21st	07:13 am	Libra
23rd	03:34 pm	Scorpio
26th	02:16 am	Sagittarius
28th	02:43 pm	Capricorn

May 1929

1st	03:19 am	Aquarius
3rd	01:51 pm	Pisces
5th	08:51 pm	Aries
8th	12:18 am	Taurus
10th	01:22 am	Gemini
12th	01:44 am	Cancer
14th	03:03 am	Leo
16th	06:33 am	Virgo
18th	12:52 pm	Libra
20th	09:53 pm	Scorpio
23rd	09:03 am	Sagittarius
25th	09:34 pm	Capricorn
28th	10:17 am	Aquarius
30th	09:37 pm	Pisces

June 1929

2nd	05:58 am	Aries
4th	10:34 am	Taurus
6th	11:57 am	Gemini
8th	11:35 am	Cancer
10th	11:25 am	Leo
12th	01:20 pm	Virgo
14th	06:38 pm	Libra
17th	03:32 am	Scorpio
19th	03:03 pm	Sagittarius
22nd	03:45 am	Capricorn
24th	04:24 pm	Aquarius
27th	03:59 am	Pisces
29th	01:21 pm	Aries

July 1929

1st	07:31 pm	Taurus
3rd	10:14 pm	Gemini
5th	10:20 pm	Cancer
7th	09:37 pm	Leo
9th	10:10 pm	Virgo
12th	01:54 am	Libra
14th	09:44 am	Scorpio
16th	09:00 pm	Sagittarius
19th	09:47 am	Capricorn
21st	10:20 pm	Aquarius
24th	09:39 am	Pisces
26th	07:13 pm	Aries
29th	02:25 am	Taurus
31st	06:43 am	Gemini

August 1929

2nd	08:15 am	Cancer
4th	08:11 am	Leo
6th	08:22 am	Virgo
8th	10:56 am	Libra
10th	05:22 pm	Scorpio
13th	03:44 am	Sagittarius
15th	04:20 pm	Capricorn
18th	04:50 am	Aquarius
20th	03:46 pm	Pisces
23rd	12:47 am	Aries
25th	07:55 am	Taurus
27th	01:03 pm	Gemini
29th	04:04 pm	Cancer
31st	05:26 pm	Leo

September 1929

2nd	06:26 pm	Virgo
4th	08:51 pm	Libra
7th	02:20 am	Scorpio
9th	11:38 am	Sagittarius
11th	11:45 pm	Capricorn
14th	12:17 pm	Aquarius
16th	11:07 pm	Pisces
19th	07:30 am	Aries
21st	01:45 pm	Taurus
23rd	06:25 pm	Gemini
25th	09:52 pm	Cancer
28th	12:28 am	Leo
30th	02:52 am	Virgo

October 1929

2nd	06:09 am	Libra
4th	11:40 am	Scorpio
6th	08:18 pm	Sagittarius
9th	07:49 am	Capricorn
11th	08:25 pm	Aquarius
14th	07:40 am	Pisces
16th	04:02 pm	Aries
18th	09:29 pm	Taurus
21st	12:54 am	Gemini
23rd	03:24 am	Cancer
25th	05:55 am	Leo
27th	09:08 am	Virgo
29th	01:39 pm	Libra
31st	08:01 pm	Scorpio

November 1929

3rd	04:47 am	Sagittarius
5th	03:57 pm	Capricorn
8th	04:33 am	Aquarius
10th	04:30 pm	Pisces
13th	01:43 am	Aries
15th	07:19 am	Taurus
17th	09:53 am	Gemini
19th	10:53 am	Cancer
21st	11:58 am	Leo
23rd	02:31 pm	Virgo
25th	07:23 pm	Libra
28th	02:40 am	Scorpio
30th	12:08 pm	Sagittarius

December 1929

2nd	11:25 pm	Capricorn
5th	11:57 am	Aquarius
8th	12:27 am	Pisces
10th	10:57 am	Aries
12th	05:49 pm	Taurus
14th	08:49 pm	Gemini
16th	09:05 pm	Cancer
18th	08:34 pm	Leo
20th	09:22 pm	Virgo
23rd	01:03 am	Libra
25th	08:11 am	Scorpio
27th	06:12 pm	Sagittarius
30th	05:56 am	Capricorn

January 1930

1st	06:29 pm	Aquarius
4th	07:04 am	Pisces
6th	06:27 pm	Aries
9th	02:59 am	Taurus
11th	07:35 am	Gemini
13th	08:35 am	Cancer
15th	07:37 am	Leo
17th	06:56 am	Virgo
19th	08:44 am	Libra
21st	02:25 pm	Scorpio
23rd	11:56 pm	Sagittarius
26th	11:53 am	Capricorn
29th	12:35 am	Aquarius
31st	12:59 pm	Pisces

February 1930

3rd	12:23 am	Aries
5th	09:48 am	Taurus
7th	04:08 pm	Gemini
9th	06:55 pm	Cancer
11th	07:00 pm	Leo
13th	06:14 pm	Virgo
15th	06:50 pm	Libra
17th	10:44 pm	Scorpio
20th	06:48 am	Sagittarius
22nd	06:13 pm	Capricorn
25th	06:57 am	Aquarius
27th	07:13 pm	Pisces

March 1930

2nd	06:08 am	Aries
4th	03:18 pm	Taurus
6th	10:16 pm	Gemini
9th	02:34 am	Cancer
11th	04:25 am	Leo
13th	04:54 am	Virgo
15th	05:43 am	Libra
17th	08:46 am	Scorpio
19th	03:23 pm	Sagittarius
22nd	01:40 am	Capricorn
24th	02:05 pm	Aquarius
27th	02:24 am	Pisces
29th	01:00 pm	Aries
31st	09:23 pm	Taurus

April 1930

3rd	03:42 am	Gemini
5th	08:11 am	Cancer
7th	11:09 am	Leo
9th	01:11 pm	Virgo
11th	03:17 pm	Libra
13th	06:45 pm	Scorpio
16th	12:49 am	Sagittarius
18th	10:07 am	Capricorn
20th	09:58 pm	Aquarius
23rd	10:23 am	Pisces
25th	09:10 pm	Aries
28th	05:08 am	Taurus
30th	10:26 am	Gemini

May 1930

2nd	01:54 pm	Cancer
4th	04:32 pm	Leo
6th	07:11 pm	Virgo
8th	10:30 pm	Libra
11th	03:06 am	Scorpio
13th	09:39 am	Sagittarius
15th	06:39 pm	Capricorn
18th	06:03 am	Aquarius
20th	06:34 pm	Pisces
23rd	05:55 am	Aries
25th	02:15 pm	Taurus
27th	07:07 pm	Gemini
29th	09:25 pm	Cancer
31st	10:45 pm	Leo

June 1930

3rd	12:37 am	Virgo
5th	04:04 am	Libra
7th	09:30 am	Scorpio
9th	04:56 pm	Sagittarius
12th	02:20 am	Capricorn
14th	01:39 pm	Aquarius
17th	02:12 am	Pisces
19th	02:15 pm	Aries
21st	11:35 pm	Taurus
24th	05:00 am	Gemini
26th	06:57 am	Cancer
28th	07:06 am	Leo
30th	07:28 am	Virgo

July 1930

2nd	09:47 am	Libra
4th	02:56 pm	Scorpio
6th	10:49 pm	Sagittarius
9th	08:49 am	Capricorn
11th	08:23 pm	Aquarius
14th	08:57 am	Pisces
16th	09:26 pm	Aries
19th	07:54 am	Taurus
21st	02:39 pm	Gemini
23rd	05:22 pm	Cancer
25th	05:19 pm	Leo
27th	04:34 pm	Virgo
29th	05:18 pm	Libra
31st	09:05 pm	Scorpio

August 1930

3rd	04:24 am	Sagittarius
5th	02:34 pm	Capricorn
8th	02:26 am	Aquarius
10th	03:03 pm	Pisces
13th	03:32 am	Aries
15th	02:38 pm	Taurus
17th	10:46 pm	Gemini
20th	03:02 am	Cancer
22nd	03:58 am	Leo
24th	03:13 am	Virgo
26th	02:58 am	Libra
28th	05:10 am	Scorpio
30th	11:04 am	Sagittarius

September 1930

1st	08:35 pm	Capricorn
4th	08:27 am	Aquarius
6th	09:06 pm	Pisces
9th	09:21 am	Aries
11th	08:18 pm	Taurus
14th	05:01 am	Gemini
16th	10:42 am	Cancer
18th	01:18 pm	Leo
20th	01:45 pm	Virgo
22nd	01:43 pm	Libra
24th	03:07 pm	Scorpio
26th	07:34 pm	Sagittarius
29th	03:48 am	Capricorn

October 1930

1st	03:09 pm	Aquarius
4th	03:48 am	Pisces
6th	03:52 pm	Aries
9th	02:14 am	Taurus
11th	10:29 am	Gemini
13th	04:29 pm	Cancer
15th	08:19 pm	Leo
17th	10:26 pm	Virgo
19th	11:43 pm	Libra
22nd	01:32 am	Scorpio
24th	05:23 am	Sagittarius
26th	12:27 pm	Capricorn
28th	10:54 pm	Aquarius
31st	11:23 am	Pisces

November 1930

2nd	11:34 pm	Aries
5th	09:37 am	Taurus
7th	04:58 pm	Gemini
9th	10:05 pm	Cancer
12th	01:45 am	Leo
14th	04:42 am	Virgo
16th	07:27 am	Libra
18th	10:36 am	Scorpio
20th	03:00 pm	Sagittarius
22nd	09:42 pm	Capricorn
25th	07:23 am	Aquarius
27th	07:32 pm	Pisces
30th	08:06 am	Aries

December 1930

2nd	06:32 pm	Taurus
5th	01:32 am	Gemini
7th	05:31 am	Cancer
9th	07:52 am	Leo
11th	10:04 am	Virgo
13th	01:05 pm	Libra
15th	05:19 pm	Scorpio
17th	10:54 pm	Sagittarius
20th	06:11 am	Capricorn
22nd	03:43 pm	Aquarius
25th	03:35 am	Pisces
27th	04:29 pm	Aries
30th	03:51 am	Taurus

January 1931

1st	11:34 am	Gemini
3rd	03:21 pm	Cancer
5th	04:32 pm	Leo
7th	05:06 pm	Virgo
9th	06:48 pm	Libra
11th	10:40 pm	Scorpio
14th	04:50 am	Sagittarius
16th	01:01 pm	Capricorn
18th	11:04 pm	Aquarius
21st	10:55 am	Pisces
23rd	11:55 pm	Aries
26th	12:10 pm	Taurus
28th	09:18 pm	Gemini
31st	02:09 am	Cancer

February 1931

2nd	03:24 am	Leo
4th	02:56 am	Virgo
6th	02:54 am	Libra
8th	05:04 am	Scorpio
10th	10:21 am	Sagittarius
12th	06:39 pm	Capricorn
15th	05:14 am	Aquarius
17th	05:23 pm	Pisces
20th	06:21 am	Aries
22nd	06:54 pm	Taurus
25th	05:13 am	Gemini
27th	11:47 am	Cancer

March 1931

1st	02:25 pm	Leo
3rd	02:21 pm	Virgo
5th	01:32 pm	Libra
7th	02:02 pm	Scorpio
9th	05:30 pm	Sagittarius
12th	12:39 am	Capricorn
14th	11:03 am	Aquarius
16th	11:26 pm	Pisces
19th	12:24 pm	Aries
22nd	12:44 am	Taurus
24th	11:19 am	Gemini
26th	07:04 pm	Cancer
28th	11:29 pm	Leo
31st	12:58 am	Virgo

April 1931

2nd	12:49 am	Libra
4th	12:50 am	Scorpio
6th	02:52 am	Sagittarius
8th	08:20 am	Capricorn
10th	05:40 pm	Aquarius
13th	05:49 am	Pisces
15th	06:48 pm	Aries
18th	06:50 am	Taurus
20th	04:56 pm	Gemini
23rd	12:42 am	Cancer
25th	06:04 am	Leo
27th	09:10 am	Virgo
29th	10:35 am	Libra

May 1931

1st	11:26 am	Scorpio
3rd	01:14 pm	Sagittarius
5th	05:35 pm	Capricorn
8th	01:36 am	Aquarius
10th	01:02 pm	Pisces
13th	01:57 am	Aries
15th	01:54 pm	Taurus
17th	11:26 pm	Gemini
20th	06:26 am	Cancer
22nd	11:27 am	Leo
24th	03:07 pm	Virgo
26th	05:51 pm	Libra
28th	08:07 pm	Scorpio
30th	10:48 pm	Sagittarius

June 1931

2nd	03:07 am	Capricorn
4th	10:23 am	Aquarius
6th	09:01 pm	Pisces
9th	09:44 am	Aries
11th	09:54 pm	Taurus
14th	07:22 am	Gemini
16th	01:38 pm	Cancer
18th	05:36 pm	Leo
20th	08:32 pm	Virgo
22nd	11:23 pm	Libra
25th	02:34 am	Scorpio
27th	06:26 am	Sagittarius
29th	11:35 am	Capricorn

July 1931

1st	06:56 pm	Aquarius
4th	05:09 am	Pisces
6th	05:40 pm	Aries
9th	06:14 am	Taurus
11th	04:14 pm	Gemini
13th	10:30 pm	Cancer
16th	01:41 am	Leo
18th	03:22 am	Virgo
20th	05:06 am	Libra
22nd	07:56 am	Scorpio
24th	12:18 pm	Sagittarius
26th	06:22 pm	Capricorn
29th	02:24 am	Aquarius
31st	12:45 pm	Pisces

August 1931

3rd	01:10 am	Aries
5th	02:05 pm	Taurus
8th	01:01 am	Gemini
10th	08:10 am	Cancer
12th	11:31 am	Leo
14th	12:25 pm	Virgo
16th	12:45 pm	Libra
18th	02:10 pm	Scorpio
20th	05:47 pm	Sagittarius
22nd	11:58 pm	Capricorn
25th	08:38 am	Aquarius
27th	07:27 pm	Pisces
30th	07:56 am	Aries

September 1931

1st	08:59 pm	Taurus
4th	08:43 am	Gemini
6th	05:15 pm	Cancer
8th	09:47 pm	Leo
10th	11:04 pm	Virgo
12th	10:43 pm	Libra
14th	10:40 pm	Scorpio
17th	12:39 am	Sagittarius
19th	05:47 am	Capricorn
21st	02:18 pm	Aquarius
24th	01:28 am	Pisces
26th	02:09 pm	Aries
29th	03:07 am	Taurus

October 1931

1st	03:03 pm	Gemini
4th	12:37 am	Cancer
6th	06:49 am	Leo
8th	09:34 am	Virgo
10th	09:50 am	Libra
12th	09:17 am	Scorpio
14th	09:51 am	Sagittarius
16th	01:18 pm	Capricorn
18th	08:39 pm	Aquarius
21st	07:32 am	Pisces
23rd	08:21 pm	Aries
26th	09:12 am	Taurus
28th	08:48 pm	Gemini
31st	06:26 am	Cancer

November 1931

2nd	01:39 pm	Leo
4th	06:08 pm	Virgo
6th	08:03 pm	Libra
8th	08:21 pm	Scorpio
10th	08:39 pm	Sagittarius
12th	10:52 pm	Capricorn
15th	04:40 am	Aquarius
17th	02:32 pm	Pisces
20th	03:08 am	Aries
22nd	04:00 pm	Taurus
25th	03:12 am	Gemini
27th	12:09 pm	Cancer
29th	07:06 pm	Leo

December 1931

2nd	12:16 am	Virgo
4th	03:44 am	Libra
6th	05:43 am	Scorpio
8th	07:04 am	Sagittarius
10th	09:17 am	Capricorn
12th	02:10 pm	Aquarius
14th	10:50 pm	Pisces
17th	10:49 am	Aries
19th	11:45 pm	Taurus
22nd	10:59 am	Gemini
24th	07:22 pm	Cancer
27th	01:16 am	Leo
29th	05:41 am	Virgo
31st	09:17 am	Libra

January 1932
2nd 12:24 pm Scorpio
4th 03:15 pm Sagittarius
6th 06:37 pm Capricorn
8th 11:43 pm Aquarius
11th 07:49 am Pisces
13th 07:07 pm Aries
16th 08:02 am Taurus
18th 07:47 pm Gemini
21st 04:22 am Cancer
23rd 09:39 am Leo
25th 12:46 pm Virgo
27th 03:07 pm Libra
29th 05:43 pm Scorpio
31st 09:07 pm Sagittarius

February 1932
3rd 01:39 am Capricorn
5th 07:48 am Aquarius
7th 04:15 pm Pisces
10th 03:17 am Aries
12th 04:05 pm Taurus
15th 04:27 am Gemini
17th 02:02 pm Cancer
19th 07:49 pm Leo
21st 10:25 pm Virgo
23rd 11:22 pm Libra
26th 12:20 am Scorpio
28th 02:38 am Sagittarius

March 1932
1st 07:06 am Capricorn
3rd 02:00 pm Aquarius
5th 11:15 pm Pisces
8th 10:35 am Aries
10th 11:19 pm Taurus
13th 12:03 pm Gemini
15th 10:46 pm Cancer
18th 05:56 am Leo
20th 09:18 am Virgo
22nd 09:56 am Libra
24th 09:35 am Scorpio
26th 10:06 am Sagittarius
28th 01:08 pm Capricorn
30th 07:30 pm Aquarius

April 1932
2nd 05:05 am Pisces
4th 04:53 pm Aries
7th 05:44 am Taurus
9th 06:27 pm Gemini
12th 05:47 am Cancer
14th 02:22 pm Leo
16th 07:21 pm Virgo
18th 09:00 pm Libra
20th 08:33 pm Scorpio
22nd 07:57 pm Sagittarius
24th 09:15 pm Capricorn
27th 02:04 am Aquarius
29th 10:55 am Pisces

May 1932
1st 10:46 pm Aries
4th 11:46 am Taurus
7th 12:20 am Gemini
9th 11:34 am Cancer
11th 08:46 pm Leo
14th 03:13 am Virgo
16th 06:32 am Libra
18th 07:15 am Scorpio
20th 06:47 am Sagittarius
22nd 07:12 am Capricorn
24th 10:30 am Aquarius
26th 05:57 pm Pisces
29th 05:09 am Aries
31st 06:04 pm Taurus

June 1932
3rd 06:32 am Gemini
5th 05:21 pm Cancer
8th 02:14 am Leo
10th 09:06 am Virgo
12th 01:41 pm Libra
14th 04:00 pm Scorpio
16th 04:45 pm Sagittarius
18th 05:31 pm Capricorn
20th 08:12 pm Aquarius
23rd 02:25 am Pisces
25th 12:34 pm Aries
28th 01:08 am Taurus
30th 01:35 pm Gemini

July 1932
3rd 12:06 am Cancer
5th 08:18 am Leo
7th 02:33 pm Virgo
9th 07:12 pm Libra
11th 10:27 pm Scorpio
14th 12:38 am Sagittarius
16th 02:35 am Capricorn
18th 05:44 am Aquarius
20th 11:34 am Pisces
22nd 08:52 pm Aries
25th 08:54 am Taurus
27th 09:26 pm Gemini
30th 08:07 am Cancer

August 1932
1st 03:57 pm Leo
3rd 09:15 pm Virgo
6th 12:56 am Libra
8th 03:49 am Scorpio
10th 06:32 am Sagittarius
12th 09:38 am Capricorn
14th 01:54 pm Aquarius
16th 08:13 pm Pisces
19th 05:18 am Aries
21st 04:56 pm Taurus
24th 05:33 am Gemini
26th 04:50 pm Cancer
29th 01:03 am Leo
31st 05:58 am Virgo

September 1932
2nd 08:32 am Libra
4th 10:06 am Scorpio
6th 11:59 am Sagittarius
8th 03:11 pm Capricorn
10th 08:16 pm Aquarius
13th 03:31 am Pisces
15th 01:01 pm Aries
18th 12:33 am Taurus
20th 01:13 pm Gemini
23rd 01:13 am Cancer
25th 10:32 am Leo
27th 04:07 pm Virgo
29th 06:22 pm Libra

October 1932
1st 06:44 pm Scorpio
3rd 07:02 pm Sagittarius
5th 09:00 pm Capricorn
8th 01:43 am Aquarius
10th 09:26 am Pisces
12th 07:35 pm Aries
15th 07:24 am Taurus
17th 08:03 pm Gemini
20th 08:26 am Cancer
22nd 06:57 pm Leo
25th 02:03 am Virgo
27th 05:15 am Libra
29th 05:30 am Scorpio
31st 04:40 am Sagittarius

November 1932
2nd 04:54 am Capricorn
4th 08:06 am Aquarius
6th 03:06 pm Pisces
9th 01:24 am Aries
11th 01:33 pm Taurus
14th 02:13 am Gemini
16th 02:32 pm Cancer
19th 01:35 am Leo
21st 10:08 am Virgo
23rd 03:08 pm Libra
25th 04:38 pm Scorpio
27th 03:58 pm Sagittarius
29th 03:16 pm Capricorn

December 1932
1st 04:46 pm Aquarius
3rd 10:08 pm Pisces
6th 07:35 am Aries
8th 07:41 pm Taurus
11th 08:26 am Gemini
13th 08:28 pm Cancer
16th 07:12 am Leo
18th 04:09 pm Virgo
20th 10:32 pm Libra
23rd 01:53 am Scorpio
25th 02:42 am Sagittarius
27th 02:31 am Capricorn
29th 03:23 am Aquarius
31st 07:16 am Pisces

January 1933

2nd	03:13 pm	Aries
5th	02:36 am	Taurus
7th	03:19 pm	Gemini
10th	03:16 am	Cancer
12th	01:26 pm	Leo
14th	09:42 pm	Virgo
17th	04:03 am	Libra
19th	08:24 am	Scorpio
21st	10:54 am	Sagittarius
23rd	12:17 pm	Capricorn
25th	01:56 pm	Aquarius
27th	05:31 pm	Pisces
30th	12:21 am	Aries

February 1933

1st	10:40 am	Taurus
3rd	11:05 pm	Gemini
6th	11:13 am	Cancer
8th	09:16 pm	Leo
11th	04:43 am	Virgo
13th	09:59 am	Libra
15th	01:46 pm	Scorpio
17th	04:42 pm	Sagittarius
19th	07:22 pm	Capricorn
21st	10:29 pm	Aquarius
24th	02:56 am	Pisces
26th	09:42 am	Aries
28th	07:20 pm	Taurus

March 1933

3rd	07:17 am	Gemini
5th	07:43 pm	Cancer
8th	06:18 am	Leo
10th	01:42 pm	Virgo
12th	06:03 pm	Libra
14th	08:27 pm	Scorpio
16th	10:18 pm	Sagittarius
19th	12:47 am	Capricorn
21st	04:39 am	Aquarius
23rd	10:15 am	Pisces
25th	05:49 pm	Aries
28th	03:31 am	Taurus
30th	03:13 pm	Gemini

April 1933

2nd	03:50 am	Cancer
4th	03:16 pm	Leo
6th	11:33 pm	Virgo
9th	04:00 am	Libra
11th	05:32 am	Scorpio
13th	05:52 am	Sagittarius
15th	06:53 am	Capricorn
17th	10:02 am	Aquarius
19th	03:54 pm	Pisces
22nd	12:14 am	Aries
24th	10:31 am	Taurus
26th	10:18 pm	Gemini
29th	10:58 am	Cancer

May 1933

1st	11:06 pm	Leo
4th	08:41 am	Virgo
6th	02:17 pm	Libra
8th	04:07 pm	Scorpio
10th	03:43 pm	Sagittarius
12th	03:15 pm	Capricorn
14th	04:45 pm	Aquarius
16th	09:33 pm	Pisces
19th	05:45 am	Aries
21st	04:26 pm	Taurus
24th	04:31 am	Gemini
26th	05:12 pm	Cancer
29th	05:33 am	Leo
31st	04:06 pm	Virgo

June 1933

2nd	11:15 pm	Libra
5th	02:25 am	Scorpio
7th	02:32 am	Sagittarius
9th	01:33 am	Capricorn
11th	01:41 am	Aquarius
13th	04:49 am	Pisces
15th	11:50 am	Aries
17th	10:12 pm	Taurus
20th	10:25 am	Gemini
22nd	11:06 pm	Cancer
25th	11:17 am	Leo
27th	10:01 pm	Virgo
30th	06:11 am	Libra

July 1933

2nd	10:57 am	Scorpio
4th	12:32 pm	Sagittarius
6th	12:15 pm	Capricorn
8th	12:05 pm	Aquarius
10th	02:01 pm	Pisces
12th	07:31 pm	Aries
15th	04:49 am	Taurus
17th	04:44 pm	Gemini
20th	05:25 am	Cancer
22nd	05:19 pm	Leo
25th	03:35 am	Virgo
27th	11:44 am	Libra
29th	05:21 pm	Scorpio
31st	08:27 pm	Sagittarius

August 1933

2nd	09:40 pm	Capricorn
4th	10:22 pm	Aquarius
7th	12:10 am	Pisces
9th	04:40 am	Aries
11th	12:44 pm	Taurus
13th	11:57 pm	Gemini
16th	12:32 pm	Cancer
19th	12:22 am	Leo
21st	10:07 am	Virgo
23rd	05:29 pm	Libra
25th	10:44 pm	Scorpio
28th	02:21 am	Sagittarius
30th	04:52 am	Capricorn

September 1933

1st	06:59 am	Aquarius
3rd	09:44 am	Pisces
5th	02:15 pm	Aries
7th	09:35 pm	Taurus
10th	08:01 am	Gemini
12th	08:25 pm	Cancer
15th	08:30 am	Leo
17th	06:13 pm	Virgo
20th	12:51 am	Libra
22nd	05:00 am	Scorpio
24th	07:49 am	Sagittarius
26th	10:23 am	Capricorn
28th	01:26 pm	Aquarius
30th	05:27 pm	Pisces

October 1933

2nd	10:51 pm	Aries
5th	06:18 am	Taurus
7th	04:18 pm	Gemini
10th	04:29 am	Cancer
12th	05:02 pm	Leo
15th	03:24 am	Virgo
17th	10:07 am	Libra
19th	01:27 pm	Scorpio
21st	02:54 pm	Sagittarius
23rd	04:13 pm	Capricorn
25th	06:48 pm	Aquarius
27th	11:17 pm	Pisces
30th	05:40 am	Aries

November 1933

1st	01:53 pm	Taurus
4th	12:02 am	Gemini
6th	12:05 pm	Cancer
9th	12:58 am	Leo
11th	12:24 pm	Virgo
13th	08:12 pm	Libra
15th	11:52 pm	Scorpio
18th	12:34 am	Sagittarius
20th	12:23 am	Capricorn
22nd	01:21 am	Aquarius
24th	04:50 am	Pisces
26th	11:12 am	Aries
28th	08:03 pm	Taurus

December 1933

1st	06:44 am	Gemini
3rd	06:53 pm	Cancer
6th	07:49 am	Leo
8th	08:00 pm	Virgo
11th	05:19 am	Libra
13th	10:27 am	Scorpio
15th	11:49 am	Sagittarius
17th	11:08 am	Capricorn
19th	10:37 am	Aquarius
21st	12:15 pm	Pisces
23rd	05:15 pm	Aries
26th	01:42 am	Taurus
28th	12:43 pm	Gemini
31st	01:06 am	Cancer

January 1934

2nd	01:56 pm	Leo
5th	02:09 am	Virgo
7th	12:20 pm	Libra
9th	07:11 pm	Scorpio
11th	10:18 pm	Sagittarius
13th	10:37 pm	Capricorn
15th	09:56 pm	Aquarius
17th	10:17 pm	Pisces
20th	01:28 am	Aries
22nd	08:26 am	Taurus
24th	06:54 pm	Gemini
27th	07:24 am	Cancer
29th	08:12 pm	Leo

February 1934

1st	08:00 am	Virgo
3rd	05:59 pm	Libra
6th	01:31 am	Scorpio
8th	06:14 am	Sagittarius
10th	08:23 am	Capricorn
12th	08:57 am	Aquarius
14th	09:27 am	Pisces
16th	11:39 am	Aries
18th	05:03 pm	Taurus
21st	02:16 am	Gemini
23rd	02:22 pm	Cancer
26th	03:13 am	Leo
28th	02:46 pm	Virgo

March 1934

3rd	12:02 am	Libra
5th	06:59 am	Scorpio
7th	11:58 am	Sagittarius
9th	03:22 pm	Capricorn
11th	05:36 pm	Aquarius
13th	07:25 pm	Pisces
15th	10:00 pm	Aries
18th	02:46 am	Taurus
20th	10:51 am	Gemini
22nd	10:13 pm	Cancer
25th	11:03 am	Leo
27th	10:44 pm	Virgo
30th	07:37 am	Libra

April 1934

1st	01:35 pm	Scorpio
3rd	05:37 pm	Sagittarius
5th	08:45 pm	Capricorn
7th	11:43 pm	Aquarius
10th	02:52 am	Pisces
12th	06:40 am	Aries
14th	11:55 am	Taurus
16th	07:41 pm	Gemini
19th	06:26 am	Cancer
21st	07:10 pm	Leo
24th	07:20 am	Virgo
26th	04:32 pm	Libra
28th	10:07 pm	Scorpio

May 1934

1st	01:02 am	Sagittarius
3rd	02:53 am	Capricorn
5th	05:06 am	Aquarius
7th	08:26 am	Pisces
9th	01:08 pm	Aries
11th	07:23 pm	Taurus
14th	03:38 am	Gemini
16th	02:17 pm	Cancer
19th	02:55 am	Leo
21st	03:35 pm	Virgo
24th	01:43 am	Libra
26th	07:52 am	Scorpio
28th	10:28 am	Sagittarius
30th	11:12 am	Capricorn

June 1934

1st	11:55 am	Aquarius
3rd	02:06 pm	Pisces
5th	06:31 pm	Aries
8th	01:17 am	Taurus
10th	10:13 am	Gemini
12th	09:14 pm	Cancer
15th	09:53 am	Leo
17th	10:51 pm	Virgo
20th	09:59 am	Libra
22nd	05:25 pm	Scorpio
24th	08:49 pm	Sagittarius
26th	09:24 pm	Capricorn
28th	09:02 pm	Aquarius
30th	09:38 pm	Pisces

July 1934

3rd	12:39 am	Aries
5th	06:47 am	Taurus
7th	03:55 pm	Gemini
10th	03:20 am	Cancer
12th	04:07 pm	Leo
15th	05:07 am	Virgo
17th	04:47 pm	Libra
20th	01:31 am	Scorpio
22nd	06:28 am	Sagittarius
24th	08:03 am	Capricorn
26th	07:43 am	Aquarius
28th	07:20 am	Pisces
30th	08:45 am	Aries

August 1934

1st	01:25 pm	Taurus
3rd	09:48 pm	Gemini
6th	09:13 am	Cancer
8th	10:08 pm	Leo
11th	10:59 am	Virgo
13th	10:33 pm	Libra
16th	07:51 am	Scorpio
18th	02:12 pm	Sagittarius
20th	05:27 pm	Capricorn
22nd	06:18 pm	Aquarius
24th	06:08 pm	Pisces
26th	06:44 pm	Aries
28th	09:54 pm	Taurus
31st	04:55 am	Gemini

September 1934

2nd	03:40 pm	Cancer
5th	04:32 am	Leo
7th	05:16 pm	Virgo
10th	04:23 am	Libra
12th	01:19 pm	Scorpio
14th	08:03 pm	Sagittarius
17th	12:36 am	Capricorn
19th	03:06 am	Aquarius
21st	04:14 am	Pisces
23rd	05:13 am	Aries
25th	07:47 am	Taurus
27th	01:33 pm	Gemini
29th	11:14 pm	Cancer

October 1934

2nd	11:44 am	Leo
5th	12:31 am	Virgo
7th	11:20 am	Libra
9th	07:31 pm	Scorpio
12th	01:32 am	Sagittarius
14th	06:04 am	Capricorn
16th	09:32 am	Aquarius
18th	12:09 pm	Pisces
20th	02:28 pm	Aries
22nd	05:34 pm	Taurus
24th	10:58 pm	Gemini
27th	07:46 am	Cancer
29th	07:42 pm	Leo

November 1934

1st	08:36 am	Virgo
3rd	07:41 pm	Libra
6th	03:32 am	Scorpio
8th	08:33 am	Sagittarius
10th	11:56 am	Capricorn
12th	02:52 pm	Aquarius
14th	05:56 pm	Pisces
16th	09:26 pm	Aries
19th	01:46 am	Taurus
21st	07:47 am	Gemini
23rd	04:25 pm	Cancer
26th	03:54 am	Leo
28th	04:52 pm	Virgo

December 1934

1st	04:39 am	Libra
3rd	01:06 pm	Scorpio
5th	05:52 pm	Sagittarius
7th	08:09 pm	Capricorn
9th	09:34 pm	Aquarius
11th	11:31 pm	Pisces
14th	02:51 am	Aries
16th	07:56 am	Taurus
18th	02:58 pm	Gemini
21st	12:11 am	Cancer
23rd	11:37 am	Leo
26th	12:32 am	Virgo
28th	12:59 pm	Libra
30th	10:41 pm	Scorpio

January 1935

2nd	04:27 am	Sagittarius
4th	06:44 am	Capricorn
6th	07:04 am	Aquarius
8th	07:17 am	Pisces
10th	09:03 am	Aries
12th	01:24 pm	Taurus
14th	08:43 pm	Gemini
17th	06:37 am	Cancer
19th	06:27 pm	Leo
22nd	07:19 am	Virgo
24th	07:59 pm	Libra
27th	06:46 am	Scorpio
29th	02:11 pm	Sagittarius
31st	05:47 pm	Capricorn

February 1935

2nd	06:26 pm	Aquarius
4th	05:47 pm	Pisces
6th	05:49 pm	Aries
8th	08:22 pm	Taurus
11th	02:35 am	Gemini
13th	12:24 pm	Cancer
16th	12:35 am	Leo
18th	01:33 pm	Virgo
21st	02:02 am	Libra
23rd	01:04 pm	Scorpio
25th	09:40 pm	Sagittarius
28th	03:04 am	Capricorn

March 1935

2nd	05:16 am	Aquarius
4th	05:13 am	Pisces
6th	04:40 am	Aries
8th	05:43 am	Taurus
10th	10:11 am	Gemini
12th	06:51 pm	Cancer
15th	06:48 am	Leo
17th	07:51 pm	Virgo
20th	08:08 am	Libra
22nd	06:44 pm	Scorpio
25th	03:24 am	Sagittarius
27th	09:48 am	Capricorn
29th	01:41 pm	Aquarius
31st	03:14 pm	Pisces

April 1935

2nd	03:31 pm	Aries
4th	04:18 pm	Taurus
6th	07:35 pm	Gemini
9th	02:49 am	Cancer
11th	01:52 pm	Leo
14th	02:47 am	Virgo
16th	03:01 pm	Libra
19th	01:09 am	Scorpio
21st	09:06 am	Sagittarius
23rd	03:13 pm	Capricorn
25th	07:43 pm	Aquarius
27th	10:39 pm	Pisces
30th	12:26 am	Aries

May 1935

2nd	02:09 am	Taurus
4th	05:26 am	Gemini
6th	11:50 am	Cancer
8th	09:55 pm	Leo
11th	10:26 am	Virgo
13th	10:48 pm	Libra
16th	08:54 am	Scorpio
18th	04:13 pm	Sagittarius
20th	09:20 pm	Capricorn
23rd	01:08 am	Aquarius
25th	04:13 am	Pisces
27th	06:59 am	Aries
29th	09:59 am	Taurus
31st	02:11 pm	Gemini

June 1935

2nd	08:43 pm	Cancer
5th	06:19 am	Leo
7th	06:25 pm	Virgo
10th	06:59 am	Libra
12th	05:35 pm	Scorpio
15th	12:57 am	Sagittarius
17th	05:21 am	Capricorn
19th	07:56 am	Aquarius
21st	09:55 am	Pisces
23rd	12:21 pm	Aries
25th	03:54 pm	Taurus
27th	09:06 pm	Gemini
30th	04:26 am	Cancer

July 1935

2nd	02:13 pm	Leo
5th	02:08 am	Virgo
7th	02:52 pm	Libra
10th	02:15 am	Scorpio
12th	10:27 am	Sagittarius
14th	03:03 pm	Capricorn
16th	04:53 pm	Aquarius
18th	05:30 pm	Pisces
20th	06:32 pm	Aries
22nd	09:21 pm	Taurus
25th	02:42 am	Gemini
27th	10:43 am	Cancer
29th	09:04 pm	Leo

August 1935

1st	09:06 am	Virgo
3rd	09:55 pm	Libra
6th	09:57 am	Scorpio
8th	07:25 pm	Sagittarius
11th	01:10 am	Capricorn
13th	03:21 am	Aquarius
15th	03:19 am	Pisces
17th	02:55 am	Aries
19th	04:07 am	Taurus
21st	08:25 am	Gemini
23rd	04:17 pm	Cancer
26th	03:00 am	Leo
28th	03:20 pm	Virgo
31st	04:08 am	Libra

September 1935

2nd	04:22 pm	Scorpio
5th	02:48 am	Sagittarius
7th	10:08 am	Capricorn
9th	01:44 pm	Aquarius
11th	02:15 pm	Pisces
13th	01:20 pm	Aries
15th	01:10 pm	Taurus
17th	03:48 pm	Gemini
19th	10:27 pm	Cancer
22nd	08:50 am	Leo
24th	09:18 pm	Virgo
27th	10:05 am	Libra
29th	10:06 pm	Scorpio

October 1935

2nd	08:41 am	Sagittarius
4th	05:02 pm	Capricorn
6th	10:20 pm	Aquarius
9th	12:27 am	Pisces
11th	12:20 am	Aries
12th	11:53 pm	Taurus
15th	01:17 am	Gemini
17th	06:21 am	Cancer
19th	03:35 pm	Leo
22nd	03:44 am	Virgo
24th	04:31 pm	Libra
27th	04:14 am	Scorpio
29th	02:17 pm	Sagittarius
31st	10:31 pm	Capricorn

November 1935

3rd	04:38 am	Aquarius
5th	08:20 am	Pisces
7th	09:54 am	Aries
9th	10:29 am	Taurus
11th	11:52 am	Gemini
13th	03:56 pm	Cancer
15th	11:51 pm	Leo
18th	11:10 am	Virgo
20th	11:52 pm	Libra
23rd	11:36 am	Scorpio
25th	09:08 pm	Sagittarius
28th	04:28 am	Capricorn
30th	10:00 am	Aquarius

December 1935

2nd	02:03 pm	Pisces
4th	04:53 pm	Aries
6th	07:03 pm	Taurus
8th	09:36 pm	Gemini
11th	01:54 am	Cancer
13th	09:06 am	Leo
15th	07:32 pm	Virgo
18th	07:58 am	Libra
20th	08:02 pm	Scorpio
23rd	05:44 am	Sagittarius
25th	12:27 pm	Capricorn
27th	04:46 pm	Aquarius
29th	07:42 pm	Pisces
31st	10:15 pm	Aries

January 1936

3rd	01:11 am	Taurus
5th	05:04 am	Gemini
7th	10:29 am	Cancer
9th	06:02 pm	Leo
12th	04:05 am	Virgo
14th	04:10 pm	Libra
17th	04:38 am	Scorpio
19th	03:11 pm	Sagittarius
21st	10:18 pm	Capricorn
24th	02:02 am	Aquarius
26th	03:35 am	Pisces
28th	04:36 am	Aries
30th	06:37 am	Taurus

February 1936

1st	10:38 am	Gemini
3rd	04:58 pm	Cancer
6th	01:26 am	Leo
8th	11:48 am	Virgo
10th	11:45 pm	Libra
13th	12:24 pm	Scorpio
15th	11:56 pm	Sagittarius
18th	08:21 am	Capricorn
20th	12:46 pm	Aquarius
22nd	01:55 pm	Pisces
24th	01:35 pm	Aries
26th	01:51 pm	Taurus
28th	04:30 pm	Gemini

March 1936

1st	10:25 pm	Cancer
4th	07:20 am	Leo
6th	06:18 pm	Virgo
9th	06:26 am	Libra
11th	07:03 pm	Scorpio
14th	07:06 am	Sagittarius
16th	04:51 pm	Capricorn
18th	10:52 pm	Aquarius
21st	12:59 am	Pisces
23rd	12:31 am	Aries
24th	11:37 pm	Taurus
27th	12:31 am	Gemini
29th	04:52 am	Cancer
31st	01:03 pm	Leo

April 1936

3rd	12:07 am	Virgo
5th	12:31 pm	Libra
8th	01:05 am	Scorpio
10th	01:03 pm	Sagittarius
12th	11:23 pm	Capricorn
15th	06:49 am	Aquarius
17th	10:37 am	Pisces
19th	11:20 am	Aries
21st	10:37 am	Taurus
23rd	10:37 am	Gemini
25th	01:22 pm	Cancer
27th	08:03 pm	Leo
30th	06:22 am	Virgo

May 1936

2nd	06:43 pm	Libra
5th	07:16 am	Scorpio
7th	06:54 pm	Sagittarius
10th	04:57 am	Capricorn
12th	12:47 pm	Aquarius
14th	05:52 pm	Pisces
16th	08:14 pm	Aries
18th	08:47 pm	Taurus
20th	09:12 pm	Gemini
22nd	11:19 pm	Cancer
25th	04:41 am	Leo
27th	01:47 pm	Virgo
30th	01:38 am	Libra

June 1936

1st	02:11 pm	Scorpio
4th	01:37 am	Sagittarius
6th	11:02 am	Capricorn
8th	06:17 pm	Aquarius
10th	11:27 pm	Pisces
13th	02:46 am	Aries
15th	04:48 am	Taurus
17th	06:29 am	Gemini
19th	09:08 am	Cancer
21st	02:06 pm	Leo
23rd	10:15 pm	Virgo
26th	09:23 am	Libra
28th	09:52 pm	Scorpio

July 1936

1st	09:27 am	Sagittarius
3rd	06:34 pm	Capricorn
6th	12:56 am	Aquarius
8th	05:10 am	Pisces
10th	08:10 am	Aries
12th	10:46 am	Taurus
14th	01:38 pm	Gemini
16th	05:27 pm	Cancer
18th	10:58 pm	Leo
21st	06:53 am	Virgo
23rd	05:30 pm	Libra
26th	05:54 am	Scorpio
28th	05:55 pm	Sagittarius
31st	03:24 am	Capricorn

August 1936

2nd	09:25 am	Aquarius
4th	12:36 pm	Pisces
6th	02:21 pm	Aries
8th	04:11 pm	Taurus
10th	07:12 pm	Gemini
12th	11:52 pm	Cancer
15th	06:20 am	Leo
17th	02:44 pm	Virgo
20th	01:17 am	Libra
22nd	01:36 pm	Scorpio
25th	02:09 am	Sagittarius
27th	12:35 pm	Capricorn
29th	07:12 pm	Aquarius
31st	10:05 pm	Pisces

September 1936

2nd	10:43 pm	Aries
4th	11:04 pm	Taurus
7th	12:54 am	Gemini
9th	05:16 am	Cancer
11th	12:13 pm	Leo
13th	09:19 pm	Virgo
16th	08:12 am	Libra
18th	08:32 pm	Scorpio
21st	09:24 am	Sagittarius
23rd	08:53 pm	Capricorn
26th	04:53 am	Aquarius
28th	08:39 am	Pisces
30th	09:10 am	Aries

October 1936

2nd	08:25 am	Taurus
4th	08:37 am	Gemini
6th	11:29 am	Cancer
8th	05:45 pm	Leo
11th	03:01 am	Virgo
13th	02:19 pm	Libra
16th	02:46 am	Scorpio
18th	03:37 pm	Sagittarius
21st	03:37 am	Capricorn
23rd	01:00 pm	Aquarius
25th	06:28 pm	Pisces
27th	08:09 pm	Aries
29th	07:34 pm	Taurus
31st	06:49 pm	Gemini

November 1936

2nd	08:00 pm	Cancer
5th	12:37 am	Leo
7th	09:00 am	Virgo
9th	08:15 pm	Libra
12th	08:52 am	Scorpio
14th	09:33 pm	Sagittarius
17th	09:20 am	Capricorn
19th	07:11 pm	Aquarius
22nd	02:04 am	Pisces
24th	05:37 am	Aries
26th	06:29 am	Taurus
28th	06:11 am	Gemini
30th	06:40 am	Cancer

December 1936

2nd	09:43 am	Leo
4th	04:30 pm	Virgo
7th	02:55 am	Libra
9th	03:28 pm	Scorpio
12th	04:07 am	Sagittarius
14th	03:25 pm	Capricorn
17th	12:42 am	Aquarius
19th	07:43 am	Pisces
21st	12:26 pm	Aries
23rd	03:05 pm	Taurus
25th	04:24 pm	Gemini
27th	05:36 pm	Cancer
29th	08:14 pm	Leo

January 1937

1st	01:45 am	Virgo
3rd	10:55 am	Libra
5th	10:58 pm	Scorpio
8th	11:43 am	Sagittarius
10th	10:53 pm	Capricorn
13th	07:25 am	Aquarius
15th	01:28 pm	Pisces
17th	05:48 pm	Aries
19th	09:07 pm	Taurus
21st	11:53 pm	Gemini
24th	02:38 am	Cancer
26th	06:08 am	Leo
28th	11:30 am	Virgo
30th	07:49 pm	Libra

February 1937

2nd	07:10 am	Scorpio
4th	07:59 pm	Sagittarius
7th	07:34 am	Capricorn
9th	04:00 pm	Aquarius
11th	09:10 pm	Pisces
14th	12:12 am	Aries
16th	02:34 am	Taurus
18th	05:22 am	Gemini
20th	09:04 am	Cancer
22nd	01:51 pm	Leo
24th	08:04 pm	Virgo
27th	04:26 am	Libra

March 1937

1st	03:23 pm	Scorpio
4th	04:08 am	Sagittarius
6th	04:23 pm	Capricorn
9th	01:35 am	Aquarius
11th	06:50 am	Pisces
13th	09:00 am	Aries
15th	09:54 am	Taurus
17th	11:19 am	Gemini
19th	02:25 pm	Cancer
21st	07:35 pm	Leo
24th	02:44 am	Virgo
26th	11:47 am	Libra
28th	10:51 pm	Scorpio
31st	11:32 am	Sagittarius

April 1937

3rd	12:16 am	Capricorn
5th	10:38 am	Aquarius
7th	04:59 pm	Pisces
9th	07:28 pm	Aries
11th	07:39 pm	Taurus
13th	07:34 pm	Gemini
15th	09:02 pm	Cancer
18th	01:11 am	Leo
20th	08:16 am	Virgo
22nd	05:51 pm	Libra
25th	05:20 am	Scorpio
27th	06:05 pm	Sagittarius
30th	06:56 am	Capricorn

May 1937

2nd	06:08 pm	Aquarius
5th	01:57 am	Pisces
7th	05:47 am	Aries
9th	06:32 am	Taurus
11th	05:56 am	Gemini
13th	06:00 am	Cancer
15th	08:27 am	Leo
17th	02:19 pm	Virgo
19th	11:34 pm	Libra
22nd	11:18 am	Scorpio
25th	12:10 am	Sagittarius
27th	12:53 pm	Capricorn
30th	12:13 am	Aquarius

June 1937

1st	08:57 am	Pisces
3rd	02:22 pm	Aries
5th	04:36 pm	Taurus
7th	04:45 pm	Gemini
9th	04:31 pm	Cancer
11th	05:44 pm	Leo
13th	10:01 pm	Virgo
16th	06:08 am	Libra
18th	05:31 pm	Scorpio
21st	06:25 am	Sagittarius
23rd	06:58 pm	Capricorn
26th	05:54 am	Aquarius
28th	02:37 pm	Pisces
30th	08:50 pm	Aries

July 1937

3rd	12:34 am	Taurus
5th	02:15 am	Gemini
7th	02:53 am	Cancer
9th	03:59 am	Leo
11th	07:15 am	Virgo
13th	02:04 pm	Libra
16th	12:36 am	Scorpio
18th	01:20 pm	Sagittarius
21st	01:50 am	Capricorn
23rd	12:20 pm	Aquarius
25th	08:21 pm	Pisces
28th	02:15 am	Aries
30th	06:31 am	Taurus

August 1937

1st	09:29 am	Gemini
3rd	11:34 am	Cancer
5th	01:35 pm	Leo
7th	04:54 pm	Virgo
9th	10:58 pm	Libra
12th	08:36 am	Scorpio
14th	08:59 pm	Sagittarius
17th	09:37 am	Capricorn
19th	08:05 pm	Aquarius
22nd	03:28 am	Pisces
24th	08:23 am	Aries
26th	11:57 am	Taurus
28th	03:01 pm	Gemini
30th	06:03 pm	Cancer

September 1937

1st	09:21 pm	Leo
4th	01:34 am	Virgo
6th	07:48 am	Libra
8th	04:59 pm	Scorpio
11th	04:59 am	Sagittarius
13th	05:51 pm	Capricorn
16th	04:51 am	Aquarius
18th	12:19 pm	Pisces
20th	04:31 pm	Aries
22nd	06:49 pm	Taurus
24th	08:46 pm	Gemini
26th	11:24 pm	Cancer
29th	03:14 am	Leo

October 1937

1st	08:28 am	Virgo
3rd	03:31 pm	Libra
6th	12:55 am	Scorpio
8th	12:44 pm	Sagittarius
11th	01:46 am	Capricorn
13th	01:37 pm	Aquarius
15th	10:03 pm	Pisces
18th	02:32 am	Aries
20th	04:09 am	Taurus
22nd	04:40 am	Gemini
24th	05:46 am	Cancer
26th	08:42 am	Leo
28th	02:01 pm	Virgo
30th	09:47 pm	Libra

November 1937

2nd	07:48 am	Scorpio
4th	07:46 pm	Sagittarius
7th	08:50 am	Capricorn
9th	09:19 pm	Aquarius
12th	07:07 am	Pisces
14th	12:59 pm	Aries
16th	03:12 pm	Taurus
18th	03:10 pm	Gemini
20th	02:47 pm	Cancer
22nd	03:55 pm	Leo
24th	07:55 pm	Virgo
27th	03:21 am	Libra
29th	01:46 pm	Scorpio

December 1937

2nd	02:05 am	Sagittarius
4th	03:07 pm	Capricorn
7th	03:40 am	Aquarius
9th	02:21 pm	Pisces
11th	09:55 pm	Aries
14th	01:50 am	Taurus
16th	02:42 am	Gemini
18th	02:03 am	Cancer
20th	01:48 am	Leo
22nd	03:57 am	Virgo
24th	09:53 am	Libra
26th	07:44 pm	Scorpio
29th	08:11 am	Sagittarius
31st	09:17 pm	Capricorn

January 1938

3rd	09:31 am	Aquarius
5th	08:06 pm	Pisces
8th	04:29 am	Aries
10th	10:06 am	Taurus
12th	12:50 pm	Gemini
14th	01:21 pm	Cancer
16th	01:09 pm	Leo
18th	02:12 pm	Virgo
20th	06:27 pm	Libra
23rd	02:55 am	Scorpio
25th	02:51 pm	Sagittarius
28th	03:58 am	Capricorn
30th	04:00 pm	Aquarius

February 1938

2nd	01:58 am	Pisces
4th	09:54 am	Aries
6th	03:58 pm	Taurus
8th	08:07 pm	Gemini
10th	10:26 pm	Cancer
12th	11:33 pm	Leo
15th	12:57 am	Virgo
17th	04:28 am	Libra
19th	11:37 am	Scorpio
21st	10:33 pm	Sagittarius
24th	11:28 am	Capricorn
26th	11:36 pm	Aquarius

March 1938

1st	09:13 am	Pisces
3rd	04:16 pm	Aries
5th	09:29 pm	Taurus
8th	01:33 am	Gemini
10th	04:46 am	Cancer
12th	07:23 am	Leo
14th	10:05 am	Virgo
16th	02:08 pm	Libra
18th	08:53 pm	Scorpio
21st	07:01 am	Sagittarius
23rd	07:32 pm	Capricorn
26th	07:56 am	Aquarius
28th	05:52 pm	Pisces
31st	12:33 am	Aries

April 1938

2nd	04:43 am	Taurus
4th	07:33 am	Gemini
6th	10:07 am	Cancer
8th	01:04 pm	Leo
10th	04:51 pm	Virgo
12th	10:02 pm	Libra
15th	05:21 am	Scorpio
17th	03:19 pm	Sagittarius
20th	03:31 am	Capricorn
22nd	04:10 pm	Aquarius
25th	02:53 am	Pisces
27th	10:08 am	Aries
29th	02:01 pm	Taurus

May 1938

1st	03:45 pm	Gemini
3rd	04:50 pm	Cancer
5th	06:42 pm	Leo
7th	10:17 pm	Virgo
10th	04:05 am	Libra
12th	12:16 pm	Scorpio
14th	10:40 pm	Sagittarius
17th	10:51 am	Capricorn
19th	11:37 pm	Aquarius
22nd	11:08 am	Pisces
24th	07:35 pm	Aries
27th	12:17 am	Taurus
29th	01:52 am	Gemini
31st	01:52 am	Cancer

June 1938

2nd	02:08 am	Leo
4th	04:21 am	Virgo
6th	09:35 am	Libra
8th	06:01 pm	Scorpio
11th	04:57 am	Sagittarius
13th	05:21 pm	Capricorn
16th	06:07 am	Aquarius
18th	06:02 pm	Pisces
21st	03:39 am	Aries
23rd	09:50 am	Taurus
25th	12:25 pm	Gemini
27th	12:27 pm	Cancer
29th	11:45 am	Leo

July 1938

1st	12:23 pm	Virgo
3rd	04:09 pm	Libra
5th	11:48 pm	Scorpio
8th	10:45 am	Sagittarius
10th	11:22 pm	Capricorn
13th	12:05 pm	Aquarius
15th	11:55 pm	Pisces
18th	10:02 am	Aries
20th	05:31 pm	Taurus
22nd	09:43 pm	Gemini
24th	10:54 pm	Cancer
26th	10:26 pm	Leo
28th	10:17 pm	Virgo
31st	12:35 am	Libra

August 1938

2nd	06:49 am	Scorpio
4th	05:02 pm	Sagittarius
7th	05:33 am	Capricorn
9th	06:15 pm	Aquarius
12th	05:45 am	Pisces
14th	03:34 pm	Aries
16th	11:25 pm	Taurus
19th	04:51 am	Gemini
21st	07:39 am	Cancer
23rd	08:27 am	Leo
25th	08:42 am	Virgo
27th	10:26 am	Libra
29th	03:26 pm	Scorpio

September 1938

1st	12:28 am	Sagittarius
3rd	12:30 pm	Capricorn
6th	01:10 am	Aquarius
8th	12:28 pm	Pisces
10th	09:40 pm	Aries
13th	04:54 am	Taurus
15th	10:23 am	Gemini
17th	02:09 pm	Cancer
19th	04:26 pm	Leo
21st	06:01 pm	Virgo
23rd	08:19 pm	Libra
26th	12:56 am	Scorpio
28th	09:02 am	Sagittarius
30th	08:20 pm	Capricorn

October 1938

3rd	08:58 am	Aquarius
5th	08:27 pm	Pisces
8th	05:22 am	Aries
10th	11:42 am	Taurus
12th	04:10 pm	Gemini
14th	07:31 pm	Cancer
16th	10:19 pm	Leo
19th	01:09 am	Virgo
21st	04:43 am	Libra
23rd	10:00 am	Scorpio
25th	05:54 pm	Sagittarius
28th	04:38 am	Capricorn
30th	05:08 pm	Aquarius

November 1938

2nd	05:09 am	Pisces
4th	02:35 pm	Aries
6th	08:41 pm	Taurus
9th	12:03 am	Gemini
11th	01:59 am	Cancer
13th	03:50 am	Leo
15th	06:38 am	Virgo
17th	11:03 am	Libra
19th	05:25 pm	Scorpio
22nd	01:56 am	Sagittarius
24th	12:37 pm	Capricorn
27th	12:58 am	Aquarius
29th	01:30 pm	Pisces

December 1938

2nd	12:02 am	Aries
4th	07:01 am	Taurus
6th	10:18 am	Gemini
8th	11:07 am	Cancer
10th	11:17 am	Leo
12th	12:37 pm	Virgo
14th	04:27 pm	Libra
16th	11:13 pm	Scorpio
19th	08:31 am	Sagittarius
21st	07:39 pm	Capricorn
24th	07:59 am	Aquarius
26th	08:41 pm	Pisces
29th	08:14 am	Aries
31st	04:47 pm	Taurus

January 1939

2nd	09:19 pm	Gemini
4th	10:20 pm	Cancer
6th	09:32 pm	Leo
8th	09:08 pm	Virgo
10th	11:10 pm	Libra
13th	04:54 am	Scorpio
15th	02:09 pm	Sagittarius
18th	01:43 am	Capricorn
20th	02:15 pm	Aquarius
23rd	02:51 am	Pisces
25th	02:42 pm	Aries
28th	12:29 am	Taurus
30th	06:50 am	Gemini

February 1939

1st	09:22 am	Cancer
3rd	09:06 am	Leo
5th	08:02 am	Virgo
7th	08:29 am	Libra
9th	12:22 pm	Scorpio
11th	08:24 pm	Sagittarius
14th	07:41 am	Capricorn
16th	08:22 pm	Aquarius
19th	08:52 am	Pisces
21st	08:23 pm	Aries
24th	06:19 am	Taurus
26th	01:47 pm	Gemini
28th	06:06 pm	Cancer

March 1939

2nd	07:30 pm	Leo
4th	07:16 pm	Virgo
6th	07:25 pm	Libra
8th	09:59 pm	Scorpio
11th	04:23 am	Sagittarius
13th	02:35 pm	Capricorn
16th	03:01 am	Aquarius
18th	03:31 pm	Pisces
21st	02:41 am	Aries
23rd	11:58 am	Taurus
25th	07:14 pm	Gemini
28th	12:19 am	Cancer
30th	03:15 am	Leo

April 1939

1st	04:39 am	Virgo
3rd	05:48 am	Libra
5th	08:21 am	Scorpio
7th	01:47 pm	Sagittarius
9th	10:46 pm	Capricorn
12th	10:33 am	Aquarius
14th	11:04 pm	Pisces
17th	10:13 am	Aries
19th	06:56 pm	Taurus
22nd	01:16 am	Gemini
24th	05:43 am	Cancer
26th	08:55 am	Leo
28th	11:26 am	Virgo
30th	02:02 pm	Libra

May 1939

2nd	05:36 pm	Scorpio
4th	11:11 pm	Sagittarius
7th	07:33 am	Capricorn
9th	06:41 pm	Aquarius
12th	07:09 am	Pisces
14th	06:41 pm	Aries
17th	03:28 am	Taurus
19th	09:06 am	Gemini
21st	12:23 pm	Cancer
23rd	02:33 pm	Leo
25th	04:51 pm	Virgo
27th	08:06 pm	Libra
30th	12:47 am	Scorpio

June 1939

1st	07:15 am	Sagittarius
3rd	03:50 pm	Capricorn
6th	02:40 am	Aquarius
8th	03:04 pm	Pisces
11th	03:10 am	Aries
13th	12:43 pm	Taurus
15th	06:32 pm	Gemini
17th	09:06 pm	Cancer
19th	09:58 pm	Leo
21st	10:56 pm	Virgo
24th	01:30 am	Libra
26th	06:25 am	Scorpio
28th	01:39 pm	Sagittarius
30th	10:53 pm	Capricorn

July 1939

3rd	09:54 am	Aquarius
5th	10:17 pm	Pisces
8th	10:50 am	Aries
10th	09:27 pm	Taurus
13th	04:20 am	Gemini
15th	07:16 am	Cancer
17th	07:30 am	Leo
19th	07:07 am	Virgo
21st	08:10 am	Libra
23rd	12:04 pm	Scorpio
25th	07:09 pm	Sagittarius
28th	04:50 am	Capricorn
30th	04:15 pm	Aquarius

August 1939

2nd	04:41 am	Pisces
4th	05:22 pm	Aries
7th	04:47 am	Taurus
9th	01:06 pm	Gemini
11th	05:21 pm	Cancer
13th	06:09 pm	Leo
15th	05:19 pm	Virgo
17th	05:03 pm	Libra
19th	07:20 pm	Scorpio
22nd	01:14 am	Sagittarius
24th	10:33 am	Capricorn
26th	10:09 pm	Aquarius
29th	10:42 am	Pisces
31st	11:15 pm	Aries

September 1939

3rd	10:47 am	Taurus
5th	08:02 pm	Gemini
8th	01:52 am	Cancer
10th	04:11 am	Leo
12th	04:09 am	Virgo
14th	03:38 am	Libra
16th	04:43 am	Scorpio
18th	09:02 am	Sagittarius
20th	05:11 pm	Capricorn
23rd	04:24 am	Aquarius
25th	05:00 pm	Pisces
28th	05:22 am	Aries
30th	04:28 pm	Taurus

October 1939

3rd	01:38 am	Gemini
5th	08:16 am	Cancer
7th	12:10 pm	Leo
9th	01:46 pm	Virgo
11th	02:15 pm	Libra
13th	03:18 pm	Scorpio
15th	06:36 pm	Sagittarius
18th	01:22 am	Capricorn
20th	11:40 am	Aquarius
23rd	12:05 am	Pisces
25th	12:28 pm	Aries
27th	11:09 pm	Taurus
30th	07:31 am	Gemini

November 1939

1st	01:41 pm	Cancer
3rd	06:01 pm	Leo
5th	08:57 pm	Virgo
7th	11:03 pm	Libra
10th	01:14 am	Scorpio
12th	04:41 am	Sagittarius
14th	10:42 am	Capricorn
16th	08:00 pm	Aquarius
19th	08:00 am	Pisces
21st	08:36 pm	Aries
24th	07:23 am	Taurus
26th	03:09 pm	Gemini
28th	08:11 pm	Cancer
30th	11:34 pm	Leo

December 1939

3rd	02:23 am	Virgo
5th	05:22 am	Libra
7th	08:57 am	Scorpio
9th	01:32 pm	Sagittarius
11th	07:51 pm	Capricorn
14th	04:42 am	Aquarius
16th	04:14 pm	Pisces
19th	05:03 am	Aries
21st	04:32 pm	Taurus
24th	12:37 am	Gemini
26th	05:03 am	Cancer
28th	07:05 am	Leo
30th	08:29 am	Virgo

January 1940

1st	10:43 am	Libra
3rd	02:36 pm	Scorpio
5th	08:12 pm	Sagittarius
8th	03:29 am	Capricorn
10th	12:42 pm	Aquarius
13th	12:03 am	Pisces
15th	12:55 pm	Aries
18th	01:15 am	Taurus
20th	10:32 am	Gemini
22nd	03:35 pm	Cancer
24th	05:10 pm	Leo
26th	05:12 pm	Virgo
28th	05:43 pm	Libra
30th	08:17 pm	Scorpio

February 1940

2nd	01:36 am	Sagittarius
4th	09:27 am	Capricorn
6th	07:21 pm	Aquarius
9th	06:58 am	Pisces
11th	07:49 pm	Aries
14th	08:36 am	Taurus
16th	07:10 pm	Gemini
19th	01:46 am	Cancer
21st	04:19 am	Leo
23rd	04:11 am	Virgo
25th	03:29 am	Libra
27th	04:13 am	Scorpio
29th	07:54 am	Sagittarius

March 1940

2nd	03:02 pm	Capricorn
5th	01:07 am	Aquarius
7th	01:07 pm	Pisces
10th	02:01 am	Aries
12th	02:44 pm	Taurus
15th	01:52 am	Gemini
17th	09:57 am	Cancer
19th	02:15 pm	Leo
21st	03:20 pm	Virgo
23rd	02:47 pm	Libra
25th	02:33 pm	Scorpio
27th	04:31 pm	Sagittarius
29th	09:59 pm	Capricorn

April 1940

1st	07:13 am	Aquarius
3rd	07:11 pm	Pisces
6th	08:10 am	Aries
8th	08:38 pm	Taurus
11th	07:32 am	Gemini
13th	04:04 pm	Cancer
15th	09:44 pm	Leo
18th	12:34 am	Virgo
20th	01:23 am	Libra
22nd	01:33 am	Scorpio
24th	02:48 am	Sagittarius
26th	06:49 am	Capricorn
28th	02:39 pm	Aquarius

May 1940

1st	01:56 am	Pisces
3rd	02:52 pm	Aries
6th	03:12 am	Taurus
8th	01:33 pm	Gemini
10th	09:33 pm	Cancer
13th	03:22 am	Leo
15th	07:17 am	Virgo
17th	09:40 am	Libra
19th	11:12 am	Scorpio
21st	01:00 pm	Sagittarius
23rd	04:34 pm	Capricorn
25th	11:19 pm	Aquarius
28th	09:39 am	Pisces
30th	10:18 pm	Aries

June 1940

2nd	10:44 am	Taurus
4th	08:49 pm	Gemini
7th	04:02 am	Cancer
9th	09:00 am	Leo
11th	12:41 pm	Virgo
13th	03:43 pm	Libra
15th	06:31 pm	Scorpio
17th	09:34 pm	Sagittarius
20th	01:44 am	Capricorn
22nd	08:15 am	Aquarius
24th	05:55 pm	Pisces
27th	06:13 am	Aries
29th	06:52 pm	Taurus

July 1940

2nd	05:15 am	Gemini
4th	12:10 pm	Cancer
6th	04:12 pm	Leo
8th	06:44 pm	Virgo
10th	09:06 pm	Libra
13th	12:07 am	Scorpio
15th	04:04 am	Sagittarius
17th	09:17 am	Capricorn
19th	04:22 pm	Aquarius
22nd	01:58 am	Pisces
24th	02:01 pm	Aries
27th	02:56 am	Taurus
29th	02:04 pm	Gemini
31st	09:32 pm	Cancer

August 1940

3rd	01:20 am	Leo
5th	02:50 am	Virgo
7th	03:49 am	Libra
9th	05:46 am	Scorpio
11th	09:29 am	Sagittarius
13th	03:15 pm	Capricorn
15th	11:07 pm	Aquarius
18th	09:10 am	Pisces
20th	09:14 pm	Aries
23rd	10:17 am	Taurus
25th	10:13 pm	Gemini
28th	06:53 am	Cancer
30th	11:31 am	Leo

September 1940

1st	12:57 pm	Virgo
3rd	12:54 pm	Libra
5th	01:16 pm	Scorpio
7th	03:36 pm	Sagittarius
9th	08:45 pm	Capricorn
12th	04:51 am	Aquarius
14th	03:25 pm	Pisces
17th	03:43 am	Aries
19th	04:45 pm	Taurus
22nd	05:05 am	Gemini
24th	02:57 pm	Cancer
26th	09:09 pm	Leo
28th	11:41 pm	Virgo
30th	11:46 pm	Libra

October 1940

2nd	11:12 pm	Scorpio
4th	11:54 pm	Sagittarius
7th	03:28 am	Capricorn
9th	10:44 am	Aquarius
11th	09:17 pm	Pisces
14th	09:50 am	Aries
16th	10:49 pm	Taurus
19th	10:59 am	Gemini
21st	09:18 pm	Cancer
24th	04:51 am	Leo
26th	09:10 am	Virgo
28th	10:37 am	Libra
30th	10:25 am	Scorpio

November 1940

1st	10:21 am	Sagittarius
3rd	12:22 pm	Capricorn
5th	06:03 pm	Aquarius
8th	03:46 am	Pisces
10th	04:13 pm	Aries
13th	05:13 am	Taurus
15th	05:00 pm	Gemini
18th	02:52 am	Cancer
20th	10:38 am	Leo
22nd	04:10 pm	Virgo
24th	07:25 pm	Libra
26th	08:44 pm	Scorpio
28th	09:18 pm	Sagittarius
30th	10:50 pm	Capricorn

December 1940

3rd	03:12 am	Aquarius
5th	11:35 am	Pisces
7th	11:26 pm	Aries
10th	12:27 pm	Taurus
13th	12:08 am	Gemini
15th	09:20 am	Cancer
17th	04:16 pm	Leo
19th	09:35 pm	Virgo
22nd	01:37 am	Libra
24th	04:30 am	Scorpio
26th	06:36 am	Sagittarius
28th	08:58 am	Capricorn
30th	01:08 pm	Aquarius

January 1941

1st	08:35 pm	Pisces
4th	07:34 am	Aries
6th	08:28 pm	Taurus
9th	08:27 am	Gemini
11th	05:33 pm	Cancer
13th	11:39 pm	Leo
16th	03:45 am	Virgo
18th	07:00 am	Libra
20th	10:04 am	Scorpio
22nd	01:16 pm	Sagittarius
24th	05:01 pm	Capricorn
26th	10:06 pm	Aquarius
29th	05:34 am	Pisces
31st	04:02 pm	Aries

February 1941

3rd	04:41 am	Taurus
5th	05:09 pm	Gemini
8th	02:57 am	Cancer
10th	09:07 am	Leo
12th	12:21 pm	Virgo
14th	02:07 pm	Libra
16th	03:52 pm	Scorpio
18th	06:37 pm	Sagittarius
20th	10:53 pm	Capricorn
23rd	05:01 am	Aquarius
25th	01:18 pm	Pisces
27th	11:54 pm	Aries

March 1941

2nd	12:23 pm	Taurus
5th	01:12 am	Gemini
7th	12:04 pm	Cancer
9th	07:19 pm	Leo
11th	10:51 pm	Virgo
13th	11:51 pm	Libra
16th	12:03 am	Scorpio
18th	01:07 am	Sagittarius
20th	04:25 am	Capricorn
22nd	10:34 am	Aquarius
24th	07:30 pm	Pisces
27th	06:39 am	Aries
29th	07:13 pm	Taurus

April 1941

1st	08:06 am	Gemini
3rd	07:43 pm	Cancer
6th	04:26 am	Leo
8th	09:21 am	Virgo
10th	10:54 am	Libra
12th	10:31 am	Scorpio
14th	10:07 am	Sagittarius
16th	11:38 am	Capricorn
18th	04:31 pm	Aquarius
21st	01:07 am	Pisces
23rd	12:34 pm	Aries
26th	01:22 am	Taurus
28th	02:11 pm	Gemini

May 1941

1st	01:56 am	Cancer
3rd	11:34 am	Leo
5th	06:05 pm	Virgo
7th	09:11 pm	Libra
9th	09:34 pm	Scorpio
11th	08:49 pm	Sagittarius
13th	09:03 pm	Capricorn
16th	12:15 am	Aquarius
18th	07:33 am	Pisces
20th	06:34 pm	Aries
23rd	07:26 am	Taurus
25th	08:10 pm	Gemini
28th	07:36 am	Cancer
30th	05:15 pm	Leo

June 1941

2nd	12:38 am	Virgo
4th	05:17 am	Libra
6th	07:13 am	Scorpio
8th	07:23 am	Sagittarius
10th	07:31 am	Capricorn
12th	09:41 am	Aquarius
14th	03:33 pm	Pisces
17th	01:30 am	Aries
19th	02:03 pm	Taurus
22nd	02:44 am	Gemini
24th	01:51 pm	Cancer
26th	10:55 pm	Leo
29th	06:03 am	Virgo

July 1941

1st	11:17 am	Libra
3rd	02:33 pm	Scorpio
5th	04:13 pm	Sagittarius
7th	05:20 pm	Capricorn
9th	07:36 pm	Aquarius
12th	12:42 am	Pisces
14th	09:34 am	Aries
16th	09:30 pm	Taurus
19th	10:09 am	Gemini
21st	09:15 pm	Cancer
24th	05:48 am	Leo
26th	12:03 pm	Virgo
28th	04:40 pm	Libra
30th	08:09 pm	Scorpio

August 1941

1st	10:49 pm	Sagittarius
4th	01:17 am	Capricorn
6th	04:32 am	Aquarius
8th	09:51 am	Pisces
10th	06:13 pm	Aries
13th	05:32 am	Taurus
15th	06:09 pm	Gemini
18th	05:37 am	Cancer
20th	02:15 pm	Leo
22nd	07:53 pm	Virgo
24th	11:21 pm	Libra
27th	01:48 am	Scorpio
29th	04:13 am	Sagittarius
31st	07:17 am	Capricorn

September 1941

2nd	11:38 am	Aquarius
4th	05:52 pm	Pisces
7th	02:28 am	Aries
9th	01:32 pm	Taurus
12th	02:05 am	Gemini
14th	02:09 pm	Cancer
16th	11:36 pm	Leo
19th	05:29 am	Virgo
21st	08:17 am	Libra
23rd	09:23 am	Scorpio
25th	10:24 am	Sagittarius
27th	12:44 pm	Capricorn
29th	05:17 pm	Aquarius

October 1941

2nd	12:18 am	Pisces
4th	09:37 am	Aries
6th	08:52 pm	Taurus
9th	09:22 am	Gemini
11th	09:53 pm	Cancer
14th	08:29 am	Leo
16th	03:36 pm	Virgo
18th	06:54 pm	Libra
20th	07:25 pm	Scorpio
22nd	07:00 pm	Sagittarius
24th	07:40 pm	Capricorn
26th	11:02 pm	Aquarius
29th	05:51 am	Pisces
31st	03:38 pm	Aries

November 1941

3rd	03:19 am	Taurus
5th	03:52 pm	Gemini
8th	04:26 am	Cancer
10th	03:49 pm	Leo
13th	12:29 am	Virgo
15th	05:21 am	Libra
17th	06:40 am	Scorpio
19th	05:53 am	Sagittarius
21st	05:11 am	Capricorn
23rd	06:46 am	Aquarius
25th	12:09 pm	Pisces
27th	09:26 pm	Aries
30th	09:18 am	Taurus

December 1941

2nd	10:00 pm	Gemini
5th	10:21 am	Cancer
7th	09:43 pm	Leo
10th	07:12 am	Virgo
12th	01:46 pm	Libra
14th	04:51 pm	Scorpio
16th	05:10 pm	Sagittarius
18th	04:26 pm	Capricorn
20th	04:53 pm	Aquarius
22nd	08:33 pm	Pisces
25th	04:24 am	Aries
27th	03:43 pm	Taurus
30th	04:27 am	Gemini

January 1942

1st	04:41 pm	Cancer
4th	03:32 am	Leo
6th	12:42 pm	Virgo
8th	07:48 pm	Libra
11th	12:24 am	Scorpio
13th	02:31 am	Sagittarius
15th	03:07 am	Capricorn
17th	03:52 am	Aquarius
19th	06:43 am	Pisces
21st	01:08 pm	Aries
23rd	11:18 pm	Taurus
26th	11:44 am	Gemini
29th	12:03 am	Cancer
31st	10:37 am	Leo

February 1942

2nd	06:57 pm	Virgo
5th	01:18 am	Libra
7th	05:56 am	Scorpio
9th	09:06 am	Sagittarius
11th	11:19 am	Capricorn
13th	01:27 pm	Aquarius
15th	04:50 pm	Pisces
17th	10:46 pm	Aries
20th	07:57 am	Taurus
22nd	07:47 pm	Gemini
25th	08:15 am	Cancer
27th	07:06 pm	Leo

March 1942

2nd	03:06 am	Virgo
4th	08:23 am	Libra
6th	11:50 am	Scorpio
8th	02:28 pm	Sagittarius
10th	05:08 pm	Capricorn
12th	08:30 pm	Aquarius
15th	01:09 am	Pisces
17th	07:41 am	Aries
19th	04:39 pm	Taurus
22nd	04:00 am	Gemini
24th	04:33 pm	Cancer
27th	04:04 am	Leo
29th	12:36 pm	Virgo
31st	05:36 pm	Libra

April 1942

2nd	07:54 pm	Scorpio
4th	09:04 pm	Sagittarius
6th	10:41 pm	Capricorn
9th	01:56 am	Aquarius
11th	07:19 am	Pisces
13th	02:49 pm	Aries
16th	12:18 am	Taurus
18th	11:36 am	Gemini
21st	12:09 am	Cancer
23rd	12:21 pm	Leo
25th	10:02 pm	Virgo
28th	03:50 am	Libra
30th	05:59 am	Scorpio

May 1942

2nd	06:03 am	Sagittarius
4th	06:04 am	Capricorn
6th	07:55 am	Aquarius
8th	12:43 pm	Pisces
10th	08:31 pm	Aries
13th	06:37 am	Taurus
15th	06:15 pm	Gemini
18th	06:49 am	Cancer
20th	07:21 pm	Leo
23rd	06:07 am	Virgo
25th	01:22 pm	Libra
27th	04:32 pm	Scorpio
29th	04:39 pm	Sagittarius
31st	03:43 pm	Capricorn

June 1942

2nd	03:59 pm	Aquarius
4th	07:14 pm	Pisces
7th	02:11 am	Aries
9th	12:16 pm	Taurus
12th	12:11 am	Gemini
14th	12:50 pm	Cancer
17th	01:19 am	Leo
19th	12:33 pm	Virgo
21st	09:04 pm	Libra
24th	01:50 am	Scorpio
26th	03:09 am	Sagittarius
28th	02:30 am	Capricorn
30th	02:00 am	Aquarius

July 1942

2nd	03:46 am	Pisces
4th	09:10 am	Aries
6th	06:22 pm	Taurus
9th	06:10 am	Gemini
11th	06:51 pm	Cancer
14th	07:08 am	Leo
16th	06:08 pm	Virgo
19th	03:02 am	Libra
21st	09:02 am	Scorpio
23rd	11:58 am	Sagittarius
25th	12:38 pm	Capricorn
27th	12:37 pm	Aquarius
29th	01:49 pm	Pisces
31st	05:55 pm	Aries

August 1942

3rd	01:47 am	Taurus
5th	12:54 pm	Gemini
8th	01:30 am	Cancer
10th	01:39 pm	Leo
13th	12:09 am	Virgo
15th	08:31 am	Libra
17th	02:38 pm	Scorpio
19th	06:35 pm	Sagittarius
21st	08:46 pm	Capricorn
23rd	10:07 pm	Aquarius
25th	11:55 pm	Pisces
28th	03:39 am	Aries
30th	10:29 am	Taurus

September 1942

1st	08:40 pm	Gemini
4th	09:00 am	Cancer
6th	09:15 pm	Leo
9th	07:31 am	Virgo
11th	03:05 pm	Libra
13th	08:18 pm	Scorpio
15th	11:58 pm	Sagittarius
18th	02:48 am	Capricorn
20th	05:27 am	Aquarius
22nd	08:34 am	Pisces
24th	12:57 pm	Aries
26th	07:34 pm	Taurus
29th	05:05 am	Gemini

October 1942

1st	05:03 pm	Cancer
4th	05:35 am	Leo
6th	04:13 pm	Virgo
8th	11:33 pm	Libra
11th	03:46 am	Scorpio
13th	06:10 am	Sagittarius
15th	08:13 am	Capricorn
17th	11:01 am	Aquarius
19th	03:05 pm	Pisces
21st	08:36 pm	Aries
24th	03:52 am	Taurus
26th	01:18 pm	Gemini
29th	01:00 am	Cancer
31st	01:48 pm	Leo

November 1942

3rd	01:19 am	Virgo
5th	09:21 am	Libra
7th	01:27 pm	Scorpio
9th	02:47 pm	Sagittarius
11th	03:18 pm	Capricorn
13th	04:48 pm	Aquarius
15th	08:28 pm	Pisces
18th	02:30 am	Aries
20th	10:37 am	Taurus
22nd	08:34 pm	Gemini
25th	08:16 am	Cancer
27th	09:09 pm	Leo
30th	09:29 am	Virgo

December 1942

2nd	06:55 pm	Libra
5th	12:06 am	Scorpio
7th	01:34 am	Sagittarius
9th	01:07 am	Capricorn
11th	12:57 am	Aquarius
13th	02:56 am	Pisces
15th	08:04 am	Aries
17th	04:16 pm	Taurus
20th	02:46 am	Gemini
22nd	02:46 pm	Cancer
25th	03:35 am	Leo
27th	04:10 pm	Virgo
30th	02:44 am	Libra

January 1943

1st	09:40 am	Scorpio
3rd	12:34 pm	Sagittarius
5th	12:35 pm	Capricorn
7th	11:42 am	Aquarius
9th	12:03 pm	Pisces
11th	03:20 pm	Aries
13th	10:21 pm	Taurus
16th	08:39 am	Gemini
18th	08:53 pm	Cancer
21st	09:44 am	Leo
23rd	10:03 pm	Virgo
26th	08:47 am	Libra
28th	04:50 pm	Scorpio
30th	09:34 pm	Sagittarius

February 1943

1st	11:15 pm	Capricorn
3rd	11:10 pm	Aquarius
5th	11:07 pm	Pisces
8th	01:00 am	Aries
10th	06:17 am	Taurus
12th	03:25 pm	Gemini
15th	03:24 am	Cancer
17th	04:18 pm	Leo
20th	04:20 am	Virgo
22nd	02:30 pm	Libra
24th	10:25 pm	Scorpio
27th	03:59 am	Sagittarius

March 1943

1st	07:19 am	Capricorn
3rd	08:56 am	Aquarius
5th	09:54 am	Pisces
7th	11:41 am	Aries
9th	03:53 pm	Taurus
11th	11:39 pm	Gemini
14th	10:51 am	Cancer
16th	11:41 pm	Leo
19th	11:43 am	Virgo
21st	09:21 pm	Libra
24th	04:23 am	Scorpio
26th	09:23 am	Sagittarius
28th	01:05 pm	Capricorn
30th	03:57 pm	Aquarius

April 1943

1st	06:27 pm	Pisces
3rd	09:17 pm	Aries
6th	01:37 am	Taurus
8th	08:41 am	Gemini
10th	07:03 pm	Cancer
13th	07:39 am	Leo
15th	07:59 pm	Virgo
18th	05:41 am	Libra
20th	12:04 pm	Scorpio
22nd	03:56 pm	Sagittarius
24th	06:39 pm	Capricorn
26th	09:21 pm	Aquarius
29th	12:36 am	Pisces

May 1943

1st	04:39 am	Aries
3rd	09:57 am	Taurus
5th	05:16 pm	Gemini
8th	03:17 am	Cancer
10th	03:38 pm	Leo
13th	04:21 am	Virgo
15th	02:44 pm	Libra
17th	09:19 pm	Scorpio
20th	12:33 am	Sagittarius
22nd	02:00 am	Capricorn
24th	03:23 am	Aquarius
26th	05:57 am	Pisces
28th	10:16 am	Aries
30th	04:25 pm	Taurus

June 1943

2nd	12:29 am	Gemini
4th	10:45 am	Cancer
6th	11:03 pm	Leo
9th	12:03 pm	Virgo
11th	11:22 pm	Libra
14th	06:59 am	Scorpio
16th	10:36 am	Sagittarius
18th	11:29 am	Capricorn
20th	11:33 am	Aquarius
22nd	12:36 pm	Pisces
24th	03:52 pm	Aries
26th	09:52 pm	Taurus
29th	06:27 am	Gemini

July 1943

1st	05:13 pm	Cancer
4th	05:39 am	Leo
6th	06:45 pm	Virgo
9th	06:44 am	Libra
11th	03:40 pm	Scorpio
13th	08:37 pm	Sagittarius
15th	10:06 pm	Capricorn
17th	09:45 pm	Aquarius
19th	09:30 pm	Pisces
21st	11:08 pm	Aries
24th	03:53 am	Taurus
26th	12:03 pm	Gemini
28th	11:04 pm	Cancer
31st	11:43 am	Leo

August 1943

3rd	12:45 am	Virgo
5th	12:51 pm	Libra
7th	10:40 pm	Scorpio
10th	05:08 am	Sagittarius
12th	08:09 am	Capricorn
14th	08:36 am	Aquarius
16th	08:06 am	Pisces
18th	08:32 am	Aries
20th	11:39 am	Taurus
22nd	06:34 pm	Gemini
25th	05:07 am	Cancer
27th	05:49 pm	Leo
30th	06:47 am	Virgo

September 1943

1st	06:33 pm	Libra
4th	04:20 am	Scorpio
6th	11:38 am	Sagittarius
8th	04:13 pm	Capricorn
10th	06:18 pm	Aquarius
12th	06:46 pm	Pisces
14th	07:08 pm	Aries
16th	09:14 pm	Taurus
19th	02:42 am	Gemini
21st	12:10 pm	Cancer
24th	12:34 am	Leo
26th	01:30 pm	Virgo
29th	12:56 am	Libra

October 1943

1st	10:04 am	Scorpio
3rd	05:03 pm	Sagittarius
5th	10:11 pm	Capricorn
8th	01:39 am	Aquarius
10th	03:44 am	Pisces
12th	05:12 am	Aries
14th	07:26 am	Taurus
16th	12:07 pm	Gemini
18th	08:28 pm	Cancer
21st	08:12 am	Leo
23rd	09:09 pm	Virgo
26th	08:38 am	Libra
28th	05:14 pm	Scorpio
30th	11:14 pm	Sagittarius

November 1943

2nd	03:36 am	Capricorn
4th	07:09 am	Aquarius
6th	10:16 am	Pisces
8th	01:10 pm	Aries
10th	04:32 pm	Taurus
12th	09:31 pm	Gemini
15th	05:22 am	Cancer
17th	04:27 pm	Leo
20th	05:21 am	Virgo
22nd	05:19 pm	Libra
25th	02:09 am	Scorpio
27th	07:35 am	Sagittarius
29th	10:43 am	Capricorn

December 1943

1st	01:01 pm	Aquarius
3rd	03:35 pm	Pisces
5th	07:00 pm	Aries
7th	11:30 pm	Taurus
10th	05:32 am	Gemini
12th	01:46 pm	Cancer
15th	12:37 am	Leo
17th	01:22 pm	Virgo
20th	01:55 am	Libra
22nd	11:46 am	Scorpio
24th	05:44 pm	Sagittarius
26th	08:24 pm	Capricorn
28th	09:21 pm	Aquarius
30th	10:17 pm	Pisces

January 1944

2nd	12:34 am	Aries
4th	04:58 am	Taurus
6th	11:44 am	Gemini
8th	08:48 pm	Cancer
11th	07:57 am	Leo
13th	08:38 pm	Virgo
16th	09:29 am	Libra
18th	08:27 pm	Scorpio
21st	03:53 am	Sagittarius
23rd	07:26 am	Capricorn
25th	08:09 am	Aquarius
27th	07:48 am	Pisces
29th	08:14 am	Aries
31st	11:07 am	Taurus

February 1944

2nd	05:17 pm	Gemini
5th	02:40 am	Cancer
7th	02:20 pm	Leo
10th	03:08 am	Virgo
12th	03:54 pm	Libra
15th	03:24 am	Scorpio
17th	12:15 pm	Sagittarius
19th	05:33 pm	Capricorn
21st	07:27 pm	Aquarius
23rd	07:09 pm	Pisces
25th	06:31 pm	Aries
27th	07:36 pm	Taurus

March 1944

1st	12:06 am	Gemini
3rd	08:38 am	Cancer
5th	08:19 pm	Leo
8th	09:18 am	Virgo
10th	09:55 pm	Libra
13th	09:12 am	Scorpio
15th	06:31 pm	Sagittarius
18th	01:13 am	Capricorn
20th	04:55 am	Aquarius
22nd	05:59 am	Pisces
24th	05:42 am	Aries
26th	06:01 am	Taurus
28th	08:58 am	Gemini
30th	03:59 pm	Cancer

April 1944

2nd	02:54 am	Leo
4th	03:49 pm	Virgo
7th	04:22 am	Libra
9th	03:12 pm	Scorpio
12th	12:02 am	Sagittarius
14th	06:56 am	Capricorn
16th	11:46 am	Aquarius
18th	02:28 pm	Pisces
20th	03:35 pm	Aries
22nd	04:28 pm	Taurus
24th	06:58 pm	Gemini
27th	12:49 am	Cancer
29th	10:36 am	Leo

May 1944

1st	11:04 pm	Virgo
4th	11:40 am	Libra
6th	10:18 pm	Scorpio
9th	06:27 am	Sagittarius
11th	12:33 pm	Capricorn
13th	05:10 pm	Aquarius
15th	08:35 pm	Pisces
17th	11:03 pm	Aries
20th	01:15 am	Taurus
22nd	04:26 am	Gemini
24th	10:04 am	Cancer
26th	07:04 pm	Leo
29th	06:58 am	Virgo
31st	07:37 pm	Libra

June 1944

3rd	06:32 am	Scorpio
5th	02:27 pm	Sagittarius
7th	07:41 pm	Capricorn
9th	11:12 pm	Aquarius
12th	01:58 am	Pisces
14th	04:41 am	Aries
16th	07:52 am	Taurus
18th	12:11 pm	Gemini
20th	06:28 pm	Cancer
23rd	03:25 am	Leo
25th	02:58 pm	Virgo
28th	03:40 am	Libra
30th	03:10 pm	Scorpio

July 1944

2nd	11:38 pm	Sagittarius
5th	04:42 am	Capricorn
7th	07:14 am	Aquarius
9th	08:39 am	Pisces
11th	10:18 am	Aries
13th	01:16 pm	Taurus
15th	06:11 pm	Gemini
18th	01:21 am	Cancer
20th	10:51 am	Leo
22nd	10:24 pm	Virgo
25th	11:08 am	Libra
27th	11:16 pm	Scorpio
30th	08:50 am	Sagittarius

August 1944

1st	02:42 pm	Capricorn
3rd	05:10 pm	Aquarius
5th	05:35 pm	Pisces
7th	05:43 pm	Aries
9th	07:19 pm	Taurus
11th	11:38 pm	Gemini
14th	07:03 am	Cancer
16th	05:08 pm	Leo
19th	05:00 am	Virgo
21st	05:45 pm	Libra
24th	06:13 am	Scorpio
26th	04:52 pm	Sagittarius
29th	12:12 am	Capricorn
31st	03:44 am	Aquarius

September 1944

2nd	04:14 am	Pisces
4th	03:27 am	Aries
6th	03:28 am	Taurus
8th	06:13 am	Gemini
10th	12:47 pm	Cancer
12th	10:50 pm	Leo
15th	11:00 am	Virgo
17th	11:48 pm	Libra
20th	12:11 pm	Scorpio
22nd	11:16 pm	Sagittarius
25th	07:55 am	Capricorn
27th	01:10 pm	Aquarius
29th	02:58 pm	Pisces

October 1944

1st	02:30 pm	Aries
3rd	01:46 pm	Taurus
5th	02:59 pm	Gemini
7th	07:56 pm	Cancer
10th	05:03 am	Leo
12th	05:04 pm	Virgo
15th	05:55 am	Libra
17th	06:03 pm	Scorpio
20th	04:50 am	Sagittarius
22nd	01:48 pm	Capricorn
24th	08:19 pm	Aquarius
26th	11:53 pm	Pisces
29th	12:54 am	Aries
31st	12:45 am	Taurus

November 1944

2nd	01:28 am	Gemini
4th	05:04 am	Cancer
6th	12:44 pm	Leo
8th	11:59 pm	Virgo
11th	12:45 pm	Libra
14th	12:48 am	Scorpio
16th	11:02 am	Sagittarius
18th	07:20 pm	Capricorn
21st	01:47 am	Aquarius
23rd	06:18 am	Pisces
25th	08:57 am	Aries
27th	10:22 am	Taurus
29th	11:55 am	Gemini

December 1944

1st	03:16 pm	Cancer
3rd	09:53 pm	Leo
6th	08:04 am	Virgo
8th	08:28 pm	Libra
11th	08:42 am	Scorpio
13th	06:50 pm	Sagittarius
16th	02:22 am	Capricorn
18th	07:44 am	Aquarius
20th	11:39 am	Pisces
22nd	02:42 pm	Aries
24th	05:24 pm	Taurus
26th	08:26 pm	Gemini
29th	12:44 am	Cancer
31st	07:19 am	Leo

January 1945

2nd	04:49 pm	Virgo
5th	04:44 am	Libra
7th	05:13 pm	Scorpio
10th	03:55 am	Sagittarius
12th	11:28 am	Capricorn
14th	03:57 pm	Aquarius
16th	06:27 pm	Pisces
18th	08:20 pm	Aries
20th	10:48 pm	Taurus
23rd	02:34 am	Gemini
25th	08:05 am	Cancer
27th	03:33 pm	Leo
30th	01:09 am	Virgo

February 1945

1st	12:46 pm	Libra
4th	01:22 am	Scorpio
6th	12:57 pm	Sagittarius
8th	09:29 pm	Capricorn
11th	02:12 am	Aquarius
13th	03:52 am	Pisces
15th	04:12 am	Aries
17th	05:05 am	Taurus
19th	08:01 am	Gemini
21st	01:42 pm	Cancer
23rd	09:58 pm	Leo
26th	08:13 am	Virgo
28th	07:57 pm	Libra

March 1945

3rd	08:32 am	Scorpio
5th	08:45 pm	Sagittarius
8th	06:37 am	Capricorn
10th	12:40 pm	Aquarius
12th	02:50 pm	Pisces
14th	02:32 pm	Aries
16th	01:54 pm	Taurus
18th	03:04 pm	Gemini
20th	07:31 pm	Cancer
23rd	03:31 am	Leo
25th	02:11 pm	Virgo
28th	02:15 am	Libra
30th	02:50 pm	Scorpio

April 1945

2nd	03:08 am	Sagittarius
4th	01:51 pm	Capricorn
6th	09:28 pm	Aquarius
9th	01:10 am	Pisces
11th	01:38 am	Aries
13th	12:40 am	Taurus
15th	12:31 am	Gemini
17th	03:13 am	Cancer
19th	09:52 am	Leo
21st	08:03 pm	Virgo
24th	08:15 am	Libra
26th	08:52 pm	Scorpio
29th	08:56 am	Sagittarius

May 1945

1st	07:40 pm	Capricorn
4th	04:06 am	Aquarius
6th	09:21 am	Pisces
8th	11:25 am	Aries
10th	11:24 am	Taurus
12th	11:12 am	Gemini
14th	12:51 pm	Cancer
16th	05:57 pm	Leo
19th	02:56 am	Virgo
21st	02:43 pm	Libra
24th	03:21 am	Scorpio
26th	03:11 pm	Sagittarius
29th	01:24 am	Capricorn
31st	09:35 am	Aquarius

June 1945

2nd	03:25 pm	Pisces
4th	06:51 pm	Aries
6th	08:23 pm	Taurus
8th	09:15 pm	Gemini
10th	11:02 pm	Cancer
13th	03:20 am	Leo
15th	11:07 am	Virgo
17th	10:06 pm	Libra
20th	10:36 am	Scorpio
22nd	10:27 pm	Sagittarius
25th	08:14 am	Capricorn
27th	03:36 pm	Aquarius
29th	08:51 pm	Pisces

July 1945

2nd	12:29 am	Aries
4th	03:04 am	Taurus
6th	05:20 am	Gemini
8th	08:10 am	Cancer
10th	12:43 pm	Leo
12th	07:58 pm	Virgo
15th	06:13 am	Libra
17th	06:29 pm	Scorpio
20th	06:36 am	Sagittarius
22nd	04:29 pm	Capricorn
24th	11:16 pm	Aquarius
27th	03:26 am	Pisces
29th	06:07 am	Aries
31st	08:29 am	Taurus

August 1945

2nd	11:23 am	Gemini
4th	03:22 pm	Cancer
6th	08:52 pm	Leo
9th	04:24 am	Virgo
11th	02:21 pm	Libra
14th	02:24 am	Scorpio
16th	02:56 pm	Sagittarius
19th	01:31 am	Capricorn
21st	08:32 am	Aquarius
23rd	12:05 pm	Pisces
25th	01:30 pm	Aries
27th	02:33 pm	Taurus
29th	04:47 pm	Gemini
31st	09:00 pm	Cancer

September 1945

3rd	03:19 am	Leo
5th	11:36 am	Virgo
7th	09:48 pm	Libra
10th	09:48 am	Scorpio
12th	10:37 pm	Sagittarius
15th	10:11 am	Capricorn
17th	06:19 pm	Aquarius
19th	10:19 pm	Pisces
21st	11:10 pm	Aries
23rd	10:53 pm	Taurus
25th	11:31 pm	Gemini
28th	02:38 am	Cancer
30th	08:47 am	Leo

October 1945

2nd	05:34 pm	Virgo
5th	04:16 am	Libra
7th	04:24 pm	Scorpio
10th	05:17 am	Sagittarius
12th	05:33 pm	Capricorn
15th	03:07 am	Aquarius
17th	08:34 am	Pisces
19th	10:09 am	Aries
21st	09:30 am	Taurus
23rd	08:49 am	Gemini
25th	10:11 am	Cancer
27th	02:55 pm	Leo
29th	11:12 pm	Virgo

November 1945

1st	10:08 am	Libra
3rd	10:29 pm	Scorpio
6th	11:18 am	Sagittarius
8th	11:35 pm	Capricorn
11th	09:59 am	Aquarius
13th	05:05 pm	Pisces
15th	08:24 pm	Aries
17th	08:48 pm	Taurus
19th	08:02 pm	Gemini
21st	08:14 pm	Cancer
23rd	11:12 pm	Leo
26th	05:59 am	Virgo
28th	04:18 pm	Libra

December 1945

1st	04:43 am	Scorpio
3rd	05:30 pm	Sagittarius
6th	05:23 am	Capricorn
8th	03:34 pm	Aquarius
10th	11:20 pm	Pisces
13th	04:15 am	Aries
15th	06:30 am	Taurus
17th	07:02 am	Gemini
19th	07:27 am	Cancer
21st	09:30 am	Leo
23rd	02:44 pm	Virgo
25th	11:45 pm	Libra
28th	11:43 am	Scorpio
31st	12:32 am	Sagittarius

January 1946

2nd	12:11 pm	Capricorn
4th	09:38 pm	Aquarius
7th	04:47 am	Pisces
9th	09:56 am	Aries
11th	01:25 pm	Taurus
13th	03:42 pm	Gemini
15th	05:32 pm	Cancer
17th	08:03 pm	Leo
20th	12:40 am	Virgo
22nd	08:31 am	Libra
24th	07:40 pm	Scorpio
27th	08:27 am	Sagittarius
29th	08:18 pm	Capricorn

February 1946

1st	05:23 am	Aquarius
3rd	11:32 am	Pisces
5th	03:38 pm	Aries
7th	06:46 pm	Taurus
9th	09:45 pm	Gemini
12th	12:59 am	Cancer
14th	04:50 am	Leo
16th	10:03 am	Virgo
18th	05:36 pm	Libra
21st	04:05 am	Scorpio
23rd	04:41 pm	Sagittarius
26th	05:01 am	Capricorn
28th	02:34 pm	Aquarius

March 1946

2nd	08:25 pm	Pisces
4th	11:23 pm	Aries
7th	01:08 am	Taurus
9th	03:12 am	Gemini
11th	06:28 am	Cancer
13th	11:14 am	Leo
15th	05:32 pm	Virgo
18th	01:40 am	Libra
20th	12:04 pm	Scorpio
23rd	12:30 am	Sagittarius
25th	01:18 pm	Capricorn
27th	11:51 pm	Aquarius
30th	06:26 am	Pisces

April 1946

1st	09:16 am	Aries
3rd	09:56 am	Taurus
5th	10:25 am	Gemini
7th	12:21 pm	Cancer
9th	04:37 pm	Leo
11th	11:20 pm	Virgo
14th	08:13 am	Libra
16th	07:03 pm	Scorpio
19th	07:30 am	Sagittarius
21st	08:28 pm	Capricorn
24th	07:56 am	Aquarius
26th	03:54 pm	Pisces
28th	07:45 pm	Aries
30th	08:31 pm	Taurus

May 1946

2nd	08:03 pm	Gemini
4th	08:22 pm	Cancer
6th	11:04 pm	Leo
9th	04:57 am	Virgo
11th	01:53 pm	Libra
14th	01:08 am	Scorpio
16th	01:46 pm	Sagittarius
19th	02:42 am	Capricorn
21st	02:31 pm	Aquarius
23rd	11:39 pm	Pisces
26th	05:05 am	Aries
28th	07:04 am	Taurus
30th	06:54 am	Gemini

June 1946

1st	06:28 am	Cancer
3rd	07:39 am	Leo
5th	11:57 am	Virgo
7th	07:57 pm	Libra
10th	07:04 am	Scorpio
12th	07:50 pm	Sagittarius
15th	08:39 am	Capricorn
17th	08:16 pm	Aquarius
20th	05:43 am	Pisces
22nd	12:19 pm	Aries
24th	03:56 pm	Taurus
26th	05:07 pm	Gemini
28th	05:10 pm	Cancer
30th	05:47 pm	Leo

July 1946

2nd	08:45 pm	Virgo
5th	03:21 am	Libra
7th	01:41 pm	Scorpio
10th	02:20 am	Sagittarius
12th	03:05 pm	Capricorn
15th	02:17 am	Aquarius
17th	11:15 am	Pisces
19th	05:59 pm	Aries
21st	10:35 pm	Taurus
24th	01:18 am	Gemini
26th	02:44 am	Cancer
28th	03:57 am	Leo
30th	06:32 am	Virgo

August 1946

1st	12:05 pm	Libra
3rd	09:23 pm	Scorpio
6th	09:36 am	Sagittarius
8th	10:23 pm	Capricorn
11th	09:23 am	Aquarius
13th	05:41 pm	Pisces
15th	11:37 pm	Aries
18th	03:59 am	Taurus
20th	07:22 am	Gemini
22nd	10:06 am	Cancer
24th	12:38 pm	Leo
26th	03:54 pm	Virgo
28th	09:15 pm	Libra
31st	05:49 am	Scorpio

September 1946

2nd	05:31 pm	Sagittarius
5th	06:24 am	Capricorn
7th	05:41 pm	Aquarius
10th	01:46 am	Pisces
12th	06:49 am	Aries
14th	10:03 am	Taurus
16th	12:45 pm	Gemini
18th	03:42 pm	Cancer
20th	07:13 pm	Leo
22nd	11:38 pm	Virgo
25th	05:40 am	Libra
27th	02:12 pm	Scorpio
30th	01:32 am	Sagittarius

October 1946

2nd	02:29 pm	Capricorn
5th	02:27 am	Aquarius
7th	11:09 am	Pisces
9th	04:05 pm	Aries
11th	06:20 pm	Taurus
13th	07:36 pm	Gemini
15th	09:23 pm	Cancer
18th	12:35 am	Leo
20th	05:35 am	Virgo
22nd	12:33 pm	Libra
24th	09:41 pm	Scorpio
27th	09:03 am	Sagittarius
29th	09:59 pm	Capricorn

November 1946

1st	10:36 am	Aquarius
3rd	08:32 pm	Pisces
6th	02:28 am	Aries
8th	04:49 am	Taurus
10th	05:07 am	Gemini
12th	05:15 am	Cancer
14th	06:53 am	Leo
16th	11:05 am	Virgo
18th	06:12 pm	Libra
21st	03:58 am	Scorpio
23rd	03:44 pm	Sagittarius
26th	04:40 am	Capricorn
28th	05:30 pm	Aquarius

December 1946

1st	04:30 am	Pisces
3rd	12:05 pm	Aries
5th	03:48 pm	Taurus
7th	04:30 pm	Gemini
9th	03:50 pm	Cancer
11th	03:46 pm	Leo
13th	06:09 pm	Virgo
16th	12:07 am	Libra
18th	09:43 am	Scorpio
20th	09:48 pm	Sagittarius
23rd	10:50 am	Capricorn
25th	11:29 pm	Aquarius
28th	10:43 am	Pisces
30th	07:31 pm	Aries

January 1947

2nd	01:06 am	Taurus
4th	03:26 am	Gemini
6th	03:28 am	Cancer
8th	02:53 am	Leo
10th	03:44 am	Virgo
12th	07:54 am	Libra
14th	04:15 pm	Scorpio
17th	04:03 am	Sagittarius
19th	05:10 pm	Capricorn
22nd	05:37 am	Aquarius
24th	04:23 pm	Pisces
27th	01:10 am	Aries
29th	07:45 am	Taurus
31st	11:52 am	Gemini

February 1947

2nd	01:38 pm	Cancer
4th	02:01 pm	Leo
6th	02:42 pm	Virgo
8th	05:39 pm	Libra
11th	12:28 am	Scorpio
13th	11:15 am	Sagittarius
16th	12:12 am	Capricorn
18th	12:38 pm	Aquarius
20th	10:57 pm	Pisces
23rd	06:57 am	Aries
25th	01:08 pm	Taurus
27th	05:47 pm	Gemini

March 1947

1st	08:59 pm	Cancer
3rd	11:00 pm	Leo
6th	12:46 am	Virgo
8th	03:51 am	Libra
10th	09:51 am	Scorpio
12th	07:34 pm	Sagittarius
15th	08:00 am	Capricorn
17th	08:35 pm	Aquarius
20th	06:57 am	Pisces
22nd	02:23 pm	Aries
24th	07:29 pm	Taurus
26th	11:16 pm	Gemini
29th	02:26 am	Cancer
31st	05:22 am	Leo

April 1947

2nd	08:30 am	Virgo
4th	12:39 pm	Libra
6th	06:56 pm	Scorpio
9th	04:12 am	Sagittarius
11th	04:08 pm	Capricorn
14th	04:51 am	Aquarius
16th	03:47 pm	Pisces
18th	11:25 pm	Aries
21st	03:56 am	Taurus
23rd	06:27 am	Gemini
25th	08:22 am	Cancer
27th	10:44 am	Leo
29th	02:15 pm	Virgo

May 1947

1st	07:24 pm	Libra
4th	02:35 am	Scorpio
6th	12:09 pm	Sagittarius
8th	11:55 pm	Capricorn
11th	12:41 pm	Aquarius
14th	12:20 am	Pisces
16th	08:56 am	Aries
18th	01:51 pm	Taurus
20th	03:51 pm	Gemini
22nd	04:27 pm	Cancer
24th	05:18 pm	Leo
26th	07:50 pm	Virgo
29th	12:54 am	Libra
31st	08:42 am	Scorpio

June 1947

2nd	06:54 pm	Sagittarius
5th	06:51 am	Capricorn
7th	07:38 pm	Aquarius
10th	07:47 am	Pisces
12th	05:34 pm	Aries
14th	11:45 pm	Taurus
17th	02:21 am	Gemini
19th	02:32 am	Cancer
21st	02:06 am	Leo
23rd	03:01 am	Virgo
25th	06:51 am	Libra
27th	02:17 pm	Scorpio
30th	12:46 am	Sagittarius

July 1947

2nd	01:03 pm	Capricorn
5th	01:50 am	Aquarius
7th	02:03 pm	Pisces
10th	12:34 am	Aries
12th	08:12 am	Taurus
14th	12:17 pm	Gemini
16th	01:14 pm	Cancer
18th	12:34 pm	Leo
20th	12:19 pm	Virgo
22nd	02:33 pm	Libra
24th	08:41 pm	Scorpio
27th	06:40 am	Sagittarius
29th	07:01 pm	Capricorn

August 1947

1st	07:50 am	Aquarius
3rd	07:49 pm	Pisces
6th	06:20 am	Aries
8th	02:43 pm	Taurus
10th	08:17 pm	Gemini
12th	10:49 pm	Cancer
14th	11:06 pm	Leo
16th	10:49 pm	Virgo
19th	12:04 am	Libra
21st	04:44 am	Scorpio
23rd	01:34 pm	Sagittarius
26th	01:31 am	Capricorn
28th	02:18 pm	Aquarius
31st	02:03 am	Pisces

September 1947

2nd	12:02 pm	Aries
4th	08:10 pm	Taurus
7th	02:18 am	Gemini
9th	06:12 am	Cancer
11th	08:03 am	Leo
13th	08:51 am	Virgo
15th	10:16 am	Libra
17th	02:10 pm	Scorpio
19th	09:49 pm	Sagittarius
22nd	08:57 am	Capricorn
24th	09:38 pm	Aquarius
27th	09:24 am	Pisces
29th	06:58 pm	Aries

October 1947

2nd	02:15 am	Taurus
4th	07:44 am	Gemini
6th	11:47 am	Cancer
8th	02:41 pm	Leo
10th	04:57 pm	Virgo
12th	07:31 pm	Libra
14th	11:45 pm	Scorpio
17th	06:53 am	Sagittarius
19th	05:14 pm	Capricorn
22nd	05:39 am	Aquarius
24th	05:46 pm	Pisces
27th	03:31 am	Aries
29th	10:16 am	Taurus
31st	02:36 pm	Gemini

November 1947

2nd	05:32 pm	Cancer
4th	08:03 pm	Leo
6th	10:55 pm	Virgo
9th	02:42 am	Libra
11th	08:02 am	Scorpio
13th	03:33 pm	Sagittarius
16th	01:37 am	Capricorn
18th	01:45 pm	Aquarius
21st	02:16 am	Pisces
23rd	12:53 pm	Aries
25th	08:06 pm	Taurus
27th	11:55 pm	Gemini
30th	01:31 am	Cancer

December 1947

2nd	02:30 am	Leo
4th	04:23 am	Virgo
6th	08:14 am	Libra
8th	02:24 pm	Scorpio
10th	10:49 pm	Sagittarius
13th	09:14 am	Capricorn
15th	09:16 pm	Aquarius
18th	09:59 am	Pisces
20th	09:37 pm	Aries
23rd	06:11 am	Taurus
25th	10:47 am	Gemini
27th	12:03 pm	Cancer
29th	11:41 am	Leo
31st	11:47 am	Virgo

January 1948

2nd	02:10 pm	Libra
4th	07:51 pm	Scorpio
7th	04:41 am	Sagittarius
9th	03:41 pm	Capricorn
12th	03:54 am	Aquarius
14th	04:35 pm	Pisces
17th	04:44 am	Aries
19th	02:42 pm	Taurus
21st	09:01 pm	Gemini
23rd	11:23 pm	Cancer
25th	11:00 pm	Leo
27th	09:56 pm	Virgo
29th	10:29 pm	Libra

February 1948

1st	02:27 am	Scorpio
3rd	10:26 am	Sagittarius
5th	09:30 pm	Capricorn
8th	09:59 am	Aquarius
10th	10:37 pm	Pisces
13th	10:37 am	Aries
15th	09:08 pm	Taurus
18th	04:56 am	Gemini
20th	09:09 am	Cancer
22nd	10:07 am	Leo
24th	09:22 am	Virgo
26th	09:05 am	Libra
28th	11:24 am	Scorpio

March 1948

1st	05:41 pm	Sagittarius
4th	03:50 am	Capricorn
6th	04:14 pm	Aquarius
9th	04:53 am	Pisces
11th	04:33 pm	Aries
14th	02:40 am	Taurus
16th	10:45 am	Gemini
18th	04:14 pm	Cancer
20th	06:58 pm	Leo
22nd	07:42 pm	Virgo
24th	08:01 pm	Libra
26th	09:49 pm	Scorpio
29th	02:46 am	Sagittarius
31st	11:34 am	Capricorn

April 1948

2nd	11:18 pm	Aquarius
5th	11:56 am	Pisces
7th	11:28 pm	Aries
10th	08:58 am	Taurus
12th	04:20 pm	Gemini
14th	09:41 pm	Cancer
17th	01:16 am	Leo
19th	03:30 am	Virgo
21st	05:16 am	Libra
23rd	07:49 am	Scorpio
25th	12:31 pm	Sagittarius
27th	08:21 pm	Capricorn
30th	07:16 am	Aquarius

May 1948

2nd	07:44 pm	Pisces
5th	07:28 am	Aries
7th	04:48 pm	Taurus
9th	11:20 pm	Gemini
12th	03:38 am	Cancer
14th	06:39 am	Leo
16th	09:14 am	Virgo
18th	12:07 pm	Libra
20th	03:55 pm	Scorpio
22nd	09:22 pm	Sagittarius
25th	05:08 am	Capricorn
27th	03:31 pm	Aquarius
30th	03:46 am	Pisces

June 1948

1st	03:55 pm	Aries
4th	01:43 am	Taurus
6th	08:06 am	Gemini
8th	11:28 am	Cancer
10th	01:11 pm	Leo
12th	02:48 pm	Virgo
14th	05:33 pm	Libra
16th	10:03 pm	Scorpio
19th	04:28 am	Sagittarius
21st	12:51 pm	Capricorn
23rd	11:15 pm	Aquarius
26th	11:23 am	Pisces
28th	11:56 pm	Aries

July 1948

1st	10:40 am	Taurus
3rd	05:48 pm	Gemini
5th	09:07 pm	Cancer
7th	09:53 pm	Leo
9th	10:03 pm	Virgo
11th	11:31 pm	Libra
14th	03:28 am	Scorpio
16th	10:11 am	Sagittarius
18th	07:13 pm	Capricorn
21st	06:02 am	Aquarius
23rd	06:13 pm	Pisces
26th	06:57 am	Aries
28th	06:34 pm	Taurus
31st	03:01 am	Gemini

August 1948

2nd	07:20 am	Cancer
4th	08:13 am	Leo
6th	07:32 am	Virgo
8th	07:29 am	Libra
10th	09:56 am	Scorpio
12th	03:49 pm	Sagittarius
15th	12:51 am	Capricorn
17th	12:02 pm	Aquarius
20th	12:23 am	Pisces
22nd	01:05 pm	Aries
25th	01:03 am	Taurus
27th	10:40 am	Gemini
29th	04:34 pm	Cancer
31st	06:41 pm	Leo

September 1948

2nd	06:20 pm	Virgo
4th	05:35 pm	Libra
6th	06:34 pm	Scorpio
8th	10:52 pm	Sagittarius
11th	06:56 am	Capricorn
13th	05:58 pm	Aquarius
16th	06:27 am	Pisces
18th	07:02 pm	Aries
21st	06:45 am	Taurus
23rd	04:40 pm	Gemini
25th	11:46 pm	Cancer
28th	03:35 am	Leo
30th	04:40 am	Virgo

October 1948

2nd	04:30 am	Libra
4th	04:58 am	Scorpio
6th	07:55 am	Sagittarius
8th	02:31 pm	Capricorn
11th	12:42 am	Aquarius
13th	01:03 pm	Pisces
16th	01:36 am	Aries
18th	12:54 pm	Taurus
20th	10:15 pm	Gemini
23rd	05:21 am	Cancer
25th	10:10 am	Leo
27th	12:53 pm	Virgo
29th	02:16 pm	Libra
31st	03:31 pm	Scorpio

November 1948

2nd	06:10 pm	Sagittarius
4th	11:39 pm	Capricorn
7th	08:41 am	Aquarius
9th	08:34 pm	Pisces
12th	09:12 am	Aries
14th	08:24 pm	Taurus
17th	05:02 am	Gemini
19th	11:11 am	Cancer
21st	03:32 pm	Leo
23rd	06:48 pm	Virgo
25th	09:33 pm	Libra
28th	12:18 am	Scorpio
30th	03:52 am	Sagittarius

December 1948

2nd	09:16 am	Capricorn
4th	05:32 pm	Aquarius
7th	04:46 am	Pisces
9th	05:30 pm	Aries
12th	05:09 am	Taurus
14th	01:44 pm	Gemini
16th	07:01 pm	Cancer
18th	10:03 pm	Leo
21st	12:19 am	Virgo
23rd	02:59 am	Libra
25th	06:39 am	Scorpio
27th	11:29 am	Sagittarius
29th	05:46 pm	Capricorn

January 1949

1st 02:07 am Aquarius
3rd 12:58 pm Pisces
6th 01:41 am Aries
8th 02:03 pm Taurus
10th 11:31 pm Gemini
13th 04:57 am Cancer
15th 07:08 am Leo
17th 07:52 am Virgo
19th 09:03 am Libra
21st 11:59 am Scorpio
23rd 05:09 pm Sagittarius
26th 12:22 am Capricorn
28th 09:26 am Aquarius
30th 08:26 pm Pisces

February 1949

2nd 09:04 am Aries
4th 09:57 pm Taurus
7th 08:40 am Gemini
9th 03:22 pm Cancer
11th 06:01 pm Leo
13th 06:05 pm Virgo
15th 05:44 pm Libra
17th 06:53 pm Scorpio
19th 10:49 pm Sagittarius
22nd 05:50 am Capricorn
24th 03:26 pm Aquarius
27th 02:54 am Pisces

March 1949

1st 03:36 pm Aries
4th 04:33 am Taurus
6th 04:05 pm Gemini
9th 12:21 am Cancer
11th 04:33 am Leo
13th 05:24 am Virgo
15th 04:40 am Libra
17th 04:25 am Scorpio
19th 06:30 am Sagittarius
21st 12:04 pm Capricorn
23rd 09:10 pm Aquarius
26th 08:50 am Pisces
28th 09:41 pm Aries
31st 10:29 am Taurus

April 1949

2nd 10:03 pm Gemini
5th 07:10 am Cancer
7th 12:59 pm Leo
9th 03:32 pm Virgo
11th 03:48 pm Libra
13th 03:27 pm Scorpio
15th 04:23 pm Sagittarius
17th 08:16 pm Capricorn
20th 03:59 am Aquarius
22nd 03:08 pm Pisces
25th 04:01 am Aries
27th 04:41 pm Taurus
30th 03:48 am Gemini

May 1949

2nd 12:43 pm Cancer
4th 07:11 pm Leo
6th 11:11 pm Virgo
9th 01:07 am Libra
11th 01:54 am Scorpio
13th 02:57 am Sagittarius
15th 05:57 am Capricorn
17th 12:19 pm Aquarius
19th 10:26 pm Pisces
22nd 11:02 am Aries
24th 11:42 pm Taurus
27th 10:27 am Gemini
29th 06:38 pm Cancer

June 1949

1st 12:36 am Leo
3rd 04:53 am Virgo
5th 07:57 am Libra
7th 10:13 am Scorpio
9th 12:24 pm Sagittarius
11th 03:40 pm Capricorn
13th 09:26 pm Aquarius
16th 06:38 am Pisces
18th 06:45 pm Aries
21st 07:30 am Taurus
23rd 06:20 pm Gemini
26th 02:01 am Cancer
28th 07:01 am Leo
30th 10:26 am Virgo

July 1949

2nd 01:22 pm Libra
4th 04:22 pm Scorpio
6th 07:45 pm Sagittarius
9th 12:02 am Capricorn
11th 06:09 am Aquarius
13th 03:01 pm Pisces
16th 02:43 am Aries
18th 03:36 pm Taurus
21st 02:57 am Gemini
23rd 10:52 am Cancer
25th 03:19 pm Leo
27th 05:36 pm Virgo
29th 07:20 pm Libra
31st 09:44 pm Scorpio

August 1949

3rd 01:25 am Sagittarius
5th 06:36 am Capricorn
7th 01:34 pm Aquarius
9th 10:45 pm Pisces
12th 10:20 am Aries
14th 11:18 pm Taurus
17th 11:23 am Gemini
19th 08:15 pm Cancer
22nd 01:08 am Leo
24th 02:55 am Virgo
26th 03:24 am Libra
28th 04:19 am Scorpio
30th 07:00 am Sagittarius

September 1949

1st 12:05 pm Capricorn
3rd 07:37 pm Aquarius
6th 05:26 am Pisces
8th 05:13 pm Aries
11th 06:12 am Taurus
13th 06:47 pm Gemini
16th 04:52 am Cancer
18th 11:05 am Leo
20th 01:34 pm Virgo
22nd 01:41 pm Libra
24th 01:20 pm Scorpio
26th 02:21 pm Sagittarius
28th 06:07 pm Capricorn

October 1949

1st 01:13 am Aquarius
3rd 11:19 am Pisces
5th 11:27 pm Aries
8th 12:26 pm Taurus
11th 01:02 am Gemini
13th 11:51 am Cancer
15th 07:35 pm Leo
17th 11:42 pm Virgo
20th 12:48 am Libra
22nd 12:18 am Scorpio
24th 12:08 am Sagittarius
26th 02:10 am Capricorn
28th 07:50 am Aquarius
30th 05:21 pm Pisces

November 1949

2nd 05:34 am Aries
4th 06:37 pm Taurus
7th 06:55 am Gemini
9th 05:35 pm Cancer
12th 02:00 am Leo
14th 07:42 am Virgo
16th 10:36 am Libra
18th 11:18 am Scorpio
20th 11:15 am Sagittarius
22nd 12:19 pm Capricorn
24th 04:24 pm Aquarius
27th 12:35 am Pisces
29th 12:18 pm Aries

December 1949

2nd 01:22 am Taurus
4th 01:28 pm Gemini
6th 11:31 pm Cancer
9th 07:27 am Leo
11th 01:31 pm Virgo
13th 05:45 pm Libra
15th 08:13 pm Scorpio
17th 09:32 pm Sagittarius
19th 11:00 pm Capricorn
22nd 02:24 am Aquarius
24th 09:20 am Pisces
26th 08:05 pm Aries
29th 08:58 am Taurus
31st 09:13 pm Gemini

January 1950

3rd	06:56 am	Cancer
5th	01:58 pm	Leo
7th	07:06 pm	Virgo
9th	11:08 pm	Libra
12th	02:28 am	Scorpio
14th	05:16 am	Sagittarius
16th	08:06 am	Capricorn
18th	12:07 pm	Aquarius
20th	06:41 pm	Pisces
23rd	04:37 am	Aries
25th	05:08 pm	Taurus
28th	05:43 am	Gemini
30th	03:50 pm	Cancer

February 1950

1st	10:34 pm	Leo
4th	02:37 am	Virgo
6th	05:19 am	Libra
8th	07:50 am	Scorpio
10th	10:51 am	Sagittarius
12th	02:45 pm	Capricorn
14th	07:57 pm	Aquarius
17th	03:11 am	Pisces
19th	01:01 pm	Aries
22nd	01:12 am	Taurus
24th	02:03 pm	Gemini
27th	01:03 am	Cancer

March 1950

1st	08:30 am	Leo
3rd	12:24 pm	Virgo
5th	02:00 pm	Libra
7th	02:55 pm	Scorpio
9th	04:37 pm	Sagittarius
11th	08:07 pm	Capricorn
14th	01:52 am	Aquarius
16th	09:59 am	Pisces
18th	08:21 pm	Aries
21st	08:32 am	Taurus
23rd	09:28 pm	Gemini
26th	09:17 am	Cancer
28th	06:04 pm	Leo
30th	11:01 pm	Virgo

April 1950

2nd	12:40 am	Libra
4th	12:35 am	Scorpio
6th	12:37 am	Sagittarius
8th	02:29 am	Capricorn
10th	07:24 am	Aquarius
12th	03:38 pm	Pisces
15th	02:32 am	Aries
17th	03:00 pm	Taurus
20th	03:54 am	Gemini
22nd	04:02 pm	Cancer
25th	01:57 am	Leo
27th	08:30 am	Virgo
29th	11:25 am	Libra

May 1950

1st	11:37 am	Scorpio
3rd	10:50 am	Sagittarius
5th	11:08 am	Capricorn
7th	02:22 pm	Aquarius
9th	09:34 pm	Pisces
12th	08:18 am	Aries
14th	08:59 pm	Taurus
17th	09:52 am	Gemini
19th	09:50 pm	Cancer
22nd	08:06 am	Leo
24th	03:50 pm	Virgo
26th	08:26 pm	Libra
28th	10:01 pm	Scorpio
30th	09:43 pm	Sagittarius

June 1950

1st	09:27 pm	Capricorn
3rd	11:18 pm	Aquarius
6th	04:57 am	Pisces
8th	02:44 pm	Aries
11th	03:12 am	Taurus
13th	04:05 pm	Gemini
16th	03:45 am	Cancer
18th	01:37 pm	Leo
20th	09:31 pm	Virgo
23rd	03:09 am	Libra
25th	06:19 am	Scorpio
27th	07:26 am	Sagittarius
29th	07:48 am	Capricorn

July 1950

1st	09:19 am	Aquarius
3rd	01:51 pm	Pisces
5th	10:24 pm	Aries
8th	10:13 am	Taurus
10th	11:02 pm	Gemini
13th	10:34 am	Cancer
15th	07:52 pm	Leo
18th	03:05 am	Virgo
20th	08:34 am	Libra
22nd	12:27 pm	Scorpio
24th	02:55 pm	Sagittarius
26th	04:39 pm	Capricorn
28th	06:55 pm	Aquarius
30th	11:19 pm	Pisces

August 1950

2nd	07:03 am	Aries
4th	06:06 pm	Taurus
7th	06:44 am	Gemini
9th	06:27 pm	Cancer
12th	03:36 am	Leo
14th	10:03 am	Virgo
16th	02:31 pm	Libra
18th	05:49 pm	Scorpio
20th	08:36 pm	Sagittarius
22nd	11:23 pm	Capricorn
25th	02:53 am	Aquarius
27th	08:02 am	Pisces
29th	03:44 pm	Aries

September 1950

1st	02:19 am	Taurus
3rd	02:45 pm	Gemini
6th	02:54 am	Cancer
8th	12:34 pm	Leo
10th	06:55 pm	Virgo
12th	10:28 pm	Libra
15th	12:27 am	Scorpio
17th	02:12 am	Sagittarius
19th	04:49 am	Capricorn
21st	08:59 am	Aquarius
23rd	03:09 pm	Pisces
25th	11:32 pm	Aries
28th	10:08 am	Taurus
30th	10:26 pm	Gemini

October 1950

3rd	10:59 am	Cancer
5th	09:40 pm	Leo
8th	04:54 am	Virgo
10th	08:29 am	Libra
12th	09:31 am	Scorpio
14th	09:44 am	Sagittarius
16th	10:55 am	Capricorn
18th	02:27 pm	Aquarius
20th	08:53 pm	Pisces
23rd	05:59 am	Aries
25th	05:03 pm	Taurus
28th	05:22 am	Gemini
30th	06:03 pm	Cancer

November 1950

2nd	05:38 am	Leo
4th	02:21 pm	Virgo
6th	07:10 pm	Libra
8th	08:29 pm	Scorpio
10th	07:51 pm	Sagittarius
12th	07:25 pm	Capricorn
14th	09:14 pm	Aquarius
17th	02:38 am	Pisces
19th	11:39 am	Aries
21st	11:08 pm	Taurus
24th	11:38 am	Gemini
27th	12:13 am	Cancer
29th	12:02 pm	Leo

December 1950

1st	09:53 pm	Virgo
4th	04:29 am	Libra
6th	07:19 am	Scorpio
8th	07:17 am	Sagittarius
10th	06:16 am	Capricorn
12th	06:34 am	Aquarius
14th	10:10 am	Pisces
16th	05:58 pm	Aries
19th	05:10 am	Taurus
21st	05:49 pm	Gemini
24th	06:18 am	Cancer
26th	05:45 pm	Leo
29th	03:41 am	Virgo
31st	11:20 am	Libra

January 1951

2nd	03:58 pm	Scorpio
4th	05:38 pm	Sagittarius
6th	05:32 pm	Capricorn
8th	05:35 pm	Aquarius
10th	07:56 pm	Pisces
13th	02:05 am	Aries
15th	12:10 pm	Taurus
18th	12:36 am	Gemini
20th	01:06 pm	Cancer
23rd	12:12 am	Leo
25th	09:26 am	Virgo
27th	04:46 pm	Libra
29th	10:04 pm	Scorpio

February 1951

1st	01:16 am	Sagittarius
3rd	02:52 am	Capricorn
5th	04:04 am	Aquarius
7th	06:29 am	Pisces
9th	11:43 am	Aries
11th	08:33 pm	Taurus
14th	08:18 am	Gemini
16th	08:51 pm	Cancer
19th	08:01 am	Leo
21st	04:43 pm	Virgo
23rd	11:01 pm	Libra
26th	03:31 am	Scorpio
28th	06:49 am	Sagittarius

March 1951

2nd	09:29 am	Capricorn
4th	12:11 pm	Aquarius
6th	03:45 pm	Pisces
8th	09:16 pm	Aries
11th	05:32 am	Taurus
13th	04:36 pm	Gemini
16th	05:06 am	Cancer
18th	04:44 pm	Leo
21st	01:39 am	Virgo
23rd	07:21 am	Libra
25th	10:36 am	Scorpio
27th	12:40 pm	Sagittarius
29th	02:51 pm	Capricorn
31st	06:02 pm	Aquarius

April 1951

2nd	10:44 pm	Pisces
5th	05:16 am	Aries
7th	01:52 pm	Taurus
10th	12:41 am	Gemini
12th	01:04 pm	Cancer
15th	01:18 am	Leo
17th	11:07 am	Virgo
19th	05:13 pm	Libra
21st	07:55 pm	Scorpio
23rd	08:40 pm	Sagittarius
25th	09:19 pm	Capricorn
27th	11:32 pm	Aquarius
30th	04:13 am	Pisces

May 1951

2nd	11:26 am	Aries
4th	08:46 pm	Taurus
7th	07:51 am	Gemini
9th	08:13 pm	Cancer
12th	08:49 am	Leo
14th	07:44 pm	Virgo
17th	03:05 am	Libra
19th	06:23 am	Scorpio
21st	06:44 am	Sagittarius
23rd	06:07 am	Capricorn
25th	06:41 am	Aquarius
27th	10:05 am	Pisces
29th	04:53 pm	Aries

June 1951

1st	02:33 am	Taurus
3rd	02:03 pm	Gemini
6th	02:31 am	Cancer
8th	03:12 pm	Leo
11th	02:47 am	Virgo
13th	11:31 am	Libra
15th	04:17 pm	Scorpio
17th	05:26 pm	Sagittarius
19th	04:38 pm	Capricorn
21st	04:04 pm	Aquarius
23rd	05:49 pm	Pisces
25th	11:13 pm	Aries
28th	08:17 am	Taurus
30th	07:51 pm	Gemini

July 1951

3rd	08:27 am	Cancer
5th	09:00 pm	Leo
8th	08:36 am	Virgo
10th	06:04 pm	Libra
13th	12:19 am	Scorpio
15th	03:03 am	Sagittarius
17th	03:14 am	Capricorn
19th	02:41 am	Aquarius
21st	03:28 am	Pisces
23rd	07:21 am	Aries
25th	03:07 pm	Taurus
28th	02:08 am	Gemini
30th	02:42 pm	Cancer

August 1951

2nd	03:08 am	Leo
4th	02:18 pm	Virgo
6th	11:34 pm	Libra
9th	06:24 am	Scorpio
11th	10:31 am	Sagittarius
13th	12:18 pm	Capricorn
15th	12:53 pm	Aquarius
17th	01:52 pm	Pisces
19th	04:58 pm	Aries
21st	11:26 pm	Taurus
24th	09:27 am	Gemini
26th	09:44 pm	Cancer
29th	10:10 am	Leo
31st	09:00 pm	Virgo

September 1951

3rd	05:32 am	Libra
5th	11:49 am	Scorpio
7th	04:11 pm	Sagittarius
9th	07:06 pm	Capricorn
11th	09:11 pm	Aquarius
13th	11:21 pm	Pisces
16th	02:47 am	Aries
18th	08:41 am	Taurus
20th	05:47 pm	Gemini
23rd	05:34 am	Cancer
25th	06:08 pm	Leo
28th	05:05 am	Virgo
30th	01:08 pm	Libra

October 1951

2nd	06:23 pm	Scorpio
4th	09:48 pm	Sagittarius
7th	12:30 am	Capricorn
9th	03:19 am	Aquarius
11th	06:46 am	Pisces
13th	11:19 am	Aries
15th	05:37 pm	Taurus
18th	02:22 am	Gemini
20th	01:42 pm	Cancer
23rd	02:25 am	Leo
25th	02:01 pm	Virgo
27th	10:25 pm	Libra
30th	03:09 am	Scorpio

November 1951

1st	05:20 am	Sagittarius
3rd	06:40 am	Capricorn
5th	08:43 am	Aquarius
7th	12:23 pm	Pisces
9th	05:52 pm	Aries
12th	01:07 am	Taurus
14th	10:15 am	Gemini
16th	09:27 pm	Cancer
19th	10:12 am	Leo
21st	10:35 pm	Virgo
24th	08:09 am	Libra
26th	01:32 pm	Scorpio
28th	03:20 pm	Sagittarius
30th	03:22 pm	Capricorn

December 1951

2nd	03:45 pm	Aquarius
4th	06:08 pm	Pisces
6th	11:18 pm	Aries
9th	07:04 am	Taurus
11th	04:54 pm	Gemini
14th	04:22 am	Cancer
16th	05:05 pm	Leo
19th	05:52 am	Virgo
21st	04:41 pm	Libra
23rd	11:38 pm	Scorpio
26th	02:27 am	Sagittarius
28th	02:24 am	Capricorn
30th	01:36 am	Aquarius

January 1952

1st	02:10 am	Pisces
3rd	05:42 am	Aries
5th	12:43 pm	Taurus
7th	10:42 pm	Gemini
10th	10:34 am	Cancer
12th	11:19 pm	Leo
15th	12:00 pm	Virgo
17th	11:19 pm	Libra
20th	07:44 am	Scorpio
22nd	12:22 pm	Sagittarius
24th	01:39 pm	Capricorn
26th	01:06 pm	Aquarius
28th	12:45 pm	Pisces
30th	02:32 pm	Aries

February 1952

1st	07:51 pm	Taurus
4th	04:55 am	Gemini
6th	04:44 pm	Cancer
9th	05:36 am	Leo
11th	06:02 pm	Virgo
14th	05:00 am	Libra
16th	01:45 pm	Scorpio
18th	07:42 pm	Sagittarius
20th	10:49 pm	Capricorn
22nd	11:48 pm	Aquarius
25th	12:01 am	Pisces
27th	01:11 am	Aries
29th	05:02 am	Taurus

March 1952

2nd	12:36 pm	Gemini
4th	11:40 pm	Cancer
7th	12:30 pm	Leo
10th	12:51 am	Virgo
12th	11:16 am	Libra
14th	07:20 pm	Scorpio
17th	01:15 am	Sagittarius
19th	05:19 am	Capricorn
21st	07:55 am	Aquarius
23rd	09:39 am	Pisces
25th	11:34 am	Aries
27th	03:05 pm	Taurus
29th	09:36 pm	Gemini

April 1952

1st	07:39 am	Cancer
3rd	08:10 pm	Leo
6th	08:40 am	Virgo
8th	06:56 pm	Libra
11th	02:13 am	Scorpio
13th	07:08 am	Sagittarius
15th	10:41 am	Capricorn
17th	01:43 pm	Aquarius
19th	04:40 pm	Pisces
21st	07:56 pm	Aries
24th	12:15 am	Taurus
26th	06:40 am	Gemini
28th	04:06 pm	Cancer

May 1952

1st	04:12 am	Leo
3rd	04:57 pm	Virgo
6th	03:39 am	Libra
8th	10:49 am	Scorpio
10th	02:50 pm	Sagittarius
12th	05:09 pm	Capricorn
14th	07:14 pm	Aquarius
16th	10:05 pm	Pisces
19th	02:07 am	Aries
21st	07:29 am	Taurus
23rd	02:37 pm	Gemini
26th	12:06 am	Cancer
28th	11:59 am	Leo
31st	12:57 am	Virgo

June 1952

2nd	12:26 pm	Libra
4th	08:19 pm	Scorpio
7th	12:21 am	Sagittarius
9th	01:46 am	Capricorn
11th	02:26 am	Aquarius
13th	04:00 am	Pisces
15th	07:29 am	Aries
17th	01:11 pm	Taurus
19th	09:03 pm	Gemini
22nd	07:04 am	Cancer
24th	07:02 pm	Leo
27th	08:06 am	Virgo
29th	08:18 pm	Libra

July 1952

2nd	05:25 am	Scorpio
4th	10:27 am	Sagittarius
6th	12:02 pm	Capricorn
8th	11:54 am	Aquarius
10th	11:59 am	Pisces
12th	01:56 pm	Aries
14th	06:45 pm	Taurus
17th	02:37 am	Gemini
19th	01:05 pm	Cancer
22nd	01:20 am	Leo
24th	02:24 pm	Virgo
27th	02:54 am	Libra
29th	01:04 pm	Scorpio
31st	07:37 pm	Sagittarius

August 1952

2nd	10:27 pm	Capricorn
4th	10:41 pm	Aquarius
6th	10:05 pm	Pisces
8th	10:33 pm	Aries
11th	01:46 am	Taurus
13th	08:36 am	Gemini
15th	06:52 pm	Cancer
18th	07:19 am	Leo
20th	08:22 pm	Virgo
23rd	08:42 am	Libra
25th	07:10 pm	Scorpio
28th	02:53 am	Sagittarius
30th	07:24 am	Capricorn

September 1952

1st	09:03 am	Aquarius
3rd	09:00 am	Pisces
5th	08:57 am	Aries
7th	10:48 am	Taurus
9th	04:06 pm	Gemini
12th	01:24 am	Cancer
14th	01:38 pm	Leo
17th	02:41 am	Virgo
19th	02:41 pm	Libra
22nd	12:43 am	Scorpio
24th	08:33 am	Sagittarius
26th	02:06 pm	Capricorn
28th	05:24 pm	Aquarius
30th	06:52 pm	Pisces

October 1952

2nd	07:34 pm	Aries
4th	09:05 pm	Taurus
7th	01:15 am	Gemini
9th	09:16 am	Cancer
11th	08:50 pm	Leo
14th	09:51 am	Virgo
16th	09:44 pm	Libra
19th	07:10 am	Scorpio
21st	02:12 pm	Sagittarius
23rd	07:28 pm	Capricorn
25th	11:28 pm	Aquarius
28th	02:23 am	Pisces
30th	04:34 am	Aries

November 1952

1st	06:58 am	Taurus
3rd	11:02 am	Gemini
5th	06:12 pm	Cancer
8th	04:56 am	Leo
10th	05:47 pm	Virgo
13th	05:57 am	Libra
15th	03:18 pm	Scorpio
17th	09:33 pm	Sagittarius
20th	01:40 am	Capricorn
22nd	04:52 am	Aquarius
24th	07:55 am	Pisces
26th	11:09 am	Aries
28th	02:54 pm	Taurus
30th	07:53 pm	Gemini

December 1952

3rd	03:08 am	Cancer
5th	01:23 pm	Leo
8th	01:57 am	Virgo
10th	02:35 pm	Libra
13th	12:39 am	Scorpio
15th	07:00 am	Sagittarius
17th	10:17 am	Capricorn
19th	12:02 pm	Aquarius
21st	01:45 pm	Pisces
23rd	04:30 pm	Aries
25th	08:46 pm	Taurus
28th	02:48 am	Gemini
30th	10:53 am	Cancer

January 1953

1st	09:17 pm	Leo
4th	09:41 am	Virgo
6th	10:36 pm	Libra
9th	09:44 am	Scorpio
11th	05:14 pm	Sagittarius
13th	08:55 pm	Capricorn
15th	09:57 pm	Aquarius
17th	10:07 pm	Pisces
19th	11:08 pm	Aries
22nd	02:20 am	Taurus
24th	08:21 am	Gemini
26th	05:07 pm	Cancer
29th	04:06 am	Leo
31st	04:35 pm	Virgo

February 1953

3rd	05:31 am	Libra
5th	05:21 pm	Scorpio
8th	02:20 am	Sagittarius
10th	07:32 am	Capricorn
12th	09:17 am	Aquarius
14th	08:58 am	Pisces
16th	08:30 am	Aries
18th	09:50 am	Taurus
20th	02:27 pm	Gemini
22nd	10:47 pm	Cancer
25th	10:05 am	Leo
27th	10:51 pm	Virgo

March 1953

2nd	11:41 am	Libra
4th	11:31 pm	Scorpio
7th	09:20 am	Sagittarius
9th	04:10 pm	Capricorn
11th	07:37 pm	Aquarius
13th	08:17 pm	Pisces
15th	07:39 pm	Aries
17th	07:44 pm	Taurus
19th	10:35 pm	Gemini
22nd	05:29 am	Cancer
24th	04:14 pm	Leo
27th	05:04 am	Virgo
29th	05:51 pm	Libra

April 1953

1st	05:19 am	Scorpio
3rd	02:58 pm	Sagittarius
5th	10:29 pm	Capricorn
8th	03:27 am	Aquarius
10th	05:49 am	Pisces
12th	06:19 am	Aries
14th	06:31 am	Taurus
16th	08:27 am	Gemini
18th	01:53 pm	Cancer
20th	11:27 pm	Leo
23rd	11:53 am	Virgo
26th	12:40 am	Libra
28th	11:52 am	Scorpio
30th	08:52 pm	Sagittarius

May 1953

3rd	03:55 am	Capricorn
5th	09:12 am	Aquarius
7th	12:46 pm	Pisces
9th	02:49 pm	Aries
11th	04:12 pm	Taurus
13th	06:27 pm	Gemini
15th	11:16 pm	Cancer
18th	07:47 am	Leo
20th	07:31 pm	Virgo
23rd	08:16 am	Libra
25th	07:32 pm	Scorpio
28th	04:08 am	Sagittarius
30th	10:17 am	Capricorn

June 1953

1st	02:45 pm	Aquarius
3rd	06:12 pm	Pisces
5th	09:01 pm	Aries
7th	11:41 pm	Taurus
10th	03:03 am	Gemini
12th	08:17 am	Cancer
14th	04:27 pm	Leo
17th	03:37 am	Virgo
19th	04:16 pm	Libra
22nd	03:57 am	Scorpio
24th	12:48 pm	Sagittarius
26th	06:29 pm	Capricorn
28th	09:51 pm	Aquarius

July 1953

1st	12:08 am	Pisces
3rd	02:23 am	Aries
5th	05:23 am	Taurus
7th	09:42 am	Gemini
9th	03:54 pm	Cancer
12th	12:28 am	Leo
14th	11:28 am	Virgo
17th	12:04 am	Libra
19th	12:17 pm	Scorpio
21st	09:59 pm	Sagittarius
24th	04:07 am	Capricorn
26th	07:03 am	Aquarius
28th	08:07 am	Pisces
30th	08:56 am	Aries

August 1953

1st	10:57 am	Taurus
3rd	03:10 pm	Gemini
5th	09:59 pm	Cancer
8th	07:16 am	Leo
10th	06:33 pm	Virgo
13th	07:08 am	Libra
15th	07:43 pm	Scorpio
18th	06:30 am	Sagittarius
20th	01:53 pm	Capricorn
22nd	05:29 pm	Aquarius
24th	06:12 pm	Pisces
26th	05:46 pm	Aries
28th	06:10 pm	Taurus
30th	09:07 pm	Gemini

September 1953

2nd	03:30 am	Cancer
4th	01:05 pm	Leo
7th	12:47 am	Virgo
9th	01:27 pm	Libra
12th	02:05 am	Scorpio
14th	01:32 pm	Sagittarius
16th	10:21 pm	Capricorn
19th	03:30 am	Aquarius
21st	05:06 am	Pisces
23rd	04:30 am	Aries
25th	03:45 am	Taurus
27th	05:01 am	Gemini
29th	09:56 am	Cancer

October 1953

1st	06:53 pm	Leo
4th	06:40 am	Virgo
6th	07:28 pm	Libra
9th	07:56 am	Scorpio
11th	07:19 pm	Sagittarius
14th	04:51 am	Capricorn
16th	11:34 am	Aquarius
18th	02:55 pm	Pisces
20th	03:27 pm	Aries
22nd	02:47 pm	Taurus
24th	03:04 pm	Gemini
26th	06:24 pm	Cancer
29th	01:55 am	Leo
31st	01:04 pm	Virgo

November 1953

3rd	01:51 am	Libra
5th	02:12 pm	Scorpio
8th	01:06 am	Sagittarius
10th	10:18 am	Capricorn
12th	05:31 pm	Aquarius
14th	10:17 pm	Pisces
17th	12:35 am	Aries
19th	01:15 am	Taurus
21st	01:54 am	Gemini
23rd	04:31 am	Cancer
25th	10:40 am	Leo
27th	08:41 pm	Virgo
30th	09:06 am	Libra

December 1953

2nd	09:30 pm	Scorpio
5th	08:09 am	Sagittarius
7th	04:33 pm	Capricorn
9th	10:59 pm	Aquarius
12th	03:46 am	Pisces
14th	07:06 am	Aries
16th	09:22 am	Taurus
18th	11:27 am	Gemini
20th	02:40 pm	Cancer
22nd	08:23 pm	Leo
25th	05:24 am	Virgo
27th	05:11 pm	Libra
30th	05:43 am	Scorpio

January 1954

1st	04:39 pm	Sagittarius
4th	12:46 am	Capricorn
6th	06:09 am	Aquarius
8th	09:43 am	Pisces
10th	12:27 pm	Aries
12th	03:10 pm	Taurus
14th	06:29 pm	Gemini
16th	11:01 pm	Cancer
19th	05:24 am	Leo
21st	02:14 pm	Virgo
24th	01:30 am	Libra
26th	02:03 pm	Scorpio
29th	01:42 am	Sagittarius
31st	10:27 am	Capricorn

February 1954

2nd	03:38 pm	Aquarius
4th	06:03 pm	Pisces
6th	07:14 pm	Aries
8th	08:47 pm	Taurus
10th	11:54 pm	Gemini
13th	05:10 am	Cancer
15th	12:35 pm	Leo
17th	10:00 pm	Virgo
20th	09:14 am	Libra
22nd	09:43 pm	Scorpio
25th	10:00 am	Sagittarius
27th	07:58 pm	Capricorn

March 1954

2nd	02:07 am	Aquarius
4th	04:32 am	Pisces
6th	04:40 am	Aries
8th	04:32 am	Taurus
10th	06:06 am	Gemini
12th	10:37 am	Cancer
14th	06:17 pm	Leo
17th	04:21 am	Virgo
19th	03:57 pm	Libra
22nd	04:26 am	Scorpio
24th	04:56 pm	Sagittarius
27th	03:55 am	Capricorn
29th	11:37 am	Aquarius
31st	03:16 pm	Pisces

April 1954

2nd	03:40 pm	Aries
4th	02:43 pm	Taurus
6th	02:40 pm	Gemini
8th	05:29 pm	Cancer
11th	12:05 am	Leo
13th	10:03 am	Virgo
15th	09:58 pm	Libra
18th	10:32 am	Scorpio
20th	10:55 pm	Sagittarius
23rd	10:11 am	Capricorn
25th	07:02 pm	Aquarius
28th	12:21 am	Pisces
30th	02:09 am	Aries

May 1954

2nd	01:42 am	Taurus
4th	01:06 am	Gemini
6th	02:30 am	Cancer
8th	07:29 am	Leo
10th	04:23 pm	Virgo
13th	04:03 am	Libra
15th	04:42 pm	Scorpio
18th	04:53 am	Sagittarius
20th	03:49 pm	Capricorn
23rd	12:48 am	Aquarius
25th	07:08 am	Pisces
27th	10:32 am	Aries
29th	11:33 am	Taurus
31st	11:41 am	Gemini

June 1954

2nd	12:46 pm	Cancer
4th	04:34 pm	Leo
7th	12:06 am	Virgo
9th	10:59 am	Libra
11th	11:30 pm	Scorpio
14th	11:37 am	Sagittarius
16th	10:05 pm	Capricorn
19th	06:26 am	Aquarius
21st	12:37 pm	Pisces
23rd	04:44 pm	Aries
25th	07:09 pm	Taurus
27th	08:41 pm	Gemini
29th	10:35 pm	Cancer

July 1954

2nd	02:16 am	Leo
4th	08:56 am	Virgo
6th	06:53 pm	Libra
9th	07:04 am	Scorpio
11th	07:19 pm	Sagittarius
14th	05:40 am	Capricorn
16th	01:19 pm	Aquarius
18th	06:33 pm	Pisces
20th	10:07 pm	Aries
23rd	12:52 am	Taurus
25th	03:30 am	Gemini
27th	06:41 am	Cancer
29th	11:10 am	Leo
31st	05:49 pm	Virgo

August 1954

3rd	03:14 am	Libra
5th	03:03 pm	Scorpio
8th	03:32 am	Sagittarius
10th	02:20 pm	Capricorn
12th	09:54 pm	Aquarius
15th	02:17 am	Pisces
17th	04:38 am	Aries
19th	06:26 am	Taurus
21st	08:56 am	Gemini
23rd	12:50 pm	Cancer
25th	06:22 pm	Leo
28th	01:44 am	Virgo
30th	11:12 am	Libra

September 1954

1st	10:48 pm	Scorpio
4th	11:32 am	Sagittarius
6th	11:10 pm	Capricorn
9th	07:31 am	Aquarius
11th	11:55 am	Pisces
13th	01:22 pm	Aries
15th	01:44 pm	Taurus
17th	02:55 pm	Gemini
19th	06:13 pm	Cancer
22nd	12:04 am	Leo
24th	08:11 am	Virgo
26th	06:11 pm	Libra
29th	05:52 am	Scorpio

October 1954

1st	06:41 pm	Sagittarius
4th	07:04 am	Capricorn
6th	04:45 pm	Aquarius
8th	10:17 pm	Pisces
10th	11:58 pm	Aries
12th	11:32 pm	Taurus
14th	11:10 pm	Gemini
17th	12:50 am	Cancer
19th	05:41 am	Leo
21st	01:44 pm	Virgo
24th	12:12 am	Libra
26th	12:11 pm	Scorpio
29th	12:59 am	Sagittarius
31st	01:36 pm	Capricorn

November 1954

3rd	12:22 am	Aquarius
5th	07:34 am	Pisces
7th	10:42 am	Aries
9th	10:48 am	Taurus
11th	09:50 am	Gemini
13th	09:59 am	Cancer
15th	01:03 pm	Leo
17th	07:52 pm	Virgo
20th	06:02 am	Libra
22nd	06:13 pm	Scorpio
25th	07:01 am	Sagittarius
27th	07:24 pm	Capricorn
30th	06:19 am	Aquarius

December 1954

2nd	02:38 pm	Pisces
4th	07:35 pm	Aries
6th	09:23 pm	Taurus
8th	09:16 pm	Gemini
10th	09:06 pm	Cancer
12th	10:48 pm	Leo
15th	03:54 am	Virgo
17th	12:51 pm	Libra
20th	12:43 am	Scorpio
22nd	01:35 pm	Sagittarius
25th	01:40 am	Capricorn
27th	12:00 pm	Aquarius
29th	08:09 pm	Pisces

January 1955

1st	01:56 am	Aries
3rd	05:24 am	Taurus
5th	07:04 am	Gemini
7th	08:00 am	Cancer
9th	09:41 am	Leo
11th	01:43 pm	Virgo
13th	09:15 pm	Libra
16th	08:15 am	Scorpio
18th	09:01 pm	Sagittarius
21st	09:09 am	Capricorn
23rd	06:58 pm	Aquarius
26th	02:11 am	Pisces
28th	07:19 am	Aries
30th	11:06 am	Taurus

February 1955

1st	02:02 pm	Gemini
3rd	04:36 pm	Cancer
5th	07:28 pm	Leo
7th	11:43 pm	Virgo
10th	06:33 am	Libra
12th	04:38 pm	Scorpio
15th	05:07 am	Sagittarius
17th	05:34 pm	Capricorn
20th	03:33 am	Aquarius
22nd	10:09 am	Pisces
24th	02:06 pm	Aries
26th	04:46 pm	Taurus
28th	07:24 pm	Gemini

March 1955

2nd	10:40 pm	Cancer
5th	02:48 am	Leo
7th	08:09 am	Virgo
9th	03:20 pm	Libra
12th	01:04 am	Scorpio
14th	01:13 pm	Sagittarius
17th	02:01 am	Capricorn
19th	12:47 pm	Aquarius
21st	07:45 pm	Pisces
23rd	11:09 pm	Aries
26th	12:31 am	Taurus
28th	01:42 am	Gemini
30th	04:05 am	Cancer

April 1955

1st	08:20 am	Leo
3rd	02:31 pm	Virgo
5th	10:34 pm	Libra
8th	08:38 am	Scorpio
10th	08:41 pm	Sagittarius
13th	09:40 am	Capricorn
15th	09:20 pm	Aquarius
18th	05:28 am	Pisces
20th	09:29 am	Aries
22nd	10:29 am	Taurus
24th	10:24 am	Gemini
26th	11:09 am	Cancer
28th	02:08 pm	Leo
30th	07:58 pm	Virgo

May 1955

3rd	04:26 am	Libra
5th	03:04 pm	Scorpio
8th	03:19 am	Sagittarius
10th	04:19 pm	Capricorn
13th	04:29 am	Aquarius
15th	01:53 pm	Pisces
17th	07:21 pm	Aries
19th	09:12 pm	Taurus
21st	08:56 pm	Gemini
23rd	08:33 pm	Cancer
25th	09:52 pm	Leo
28th	02:16 am	Virgo
30th	10:08 am	Libra

June 1955

1st	08:54 pm	Scorpio
4th	09:24 am	Sagittarius
6th	10:21 pm	Capricorn
9th	10:30 am	Aquarius
11th	08:32 pm	Pisces
14th	03:24 am	Aries
16th	06:50 am	Taurus
18th	07:36 am	Gemini
20th	07:15 am	Cancer
22nd	07:36 am	Leo
24th	10:26 am	Virgo
26th	04:55 pm	Libra
29th	03:04 am	Scorpio

July 1955

1st	03:34 pm	Sagittarius
4th	04:29 am	Capricorn
6th	04:18 pm	Aquarius
9th	02:09 am	Pisces
11th	09:33 am	Aries
13th	02:20 pm	Taurus
15th	04:43 pm	Gemini
17th	05:30 pm	Cancer
19th	06:03 pm	Leo
21st	08:06 pm	Virgo
24th	01:16 am	Libra
26th	10:19 am	Scorpio
28th	10:24 pm	Sagittarius
31st	11:18 am	Capricorn

August 1955

2nd	10:52 pm	Aquarius
5th	08:04 am	Pisces
7th	03:00 pm	Aries
9th	08:03 pm	Taurus
11th	11:33 pm	Gemini
14th	01:50 am	Cancer
16th	03:34 am	Leo
18th	05:57 am	Virgo
20th	10:34 am	Libra
22nd	06:37 pm	Scorpio
25th	06:03 am	Sagittarius
27th	06:57 pm	Capricorn
30th	06:35 am	Aquarius

September 1955

1st	03:23 pm	Pisces
3rd	09:24 pm	Aries
6th	01:36 am	Taurus
8th	04:58 am	Gemini
10th	08:01 am	Cancer
12th	11:02 am	Leo
14th	02:33 pm	Virgo
16th	07:35 pm	Libra
19th	03:18 am	Scorpio
21st	02:11 pm	Sagittarius
24th	03:01 am	Capricorn
26th	03:07 pm	Aquarius
29th	12:12 am	Pisces

October 1955

1st	05:46 am	Aries
3rd	08:52 am	Taurus
5th	10:59 am	Gemini
7th	01:23 pm	Cancer
9th	04:41 pm	Leo
11th	09:11 pm	Virgo
14th	03:13 am	Libra
16th	11:23 am	Scorpio
18th	10:07 pm	Sagittarius
21st	10:52 am	Capricorn
23rd	11:33 pm	Aquarius
26th	09:37 am	Pisces
28th	03:46 pm	Aries
30th	06:30 pm	Taurus

November 1955

1st	07:23 pm	Gemini
3rd	08:11 pm	Cancer
5th	10:20 pm	Leo
8th	02:36 am	Virgo
10th	09:15 am	Libra
12th	06:12 pm	Scorpio
15th	05:17 am	Sagittarius
17th	05:59 pm	Capricorn
20th	06:58 am	Aquarius
22nd	06:10 pm	Pisces
25th	01:47 am	Aries
27th	05:27 am	Taurus
29th	06:11 am	Gemini

December 1955

1st	05:46 am	Cancer
3rd	06:07 am	Leo
5th	08:50 am	Virgo
7th	02:48 pm	Libra
9th	11:59 pm	Scorpio
12th	11:34 am	Sagittarius
15th	12:23 am	Capricorn
17th	01:19 pm	Aquarius
20th	01:02 am	Pisces
22nd	10:05 am	Aries
24th	03:33 pm	Taurus
26th	05:33 pm	Gemini
28th	05:17 pm	Cancer
30th	04:36 pm	Leo

January 1956

1st	05:31 pm	Virgo
3rd	09:44 pm	Libra
6th	06:00 am	Scorpio
8th	05:33 pm	Sagittarius
11th	06:34 am	Capricorn
13th	07:19 pm	Aquarius
16th	06:47 am	Pisces
18th	04:17 pm	Aries
20th	11:11 pm	Taurus
23rd	03:06 am	Gemini
25th	04:20 am	Cancer
27th	04:06 am	Leo
29th	04:17 am	Virgo
31st	06:56 am	Libra

February 1956

2nd	01:33 pm	Scorpio
5th	12:13 am	Sagittarius
7th	01:08 pm	Capricorn
10th	01:52 am	Aquarius
12th	12:52 pm	Pisces
14th	09:48 pm	Aries
17th	04:48 am	Taurus
19th	09:50 am	Gemini
21st	12:50 pm	Cancer
23rd	02:10 pm	Leo
25th	03:05 pm	Virgo
27th	05:20 pm	Libra
29th	10:45 pm	Scorpio

March 1956

3rd	08:09 am	Sagittarius
5th	08:32 pm	Capricorn
8th	09:19 am	Aquarius
10th	08:11 pm	Pisces
13th	04:26 am	Aries
15th	10:32 am	Taurus
17th	03:12 pm	Gemini
19th	06:47 pm	Cancer
21st	09:31 pm	Leo
23rd	11:53 pm	Virgo
26th	03:00 am	Libra
28th	08:18 am	Scorpio
30th	04:56 pm	Sagittarius

April 1956

2nd	04:37 am	Capricorn
4th	05:24 pm	Aquarius
7th	04:37 am	Pisces
9th	12:46 pm	Aries
11th	06:03 pm	Taurus
13th	09:30 pm	Gemini
16th	12:15 am	Cancer
18th	03:00 am	Leo
20th	06:17 am	Virgo
22nd	10:36 am	Libra
24th	04:44 pm	Scorpio
27th	01:25 am	Sagittarius
29th	12:44 pm	Capricorn

May 1956

2nd	01:27 am	Aquarius
4th	01:15 pm	Pisces
6th	10:05 pm	Aries
9th	03:24 am	Taurus
11th	06:00 am	Gemini
13th	07:21 am	Cancer
15th	08:52 am	Leo
17th	11:40 am	Virgo
19th	04:25 pm	Libra
21st	11:26 pm	Scorpio
24th	08:46 am	Sagittarius
26th	08:11 pm	Capricorn
29th	08:52 am	Aquarius
31st	09:09 pm	Pisces

June 1956

3rd	07:05 am	Aries
5th	01:22 pm	Taurus
7th	04:09 pm	Gemini
9th	04:42 pm	Cancer
11th	04:45 pm	Leo
13th	06:03 pm	Virgo
15th	09:58 pm	Libra
18th	05:03 am	Scorpio
20th	02:55 pm	Sagittarius
23rd	02:43 am	Capricorn
25th	03:26 pm	Aquarius
28th	03:54 am	Pisces
30th	02:43 pm	Aries

July 1956

2nd	10:26 pm	Taurus
5th	02:26 am	Gemini
7th	03:20 am	Cancer
9th	02:42 am	Leo
11th	02:34 am	Virgo
13th	04:54 am	Libra
15th	10:56 am	Scorpio
17th	08:38 pm	Sagittarius
20th	08:41 am	Capricorn
22nd	09:28 pm	Aquarius
25th	09:50 am	Pisces
27th	08:54 pm	Aries
30th	05:40 am	Taurus

August 1956

1st	11:16 am	Gemini
3rd	01:32 pm	Cancer
5th	01:27 pm	Leo
7th	12:50 pm	Virgo
9th	01:50 pm	Libra
11th	06:20 pm	Scorpio
14th	03:00 am	Sagittarius
16th	02:47 pm	Capricorn
19th	03:38 am	Aquarius
21st	03:47 pm	Pisces
24th	02:30 am	Aries
26th	11:23 am	Taurus
28th	05:59 pm	Gemini
30th	09:51 pm	Cancer

September 1956

1st	11:14 pm	Leo
3rd	11:20 pm	Virgo
6th	12:04 am	Libra
8th	03:26 am	Scorpio
10th	10:46 am	Sagittarius
12th	09:46 pm	Capricorn
15th	10:28 am	Aquarius
17th	10:34 pm	Pisces
20th	08:47 am	Aries
22nd	05:01 pm	Taurus
24th	11:25 pm	Gemini
27th	04:00 am	Cancer
29th	06:49 am	Leo

October 1956

1st	08:24 am	Virgo
3rd	10:01 am	Libra
5th	01:19 pm	Scorpio
7th	07:46 pm	Sagittarius
10th	05:48 am	Capricorn
12th	06:09 pm	Aquarius
15th	06:25 am	Pisces
17th	04:35 pm	Aries
20th	12:07 am	Taurus
22nd	05:29 am	Gemini
24th	09:23 am	Cancer
26th	12:27 pm	Leo
28th	03:09 pm	Virgo
30th	06:10 pm	Libra

November 1956

1st	10:24 pm	Scorpio
4th	04:56 am	Sagittarius
6th	02:24 pm	Capricorn
9th	02:19 am	Aquarius
11th	02:51 pm	Pisces
14th	01:36 am	Aries
16th	09:12 am	Taurus
18th	01:45 pm	Gemini
20th	04:17 pm	Cancer
22nd	06:10 pm	Leo
24th	08:32 pm	Virgo
27th	12:11 am	Libra
29th	05:34 am	Scorpio

December 1956

1st	12:59 pm	Sagittarius
3rd	10:36 pm	Capricorn
6th	10:16 am	Aquarius
8th	10:57 pm	Pisces
11th	10:37 am	Aries
13th	07:15 pm	Taurus
16th	12:06 am	Gemini
18th	01:52 am	Cancer
20th	02:11 am	Leo
22nd	02:56 am	Virgo
24th	05:39 am	Libra
26th	11:09 am	Scorpio
28th	07:20 pm	Sagittarius
31st	05:37 am	Capricorn

January 1957

2nd	05:24 pm	Aquarius
5th	06:04 am	Pisces
7th	06:23 pm	Aries
10th	04:27 am	Taurus
12th	10:44 am	Gemini
14th	01:06 pm	Cancer
16th	12:50 pm	Leo
18th	12:03 pm	Virgo
20th	12:55 pm	Libra
22nd	05:02 pm	Scorpio
25th	12:52 am	Sagittarius
27th	11:32 am	Capricorn
29th	11:42 pm	Aquarius

February 1957

1st	12:20 pm	Pisces
4th	12:42 am	Aries
6th	11:37 am	Taurus
8th	07:34 pm	Gemini
10th	11:39 pm	Cancer
13th	12:19 am	Leo
14th	11:17 pm	Virgo
16th	10:50 pm	Libra
19th	01:06 am	Scorpio
21st	07:23 am	Sagittarius
23rd	05:27 pm	Capricorn
26th	05:42 am	Aquarius
28th	06:25 pm	Pisces

March 1957

3rd	06:31 am	Aries
5th	05:20 pm	Taurus
8th	02:03 am	Gemini
10th	07:45 am	Cancer
12th	10:12 am	Leo
14th	10:20 am	Virgo
16th	09:59 am	Libra
18th	11:15 am	Scorpio
20th	03:54 pm	Sagittarius
23rd	12:34 am	Capricorn
25th	12:17 pm	Aquarius
28th	01:00 am	Pisces
30th	12:55 pm	Aries

April 1957

1st	11:11 pm	Taurus
4th	07:30 am	Gemini
6th	01:37 pm	Cancer
8th	05:24 pm	Leo
10th	07:13 pm	Virgo
12th	08:08 pm	Libra
14th	09:45 pm	Scorpio
17th	01:43 am	Sagittarius
19th	09:08 am	Capricorn
21st	07:53 pm	Aquarius
24th	08:23 am	Pisces
26th	08:22 pm	Aries
29th	06:18 am	Taurus

May 1957

1st	01:47 pm	Gemini
3rd	07:08 pm	Cancer
5th	10:54 pm	Leo
8th	01:37 am	Virgo
10th	03:57 am	Libra
12th	06:48 am	Scorpio
14th	11:13 am	Sagittarius
16th	06:13 pm	Capricorn
19th	04:12 am	Aquarius
21st	04:20 pm	Pisces
24th	04:34 am	Aries
26th	02:43 pm	Taurus
28th	09:47 pm	Gemini
31st	02:06 am	Cancer

June 1957

2nd	04:45 am	Leo
4th	06:59 am	Virgo
6th	09:46 am	Libra
8th	01:41 pm	Scorpio
10th	07:09 pm	Sagittarius
13th	02:36 am	Capricorn
15th	12:23 pm	Aquarius
18th	12:15 am	Pisces
20th	12:46 pm	Aries
22nd	11:38 pm	Taurus
25th	07:07 am	Gemini
27th	11:01 am	Cancer
29th	12:31 pm	Leo

July 1957

1st	01:23 pm	Virgo
3rd	03:16 pm	Libra
5th	07:10 pm	Scorpio
8th	01:20 am	Sagittarius
10th	09:35 am	Capricorn
12th	07:43 pm	Aquarius
15th	07:32 am	Pisces
17th	08:14 pm	Aries
20th	07:58 am	Taurus
22nd	04:34 pm	Gemini
24th	09:05 pm	Cancer
26th	10:16 pm	Leo
28th	09:59 pm	Virgo
30th	10:20 pm	Libra

August 1957

2nd	01:01 am	Scorpio
4th	06:47 am	Sagittarius
6th	03:23 pm	Capricorn
9th	02:02 am	Aquarius
11th	02:02 pm	Pisces
14th	02:46 am	Aries
16th	03:00 pm	Taurus
19th	12:51 am	Gemini
21st	06:48 am	Cancer
23rd	08:51 am	Leo
25th	08:26 am	Virgo
27th	07:41 am	Libra
29th	08:45 am	Scorpio
31st	01:07 pm	Sagittarius

September 1957

2nd	09:05 pm	Capricorn
5th	07:50 am	Aquarius
7th	08:04 pm	Pisces
10th	08:45 am	Aries
12th	08:57 pm	Taurus
15th	07:26 am	Gemini
17th	02:50 pm	Cancer
19th	06:31 pm	Leo
21st	07:11 pm	Virgo
23rd	06:33 pm	Libra
25th	06:40 pm	Scorpio
27th	09:27 pm	Sagittarius
30th	03:59 am	Capricorn

October 1957

2nd	02:04 pm	Aquarius
5th	02:17 am	Pisces
7th	02:57 pm	Aries
10th	02:48 am	Taurus
12th	01:01 pm	Gemini
14th	08:54 pm	Cancer
17th	01:59 am	Leo
19th	04:24 am	Virgo
21st	05:03 am	Libra
23rd	05:31 am	Scorpio
25th	07:33 am	Sagittarius
27th	12:41 pm	Capricorn
29th	09:32 pm	Aquarius

November 1957

1st	09:18 am	Pisces
3rd	10:00 pm	Aries
6th	09:38 am	Taurus
8th	07:09 pm	Gemini
11th	02:24 am	Cancer
13th	07:36 am	Leo
15th	11:07 am	Virgo
17th	01:25 pm	Libra
19th	03:17 pm	Scorpio
21st	05:52 pm	Sagittarius
23rd	10:29 pm	Capricorn
26th	06:16 am	Aquarius
28th	05:16 pm	Pisces

December 1957

1st	05:56 am	Aries
3rd	05:48 pm	Taurus
6th	03:00 am	Gemini
8th	09:16 am	Cancer
10th	01:23 pm	Leo
12th	04:28 pm	Virgo
14th	07:23 pm	Libra
16th	10:35 pm	Scorpio
19th	02:30 am	Sagittarius
21st	07:47 am	Capricorn
23rd	03:19 pm	Aquarius
26th	01:41 am	Pisces
28th	02:13 pm	Aries
31st	02:37 am	Taurus

January 1958

2nd	12:21 pm	Gemini
4th	06:22 pm	Cancer
6th	09:21 pm	Leo
8th	10:59 pm	Virgo
11th	12:52 am	Libra
13th	04:02 am	Scorpio
15th	08:49 am	Sagittarius
17th	03:13 pm	Capricorn
19th	11:22 pm	Aquarius
22nd	09:42 am	Pisces
24th	10:03 pm	Aries
27th	10:56 am	Taurus
29th	09:47 pm	Gemini

February 1958

1st	04:41 am	Cancer
3rd	07:38 am	Leo
5th	08:11 am	Virgo
7th	08:23 am	Libra
9th	10:03 am	Scorpio
11th	02:11 pm	Sagittarius
13th	08:55 pm	Capricorn
16th	05:51 am	Aquarius
18th	04:39 pm	Pisces
21st	05:02 am	Aries
23rd	06:05 pm	Taurus
26th	05:52 am	Gemini
28th	02:17 pm	Cancer

March 1958

2nd	06:27 pm	Leo
4th	07:15 pm	Virgo
6th	06:35 pm	Libra
8th	06:34 pm	Scorpio
10th	08:56 pm	Sagittarius
13th	02:36 am	Capricorn
15th	11:28 am	Aquarius
17th	10:41 pm	Pisces
20th	11:17 am	Aries
23rd	12:16 am	Taurus
25th	12:20 pm	Gemini
27th	09:53 pm	Cancer
30th	03:46 am	Leo

April 1958

1st	06:01 am	Virgo
3rd	05:54 am	Libra
5th	05:16 am	Scorpio
7th	06:07 am	Sagittarius
9th	10:01 am	Capricorn
11th	05:41 pm	Aquarius
14th	04:38 am	Pisces
16th	05:23 pm	Aries
19th	06:16 am	Taurus
21st	06:03 pm	Gemini
24th	03:46 am	Cancer
26th	10:44 am	Leo
28th	02:41 pm	Virgo
30th	04:06 pm	Libra

May 1958

2nd	04:14 pm	Scorpio
4th	04:43 pm	Sagittarius
6th	07:21 pm	Capricorn
9th	01:29 am	Aquarius
11th	11:27 am	Pisces
13th	11:58 pm	Aries
16th	12:50 pm	Taurus
19th	12:14 am	Gemini
21st	09:23 am	Cancer
23rd	04:15 pm	Leo
25th	09:00 pm	Virgo
27th	11:55 pm	Libra
30th	01:33 am	Scorpio

June 1958

1st	02:54 am	Sagittarius
3rd	05:23 am	Capricorn
5th	10:34 am	Aquarius
7th	07:24 pm	Pisces
10th	07:20 am	Aries
12th	08:12 pm	Taurus
15th	07:31 am	Gemini
17th	04:04 pm	Cancer
19th	10:04 pm	Leo
22nd	02:22 am	Virgo
24th	05:42 am	Libra
26th	08:30 am	Scorpio
28th	11:12 am	Sagittarius
30th	02:32 pm	Capricorn

July 1958

2nd	07:44 pm	Aquarius
5th	03:57 am	Pisces
7th	03:18 pm	Aries
10th	04:09 am	Taurus
12th	03:47 pm	Gemini
15th	12:15 am	Cancer
17th	05:31 am	Leo
19th	08:42 am	Virgo
21st	11:11 am	Libra
23rd	01:57 pm	Scorpio
25th	05:25 pm	Sagittarius
27th	09:53 pm	Capricorn
30th	03:52 am	Aquarius

August 1958

1st	12:11 pm	Pisces
3rd	11:14 pm	Aries
6th	12:04 pm	Taurus
9th	12:16 am	Gemini
11th	09:25 am	Cancer
13th	02:43 pm	Leo
15th	05:07 pm	Virgo
17th	06:17 pm	Libra
19th	07:50 pm	Scorpio
21st	10:48 pm	Sagittarius
24th	03:38 am	Capricorn
26th	10:28 am	Aquarius
28th	07:25 pm	Pisces
31st	06:35 am	Aries

September 1958

2nd	07:24 pm	Taurus
5th	08:07 am	Gemini
7th	06:22 pm	Cancer
10th	12:42 am	Leo
12th	03:19 am	Virgo
14th	03:44 am	Libra
16th	03:49 am	Scorpio
18th	05:16 am	Sagittarius
20th	09:13 am	Capricorn
22nd	04:03 pm	Aquarius
25th	01:33 am	Pisces
27th	01:07 pm	Aries
30th	01:58 am	Taurus

October 1958

2nd	02:50 pm	Gemini
5th	02:00 am	Cancer
7th	09:51 am	Leo
9th	01:50 pm	Virgo
11th	02:44 pm	Libra
13th	02:11 pm	Scorpio
15th	02:09 pm	Sagittarius
17th	04:23 pm	Capricorn
19th	10:04 pm	Aquarius
22nd	07:20 am	Pisces
24th	07:10 pm	Aries
27th	08:07 am	Taurus
29th	08:50 pm	Gemini

November 1958

1st	08:09 am	Cancer
3rd	05:03 pm	Leo
5th	10:45 pm	Virgo
8th	01:16 am	Libra
10th	01:30 am	Scorpio
12th	01:03 am	Sagittarius
14th	01:54 am	Capricorn
16th	05:53 am	Aquarius
18th	01:56 pm	Pisces
21st	01:28 am	Aries
23rd	02:30 pm	Taurus
26th	03:00 am	Gemini
28th	01:51 pm	Cancer
30th	10:41 pm	Leo

December 1958

3rd	05:18 am	Virgo
5th	09:31 am	Libra
7th	11:28 am	Scorpio
9th	12:02 pm	Sagittarius
11th	12:46 pm	Capricorn
13th	03:38 pm	Aquarius
15th	10:12 pm	Pisces
18th	08:45 am	Aries
20th	09:38 pm	Taurus
23rd	10:09 am	Gemini
25th	08:33 pm	Cancer
28th	04:33 am	Leo
30th	10:41 am	Virgo

January 1959

1st	03:21 pm	Libra
3rd	06:42 pm	Scorpio
5th	08:56 pm	Sagittarius
7th	10:50 pm	Capricorn
10th	01:52 am	Aquarius
12th	07:39 am	Pisces
14th	05:10 pm	Aries
17th	05:33 am	Taurus
19th	06:16 pm	Gemini
22nd	04:47 am	Cancer
24th	12:13 pm	Leo
26th	05:13 pm	Virgo
28th	08:54 pm	Libra
31st	12:05 am	Scorpio

February 1959

2nd	03:11 am	Sagittarius
4th	06:29 am	Capricorn
6th	10:40 am	Aquarius
8th	04:50 pm	Pisces
11th	01:55 am	Aries
13th	01:47 pm	Taurus
16th	02:39 am	Gemini
18th	01:51 pm	Cancer
20th	09:38 pm	Leo
23rd	02:06 am	Virgo
25th	04:29 am	Libra
27th	06:15 am	Scorpio

March 1959

1st	08:33 am	Sagittarius
3rd	12:06 pm	Capricorn
5th	05:16 pm	Aquarius
8th	12:25 am	Pisces
10th	09:54 am	Aries
12th	09:37 pm	Taurus
15th	10:30 am	Gemini
17th	10:28 pm	Cancer
20th	07:22 am	Leo
22nd	12:28 pm	Virgo
24th	02:27 pm	Libra
26th	02:54 pm	Scorpio
28th	03:31 pm	Sagittarius
30th	05:49 pm	Capricorn

April 1959

1st	10:42 pm	Aquarius
4th	06:23 am	Pisces
6th	04:33 pm	Aries
9th	04:32 am	Taurus
11th	05:25 pm	Gemini
14th	05:48 am	Cancer
16th	03:55 pm	Leo
18th	10:28 pm	Virgo
21st	01:19 am	Libra
23rd	01:34 am	Scorpio
25th	12:59 am	Sagittarius
27th	01:32 am	Capricorn
29th	04:55 am	Aquarius

May 1959

1st	11:58 am	Pisces
3rd	10:19 pm	Aries
6th	10:39 am	Taurus
8th	11:34 pm	Gemini
11th	11:57 am	Cancer
13th	10:40 pm	Leo
16th	06:38 am	Virgo
18th	11:06 am	Libra
20th	12:24 pm	Scorpio
22nd	11:51 am	Sagittarius
24th	11:24 am	Capricorn
26th	01:09 pm	Aquarius
28th	06:42 pm	Pisces
31st	04:18 am	Aries

June 1959

2nd	04:37 pm	Taurus
5th	05:35 am	Gemini
7th	05:44 pm	Cancer
10th	04:19 am	Leo
12th	12:50 pm	Virgo
14th	06:42 pm	Libra
16th	09:38 pm	Scorpio
18th	10:14 pm	Sagittarius
20th	10:01 pm	Capricorn
22nd	11:00 pm	Aquarius
25th	03:09 am	Pisces
27th	11:28 am	Aries
29th	11:11 pm	Taurus

July 1959

2nd	12:05 pm	Gemini
5th	12:03 am	Cancer
7th	10:08 am	Leo
9th	06:15 pm	Virgo
12th	12:26 am	Libra
14th	04:33 am	Scorpio
16th	06:42 am	Sagittarius
18th	07:42 am	Capricorn
20th	09:05 am	Aquarius
22nd	12:41 pm	Pisces
24th	07:53 pm	Aries
27th	06:43 am	Taurus
29th	07:23 pm	Gemini

August 1959

1st	07:24 am	Cancer
3rd	05:09 pm	Leo
6th	12:30 am	Virgo
8th	05:56 am	Libra
10th	10:00 am	Scorpio
12th	12:58 pm	Sagittarius
14th	03:19 pm	Capricorn
16th	05:53 pm	Aquarius
18th	09:59 pm	Pisces
21st	04:51 am	Aries
23rd	02:58 pm	Taurus
26th	03:18 am	Gemini
28th	03:33 pm	Cancer
31st	01:33 am	Leo

September 1959

2nd	08:31 am	Virgo
4th	12:56 pm	Libra
6th	03:53 pm	Scorpio
8th	06:20 pm	Sagittarius
10th	09:04 pm	Capricorn
13th	12:43 am	Aquarius
15th	05:54 am	Pisces
17th	01:16 pm	Aries
19th	11:12 pm	Taurus
22nd	11:16 am	Gemini
24th	11:49 pm	Cancer
27th	10:36 am	Leo
29th	06:04 pm	Virgo

October 1959

1st	10:08 pm	Libra
3rd	11:54 pm	Scorpio
6th	12:54 am	Sagittarius
8th	02:38 am	Capricorn
10th	06:12 am	Aquarius
12th	12:06 pm	Pisces
14th	08:20 pm	Aries
17th	06:40 am	Taurus
19th	06:40 pm	Gemini
22nd	07:22 am	Cancer
24th	07:03 pm	Leo
27th	03:49 am	Virgo
29th	08:42 am	Libra
31st	10:14 am	Scorpio

November 1959

2nd	10:02 am	Sagittarius
4th	10:05 am	Capricorn
6th	12:14 pm	Aquarius
8th	05:36 pm	Pisces
11th	02:10 am	Aries
13th	01:04 pm	Taurus
16th	01:16 am	Gemini
18th	01:57 pm	Cancer
21st	02:04 am	Leo
23rd	12:08 pm	Virgo
25th	06:41 pm	Libra
27th	09:22 pm	Scorpio
29th	09:12 pm	Sagittarius

December 1959

1st	08:11 pm	Capricorn
3rd	08:35 pm	Aquarius
6th	12:16 am	Pisces
8th	07:59 am	Aries
10th	06:56 pm	Taurus
13th	07:24 am	Gemini
15th	08:00 pm	Cancer
18th	07:58 am	Leo
20th	06:30 pm	Virgo
23rd	02:29 am	Libra
25th	07:01 am	Scorpio
27th	08:16 am	Sagittarius
29th	07:38 am	Capricorn
31st	07:15 am	Aquarius

January 1960

2nd	09:19 am	Pisces
4th	03:21 pm	Aries
7th	01:22 am	Taurus
9th	01:45 pm	Gemini
12th	02:23 am	Cancer
14th	01:59 pm	Leo
17th	12:03 am	Virgo
19th	08:14 am	Libra
21st	01:59 pm	Scorpio
23rd	05:03 pm	Sagittarius
25th	06:00 pm	Capricorn
27th	06:19 pm	Aquarius
29th	07:56 pm	Pisces

February 1960

1st	12:39 am	Aries
3rd	09:16 am	Taurus
5th	08:58 pm	Gemini
8th	09:37 am	Cancer
10th	09:08 pm	Leo
13th	06:35 am	Virgo
15th	01:55 pm	Libra
17th	07:24 pm	Scorpio
19th	11:12 pm	Sagittarius
22nd	01:39 am	Capricorn
24th	03:32 am	Aquarius
26th	06:04 am	Pisces
28th	10:37 am	Aries

March 1960

1st	06:18 pm	Taurus
4th	05:08 am	Gemini
6th	05:37 pm	Cancer
9th	05:25 am	Leo
11th	02:47 pm	Virgo
13th	09:19 pm	Libra
16th	01:37 am	Scorpio
18th	04:37 am	Sagittarius
20th	07:14 am	Capricorn
22nd	10:10 am	Aquarius
24th	02:02 pm	Pisces
26th	07:30 pm	Aries
29th	03:13 am	Taurus
31st	01:32 pm	Gemini

April 1960

3rd	01:46 am	Cancer
5th	02:01 pm	Leo
8th	12:02 am	Virgo
10th	06:36 am	Libra
12th	10:01 am	Scorpio
14th	11:37 am	Sagittarius
16th	01:01 pm	Capricorn
18th	03:32 pm	Aquarius
20th	07:55 pm	Pisces
23rd	02:23 am	Aries
25th	10:51 am	Taurus
27th	09:16 pm	Gemini
30th	09:22 am	Cancer

May 1960

2nd	09:59 pm	Leo
5th	08:59 am	Virgo
7th	04:30 pm	Libra
9th	08:07 pm	Scorpio
11th	08:55 pm	Sagittarius
13th	08:50 pm	Capricorn
15th	09:51 pm	Aquarius
18th	01:23 am	Pisces
20th	07:55 am	Aries
22nd	05:00 pm	Taurus
25th	03:55 am	Gemini
27th	04:06 pm	Cancer
30th	04:50 am	Leo

June 1960

1st	04:38 pm	Virgo
4th	01:31 am	Libra
6th	06:20 am	Scorpio
8th	07:31 am	Sagittarius
10th	06:48 am	Capricorn
12th	06:23 am	Aquarius
14th	08:17 am	Pisces
16th	01:42 pm	Aries
18th	10:33 pm	Taurus
21st	09:46 am	Gemini
23rd	10:10 pm	Cancer
26th	10:51 am	Leo
28th	10:53 pm	Virgo

July 1960

1st	08:46 am	Libra
3rd	03:09 pm	Scorpio
5th	05:42 pm	Sagittarius
7th	05:34 pm	Capricorn
9th	04:43 pm	Aquarius
11th	05:19 pm	Pisces
13th	09:07 pm	Aries
16th	04:48 am	Taurus
18th	03:40 pm	Gemini
21st	04:09 am	Cancer
23rd	04:46 pm	Leo
26th	04:31 am	Virgo
28th	02:33 pm	Libra
30th	09:55 pm	Scorpio

August 1960

2nd	02:04 am	Sagittarius
4th	03:26 am	Capricorn
6th	03:21 am	Aquarius
8th	03:42 am	Pisces
10th	06:21 am	Aries
12th	12:36 pm	Taurus
14th	10:29 pm	Gemini
17th	10:43 am	Cancer
19th	11:18 pm	Leo
22nd	10:41 am	Virgo
24th	08:09 pm	Libra
27th	03:24 am	Scorpio
29th	08:19 am	Sagittarius
31st	11:09 am	Capricorn

September 1960

2nd	12:35 pm	Aquarius
4th	01:51 pm	Pisces
6th	04:26 pm	Aries
8th	09:44 pm	Taurus
11th	06:31 am	Gemini
13th	06:10 pm	Cancer
16th	06:46 am	Leo
18th	06:07 pm	Virgo
21st	02:58 am	Libra
23rd	09:18 am	Scorpio
25th	01:42 pm	Sagittarius
27th	04:54 pm	Capricorn
29th	07:32 pm	Aquarius

October 1960

1st	10:14 pm	Pisces
4th	01:46 am	Aries
6th	07:09 am	Taurus
8th	03:16 pm	Gemini
11th	02:18 am	Cancer
13th	02:55 pm	Leo
16th	02:40 am	Virgo
18th	11:32 am	Libra
20th	05:06 pm	Scorpio
22nd	08:16 pm	Sagittarius
24th	10:28 pm	Capricorn
27th	12:57 am	Aquarius
29th	04:26 am	Pisces
31st	09:11 am	Aries

November 1960

2nd	03:27 pm	Taurus
4th	11:44 pm	Gemini
7th	10:26 am	Cancer
9th	10:59 pm	Leo
12th	11:24 am	Virgo
14th	09:07 pm	Libra
17th	02:53 am	Scorpio
19th	05:17 am	Sagittarius
21st	06:02 am	Capricorn
23rd	07:04 am	Aquarius
25th	09:49 am	Pisces
27th	02:51 pm	Aries
29th	10:00 pm	Taurus

December 1960

2nd	07:01 am	Gemini
4th	05:52 pm	Cancer
7th	06:21 am	Leo
9th	07:13 pm	Virgo
12th	06:10 am	Libra
14th	01:13 pm	Scorpio
16th	04:07 pm	Sagittarius
18th	04:16 pm	Capricorn
20th	03:49 pm	Aquarius
22nd	04:47 pm	Pisces
24th	08:34 pm	Aries
27th	03:30 am	Taurus
29th	01:01 pm	Gemini

January 1961

1st	12:22 am	Cancer
3rd	12:54 pm	Leo
6th	01:48 am	Virgo
8th	01:31 pm	Libra
10th	10:09 pm	Scorpio
13th	02:40 am	Sagittarius
15th	03:41 am	Capricorn
17th	02:55 am	Aquarius
19th	02:32 am	Pisces
21st	04:26 am	Aries
23rd	09:51 am	Taurus
25th	06:50 pm	Gemini
28th	06:22 am	Cancer
30th	07:05 pm	Leo

February 1961

2nd	07:48 am	Virgo
4th	07:27 pm	Libra
7th	04:51 am	Scorpio
9th	11:01 am	Sagittarius
11th	01:51 pm	Capricorn
13th	02:15 pm	Aquarius
15th	01:53 pm	Pisces
17th	02:41 pm	Aries
19th	06:21 pm	Taurus
22nd	01:51 am	Gemini
24th	12:49 pm	Cancer
27th	01:34 am	Leo

March 1961

1st	02:12 pm	Virgo
4th	01:21 am	Libra
6th	10:24 am	Scorpio
8th	05:04 pm	Sagittarius
10th	09:19 pm	Capricorn
12th	11:29 pm	Aquarius
15th	12:26 am	Pisces
17th	01:32 am	Aries
19th	04:25 am	Taurus
21st	10:32 am	Gemini
23rd	08:22 pm	Cancer
26th	08:49 am	Leo
28th	09:30 pm	Virgo
31st	08:21 am	Libra

April 1961

2nd	04:37 pm	Scorpio
4th	10:34 pm	Sagittarius
7th	02:52 am	Capricorn
9th	06:03 am	Aquarius
11th	08:31 am	Pisces
13th	10:55 am	Aries
15th	02:16 pm	Taurus
17th	07:55 pm	Gemini
20th	04:50 am	Cancer
22nd	04:43 pm	Leo
25th	05:31 am	Virgo
27th	04:34 pm	Libra
30th	12:27 am	Scorpio

May 1961

2nd	05:25 am	Sagittarius
4th	08:40 am	Capricorn
6th	11:24 am	Aquarius
8th	02:23 pm	Pisces
10th	05:56 pm	Aries
12th	10:25 pm	Taurus
15th	04:34 am	Gemini
17th	01:17 pm	Cancer
20th	12:45 am	Leo
22nd	01:38 pm	Virgo
25th	01:18 am	Libra
27th	09:35 am	Scorpio
29th	02:11 pm	Sagittarius
31st	04:20 pm	Capricorn

June 1961

2nd	05:45 pm	Aquarius
4th	07:50 pm	Pisces
6th	11:23 pm	Aries
9th	04:38 am	Taurus
11th	11:40 am	Gemini
13th	08:50 pm	Cancer
16th	08:16 am	Leo
18th	09:12 pm	Virgo
21st	09:32 am	Libra
23rd	06:51 pm	Scorpio
26th	12:05 am	Sagittarius
28th	02:00 am	Capricorn
30th	02:18 am	Aquarius

July 1961

2nd	02:53 am	Pisces
4th	05:12 am	Aries
6th	10:02 am	Taurus
8th	05:27 pm	Gemini
11th	03:13 am	Cancer
13th	02:56 pm	Leo
16th	03:55 am	Virgo
18th	04:39 pm	Libra
21st	03:05 am	Scorpio
23rd	09:42 am	Sagittarius
25th	12:29 pm	Capricorn
27th	12:41 pm	Aquarius
29th	12:13 pm	Pisces
31st	12:56 pm	Aries

August 1961

2nd	04:19 pm	Taurus
4th	11:04 pm	Gemini
7th	08:56 am	Cancer
9th	08:59 pm	Leo
12th	10:00 am	Virgo
14th	10:44 pm	Libra
17th	09:44 am	Scorpio
19th	05:44 pm	Sagittarius
21st	10:07 pm	Capricorn
23rd	11:25 pm	Aquarius
25th	11:02 pm	Pisces
27th	10:49 pm	Aries
30th	12:37 am	Taurus

September 1961

1st	05:53 am	Gemini
3rd	03:00 pm	Cancer
6th	03:01 am	Leo
8th	04:05 pm	Virgo
11th	04:33 am	Libra
13th	03:23 pm	Scorpio
15th	11:54 pm	Sagittarius
18th	05:42 am	Capricorn
20th	08:43 am	Aquarius
22nd	09:36 am	Pisces
24th	09:40 am	Aries
26th	10:42 am	Taurus
28th	02:31 pm	Gemini
30th	10:19 pm	Cancer

October 1961

3rd	09:44 am	Leo
5th	10:46 pm	Virgo
8th	11:04 am	Libra
10th	09:19 pm	Scorpio
13th	05:21 am	Sagittarius
15th	11:24 am	Capricorn
17th	03:37 pm	Aquarius
19th	06:10 pm	Pisces
21st	07:36 pm	Aries
23rd	09:07 pm	Taurus
26th	12:24 am	Gemini
28th	07:03 am	Cancer
30th	05:30 pm	Leo

November 1961

2nd	06:18 am	Virgo
4th	06:42 pm	Libra
7th	04:40 am	Scorpio
9th	11:51 am	Sagittarius
11th	04:59 pm	Capricorn
13th	08:59 pm	Aquarius
16th	12:18 am	Pisces
18th	03:10 am	Aries
20th	06:03 am	Taurus
22nd	09:59 am	Gemini
24th	04:20 pm	Cancer
27th	02:01 am	Leo
29th	02:25 pm	Virgo

December 1961

2nd	03:08 am	Libra
4th	01:30 pm	Scorpio
6th	08:25 pm	Sagittarius
9th	12:31 am	Capricorn
11th	03:11 am	Aquarius
13th	05:41 am	Pisces
15th	08:44 am	Aries
17th	12:39 pm	Taurus
19th	05:47 pm	Gemini
22nd	12:50 am	Cancer
24th	10:26 am	Leo
26th	10:29 pm	Virgo
29th	11:26 am	Libra
31st	10:42 pm	Scorpio

January 1962

3rd	06:23 am	Sagittarius
5th	10:24 am	Capricorn
7th	12:00 pm	Aquarius
9th	12:53 pm	Pisces
11th	02:34 pm	Aries
13th	06:01 pm	Taurus
15th	11:42 pm	Gemini
18th	07:40 am	Cancer
20th	05:50 pm	Leo
23rd	05:53 am	Virgo
25th	06:52 pm	Libra
28th	06:54 am	Scorpio
30th	03:59 pm	Sagittarius

February 1962

1st	09:10 pm	Capricorn
3rd	10:57 pm	Aquarius
5th	10:53 pm	Pisces
7th	10:50 pm	Aries
10th	12:35 am	Taurus
12th	05:18 am	Gemini
14th	01:20 pm	Cancer
17th	12:04 am	Leo
19th	12:27 pm	Virgo
22nd	01:22 am	Libra
24th	01:36 pm	Scorpio
26th	11:46 pm	Sagittarius

March 1962

1st	06:38 am	Capricorn
3rd	09:52 am	Aquarius
5th	10:16 am	Pisces
7th	09:32 am	Aries
9th	09:40 am	Taurus
11th	12:35 pm	Gemini
13th	07:26 pm	Cancer
16th	05:56 am	Leo
18th	06:33 pm	Virgo
21st	07:28 am	Libra
23rd	07:29 pm	Scorpio
26th	05:49 am	Sagittarius
28th	01:46 pm	Capricorn
30th	06:43 pm	Aquarius

April 1962

1st	08:42 pm	Pisces
3rd	08:41 pm	Aries
5th	08:25 pm	Taurus
7th	10:00 pm	Gemini
10th	03:12 am	Cancer
12th	12:36 pm	Leo
15th	12:57 am	Virgo
17th	01:54 pm	Libra
20th	01:37 am	Scorpio
22nd	11:27 am	Sagittarius
24th	07:20 pm	Capricorn
27th	01:08 am	Aquarius
29th	04:40 am	Pisces

May 1962

1st	06:12 am	Aries
3rd	06:49 am	Taurus
5th	08:16 am	Gemini
7th	12:28 pm	Cancer
9th	08:35 pm	Leo
12th	08:11 am	Virgo
14th	09:03 pm	Libra
17th	08:43 am	Scorpio
19th	06:02 pm	Sagittarius
22nd	01:08 am	Capricorn
24th	06:31 am	Aquarius
26th	10:29 am	Pisces
28th	01:15 pm	Aries
30th	03:17 pm	Taurus

June 1962

1st	05:40 pm	Gemini
3rd	09:56 pm	Cancer
6th	05:23 am	Leo
8th	04:12 pm	Virgo
11th	04:51 am	Libra
13th	04:45 pm	Scorpio
16th	02:04 am	Sagittarius
18th	08:30 am	Capricorn
20th	12:49 pm	Aquarius
22nd	03:59 pm	Pisces
24th	06:43 pm	Aries
26th	09:34 pm	Taurus
29th	01:09 am	Gemini

July 1962

1st	06:19 am	Cancer
3rd	01:55 pm	Leo
6th	12:22 am	Virgo
8th	12:48 pm	Libra
11th	01:05 am	Scorpio
13th	11:00 am	Sagittarius
15th	05:32 pm	Capricorn
17th	09:07 pm	Aquarius
19th	11:00 pm	Pisces
22nd	12:34 am	Aries
24th	02:57 am	Taurus
26th	06:57 am	Gemini
28th	01:00 pm	Cancer
30th	09:21 pm	Leo

August 1962

2nd	07:57 am	Virgo
4th	08:18 pm	Libra
7th	08:56 am	Scorpio
9th	07:48 pm	Sagittarius
12th	03:18 am	Capricorn
14th	07:07 am	Aquarius
16th	08:17 am	Pisces
18th	08:25 am	Aries
20th	09:20 am	Taurus
22nd	12:28 pm	Gemini
24th	06:34 pm	Cancer
27th	03:30 am	Leo
29th	02:36 pm	Virgo

September 1962

1st	03:01 am	Libra
3rd	03:46 pm	Scorpio
6th	03:26 am	Sagittarius
8th	12:20 pm	Capricorn
10th	05:26 pm	Aquarius
12th	07:02 pm	Pisces
14th	06:33 pm	Aries
16th	06:01 pm	Taurus
18th	07:29 pm	Gemini
21st	12:26 am	Cancer
23rd	09:07 am	Leo
25th	08:31 pm	Virgo
28th	09:08 am	Libra
30th	09:49 pm	Scorpio

October 1962

3rd	09:40 am	Sagittarius
5th	07:35 pm	Capricorn
8th	02:22 am	Aquarius
10th	05:29 am	Pisces
12th	05:41 am	Aries
14th	04:43 am	Taurus
16th	04:50 am	Gemini
18th	08:05 am	Cancer
20th	03:30 pm	Leo
23rd	02:31 am	Virgo
25th	03:14 pm	Libra
28th	03:49 am	Scorpio
30th	03:20 pm	Sagittarius

November 1962

2nd	01:17 am	Capricorn
4th	09:02 am	Aquarius
6th	01:52 pm	Pisces
8th	03:45 pm	Aries
10th	03:45 pm	Taurus
12th	03:43 pm	Gemini
14th	05:49 pm	Cancer
16th	11:40 pm	Leo
19th	09:33 am	Virgo
21st	09:58 pm	Libra
24th	10:33 am	Scorpio
26th	09:43 pm	Sagittarius
29th	07:00 am	Capricorn

December 1962

1st	02:26 pm	Aquarius
3rd	07:53 pm	Pisces
5th	11:17 pm	Aries
8th	12:59 am	Taurus
10th	02:07 am	Gemini
12th	04:21 am	Cancer
14th	09:20 am	Leo
16th	05:59 pm	Virgo
19th	05:41 am	Libra
21st	06:18 pm	Scorpio
24th	05:33 am	Sagittarius
26th	02:19 pm	Capricorn
28th	08:42 pm	Aquarius
31st	01:20 am	Pisces

January 1963

2nd	04:48 am	Aries
4th	07:34 am	Taurus
6th	10:14 am	Gemini
8th	01:41 pm	Cancer
10th	07:01 pm	Leo
13th	03:07 am	Virgo
15th	02:05 pm	Libra
18th	02:36 am	Scorpio
20th	02:21 pm	Sagittarius
22nd	11:24 pm	Capricorn
25th	05:14 am	Aquarius
27th	08:35 am	Pisces
29th	10:44 am	Aries
31st	12:55 pm	Taurus

February 1963

2nd	04:03 pm	Gemini
4th	08:40 pm	Cancer
7th	03:06 am	Leo
9th	11:36 am	Virgo
11th	10:18 pm	Libra
14th	10:38 am	Scorpio
16th	10:57 pm	Sagittarius
19th	09:00 am	Capricorn
21st	03:23 pm	Aquarius
23rd	06:17 pm	Pisces
25th	07:05 pm	Aries
27th	07:38 pm	Taurus

March 1963

1st	09:39 pm	Gemini
4th	02:08 am	Cancer
6th	09:15 am	Leo
8th	06:34 pm	Virgo
11th	05:35 am	Libra
13th	05:51 pm	Scorpio
16th	06:27 am	Sagittarius
18th	05:35 pm	Capricorn
21st	01:21 am	Aquarius
23rd	05:04 am	Pisces
25th	05:38 am	Aries
27th	04:57 am	Taurus
29th	05:13 am	Gemini
31st	08:14 am	Cancer

April 1963

2nd	02:45 pm	Leo
5th	12:20 am	Virgo
7th	11:50 am	Libra
10th	12:14 am	Scorpio
12th	12:48 pm	Sagittarius
15th	12:27 am	Capricorn
17th	09:34 am	Aquarius
19th	02:53 pm	Pisces
21st	04:30 pm	Aries
23rd	03:51 pm	Taurus
25th	03:06 pm	Gemini
27th	04:27 pm	Cancer
29th	09:25 pm	Leo

May 1963

2nd	06:13 am	Virgo
4th	05:42 pm	Libra
7th	06:16 am	Scorpio
9th	06:42 pm	Sagittarius
12th	06:13 am	Capricorn
14th	03:51 pm	Aquarius
16th	10:32 pm	Pisces
19th	01:48 am	Aries
21st	02:21 am	Taurus
23rd	01:53 am	Gemini
25th	02:29 am	Cancer
27th	05:58 am	Leo
29th	01:22 pm	Virgo

June 1963

1st	12:09 am	Libra
3rd	12:39 pm	Scorpio
6th	01:01 am	Sagittarius
8th	12:07 pm	Capricorn
10th	09:22 pm	Aquarius
13th	04:21 am	Pisces
15th	08:46 am	Aries
17th	10:54 am	Taurus
19th	11:44 am	Gemini
21st	12:46 pm	Cancer
23rd	03:44 pm	Leo
25th	09:56 pm	Virgo
28th	07:41 am	Libra
30th	07:48 pm	Scorpio

July 1963

3rd	08:11 am	Sagittarius
5th	07:03 pm	Capricorn
8th	03:36 am	Aquarius
10th	09:53 am	Pisces
12th	02:16 pm	Aries
14th	05:15 pm	Taurus
16th	07:27 pm	Gemini
18th	09:45 pm	Cancer
21st	01:15 am	Leo
23rd	07:06 am	Virgo
25th	04:02 pm	Libra
28th	03:38 am	Scorpio
30th	04:08 pm	Sagittarius

August 1963

2nd	03:12 am	Capricorn
4th	11:25 am	Aquarius
6th	04:46 pm	Pisces
8th	08:07 pm	Aries
10th	10:37 pm	Taurus
13th	01:16 am	Gemini
15th	04:39 am	Cancer
17th	09:17 am	Leo
19th	03:40 pm	Virgo
22nd	12:25 am	Libra
24th	11:39 am	Scorpio
27th	12:15 am	Sagittarius
29th	11:57 am	Capricorn
31st	08:37 pm	Aquarius

September 1963

3rd	01:37 am	Pisces
5th	03:52 am	Aries
7th	05:02 am	Taurus
9th	06:46 am	Gemini
11th	10:08 am	Cancer
13th	03:30 pm	Leo
15th	10:47 pm	Virgo
18th	08:00 am	Libra
20th	07:10 pm	Scorpio
23rd	07:50 am	Sagittarius
25th	08:15 pm	Capricorn
28th	06:03 am	Aquarius
30th	11:47 am	Pisces

October 1963

2nd	01:48 pm	Aries
4th	01:50 pm	Taurus
6th	01:58 pm	Gemini
8th	04:01 pm	Cancer
10th	08:54 pm	Leo
13th	04:34 am	Virgo
15th	02:24 pm	Libra
18th	01:53 am	Scorpio
20th	02:32 pm	Sagittarius
23rd	03:21 am	Capricorn
25th	02:20 pm	Aquarius
27th	09:36 pm	Pisces
30th	12:40 am	Aries

November 1963

1st	12:42 am	Taurus
2nd	11:48 pm	Gemini
5th	12:08 am	Cancer
7th	03:24 am	Leo
9th	10:14 am	Virgo
11th	08:08 pm	Libra
14th	07:57 am	Scorpio
16th	08:40 pm	Sagittarius
19th	09:23 am	Capricorn
21st	08:51 pm	Aquarius
24th	05:32 am	Pisces
26th	10:25 am	Aries
28th	11:49 am	Taurus
30th	11:15 am	Gemini

December 1963

2nd	10:45 am	Cancer
4th	12:20 pm	Leo
6th	05:26 pm	Virgo
9th	02:21 am	Libra
11th	02:04 pm	Scorpio
14th	02:53 am	Sagittarius
16th	03:21 pm	Capricorn
19th	02:29 am	Aquarius
21st	11:28 am	Pisces
23rd	05:41 pm	Aries
25th	08:57 pm	Taurus
27th	09:58 pm	Gemini
29th	10:07 pm	Cancer
31st	11:09 pm	Leo

January 1964

3rd	02:48 am	Virgo
5th	10:10 am	Libra
7th	09:04 pm	Scorpio
10th	09:49 am	Sagittarius
12th	10:14 pm	Capricorn
15th	08:48 am	Aquarius
17th	05:04 pm	Pisces
19th	11:10 pm	Aries
22nd	03:23 am	Taurus
24th	06:05 am	Gemini
26th	07:51 am	Cancer
28th	09:45 am	Leo
30th	01:09 pm	Virgo

February 1964

1st	07:25 pm	Libra
4th	05:13 am	Scorpio
6th	05:35 pm	Sagittarius
9th	06:11 am	Capricorn
11th	04:39 pm	Aquarius
14th	12:09 am	Pisces
16th	05:10 am	Aries
18th	08:45 am	Taurus
20th	11:48 am	Gemini
22nd	02:49 pm	Cancer
24th	06:11 pm	Leo
26th	10:30 pm	Virgo
29th	04:46 am	Libra

March 1964

2nd	01:54 pm	Scorpio
5th	01:47 am	Sagittarius
7th	02:35 pm	Capricorn
10th	01:36 am	Aquarius
12th	09:05 am	Pisces
14th	01:15 pm	Aries
16th	03:30 pm	Taurus
18th	05:26 pm	Gemini
20th	08:11 pm	Cancer
23rd	12:15 am	Leo
25th	05:42 am	Virgo
27th	12:48 pm	Libra
29th	10:03 pm	Scorpio

April 1964

1st	09:41 am	Sagittarius
3rd	10:36 pm	Capricorn
6th	10:24 am	Aquarius
8th	06:47 pm	Pisces
10th	11:08 pm	Aries
13th	12:37 am	Taurus
15th	01:06 am	Gemini
17th	02:23 am	Cancer
19th	05:40 am	Leo
21st	11:17 am	Virgo
23rd	07:08 pm	Libra
26th	05:01 am	Scorpio
28th	04:46 pm	Sagittarius

May 1964

1st	05:42 am	Capricorn
3rd	06:06 pm	Aquarius
6th	03:43 am	Pisces
8th	09:16 am	Aries
10th	11:09 am	Taurus
12th	11:01 am	Gemini
14th	10:53 am	Cancer
16th	12:31 pm	Leo
18th	05:02 pm	Virgo
21st	12:41 am	Libra
23rd	10:58 am	Scorpio
25th	11:03 pm	Sagittarius
28th	12:00 pm	Capricorn
31st	12:33 am	Aquarius

June 1964

2nd	11:01 am	Pisces
4th	06:03 pm	Aries
6th	09:20 pm	Taurus
8th	09:50 pm	Gemini
10th	09:16 pm	Cancer
12th	09:35 pm	Leo
15th	12:27 am	Virgo
17th	06:54 am	Libra
19th	04:49 pm	Scorpio
22nd	05:03 am	Sagittarius
24th	06:02 pm	Capricorn
27th	06:22 am	Aquarius
29th	04:56 pm	Pisces

July 1964

2nd	12:52 am	Aries
4th	05:42 am	Taurus
6th	07:43 am	Gemini
8th	07:57 am	Cancer
10th	08:01 am	Leo
12th	09:44 am	Virgo
14th	02:41 pm	Libra
16th	11:32 pm	Scorpio
19th	11:28 am	Sagittarius
22nd	12:27 am	Capricorn
24th	12:31 pm	Aquarius
26th	10:36 pm	Pisces
29th	06:25 am	Aries
31st	12:00 pm	Taurus

August 1964

2nd	03:28 pm	Gemini
4th	05:13 pm	Cancer
6th	06:11 pm	Leo
8th	07:50 pm	Virgo
10th	11:51 pm	Libra
13th	07:31 am	Scorpio
15th	06:44 pm	Sagittarius
18th	07:38 am	Capricorn
20th	07:39 pm	Aquarius
23rd	05:13 am	Pisces
25th	12:15 pm	Aries
27th	05:24 pm	Taurus
29th	09:16 pm	Gemini

September 1964

1st	12:13 am	Cancer
3rd	02:36 am	Leo
5th	05:12 am	Virgo
7th	09:19 am	Libra
9th	04:20 pm	Scorpio
12th	02:47 am	Sagittarius
14th	03:30 pm	Capricorn
17th	03:47 am	Aquarius
19th	01:22 pm	Pisces
21st	07:44 pm	Aries
23rd	11:46 pm	Taurus
26th	02:46 am	Gemini
28th	05:40 am	Cancer
30th	08:53 am	Leo

October 1964

2nd	12:42 pm	Virgo
4th	05:45 pm	Libra
7th	12:57 am	Scorpio
9th	11:02 am	Sagittarius
11th	11:32 pm	Capricorn
14th	12:16 pm	Aquarius
16th	10:33 pm	Pisces
19th	05:05 am	Aries
21st	08:24 am	Taurus
23rd	10:03 am	Gemini
25th	11:37 am	Cancer
27th	02:14 pm	Leo
29th	06:25 pm	Virgo

November 1964

1st	12:24 am	Libra
3rd	08:25 am	Scorpio
5th	06:43 pm	Sagittarius
8th	07:06 am	Capricorn
10th	08:08 pm	Aquarius
13th	07:28 am	Pisces
15th	03:10 pm	Aries
17th	06:57 pm	Taurus
19th	07:59 pm	Gemini
21st	08:04 pm	Cancer
23rd	08:59 pm	Leo
26th	12:03 am	Virgo
28th	05:54 am	Libra
30th	02:31 pm	Scorpio

December 1964

3rd	01:24 am	Sagittarius
5th	01:53 pm	Capricorn
8th	02:57 am	Aquarius
10th	03:00 pm	Pisces
13th	12:12 am	Aries
15th	05:33 am	Taurus
17th	07:21 am	Gemini
19th	07:02 am	Cancer
21st	06:31 am	Leo
23rd	07:41 am	Virgo
25th	12:04 pm	Libra
27th	08:11 pm	Scorpio
30th	07:21 am	Sagittarius

January 1965

1st	08:06 pm	Capricorn
4th	09:04 am	Aquarius
6th	09:06 pm	Pisces
9th	07:08 am	Aries
11th	02:11 pm	Taurus
13th	05:48 pm	Gemini
15th	06:35 pm	Cancer
17th	05:57 pm	Leo
19th	05:55 pm	Virgo
21st	08:28 pm	Libra
24th	03:01 am	Scorpio
26th	01:32 pm	Sagittarius
29th	02:21 am	Capricorn
31st	03:18 pm	Aquarius

February 1965

3rd	02:56 am	Pisces
5th	12:43 pm	Aries
7th	08:24 pm	Taurus
10th	01:36 am	Gemini
12th	04:14 am	Cancer
14th	04:54 am	Leo
16th	05:05 am	Virgo
18th	06:45 am	Libra
20th	11:45 am	Scorpio
22nd	08:57 pm	Sagittarius
25th	09:17 am	Capricorn
27th	10:14 pm	Aquarius

March 1965

2nd	09:38 am	Pisces
4th	06:45 pm	Aries
7th	01:49 am	Taurus
9th	07:14 am	Gemini
11th	11:03 am	Cancer
13th	01:23 pm	Leo
15th	02:55 pm	Virgo
17th	05:04 pm	Libra
19th	09:32 pm	Scorpio
22nd	05:37 am	Sagittarius
24th	05:07 pm	Capricorn
27th	05:59 am	Aquarius
29th	05:32 pm	Pisces

April 1965

1st	02:19 am	Aries
3rd	08:29 am	Taurus
5th	12:55 pm	Gemini
7th	04:24 pm	Cancer
9th	07:24 pm	Leo
11th	10:14 pm	Virgo
14th	01:38 am	Libra
16th	06:42 am	Scorpio
18th	02:31 pm	Sagittarius
21st	01:24 am	Capricorn
23rd	02:04 pm	Aquarius
26th	02:02 am	Pisces
28th	11:12 am	Aries
30th	05:04 pm	Taurus

May 1965

2nd	08:27 pm	Gemini
4th	10:39 pm	Cancer
7th	12:50 am	Leo
9th	03:47 am	Virgo
11th	08:04 am	Libra
13th	02:10 pm	Scorpio
15th	10:32 pm	Sagittarius
18th	09:20 am	Capricorn
20th	09:51 pm	Aquarius
23rd	10:14 am	Pisces
25th	08:19 pm	Aries
28th	02:48 am	Taurus
30th	05:58 am	Gemini

June 1965

1st	07:05 am	Cancer
3rd	07:47 am	Leo
5th	09:33 am	Virgo
7th	01:30 pm	Libra
9th	08:04 pm	Scorpio
12th	05:10 am	Sagittarius
14th	04:20 pm	Capricorn
17th	04:51 am	Aquarius
19th	05:29 pm	Pisces
22nd	04:29 am	Aries
24th	12:16 pm	Taurus
26th	04:18 pm	Gemini
28th	05:20 pm	Cancer
30th	04:59 pm	Leo

July 1965

2nd	05:11 pm	Virgo
4th	07:43 pm	Libra
7th	01:38 am	Scorpio
9th	10:53 am	Sagittarius
11th	10:29 pm	Capricorn
14th	11:08 am	Aquarius
16th	11:45 pm	Pisces
19th	11:13 am	Aries
21st	08:14 pm	Taurus
24th	01:48 am	Gemini
26th	03:53 am	Cancer
28th	03:37 am	Leo
30th	02:55 am	Virgo

August 1965

1st	03:54 am	Libra
3rd	08:20 am	Scorpio
5th	04:49 pm	Sagittarius
8th	04:22 am	Capricorn
10th	05:09 pm	Aquarius
13th	05:38 am	Pisces
15th	04:57 pm	Aries
18th	02:27 am	Taurus
20th	09:21 am	Gemini
22nd	01:04 pm	Cancer
24th	02:01 pm	Leo
26th	01:36 pm	Virgo
28th	01:52 pm	Libra
30th	04:54 pm	Scorpio

September 1965

2nd	12:00 am	Sagittarius
4th	10:51 am	Capricorn
6th	11:34 pm	Aquarius
9th	11:57 am	Pisces
11th	10:50 pm	Aries
14th	07:56 am	Taurus
16th	03:06 pm	Gemini
18th	08:01 pm	Cancer
20th	10:35 pm	Leo
22nd	11:30 pm	Virgo
25th	12:16 am	Libra
27th	02:47 am	Scorpio
29th	08:42 am	Sagittarius

October 1965

1st	06:29 pm	Capricorn
4th	06:48 am	Aquarius
6th	07:14 pm	Pisces
9th	05:54 am	Aries
11th	02:16 pm	Taurus
13th	08:40 pm	Gemini
16th	01:27 am	Cancer
18th	04:51 am	Leo
20th	07:13 am	Virgo
22nd	09:21 am	Libra
24th	12:31 pm	Scorpio
26th	06:09 pm	Sagittarius
29th	03:05 am	Capricorn
31st	02:50 pm	Aquarius

November 1965

3rd	03:23 am	Pisces
5th	02:22 pm	Aries
7th	10:30 pm	Taurus
10th	03:54 am	Gemini
12th	07:29 am	Cancer
14th	10:14 am	Leo
16th	12:55 pm	Virgo
18th	04:10 pm	Libra
20th	08:37 pm	Scorpio
23rd	02:57 am	Sagittarius
25th	11:45 am	Capricorn
27th	11:03 pm	Aquarius
30th	11:40 am	Pisces

December 1965

2nd	11:22 pm	Aries
5th	08:11 am	Taurus
7th	01:28 pm	Gemini
9th	03:57 pm	Cancer
11th	05:08 pm	Leo
13th	06:36 pm	Virgo
15th	09:33 pm	Libra
18th	02:40 am	Scorpio
20th	10:01 am	Sagittarius
22nd	07:27 pm	Capricorn
25th	06:44 am	Aquarius
27th	07:17 pm	Pisces
30th	07:40 am	Aries

January 1966

1st	05:46 pm	Taurus
4th	12:06 am	Gemini
6th	02:40 am	Cancer
8th	02:50 am	Leo
10th	02:34 am	Virgo
12th	03:53 am	Libra
14th	08:08 am	Scorpio
16th	03:40 pm	Sagittarius
19th	01:45 am	Capricorn
21st	01:26 pm	Aquarius
24th	01:59 am	Pisces
26th	02:33 pm	Aries
29th	01:43 am	Taurus
31st	09:43 am	Gemini

February 1966

2nd	01:41 pm	Cancer
4th	02:14 pm	Leo
6th	01:11 pm	Virgo
8th	12:50 pm	Libra
10th	03:15 pm	Scorpio
12th	09:33 pm	Sagittarius
15th	07:26 am	Capricorn
17th	07:26 pm	Aquarius
20th	08:05 am	Pisces
22nd	08:30 pm	Aries
25th	07:53 am	Taurus
27th	05:03 pm	Gemini

March 1966

1st	10:48 pm	Cancer
4th	12:57 am	Leo
6th	12:37 am	Virgo
7th	11:49 pm	Libra
10th	12:47 am	Scorpio
12th	05:18 am	Sagittarius
14th	01:55 pm	Capricorn
17th	01:35 am	Aquarius
19th	02:19 pm	Pisces
22nd	02:33 am	Aries
24th	01:32 pm	Taurus
26th	10:41 pm	Gemini
29th	05:23 am	Cancer
31st	09:12 am	Leo

April 1966

2nd	10:31 am	Virgo
4th	10:40 am	Libra
6th	11:30 am	Scorpio
8th	02:54 pm	Sagittarius
10th	10:02 pm	Capricorn
13th	08:42 am	Aquarius
15th	09:13 pm	Pisces
18th	09:27 am	Aries
20th	08:00 pm	Taurus
23rd	04:27 am	Gemini
25th	10:48 am	Cancer
27th	03:09 pm	Leo
29th	05:50 pm	Virgo

May 1966

1st	07:31 pm	Libra
3rd	09:23 pm	Scorpio
6th	12:52 am	Sagittarius
8th	07:12 am	Capricorn
10th	04:52 pm	Aquarius
13th	04:55 am	Pisces
15th	05:15 pm	Aries
18th	03:49 am	Taurus
20th	11:40 am	Gemini
22nd	05:00 pm	Cancer
24th	08:37 pm	Leo
26th	11:22 pm	Virgo
29th	02:00 am	Libra
31st	05:11 am	Scorpio

June 1966

2nd	09:39 am	Sagittarius
4th	04:10 pm	Capricorn
7th	01:21 am	Aquarius
9th	12:57 pm	Pisces
12th	01:26 am	Aries
14th	12:30 pm	Taurus
16th	08:26 pm	Gemini
19th	01:05 am	Cancer
21st	03:29 am	Leo
23rd	05:08 am	Virgo
25th	07:23 am	Libra
27th	11:04 am	Scorpio
29th	04:31 pm	Sagittarius

July 1966

1st	11:51 pm	Capricorn
4th	09:14 am	Aquarius
6th	08:39 pm	Pisces
9th	09:16 am	Aries
11th	09:04 pm	Taurus
14th	05:51 am	Gemini
16th	10:44 am	Cancer
18th	12:28 pm	Leo
20th	12:47 pm	Virgo
22nd	01:38 pm	Libra
24th	04:32 pm	Scorpio
26th	10:05 pm	Sagittarius
29th	06:04 am	Capricorn
31st	04:02 pm	Aquarius

August 1966

3rd	03:36 am	Pisces
5th	04:15 pm	Aries
8th	04:38 am	Taurus
10th	02:38 pm	Gemini
12th	08:42 pm	Cancer
14th	10:50 pm	Leo
16th	10:35 pm	Virgo
18th	10:05 pm	Libra
20th	11:24 pm	Scorpio
23rd	03:51 am	Sagittarius
25th	11:37 am	Capricorn
27th	09:56 pm	Aquarius
30th	09:48 am	Pisces

September 1966

1st	10:28 pm	Aries
4th	10:59 am	Taurus
6th	09:52 pm	Gemini
9th	05:27 am	Cancer
11th	09:01 am	Leo
13th	09:26 am	Virgo
15th	08:33 am	Libra
17th	08:34 am	Scorpio
19th	11:21 am	Sagittarius
21st	05:53 pm	Capricorn
24th	03:48 am	Aquarius
26th	03:49 pm	Pisces
29th	04:29 am	Aries

October 1966

1st	04:47 pm	Taurus
4th	03:43 am	Gemini
6th	12:12 pm	Cancer
8th	05:25 pm	Leo
10th	07:27 pm	Virgo
12th	07:29 pm	Libra
14th	07:21 pm	Scorpio
16th	08:59 pm	Sagittarius
19th	01:55 am	Capricorn
21st	10:41 am	Aquarius
23rd	10:20 pm	Pisces
26th	11:03 am	Aries
28th	11:06 pm	Taurus
31st	09:28 am	Gemini

November 1966

2nd	05:43 pm	Cancer
4th	11:36 pm	Leo
7th	03:10 am	Virgo
9th	04:54 am	Libra
11th	05:53 am	Scorpio
13th	07:36 am	Sagittarius
15th	11:37 am	Capricorn
17th	07:03 pm	Aquarius
20th	05:53 am	Pisces
22nd	06:31 pm	Aries
25th	06:37 am	Taurus
27th	04:31 pm	Gemini
29th	11:50 pm	Cancer

December 1966

2nd	05:02 am	Leo
4th	08:48 am	Virgo
6th	11:43 am	Libra
8th	02:18 pm	Scorpio
10th	05:13 pm	Sagittarius
12th	09:30 pm	Capricorn
15th	04:19 am	Aquarius
17th	02:17 pm	Pisces
20th	02:39 am	Aries
22nd	03:07 pm	Taurus
25th	01:14 am	Gemini
27th	07:58 am	Cancer
29th	11:57 am	Leo
31st	02:33 pm	Virgo

January 1967

2nd	05:04 pm	Libra
4th	08:16 pm	Scorpio
7th	12:28 am	Sagittarius
9th	05:53 am	Capricorn
11th	01:05 pm	Aquarius
13th	10:45 pm	Pisces
16th	10:48 am	Aries
18th	11:39 pm	Taurus
21st	10:38 am	Gemini
23rd	05:51 pm	Cancer
25th	09:21 pm	Leo
27th	10:36 pm	Virgo
29th	11:33 pm	Libra

February 1967

1st	01:44 am	Scorpio
3rd	05:56 am	Sagittarius
5th	12:10 pm	Capricorn
7th	08:17 pm	Aquarius
10th	06:19 am	Pisces
12th	06:17 pm	Aries
15th	07:19 am	Taurus
17th	07:16 pm	Gemini
20th	03:48 am	Cancer
22nd	08:04 am	Leo
24th	09:04 am	Virgo
26th	08:44 am	Libra
28th	09:09 am	Scorpio

March 1967

2nd	11:53 am	Sagittarius
4th	05:35 pm	Capricorn
7th	02:04 am	Aquarius
9th	12:41 pm	Pisces
12th	12:53 am	Aries
14th	01:54 pm	Taurus
17th	02:19 am	Gemini
19th	12:10 pm	Cancer
21st	06:04 pm	Leo
23rd	08:08 pm	Virgo
25th	07:50 pm	Libra
27th	07:10 pm	Scorpio
29th	08:08 pm	Sagittarius

April 1967

1st	12:11 am	Capricorn
3rd	07:49 am	Aquarius
5th	06:29 pm	Pisces
8th	06:57 am	Aries
10th	07:56 pm	Taurus
13th	08:15 am	Gemini
15th	06:37 pm	Cancer
18th	01:54 am	Leo
20th	05:43 am	Virgo
22nd	06:41 am	Libra
24th	06:19 am	Scorpio
26th	06:27 am	Sagittarius
28th	08:54 am	Capricorn
30th	02:57 pm	Aquarius

May 1967

3rd	12:47 am	Pisces
5th	01:10 pm	Aries
8th	02:09 am	Taurus
10th	02:08 pm	Gemini
13th	12:11 am	Cancer
15th	07:49 am	Leo
17th	12:52 pm	Virgo
19th	03:31 pm	Libra
21st	04:30 pm	Scorpio
23rd	05:06 pm	Sagittarius
25th	06:58 pm	Capricorn
27th	11:44 pm	Aquarius
30th	08:18 am	Pisces

June 1967

1st	08:07 pm	Aries
4th	09:04 am	Taurus
6th	08:52 pm	Gemini
9th	06:18 am	Cancer
11th	01:19 pm	Leo
13th	06:24 pm	Virgo
15th	09:58 pm	Libra
18th	12:25 am	Scorpio
20th	02:20 am	Sagittarius
22nd	04:46 am	Capricorn
24th	09:11 am	Aquarius
26th	04:50 pm	Pisces
29th	03:53 am	Aries

July 1967

1st	04:43 pm	Taurus
4th	04:39 am	Gemini
6th	01:48 pm	Cancer
8th	07:59 pm	Leo
11th	12:08 am	Virgo
13th	03:20 am	Libra
15th	06:17 am	Scorpio
17th	09:22 am	Sagittarius
19th	12:59 pm	Capricorn
21st	05:59 pm	Aquarius
24th	01:28 am	Pisces
26th	12:00 pm	Aries
29th	12:41 am	Taurus
31st	01:01 pm	Gemini

August 1967

2nd	10:32 pm	Cancer
5th	04:26 am	Leo
7th	07:36 am	Virgo
9th	09:35 am	Libra
11th	11:44 am	Scorpio
13th	02:52 pm	Sagittarius
15th	07:18 pm	Capricorn
18th	01:17 am	Aquarius
20th	09:18 am	Pisces
22nd	07:48 pm	Aries
25th	08:21 am	Taurus
27th	09:08 pm	Gemini
30th	07:35 am	Cancer

September 1967

1st	02:08 pm	Leo
3rd	05:07 pm	Virgo
5th	06:03 pm	Libra
7th	06:44 pm	Scorpio
9th	08:40 pm	Sagittarius
12th	12:43 am	Capricorn
14th	07:08 am	Aquarius
16th	03:53 pm	Pisces
19th	02:46 am	Aries
21st	03:21 pm	Taurus
24th	04:21 am	Gemini
26th	03:45 pm	Cancer
28th	11:41 pm	Leo

October 1967

1st	03:39 am	Virgo
3rd	04:34 am	Libra
5th	04:14 am	Scorpio
7th	04:32 am	Sagittarius
9th	07:04 am	Capricorn
11th	12:45 pm	Aquarius
13th	09:38 pm	Pisces
16th	08:58 am	Aries
18th	09:41 pm	Taurus
21st	10:38 am	Gemini
23rd	10:27 pm	Cancer
26th	07:40 am	Leo
28th	01:19 pm	Virgo
30th	03:31 pm	Libra

November 1967

1st	03:26 pm	Scorpio
3rd	02:51 pm	Sagittarius
5th	03:44 pm	Capricorn
7th	07:45 pm	Aquarius
10th	03:43 am	Pisces
12th	02:58 pm	Aries
15th	03:52 am	Taurus
17th	04:40 pm	Gemini
20th	04:13 am	Cancer
22nd	01:47 pm	Leo
24th	08:46 pm	Virgo
27th	12:48 am	Libra
29th	02:13 am	Scorpio

December 1967

1st	02:10 am	Sagittarius
3rd	02:25 am	Capricorn
5th	04:57 am	Aquarius
7th	11:19 am	Pisces
9th	09:43 pm	Aries
12th	10:32 am	Taurus
14th	11:18 pm	Gemini
17th	10:23 am	Cancer
19th	07:21 pm	Leo
22nd	02:21 am	Virgo
24th	07:27 am	Libra
26th	10:36 am	Scorpio
28th	12:09 pm	Sagittarius
30th	01:11 pm	Capricorn

January 1968

1st	03:24 pm	Aquarius
3rd	08:36 pm	Pisces
6th	05:45 am	Aries
8th	06:03 pm	Taurus
11th	06:54 am	Gemini
13th	05:54 pm	Cancer
16th	02:10 am	Leo
18th	08:11 am	Virgo
20th	12:47 pm	Libra
22nd	04:28 pm	Scorpio
24th	07:24 pm	Sagittarius
26th	09:57 pm	Capricorn
29th	01:06 am	Aquarius
31st	06:16 am	Pisces

February 1968

2nd	02:39 pm	Aries
5th	02:15 am	Taurus
7th	03:09 pm	Gemini
10th	02:34 am	Cancer
12th	10:50 am	Leo
14th	04:03 pm	Virgo
16th	07:21 pm	Libra
18th	10:00 pm	Scorpio
21st	12:48 am	Sagittarius
23rd	04:12 am	Capricorn
25th	08:37 am	Aquarius
27th	02:42 pm	Pisces
29th	11:15 pm	Aries

March 1968

3rd	10:28 am	Taurus
5th	11:17 pm	Gemini
8th	11:21 am	Cancer
10th	08:27 pm	Leo
13th	01:51 am	Virgo
15th	04:23 am	Libra
17th	05:33 am	Scorpio
19th	06:54 am	Sagittarius
21st	09:35 am	Capricorn
23rd	02:17 pm	Aquarius
25th	09:15 pm	Pisces
28th	06:32 am	Aries
30th	05:55 pm	Taurus

April 1968

2nd	06:40 am	Gemini
4th	07:13 pm	Cancer
7th	05:28 am	Leo
9th	12:04 pm	Virgo
11th	03:01 pm	Libra
13th	03:32 pm	Scorpio
15th	03:23 pm	Sagittarius
17th	04:23 pm	Capricorn
19th	07:57 pm	Aquarius
22nd	02:46 am	Pisces
24th	12:32 pm	Aries
27th	12:22 am	Taurus
29th	01:11 pm	Gemini

May 1968

2nd	01:50 am	Cancer
4th	12:54 pm	Leo
6th	08:58 pm	Virgo
9th	01:21 am	Libra
11th	02:30 am	Scorpio
13th	01:53 am	Sagittarius
15th	01:31 am	Capricorn
17th	03:22 am	Aquarius
19th	08:53 am	Pisces
21st	06:14 pm	Aries
24th	06:16 am	Taurus
26th	07:12 pm	Gemini
29th	07:43 am	Cancer
31st	06:53 pm	Leo

June 1968

3rd	03:52 am	Virgo
5th	09:49 am	Libra
7th	12:30 pm	Scorpio
9th	12:42 pm	Sagittarius
11th	12:05 pm	Capricorn
13th	12:46 pm	Aquarius
15th	04:42 pm	Pisces
18th	12:50 am	Aries
20th	12:25 pm	Taurus
23rd	01:22 am	Gemini
25th	01:43 pm	Cancer
28th	12:31 am	Leo
30th	09:26 am	Virgo

July 1968

2nd	04:10 pm	Libra
4th	08:20 pm	Scorpio
6th	10:05 pm	Sagittarius
8th	10:24 pm	Capricorn
10th	11:03 pm	Aquarius
13th	02:03 am	Pisces
15th	08:52 am	Aries
17th	07:31 pm	Taurus
20th	08:13 am	Gemini
22nd	08:31 pm	Cancer
25th	06:55 am	Leo
27th	03:10 pm	Virgo
29th	09:32 pm	Libra

August 1968

1st	02:11 am	Scorpio
3rd	05:11 am	Sagittarius
5th	06:57 am	Capricorn
7th	08:37 am	Aquarius
9th	11:46 am.	Pisces
11th	05:53 pm	Aries
14th	03:36 am	Taurus
16th	03:51 pm	Gemini
19th	04:15 am	Cancer
21st	02:40 pm	Leo
23rd	10:21 pm	Virgo
26th	03:45 am	Libra
28th	07:38 am	Scorpio
30th	10:41 am	Sagittarius

September 1968

1st	01:22 pm	Capricorn
3rd	04:19 pm	Aquarius
5th	08:27 pm	Pisces
8th	02:49 am	Aries
10th	12:06 pm	Taurus
12th	11:54 pm	Gemini
15th	12:28 pm	Cancer
17th	11:25 pm	Leo
20th	07:16 am	Virgo
22nd	12:00 pm	Libra
24th	02:39 pm	Scorpio
26th	04:30 pm	Sagittarius
28th	06:44 pm	Capricorn
30th	10:11 pm	Aquarius

October 1968

3rd	03:21 am	Pisces
5th	10:35 am	Aries
7th	08:07 pm	Taurus
10th	07:44 am	Gemini
12th	08:23 pm	Cancer
15th	08:08 am	Leo
17th	04:59 pm	Virgo
19th	10:05 pm	Libra
22nd	12:06 am	Scorpio
24th	12:32 am	Sagittarius
26th	01:13 am	Capricorn
28th	03:43 am	Aquarius
30th	08:54 am	Pisces

November 1968

1st	04:51 pm	Aries
4th	03:01 am	Taurus
6th	02:48 pm	Gemini
9th	03:27 am	Cancer
11th	03:45 pm	Leo
14th	01:55 am	Virgo
16th	08:26 am	Libra
18th	11:06 am	Scorpio
20th	11:04 am	Sagittarius
22nd	10:20 am	Capricorn
24th	11:02 am	Aquarius
26th	02:53 pm	Pisces
28th	10:26 pm	Aries

December 1968

1st	08:58 am	Taurus
3rd	09:06 pm	Gemini
6th	09:43 am	Cancer
8th	10:03 pm	Leo
11th	09:00 am	Virgo
13th	05:09 pm	Libra
15th	09:31 pm	Scorpio
17th	10:28 pm	Sagittarius
19th	09:32 pm	Capricorn
21st	08:59 pm	Aquarius
23rd	11:01 pm	Pisces
26th	05:02 am	Aries
28th	02:57 pm	Taurus
31st	03:11 am	Gemini

January 1969

2nd	03:53 pm	Cancer
5th	03:55 am	Leo
7th	02:42 pm	Virgo
9th	11:33 pm	Libra
12th	05:32 am	Scorpio
14th	08:19 am	Sagittarius
16th	08:39 am	Capricorn
18th	08:17 am	Aquarius
20th	09:21 am	Pisces
22nd	01:43 pm	Aries
24th	10:13 pm	Taurus
27th	09:53 am	Gemini
29th	10:36 pm	Cancer

February 1969

1st	10:29 am	Leo
3rd	08:41 pm	Virgo
6th	05:00 am	Libra
8th	11:18 am	Scorpio
10th	03:23 pm	Sagittarius
12th	05:28 pm	Capricorn
14th	06:31 pm	Aquarius
16th	08:03 pm	Pisces
18th	11:49 pm	Aries
21st	07:02 am	Taurus
23rd	05:41 pm	Gemini
26th	06:11 am	Cancer
28th	06:12 pm	Leo

March 1969

3rd	04:07 am	Virgo
5th	11:34 am	Libra
7th	04:56 pm	Scorpio
9th	08:48 pm	Sagittarius
11th	11:40 pm	Capricorn
14th	02:09 am	Aquarius
16th	05:04 am	Pisces
18th	09:27 am	Aries
20th	04:20 pm	Taurus
23rd	02:13 am	Gemini
25th	02:19 pm	Cancer
28th	02:37 am	Leo
30th	12:54 pm	Virgo

April 1969

1st	08:03 pm	Libra
4th	12:22 am	Scorpio
6th	02:57 am	Sagittarius
8th	05:05 am	Capricorn
10th	07:46 am	Aquarius
12th	11:41 am	Pisces
14th	05:13 pm	Aries
17th	12:43 am	Taurus
19th	10:28 am	Gemini
21st	10:17 pm	Cancer
24th	10:51 am	Leo
26th	09:57 pm	Virgo
29th	05:44 am	Libra

May 1969

1st	09:50 am	Scorpio
3rd	11:19 am	Sagittarius
5th	11:57 am	Capricorn
7th	01:28 pm	Aquarius
9th	05:04 pm	Pisces
11th	11:09 pm	Aries
14th	07:28 am	Taurus
16th	05:41 pm	Gemini
19th	05:31 am	Cancer
21st	06:12 pm	Leo
24th	06:07 am	Virgo
26th	03:08 pm	Libra
28th	08:05 pm	Scorpio
30th	09:30 pm	Sagittarius

June 1969

1st	09:07 pm	Capricorn
3rd	09:04 pm	Aquarius
5th	11:13 pm	Pisces
8th	04:37 am	Aries
10th	01:06 pm	Taurus
12th	11:49 pm	Gemini
15th	11:52 am	Cancer
18th	12:35 am	Leo
20th	12:54 pm	Virgo
22nd	11:04 pm	Libra
25th	05:31 am	Scorpio
27th	08:00 am	Sagittarius
29th	07:44 am	Capricorn

July 1969

1st	06:49 am	Aquarius
3rd	07:26 am	Pisces
5th	11:16 am	Aries
7th	06:53 pm	Taurus
10th	05:31 am	Gemini
12th	05:47 pm	Cancer
15th	06:29 am	Leo
17th	06:42 pm	Virgo
20th	05:20 am	Libra
22nd	01:04 pm	Scorpio
24th	05:11 pm	Sagittarius
26th	06:09 pm	Capricorn
28th	05:35 pm	Aquarius
30th	05:31 pm	Pisces

August 1969

1st	07:55 pm	Aries
4th	02:02 am	Taurus
6th	11:49 am	Gemini
8th	11:57 pm	Cancer
11th	12:38 pm	Leo
14th	12:33 am	Virgo
16th	10:51 am	Libra
18th	06:54 pm	Scorpio
21st	12:12 am	Sagittarius
23rd	02:49 am	Capricorn
25th	03:36 am	Aquarius
27th	04:03 am	Pisces
29th	05:57 am	Aries
31st	10:50 am	Taurus

September 1969

2nd	07:24 pm	Gemini
5th	06:57 am	Cancer
7th	07:36 pm	Leo
10th	07:20 am	Virgo
12th	05:02 pm	Libra
15th	12:25 am	Scorpio
17th	05:42 am	Sagittarius
19th	09:14 am	Capricorn
21st	11:31 am	Aquarius
23rd	01:22 pm	Pisces
25th	03:56 pm	Aries
27th	08:29 pm	Taurus
30th	04:06 am	Gemini

October 1969

2nd	02:52 pm	Cancer
5th	03:25 am	Leo
7th	03:21 pm	Virgo
10th	12:48 am	Libra
12th	07:19 am	Scorpio
14th	11:33 am	Sagittarius
16th	02:35 pm	Capricorn
18th	05:21 pm	Aquarius
20th	08:26 pm	Pisces
23rd	12:17 am	Aries
25th	05:33 am	Taurus
27th	01:00 pm	Gemini
29th	11:13 pm	Cancer

November 1969

1st	11:35 am	Leo
4th	12:00 am	Virgo
6th	09:59 am	Libra
8th	04:18 pm	Scorpio
10th	07:30 pm	Sagittarius
12th	09:09 pm	Capricorn
14th	10:53 pm	Aquarius
17th	01:52 am	Pisces
19th	06:32 am	Aries
21st	12:52 pm	Taurus
23rd	08:59 pm	Gemini
26th	07:10 am	Cancer
28th	07:22 pm	Leo

December 1969

1st	08:14 am	Virgo
3rd	07:17 pm	Libra
6th	02:30 am	Scorpio
8th	05:43 am	Sagittarius
10th	06:20 am	Capricorn
12th	06:27 am	Aquarius
14th	07:56 am	Pisces
16th	11:56 am	Aries
18th	06:35 pm	Taurus
21st	03:28 am	Gemini
23rd	02:09 pm	Cancer
26th	02:21 am	Leo
28th	03:20 pm	Virgo
31st	03:18 am	Libra

January 1970

2nd	12:03 pm	Scorpio
4th	04:33 pm	Sagittarius
6th	05:30 pm	Capricorn
8th	04:48 pm	Aquarius
10th	04:37 pm	Pisces
12th	06:48 pm	Aries
15th	12:20 am	Taurus
17th	09:07 am	Gemini
19th	08:14 pm	Cancer
22nd	08:40 am	Leo
24th	09:33 pm	Virgo
27th	09:42 am	Libra
29th	07:34 pm	Scorpio

February 1970

1st	01:50 am	Sagittarius
3rd	04:22 am	Capricorn
5th	04:20 am	Aquarius
7th	03:37 am	Pisces
9th	04:17 am	Aries
11th	07:59 am	Taurus
13th	03:29 pm	Gemini
16th	02:17 am	Cancer
18th	02:53 pm	Leo
21st	03:42 am	Virgo
23rd	03:30 pm	Libra
26th	01:23 am	Scorpio
28th	08:38 am	Sagittarius

March 1970

2nd	12:54 pm	Capricorn
4th	02:35 pm	Aquarius
6th	02:49 pm	Pisces
8th	03:16 pm	Aries
10th	05:43 pm	Taurus
12th	11:37 pm	Gemini
15th	09:19 am	Cancer
17th	09:40 pm	Leo
20th	10:30 am	Virgo
22nd	09:57 pm	Libra
25th	07:10 am	Scorpio
27th	02:07 pm	Sagittarius
29th	07:00 pm	Capricorn
31st	10:08 pm	Aquarius

April 1970

3rd	12:01 am	Pisces
5th	01:32 am	Aries
7th	04:02 am	Taurus
9th	09:02 am	Gemini
11th	05:33 pm	Cancer
14th	05:16 am	Leo
16th	06:07 pm	Virgo
19th	05:35 am	Libra
21st	02:15 pm	Scorpio
23rd	08:15 pm	Sagittarius
26th	12:26 am	Capricorn
28th	03:43 am	Aquarius
30th	06:38 am	Pisces

May 1970

2nd	09:32 am	Aries
4th	01:05 pm	Taurus
6th	06:18 pm	Gemini
9th	02:17 am	Cancer
11th	01:22 pm	Leo
14th	02:11 am	Virgo
16th	02:03 pm	Libra
18th	10:49 pm	Scorpio
21st	04:11 am	Sagittarius
23rd	07:13 am	Capricorn
25th	09:26 am	Aquarius
27th	11:59 am	Pisces
29th	03:27 pm	Aries
31st	08:03 pm	Taurus

June 1970

3rd	02:10 am	Gemini
5th	10:25 am	Cancer
7th	09:17 pm	Leo
10th	10:02 am	Virgo
12th	10:28 pm	Libra
15th	08:02 am	Scorpio
17th	01:39 pm	Sagittarius
19th	04:05 pm	Capricorn
21st	05:01 pm	Aquarius
23rd	06:12 pm	Pisces
25th	08:52 pm	Aries
28th	01:35 am	Taurus
30th	08:24 am	Gemini

July 1970

2nd	05:21 pm	Cancer
5th	04:26 am	Leo
7th	05:11 pm	Virgo
10th	06:03 am	Libra
12th	04:41 pm	Scorpio
14th	11:26 pm	Sagittarius
17th	02:19 am	Capricorn
19th	02:45 am	Aquarius
21st	02:37 am	Pisces
23rd	03:43 am	Aries
25th	07:18 am	Taurus
27th	01:53 pm	Gemini
29th	11:14 pm	Cancer

August 1970

1st	10:44 am	Leo
3rd	11:34 pm	Virgo
6th	12:33 pm	Libra
8th	11:57 pm	Scorpio
11th	08:07 am	Sagittarius
13th	12:25 pm	Capricorn
15th	01:31 pm	Aquarius
17th	01:01 pm	Pisces
19th	12:50 pm	Aries
21st	02:46 pm	Taurus
23rd	08:03 pm	Gemini
26th	04:58 am	Cancer
28th	04:38 pm	Leo
31st	05:36 am	Virgo

September 1970

2nd	06:26 pm	Libra
5th	05:54 am	Scorpio
7th	02:58 pm	Sagittarius
9th	08:52 pm	Capricorn
11th	11:34 pm	Aquarius
13th	11:57 pm	Pisces
15th	11:35 pm	Aries
18th	12:21 am	Taurus
20th	04:02 am	Gemini
22nd	11:41 am	Cancer
24th	10:54 pm	Leo
27th	11:54 am	Virgo
30th	12:33 am	Libra

October 1970

2nd	11:35 am	Scorpio
4th	08:31 pm	Sagittarius
7th	03:10 am	Capricorn
9th	07:26 am	Aquarius
11th	09:30 am	Pisces
13th	10:12 am	Aries
15th	11:00 am	Taurus
17th	01:43 pm	Gemini
19th	07:59 pm	Cancer
22nd	06:12 am	Leo
24th	06:57 pm	Virgo
27th	07:37 am	Libra
29th	06:15 pm	Scorpio

November 1970

1st	02:24 am	Sagittarius
3rd	08:33 am	Capricorn
5th	01:11 pm	Aquarius
7th	04:33 pm	Pisces
9th	06:52 pm	Aries
11th	08:50 pm	Taurus
13th	11:48 pm	Gemini
16th	05:23 am	Cancer
18th	02:36 pm	Leo
21st	02:50 am	Virgo
23rd	03:39 pm	Libra
26th	02:25 am	Scorpio
28th	10:02 am	Sagittarius
30th	03:06 pm	Capricorn

December 1970

2nd	06:45 pm	Aquarius
4th	09:55 pm	Pisces
7th	01:03 am	Aries
9th	04:24 am	Taurus
11th	08:33 am	Gemini
13th	02:32 pm	Cancer
15th	11:22 pm	Leo
18th	11:05 am	Virgo
21st	12:01 am	Libra
23rd	11:27 am	Scorpio
25th	07:28 pm	Sagittarius
28th	12:01 am	Capricorn
30th	02:24 am	Aquarius

January 1971
1st 04:08 am Pisces
3rd 06:26 am Aries
5th 10:00 am Taurus
7th 03:08 pm Gemini
9th 10:09 pm Cancer
12th 07:24 am Leo
14th 06:58 pm Virgo
17th 07:53 am Libra
19th 08:04 pm Scorpio
22nd 05:16 am Sagittarius
24th 10:33 am Capricorn
26th 12:36 pm Aquarius
28th 01:02 pm Pisces
30th 01:36 pm Aries

February 1971
1st 03:49 pm Taurus
3rd 08:35 pm Gemini
6th 04:07 am Cancer
8th 02:06 pm Leo
11th 01:58 am Virgo
13th 02:50 pm Libra
16th 03:22 am Scorpio
18th 01:46 pm Sagittarius
20th 08:37 pm Capricorn
22nd 11:43 pm Aquarius
25th 12:05 am Pisces
26th 11:30 pm Aries
28th 11:54 pm Taurus

March 1971
3rd 03:02 am Gemini
5th 09:47 am Cancer
7th 07:55 pm Leo
10th 08:10 am Virgo
12th 09:06 pm Libra
15th 09:31 am Scorpio
17th 08:24 pm Sagittarius
20th 04:37 am Capricorn
22nd 09:29 am Aquarius
24th 11:08 am Pisces
26th 10:46 am Aries
28th 10:16 am Taurus
30th 11:44 am Gemini

April 1971
1st 04:51 pm Cancer
4th 02:06 am Leo
6th 02:16 pm Virgo
9th 03:17 am Libra
11th 03:28 pm Scorpio
14th 02:03 am Sagittarius
16th 10:38 am Capricorn
18th 04:46 pm Aquarius
20th 08:08 pm Pisces
22nd 09:08 pm Aries
24th 09:07 pm Taurus
26th 09:58 pm Gemini
29th 01:43 am Cancer

May 1971
1st 09:35 am Leo
3rd 09:03 pm Virgo
6th 09:59 am Libra
8th 10:04 pm Scorpio
11th 08:08 am Sagittarius
13th 04:09 pm Capricorn
15th 10:20 pm Aquarius
18th 02:39 am Pisces
20th 05:11 am Aries
22nd 06:31 am Taurus
24th 08:01 am Gemini
26th 11:26 am Cancer
28th 06:16 pm Leo
31st 04:48 am Virgo

June 1971
2nd 05:27 pm Libra
5th 05:36 am Scorpio
7th 03:28 pm Sagittarius
9th 10:45 pm Capricorn
12th 04:03 am Aquarius
14th 08:01 am Pisces
16th 11:06 am Aries
18th 01:39 pm Taurus
20th 04:24 pm Gemini
22nd 08:30 pm Cancer
25th 03:12 am Leo
27th 01:06 pm Virgo
30th 01:22 am Libra

July 1971
2nd 01:46 pm Scorpio
4th 11:59 pm Sagittarius
7th 07:03 am Capricorn
9th 11:27 am Aquarius
11th 02:14 pm Pisces
13th 04:32 pm Aries
15th 07:10 pm Taurus
17th 10:47 pm Gemini
20th 03:57 am Cancer
22nd 11:17 am Leo
24th 09:09 pm Virgo
27th 09:12 am Libra
29th 09:50 pm Scorpio

August 1971
1st 08:50 am Sagittarius
3rd 04:32 pm Capricorn
5th 08:47 pm Aquarius
7th 10:34 pm Pisces
9th 11:27 pm Aries
12th 12:55 am Taurus
14th 04:11 am Gemini
16th 09:50 am Cancer
18th 05:58 pm Leo
21st 04:19 am Virgo
23rd 04:23 pm Libra
26th 05:09 am Scorpio
28th 04:57 pm Sagittarius
31st 01:54 am Capricorn

September 1971
2nd 07:04 am Aquarius
4th 08:51 am Pisces
6th 08:43 am Aries
8th 08:38 am Taurus
10th 10:25 am Gemini
12th 03:21 pm Cancer
14th 11:38 pm Leo
17th 10:29 am Virgo
19th 10:47 pm Libra
22nd 11:33 am Scorpio
24th 11:43 pm Sagittarius
27th 09:53 am Capricorn
29th 04:39 pm Aquarius

October 1971
1st 07:37 pm Pisces
3rd 07:41 pm Aries
5th 06:42 pm Taurus
7th 06:53 pm Gemini
9th 10:11 pm Cancer
12th 05:30 am Leo
14th 04:16 pm Virgo
17th 04:47 am Libra
19th 05:31 pm Scorpio
22nd 05:32 am Sagittarius
24th 04:05 pm Capricorn
27th 12:11 am Aquarius
29th 04:57 am Pisces
31st 06:26 am Aries

November 1971
2nd 05:55 am Taurus
4th 05:27 am Gemini
6th 07:15 am Cancer
8th 12:57 pm Leo
10th 10:44 pm Virgo
13th 11:06 am Libra
15th 11:50 pm Scorpio
18th 11:30 am Sagittarius
20th 09:36 pm Capricorn
23rd 05:52 am Aquarius
25th 11:48 am Pisces
27th 03:04 pm Aries
29th 04:08 pm Taurus

December 1971
1st 04:25 pm Gemini
3rd 05:51 pm Cancer
5th 10:17 pm Leo
8th 06:41 am Virgo
10th 06:19 pm Libra
13th 07:02 am Scorpio
15th 06:37 pm Sagittarius
18th 04:07 am Capricorn
20th 11:33 am Aquarius
22nd 05:10 pm Pisces
24th 09:09 pm Aries
26th 11:45 pm Taurus
29th 01:38 am Gemini
31st 04:01 am Cancer

January 1972		
2nd	08:22 am	Leo
4th	03:50 pm	Virgo
7th	02:33 am	Libra
9th	03:03 pm	Scorpio
12th	02:57 am	Sagittarius
14th	12:26 pm	Capricorn
16th	07:04 pm	Aquarius
18th	11:28 pm	Pisces
21st	02:35 am	Aries
23rd	05:17 am	Taurus
25th	08:14 am	Gemini
27th	12:02 pm	Cancer
29th	05:21 pm	Leo

February 1972		
1st	12:56 am	Virgo
3rd	11:07 am	Libra
5th	11:18 pm	Scorpio
8th	11:38 am	Sagittarius
10th	09:50 pm	Capricorn
13th	04:36 am	Aquarius
15th	08:11 am	Pisces
17th	09:51 am	Aries
19th	11:11 am	Taurus
21st	01:36 pm	Gemini
23rd	05:52 pm	Cancer
26th	12:15 am	Leo
28th	08:39 am	Virgo

March 1972		
1st	07:00 pm	Libra
4th	07:00 am	Scorpio
6th	07:37 pm	Sagittarius
9th	06:50 am	Capricorn
11th	02:43 pm	Aquarius
13th	06:39 pm	Pisces
15th	07:37 pm	Aries
17th	07:28 pm	Taurus
19th	08:13 pm	Gemini
21st	11:26 pm	Cancer
24th	05:46 am	Leo
26th	02:48 pm	Virgo
29th	01:42 am	Libra
31st	01:49 pm	Scorpio

April 1972		
3rd	02:27 am	Sagittarius
5th	02:21 pm	Capricorn
7th	11:38 pm	Aquarius
10th	04:58 am	Pisces
12th	06:32 am	Aries
14th	05:55 am	Taurus
16th	05:17 am	Gemini
18th	06:46 am	Cancer
20th	11:47 am	Leo
22nd	08:24 pm	Virgo
25th	07:34 am	Libra
27th	07:56 pm	Scorpio
30th	08:31 am	Sagittarius

May 1972		
2nd	08:29 pm	Capricorn
5th	06:35 am	Aquarius
7th	01:28 pm	Pisces
9th	04:35 pm	Aries
11th	04:48 pm	Taurus
13th	03:57 pm	Gemini
15th	04:16 pm	Cancer
17th	07:38 pm	Leo
20th	02:56 am	Virgo
22nd	01:36 pm	Libra
25th	02:01 am	Scorpio
27th	02:33 pm	Sagittarius
30th	02:13 am	Capricorn

June 1972		
1st	12:15 pm	Aquarius
3rd	07:52 pm	Pisces
6th	12:28 am	Aries
8th	02:15 am	Taurus
10th	02:24 am	Gemini
12th	02:45 am	Cancer
14th	05:10 am	Leo
16th	11:03 am	Virgo
18th	08:39 pm	Libra
21st	08:43 am	Scorpio
23rd	09:14 pm	Sagittarius
26th	08:36 am	Capricorn
28th	06:03 pm	Aquarius

July 1972		
1st	01:19 am	Pisces
3rd	06:22 am	Aries
5th	09:25 am	Taurus
7th	11:05 am	Gemini
9th	12:29 pm	Cancer
11th	03:05 pm	Leo
13th	08:16 pm	Virgo
16th	04:49 am	Libra
18th	04:15 pm	Scorpio
21st	04:46 am	Sagittarius
23rd	04:10 pm	Capricorn
26th	01:07 am	Aquarius
28th	07:29 am	Pisces
30th	11:50 am	Aries

August 1972		
1st	02:58 pm	Taurus
3rd	05:33 pm	Gemini
5th	08:18 pm	Cancer
7th	11:56 pm	Leo
10th	05:23 am	Virgo
12th	01:27 pm	Libra
15th	12:20 am	Scorpio
17th	12:49 pm	Sagittarius
20th	12:38 am	Capricorn
22nd	09:43 am	Aquarius
24th	03:29 pm	Pisces
26th	06:41 pm	Aries
28th	08:43 pm	Taurus
30th	10:56 pm	Gemini

September 1972		
2nd	02:12 am	Cancer
4th	06:54 am	Leo
6th	01:15 pm	Virgo
8th	09:37 pm	Libra
11th	08:15 am	Scorpio
13th	08:42 pm	Sagittarius
16th	09:08 am	Capricorn
18th	07:05 pm	Aquarius
21st	01:09 am	Pisces
23rd	03:45 am	Aries
25th	04:28 am	Taurus
27th	05:14 am	Gemini
29th	07:39 am	Cancer

October 1972		
1st	12:25 pm	Leo
3rd	07:31 pm	Virgo
6th	04:35 am	Libra
8th	03:27 pm	Scorpio
11th	03:53 am	Sagittarius
13th	04:44 pm	Capricorn
16th	03:51 am	Aquarius
18th	11:13 am	Pisces
20th	02:23 pm	Aries
22nd	02:37 pm	Taurus
24th	02:02 pm	Gemini
26th	02:44 pm	Cancer
28th	06:14 pm	Leo
31st	12:59 am	Virgo

November 1972		
2nd	10:27 am	Libra
4th	09:46 pm	Scorpio
7th	10:17 am	Sagittarius
9th	11:11 pm	Capricorn
12th	11:03 am	Aquarius
14th	07:56 pm	Pisces
17th	12:44 am	Aries
19th	01:53 am	Taurus
21st	01:05 am	Gemini
23rd	12:31 am	Cancer
25th	02:12 am	Leo
27th	07:24 am	Virgo
29th	04:15 pm	Libra

December 1972		
2nd	03:42 am	Scorpio
4th	04:23 pm	Sagittarius
7th	05:07 am	Capricorn
9th	04:54 pm	Aquarius
12th	02:33 am	Pisces
14th	09:00 am	Aries
16th	11:59 am	Taurus
18th	12:24 pm	Gemini
20th	11:57 am	Cancer
22nd	12:34 pm	Leo
24th	04:03 pm	Virgo
26th	11:22 pm	Libra
29th	10:10 am	Scorpio
31st	10:52 pm	Sagittarius

January 1973

3rd	11:30 am	Capricorn
5th	10:47 pm	Aquarius
8th	08:03 am	Pisces
10th	02:58 pm	Aries
12th	07:25 pm	Taurus
14th	09:41 pm	Gemini
16th	10:39 pm	Cancer
18th	11:40 pm	Leo
21st	02:24 am	Virgo
23rd	08:16 am	Libra
25th	05:52 pm	Scorpio
28th	06:11 am	Sagittarius
30th	06:54 pm	Capricorn

February 1973

2nd	05:55 am	Aquarius
4th	02:22 pm	Pisces
6th	08:29 pm	Aries
9th	12:54 am	Taurus
11th	04:10 am	Gemini
13th	06:44 am	Cancer
15th	09:12 am	Leo
17th	12:31 pm	Virgo
19th	05:58 pm	Libra
22nd	02:35 am	Scorpio
24th	02:14 pm	Sagittarius
27th	03:04 am	Capricorn

March 1973

1st	02:22 pm	Aquarius
3rd	10:31 pm	Pisces
6th	03:37 am	Aries
8th	06:51 am	Taurus
10th	09:31 am	Gemini
12th	12:29 pm	Cancer
14th	04:08 pm	Leo
16th	08:42 pm	Virgo
19th	02:48 am	Libra
21st	11:16 am	Scorpio
23rd	10:26 pm	Sagittarius
26th	11:16 am	Capricorn
28th	11:13 pm	Aquarius
31st	07:55 am	Pisces

April 1973

2nd	12:48 pm	Aries
4th	02:58 pm	Taurus
6th	04:12 pm	Gemini
8th	06:05 pm	Cancer
10th	09:31 pm	Leo
13th	02:47 am	Virgo
15th	09:50 am	Libra
17th	06:51 pm	Scorpio
20th	06:02 am	Sagittarius
22nd	06:49 pm	Capricorn
25th	07:21 am	Aquarius
27th	05:10 pm	Pisces
29th	10:53 pm	Aries

May 1973

2nd	01:02 am	Taurus
4th	01:16 am	Gemini
6th	01:35 am	Cancer
8th	03:36 am	Leo
10th	08:13 am	Virgo
12th	03:31 pm	Libra
15th	01:09 am	Scorpio
17th	12:42 pm	Sagittarius
20th	01:30 am	Capricorn
22nd	02:17 pm	Aquarius
25th	01:05 am	Pisces
27th	08:15 am	Aries
29th	11:28 am	Taurus
31st	11:53 am	Gemini

June 1973

2nd	11:21 am	Cancer
4th	11:49 am	Leo
6th	02:51 pm	Virgo
8th	09:16 pm	Libra
11th	06:52 am	Scorpio
13th	06:43 pm	Sagittarius
16th	07:37 am	Capricorn
18th	08:19 pm	Aquarius
21st	07:29 am	Pisces
23rd	03:48 pm	Aries
25th	08:37 pm	Taurus
27th	10:18 pm	Gemini
29th	10:08 pm	Cancer

July 1973

1st	09:56 pm	Leo
3rd	11:31 pm	Virgo
6th	04:24 am	Libra
8th	01:05 pm	Scorpio
11th	12:48 am	Sagittarius
13th	01:46 pm	Capricorn
16th	02:15 am	Aquarius
18th	01:07 pm	Pisces
20th	09:44 pm	Aries
23rd	03:41 am	Taurus
25th	06:58 am	Gemini
27th	08:10 am	Cancer
29th	08:29 am	Leo
31st	09:35 am	Virgo

August 1973

2nd	01:12 pm	Libra
4th	08:36 pm	Scorpio
7th	07:37 am	Sagittarius
9th	08:30 pm	Capricorn
12th	08:52 am	Aquarius
14th	07:14 pm	Pisces
17th	03:16 am	Aries
19th	09:14 am	Taurus
21st	01:26 pm	Gemini
23rd	04:08 pm	Cancer
25th	05:49 pm	Leo
27th	07:33 pm	Virgo
29th	10:52 pm	Libra

September 1973

1st	05:18 am	Scorpio
3rd	03:24 pm	Sagittarius
6th	04:01 am	Capricorn
8th	04:31 pm	Aquarius
11th	02:40 am	Pisces
13th	09:56 am	Aries
15th	02:59 pm	Taurus
17th	06:48 pm	Gemini
19th	10:01 pm	Cancer
22nd	12:56 am	Leo
24th	03:59 am	Virgo
26th	08:01 am	Libra
28th	02:18 pm	Scorpio
30th	11:47 pm	Sagittarius

October 1973

3rd	12:02 pm	Capricorn
6th	12:49 am	Aquarius
8th	11:24 am	Pisces
10th	06:29 pm	Aries
12th	10:36 pm	Taurus
15th	01:09 am	Gemini
17th	03:29 am	Cancer
19th	06:25 am	Leo
21st	10:19 am	Virgo
23rd	03:28 pm	Libra
25th	10:28 pm	Scorpio
28th	07:58 am	Sagittarius
30th	07:57 pm	Capricorn

November 1973

2nd	08:58 am	Aquarius
4th	08:26 pm	Pisces
7th	04:19 am	Aries
9th	08:26 am	Taurus
11th	10:00 am	Gemini
13th	10:46 am	Cancer
15th	12:20 pm	Leo
17th	03:41 pm	Virgo
19th	09:16 pm	Libra
22nd	05:07 am	Scorpio
24th	03:11 pm	Sagittarius
27th	03:13 am	Capricorn
29th	04:17 pm	Aquarius

December 1973

2nd	04:32 am	Pisces
4th	01:50 pm	Aries
6th	07:09 pm	Taurus
8th	08:58 pm	Gemini
10th	08:52 pm	Cancer
12th	08:44 pm	Leo
14th	10:21 pm	Virgo
17th	02:53 am	Libra
19th	10:44 am	Scorpio
21st	09:20 pm	Sagittarius
24th	09:41 am	Capricorn
26th	10:43 pm	Aquarius
29th	11:10 am	Pisces
31st	09:34 pm	Aries

January 1974

3rd	04:38 am	Taurus
5th	08:00 am	Gemini
7th	08:28 am	Cancer
9th	07:42 am	Leo
11th	07:42 am	Virgo
13th	10:21 am	Libra
15th	04:54 pm	Scorpio
18th	03:12 am	Sagittarius
20th	03:47 pm	Capricorn
23rd	04:50 am	Aquarius
25th	05:01 pm	Pisces
28th	03:32 am	Aries
30th	11:42 am	Taurus

February 1974

1st	04:53 pm	Gemini
3rd	07:06 pm	Cancer
5th	07:12 pm	Leo
7th	06:52 pm	Virgo
9th	08:10 pm	Libra
12th	12:58 am	Scorpio
14th	10:01 am	Sagittarius
16th	10:16 pm	Capricorn
19th	11:21 am	Aquarius
21st	11:15 pm	Pisces
24th	09:13 am	Aries
26th	05:11 pm	Taurus
28th	11:10 pm	Gemini

March 1974

3rd	03:00 am	Cancer
5th	04:49 am	Leo
7th	05:33 am	Virgo
9th	06:52 am	Libra
11th	10:40 am	Scorpio
13th	06:20 pm	Sagittarius
16th	05:41 am	Capricorn
18th	06:38 pm	Aquarius
21st	06:34 am	Pisces
23rd	04:03 pm	Aries
25th	11:10 pm	Taurus
28th	04:33 am	Gemini
30th	08:40 am	Cancer

April 1974

1st	11:41 am	Leo
3rd	01:57 pm	Virgo
5th	04:23 pm	Libra
7th	08:25 pm	Scorpio
10th	03:27 am	Sagittarius
12th	01:56 pm	Capricorn
15th	02:34 am	Aquarius
17th	02:44 pm	Pisces
20th	12:20 am	Aries
22nd	06:54 am	Taurus
24th	11:11 am	Gemini
26th	02:18 pm	Cancer
28th	05:04 pm	Leo
30th	08:01 pm	Virgo

May 1974

2nd	11:39 pm	Libra
5th	04:43 am	Scorpio
7th	12:05 pm	Sagittarius
9th	10:15 pm	Capricorn
12th	10:34 am	Aquarius
14th	11:03 pm	Pisces
17th	09:20 am	Aries
19th	04:10 pm	Taurus
21st	07:54 pm	Gemini
23rd	09:46 pm	Cancer
25th	11:12 pm	Leo
28th	01:26 am	Virgo
30th	05:16 am	Libra

June 1974

1st	11:10 am	Scorpio
3rd	07:22 pm	Sagittarius
6th	05:48 am	Capricorn
8th	06:02 pm	Aquarius
11th	06:44 am	Pisces
13th	05:53 pm	Aries
16th	01:47 am	Taurus
18th	05:59 am	Gemini
20th	07:21 am	Cancer
22nd	07:30 am	Leo
24th	08:11 am	Virgo
26th	10:57 am	Libra
28th	04:40 pm	Scorpio

July 1974

1st	01:21 am	Sagittarius
3rd	12:19 pm	Capricorn
6th	12:41 am	Aquarius
8th	01:26 pm	Pisces
11th	01:10 am	Aries
13th	10:21 am	Taurus
15th	03:54 pm	Gemini
17th	05:56 pm	Cancer
19th	05:43 pm	Leo
21st	05:10 pm	Virgo
23rd	06:19 pm	Libra
25th	10:46 pm	Scorpio
28th	07:00 am	Sagittarius
30th	06:11 pm	Capricorn

August 1974

2nd	06:46 am	Aquarius
4th	07:27 pm	Pisces
7th	07:15 am	Aries
9th	05:13 pm	Taurus
12th	12:15 am	Gemini
14th	03:49 am	Cancer
16th	04:27 am	Leo
18th	03:43 am	Virgo
20th	03:45 am	Libra
22nd	06:37 am	Scorpio
24th	01:34 pm	Sagittarius
27th	12:15 am	Capricorn
29th	12:53 pm	Aquarius

September 1974

1st	01:29 am	Pisces
3rd	12:58 pm	Aries
5th	10:50 pm	Taurus
8th	06:36 am	Gemini
10th	11:40 am	Cancer
12th	01:54 pm	Leo
14th	02:12 pm	Virgo
16th	02:17 pm	Libra
18th	04:14 pm	Scorpio
20th	09:46 pm	Sagittarius
23rd	07:22 am	Capricorn
25th	07:39 pm	Aquarius
28th	08:15 am	Pisces
30th	07:26 pm	Aries

October 1974

3rd	04:39 am	Taurus
5th	12:01 pm	Gemini
7th	05:30 pm	Cancer
9th	09:03 pm	Leo
11th	10:56 pm	Virgo
14th	12:11 am	Libra
16th	02:23 am	Scorpio
18th	07:14 am	Sagittarius
20th	03:44 pm	Capricorn
23rd	03:20 am	Aquarius
25th	03:57 pm	Pisces
28th	03:14 am	Aries
30th	12:00 pm	Taurus

November 1974

1st	06:23 pm	Gemini
3rd	11:01 pm	Cancer
6th	02:30 am	Leo
8th	05:18 am	Virgo
10th	07:59 am	Libra
12th	11:23 am	Scorpio
14th	04:39 pm	Sagittarius
17th	12:42 am	Capricorn
19th	11:39 am	Aquarius
22nd	12:11 am	Pisces
24th	11:59 am	Aries
26th	09:05 pm	Taurus
29th	02:58 am	Gemini

December 1974

1st	06:22 am	Cancer
3rd	08:31 am	Leo
5th	10:40 am	Virgo
7th	01:43 pm	Libra
9th	06:14 pm	Scorpio
12th	12:35 am	Sagittarius
14th	09:04 am	Capricorn
16th	07:48 pm	Aquarius
19th	08:12 am	Pisces
21st	08:35 pm	Aries
24th	06:45 am	Taurus
26th	01:16 pm	Gemini
28th	04:16 pm	Cancer
30th	05:05 pm	Leo

January 1975

1st	05:33 pm	Virgo
3rd	07:22 pm	Libra
5th	11:39 pm	Scorpio
8th	06:39 am	Sagittarius
10th	03:58 pm	Capricorn
13th	03:03 am	Aquarius
15th	03:23 pm	Pisces
18th	04:04 am	Aries
20th	03:21 pm	Taurus
22nd	11:23 pm	Gemini
25th	03:20 am	Cancer
27th	04:00 am	Leo
29th	03:14 am	Virgo
31st	03:13 am	Libra

February 1975

2nd	05:53 am	Scorpio
4th	12:10 pm	Sagittarius
6th	09:42 pm	Capricorn
9th	09:17 am	Aquarius
11th	09:45 pm	Pisces
14th	10:22 am	Aries
16th	10:09 pm	Taurus
19th	07:35 am	Gemini
21st	01:19 pm	Cancer
23rd	03:13 pm	Leo
25th	02:37 pm	Virgo
27th	01:38 pm	Libra

March 1975

1st	02:34 pm	Scorpio
3rd	07:06 pm	Sagittarius
6th	03:40 am	Capricorn
8th	03:10 pm	Aquarius
11th	03:49 am	Pisces
13th	04:19 pm	Aries
16th	03:53 am	Taurus
18th	01:43 pm	Gemini
20th	08:48 pm	Cancer
23rd	12:31 am	Leo
25th	01:21 am	Virgo
27th	12:51 am	Libra
29th	01:08 am	Scorpio
31st	04:10 am	Sagittarius

April 1975

2nd	11:08 am	Capricorn
4th	09:45 pm	Aquarius
7th	10:17 am	Pisces
9th	10:44 pm	Aries
12th	09:53 am	Taurus
14th	07:14 pm	Gemini
17th	02:27 am	Cancer
19th	07:14 am	Leo
21st	09:43 am	Virgo
23rd	10:42 am	Libra
25th	11:40 am	Scorpio
27th	02:20 pm	Sagittarius
29th	08:09 pm	Capricorn

May 1975

2nd	05:34 am	Aquarius
4th	05:34 pm	Pisces
7th	06:03 am	Aries
9th	05:04 pm	Taurus
12th	01:44 am	Gemini
14th	08:08 am	Cancer
16th	12:39 pm	Leo
18th	03:46 pm	Virgo
20th	06:05 pm	Libra
22nd	08:26 pm	Scorpio
24th	11:52 pm	Sagittarius
27th	05:31 am	Capricorn
29th	02:09 pm	Aquarius

June 1975

1st	01:32 am	Pisces
3rd	02:01 pm	Aries
6th	01:19 am	Taurus
8th	09:49 am	Gemini
10th	03:22 pm	Cancer
12th	06:45 pm	Leo
14th	09:11 pm	Virgo
16th	11:41 pm	Libra
19th	02:59 am	Scorpio
21st	07:35 am	Sagittarius
23rd	01:56 pm	Capricorn
25th	10:33 pm	Aquarius
28th	09:33 am	Pisces
30th	10:02 pm	Aries

July 1975

3rd	09:54 am	Taurus
5th	06:59 pm	Gemini
8th	12:23 am	Cancer
10th	02:50 am	Leo
12th	03:56 am	Virgo
14th	05:21 am	Libra
16th	08:23 am	Scorpio
18th	01:32 pm	Sagittarius
20th	08:46 pm	Capricorn
23rd	05:56 am	Aquarius
25th	04:59 pm	Pisces
28th	05:27 am	Aries
30th	05:54 pm	Taurus

August 1975

2nd	04:02 am	Gemini
4th	10:17 am	Cancer
6th	12:44 pm	Leo
8th	12:54 pm	Virgo
10th	12:51 pm	Libra
12th	02:30 pm	Scorpio
14th	07:00 pm	Sagittarius
17th	02:25 am	Capricorn
19th	12:09 pm	Aquarius
21st	11:32 pm	Pisces
24th	12:03 pm	Aries
27th	12:45 am	Taurus
29th	11:54 am	Gemini
31st	07:35 pm	Cancer

September 1975

2nd	11:08 pm	Leo
4th	11:29 pm	Virgo
6th	10:38 pm	Libra
8th	10:46 pm	Scorpio
11th	01:41 am	Sagittarius
13th	08:11 am	Capricorn
15th	05:51 pm	Aquarius
18th	05:32 am	Pisces
20th	06:07 pm	Aries
23rd	06:43 am	Taurus
25th	06:13 pm	Gemini
28th	03:07 am	Cancer
30th	08:21 am	Leo

October 1975

2nd	10:03 am	Virgo
4th	09:39 am	Libra
6th	09:09 am	Scorpio
8th	10:36 am	Sagittarius
10th	03:29 pm	Capricorn
13th	12:10 am	Aquarius
15th	11:40 am	Pisces
18th	12:20 am	Aries
20th	12:43 pm	Taurus
22nd	11:51 pm	Gemini
25th	08:57 am	Cancer
27th	03:20 pm	Leo
29th	06:47 pm	Virgo
31st	07:55 pm	Libra

November 1975

2nd	08:08 pm	Scorpio
4th	09:10 pm	Sagittarius
7th	12:45 am	Capricorn
9th	07:59 am	Aquarius
11th	06:42 pm	Pisces
14th	07:17 am	Aries
16th	07:38 pm	Taurus
19th	06:14 am	Gemini
21st	02:36 pm	Cancer
23rd	08:48 pm	Leo
26th	01:05 am	Virgo
28th	03:48 am	Libra
30th	05:37 am	Scorpio

December 1975

2nd	07:33 am	Sagittarius
4th	10:58 am	Capricorn
6th	05:12 pm	Aquarius
9th	02:52 am	Pisces
11th	03:06 pm	Aries
14th	03:39 am	Taurus
16th	02:13 pm	Gemini
18th	09:49 pm	Cancer
21st	02:54 am	Leo
23rd	06:28 am	Virgo
25th	09:27 am	Libra
27th	12:28 pm	Scorpio
29th	03:53 pm	Sagittarius
31st	08:17 pm	Capricorn

January 1976

3rd	02:33 am	Aquarius
5th	11:35 am	Pisces
7th	11:21 pm	Aries
10th	12:10 pm	Taurus
12th	11:20 pm	Gemini
15th	07:01 am	Cancer
17th	11:15 am	Leo
19th	01:25 pm	Virgo
21st	03:11 pm	Libra
23rd	05:48 pm	Scorpio
25th	09:51 pm	Sagittarius
28th	03:24 am	Capricorn
30th	10:34 am	Aquarius

February 1976

1st	07:47 pm	Pisces
4th	07:17 am	Aries
6th	08:13 pm	Taurus
9th	08:16 am	Gemini
11th	04:59 pm	Cancer
13th	09:33 pm	Leo
15th	10:59 pm	Virgo
17th	11:14 pm	Libra
20th	12:14 am	Scorpio
22nd	03:18 am	Sagittarius
24th	08:54 am	Capricorn
26th	04:49 pm	Aquarius
29th	02:42 am	Pisces

March 1976

2nd	02:22 pm	Aries
5th	03:18 am	Taurus
7th	03:56 pm	Gemini
10th	01:59 am	Cancer
12th	07:56 am	Leo
14th	09:59 am	Virgo
16th	09:44 am	Libra
18th	09:18 am	Scorpio
20th	10:34 am	Sagittarius
22nd	02:48 pm	Capricorn
24th	10:20 pm	Aquarius
27th	08:34 am	Pisces
29th	08:37 pm	Aries

April 1976

1st	09:34 am	Taurus
3rd	10:16 pm	Gemini
6th	09:07 am	Cancer
8th	04:37 pm	Leo
10th	08:16 pm	Virgo
12th	08:55 pm	Libra
14th	08:15 pm	Scorpio
16th	08:15 pm	Sagittarius
18th	10:44 pm	Capricorn
21st	04:48 am	Aquarius
23rd	02:28 pm	Pisces
26th	02:37 am	Aries
28th	03:38 pm	Taurus

May 1976

1st	04:05 am	Gemini
3rd	02:54 pm	Cancer
5th	11:09 pm	Leo
8th	04:21 am	Virgo
10th	06:40 am	Libra
12th	07:03 am	Scorpio
14th	07:04 am	Sagittarius
16th	08:32 am	Capricorn
18th	01:03 pm	Aquarius
20th	09:27 pm	Pisces
23rd	09:07 am	Aries
25th	10:07 pm	Taurus
28th	10:22 am	Gemini
30th	08:39 pm	Cancer

June 1976

2nd	04:38 am	Leo
4th	10:21 am	Virgo
6th	02:00 pm	Libra
8th	03:58 pm	Scorpio
10th	05:07 pm	Sagittarius
12th	06:45 pm	Capricorn
14th	10:31 pm	Aquarius
17th	05:44 am	Pisces
19th	04:32 pm	Aries
22nd	05:22 am	Taurus
24th	05:37 pm	Gemini
27th	03:29 am	Cancer
29th	10:40 am	Leo

July 1976

1st	03:46 pm	Virgo
3rd	07:35 pm	Libra
5th	10:34 pm	Scorpio
8th	01:06 am	Sagittarius
10th	03:49 am	Capricorn
12th	07:53 am	Aquarius
14th	02:36 pm	Pisces
17th	12:40 am	Aries
19th	01:11 pm	Taurus
22nd	01:41 am	Gemini
24th	11:40 am	Cancer
26th	06:19 pm	Leo
28th	10:24 pm	Virgo
31st	01:14 am	Libra

August 1976

2nd	03:56 am	Scorpio
4th	07:03 am	Sagittarius
6th	10:55 am	Capricorn
8th	03:57 pm	Aquarius
10th	11:01 pm	Pisces
13th	08:49 am	Aries
15th	09:05 pm	Taurus
18th	09:54 am	Gemini
20th	08:34 pm	Cancer
23rd	03:31 am	Leo
25th	07:04 am	Virgo
27th	08:42 am	Libra
29th	10:05 am	Scorpio
31st	12:28 pm	Sagittarius

September 1976

2nd	04:29 pm	Capricorn
4th	10:20 pm	Aquarius
7th	06:12 am	Pisces
9th	04:18 pm	Aries
12th	04:30 am	Taurus
14th	05:32 pm	Gemini
17th	05:07 am	Cancer
19th	01:11 pm	Leo
21st	05:16 pm	Virgo
23rd	06:28 pm	Libra
25th	06:34 pm	Scorpio
27th	07:22 pm	Sagittarius
29th	10:13 pm	Capricorn

October 1976

2nd	03:49 am	Aquarius
4th	12:10 pm	Pisces
6th	10:50 pm	Aries
9th	11:11 am	Taurus
12th	12:15 am	Gemini
14th	12:24 pm	Cancer
16th	09:49 pm	Leo
19th	03:25 am	Virgo
21st	05:27 am	Libra
23rd	05:17 am	Scorpio
25th	04:49 am	Sagittarius
27th	05:56 am	Capricorn
29th	10:05 am	Aquarius
31st	05:53 pm	Pisces

November 1976

3rd	04:46 am	Aries
5th	05:23 pm	Taurus
8th	06:21 am	Gemini
10th	06:28 pm	Cancer
13th	04:36 am	Leo
15th	11:46 am	Virgo
17th	03:34 pm	Libra
19th	04:32 pm	Scorpio
21st	04:04 pm	Sagittarius
23rd	04:04 pm	Capricorn
25th	06:30 pm	Aquarius
28th	12:48 am	Pisces
30th	11:02 am	Aries

December 1976

2nd	11:42 pm	Taurus
5th	12:38 pm	Gemini
8th	12:21 am	Cancer
10th	10:12 am	Leo
12th	05:55 pm	Virgo
14th	11:13 pm	Libra
17th	02:02 am	Scorpio
19th	02:54 am	Sagittarius
21st	03:12 am	Capricorn
23rd	04:48 am	Aquarius
25th	09:36 am	Pisces
27th	06:32 pm	Aries
30th	06:43 am	Taurus

January 1977

1st	07:43 pm	Gemini
4th	07:13 am	Cancer
6th	04:21 pm	Leo
8th	11:23 pm	Virgo
11th	04:48 am	Libra
13th	08:44 am	Scorpio
15th	11:18 am	Sagittarius
17th	01:02 pm	Capricorn
19th	03:12 pm	Aquarius
21st	07:30 pm	Pisces
24th	03:20 am	Aries
26th	02:41 pm	Taurus
29th	03:37 am	Gemini
31st	03:20 pm	Cancer

February 1977

3rd	12:12 am	Leo
5th	06:17 am	Virgo
7th	10:36 am	Libra
9th	02:04 pm	Scorpio
11th	05:11 pm	Sagittarius
13th	08:14 pm	Capricorn
15th	11:45 pm	Aquarius
18th	04:45 am	Pisces
20th	12:23 pm	Aries
22nd	11:06 pm	Taurus
25th	11:50 am	Gemini
28th	12:02 am	Cancer

March 1977

2nd	09:25 am	Leo
4th	03:19 pm	Virgo
6th	06:35 pm	Libra
8th	08:37 pm	Scorpio
10th	10:42 pm	Sagittarius
13th	01:40 am	Capricorn
15th	06:00 am	Aquarius
17th	12:06 pm	Pisces
19th	08:23 pm	Aries
22nd	07:06 am	Taurus
24th	07:39 pm	Gemini
27th	08:17 am	Cancer
29th	06:41 pm	Leo

April 1977

1st	01:25 am	Virgo
3rd	04:39 am	Libra
5th	05:40 am	Scorpio
7th	06:09 am	Sagittarius
9th	07:41 am	Capricorn
11th	11:24 am	Aquarius
13th	05:50 pm	Pisces
16th	02:52 am	Aries
18th	02:03 pm	Taurus
21st	02:37 am	Gemini
23rd	03:25 pm	Cancer
26th	02:43 am	Leo
28th	10:52 am	Virgo
30th	03:13 pm	Libra

May 1977

2nd	04:24 pm	Scorpio
4th	03:59 pm	Sagittarius
6th	03:54 pm	Capricorn
8th	06:00 pm	Aquarius
10th	11:29 pm	Pisces
13th	08:30 am	Aries
15th	08:04 pm	Taurus
18th	08:50 am	Gemini
20th	09:36 pm	Cancer
23rd	09:13 am	Leo
25th	06:31 pm	Virgo
28th	12:29 am	Libra
30th	02:57 am	Scorpio

June 1977

1st	02:54 am	Sagittarius
3rd	02:07 am	Capricorn
5th	02:44 am	Aquarius
7th	06:36 am	Pisces
9th	02:34 pm	Aries
12th	01:57 am	Taurus
14th	02:50 pm	Gemini
17th	03:29 am	Cancer
19th	02:54 pm	Leo
22nd	12:29 am	Virgo
24th	07:36 am	Libra
26th	11:42 am	Scorpio
28th	01:02 pm	Sagittarius
30th	12:48 pm	Capricorn

July 1977

2nd	12:56 pm	Aquarius
4th	03:31 pm	Pisces
6th	10:03 pm	Aries
9th	08:33 am	Taurus
11th	09:15 pm	Gemini
14th	09:50 am	Cancer
16th	08:51 pm	Leo
19th	05:59 am	Virgo
21st	01:10 pm	Libra
23rd	06:14 pm	Scorpio
25th	09:05 pm	Sagittarius
27th	10:15 pm	Capricorn
29th	11:05 pm	Aquarius

August 1977

1st	01:24 am	Pisces
3rd	06:54 am	Aries
5th	04:18 pm	Taurus
8th	04:30 am	Gemini
10th	05:04 pm	Cancer
13th	03:57 am	Leo
15th	12:26 pm	Virgo
17th	06:49 pm	Libra
19th	11:35 pm	Scorpio
22nd	03:03 am	Sagittarius
24th	05:31 am	Capricorn
26th	07:41 am	Aquarius
28th	10:47 am	Pisces
30th	04:12 pm	Aries

September 1977

2nd	12:52 am	Taurus
4th	12:27 pm	Gemini
7th	01:03 am	Cancer
9th	12:14 pm	Leo
11th	08:35 pm	Virgo
14th	02:08 am	Libra
16th	05:46 am	Scorpio
18th	08:28 am	Sagittarius
20th	11:04 am	Capricorn
22nd	02:12 pm	Aquarius
24th	06:30 pm	Pisces
27th	12:41 am	Aries
29th	09:22 am	Taurus

October 1977

1st	08:34 pm	Gemini
4th	09:09 am	Cancer
6th	08:58 pm	Leo
9th	05:59 am	Virgo
11th	11:30 am	Libra
13th	02:11 pm	Scorpio
15th	03:27 pm	Sagittarius
17th	04:51 pm	Capricorn
19th	07:36 pm	Aquarius
22nd	12:27 am	Pisces
24th	07:34 am	Aries
26th	04:53 pm	Taurus
29th	04:08 am	Gemini
31st	04:40 pm	Cancer

November 1977

3rd	05:03 am	Leo
5th	03:17 pm	Virgo
7th	09:51 pm	Libra
10th	12:42 am	Scorpio
12th	01:04 am	Sagittarius
14th	12:51 am	Capricorn
16th	02:00 am	Aquarius
18th	05:59 am	Pisces
20th	01:13 pm	Aries
22nd	11:10 pm	Taurus
25th	10:49 am	Gemini
27th	11:20 pm	Cancer
30th	11:53 am	Leo

December 1977

2nd	11:06 pm	Virgo
5th	07:18 am	Libra
7th	11:33 am	Scorpio
9th	12:22 pm	Sagittarius
11th	11:26 am	Capricorn
13th	11:00 am	Aquarius
15th	01:09 pm	Pisces
17th	07:11 pm	Aries
20th	04:54 am	Taurus
22nd	04:52 pm	Gemini
25th	05:30 am	Cancer
27th	05:52 pm	Leo
30th	05:14 am	Virgo

January 1978

1st	02:32 pm	Libra
3rd	08:35 pm	Scorpio
5th	11:04 pm	Sagittarius
7th	10:55 pm	Capricorn
9th	10:05 pm	Aquarius
11th	10:51 pm	Pisces
14th	03:05 am	Aries
16th	11:31 am	Taurus
18th	11:07 pm	Gemini
21st	11:51 am	Cancer
24th	12:02 am	Leo
26th	10:56 am	Virgo
28th	08:08 pm	Libra
31st	03:04 am	Scorpio

February 1978

2nd	07:14 am	Sagittarius
4th	08:50 am	Capricorn
6th	09:04 am	Aquarius
8th	09:48 am	Pisces
10th	12:57 pm	Aries
12th	07:51 pm	Taurus
15th	06:24 am	Gemini
17th	06:56 pm	Cancer
20th	07:10 am	Leo
22nd	05:40 pm	Virgo
25th	02:04 am	Libra
27th	08:28 am	Scorpio

March 1978

1st	01:02 pm	Sagittarius
3rd	03:58 pm	Capricorn
5th	05:51 pm	Aquarius
7th	07:46 pm	Pisces
9th	11:08 pm	Aries
12th	05:18 am	Taurus
14th	02:49 pm	Gemini
17th	02:49 am	Cancer
19th	03:12 pm	Leo
22nd	01:50 am	Virgo
24th	09:42 am	Libra
26th	03:01 pm	Scorpio
28th	06:38 pm	Sagittarius
30th	09:24 pm	Capricorn

April 1978

2nd	12:05 am	Aquarius
4th	03:21 am	Pisces
6th	07:51 am	Aries
8th	02:22 pm	Taurus
10th	11:28 pm	Gemini
13th	10:59 am	Cancer
15th	11:31 pm	Leo
18th	10:44 am	Virgo
20th	06:53 pm	Libra
22nd	11:39 pm	Scorpio
25th	02:00 am	Sagittarius
27th	03:28 am	Capricorn
29th	05:28 am	Aquarius

May 1978

1st	09:00 am	Pisces
3rd	02:27 pm	Aries
5th	09:52 pm	Taurus
8th	07:19 am	Gemini
10th	06:42 pm	Cancer
13th	07:17 am	Leo
15th	07:15 pm	Virgo
18th	04:25 am	Libra
20th	09:39 am	Scorpio
22nd	11:31 am	Sagittarius
24th	11:42 am	Capricorn
26th	12:10 pm	Aquarius
28th	02:37 pm	Pisces
30th	07:52 pm	Aries

June 1978

2nd	03:50 am	Taurus
4th	01:54 pm	Gemini
7th	01:30 am	Cancer
9th	02:08 pm	Leo
12th	02:35 am	Virgo
14th	12:56 pm	Libra
16th	07:29 pm	Scorpio
18th	10:01 pm	Sagittarius
20th	09:52 pm	Capricorn
22nd	09:08 pm	Aquarius
24th	09:57 pm	Pisces
27th	01:53 am	Aries
29th	09:21 am	Taurus

July 1978

1st	07:38 pm	Gemini
4th	07:34 am	Cancer
6th	08:13 pm	Leo
9th	08:45 am	Virgo
11th	07:48 pm	Libra
14th	03:47 am	Scorpio
16th	07:50 am	Sagittarius
18th	08:33 am	Capricorn
20th	07:42 am	Aquarius
22nd	07:26 am	Pisces
24th	09:46 am	Aries
26th	03:51 pm	Taurus
29th	01:31 am	Gemini
31st	01:28 pm	Cancer

August 1978

3rd	02:10 am	Leo
5th	02:29 pm	Virgo
8th	01:30 am	Libra
10th	10:12 am	Scorpio
12th	03:43 pm	Sagittarius
14th	06:03 pm	Capricorn
16th	06:15 pm	Aquarius
18th	06:05 pm	Pisces
20th	07:30 pm	Aries
23rd	12:06 am	Taurus
25th	08:31 am	Gemini
27th	07:59 pm	Cancer
30th	08:40 am	Leo

September 1978

1st	08:47 pm	Virgo
4th	07:16 am	Libra
6th	03:38 pm	Scorpio
8th	09:39 pm	Sagittarius
11th	01:20 am	Capricorn
13th	03:09 am	Aquarius
15th	04:10 am	Pisces
17th	05:50 am	Aries
19th	09:43 am	Taurus
21st	04:56 pm	Gemini
24th	03:32 am	Cancer
26th	04:02 pm	Leo
29th	04:11 am	Virgo

October 1978

1st	02:17 pm	Libra
3rd	09:48 pm	Scorpio
6th	03:07 am	Sagittarius
8th	06:53 am	Capricorn
10th	09:43 am	Aquarius
12th	12:13 pm	Pisces
14th	03:06 pm	Aries
16th	07:22 pm	Taurus
19th	02:06 am	Gemini
21st	11:53 am	Cancer
24th	12:04 am	Leo
26th	12:32 pm	Virgo
28th	10:51 pm	Libra
31st	05:53 am	Scorpio

November 1978

2nd	10:04 am	Sagittarius
4th	12:41 pm	Capricorn
6th	03:04 pm	Aquarius
8th	06:06 pm	Pisces
10th	10:12 pm	Aries
13th	03:35 am	Taurus
15th	10:45 am	Gemini
17th	08:16 pm	Cancer
20th	08:09 am	Leo
22nd	08:57 pm	Virgo
25th	08:07 am	Libra
27th	03:39 pm	Scorpio
29th	07:24 pm	Sagittarius

December 1978

1st	08:44 pm	Capricorn
3rd	09:36 pm	Aquarius
5th	11:36 pm	Pisces
8th	03:40 am	Aries
10th	09:51 am	Taurus
12th	05:55 pm	Gemini
15th	03:50 am	Cancer
17th	03:38 pm	Leo
20th	04:34 am	Virgo
22nd	04:40 pm	Libra
25th	01:32 am	Scorpio
27th	06:08 am	Sagittarius
29th	07:16 am	Capricorn
31st	06:53 am	Aquarius

January 1979

2nd	07:08 am	Pisces
4th	09:41 am	Aries
6th	03:18 pm	Taurus
8th	11:43 pm	Gemini
11th	10:15 am	Cancer
13th	10:16 pm	Leo
16th	11:10 am	Virgo
18th	11:41 pm	Libra
21st	09:51 am	Scorpio
23rd	04:08 pm	Sagittarius
25th	06:28 pm	Capricorn
27th	06:12 pm	Aquarius
29th	05:25 pm	Pisces
31st	06:12 pm	Aries

February 1979

2nd	10:03 pm	Taurus
5th	05:33 am	Gemini
7th	04:06 pm	Cancer
10th	04:26 am	Leo
12th	05:18 pm	Virgo
15th	05:37 am	Libra
17th	04:12 pm	Scorpio
19th	11:51 pm	Sagittarius
22nd	04:01 am	Capricorn
24th	05:12 am	Aquarius
26th	04:53 am	Pisces
28th	04:54 am	Aries

March 1979

2nd	07:09 am	Taurus
4th	12:58 pm	Gemini
6th	10:34 pm	Cancer
9th	10:48 am	Leo
11th	11:43 pm	Virgo
14th	11:42 am	Libra
16th	09:49 pm	Scorpio
19th	05:38 am	Sagittarius
21st	10:57 am	Capricorn
23rd	01:52 pm	Aquarius
25th	03:05 pm	Pisces
27th	03:48 pm	Aries
29th	05:36 pm	Taurus
31st	10:09 pm	Gemini

April 1979

3rd	06:24 am	Cancer
5th	05:58 pm	Leo
8th	06:52 am	Virgo
10th	06:45 pm	Libra
13th	04:16 am	Scorpio
15th	11:18 am	Sagittarius
17th	04:23 pm	Capricorn
19th	08:02 pm	Aquarius
21st	10:41 pm	Pisces
24th	12:51 am	Aries
26th	03:28 am	Taurus
28th	07:49 am	Gemini
30th	03:12 pm	Cancer

May 1979

3rd	01:57 am	Leo
5th	02:42 pm	Virgo
8th	02:48 am	Libra
10th	12:10 pm	Scorpio
12th	06:25 pm	Sagittarius
14th	10:26 pm	Capricorn
17th	01:26 am	Aquarius
19th	04:19 am	Pisces
21st	07:30 am	Aries
23rd	11:21 am	Taurus
25th	04:28 pm	Gemini
27th	11:51 pm	Cancer
30th	10:08 am	Leo

June 1979

1st	10:41 pm	Virgo
4th	11:12 am	Libra
6th	09:05 pm	Scorpio
9th	03:15 am	Sagittarius
11th	06:24 am	Capricorn
13th	08:06 am	Aquarius
15th	09:56 am	Pisces
17th	12:53 pm	Aries
19th	05:18 pm	Taurus
21st	11:23 pm	Gemini
24th	07:25 am	Cancer
26th	05:47 pm	Leo
29th	06:14 am	Virgo

July 1979

1st	07:08 pm	Libra
4th	05:57 am	Scorpio
6th	12:56 pm	Sagittarius
8th	04:08 pm	Capricorn
10th	04:59 pm	Aquarius
12th	05:23 pm	Pisces
14th	06:57 pm	Aries
16th	10:43 pm	Taurus
19th	05:00 am	Gemini
21st	01:41 pm	Cancer
24th	12:30 am	Leo
26th	01:01 pm	Virgo
29th	02:06 am	Libra
31st	01:47 pm	Scorpio

August 1979

2nd	10:06 pm	Sagittarius
5th	02:23 am	Capricorn
7th	03:28 am	Aquarius
9th	03:06 am	Pisces
11th	03:10 am	Aries
13th	05:22 am	Taurus
15th	10:41 am	Gemini
17th	07:17 pm	Cancer
20th	06:29 am	Leo
22nd	07:12 pm	Virgo
25th	08:14 am	Libra
27th	08:13 pm	Scorpio
30th	05:40 am	Sagittarius

September 1979

1st	11:34 am	Capricorn
3rd	01:59 pm	Aquarius
5th	02:03 pm	Pisces
7th	01:29 pm	Aries
9th	02:13 pm	Taurus
11th	05:54 pm	Gemini
14th	01:27 am	Cancer
16th	12:25 pm	Leo
19th	01:16 am	Virgo
21st	02:11 pm	Libra
24th	01:54 am	Scorpio
26th	11:36 am	Sagittarius
28th	06:40 pm	Capricorn
30th	10:49 pm	Aquarius

October 1979

3rd	12:23 am	Pisces
5th	12:28 am	Aries
7th	12:45 am	Taurus
9th	03:07 am	Gemini
11th	09:09 am	Cancer
13th	07:12 pm	Leo
16th	07:52 am	Virgo
18th	08:45 pm	Libra
21st	08:02 am	Scorpio
23rd	05:09 pm	Sagittarius
26th	12:11 am	Capricorn
28th	05:17 am	Aquarius
30th	08:29 am	Pisces

November 1979

1st	10:09 am	Aries
3rd	11:16 am	Taurus
5th	01:26 pm	Gemini
7th	06:24 pm	Cancer
10th	03:15 am	Leo
12th	03:21 pm	Virgo
15th	04:17 am	Libra
17th	03:30 pm	Scorpio
19th	11:57 pm	Sagittarius
22nd	06:02 am	Capricorn
24th	10:37 am	Aquarius
26th	02:17 pm	Pisces
28th	05:17 pm	Aries
30th	07:55 pm	Taurus

December 1979

2nd	11:02 pm	Gemini
5th	04:02 am	Cancer
7th	12:09 pm	Leo
9th	11:33 pm	Virgo
12th	12:29 pm	Libra
15th	12:08 am	Scorpio
17th	08:37 am	Sagittarius
19th	01:55 pm	Capricorn
21st	05:13 pm	Aquarius
23rd	07:50 pm	Pisces
25th	10:40 pm	Aries
28th	02:08 am	Taurus
30th	06:32 am	Gemini

January 1980

1st	12:29 pm	Cancer
3rd	08:47 pm	Leo
6th	07:49 am	Virgo
8th	08:38 pm	Libra
11th	08:56 am	Scorpio
13th	06:17 pm	Sagittarius
15th	11:52 pm	Capricorn
18th	02:25 am	Aquarius
20th	03:33 am	Pisces
22nd	04:52 am	Aries
24th	07:32 am	Taurus
26th	12:11 pm	Gemini
28th	07:03 pm	Cancer
31st	04:09 am	Leo

February 1980

2nd	03:21 pm	Virgo
5th	04:04 am	Libra
7th	04:46 pm	Scorpio
10th	03:19 am	Sagittarius
12th	10:12 am	Capricorn
14th	01:20 pm	Aquarius
16th	01:54 pm	Pisces
18th	01:43 pm	Aries
20th	02:35 pm	Taurus
22nd	05:58 pm	Gemini
25th	12:35 am	Cancer
27th	10:10 am	Leo
29th	09:53 pm	Virgo

March 1980

3rd	10:40 am	Libra
5th	11:23 pm	Scorpio
8th	10:39 am	Sagittarius
10th	07:02 pm	Capricorn
12th	11:45 pm	Aquarius
15th	01:11 am	Pisces
17th	12:41 am	Aries
19th	12:13 am	Taurus
21st	01:48 am	Gemini
23rd	06:56 am	Cancer
25th	03:59 pm	Leo
28th	03:52 am	Virgo
30th	04:49 pm	Libra

April 1980

2nd	05:22 am	Scorpio
4th	04:35 pm	Sagittarius
7th	01:43 am	Capricorn
9th	08:00 am	Aquarius
11th	11:07 am	Pisces
13th	11:40 am	Aries
15th	11:11 am	Taurus
17th	11:41 am	Gemini
19th	03:12 pm	Cancer
21st	10:52 pm	Leo
24th	10:12 am	Virgo
26th	11:10 pm	Libra
29th	11:35 am	Scorpio

May 1980

1st	10:22 pm	Sagittarius
4th	07:14 am	Capricorn
6th	02:04 pm	Aquarius
8th	06:34 pm	Pisces
10th	08:45 pm	Aries
12th	09:24 pm	Taurus
14th	10:08 pm	Gemini
17th	12:52 am	Cancer
19th	07:15 am	Leo
21st	05:33 pm	Virgo
24th	06:11 am	Libra
26th	06:37 pm	Scorpio
29th	05:05 am	Sagittarius
31st	01:15 pm	Capricorn

June 1980

2nd	07:30 pm	Aquarius
5th	12:10 am	Pisces
7th	03:24 am	Aries
9th	05:30 am	Taurus
11th	07:23 am	Gemini
13th	10:30 am	Cancer
15th	04:22 pm	Leo
18th	01:47 am	Virgo
20th	01:55 pm	Libra
23rd	02:27 am	Scorpio
25th	01:02 pm	Sagittarius
27th	08:46 pm	Capricorn
30th	02:04 am	Aquarius

July 1980

2nd	05:49 am	Pisces
4th	08:47 am	Aries
6th	11:30 am	Taurus
8th	02:34 pm	Gemini
10th	06:45 pm	Cancer
13th	01:03 am	Leo
15th	10:11 am	Virgo
17th	09:55 pm	Libra
20th	10:33 am	Scorpio
22nd	09:42 pm	Sagittarius
25th	05:45 am	Capricorn
27th	10:35 am	Aquarius
29th	01:11 pm	Pisces
31st	02:53 pm	Aries

August 1980

2nd	04:55 pm	Taurus
4th	08:10 pm	Gemini
7th	01:12 am	Cancer
9th	08:24 am	Leo
11th	05:55 pm	Virgo
14th	05:32 am	Libra
16th	06:15 pm	Scorpio
19th	06:08 am	Sagittarius
21st	03:12 pm	Capricorn
23rd	08:33 pm	Aquarius
25th	10:44 pm	Pisces
27th	11:11 pm	Aries
29th	11:41 pm	Taurus

September 1980

1st	01:50 am	Gemini
3rd	06:40 am	Cancer
5th	02:22 pm	Leo
8th	12:31 am	Virgo
10th	12:22 pm	Libra
13th	01:06 am	Scorpio
15th	01:28 pm	Sagittarius
17th	11:45 pm	Capricorn
20th	06:31 am	Aquarius
22nd	09:28 am	Pisces
24th	09:38 am	Aries
26th	08:53 am	Taurus
28th	09:21 am	Gemini
30th	12:47 pm	Cancer

October 1980

2nd	07:57 pm	Leo
5th	06:19 am	Virgo
7th	06:31 pm	Libra
10th	07:15 am	Scorpio
12th	07:38 pm	Sagittarius
15th	06:37 am	Capricorn
17th	02:54 pm	Aquarius
19th	07:32 pm	Pisces
21st	08:43 pm	Aries
23rd	07:56 pm	Taurus
25th	07:17 pm	Gemini
27th	09:00 pm	Cancer
30th	02:39 am	Leo

November 1980

1st	12:19 pm	Virgo
4th	12:32 am	Libra
6th	01:19 pm	Scorpio
9th	01:26 am	Sagittarius
11th	12:15 pm	Capricorn
13th	09:11 pm	Aquarius
16th	03:21 am	Pisces
18th	06:22 am	Aries
20th	06:51 am	Taurus
22nd	06:27 am	Gemini
24th	07:19 am	Cancer
26th	11:23 am	Leo
28th	07:38 pm	Virgo

December 1980

1st	07:14 am	Libra
3rd	08:00 pm	Scorpio
6th	07:58 am	Sagittarius
8th	06:12 pm	Capricorn
11th	02:36 am	Aquarius
13th	09:04 am	Pisces
15th	01:22 pm	Aries
17th	03:37 pm	Taurus
19th	04:40 pm	Gemini
21st	06:03 pm	Cancer
23rd	09:34 pm	Leo
26th	04:33 am	Virgo
28th	03:05 pm	Libra
31st	03:36 am	Scorpio

January 1981

2nd	03:42 pm	Sagittarius
5th	01:41 am	Capricorn
7th	09:13 am	Aquarius
9th	02:42 pm	Pisces
11th	06:44 pm	Aries
13th	09:45 pm	Taurus
16th	12:18 am	Gemini
18th	03:08 am	Cancer
20th	07:21 am	Leo
22nd	02:03 pm	Virgo
24th	11:45 pm	Libra
27th	11:49 am	Scorpio
30th	12:12 am	Sagittarius

February 1981

1st	10:37 am	Capricorn
3rd	05:55 pm	Aquarius
5th	10:22 pm	Pisces
8th	01:02 am	Aries
10th	03:11 am	Taurus
12th	05:51 am	Gemini
14th	09:43 am	Cancer
16th	03:10 pm	Leo
18th	10:34 pm	Virgo
21st	08:12 am	Libra
23rd	07:55 pm	Scorpio
26th	08:29 am	Sagittarius
28th	07:47 pm	Capricorn

March 1981

3rd	03:51 am	Aquarius
5th	08:12 am	Pisces
7th	09:49 am	Aries
9th	10:23 am	Taurus
11th	11:42 am	Gemini
13th	03:06 pm	Cancer
15th	09:03 pm	Leo
18th	05:20 am	Virgo
20th	03:31 pm	Libra
23rd	03:14 am	Scorpio
25th	03:51 pm	Sagittarius
28th	03:53 am	Capricorn
30th	01:16 pm	Aquarius

April 1981

1st	06:41 pm	Pisces
3rd	08:25 pm	Aries
5th	08:04 pm	Taurus
7th	07:47 pm	Gemini
9th	09:34 pm	Cancer
12th	02:37 am	Leo
14th	10:57 am	Virgo
16th	09:38 pm	Libra
19th	09:39 am	Scorpio
21st	10:15 pm	Sagittarius
24th	10:31 am	Capricorn
26th	08:57 pm	Aquarius
29th	03:56 am	Pisces

May 1981

1st	06:58 am	Aries
3rd	07:00 am	Taurus
5th	06:01 am	Gemini
7th	06:18 am	Cancer
9th	09:40 am	Leo
11th	04:55 pm	Virgo
14th	03:24 am	Libra
16th	03:38 pm	Scorpio
19th	04:14 am	Sagittarius
21st	04:20 pm	Capricorn
24th	03:01 am	Aquarius
26th	11:06 am	Pisces
28th	03:44 pm	Aries
30th	05:11 pm	Taurus

June 1981

1st	04:49 pm	Gemini
3rd	04:39 pm	Cancer
5th	06:43 pm	Leo
8th	12:26 am	Virgo
10th	09:55 am	Libra
12th	09:55 pm	Scorpio
15th	10:32 am	Sagittarius
17th	10:21 pm	Capricorn
20th	08:36 am	Aquarius
22nd	04:44 pm	Pisces
24th	10:18 pm	Aries
27th	01:17 am	Taurus
29th	02:21 am	Gemini

July 1981

1st	02:57 am	Cancer
3rd	04:47 am	Leo
5th	09:26 am	Virgo
7th	05:42 pm	Libra
10th	05:02 am	Scorpio
12th	05:35 pm	Sagittarius
15th	05:20 am	Capricorn
17th	03:02 pm	Aquarius
19th	10:26 pm	Pisces
22nd	03:44 am	Aries
24th	07:19 am	Taurus
26th	09:42 am	Gemini
28th	11:41 am	Cancer
30th	02:21 pm	Leo

August 1981

1st	06:55 pm	Virgo
4th	02:24 am	Libra
6th	12:59 pm	Scorpio
9th	01:23 am	Sagittarius
11th	01:20 pm	Capricorn
13th	10:56 pm	Aquarius
16th	05:35 am	Pisces
18th	09:49 am	Aries
20th	12:44 pm	Taurus
22nd	03:18 pm	Gemini
24th	06:17 pm	Cancer
26th	10:10 pm	Leo
29th	03:32 am	Virgo
31st	11:03 am	Libra

September 1981

2nd	09:10 pm	Scorpio
5th	09:24 am	Sagittarius
7th	09:49 pm	Capricorn
10th	07:59 am	Aquarius
12th	02:34 pm	Pisces
14th	05:56 pm	Aries
16th	07:30 pm	Taurus
18th	08:59 pm	Gemini
20th	11:40 pm	Cancer
23rd	04:09 am	Leo
25th	10:29 am	Virgo
27th	06:40 pm	Libra
30th	04:53 am	Scorpio

October 1981

2nd	05:00 pm	Sagittarius
5th	05:49 am	Capricorn
7th	05:01 pm	Aquarius
10th	12:33 am	Pisces
12th	04:01 am	Aries
14th	04:44 am	Taurus
16th	04:41 am	Gemini
18th	05:53 am	Cancer
20th	09:35 am	Leo
22nd	04:05 pm	Virgo
25th	12:57 am	Libra
27th	11:38 am	Scorpio
29th	11:49 pm	Sagittarius

November 1981

1st	12:46 pm	Capricorn
4th	12:51 am	Aquarius
6th	09:52 am	Pisces
8th	02:39 pm	Aries
10th	03:45 pm	Taurus
12th	03:00 pm	Gemini
14th	02:37 pm	Cancer
16th	04:33 pm	Leo
18th	09:53 pm	Virgo
21st	06:33 am	Libra
23rd	05:37 pm	Scorpio
26th	06:01 am	Sagittarius
28th	06:53 pm	Capricorn

December 1981

1st	07:09 am	Aquarius
3rd	05:16 pm	Pisces
5th	11:49 pm	Aries
8th	02:32 am	Taurus
10th	02:30 am	Gemini
12th	01:41 am	Cancer
14th	02:09 am	Leo
16th	05:38 am	Virgo
18th	12:58 pm	Libra
20th	11:39 pm	Scorpio
23rd	12:11 pm	Sagittarius
26th	01:00 am	Capricorn
28th	12:54 pm	Aquarius
30th	11:01 pm	Pisces

January 1982

2nd	06:33 am	Aries
4th	11:03 am	Taurus
6th	12:49 pm	Gemini
8th	01:01 pm	Cancer
10th	01:21 pm	Leo
12th	03:37 pm	Virgo
14th	09:17 pm	Libra
17th	06:47 am	Scorpio
19th	07:00 pm	Sagittarius
22nd	07:51 am	Capricorn
24th	07:25 pm	Aquarius
27th	04:50 am	Pisces
29th	11:59 am	Aries
31st	05:04 pm	Taurus

February 1982

2nd	08:20 pm	Gemini
4th	10:18 pm	Cancer
6th	11:50 pm	Leo
9th	02:15 am	Virgo
11th	07:02 am	Libra
13th	03:16 pm	Scorpio
16th	02:45 am	Sagittarius
18th	03:36 pm	Capricorn
21st	03:15 am	Aquarius
23rd	12:09 pm	Pisces
25th	06:17 pm	Aries
27th	10:32 pm	Taurus

March 1982

2nd	01:50 am	Gemini
4th	04:49 am	Cancer
6th	07:50 am	Leo
8th	11:27 am	Virgo
10th	04:34 pm	Libra
13th	12:17 am	Scorpio
15th	11:03 am	Sagittarius
17th	11:47 pm	Capricorn
20th	11:53 am	Aquarius
22nd	09:02 pm	Pisces
25th	02:37 am	Aries
27th	05:40 am	Taurus
29th	07:44 am	Gemini
31st	10:09 am	Cancer

April 1982

2nd	01:37 pm	Leo
4th	06:18 pm	Virgo
7th	12:27 am	Libra
9th	08:33 am	Scorpio
11th	07:07 pm	Sagittarius
14th	07:42 am	Capricorn
16th	08:18 pm	Aquarius
19th	06:20 am	Pisces
21st	12:23 pm	Aries
23rd	02:59 pm	Taurus
25th	03:48 pm	Gemini
27th	04:44 pm	Cancer
29th	07:10 pm	Leo

May 1982

1st	11:45 pm	Virgo
4th	06:33 am	Libra
6th	03:24 pm	Scorpio
9th	02:17 am	Sagittarius
11th	02:50 pm	Capricorn
14th	03:44 am	Aquarius
16th	02:47 pm	Pisces
18th	10:04 pm	Aries
21st	01:22 am	Taurus
23rd	01:55 am	Gemini
25th	01:39 am	Cancer
27th	02:27 am	Leo
29th	05:43 am	Virgo
31st	12:03 pm	Libra

June 1982

2nd	09:12 pm	Scorpio
5th	08:32 am	Sagittarius
7th	09:12 pm	Capricorn
10th	10:08 am	Aquarius
12th	09:44 pm	Pisces
15th	06:20 am	Aries
17th	11:07 am	Taurus
19th	12:34 pm	Gemini
21st	12:13 pm	Cancer
23rd	11:57 am	Leo
25th	01:36 pm	Virgo
27th	06:30 pm	Libra
30th	03:02 am	Scorpio

July 1982

2nd	02:26 pm	Sagittarius
5th	03:15 am	Capricorn
7th	04:03 pm	Aquarius
10th	03:36 am	Pisces
12th	12:49 pm	Aries
14th	07:00 pm	Taurus
16th	10:04 pm	Gemini
18th	10:46 pm	Cancer
20th	10:36 pm	Leo
22nd	11:20 pm	Virgo
25th	02:45 am	Libra
27th	09:58 am	Scorpio
29th	08:48 pm	Sagittarius

August 1982

1st	09:36 am	Capricorn
3rd	10:17 pm	Aquarius
6th	09:24 am	Pisces
8th	06:21 pm	Aries
11th	01:00 am	Taurus
13th	05:22 am	Gemini
15th	07:41 am	Cancer
17th	08:40 am	Leo
19th	09:40 am	Virgo
21st	12:22 pm	Libra
23rd	06:21 pm	Scorpio
26th	04:11 am	Sagittarius
28th	04:42 pm	Capricorn
31st	05:24 am	Aquarius

September 1982

2nd	04:11 pm	Pisces
5th	12:24 am	Aries
7th	06:27 am	Taurus
9th	10:58 am	Gemini
11th	02:18 pm	Cancer
13th	04:46 pm	Leo
15th	06:58 pm	Virgo
17th	10:03 pm	Libra
20th	03:33 am	Scorpio
22nd	12:30 pm	Sagittarius
25th	12:32 am	Capricorn
27th	01:22 pm	Aquarius
30th	12:19 am	Pisces

October 1982

2nd	08:06 am	Aries
4th	01:09 pm	Taurus
6th	04:39 pm	Gemini
8th	07:40 pm	Cancer
10th	10:44 pm	Leo
13th	02:09 am	Virgo
15th	06:23 am	Libra
17th	12:21 pm	Scorpio
19th	09:03 pm	Sagittarius
22nd	08:38 am	Capricorn
24th	09:36 pm	Aquarius
27th	09:13 am	Pisces
29th	05:25 pm	Aries
31st	10:04 pm	Taurus

November 1982

3rd	12:23 am	Gemini
5th	01:59 am	Cancer
7th	04:10 am	Leo
9th	07:40 am	Virgo
11th	12:46 pm	Libra
13th	07:43 pm	Scorpio
16th	04:52 am	Sagittarius
18th	04:22 pm	Capricorn
21st	05:21 am	Aquarius
23rd	05:43 pm	Pisces
26th	03:07 am	Aries
28th	08:32 am	Taurus
30th	10:36 am	Gemini

December 1982

2nd	10:58 am	Cancer
4th	11:26 am	Leo
6th	01:32 pm	Virgo
8th	06:11 pm	Libra
11th	01:35 am	Scorpio
13th	11:27 am	Sagittarius
15th	11:16 pm	Capricorn
18th	12:13 pm	Aquarius
21st	12:56 am	Pisces
23rd	11:34 am	Aries
25th	06:37 pm	Taurus
27th	09:49 pm	Gemini
29th	10:12 pm	Cancer
31st	09:33 pm	Leo

January 1983

2nd	09:50 pm	Virgo
5th	12:45 am	Libra
7th	07:16 am	Scorpio
9th	05:14 pm	Sagittarius
12th	05:26 am	Capricorn
14th	06:27 pm	Aquarius
17th	07:03 am	Pisces
19th	06:08 pm	Aries
22nd	02:36 am	Taurus
24th	07:40 am	Gemini
26th	09:29 am	Cancer
28th	09:10 am	Leo
30th	08:35 am	Virgo

February 1983

1st	09:47 am	Libra
3rd	02:32 pm	Scorpio
5th	11:29 pm	Sagittarius
8th	11:34 am	Capricorn
11th	12:41 am	Aquarius
13th	01:02 pm	Pisces
15th	11:46 pm	Aries
18th	08:31 am	Taurus
20th	02:52 pm	Gemini
22nd	06:31 pm	Cancer
24th	07:47 pm	Leo
26th	07:49 pm	Virgo
28th	08:30 pm	Libra

March 1983

2nd	11:51 pm	Scorpio
5th	07:15 am	Sagittarius
7th	06:29 pm	Capricorn
10th	07:30 am	Aquarius
12th	07:47 pm	Pisces
15th	06:00 am	Aries
17th	02:05 pm	Taurus
19th	08:20 pm	Gemini
22nd	12:53 am	Cancer
24th	03:43 am	Leo
26th	05:18 am	Virgo
28th	06:49 am	Libra
30th	09:57 am	Scorpio

April 1983

1st	04:20 pm	Sagittarius
4th	02:30 am	Capricorn
6th	03:07 pm	Aquarius
9th	03:31 am	Pisces
11th	01:37 pm	Aries
13th	08:59 pm	Taurus
16th	02:15 am	Gemini
18th	06:14 am	Cancer
20th	09:27 am	Leo
22nd	12:12 pm	Virgo
24th	03:04 pm	Libra
26th	07:05 pm	Scorpio
29th	01:29 am	Sagittarius

May 1983

1st	11:02 am	Capricorn
3rd	11:09 pm	Aquarius
6th	11:44 am	Pisces
8th	10:17 pm	Aries
11th	05:36 am	Taurus
13th	10:04 am	Gemini
15th	12:48 pm	Cancer
17th	03:01 pm	Leo
19th	05:37 pm	Virgo
21st	09:12 pm	Libra
24th	02:17 am	Scorpio
26th	09:28 am	Sagittarius
28th	07:07 pm	Capricorn
31st	07:00 am	Aquarius

June 1983

2nd	07:42 pm	Pisces
5th	06:59 am	Aries
7th	03:05 pm	Taurus
9th	07:38 pm	Gemini
11th	09:33 pm	Cancer
13th	10:22 pm	Leo
15th	11:38 pm	Virgo
18th	02:37 am	Libra
20th	08:00 am	Scorpio
22nd	03:55 pm	Sagittarius
25th	02:09 am	Capricorn
27th	02:07 pm	Aquarius
30th	02:52 am	Pisces

July 1983

2nd	02:48 pm	Aries
5th	12:06 am	Taurus
7th	05:41 am	Gemini
9th	07:51 am	Cancer
11th	07:54 am	Leo
13th	07:43 am	Virgo
15th	09:10 am	Libra
17th	01:38 pm	Scorpio
19th	09:32 pm	Sagittarius
22nd	08:11 am	Capricorn
24th	08:27 pm	Aquarius
27th	09:12 am	Pisces
29th	09:21 pm	Aries

August 1983

1st	07:37 am	Taurus
3rd	02:43 pm	Gemini
5th	06:09 pm	Cancer
7th	06:37 pm	Leo
9th	05:49 pm	Virgo
11th	05:52 pm	Libra
13th	08:44 pm	Scorpio
16th	03:34 am	Sagittarius
18th	02:00 pm	Capricorn
21st	02:26 am	Aquarius
23rd	03:10 pm	Pisces
26th	03:08 am	Aries
28th	01:38 pm	Taurus
30th	09:49 pm	Gemini

September 1983

2nd	02:53 am	Cancer
4th	04:48 am	Leo
6th	04:36 am	Virgo
8th	04:14 am	Libra
10th	05:49 am	Scorpio
12th	11:08 am	Sagittarius
14th	08:34 pm	Capricorn
17th	08:46 am	Aquarius
19th	09:30 pm	Pisces
22nd	09:11 am	Aries
24th	07:13 pm	Taurus
27th	03:25 am	Gemini
29th	09:25 am	Cancer

October 1983

1st	12:55 pm	Leo
3rd	02:15 pm	Virgo
5th	02:42 pm	Libra
7th	04:06 pm	Scorpio
9th	08:21 pm	Sagittarius
12th	04:30 am	Capricorn
14th	04:00 pm	Aquarius
17th	04:42 am	Pisces
19th	04:19 pm	Aries
22nd	01:48 am	Taurus
24th	09:10 am	Gemini
26th	02:47 pm	Cancer
28th	06:51 pm	Leo
30th	09:33 pm	Virgo

November 1983

1st	11:31 pm	Libra
4th	01:53 am	Scorpio
6th	06:09 am	Sagittarius
8th	01:32 pm	Capricorn
11th	12:11 am	Aquarius
13th	12:41 pm	Pisces
16th	12:37 am	Aries
18th	10:07 am	Taurus
20th	04:45 pm	Gemini
22nd	09:11 pm	Cancer
25th	12:20 am	Leo
27th	03:02 am	Virgo
29th	05:57 am	Libra

December 1983

1st	09:41 am	Scorpio
3rd	02:56 pm	Sagittarius
5th	10:28 pm	Capricorn
8th	08:40 am	Aquarius
10th	08:53 pm	Pisces
13th	09:17 am	Aries
15th	07:33 pm	Taurus
18th	02:24 am	Gemini
20th	06:03 am	Cancer
22nd	07:44 am	Leo
24th	09:02 am	Virgo
26th	11:19 am	Libra
28th	03:27 pm	Scorpio
30th	09:44 pm	Sagittarius

January 1984

2nd	06:08 am	Capricorn
4th	04:31 pm	Aquarius
7th	04:35 am	Pisces
9th	05:16 pm	Aries
12th	04:36 am	Taurus
14th	12:41 pm	Gemini
16th	04:48 pm	Cancer
18th	05:50 pm	Leo
20th	05:36 pm	Virgo
22nd	06:07 pm	Libra
24th	09:04 pm	Scorpio
27th	03:13 am	Sagittarius
29th	12:13 pm	Capricorn
31st	11:11 pm	Aquarius

February 1984

3rd	11:22 am	Pisces
6th	12:04 am	Aries
8th	12:06 pm	Taurus
10th	09:40 pm	Gemini
13th	03:21 am	Cancer
15th	05:10 am	Leo
17th	04:32 am	Virgo
19th	03:40 am	Libra
21st	04:45 am	Scorpio
23rd	09:23 am	Sagittarius
25th	05:50 pm	Capricorn
28th	05:02 am	Aquarius

March 1984

1st	05:30 pm	Pisces
4th	06:07 am	Aries
6th	06:09 pm	Taurus
9th	04:30 am	Gemini
11th	11:48 am	Cancer
13th	03:21 pm	Leo
15th	03:47 pm	Virgo
17th	02:52 pm	Libra
19th	02:49 pm	Scorpio
21st	05:41 pm	Sagittarius
24th	12:36 am	Capricorn
26th	11:09 am	Aquarius
28th	11:37 pm	Pisces
31st	12:14 pm	Aries

April 1984

2nd	11:56 pm	Taurus
5th	10:05 am	Gemini
7th	06:00 pm	Cancer
9th	11:02 pm	Leo
12th	01:11 am	Virgo
14th	01:30 am	Libra
16th	01:41 am	Scorpio
18th	03:44 am	Sagittarius
20th	09:11 am	Capricorn
22nd	06:27 pm	Aquarius
25th	06:27 am	Pisces
27th	07:03 pm	Aries
30th	06:31 am	Taurus

May 1984

2nd	04:02 pm	Gemini
4th	11:26 pm	Cancer
7th	04:43 am	Leo
9th	08:02 am	Virgo
11th	09:54 am	Libra
13th	11:22 am	Scorpio
15th	01:50 pm	Sagittarius
17th	06:44 pm	Capricorn
20th	02:56 am	Aquarius
22nd	02:09 pm	Pisces
25th	02:40 am	Aries
27th	02:14 pm	Taurus
29th	11:23 pm	Gemini

June 1984

1st	05:54 am	Cancer
3rd	10:19 am	Leo
5th	01:27 pm	Virgo
7th	04:04 pm	Libra
9th	06:49 pm	Scorpio
11th	10:27 pm	Sagittarius
14th	03:48 am	Capricorn
16th	11:41 am	Aquarius
18th	10:18 pm	Pisces
21st	10:41 am	Aries
23rd	10:38 pm	Taurus
26th	08:04 am	Gemini
28th	02:10 pm	Cancer
30th	05:30 pm	Leo

July 1984

2nd	07:28 pm	Virgo
4th	09:27 pm	Libra
7th	12:29 am	Scorpio
9th	05:03 am	Sagittarius
11th	11:23 am	Capricorn
13th	07:42 pm	Aquarius
16th	06:11 am	Pisces
18th	06:26 pm	Aries
21st	06:53 am	Taurus
23rd	05:10 pm	Gemini
25th	11:44 pm	Cancer
28th	02:42 am	Leo
30th	03:29 am	Virgo

August 1984

1st	04:03 am	Libra
3rd	06:04 am	Scorpio
5th	10:30 am	Sagittarius
7th	05:25 pm	Capricorn
10th	02:26 am	Aquarius
12th	01:13 pm	Pisces
15th	01:28 am	Aries
17th	02:14 pm	Taurus
20th	01:32 am	Gemini
22nd	09:21 am	Cancer
24th	01:00 pm	Leo
26th	01:33 pm	Virgo
28th	12:57 pm	Libra
30th	01:23 pm	Scorpio

September 1984

1st	04:30 pm	Sagittarius
3rd	10:55 pm	Capricorn
6th	08:12 am	Aquarius
8th	07:25 pm	Pisces
11th	07:47 am	Aries
13th	08:33 pm	Taurus
16th	08:26 am	Gemini
18th	05:36 pm	Cancer
20th	10:49 pm	Leo
23rd	12:19 am	Virgo
24th	11:41 pm	Libra
26th	11:04 pm	Scorpio
29th	12:32 am	Sagittarius

October 1984

1st	05:28 am	Capricorn
3rd	02:04 pm	Aquarius
6th	01:20 am	Pisces
8th	01:51 pm	Aries
11th	02:29 am	Taurus
13th	02:14 pm	Gemini
16th	12:00 am	Cancer
18th	06:41 am	Leo
20th	09:56 am	Virgo
22nd	10:32 am	Libra
24th	10:08 am	Scorpio
26th	10:43 am	Sagittarius
28th	02:05 pm	Capricorn
30th	09:13 pm	Aquarius

November 1984

2nd	07:50 am	Pisces
4th	08:21 pm	Aries
7th	08:54 am	Taurus
9th	08:11 pm	Gemini
12th	05:32 am	Cancer
14th	12:34 pm	Leo
16th	05:08 pm	Virgo
18th	07:30 pm	Libra
20th	08:31 pm	Scorpio
22nd	09:34 pm	Sagittarius
25th	12:18 am	Capricorn
27th	06:06 am	Aquarius
29th	03:34 pm	Pisces

December 1984

2nd	03:42 am	Aries
4th	04:21 pm	Taurus
7th	03:24 am	Gemini
9th	11:57 am	Cancer
11th	06:09 pm	Leo
13th	10:36 pm	Virgo
16th	01:52 am	Libra
18th	04:28 am	Scorpio
20th	06:59 am	Sagittarius
22nd	10:21 am	Capricorn
24th	03:48 pm	Aquarius
27th	12:19 am	Pisces
29th	11:50 am	Aries

January 1985

1st	12:37 am	Taurus
3rd	12:01 pm	Gemini
5th	08:18 pm	Cancer
8th	01:28 am	Leo
10th	04:40 am	Virgo
12th	07:14 am	Libra
14th	10:08 am	Scorpio
16th	01:48 pm	Sagittarius
18th	06:29 pm	Capricorn
21st	12:39 am	Aquarius
23rd	09:02 am	Pisces
25th	08:06 pm	Aries
28th	08:54 am	Taurus
30th	09:01 pm	Gemini

February 1985

2nd	05:59 am	Cancer
4th	11:02 am	Leo
6th	01:10 pm	Virgo
8th	02:11 pm	Libra
10th	03:49 pm	Scorpio
12th	07:09 pm	Sagittarius
15th	12:27 am	Capricorn
17th	07:37 am	Aquarius
19th	04:38 pm	Pisces
22nd	03:43 am	Aries
24th	04:28 pm	Taurus
27th	05:12 am	Gemini

March 1985

1st	03:24 pm	Cancer
3rd	09:28 pm	Leo
5th	11:43 pm	Virgo
7th	11:48 pm	Libra
9th	11:47 pm	Scorpio
12th	01:29 am	Sagittarius
14th	05:55 am	Capricorn
16th	01:11 pm	Aquarius
18th	10:51 pm	Pisces
21st	10:21 am	Aries
23rd	11:07 pm	Taurus
26th	12:02 pm	Gemini
28th	11:14 pm	Cancer
31st	06:52 am	Leo

April 1985

2nd	10:25 am	Virgo
4th	10:54 am	Libra
6th	10:11 am	Scorpio
8th	10:18 am	Sagittarius
10th	12:57 pm	Capricorn
12th	07:04 pm	Aquarius
15th	04:31 am	Pisces
17th	04:19 pm	Aries
20th	05:13 am	Taurus
22nd	06:01 pm	Gemini
25th	05:27 am	Cancer
27th	02:10 pm	Leo
29th	07:24 pm	Virgo

May 1985

1st	09:22 pm	Libra
3rd	09:17 pm	Scorpio
5th	08:56 pm	Sagittarius
7th	10:12 pm	Capricorn
10th	02:38 am	Aquarius
12th	10:56 am	Pisces
14th	10:26 pm	Aries
17th	11:24 am	Taurus
20th	12:01 am	Gemini
22nd	11:05 am	Cancer
24th	07:54 pm	Leo
27th	02:07 am	Virgo
29th	05:41 am	Libra
31st	07:08 am	Scorpio

June 1985

2nd	07:34 am	Sagittarius
4th	08:34 am	Capricorn
6th	11:52 am	Aquarius
8th	06:47 pm	Pisces
11th	05:24 am	Aries
13th	06:12 pm	Taurus
16th	06:46 am	Gemini
18th	05:22 pm	Cancer
21st	01:32 am	Leo
23rd	07:33 am	Virgo
25th	11:48 am	Libra
27th	02:38 pm	Scorpio
29th	04:31 pm	Sagittarius

July 1985

1st	06:22 pm	Capricorn
3rd	09:36 pm	Aquarius
6th	03:40 am	Pisces
8th	01:21 pm	Aries
11th	01:44 am	Taurus
13th	02:24 pm	Gemini
16th	12:55 am	Cancer
18th	08:25 am	Leo
20th	01:30 pm	Virgo
22nd	05:10 pm	Libra
24th	08:16 pm	Scorpio
26th	11:13 pm	Sagittarius
29th	02:21 am	Capricorn
31st	06:26 am	Aquarius

August 1985

2nd	12:34 pm	Pisces
4th	09:43 pm	Aries
7th	09:42 am	Taurus
9th	10:32 pm	Gemini
12th	09:29 am	Cancer
14th	04:57 pm	Leo
16th	09:15 pm	Virgo
18th	11:44 pm	Libra
21st	01:52 am	Scorpio
23rd	04:36 am	Sagittarius
25th	08:25 am	Capricorn
27th	01:32 pm	Aquarius
29th	08:25 pm	Pisces

September 1985

1st	05:42 am	Aries
3rd	05:28 pm	Taurus
6th	06:27 am	Gemini
8th	06:11 pm	Cancer
11th	02:28 am	Leo
13th	06:53 am	Virgo
15th	08:34 am	Libra
17th	09:17 am	Scorpio
19th	10:41 am	Sagittarius
21st	01:50 pm	Capricorn
23rd	07:12 pm	Aquarius
26th	02:51 am	Pisces
28th	12:43 pm	Aries

October 1985

1st	12:35 am	Taurus
3rd	01:37 pm	Gemini
6th	01:59 am	Cancer
8th	11:34 am	Leo
10th	05:10 pm	Virgo
12th	07:12 pm	Libra
14th	07:13 pm	Scorpio
16th	07:06 pm	Sagittarius
18th	08:35 pm	Capricorn
21st	12:55 am	Aquarius
23rd	08:28 am	Pisces
25th	06:48 pm	Aries
28th	07:00 am	Taurus
30th	07:59 pm	Gemini

November 1985

2nd	08:31 am	Cancer
4th	07:04 pm	Leo
7th	02:19 am	Virgo
9th	05:52 am	Libra
11th	06:31 am	Scorpio
13th	05:53 am	Sagittarius
15th	05:54 am	Capricorn
17th	08:26 am	Aquarius
19th	02:43 pm	Pisces
22nd	12:43 am	Aries
24th	01:07 pm	Taurus
27th	02:08 am	Gemini
29th	02:23 pm	Cancer

December 1985

2nd	01:00 am	Leo
4th	09:14 am	Virgo
6th	02:34 pm	Libra
8th	04:57 pm	Scorpio
10th	05:14 pm	Sagittarius
12th	05:00 pm	Capricorn
14th	06:15 pm	Aquarius
16th	10:50 pm	Pisces
19th	07:37 am	Aries
21st	07:41 pm	Taurus
24th	08:45 am	Gemini
26th	08:44 pm	Cancer
29th	06:45 am	Leo
31st	02:44 pm	Virgo

January 1986

2nd 08:46 pm Libra
5th 12:44 am Scorpio
7th 02:47 am Sagittarius
9th 03:42 am Capricorn
11th 05:02 am Aquarius
13th 08:39 am Pisces
15th 04:03 pm Aries
18th 03:14 am Taurus
20th 04:12 pm Gemini
23rd 04:15 am Cancer
25th 01:48 pm Leo
27th 08:51 pm Virgo
30th 02:10 am Libra

February 1986

1st 06:19 am Scorpio
3rd 09:32 am Sagittarius
5th 12:02 pm Capricorn
7th 02:35 pm Aquarius
9th 06:33 pm Pisces
12th 01:21 am Aries
14th 11:38 am Taurus
17th 12:17 am Gemini
19th 12:39 pm Cancer
21st 10:25 pm Leo
24th 04:58 am Virgo
26th 09:07 am Libra
28th 12:06 pm Scorpio

March 1986

2nd 02:52 pm Sagittarius
4th 05:56 pm Capricorn
6th 09:43 pm Aquarius
9th 02:48 am Pisces
11th 10:04 am Aries
13th 08:04 pm Taurus
16th 08:23 am Gemini
18th 09:05 pm Cancer
21st 07:39 am Leo
23rd 02:40 pm Virgo
25th 06:23 pm Libra
27th 08:06 pm Scorpio
29th 09:21 pm Sagittarius
31st 11:26 pm Capricorn

April 1986

3rd 03:11 am Aquarius
5th 09:04 am Pisces
7th 05:12 pm Aries
10th 03:37 am Taurus
12th 03:51 pm Gemini
15th 04:42 am Cancer
17th 04:10 pm Leo
20th 12:24 am Virgo
22nd 04:50 am Libra
24th 06:16 am Scorpio
26th 06:16 am Sagittarius
28th 06:41 am Capricorn
30th 09:06 am Aquarius

May 1986

2nd 02:31 pm Pisces
4th 11:01 pm Aries
7th 09:59 am Taurus
9th 10:26 pm Gemini
12th 11:18 am Cancer
14th 11:15 pm Leo
17th 08:46 am Virgo
19th 02:41 pm Libra
21st 05:03 pm Scorpio
23rd 04:57 pm Sagittarius
25th 04:15 pm Capricorn
27th 05:00 pm Aquarius
29th 08:55 pm Pisces

June 1986

1st 04:43 am Aries
3rd 03:46 pm Taurus
6th 04:27 am Gemini
8th 05:16 pm Cancer
11th 05:12 am Leo
13th 03:18 pm Virgo
15th 10:38 pm Libra
18th 02:37 am Scorpio
20th 03:36 am Sagittarius
22nd 03:00 am Capricorn
24th 02:50 am Aquarius
26th 05:13 am Pisces
28th 11:35 am Aries
30th 09:55 pm Taurus

July 1986

3rd 10:32 am Gemini
5th 11:20 pm Cancer
8th 10:56 am Leo
10th 08:50 pm Virgo
13th 04:40 am Libra
15th 09:59 am Scorpio
17th 12:35 pm Sagittarius
19th 01:10 pm Capricorn
21st 01:18 pm Aquarius
23rd 02:59 pm Pisces
25th 08:03 pm Aries
28th 05:11 am Taurus
30th 05:19 pm Gemini

August 1986

2nd 06:04 am Cancer
4th 05:27 pm Leo
7th 02:45 am Virgo
9th 10:05 am Libra
11th 03:36 pm Scorpio
13th 07:17 pm Sagittarius
15th 09:23 pm Capricorn
17th 10:44 pm Aquarius
20th 12:52 am Pisces
22nd 05:27 am Aries
24th 01:37 pm Taurus
27th 01:01 am Gemini
29th 01:40 pm Cancer

September 1986

1st 01:09 am Leo
3rd 10:06 am Virgo
5th 04:34 pm Libra
7th 09:12 pm Scorpio
10th 12:41 am Sagittarius
12th 03:28 am Capricorn
14th 06:07 am Aquarius
16th 09:27 am Pisces
18th 02:34 pm Aries
20th 10:26 pm Taurus
23rd 09:14 am Gemini
25th 09:45 pm Cancer
28th 09:40 am Leo
30th 06:58 pm Virgo

October 1986

3rd 01:03 am Libra
5th 04:36 am Scorpio
7th 06:48 am Sagittarius
9th 08:53 am Capricorn
11th 11:45 am Aquarius
13th 04:04 pm Pisces
15th 10:13 pm Aries
18th 06:36 am Taurus
20th 05:16 pm Gemini
23rd 05:38 am Cancer
25th 06:03 pm Leo
28th 04:20 am Virgo
30th 11:05 am Libra

November 1986

1st 02:20 pm Scorpio
3rd 03:19 pm Sagittarius
5th 03:49 pm Capricorn
7th 05:29 pm Aquarius
9th 09:30 pm Pisces
12th 04:15 am Aries
14th 01:25 pm Taurus
17th 12:27 am Gemini
19th 12:46 pm Cancer
22nd 01:26 am Leo
24th 12:46 pm Virgo
26th 08:59 pm Libra
29th 01:14 am Scorpio

December 1986

1st 02:08 am Sagittarius
3rd 01:29 am Capricorn
5th 01:23 am Aquarius
7th 03:49 am Pisces
9th 09:49 am Aries
11th 07:11 pm Taurus
14th 06:42 am Gemini
16th 07:10 pm Cancer
19th 07:44 am Leo
21st 07:31 pm Virgo
24th 05:05 am Libra
26th 11:07 am Scorpio
28th 01:20 pm Sagittarius
30th 12:54 pm Capricorn

January 1987

1st	11:54 am	Aquarius
3rd	12:36 pm	Pisces
5th	04:51 pm	Aries
8th	01:13 am	Taurus
10th	12:40 pm	Gemini
13th	01:19 am	Cancer
15th	01:45 pm	Leo
18th	01:15 am	Virgo
20th	11:10 am	Libra
22nd	06:31 pm	Scorpio
24th	10:36 pm	Sagittarius
26th	11:43 pm	Capricorn
28th	11:17 pm	Aquarius
30th	11:25 pm	Pisces

February 1987

2nd	02:10 am	Aries
4th	08:53 am	Taurus
6th	07:24 pm	Gemini
9th	07:55 am	Cancer
11th	08:22 pm	Leo
14th	07:26 am	Virgo
16th	04:45 pm	Libra
19th	12:05 am	Scorpio
21st	05:09 am	Sagittarius
23rd	07:57 am	Capricorn
25th	09:09 am	Aquarius
27th	10:07 am	Pisces

March 1987

1st	12:37 pm	Aries
3rd	06:12 pm	Taurus
6th	03:27 am	Gemini
8th	03:25 pm	Cancer
11th	03:55 am	Leo
13th	02:55 pm	Virgo
15th	11:34 pm	Libra
18th	05:57 am	Scorpio
20th	10:32 am	Sagittarius
22nd	01:49 pm	Capricorn
24th	04:18 pm	Aquarius
26th	06:46 pm	Pisces
28th	10:13 pm	Aries
31st	03:46 am	Taurus

April 1987

2nd	12:17 pm	Gemini
4th	11:34 pm	Cancer
7th	12:04 pm	Leo
9th	11:28 pm	Virgo
12th	08:06 am	Libra
14th	01:41 pm	Scorpio
16th	05:02 pm	Sagittarius
18th	07:21 pm	Capricorn
20th	09:46 pm	Aquarius
23rd	01:02 am	Pisces
25th	05:41 am	Aries
27th	12:06 pm	Taurus
29th	08:43 pm	Gemini

May 1987

2nd	07:39 am	Cancer
4th	08:07 pm	Leo
7th	08:08 am	Virgo
9th	05:29 pm	Libra
11th	11:10 pm	Scorpio
14th	01:41 am	Sagittarius
16th	02:37 am	Capricorn
18th	03:43 am	Aquarius
20th	06:24 am	Pisces
22nd	11:23 am	Aries
24th	06:39 pm	Taurus
27th	03:56 am	Gemini
29th	03:00 pm	Cancer

June 1987

1st	03:26 am	Leo
3rd	03:57 pm	Virgo
6th	02:25 am	Libra
8th	09:07 am	Scorpio
10th	11:53 am	Sagittarius
12th	12:05 pm	Capricorn
14th	11:45 am	Aquarius
16th	12:55 pm	Pisces
18th	04:57 pm	Aries
21st	12:09 am	Taurus
23rd	09:55 am	Gemini
25th	09:23 pm	Cancer
28th	09:52 am	Leo
30th	10:34 pm	Virgo

July 1987

3rd	09:55 am	Libra
5th	06:03 pm	Scorpio
7th	10:05 pm	Sagittarius
9th	10:44 pm	Capricorn
11th	09:50 pm	Aquarius
13th	09:36 pm	Pisces
16th	12:01 am	Aries
18th	06:05 am	Taurus
20th	03:33 pm	Gemini
23rd	03:13 am	Cancer
25th	03:50 pm	Leo
28th	04:26 am	Virgo
30th	04:00 pm	Libra

August 1987

2nd	01:10 am	Scorpio
4th	06:48 am	Sagittarius
6th	08:52 am	Capricorn
8th	08:37 am	Aquarius
10th	08:01 am	Pisces
12th	09:10 am	Aries
14th	01:38 pm	Taurus
16th	09:59 pm	Gemini
19th	09:19 am	Cancer
21st	09:58 pm	Leo
24th	10:24 am	Virgo
26th	09:36 pm	Libra
29th	06:50 am	Scorpio
31st	01:24 pm	Sagittarius

September 1987

2nd	05:04 pm	Capricorn
4th	06:22 pm	Aquarius
6th	06:37 pm	Pisces
8th	07:34 pm	Aries
10th	10:57 pm	Taurus
13th	05:55 am	Gemini
15th	04:22 pm	Cancer
18th	04:51 am	Leo
20th	05:13 pm	Virgo
23rd	03:59 am	Libra
25th	12:31 pm	Scorpio
27th	06:49 pm	Sagittarius
29th	11:09 pm	Capricorn

October 1987

2nd	01:52 am	Aquarius
4th	03:40 am	Pisces
6th	05:35 am	Aries
8th	08:58 am	Taurus
10th	03:04 pm	Gemini
13th	12:31 am	Cancer
15th	12:35 pm	Leo
18th	01:06 am	Virgo
20th	11:50 am	Libra
22nd	07:42 pm	Scorpio
25th	12:57 am	Sagittarius
27th	04:33 am	Capricorn
29th	07:27 am	Aquarius
31st	10:20 am	Pisces

November 1987

2nd	01:40 pm	Aries
4th	06:02 pm	Taurus
7th	12:16 am	Gemini
9th	09:10 am	Cancer
11th	08:45 pm	Leo
14th	09:30 am	Virgo
16th	08:49 pm	Libra
19th	04:47 am	Scorpio
21st	09:17 am	Sagittarius
23rd	11:32 am	Capricorn
25th	01:13 pm	Aquarius
27th	03:41 pm	Pisces
29th	07:36 pm	Aries

December 1987

2nd	01:06 am	Taurus
4th	08:14 am	Gemini
6th	05:20 pm	Cancer
9th	04:41 am	Leo
11th	05:30 pm	Virgo
14th	05:40 am	Libra
16th	02:42 pm	Scorpio
18th	07:33 pm	Sagittarius
20th	09:08 pm	Capricorn
22nd	09:20 pm	Aquarius
24th	10:10 pm	Pisces
27th	01:06 am	Aries
29th	06:37 am	Taurus
31st	02:29 pm	Gemini

January 1988

3rd	12:17 am	Cancer
5th	11:48 am	Leo
8th	12:35 am	Virgo
10th	01:18 pm	Libra
12th	11:40 pm	Scorpio
15th	05:59 am	Sagittarius
17th	08:16 am	Capricorn
19th	08:02 am	Aquarius
21st	07:27 am	Pisces
23rd	08:31 am	Aries
25th	12:37 pm	Taurus
27th	08:03 pm	Gemini
30th	06:12 am	Cancer

February 1988

1st	06:06 pm	Leo
4th	06:55 am	Virgo
6th	07:36 pm	Libra
9th	06:42 am	Scorpio
11th	02:36 pm	Sagittarius
13th	06:37 pm	Capricorn
15th	07:26 pm	Aquarius
17th	06:44 pm	Pisces
19th	06:35 pm	Aries
21st	08:51 pm	Taurus
24th	02:42 am	Gemini
26th	12:12 pm	Cancer
29th	12:12 am	Leo

March 1988

2nd	01:07 pm	Virgo
5th	01:32 am	Libra
7th	12:27 pm	Scorpio
9th	08:59 pm	Sagittarius
12th	02:31 am	Capricorn
14th	05:08 am	Aquarius
16th	05:42 am	Pisces
18th	05:45 am	Aries
20th	07:05 am	Taurus
22nd	11:21 am	Gemini
24th	07:28 pm	Cancer
27th	06:54 am	Leo
29th	07:49 pm	Virgo

April 1988

1st	08:05 am	Libra
3rd	06:26 pm	Scorpio
6th	02:29 am	Sagittarius
8th	08:20 am	Capricorn
10th	12:11 pm	Aquarius
12th	02:25 pm	Pisces
14th	03:47 pm	Aries
16th	05:32 pm	Taurus
18th	09:10 pm	Gemini
21st	04:05 am	Cancer
23rd	02:35 pm	Leo
26th	03:16 am	Virgo
28th	03:38 pm	Libra

May 1988

1st	01:40 am	Scorpio
3rd	08:53 am	Sagittarius
5th	01:54 pm	Capricorn
7th	05:37 pm	Aquarius
9th	08:39 pm	Pisces
11th	11:24 pm	Aries
14th	02:22 am	Taurus
16th	06:32 am	Gemini
18th	01:06 pm	Cancer
20th	10:52 pm	Leo
23rd	11:13 am	Virgo
25th	11:50 pm	Libra
28th	10:07 am	Scorpio
30th	04:58 pm	Sagittarius

June 1988

1st	08:59 pm	Capricorn
3rd	11:34 pm	Aquarius
6th	02:01 am	Pisces
8th	05:04 am	Aries
10th	09:03 am	Taurus
12th	02:15 pm	Gemini
14th	09:19 pm	Cancer
17th	06:58 am	Leo
19th	07:04 pm	Virgo
22nd	07:57 am	Libra
24th	06:59 pm	Scorpio
27th	02:18 am	Sagittarius
29th	06:00 am	Capricorn

July 1988

1st	07:30 am	Aquarius
3rd	08:34 am	Pisces
5th	10:37 am	Aries
7th	02:27 pm	Taurus
9th	08:17 pm	Gemini
12th	04:09 am	Cancer
14th	02:12 pm	Leo
17th	02:18 am	Virgo
19th	03:22 pm	Libra
22nd	03:13 am	Scorpio
24th	11:42 am	Sagittarius
26th	04:07 pm	Capricorn
28th	05:25 pm	Aquarius
30th	05:23 pm	Pisces

August 1988

1st	05:53 pm	Aries
3rd	08:24 pm	Taurus
6th	01:43 am	Gemini
8th	09:53 am	Cancer
10th	08:27 pm	Leo
13th	08:46 am	Virgo
15th	09:52 pm	Libra
18th	10:12 am	Scorpio
20th	07:55 pm	Sagittarius
23rd	01:49 am	Capricorn
25th	04:05 am	Aquarius
27th	04:01 am	Pisces
29th	03:29 am	Aries
31st	04:23 am	Taurus

September 1988

2nd	08:12 am	Gemini
4th	03:37 pm	Cancer
7th	02:15 am	Leo
9th	02:48 pm	Virgo
12th	03:51 am	Libra
14th	04:08 pm	Scorpio
17th	02:26 am	Sagittarius
19th	09:45 am	Capricorn
21st	01:43 pm	Aquarius
23rd	02:51 pm	Pisces
25th	02:30 pm	Aries
27th	02:29 pm	Taurus
29th	04:43 pm	Gemini

October 1988

1st	10:39 pm	Cancer
4th	08:31 am	Leo
6th	09:02 pm	Virgo
9th	10:04 am	Libra
11th	09:58 pm	Scorpio
14th	07:58 am	Sagittarius
16th	03:45 pm	Capricorn
18th	09:05 pm	Aquarius
20th	11:59 pm	Pisces
23rd	12:59 am	Aries
25th	01:23 am	Taurus
27th	02:56 am	Gemini
29th	07:29 am	Cancer
31st	04:04 pm	Leo

November 1988

3rd	04:02 am	Virgo
5th	05:04 pm	Libra
8th	04:47 am	Scorpio
10th	02:06 pm	Sagittarius
12th	09:13 pm	Capricorn
15th	02:37 am	Aquarius
17th	06:34 am	Pisces
19th	09:13 am	Aries
21st	11:02 am	Taurus
23rd	01:12 pm	Gemini
25th	05:20 pm	Cancer
28th	12:52 am	Leo
30th	12:00 pm	Virgo

December 1988

3rd	12:56 am	Libra
5th	12:52 pm	Scorpio
7th	09:56 pm	Sagittarius
10th	04:07 am	Capricorn
12th	08:26 am	Aquarius
14th	11:53 am	Pisces
16th	03:03 pm	Aries
18th	06:11 pm	Taurus
20th	09:43 pm	Gemini
23rd	02:35 am	Cancer
25th	09:58 am	Leo
27th	08:28 pm	Virgo
30th	09:10 am	Libra

January 1989

1st	09:34 pm	Scorpio
4th	07:12 am	Sagittarius
6th	01:14 pm	Capricorn
8th	04:31 pm	Aquarius
10th	06:31 pm	Pisces
12th	08:36 pm	Aries
14th	11:36 pm	Taurus
17th	03:57 am	Gemini
19th	09:57 am	Cancer
21st	06:03 pm	Leo
24th	04:33 am	Virgo
26th	05:02 pm	Libra
29th	05:49 am	Scorpio
31st	04:31 pm	Sagittarius

February 1989

2nd	11:30 pm	Capricorn
5th	02:51 am	Aquarius
7th	03:52 am	Pisces
9th	04:18 am	Aries
11th	05:45 am	Taurus
13th	09:23 am	Gemini
15th	03:40 pm	Cancer
18th	12:33 am	Leo
20th	11:35 am	Virgo
23rd	12:05 am	Libra
25th	12:57 pm	Scorpio
28th	12:30 am	Sagittarius

March 1989

2nd	08:58 am	Capricorn
4th	01:37 pm	Aquarius
6th	02:59 pm	Pisces
8th	02:37 pm	Aries
10th	02:25 pm	Taurus
12th	04:16 pm	Gemini
14th	09:28 pm	Cancer
17th	06:13 am	Leo
19th	05:40 pm	Virgo
22nd	06:24 am	Libra
24th	07:11 pm	Scorpio
27th	06:54 am	Sagittarius
29th	04:26 pm	Capricorn
31st	10:45 pm	Aquarius

April 1989

3rd	01:37 am	Pisces
5th	01:51 am	Aries
7th	01:08 am	Taurus
9th	01:31 am	Gemini
11th	04:58 am	Cancer
13th	12:31 pm	Leo
15th	11:40 pm	Virgo
18th	12:32 pm	Libra
21st	01:14 am	Scorpio
23rd	12:39 pm	Sagittarius
25th	10:16 pm	Capricorn
28th	05:33 am	Aquarius
30th	10:04 am	Pisces

May 1989

2nd	11:51 am	Aries
4th	11:55 am	Taurus
6th	12:04 pm	Gemini
8th	02:20 pm	Cancer
10th	08:23 pm	Leo
13th	06:31 am	Virgo
15th	07:08 pm	Libra
18th	07:48 am	Scorpio
20th	06:52 pm	Sagittarius
23rd	03:54 am	Capricorn
25th	11:01 am	Aquarius
27th	04:13 pm	Pisces
29th	07:26 pm	Aries
31st	09:00 pm	Taurus

June 1989

2nd	10:03 pm	Gemini
5th	12:17 am	Cancer
7th	05:28 am	Leo
9th	02:30 pm	Virgo
12th	02:31 am	Libra
14th	03:12 pm	Scorpio
17th	02:13 am	Sagittarius
19th	10:42 am	Capricorn
21st	04:57 pm	Aquarius
23rd	09:37 pm	Pisces
26th	01:06 am	Aries
28th	03:45 am	Taurus
30th	06:09 am	Gemini

July 1989

2nd	09:19 am	Cancer
4th	02:38 pm	Leo
6th	11:05 pm	Virgo
9th	10:31 am	Libra
11th	11:09 pm	Scorpio
14th	10:31 am	Sagittarius
16th	07:02 pm	Capricorn
19th	12:36 am	Aquarius
21st	04:07 am	Pisces
23rd	06:41 am	Aries
25th	09:10 am	Taurus
27th	12:15 pm	Gemini
29th	04:32 pm	Cancer
31st	10:41 pm	Leo

August 1989

3rd	07:19 am	Virgo
5th	06:28 pm	Libra
8th	07:05 am	Scorpio
10th	07:03 pm	Sagittarius
13th	04:17 am	Capricorn
15th	09:59 am	Aquarius
17th	12:46 pm	Pisces
19th	01:59 pm	Aries
21st	03:11 pm	Taurus
23rd	05:39 pm	Gemini
25th	10:13 pm	Cancer
28th	05:12 am	Leo
30th	02:30 pm	Virgo

September 1989

2nd	01:48 am	Libra
4th	02:23 pm	Scorpio
7th	02:51 am	Sagittarius
9th	01:14 pm	Capricorn
11th	08:02 pm	Aquarius
13th	11:08 pm	Pisces
15th	11:39 pm	Aries
17th	11:23 pm	Taurus
20th	12:16 am	Gemini
22nd	03:51 am	Cancer
24th	10:44 am	Leo
26th	08:33 pm	Virgo
29th	08:15 am	Libra

October 1989

1st	08:53 pm	Scorpio
4th	09:30 am	Sagittarius
6th	08:46 pm	Capricorn
9th	05:07 am	Aquarius
11th	09:38 am	Pisces
13th	10:42 am	Aries
15th	09:53 am	Taurus
17th	09:19 am	Gemini
19th	11:10 am	Cancer
21st	04:48 pm	Leo
24th	02:15 am	Virgo
26th	02:11 pm	Libra
29th	02:56 am	Scorpio
31st	03:23 pm	Sagittarius

November 1989

3rd	02:47 am	Capricorn
5th	12:10 pm	Aquarius
7th	06:25 pm	Pisces
9th	09:08 pm	Aries
11th	09:10 pm	Taurus
13th	08:19 pm	Gemini
15th	08:51 pm	Cancer
18th	12:46 am	Leo
20th	08:55 am	Virgo
22nd	08:26 pm	Libra
25th	09:14 am	Scorpio
27th	09:30 pm	Sagittarius
30th	08:27 am	Capricorn

December 1989

2nd	05:42 pm	Aquarius
5th	12:48 am	Pisces
7th	05:12 am	Aries
9th	06:59 am	Taurus
11th	07:15 am	Gemini
13th	07:49 am	Cancer
15th	10:42 am	Leo
17th	05:20 pm	Virgo
20th	03:46 am	Libra
22nd	04:19 pm	Scorpio
25th	04:38 am	Sagittarius
27th	03:11 pm	Capricorn
29th	11:38 pm	Aquarius

January 1990

1st	06:10 am	Pisces
3rd	10:57 am	Aries
5th	02:04 pm	Taurus
7th	04:02 pm	Gemini
9th	05:52 pm	Cancer
11th	09:03 pm	Leo
14th	02:58 am	Virgo
16th	12:18 pm	Libra
19th	12:16 am	Scorpio
21st	12:44 pm	Sagittarius
23rd	11:28 pm	Capricorn
26th	07:25 am	Aquarius
28th	12:51 pm	Pisces
30th	04:34 pm	Aries

February 1990

1st	07:27 pm	Taurus
3rd	10:13 pm	Gemini
6th	01:27 am	Cancer
8th	05:52 am	Leo
10th	12:13 pm	Virgo
12th	09:10 pm	Libra
15th	08:35 am	Scorpio
17th	09:07 pm	Sagittarius
20th	08:31 am	Capricorn
22nd	04:53 pm	Aquarius
24th	09:50 pm	Pisces
27th	12:17 am	Aries

March 1990

1st	01:43 am	Taurus
3rd	03:38 am	Gemini
5th	07:03 am	Cancer
7th	12:25 pm	Leo
9th	07:47 pm	Virgo
12th	05:09 am	Libra
14th	04:25 pm	Scorpio
17th	04:56 am	Sagittarius
19th	05:02 pm	Capricorn
22nd	02:32 am	Aquarius
24th	08:09 am	Pisces
26th	10:16 am	Aries
28th	10:27 am	Taurus
30th	10:42 am	Gemini

April 1990

1st	12:50 pm	Cancer
3rd	05:50 pm	Leo
6th	01:42 am	Virgo
8th	11:45 am	Libra
10th	11:18 pm	Scorpio
13th	11:48 am	Sagittarius
16th	12:15 am	Capricorn
18th	10:53 am	Aquarius
20th	05:57 pm	Pisces
22nd	08:59 pm	Aries
24th	09:03 pm	Taurus
26th	08:12 pm	Gemini
28th	08:39 pm	Cancer

May 1990

1st	12:09 am	Leo
3rd	07:18 am	Virgo
5th	05:29 pm	Libra
8th	05:23 am	Scorpio
10th	05:56 pm	Sagittarius
13th	06:21 am	Capricorn
15th	05:31 pm	Aquarius
18th	01:54 am	Pisces
20th	06:32 am	Aries
22nd	07:43 am	Taurus
24th	07:00 am	Gemini
26th	06:34 am	Cancer
28th	08:29 am	Leo
30th	02:08 pm	Virgo

June 1990

1st	11:31 pm	Libra
4th	11:22 am	Scorpio
7th	12:00 am	Sagittarius
9th	12:12 pm	Capricorn
11th	11:09 pm	Aquarius
14th	08:00 am	Pisces
16th	01:55 pm	Aries
18th	04:43 pm	Taurus
20th	05:15 pm	Gemini
22nd	05:10 pm	Cancer
24th	06:25 pm	Leo
26th	10:42 pm	Virgo
29th	06:47 am	Libra

July 1990

1st	06:01 pm	Scorpio
4th	06:36 am	Sagittarius
6th	06:40 pm	Capricorn
9th	05:07 am	Aquarius
11th	01:30 pm	Pisces
13th	07:37 pm	Aries
15th	11:29 pm	Taurus
18th	01:32 am	Gemini
20th	02:44 am	Cancer
22nd	04:29 am	Leo
24th	08:18 am	Virgo
26th	03:19 pm	Libra
29th	01:40 am	Scorpio
31st	02:00 pm	Sagittarius

August 1990

3rd	02:09 am	Capricorn
5th	12:19 pm	Aquarius
7th	07:55 pm	Pisces
10th	01:13 am	Aries
12th	04:55 am	Taurus
14th	07:42 am	Gemini
16th	10:13 am	Cancer
18th	01:12 pm	Leo
20th	05:33 pm	Virgo
23rd	12:17 am	Libra
25th	09:56 am	Scorpio
27th	09:58 pm	Sagittarius
30th	10:23 am	Capricorn

September 1990

1st	08:51 pm	Aquarius
4th	04:06 am	Pisces
6th	08:23 am	Aries
8th	10:56 am	Taurus
10th	01:05 pm	Gemini
12th	03:53 pm	Cancer
14th	07:52 pm	Leo
17th	01:19 am	Virgo
19th	08:34 am	Libra
21st	06:06 pm	Scorpio
24th	05:52 am	Sagittarius
26th	06:37 pm	Capricorn
29th	05:54 am	Aquarius

October 1990

1st	01:43 pm	Pisces
3rd	05:42 pm	Aries
5th	07:06 pm	Taurus
7th	07:47 pm	Gemini
9th	09:30 pm	Cancer
12th	01:17 am	Leo
14th	07:21 am	Virgo
16th	03:27 pm	Libra
19th	01:24 am	Scorpio
21st	01:10 pm	Sagittarius
24th	02:03 am	Capricorn
26th	02:14 pm	Aquarius
28th	11:22 pm	Pisces
31st	04:15 am	Aries

November 1990

2nd	05:32 am	Taurus
4th	05:06 am	Gemini
6th	05:08 am	Cancer
8th	07:24 am	Leo
10th	12:48 pm	Virgo
12th	09:09 pm	Libra
15th	07:40 am	Scorpio
17th	07:40 pm	Sagittarius
20th	08:32 am	Capricorn
22nd	09:07 pm	Aquarius
25th	07:32 am	Pisces
27th	02:07 pm	Aries
29th	04:38 pm	Taurus

December 1990

1st	04:23 pm	Gemini
3rd	03:28 pm	Cancer
5th	04:00 pm	Leo
7th	07:39 pm	Virgo
10th	03:00 am	Libra
12th	01:28 pm	Scorpio
15th	01:44 am	Sagittarius
17th	02:35 pm	Capricorn
20th	02:59 am	Aquarius
22nd	01:48 pm	Pisces
24th	09:45 pm	Aries
27th	02:09 am	Taurus
29th	03:26 am	Gemini
31st	03:03 am	Cancer

January 1991

2nd	02:55 am	Leo
4th	04:57 am	Virgo
6th	10:34 am	Libra
8th	08:00 pm	Scorpio
11th	08:07 am	Sagittarius
13th	09:01 pm	Capricorn
16th	09:05 am	Aquarius
18th	07:24 pm	Pisces
21st	03:28 am	Aries
23rd	09:01 am	Taurus
25th	12:07 pm	Gemini
27th	01:23 pm	Cancer
29th	02:04 pm	Leo
31st	03:44 pm	Virgo

February 1991

2nd	08:03 pm	Libra
5th	04:02 am	Scorpio
7th	03:24 pm	Sagittarius
10th	04:16 am	Capricorn
12th	04:17 pm	Aquarius
15th	01:59 am	Pisces
17th	09:12 am	Aries
19th	02:25 pm	Taurus
21st	06:11 pm	Gemini
23rd	08:57 pm	Cancer
25th	11:13 pm	Leo
28th	01:50 am	Virgo

March 1991

2nd	06:04 am	Libra
4th	01:09 pm	Scorpio
6th	11:35 pm	Sagittarius
9th	12:14 pm	Capricorn
12th	12:31 am	Aquarius
14th	10:11 am	Pisces
16th	04:38 pm	Aries
18th	08:41 pm	Taurus
20th	11:37 pm	Gemini
23rd	02:28 am	Cancer
25th	05:44 am	Leo
27th	09:41 am	Virgo
29th	02:50 pm	Libra
31st	10:01 pm	Scorpio

April 1991

3rd	07:59 am	Sagittarius
5th	08:20 pm	Capricorn
8th	09:00 am	Aquarius
10th	07:18 pm	Pisces
13th	01:50 am	Aries
15th	05:06 am	Taurus
17th	06:41 am	Gemini
19th	08:18 am	Cancer
21st	11:05 am	Leo
23rd	03:30 pm	Virgo
25th	09:36 pm	Libra
28th	05:34 am	Scorpio
30th	03:42 pm	Sagittarius

May 1991

3rd	03:55 am	Capricorn
5th	04:51 pm	Aquarius
8th	04:05 am	Pisces
10th	11:35 am	Aries
12th	03:08 pm	Taurus
14th	04:02 pm	Gemini
16th	04:14 pm	Cancer
18th	05:30 pm	Leo
20th	09:01 pm	Virgo
23rd	03:08 am	Libra
25th	11:42 am	Scorpio
27th	10:21 pm	Sagittarius
30th	10:41 am	Capricorn

June 1991

1st	11:42 pm	Aquarius
4th	11:37 am	Pisces
6th	08:26 pm	Aries
9th	01:13 am	Taurus
11th	02:37 am	Gemini
13th	02:17 am	Cancer
15th	02:11 am	Leo
17th	04:03 am	Virgo
19th	09:02 am	Libra
21st	05:19 pm	Scorpio
24th	04:16 am	Sagittarius
26th	04:50 pm	Capricorn
29th	05:48 am	Aquarius

July 1991

1st	05:51 pm	Pisces
4th	03:34 am	Aries
6th	09:52 am	Taurus
8th	12:42 pm	Gemini
10th	01:03 pm	Cancer
12th	12:35 pm	Leo
14th	01:12 pm	Virgo
16th	04:34 pm	Libra
18th	11:41 pm	Scorpio
21st	10:17 am	Sagittarius
23rd	10:56 pm	Capricorn
26th	11:49 am	Aquarius
28th	11:35 pm	Pisces
31st	09:21 am	Aries

August 1991

2nd	04:32 pm	Taurus
4th	08:55 pm	Gemini
6th	10:47 pm	Cancer
8th	11:10 pm	Leo
10th	11:35 pm	Virgo
13th	01:52 am	Libra
15th	07:34 am	Scorpio
17th	05:11 pm	Sagittarius
20th	05:35 am	Capricorn
22nd	06:27 pm	Aquarius
25th	05:52 am	Pisces
27th	03:01 pm	Aries
29th	10:00 pm	Taurus

September 1991

1st	03:03 am	Gemini
3rd	06:20 am	Cancer
5th	08:14 am	Leo
7th	09:35 am	Virgo
9th	11:52 am	Libra
11th	04:42 pm	Scorpio
14th	01:15 am	Sagittarius
16th	01:04 pm	Capricorn
19th	01:58 am	Aquarius
21st	01:21 pm	Pisces
23rd	09:56 pm	Aries
26th	04:00 am	Taurus
28th	08:26 am	Gemini
30th	11:59 am	Cancer

October 1991

2nd	02:59 pm	Leo
4th	05:45 pm	Virgo
6th	09:01 pm	Libra
9th	02:00 am	Scorpio
11th	09:58 am	Sagittarius
13th	09:11 pm	Capricorn
16th	10:05 am	Aquarius
18th	09:53 pm	Pisces
21st	06:33 am	Aries
23rd	11:56 am	Taurus
25th	03:09 pm	Gemini
27th	05:37 pm	Cancer
29th	08:21 pm	Leo
31st	11:47 pm	Virgo

November 1991

3rd	04:13 am	Libra
5th	10:09 am	Scorpio
7th	06:22 pm	Sagittarius
10th	05:17 am	Capricorn
12th	06:07 pm	Aquarius
15th	06:34 am	Pisces
17th	04:08 pm	Aries
19th	09:49 pm	Taurus
22nd	12:23 am	Gemini
24th	01:26 am	Cancer
26th	02:38 am	Leo
28th	05:12 am	Virgo
30th	09:47 am	Libra

December 1991

2nd	04:34 pm	Scorpio
5th	01:33 am	Sagittarius
7th	12:41 pm	Capricorn
10th	01:27 am	Aquarius
12th	02:20 pm	Pisces
15th	01:07 am	Aries
17th	08:10 am	Taurus
19th	11:22 am	Gemini
21st	11:55 am	Cancer
23rd	11:39 am	Leo
25th	12:24 pm	Virgo
27th	03:38 pm	Libra
29th	10:04 pm	Scorpio

January 1992

1st	07:31 am	Sagittarius
3rd	07:10 pm	Capricorn
6th	08:00 am	Aquarius
8th	08:52 pm	Pisces
11th	08:23 am	Aries
13th	05:01 pm	Taurus
15th	09:55 pm	Gemini
17th	11:26 pm	Cancer
19th	10:57 pm	Leo
21st	10:22 pm	Virgo
23rd	11:43 pm	Libra
26th	04:32 am	Scorpio
28th	01:20 pm	Sagittarius
31st	01:08 am	Capricorn

February 1992

2nd	02:09 pm	Aquarius
5th	02:51 am	Pisces
7th	02:15 pm	Aries
9th	11:36 pm	Taurus
12th	06:08 am	Gemini
14th	09:31 am	Cancer
16th	10:16 am	Leo
18th	09:47 am	Virgo
20th	10:05 am	Libra
22nd	01:12 pm	Scorpio
24th	08:27 pm	Sagittarius
27th	07:34 am	Capricorn
29th	08:34 pm	Aquarius

March 1992

3rd	09:11 am	Pisces
5th	08:07 pm	Aries
8th	05:05 am	Taurus
10th	12:04 pm	Gemini
12th	04:50 pm	Cancer
14th	07:21 pm	Leo
16th	08:14 pm	Virgo
18th	08:55 pm	Libra
20th	11:20 pm	Scorpio
23rd	05:13 am	Sagittarius
25th	03:09 pm	Capricorn
28th	03:45 am	Aquarius
30th	04:24 pm	Pisces

April 1992

2nd	03:04 am	Aries
4th	11:18 am	Taurus
6th	05:33 pm	Gemini
8th	10:19 pm	Cancer
11th	01:46 am	Leo
13th	04:09 am	Virgo
15th	06:11 am	Libra
17th	09:10 am	Scorpio
19th	02:41 pm	Sagittarius
21st	11:41 pm	Capricorn
24th	11:39 am	Aquarius
27th	12:20 am	Pisces
29th	11:14 am	Aries

May 1992

1st	07:10 pm	Taurus
4th	12:29 am	Gemini
6th	04:10 am	Cancer
8th	07:08 am	Leo
10th	09:56 am	Virgo
12th	01:05 pm	Libra
14th	05:15 pm	Scorpio
16th	11:22 pm	Sagittarius
19th	08:13 am	Capricorn
21st	07:44 pm	Aquarius
24th	08:26 am	Pisces
26th	07:53 pm	Aries
29th	04:17 am	Taurus
31st	09:19 am	Gemini

June 1992

2nd	11:58 am	Cancer
4th	01:35 pm	Leo
6th	03:28 pm	Virgo
8th	06:34 pm	Libra
10th	11:27 pm	Scorpio
13th	06:29 am	Sagittarius
15th	03:50 pm	Capricorn
18th	03:19 am	Aquarius
20th	04:00 pm	Pisces
23rd	04:04 am	Aries
25th	01:29 pm	Taurus
27th	07:14 pm	Gemini
29th	09:42 pm	Cancer

July 1992

1st	10:15 pm	Leo
3rd	10:38 pm	Virgo
6th	12:28 am	Libra
8th	04:54 am	Scorpio
10th	12:18 pm	Sagittarius
12th	10:16 pm	Capricorn
15th	10:03 am	Aquarius
17th	10:45 pm	Pisces
20th	11:08 am	Aries
22nd	09:36 pm	Taurus
25th	04:45 am	Gemini
27th	08:09 am	Cancer
29th	08:40 am	Leo
31st	08:02 am	Virgo

August 1992

2nd	08:17 am	Libra
4th	11:16 am	Scorpio
6th	05:57 pm	Sagittarius
9th	04:01 am	Capricorn
11th	04:07 pm	Aquarius
14th	04:51 am	Pisces
16th	05:12 pm	Aries
19th	04:10 am	Taurus
21st	12:37 pm	Gemini
23rd	05:37 pm	Cancer
25th	07:16 pm	Leo
27th	06:47 pm	Virgo
29th	06:11 pm	Libra
31st	07:39 pm	Scorpio

September 1992

3rd	12:50 am	Sagittarius
5th	10:06 am	Capricorn
7th	10:09 pm	Aquarius
10th	10:56 am	Pisces
12th	11:03 pm	Aries
15th	09:47 am	Taurus
17th	06:40 pm	Gemini
20th	12:59 am	Cancer
22nd	04:19 am	Leo
24th	05:09 am	Virgo
26th	04:56 am	Libra
28th	05:44 am	Scorpio
30th	09:34 am	Sagittarius

October 1992

2nd	05:29 pm	Capricorn
5th	04:53 am	Aquarius
7th	05:38 pm	Pisces
10th	05:36 am	Aries
12th	03:49 pm	Taurus
15th	12:09 am	Gemini
17th	06:36 am	Cancer
19th	11:01 am	Leo
21st	01:28 pm	Virgo
23rd	02:40 pm	Libra
25th	04:05 pm	Scorpio
27th	07:29 pm	Sagittarius
30th	02:18 am	Capricorn

November 1992

1st	12:44 pm	Aquarius
4th	01:13 am	Pisces
6th	01:20 pm	Aries
8th	11:19 pm	Taurus
11th	06:50 am	Gemini
13th	12:19 pm	Cancer
15th	04:23 pm	Leo
17th	07:29 pm	Virgo
19th	10:03 pm	Libra
22nd	12:52 am	Scorpio
24th	05:01 am	Sagittarius
26th	11:39 am	Capricorn
28th	09:19 pm	Aquarius

December 1992

1st	09:24 am	Pisces
3rd	09:49 pm	Aries
6th	08:17 am	Taurus
8th	03:37 pm	Gemini
10th	08:06 pm	Cancer
12th	10:47 pm	Leo
15th	12:56 am	Virgo
17th	03:33 am	Libra
19th	07:20 am	Scorpio
21st	12:43 pm	Sagittarius
23rd	08:05 pm	Capricorn
26th	05:43 am	Aquarius
28th	05:28 pm	Pisces
31st	06:07 am	Aries

January 1993
2nd	05:30 pm	Taurus
5th	01:42 am	Gemini
7th	06:11 am	Cancer
9th	07:50 am	Leo
11th	08:21 am	Virgo
13th	09:31 am	Libra
15th	12:42 pm	Scorpio
17th	06:31 pm	Sagittarius
20th	02:47 am	Capricorn
22nd	01:01 pm	Aquarius
25th	12:48 am	Pisces
27th	01:28 pm	Aries
30th	01:37 am	Taurus

February 1993
1st	11:15 am	Gemini
3rd	04:57 pm	Cancer
5th	06:52 pm	Leo
7th	06:29 pm	Virgo
9th	05:59 pm	Libra
11th	07:24 pm	Scorpio
14th	12:08 am	Sagittarius
16th	08:21 am	Capricorn
18th	07:06 pm	Aquarius
21st	07:12 am	Pisces
23rd	07:51 pm	Aries
26th	08:12 am	Taurus
28th	06:53 pm	Gemini

March 1993
3rd	02:17 am	Cancer
5th	05:41 am	Leo
7th	05:53 am	Virgo
9th	04:47 am	Libra
11th	04:40 am	Scorpio
13th	07:34 am	Sagittarius
15th	02:28 pm	Capricorn
18th	12:53 am	Aquarius
20th	01:11 pm	Pisces
23rd	01:52 am	Aries
25th	02:00 pm	Taurus
28th	12:48 am	Gemini
30th	09:14 am	Cancer

April 1993
1st	02:22 pm	Leo
3rd	04:11 pm	Virgo
5th	03:55 pm	Libra
7th	03:32 pm	Scorpio
9th	05:10 pm	Sagittarius
11th	10:24 pm	Capricorn
14th	07:36 am	Aquarius
16th	07:33 pm	Pisces
19th	08:15 am	Aries
21st	08:08 pm	Taurus
24th	06:27 am	Gemini
26th	02:46 pm	Cancer
28th	08:40 pm	Leo

May 1993
1st	12:00 am	Virgo
3rd	01:20 am	Libra
5th	01:58 am	Scorpio
7th	03:35 am	Sagittarius
9th	07:51 am	Capricorn
11th	03:44 pm	Aquarius
14th	02:51 am	Pisces
16th	03:25 pm	Aries
19th	03:17 am	Taurus
21st	01:08 pm	Gemini
23rd	08:38 pm	Cancer
26th	02:04 am	Leo
28th	05:47 am	Virgo
30th	08:19 am	Libra

June 1993
1st	10:23 am	Scorpio
3rd	01:01 pm	Sagittarius
5th	05:27 pm	Capricorn
8th	12:40 am	Aquarius
10th	10:57 am	Pisces
12th	11:14 pm	Aries
15th	11:20 am	Taurus
17th	09:12 pm	Gemini
20th	04:05 am	Cancer
22nd	08:27 am	Leo
24th	11:19 am	Virgo
26th	01:46 pm	Libra
28th	04:38 pm	Scorpio
30th	08:28 pm	Sagittarius

July 1993
3rd	01:49 am	Capricorn
5th	09:15 am	Aquarius
7th	07:10 pm	Pisces
10th	07:12 am	Aries
12th	07:38 pm	Taurus
15th	06:07 am	Gemini
17th	01:08 pm	Cancer
19th	04:48 pm	Leo
21st	06:24 pm	Virgo
23rd	07:40 pm	Libra
25th	10:00 pm	Scorpio
28th	02:13 am	Sagittarius
30th	08:27 am	Capricorn

August 1993
1st	04:37 pm	Aquarius
4th	02:44 am	Pisces
6th	02:40 pm	Aries
9th	03:23 am	Taurus
11th	02:47 pm	Gemini
13th	10:47 pm	Cancer
16th	02:44 am	Leo
18th	03:41 am	Virgo
20th	03:36 am	Libra
22nd	04:28 am	Scorpio
24th	07:46 am	Sagittarius
26th	01:58 pm	Capricorn
28th	10:42 pm	Aquarius
31st	09:19 am	Pisces

September 1993
2nd	09:21 pm	Aries
5th	10:10 am	Taurus
7th	10:16 pm	Gemini
10th	07:37 am	Cancer
12th	12:52 pm	Leo
14th	02:21 pm	Virgo
16th	01:44 pm	Libra
18th	01:15 pm	Scorpio
20th	02:54 pm	Sagittarius
22nd	07:54 pm	Capricorn
25th	04:19 am	Aquarius
27th	03:13 pm	Pisces
30th	03:29 am	Aries

October 1993
2nd	04:14 pm	Taurus
5th	04:27 am	Gemini
7th	02:43 pm	Cancer
9th	09:34 pm	Leo
12th	12:36 am	Virgo
14th	12:48 am	Libra
16th	12:01 am	Scorpio
18th	12:24 am	Sagittarius
20th	03:42 am	Capricorn
22nd	10:49 am	Aquarius
24th	09:18 pm	Pisces
27th	09:40 am	Aries
29th	10:21 pm	Taurus

November 1993
1st	10:13 am	Gemini
3rd	08:25 pm	Cancer
6th	04:07 am	Leo
8th	08:48 am	Virgo
10th	10:43 am	Libra
12th	11:00 am	Scorpio
14th	11:21 am	Sagittarius
16th	01:35 pm	Capricorn
18th	07:08 pm	Aquarius
21st	04:28 am	Pisces
23rd	04:31 pm	Aries
26th	05:15 am	Taurus
28th	04:48 pm	Gemini

December 1993
1st	02:17 am	Cancer
3rd	09:33 am	Leo
5th	02:44 pm	Virgo
7th	06:04 pm	Libra
9th	08:05 pm	Scorpio
11th	09:40 pm	Sagittarius
14th	12:06 am	Capricorn
16th	04:52 am	Aquarius
18th	12:59 pm	Pisces
21st	12:19 am	Aries
23rd	01:05 pm	Taurus
26th	12:46 am	Gemini
28th	09:46 am	Cancer
30th	04:00 pm	Leo

January 1994

1st	08:15 pm	Virgo
3rd	11:31 pm	Libra
6th	02:29 am	Scorpio
8th	05:34 am	Sagittarius
10th	09:16 am	Capricorn
12th	02:25 pm	Aquarius
14th	10:04 pm	Pisces
17th	08:42 am	Aries
19th	09:22 pm	Taurus
22nd	09:35 am	Gemini
24th	06:55 pm	Cancer
27th	12:39 am	Leo
29th	03:39 am	Virgo
31st	05:34 am	Libra

February 1994

2nd	07:50 am	Scorpio
4th	11:15 am	Sagittarius
6th	04:02 pm	Capricorn
8th	10:17 pm	Aquarius
11th	06:23 am	Pisces
13th	04:50 pm	Aries
16th	05:20 am	Taurus
18th	06:06 pm	Gemini
21st	04:28 am	Cancer
23rd	10:48 am	Leo
25th	01:28 pm	Virgo
27th	02:06 pm	Libra

March 1994

1st	02:44 pm	Scorpio
3rd	04:54 pm	Sagittarius
5th	09:25 pm	Capricorn
8th	04:15 am	Aquarius
10th	01:10 pm	Pisces
12th	11:59 pm	Aries
15th	12:28 pm	Taurus
18th	01:29 am	Gemini
20th	12:54 pm	Cancer
22nd	08:40 pm	Leo
25th	12:14 am	Virgo
27th	12:47 am	Libra
29th	12:15 am	Scorpio
31st	12:42 am	Sagittarius

April 1994

2nd	03:38 am	Capricorn
4th	09:46 am	Aquarius
6th	06:51 pm	Pisces
9th	06:09 am	Aries
11th	06:48 pm	Taurus
14th	07:48 am	Gemini
16th	07:41 pm	Cancer
19th	04:45 am	Leo
21st	09:58 am	Virgo
23rd	11:41 am	Libra
25th	11:19 am	Scorpio
27th	10:49 am	Sagittarius
29th	12:05 pm	Capricorn

May 1994

1st	04:35 pm	Aquarius
4th	12:47 am	Pisces
6th	12:02 pm	Aries
9th	12:51 am	Taurus
11th	01:44 pm	Gemini
14th	01:27 am	Cancer
16th	10:59 am	Leo
18th	05:31 pm	Virgo
20th	08:55 pm	Libra
22nd	09:51 pm	Scorpio
24th	09:43 pm	Sagittarius
26th	10:17 pm	Capricorn
29th	01:19 am	Aquarius
31st	08:04 am	Pisces

June 1994

2nd	06:32 pm	Aries
5th	07:14 am	Taurus
7th	08:04 pm	Gemini
10th	07:22 am	Cancer
12th	04:29 pm	Leo
14th	11:17 pm	Virgo
17th	03:48 am	Libra
19th	06:20 am	Scorpio
21st	07:33 am	Sagittarius
23rd	08:37 am	Capricorn
25th	11:10 am	Aquarius
27th	04:45 pm	Pisces
30th	02:07 am	Aries

July 1994

2nd	02:24 pm	Taurus
5th	03:13 am	Gemini
7th	02:18 pm	Cancer
9th	10:44 pm	Leo
12th	04:49 am	Virgo
14th	09:15 am	Libra
16th	12:35 pm	Scorpio
18th	03:10 pm	Sagittarius
20th	05:31 pm	Capricorn
22nd	08:39 pm	Aquarius
25th	01:57 am	Pisces
27th	10:31 am	Aries
29th	10:13 pm	Taurus

August 1994

1st	11:05 am	Gemini
3rd	10:23 pm	Cancer
6th	06:31 am	Leo
8th	11:43 am	Virgo
10th	03:07 pm	Libra
12th	05:56 pm	Scorpio
14th	08:53 pm	Sagittarius
17th	12:18 am	Capricorn
19th	04:34 am	Aquarius
21st	10:28 am	Pisces
23rd	06:55 pm	Aries
26th	06:14 am	Taurus
28th	07:08 pm	Gemini
31st	07:00 am	Cancer

September 1994

2nd	03:38 pm	Leo
4th	08:34 pm	Virgo
6th	10:57 pm	Libra
9th	12:26 am	Scorpio
11th	02:26 am	Sagittarius
13th	05:45 am	Capricorn
15th	10:43 am	Aquarius
17th	05:32 pm	Pisces
20th	02:30 am	Aries
22nd	01:48 pm	Taurus
25th	02:42 am	Gemini
27th	03:12 pm	Cancer
30th	12:56 am	Leo

October 1994

2nd	06:40 am	Virgo
4th	08:57 am	Libra
6th	09:22 am	Scorpio
8th	09:47 am	Sagittarius
10th	11:44 am	Capricorn
12th	04:10 pm	Aquarius
14th	11:19 pm	Pisces
17th	08:57 am	Aries
19th	08:35 pm	Taurus
22nd	09:28 am	Gemini
24th	10:16 pm	Cancer
27th	09:05 am	Leo
29th	04:22 pm	Virgo
31st	07:47 pm	Libra

November 1994

2nd	08:20 pm	Scorpio
4th	07:46 pm	Sagittarius
6th	08:02 pm	Capricorn
8th	10:48 pm	Aquarius
11th	05:04 am	Pisces
13th	02:44 pm	Aries
16th	02:44 am	Taurus
18th	03:42 pm	Gemini
21st	04:21 am	Cancer
23rd	03:33 pm	Leo
26th	12:09 am	Virgo
28th	05:23 am	Libra
30th	07:22 am	Scorpio

December 1994

2nd	07:13 am	Sagittarius
4th	06:43 am	Capricorn
6th	07:52 am	Aquarius
8th	12:25 pm	Pisces
10th	09:04 pm	Aries
13th	08:56 am	Taurus
15th	10:00 pm	Gemini
18th	10:25 am	Cancer
20th	09:13 pm	Leo
23rd	06:01 am	Virgo
25th	12:28 pm	Libra
27th	04:18 pm	Scorpio
29th	05:46 pm	Sagittarius
31st	05:58 pm	Capricorn

January 1995

2nd	06:39 pm	Aquarius
4th	09:49 pm	Pisces
7th	04:57 am	Aries
9th	03:59 pm	Taurus
12th	04:58 am	Gemini
14th	05:20 pm	Cancer
17th	03:37 am	Leo
19th	11:40 am	Virgo
21st	05:54 pm	Libra
23rd	10:33 pm	Scorpio
26th	01:37 am	Sagittarius
28th	03:27 am	Capricorn
30th	05:03 am	Aquarius

February 1995

1st	08:05 am	Pisces
3rd	02:13 pm	Aries
6th	12:09 am	Taurus
8th	12:44 pm	Gemini
11th	01:17 am	Cancer
13th	11:32 am	Leo
15th	06:52 pm	Virgo
18th	12:01 am	Libra
20th	03:56 am	Scorpio
22nd	07:13 am	Sagittarius
24th	10:11 am	Capricorn
26th	01:14 pm	Aquarius
28th	05:16 pm	Pisces

March 1995

2nd	11:30 pm	Aries
5th	08:51 am	Taurus
7th	08:55 pm	Gemini
10th	09:41 am	Cancer
12th	08:29 pm	Leo
15th	03:55 am	Virgo
17th	08:18 am	Libra
19th	10:53 am	Scorpio
21st	12:58 pm	Sagittarius
23rd	03:32 pm	Capricorn
25th	07:10 pm	Aquarius
28th	12:18 am	Pisces
30th	07:26 am	Aries

April 1995

1st	04:59 pm	Taurus
4th	04:49 am	Gemini
6th	05:40 pm	Cancer
9th	05:16 am	Leo
11th	01:39 pm	Virgo
13th	06:21 pm	Libra
15th	08:13 pm	Scorpio
17th	08:52 pm	Sagittarius
19th	09:54 pm	Capricorn
22nd	12:38 am	Aquarius
24th	05:51 am	Pisces
26th	01:42 pm	Aries
28th	11:53 pm	Taurus

May 1995

1st	11:54 am	Gemini
4th	12:45 am	Cancer
6th	12:55 pm	Leo
8th	10:34 pm	Virgo
11th	04:31 am	Libra
13th	06:54 am	Scorpio
15th	06:59 am	Sagittarius
17th	06:36 am	Capricorn
19th	07:40 am	Aquarius
21st	11:40 am	Pisces
23rd	07:13 pm	Aries
26th	05:47 am	Taurus
28th	06:07 pm	Gemini
31st	07:00 am	Cancer

June 1995

2nd	07:17 pm	Leo
5th	05:47 am	Virgo
7th	01:14 pm	Libra
9th	05:04 pm	Scorpio
11th	05:50 pm	Sagittarius
13th	05:05 pm	Capricorn
15th	04:52 pm	Aquarius
17th	07:13 pm	Pisces
20th	01:29 am	Aries
22nd	11:36 am	Taurus
25th	12:03 am	Gemini
27th	12:57 pm	Cancer
30th	01:02 am	Leo

July 1995

2nd	11:36 am	Virgo
4th	07:56 pm	Libra
7th	01:19 am	Scorpio
9th	03:38 am	Sagittarius
11th	03:44 am	Capricorn
13th	03:21 am	Aquarius
15th	04:37 am	Pisces
17th	09:23 am	Aries
19th	06:21 pm	Taurus
22nd	06:24 am	Gemini
24th	07:16 pm	Cancer
27th	07:07 am	Leo
29th	05:12 pm	Virgo

August 1995

1st	01:24 am	Libra
3rd	07:30 am	Scorpio
5th	11:14 am	Sagittarius
7th	12:52 pm	Capricorn
9th	01:28 pm	Aquarius
11th	02:47 pm	Pisces
13th	06:41 pm	Aries
16th	02:26 am	Taurus
18th	01:40 pm	Gemini
21st	02:24 am	Cancer
23rd	02:13 pm	Leo
25th	11:51 pm	Virgo
28th	07:15 am	Libra
30th	12:52 pm	Scorpio

September 1995

1st	04:57 pm	Sagittarius
3rd	07:45 pm	Capricorn
5th	09:48 pm	Aquarius
8th	12:08 am	Pisces
10th	04:14 am	Aries
12th	11:22 am	Taurus
14th	09:48 pm	Gemini
17th	10:16 am	Cancer
19th	10:20 pm	Leo
22nd	08:02 am	Virgo
24th	02:50 pm	Libra
26th	07:21 pm	Scorpio
28th	10:31 pm	Sagittarius

October 1995

1st	01:11 am	Capricorn
3rd	04:00 am	Aquarius
5th	07:36 am	Pisces
7th	12:42 pm	Aries
9th	08:05 pm	Taurus
12th	06:10 am	Gemini
14th	06:20 pm	Cancer
17th	06:47 am	Leo
19th	05:12 pm	Virgo
22nd	12:16 am	Libra
24th	04:07 am	Scorpio
26th	05:57 am	Sagittarius
28th	07:15 am	Capricorn
30th	09:24 am	Aquarius

November 1995

1st	01:18 pm	Pisces
3rd	07:21 pm	Aries
6th	03:36 am	Taurus
8th	01:55 pm	Gemini
11th	01:57 am	Cancer
13th	02:38 pm	Leo
16th	02:03 am	Virgo
18th	10:18 am	Libra
20th	02:41 pm	Scorpio
22nd	03:57 pm	Sagittarius
24th	03:49 pm	Capricorn
26th	04:16 pm	Aquarius
28th	06:59 pm	Pisces

December 1995

1st	12:51 am	Aries
3rd	09:40 am	Taurus
5th	08:35 pm	Gemini
8th	08:45 am	Cancer
10th	09:25 pm	Leo
13th	09:27 am	Virgo
15th	07:10 pm	Libra
18th	01:07 am	Scorpio
20th	03:14 am	Sagittarius
22nd	02:46 am	Capricorn
24th	01:52 am	Aquarius
26th	02:45 am	Pisces
28th	07:06 am	Aries
30th	03:21 pm	Taurus

January 1996

2nd	02:30 am	Gemini
4th	02:56 pm	Cancer
7th	03:31 am	Leo
9th	03:30 pm	Virgo
12th	01:55 am	Libra
14th	09:30 am	Scorpio
16th	01:25 pm	Sagittarius
18th	02:07 pm	Capricorn
20th	01:15 pm	Aquarius
22nd	01:02 pm	Pisces
24th	03:37 pm	Aries
26th	10:17 pm	Taurus
29th	08:43 am	Gemini
31st	09:11 pm	Cancer

February 1996

3rd	09:46 am	Leo
5th	09:23 pm	Virgo
8th	07:30 am	Libra
10th	03:36 pm	Scorpio
12th	08:59 pm	Sagittarius
14th	11:30 pm	Capricorn
17th	12:00 am	Aquarius
19th	12:10 am	Pisces
21st	01:59 am	Aries
23rd	07:09 am	Taurus
25th	04:14 pm	Gemini
28th	04:11 am	Cancer

March 1996

1st	04:48 pm	Leo
4th	04:13 am	Virgo
6th	01:41 pm	Libra
8th	09:06 pm	Scorpio
11th	02:33 am	Sagittarius
13th	06:08 am	Capricorn
15th	08:16 am	Aquarius
17th	09:51 am	Pisces
19th	12:16 pm	Aries
21st	04:59 pm	Taurus
24th	01:00 am	Gemini
26th	12:06 pm	Cancer
29th	12:37 am	Leo
31st	12:15 pm	Virgo

April 1996

2nd	09:27 pm	Libra
5th	03:57 am	Scorpio
7th	08:22 am	Sagittarius
9th	11:31 am	Capricorn
11th	02:10 pm	Aquarius
13th	05:00 pm	Pisces
15th	08:43 pm	Aries
18th	02:06 am	Taurus
20th	09:55 am	Gemini
22nd	08:25 pm	Cancer
25th	08:45 am	Leo
27th	08:49 pm	Virgo
30th	06:28 am	Libra

May 1996

2nd	12:43 pm	Scorpio
4th	04:05 pm	Sagittarius
6th	05:54 pm	Capricorn
8th	07:39 pm	Aquarius
10th	10:29 pm	Pisces
13th	03:01 am	Aries
15th	09:25 am	Taurus
17th	05:48 pm	Gemini
20th	04:17 am	Cancer
22nd	04:28 pm	Leo
25th	04:59 am	Virgo
27th	03:34 pm	Libra
29th	10:31 pm	Scorpio

June 1996

1st	01:43 am	Sagittarius
3rd	02:29 am	Capricorn
5th	02:45 am	Aquarius
7th	04:19 am	Pisces
9th	08:23 am	Aries
11th	03:11 pm	Taurus
14th	12:16 am	Gemini
16th	11:08 am	Cancer
18th	11:22 pm	Leo
21st	12:07 pm	Virgo
23rd	11:38 pm	Libra
26th	07:54 am	Scorpio
28th	12:02 pm	Sagittarius
30th	12:47 pm	Capricorn

July 1996

2nd	12:05 pm	Aquarius
4th	12:07 pm	Pisces
6th	02:42 pm	Aries
8th	08:44 pm	Taurus
11th	05:53 am	Gemini
13th	05:08 pm	Cancer
16th	05:32 am	Leo
18th	06:17 pm	Virgo
21st	06:14 am	Libra
23rd	03:43 pm	Scorpio
25th	09:24 pm	Sagittarius
27th	11:18 pm	Capricorn
29th	10:48 pm	Aquarius
31st	10:01 pm	Pisces

August 1996

2nd	11:05 pm	Aries
5th	03:34 am	Taurus
7th	11:49 am	Gemini
9th	10:58 pm	Cancer
12th	11:29 am	Leo
15th	12:08 am	Virgo
17th	11:55 am	Libra
19th	09:51 pm	Scorpio
22nd	04:49 am	Sagittarius
24th	08:22 am	Capricorn
26th	09:11 am	Aquarius
28th	08:49 am	Pisces
30th	09:15 am	Aries

September 1996

1st	12:20 pm	Taurus
3rd	07:09 pm	Gemini
6th	05:30 am	Cancer
8th	05:54 pm	Leo
11th	06:29 am	Virgo
13th	05:52 pm	Libra
16th	03:20 am	Scorpio
18th	10:31 am	Sagittarius
20th	03:13 pm	Capricorn
22nd	05:40 pm	Aquarius
24th	06:43 pm	Pisces
26th	07:46 pm	Aries
28th	10:24 pm	Taurus

October 1996

1st	04:02 am	Gemini
3rd	01:15 pm	Cancer
6th	01:12 am	Leo
8th	01:49 pm	Virgo
11th	01:01 am	Libra
13th	09:46 am	Scorpio
15th	04:08 pm	Sagittarius
17th	08:38 pm	Capricorn
19th	11:51 pm	Aquarius
22nd	02:22 am	Pisces
24th	04:51 am	Aries
26th	08:12 am	Taurus
28th	01:35 pm	Gemini
30th	09:57 pm	Cancer

November 1996

2nd	09:16 am	Leo
4th	09:58 pm	Virgo
7th	09:29 am	Libra
9th	06:02 pm	Scorpio
11th	11:27 pm	Sagittarius
14th	02:44 am	Capricorn
16th	05:14 am	Aquarius
18th	08:00 am	Pisces
20th	11:34 am	Aries
22nd	04:12 pm	Taurus
24th	10:20 pm	Gemini
27th	06:38 am	Cancer
29th	05:30 pm	Leo

December 1996

2nd	06:11 am	Virgo
4th	06:24 pm	Libra
7th	03:39 am	Scorpio
9th	08:59 am	Sagittarius
11th	11:15 am	Capricorn
13th	12:14 pm	Aquarius
15th	01:44 pm	Pisces
17th	04:56 pm	Aries
19th	10:10 pm	Taurus
22nd	05:18 am	Gemini
24th	02:15 pm	Cancer
27th	01:09 am	Leo
29th	01:45 pm	Virgo

January 1997

1st	02:32 am	Libra
3rd	01:02 pm	Scorpio
5th	07:28 pm	Sagittarius
7th	09:55 pm	Capricorn
9th	10:00 pm	Aquarius
11th	09:51 pm	Pisces
13th	11:22 pm	Aries
16th	03:40 am	Taurus
18th	10:54 am	Gemini
20th	08:29 pm	Cancer
23rd	07:50 am	Leo
25th	08:27 pm	Virgo
28th	09:22 am	Libra
30th	08:48 pm	Scorpio

February 1997

2nd	04:51 am	Sagittarius
4th	08:45 am	Capricorn
6th	09:22 am	Aquarius
8th	08:34 am	Pisces
10th	08:30 am	Aries
12th	10:57 am	Taurus
14th	04:54 pm	Gemini
17th	02:13 am	Cancer
19th	01:53 pm	Leo
22nd	02:39 am	Virgo
24th	03:24 pm	Libra
27th	02:57 am	Scorpio

March 1997

1st	12:01 pm	Sagittarius
3rd	05:39 pm	Capricorn
5th	07:55 pm	Aquarius
7th	07:57 pm	Pisces
9th	07:33 pm	Aries
11th	08:38 pm	Taurus
14th	12:49 am	Gemini
16th	08:51 am	Cancer
18th	08:09 pm	Leo
21st	09:00 am	Virgo
23rd	09:36 pm	Libra
26th	08:43 am	Scorpio
28th	05:40 pm	Sagittarius
31st	12:07 am	Capricorn

April 1997

2nd	03:59 am	Aquarius
4th	05:43 am	Pisces
6th	06:20 am	Aries
8th	07:21 am	Taurus
10th	10:28 am	Gemini
12th	05:04 pm	Cancer
15th	03:22 am	Leo
17th	04:01 pm	Virgo
20th	04:37 am	Libra
22nd	03:19 pm	Scorpio
24th	11:32 pm	Sagittarius
27th	05:33 am	Capricorn
29th	09:51 am	Aquarius

May 1997

1st	12:51 pm	Pisces
3rd	03:00 pm	Aries
5th	05:05 pm	Taurus
7th	08:21 pm	Gemini
10th	02:13 am	Cancer
12th	11:33 am	Leo
14th	11:44 pm	Virgo
17th	12:27 pm	Libra
19th	11:12 pm	Scorpio
22nd	06:51 am	Sagittarius
24th	11:52 am	Capricorn
26th	03:21 pm	Aquarius
28th	06:18 pm	Pisces
30th	09:18 pm	Aries

June 1997

2nd	12:39 am	Taurus
4th	04:55 am	Gemini
6th	11:02 am	Cancer
8th	07:58 pm	Leo
11th	07:43 am	Virgo
13th	08:36 pm	Libra
16th	07:51 am	Scorpio
18th	03:40 pm	Sagittarius
20th	08:03 pm	Capricorn
22nd	10:21 pm	Aquarius
25th	12:09 am	Pisces
27th	02:39 am	Aries
29th	06:24 am	Taurus

July 1997

1st	11:36 am	Gemini
3rd	06:33 pm	Cancer
6th	03:45 am	Leo
8th	03:22 pm	Virgo
11th	04:21 am	Libra
13th	04:21 pm	Scorpio
16th	01:03 am	Sagittarius
18th	05:46 am	Capricorn
20th	07:29 am	Aquarius
22nd	08:00 am	Pisces
24th	09:03 am	Aries
26th	11:54 am	Taurus
28th	05:05 pm	Gemini
31st	12:39 am	Cancer

August 1997

2nd	10:27 am	Leo
4th	10:16 pm	Virgo
7th	11:17 am	Libra
9th	11:51 pm	Scorpio
12th	09:45 am	Sagittarius
14th	03:43 pm	Capricorn
16th	05:59 pm	Aquarius
18th	06:01 pm	Pisces
20th	05:45 pm	Aries
22nd	06:58 pm	Taurus
24th	10:57 pm	Gemini
27th	06:11 am	Cancer
29th	04:19 pm	Leo

September 1997

1st	04:27 am	Virgo
3rd	05:30 pm	Libra
6th	06:10 am	Scorpio
8th	04:55 pm	Sagittarius
11th	12:24 am	Capricorn
13th	04:11 am	Aquarius
15th	05:00 am	Pisces
17th	04:25 am	Aries
19th	04:22 am	Taurus
21st	06:39 am	Gemini
23rd	12:33 pm	Cancer
25th	10:13 pm	Leo
28th	10:28 am	Virgo
30th	11:33 pm	Libra

October 1997

3rd	11:58 am	Scorpio
5th	10:43 pm	Sagittarius
8th	07:04 am	Capricorn
10th	12:29 pm	Aquarius
12th	03:00 pm	Pisces
14th	03:25 pm	Aries
16th	03:16 pm	Taurus
18th	04:27 pm	Gemini
20th	08:46 pm	Cancer
23rd	05:10 am	Leo
25th	05:00 pm	Virgo
28th	06:05 am	Libra
30th	06:16 pm	Scorpio

November 1997

2nd	04:27 am	Sagittarius
4th	12:31 pm	Capricorn
6th	06:34 pm	Aquarius
8th	10:35 pm	Pisces
11th	12:44 am	Aries
13th	01:45 am	Taurus
15th	03:05 am	Gemini
17th	06:33 am	Cancer
19th	01:38 pm	Leo
22nd	12:33 am	Virgo
24th	01:30 pm	Libra
27th	01:44 am	Scorpio
29th	11:29 am	Sagittarius

December 1997

1st	06:39 pm	Capricorn
3rd	11:58 pm	Aquarius
6th	04:08 am	Pisces
8th	07:24 am	Aries
10th	10:00 am	Taurus
12th	12:35 pm	Gemini
14th	04:25 pm	Cancer
16th	10:58 pm	Leo
19th	09:00 am	Virgo
21st	09:35 pm	Libra
24th	10:08 am	Scorpio
26th	08:08 pm	Sagittarius
29th	02:49 am	Capricorn
31st	06:59 am	Aquarius

January 1998

2nd	09:56 am	Pisces
4th	12:44 pm	Aries
6th	03:53 pm	Taurus
8th	07:43 pm	Gemini
11th	12:43 am	Cancer
13th	07:46 am	Leo
15th	05:32 pm	Virgo
18th	05:45 am	Libra
20th	06:35 pm	Scorpio
23rd	05:26 am	Sagittarius
25th	12:40 pm	Capricorn
27th	04:27 pm	Aquarius
29th	06:09 pm	Pisces
31st	07:21 pm	Aries

February 1998

2nd	09:25 pm	Taurus
5th	01:10 am	Gemini
7th	06:58 am	Cancer
9th	02:57 pm	Leo
12th	01:10 am	Virgo
14th	01:18 pm	Libra
17th	02:13 am	Scorpio
19th	01:57 pm	Sagittarius
21st	10:30 pm	Capricorn
24th	03:11 am	Aquarius
26th	04:43 am	Pisces
28th	04:43 am	Aries

March 1998

2nd	05:01 am	Taurus
4th	07:15 am	Gemini
6th	12:27 pm	Cancer
8th	08:46 pm	Leo
11th	07:36 am	Virgo
13th	07:58 pm	Libra
16th	08:51 am	Scorpio
18th	08:57 pm	Sagittarius
21st	06:44 am	Capricorn
23rd	01:02 pm	Aquarius
25th	03:43 pm	Pisces
27th	03:49 pm	Aries
29th	03:07 pm	Taurus
31st	03:38 pm	Gemini

April 1998

2nd	07:10 pm	Cancer
5th	02:36 am	Leo
7th	01:26 pm	Virgo
10th	02:05 am	Libra
12th	02:56 pm	Scorpio
15th	02:53 am	Sagittarius
17th	01:05 pm	Capricorn
19th	08:42 pm	Aquarius
22nd	01:06 am	Pisces
24th	02:31 am	Aries
26th	02:09 am	Taurus
28th	01:56 am	Gemini
30th	03:57 am	Cancer

May 1998

2nd	09:50 am	Leo
4th	07:47 pm	Virgo
7th	08:19 am	Libra
9th	09:11 pm	Scorpio
12th	08:48 am	Sagittarius
14th	06:39 pm	Capricorn
17th	02:31 am	Aquarius
19th	08:04 am	Pisces
21st	11:06 am	Aries
23rd	12:07 pm	Taurus
25th	12:26 pm	Gemini
27th	01:59 pm	Cancer
29th	06:38 pm	Leo

June 1998

1st	03:21 am	Virgo
3rd	03:17 pm	Libra
6th	04:06 am	Scorpio
8th	03:35 pm	Sagittarius
11th	12:51 am	Capricorn
13th	08:03 am	Aquarius
15th	01:32 pm	Pisces
17th	05:23 pm	Aries
19th	07:48 pm	Taurus
21st	09:27 pm	Gemini
23rd	11:39 pm	Cancer
26th	04:04 am	Leo
28th	11:55 am	Virgo
30th	11:05 pm	Libra

July 1998

3rd	11:46 am	Scorpio
5th	11:24 pm	Sagittarius
8th	08:28 am	Capricorn
10th	02:53 pm	Aquarius
12th	07:23 pm	Pisces
14th	10:45 pm	Aries
17th	01:34 am	Taurus
19th	04:19 am	Gemini
21st	07:43 am	Cancer
23rd	12:49 pm	Leo
25th	08:34 pm	Virgo
28th	07:15 am	Libra
30th	07:45 pm	Scorpio

August 1998

2nd	07:48 am	Sagittarius
4th	05:18 pm	Capricorn
6th	11:32 pm	Aquarius
9th	03:05 am	Pisces
11th	05:11 am	Aries
13th	07:05 am	Taurus
15th	09:46 am	Gemini
17th	01:56 pm	Cancer
19th	08:01 pm	Leo
22nd	04:22 am	Virgo
24th	03:02 pm	Libra
27th	03:26 am	Scorpio
29th	03:56 pm	Sagittarius

September 1998

1st	02:23 am	Capricorn
3rd	09:21 am	Aquarius
5th	12:48 pm	Pisces
7th	01:53 pm	Aries
9th	02:17 pm	Taurus
11th	03:41 pm	Gemini
13th	07:21 pm	Cancer
16th	01:48 am	Leo
18th	10:52 am	Virgo
20th	09:58 pm	Libra
23rd	10:22 am	Scorpio
25th	11:05 pm	Sagittarius
28th	10:31 am	Capricorn
30th	06:54 pm	Aquarius

October 1998

2nd	11:24 pm	Pisces
5th	12:33 am	Aries
6th	11:58 pm	Taurus
8th	11:44 pm	Gemini
11th	01:49 am	Cancer
13th	07:26 am	Leo
15th	04:32 pm	Virgo
18th	04:03 am	Libra
20th	04:37 pm	Scorpio
23rd	05:17 am	Sagittarius
25th	05:05 pm	Capricorn
28th	02:45 am	Aquarius
30th	08:59 am	Pisces

November 1998

1st	11:28 am	Aries
3rd	11:13 am	Taurus
5th	10:11 am	Gemini
7th	10:40 am	Cancer
9th	02:33 pm	Leo
11th	10:37 pm	Virgo
14th	09:58 am	Libra
16th	10:41 pm	Scorpio
19th	11:13 am	Sagittarius
21st	10:46 pm	Capricorn
24th	08:44 am	Aquarius
26th	04:15 pm	Pisces
28th	08:34 pm	Aries
30th	09:53 pm	Taurus

December 1998

2nd	09:30 pm	Gemini
4th	09:28 pm	Cancer
6th	11:56 pm	Leo
9th	06:22 am	Virgo
11th	04:44 pm	Libra
14th	05:17 am	Scorpio
16th	05:48 pm	Sagittarius
19th	04:56 am	Capricorn
21st	02:17 pm	Aquarius
23rd	09:45 pm	Pisces
26th	03:04 am	Aries
28th	06:05 am	Taurus
30th	07:22 am	Gemini

January 1999

1st	08:15 am	Cancer
3rd	10:31 am	Leo
5th	03:49 pm	Virgo
8th	12:53 am	Libra
10th	12:49 pm	Scorpio
13th	01:24 am	Sagittarius
15th	12:29 pm	Capricorn
17th	09:12 pm	Aquarius
20th	03:40 am	Pisces
22nd	08:25 am	Aries
24th	11:53 am	Taurus
26th	02:30 pm	Gemini
28th	04:57 pm	Cancer
30th	08:16 pm	Leo

February 1999

2nd	01:38 am	Virgo
4th	09:56 am	Libra
6th	09:07 pm	Scorpio
9th	09:39 am	Sagittarius
11th	09:10 pm	Capricorn
14th	05:57 am	Aquarius
16th	11:40 am	Pisces
18th	03:07 pm	Aries
20th	05:29 pm	Taurus
22nd	07:54 pm	Gemini
24th	11:09 pm	Cancer
27th	03:45 am	Leo

March 1999

1st	10:05 am	Virgo
3rd	06:35 pm	Libra
6th	05:23 am	Scorpio
8th	05:46 pm	Sagittarius
11th	05:54 am	Capricorn
13th	03:32 pm	Aquarius
15th	09:31 pm	Pisces
18th	12:13 am	Aries
20th	01:09 am	Taurus
22nd	02:06 am	Gemini
24th	04:34 am	Cancer
26th	09:23 am	Leo
28th	04:35 pm	Virgo
31st	01:50 am	Libra

April 1999

2nd	12:49 pm	Scorpio
5th	01:08 am	Sagittarius
7th	01:39 pm	Capricorn
10th	12:25 am	Aquarius
12th	07:35 am	Pisces
14th	10:47 am	Aries
16th	11:08 am	Taurus
18th	10:39 am	Gemini
20th	11:28 am	Cancer
22nd	03:06 pm	Leo
24th	10:05 pm	Virgo
27th	07:47 am	Libra
29th	07:13 pm	Scorpio

May 1999

2nd	07:37 am	Sagittarius
4th	08:12 pm	Capricorn
7th	07:41 am	Aquarius
9th	04:17 pm	Pisces
11th	08:54 pm	Aries
13th	09:57 pm	Taurus
15th	09:08 pm	Gemini
17th	08:40 pm	Cancer
19th	10:37 pm	Leo
22nd	04:16 am	Virgo
24th	01:30 pm	Libra
27th	01:05 am	Scorpio
29th	01:38 pm	Sagittarius

June 1999

1st	02:06 am	Capricorn
3rd	01:37 pm	Aquarius
5th	11:01 pm	Pisces
8th	05:08 am	Aries
10th	07:44 am	Taurus
12th	07:49 am	Gemini
14th	07:14 am	Cancer
16th	08:08 am	Leo
18th	12:12 pm	Virgo
20th	08:11 pm	Libra
23rd	07:19 am	Scorpio
25th	07:52 pm	Sagittarius
28th	08:12 am	Capricorn
30th	07:20 pm	Aquarius

July 1999

3rd	04:35 am	Pisces
5th	11:22 am	Aries
7th	03:22 pm	Taurus
9th	05:00 pm	Gemini
11th	05:28 pm	Cancer
13th	06:26 pm	Leo
15th	09:39 pm	Virgo
18th	04:20 am	Libra
20th	02:31 pm	Scorpio
23rd	02:49 am	Sagittarius
25th	03:09 pm	Capricorn
28th	01:55 am	Aquarius
30th	10:28 am	Pisces

August 1999

1st	04:47 pm	Aries
3rd	09:09 pm	Taurus
5th	11:58 pm	Gemini
8th	01:53 am	Cancer
10th	03:56 am	Leo
12th	07:22 am	Virgo
14th	01:24 pm	Libra
16th	10:40 pm	Scorpio
19th	10:32 am	Sagittarius
21st	11:00 pm	Capricorn
24th	09:50 am	Aquarius
26th	05:50 pm	Pisces
28th	11:10 pm	Aries
31st	02:41 am	Taurus

September 1999

2nd	05:25 am	Gemini
4th	08:10 am	Cancer
6th	11:29 am	Leo
8th	03:57 pm	Virgo
10th	10:16 pm	Libra
13th	07:09 am	Scorpio
15th	06:35 pm	Sagittarius
18th	07:14 am	Capricorn
20th	06:39 pm	Aquarius
23rd	02:52 am	Pisces
25th	07:34 am	Aries
27th	09:51 am	Taurus
29th	11:21 am	Gemini

October 1999

1st	01:32 pm	Cancer
3rd	05:14 pm	Leo
5th	10:40 pm	Virgo
8th	05:52 am	Libra
10th	03:02 pm	Scorpio
13th	02:19 am	Sagittarius
15th	03:04 pm	Capricorn
18th	03:17 am	Aquarius
20th	12:33 pm	Pisces
22nd	05:42 pm	Aries
24th	07:26 pm	Taurus
26th	07:34 pm	Gemini
28th	08:10 pm	Cancer
30th	10:48 pm	Leo

November 1999

2nd	04:08 am	Virgo
4th	11:57 am	Libra
6th	09:46 pm	Scorpio
9th	09:15 am	Sagittarius
11th	10:01 pm	Capricorn
14th	10:46 am	Aquarius
16th	09:21 pm	Pisces
19th	03:58 am	Aries
21st	06:27 am	Taurus
23rd	06:14 am	Gemini
25th	05:29 am	Cancer
27th	06:19 am	Leo
29th	10:11 am	Virgo

December 1999

1st	05:30 pm	Libra
4th	03:36 am	Scorpio
6th	03:28 pm	Sagittarius
9th	04:14 am	Capricorn
11th	04:59 pm	Aquarius
14th	04:18 am	Pisces
16th	12:31 pm	Aries
18th	04:46 pm	Taurus
20th	05:39 pm	Gemini
22nd	04:53 pm	Cancer
24th	04:32 pm	Leo
26th	06:35 pm	Virgo
29th	12:15 am	Libra
31st	09:37 am	Scorpio

January 2000

2nd	09:32 pm	Sagittarius
5th	10:24 am	Capricorn
7th	10:53 pm	Aquarius
10th	10:00 am	Pisces
12th	06:49 pm	Aries
15th	12:38 am	Taurus
17th	03:25 am	Gemini
19th	04:01 am	Cancer
21st	03:59 am	Leo
23rd	05:08 am	Virgo
25th	09:10 am	Libra
27th	05:02 pm	Scorpio
30th	04:18 am	Sagittarius

February 2000

1st	05:10 pm	Capricorn
4th	05:32 am	Aquarius
6th	04:02 pm	Pisces
9th	12:18 am	Aries
11th	06:21 am	Taurus
13th	10:23 am	Gemini
15th	12:45 pm	Cancer
17th	02:12 pm	Leo
19th	03:54 pm	Virgo
21st	07:22 pm	Libra
24th	01:58 am	Scorpio
26th	12:10 pm	Sagittarius
29th	12:46 am	Capricorn

March 2000

2nd	01:15 pm	Aquarius
4th	11:31 pm	Pisces
7th	06:55 am	Aries
9th	12:01 pm	Taurus
11th	03:46 pm	Gemini
13th	06:52 pm	Cancer
15th	09:44 pm	Leo
18th	12:49 am	Virgo
20th	04:57 am	Libra
22nd	11:18 am	Scorpio
24th	08:43 pm	Sagittarius
27th	08:51 am	Capricorn
29th	09:35 pm	Aquarius

April 2000

1st	08:13 am	Pisces
3rd	03:22 pm	Aries
5th	07:29 pm	Taurus
7th	09:59 pm	Gemini
10th	12:16 am	Cancer
12th	03:16 am	Leo
14th	07:19 am	Virgo
16th	12:36 pm	Libra
18th	07:36 pm	Scorpio
21st	04:58 am	Sagittarius
23rd	04:48 pm	Capricorn
26th	05:42 am	Aquarius
28th	05:07 pm	Pisces

May 2000

1st	12:55 am	Aries
3rd	04:54 am	Taurus
5th	06:24 am	Gemini
7th	07:14 am	Cancer
9th	09:02 am	Leo
11th	12:42 pm	Virgo
13th	06:28 pm	Libra
16th	02:17 am	Scorpio
18th	12:10 pm	Sagittarius
21st	12:02 am	Capricorn
23rd	01:01 pm	Aquarius
26th	01:08 am	Pisces
28th	10:08 am	Aries
30th	03:03 pm	Taurus

June 2000

1st	04:35 pm	Gemini
3rd	04:30 pm	Cancer
5th	04:46 pm	Leo
7th	06:58 pm	Virgo
9th	11:59 pm	Libra
12th	07:55 am	Scorpio
14th	06:18 pm	Sagittarius
17th	06:27 am	Capricorn
19th	07:27 pm	Aquarius
22nd	07:52 am	Pisces
24th	05:56 pm	Aries
27th	12:19 am	Taurus
29th	03:00 am	Gemini

July 2000

1st	03:10 am	Cancer
3rd	02:38 am	Leo
5th	03:19 am	Virgo
7th	06:47 am	Libra
9th	01:49 pm	Scorpio
12th	12:06 am	Sagittarius
14th	12:28 pm	Capricorn
17th	01:27 am	Aquarius
19th	01:45 pm	Pisces
22nd	12:10 am	Aries
24th	07:44 am	Taurus
26th	12:02 pm	Gemini
28th	01:30 pm	Cancer
30th	01:24 pm	Leo

August 2000

1st	01:28 pm	Virgo
3rd	03:32 pm	Libra
5th	09:05 pm	Scorpio
8th	06:31 am	Sagittarius
10th	06:44 pm	Capricorn
13th	07:43 am	Aquarius
15th	07:42 pm	Pisces
18th	05:44 am	Aries
20th	01:31 pm	Taurus
22nd	06:55 pm	Gemini
24th	10:00 pm	Cancer
26th	11:17 pm	Leo
28th	11:56 pm	Virgo
31st	01:33 am	Libra

September 2000

2nd	05:56 am	Scorpio
4th	02:09 pm	Sagittarius
7th	01:48 am	Capricorn
9th	02:45 pm	Aquarius
12th	02:35 am	Pisces
14th	12:01 pm	Aries
16th	07:06 pm	Taurus
19th	12:23 am	Gemini
21st	04:16 am	Cancer
23rd	07:00 am	Leo
25th	09:02 am	Virgo
27th	11:22 am	Libra
29th	03:30 pm	Scorpio

October 2000

1st	10:50 pm	Sagittarius
4th	09:43 am	Capricorn
6th	10:34 pm	Aquarius
9th	10:37 am	Pisces
11th	07:52 pm	Aries
14th	02:07 am	Taurus
16th	06:19 am	Gemini
18th	09:37 am	Cancer
20th	12:43 pm	Leo
22nd	03:53 pm	Virgo
24th	07:30 pm	Libra
27th	12:24 am	Scorpio
29th	07:41 am	Sagittarius
31st	06:02 pm	Capricorn

November 2000

3rd	06:41 am	Aquarius
5th	07:13 pm	Pisces
8th	05:03 am	Aries
10th	11:12 am	Taurus
12th	02:28 pm	Gemini
14th	04:21 pm	Cancer
16th	06:19 pm	Leo
18th	09:16 pm	Virgo
21st	01:35 am	Libra
23rd	07:33 am	Scorpio
25th	03:33 pm	Sagittarius
28th	01:58 am	Capricorn
30th	02:27 pm	Aquarius

December 2000

3rd	03:23 am	Pisces
5th	02:18 pm	Aries
7th	09:27 pm	Taurus
10th	12:51 am	Gemini
12th	01:49 am	Cancer
14th	02:09 am	Leo
16th	03:30 am	Virgo
18th	07:01 am	Libra
20th	01:12 pm	Scorpio
22nd	09:58 pm	Sagittarius
25th	08:54 am	Capricorn
27th	09:26 pm	Aquarius
30th	10:28 am	Pisces

January 2001

1st	10:15 pm	Aries
4th	06:57 am	Taurus
6th	11:44 am	Gemini
8th	01:09 pm	Cancer
10th	12:45 pm	Leo
12th	12:26 pm	Virgo
14th	02:06 pm	Libra
16th	07:03 pm	Scorpio
19th	03:36 am	Sagittarius
21st	02:57 pm	Capricorn
24th	03:44 am	Aquarius
26th	04:39 pm	Pisces
29th	04:35 am	Aries
31st	02:22 pm	Taurus

February 2001

2nd	08:56 pm	Gemini
5th	12:01 am	Cancer
7th	12:21 am	Leo
8th	11:36 pm	Virgo
10th	11:46 pm	Libra
13th	02:52 am	Scorpio
15th	10:03 am	Sagittarius
17th	08:59 pm	Capricorn
20th	09:54 am	Aquarius
22nd	10:45 pm	Pisces
25th	10:20 am	Aries
27th	08:06 pm	Taurus

March 2001

2nd	03:37 am	Gemini
4th	08:25 am	Cancer
6th	10:30 am	Leo
8th	10:45 am	Virgo
10th	10:48 am	Libra
12th	12:43 pm	Scorpio
14th	06:17 pm	Sagittarius
17th	04:02 am	Capricorn
19th	04:37 pm	Aquarius
22nd	05:29 am	Pisces
24th	04:44 pm	Aries
27th	01:51 am	Taurus
29th	09:01 am	Gemini
31st	02:24 pm	Cancer

April 2001

2nd	05:54 pm	Leo
4th	07:47 pm	Virgo
6th	08:57 pm	Libra
8th	11:02 pm	Scorpio
11th	03:47 am	Sagittarius
13th	12:21 pm	Capricorn
16th	12:11 am	Aquarius
18th	01:01 pm	Pisces
21st	12:18 am	Aries
23rd	08:57 am	Taurus
25th	03:12 pm	Gemini
27th	07:50 pm	Cancer
29th	11:25 pm	Leo

May 2001

2nd	02:17 am	Virgo
4th	04:50 am	Libra
6th	08:01 am	Scorpio
8th	01:06 pm	Sagittarius
10th	09:10 pm	Capricorn
13th	08:20 am	Aquarius
15th	09:02 pm	Pisces
18th	08:42 am	Aries
20th	05:30 pm	Taurus
22nd	11:12 pm	Gemini
25th	02:43 am	Cancer
27th	05:12 am	Leo
29th	07:38 am	Virgo
31st	10:42 am	Libra

June 2001

2nd	02:56 pm	Scorpio
4th	08:58 pm	Sagittarius
7th	05:24 am	Capricorn
9th	04:20 pm	Aquarius
12th	04:54 am	Pisces
14th	05:04 pm	Aries
17th	02:40 am	Taurus
19th	08:43 am	Gemini
21st	11:41 am	Cancer
23rd	12:55 pm	Leo
25th	01:58 pm	Virgo
27th	04:11 pm	Libra
29th	08:29 pm	Scorpio

July 2001

2nd	03:14 am	Sagittarius
4th	12:22 pm	Capricorn
6th	11:34 pm	Aquarius
9th	12:06 pm	Pisces
12th	12:36 am	Aries
14th	11:14 am	Taurus
16th	06:26 pm	Gemini
18th	09:57 pm	Cancer
20th	10:43 pm	Leo
22nd	10:29 pm	Virgo
24th	11:08 pm	Libra
27th	02:17 am	Scorpio
29th	08:45 am	Sagittarius
31st	06:17 pm	Capricorn

August 2001

3rd	05:54 am	Aquarius
5th	06:31 pm	Pisces
8th	07:05 am	Aries
10th	06:24 pm	Taurus
13th	02:59 am	Gemini
15th	07:55 am	Cancer
17th	09:26 am	Leo
19th	08:53 am	Virgo
21st	08:19 am	Libra
23rd	09:51 am	Scorpio
25th	03:00 pm	Sagittarius
28th	12:02 am	Capricorn
30th	11:48 am	Aquarius

September 2001

2nd	12:33 am	Pisces
4th	12:59 pm	Aries
7th	12:18 am	Taurus
9th	09:41 am	Gemini
11th	04:10 pm	Cancer
13th	07:16 pm	Leo
15th	07:40 pm	Virgo
17th	07:00 pm	Libra
19th	07:28 pm	Scorpio
21st	11:03 pm	Sagittarius
24th	06:49 am	Capricorn
26th	06:05 pm	Aquarius
29th	06:51 am	Pisces

October 2001

1st	07:08 pm	Aries
4th	06:02 am	Taurus
6th	03:13 pm	Gemini
8th	10:20 pm	Cancer
11th	02:55 am	Leo
13th	04:59 am	Virgo
15th	05:27 am	Libra
17th	06:03 am	Scorpio
19th	08:47 am	Sagittarius
21st	03:12 pm	Capricorn
24th	01:27 am	Aquarius
26th	01:56 pm	Pisces
29th	02:16 am	Aries
31st	12:48 pm	Taurus

November 2001

2nd	09:13 pm	Gemini
5th	03:45 am	Cancer
7th	08:34 am	Leo
9th	11:49 am	Virgo
11th	01:53 pm	Libra
13th	03:45 pm	Scorpio
15th	06:51 pm	Sagittarius
18th	12:40 am	Capricorn
20th	09:55 am	Aquarius
22nd	09:53 pm	Pisces
25th	10:22 am	Aries
27th	09:06 pm	Taurus
30th	05:04 am	Gemini

December 2001

2nd	10:31 am	Cancer
4th	02:16 pm	Leo
6th	05:11 pm	Virgo
8th	07:57 pm	Libra
10th	11:10 pm	Scorpio
13th	03:30 am	Sagittarius
15th	09:48 am	Capricorn
17th	06:43 pm	Aquarius
20th	06:10 am	Pisces
22nd	06:46 pm	Aries
25th	06:13 am	Taurus
27th	02:39 pm	Gemini
29th	07:41 pm	Cancer
31st	10:10 pm	Leo

January 2002

2nd	11:35 pm	Virgo
5th	01:24 am	Libra
7th	04:42 am	Scorpio
9th	09:58 am	Sagittarius
11th	05:19 pm	Capricorn
14th	02:42 am	Aquarius
16th	02:01 pm	Pisces
19th	02:35 am	Aries
21st	02:48 pm	Taurus
24th	12:28 am	Gemini
26th	06:17 am	Cancer
28th	08:31 am	Leo
30th	08:40 am	Virgo

February 2002

1st	08:45 am	Libra
3rd	10:36 am	Scorpio
5th	03:22 pm	Sagittarius
7th	11:09 pm	Capricorn
10th	09:15 am	Aquarius
12th	08:53 pm	Pisces
15th	09:26 am	Aries
17th	09:58 pm	Taurus
20th	08:51 am	Gemini
22nd	04:16 pm	Cancer
24th	07:37 pm	Leo
26th	07:48 pm	Virgo
28th	06:47 pm	Libra

March 2002

2nd	06:52 pm	Scorpio
4th	09:55 pm	Sagittarius
7th	04:48 am	Capricorn
9th	02:57 pm	Aquarius
12th	02:57 am	Pisces
14th	03:35 pm	Aries
17th	04:02 am	Taurus
19th	03:20 pm	Gemini
22nd	12:07 am	Cancer
24th	05:13 am	Leo
26th	06:44 am	Virgo
28th	06:04 am	Libra
30th	05:22 am	Scorpio

April 2002

1st	06:49 am	Sagittarius
3rd	11:59 am	Capricorn
5th	09:07 pm	Aquarius
8th	08:58 am	Pisces
10th	09:41 pm	Aries
13th	09:56 am	Taurus
15th	08:57 pm	Gemini
18th	06:01 am	Cancer
20th	12:21 pm	Leo
22nd	03:35 pm	Virgo
24th	04:22 pm	Libra
26th	04:16 pm	Scorpio
28th	05:13 pm	Sagittarius
30th	09:03 pm	Capricorn

May 2002

3rd	04:44 am	Aquarius
5th	03:47 pm	Pisces
8th	04:23 am	Aries
10th	04:33 pm	Taurus
13th	03:05 am	Gemini
15th	11:34 am	Cancer
17th	05:53 pm	Leo
19th	10:01 pm	Virgo
22nd	12:19 am	Libra
24th	01:39 am	Scorpio
26th	03:20 am	Sagittarius
28th	06:55 am	Capricorn
30th	01:35 pm	Aquarius

June 2002

1st	11:38 pm	Pisces
4th	11:52 am	Aries
7th	12:07 am	Taurus
9th	10:30 am	Gemini
11th	06:16 pm	Cancer
13th	11:40 pm	Leo
16th	03:24 am	Virgo
18th	06:11 am	Libra
20th	08:43 am	Scorpio
22nd	11:42 am	Sagittarius
24th	04:02 pm	Capricorn
26th	10:37 pm	Aquarius
29th	08:01 am	Pisces

July 2002

1st	07:50 pm	Aries
4th	08:17 am	Taurus
6th	07:01 pm	Gemini
9th	02:37 am	Cancer
11th	07:08 am	Leo
13th	09:41 am	Virgo
15th	11:40 am	Libra
17th	02:13 pm	Scorpio
19th	06:03 pm	Sagittarius
21st	11:26 pm	Capricorn
24th	06:40 am	Aquarius
26th	04:05 pm	Pisces
29th	03:39 am	Aries
31st	04:17 pm	Taurus

August 2002

3rd	03:47 am	Gemini
5th	12:02 pm	Cancer
7th	04:28 pm	Leo
9th	06:04 pm	Virgo
11th	06:38 pm	Libra
13th	08:01 pm	Scorpio
15th	11:26 pm	Sagittarius
18th	05:16 am	Capricorn
20th	01:17 pm	Aquarius
22nd	11:11 pm	Pisces
25th	10:48 am	Aries
27th	11:32 pm	Taurus
30th	11:46 am	Gemini

September 2002

1st	09:15 pm	Cancer
4th	02:37 am	Leo
6th	04:17 am	Virgo
8th	03:57 am	Libra
10th	03:49 am	Scorpio
12th	05:45 am	Sagittarius
14th	10:48 am	Capricorn
16th	06:55 pm	Aquarius
19th	05:19 am	Pisces
21st	05:11 pm	Aries
24th	05:55 am	Taurus
26th	06:27 pm	Gemini
29th	05:02 am	Cancer

October 2002

1st	11:59 am	Leo
3rd	02:53 pm	Virgo
5th	02:52 pm	Libra
7th	01:58 pm	Scorpio
9th	02:21 pm	Sagittarius
11th	05:45 pm	Capricorn
14th	12:52 am	Aquarius
16th	11:07 am	Pisces
18th	11:14 pm	Aries
21st	11:57 am	Taurus
24th	12:18 am	Gemini
26th	11:11 am	Cancer
28th	07:20 pm	Leo
31st	12:00 am	Virgo

November 2002

2nd	01:29 am	Libra
4th	01:11 am	Scorpio
6th	01:02 am	Sagittarius
8th	02:59 am	Capricorn
10th	08:27 am	Aquarius
12th	05:42 pm	Pisces
15th	05:38 am	Aries
17th	06:24 pm	Taurus
20th	06:26 am	Gemini
22nd	04:48 pm	Cancer
25th	01:00 am	Leo
27th	06:42 am	Virgo
29th	09:55 am	Libra

December 2002

1st	11:16 am	Scorpio
3rd	11:58 am	Sagittarius
5th	01:39 pm	Capricorn
7th	05:55 pm	Aquarius
10th	01:46 am	Pisces
12th	12:59 pm	Aries
15th	01:44 am	Taurus
17th	01:44 pm	Gemini
19th	11:30 pm	Cancer
22nd	06:49 am	Leo
24th	12:06 pm	Virgo
26th	03:54 pm	Libra
28th	06:42 pm	Scorpio
30th	09:02 pm	Sagittarius

January 2003

1st	11:43 pm	Capricorn
4th	03:57 am	Aquarius
6th	10:57 am	Pisces
8th	09:15 pm	Aries
11th	09:48 am	Taurus
13th	10:08 pm	Gemini
16th	07:56 am	Cancer
18th	02:30 pm	Leo
20th	06:32 pm	Virgo
22nd	09:23 pm	Libra
25th	12:09 am	Scorpio
27th	03:26 am	Sagittarius
29th	07:30 am	Capricorn
31st	12:45 pm	Aquarius

February 2003

2nd	07:55 pm	Pisces
5th	05:45 am	Aries
7th	06:00 pm	Taurus
10th	06:46 am	Gemini
12th	05:20 pm	Cancer
15th	12:05 am	Leo
17th	03:23 am	Virgo
19th	04:49 am	Libra
21st	06:10 am	Scorpio
23rd	08:46 am	Sagittarius
25th	01:12 pm	Capricorn
27th	07:25 pm	Aquarius

March 2003

2nd	03:26 am	Pisces
4th	01:30 pm	Aries
7th	01:37 am	Taurus
9th	02:38 pm	Gemini
12th	02:12 am	Cancer
14th	10:07 am	Leo
16th	01:53 pm	Virgo
18th	02:44 pm	Libra
20th	02:38 pm	Scorpio
22nd	03:33 pm	Sagittarius
24th	06:49 pm	Capricorn
27th	12:51 am	Aquarius
29th	09:26 am	Pisces
31st	08:05 pm	Aries

April 2003

3rd	08:21 am	Taurus
5th	09:24 pm	Gemini
8th	09:37 am	Cancer
10th	06:54 pm	Leo
13th	12:07 am	Virgo
15th	01:42 am	Libra
17th	01:16 am	Scorpio
19th	12:52 am	Sagittarius
21st	02:21 am	Capricorn
23rd	06:58 am	Aquarius
25th	03:03 pm	Pisces
28th	01:55 am	Aries
30th	02:27 pm	Taurus

May 2003

3rd	03:28 am	Gemini
5th	03:43 pm	Cancer
8th	01:47 am	Leo
10th	08:32 am	Virgo
12th	11:43 am	Libra
14th	12:14 pm	Scorpio
16th	11:43 am	Sagittarius
18th	12:04 pm	Capricorn
20th	03:01 pm	Aquarius
22nd	09:42 pm	Pisces
25th	07:59 am	Aries
27th	08:33 pm	Taurus
30th	09:32 am	Gemini

June 2003

1st	09:28 pm	Cancer
4th	07:26 am	Leo
6th	02:51 pm	Virgo
8th	07:31 pm	Libra
10th	09:39 pm	Scorpio
12th	10:13 pm	Sagittarius
14th	10:39 pm	Capricorn
17th	12:42 am	Aquarius
19th	05:57 am	Pisces
21st	03:06 pm	Aries
24th	03:16 am	Taurus
26th	04:14 pm	Gemini
29th	03:52 am	Cancer

July 2003

1st	01:14 pm	Leo
3rd	08:16 pm	Virgo
6th	01:21 am	Libra
8th	04:44 am	Scorpio
10th	06:49 am	Sagittarius
12th	08:21 am	Capricorn
14th	10:39 am	Aquarius
16th	03:14 pm	Pisces
18th	11:20 pm	Aries
21st	10:49 am	Taurus
23rd	11:43 pm	Gemini
26th	11:23 am	Cancer
28th	08:17 pm	Leo
31st	02:27 am	Virgo

August 2003

2nd	06:48 am	Libra
4th	10:13 am	Scorpio
6th	01:11 pm	Sagittarius
8th	04:03 pm	Capricorn
10th	07:24 pm	Aquarius
13th	12:19 am	Pisces
15th	08:00 am	Aries
17th	06:53 pm	Taurus
20th	07:41 am	Gemini
22nd	07:45 pm	Cancer
25th	04:49 am	Leo
27th	10:27 am	Virgo
29th	01:42 pm	Libra
31st	04:01 pm	Scorpio

September 2003

2nd	06:32 pm	Sagittarius
4th	09:52 pm	Capricorn
7th	02:15 am	Aquarius
9th	08:07 am	Pisces
11th	04:10 pm	Aries
14th	02:50 am	Taurus
16th	03:32 pm	Gemini
19th	04:08 am	Cancer
21st	02:03 pm	Leo
23rd	08:05 pm	Virgo
25th	10:49 pm	Libra
27th	11:53 pm	Scorpio
30th	12:58 am	Sagittarius

October 2003

2nd	03:22 am	Capricorn
4th	07:46 am	Aquarius
6th	02:21 pm	Pisces
8th	11:08 pm	Aries
11th	10:06 am	Taurus
13th	10:45 pm	Gemini
16th	11:41 am	Cancer
18th	10:42 pm	Leo
21st	06:02 am	Virgo
23rd	09:28 am	Libra
25th	10:09 am	Scorpio
27th	09:55 am	Sagittarius
29th	10:37 am	Capricorn
31st	01:42 pm	Aquarius

November 2003

2nd	07:53 pm	Pisces
5th	05:03 am	Aries
7th	04:30 pm	Taurus
10th	05:15 am	Gemini
12th	06:11 pm	Cancer
15th	05:49 am	Leo
17th	02:37 pm	Virgo
19th	07:42 pm	Libra
21st	09:24 pm	Scorpio
23rd	09:03 pm	Sagittarius
25th	08:32 pm	Capricorn
27th	09:49 pm	Aquarius
30th	02:26 am	Pisces

December 2003

2nd	10:56 am	Aries
4th	10:30 pm	Taurus
7th	11:27 am	Gemini
10th	12:11 am	Cancer
12th	11:41 am	Leo
14th	09:07 pm	Virgo
17th	03:47 am	Libra
19th	07:20 am	Scorpio
21st	08:16 am	Sagittarius
23rd	07:56 am	Capricorn
25th	08:14 am	Aquarius
27th	11:10 am	Pisces
29th	06:09 pm	Aries

January 2004

1st	05:02 am	Taurus
3rd	05:59 pm	Gemini
6th	06:39 am	Cancer
8th	05:39 pm	Leo
11th	02:38 am	Virgo
13th	09:39 am	Libra
15th	02:33 pm	Scorpio
17th	05:18 pm	Sagittarius
19th	06:25 pm	Capricorn
21st	07:11 pm	Aquarius
23rd	09:29 pm	Pisces
26th	03:06 am	Aries
28th	12:47 pm	Taurus
31st	01:19 am	Gemini

February 2004

2nd	02:04 pm	Cancer
5th	12:50 am	Leo
7th	09:03 am	Virgo
9th	03:13 pm	Libra
11th	07:58 pm	Scorpio
13th	11:36 pm	Sagittarius
16th	02:14 am	Capricorn
18th	04:28 am	Aquarius
20th	07:27 am	Pisces
22nd	12:46 pm	Aries
24th	09:31 pm	Taurus
27th	09:23 am	Gemini
29th	10:13 pm	Cancer

March 2004

3rd	09:18 am	Leo
5th	05:18 pm	Virgo
7th	10:31 pm	Libra
10th	02:03 am	Scorpio
12th	04:58 am	Sagittarius
14th	07:52 am	Capricorn
16th	11:11 am	Aquarius
18th	03:26 pm	Pisces
20th	09:29 pm	Aries
23rd	06:10 am	Taurus
25th	05:35 pm	Gemini
28th	06:24 am	Cancer
30th	06:08 pm	Leo

April 2004

2nd	02:46 am	Virgo
4th	07:53 am	Libra
6th	10:25 am	Scorpio
8th	11:51 am	Sagittarius
10th	01:34 pm	Capricorn
12th	04:33 pm	Aquarius
14th	09:24 pm	Pisces
17th	04:25 am	Aries
19th	01:43 pm	Taurus
22nd	01:10 am	Gemini
24th	01:56 pm	Cancer
27th	02:15 am	Leo
29th	12:01 pm	Virgo

May 2004

1st	06:03 pm	Libra
3rd	08:39 pm	Scorpio
5th	09:09 pm	Sagittarius
7th	09:17 pm	Capricorn
9th	10:47 pm	Aquarius
12th	02:53 am	Pisces
14th	10:03 am	Aries
16th	07:58 pm	Taurus
19th	07:48 am	Gemini
21st	08:35 pm	Cancer
24th	09:08 am	Leo
26th	07:52 pm	Virgo
29th	03:23 am	Libra
31st	07:09 am	Scorpio

June 2004

2nd	07:53 am	Sagittarius
4th	07:13 am	Capricorn
6th	07:10 am	Aquarius
8th	09:39 am	Pisces
10th	03:50 pm	Aries
13th	01:37 am	Taurus
15th	01:45 pm	Gemini
18th	02:38 am	Cancer
20th	03:05 pm	Leo
23rd	02:10 am	Virgo
25th	10:50 am	Libra
27th	04:13 pm	Scorpio
29th	06:16 pm	Sagittarius

July 2004

1st	06:02 pm	Capricorn
3rd	05:22 pm	Aquarius
5th	06:27 pm	Pisces
7th	11:04 pm	Aries
10th	07:51 am	Taurus
12th	07:45 pm	Gemini
15th	08:41 am	Cancer
17th	08:57 pm	Leo
20th	07:44 am	Virgo
22nd	04:39 pm	Libra
24th	11:09 pm	Scorpio
27th	02:49 am	Sagittarius
29th	03:58 am	Capricorn
31st	03:55 am	Aquarius

August 2004

2nd	04:35 am	Pisces
4th	08:00 am	Aries
6th	03:26 pm	Taurus
9th	02:33 am	Gemini
11th	03:21 pm	Cancer
14th	03:30 am	Leo
16th	01:50 pm	Virgo
18th	10:10 pm	Libra
21st	04:37 am	Scorpio
23rd	09:09 am	Sagittarius
25th	11:47 am	Capricorn
27th	01:09 pm	Aquarius
29th	02:34 pm	Pisces
31st	05:46 pm	Aries

September 2004

3rd	12:16 am	Taurus
5th	10:25 am	Gemini
7th	10:51 pm	Cancer
10th	11:06 am	Leo
12th	09:17 pm	Virgo
15th	04:54 am	Libra
17th	10:26 am	Scorpio
19th	02:30 pm	Sagittarius
21st	05:36 pm	Capricorn
23rd	08:10 pm	Aquarius
25th	10:56 pm	Pisces
28th	02:58 am	Aries
30th	09:24 am	Taurus

October 2004

2nd	06:55 pm	Gemini
5th	06:55 am	Cancer
7th	07:23 pm	Leo
10th	06:01 am	Virgo
12th	01:33 pm	Libra
14th	06:11 pm	Scorpio
16th	08:58 pm	Sagittarius
18th	11:07 pm	Capricorn
21st	01:38 am	Aquarius
23rd	05:14 am	Pisces
25th	10:25 am	Aries
27th	05:38 pm	Taurus
30th	03:11 am	Gemini

November 2004

1st	02:54 pm	Cancer
4th	03:32 am	Leo
6th	03:01 pm	Virgo
8th	11:23 pm	Libra
11th	04:06 am	Scorpio
13th	05:57 am	Sagittarius
15th	06:33 am	Capricorn
17th	07:39 am	Aquarius
19th	10:38 am	Pisces
21st	04:12 pm	Aries
24th	12:16 am	Taurus
26th	10:26 am	Gemini
28th	10:11 pm	Cancer

December 2004

1st	10:50 am	Leo
3rd	11:01 pm	Virgo
6th	08:47 am	Libra
8th	02:44 pm	Scorpio
10th	04:55 pm	Sagittarius
12th	04:42 pm	Capricorn
14th	04:10 pm	Aquarius
16th	05:24 pm	Pisces
18th	09:53 pm	Aries
21st	05:53 am	Taurus
23rd	04:33 pm	Gemini
26th	04:38 am	Cancer
28th	05:15 pm	Leo
31st	05:34 am	Virgo

January 2005

2nd	04:20 pm	Libra
5th	12:00 am	Scorpio
7th	03:45 am	Sagittarius
9th	04:11 am	Capricorn
11th	03:07 am	Aquarius
13th	02:51 am	Pisces
15th	05:27 am	Aries
17th	12:07 pm	Taurus
19th	10:25 pm	Gemini
22nd	10:43 am	Cancer
24th	11:22 pm	Leo
27th	11:25 am	Virgo
29th	10:13 pm	Libra

February 2005

1st	06:52 am	Scorpio
3rd	12:22 pm	Sagittarius
5th	02:33 pm	Capricorn
7th	02:27 pm	Aquarius
9th	02:00 pm	Pisces
11th	03:22 pm	Aries
13th	08:18 pm	Taurus
16th	05:19 am	Gemini
18th	05:13 pm	Cancer
21st	05:55 am	Leo
23rd	05:45 pm	Virgo
26th	03:59 am	Libra
28th	12:21 pm	Scorpio

March 2005

2nd	06:30 pm	Sagittarius
4th	10:12 pm	Capricorn
6th	11:50 pm	Aquarius
9th	12:33 am	Pisces
11th	02:04 am	Aries
13th	06:06 am	Taurus
15th	01:45 pm	Gemini
18th	12:44 am	Cancer
20th	01:18 pm	Leo
23rd	01:11 am	Virgo
25th	11:00 am	Libra
27th	06:30 pm	Scorpio
29th	11:57 pm	Sagittarius

April 2005

1st	03:49 am	Capricorn
3rd	06:32 am	Aquarius
5th	08:46 am	Pisces
7th	11:28 am	Aries
9th	03:50 pm	Taurus
11th	10:55 pm	Gemini
14th	09:04 am	Cancer
16th	09:18 pm	Leo
19th	09:28 am	Virgo
21st	07:28 pm	Libra
24th	02:26 am	Scorpio
26th	06:46 am	Sagittarius
28th	09:33 am	Capricorn
30th	11:54 am	Aquarius

May 2005

2nd	02:43 pm	Pisces
4th	06:36 pm	Aries
7th	12:02 am	Taurus
9th	07:29 am	Gemini
11th	05:21 pm	Cancer
14th	05:18 am	Leo
16th	05:47 pm	Virgo
19th	04:30 am	Libra
21st	11:49 am	Scorpio
23rd	03:39 pm	Sagittarius
25th	05:11 pm	Capricorn
27th	06:10 pm	Aquarius
29th	08:10 pm	Pisces

June 2005

1st	12:08 am	Aries
3rd	06:20 am	Taurus
5th	02:36 pm	Gemini
8th	12:47 am	Cancer
10th	12:40 pm	Leo
13th	01:23 am	Virgo
15th	12:59 pm	Libra
17th	09:24 pm	Scorpio
20th	01:45 am	Sagittarius
22nd	02:52 am	Capricorn
24th	02:37 am	Aquarius
26th	03:03 am	Pisces
28th	05:52 am	Aries
30th	11:45 am	Taurus

July 2005

2nd	08:26 pm	Gemini
5th	07:08 am	Cancer
7th	07:12 pm	Leo
10th	07:58 am	Virgo
12th	08:10 pm	Libra
15th	05:51 am	Scorpio
17th	11:35 am	Sagittarius
19th	01:27 pm	Capricorn
21st	12:56 pm	Aquarius
23rd	12:12 pm	Pisces
25th	01:23 pm	Aries
27th	05:55 pm	Taurus
30th	02:03 am	Gemini

August 2005

1st	12:53 pm	Cancer
4th	01:10 am	Leo
6th	01:54 pm	Virgo
9th	02:09 am	Libra
11th	12:35 pm	Scorpio
13th	07:48 pm	Sagittarius
15th	11:13 pm	Capricorn
17th	11:39 pm	Aquarius
19th	10:53 pm	Pisces
21st	11:02 pm	Aries
24th	01:58 am	Taurus
26th	08:43 am	Gemini
28th	06:57 pm	Cancer
31st	07:15 am	Leo

September 2005

2nd	07:57 pm	Virgo
5th	07:52 am	Libra
7th	06:11 pm	Scorpio
10th	02:03 am	Sagittarius
12th	06:57 am	Capricorn
14th	09:03 am	Aquarius
16th	09:25 am	Pisces
18th	09:43 am	Aries
20th	11:48 am	Taurus
22nd	05:07 pm	Gemini
25th	02:11 am	Cancer
27th	02:03 pm	Leo
30th	02:45 am	Virgo

October 2005

2nd	02:24 pm	Libra
5th	12:04 am	Scorpio
7th	07:28 am	Sagittarius
9th	12:44 pm	Capricorn
11th	04:06 pm	Aquarius
13th	06:06 pm	Pisces
15th	07:40 pm	Aries
17th	10:05 pm	Taurus
20th	02:45 am	Gemini
22nd	10:41 am	Cancer
24th	09:49 pm	Leo
27th	10:29 am	Virgo
29th	10:16 pm	Libra

November 2005

1st	07:30 am	Scorpio
3rd	01:56 pm	Sagittarius
5th	06:17 pm	Capricorn
7th	09:31 pm	Aquarius
10th	12:23 am	Pisces
12th	03:23 am	Aries
14th	07:03 am	Taurus
16th	12:10 pm	Gemini
18th	07:43 pm	Cancer
21st	06:10 am	Leo
23rd	06:42 pm	Virgo
26th	06:58 am	Libra
28th	04:33 pm	Scorpio
30th	10:33 pm	Sagittarius

December 2005

3rd	01:43 am	Capricorn
5th	03:37 am	Aquarius
7th	05:45 am	Pisces
9th	09:03 am	Aries
11th	01:46 pm	Taurus
13th	08:00 pm	Gemini
16th	04:02 am	Cancer
18th	02:19 pm	Leo
21st	02:39 am	Virgo
23rd	03:27 pm	Libra
26th	02:04 am	Scorpio
28th	08:44 am	Sagittarius
30th	11:36 am	Capricorn

January 2006

1st	12:15 pm	Aquarius
3rd	12:44 pm	Pisces
5th	02:45 pm	Aries
7th	07:10 pm	Taurus
10th	01:59 am	Gemini
12th	10:51 am	Cancer
14th	09:31 pm	Leo
17th	09:49 am	Virgo
19th	10:49 pm	Libra
22nd	10:29 am	Scorpio
24th	06:38 pm	Sagittarius
26th	10:32 pm	Capricorn
28th	11:10 pm	Aquarius
30th	10:32 pm	Pisces

February 2006

1st	10:46 pm	Aries
4th	01:32 am	Taurus
6th	07:33 am	Gemini
8th	04:34 pm	Cancer
11th	03:45 am	Leo
13th	04:14 pm	Virgo
16th	05:09 am	Libra
18th	05:12 pm	Scorpio
21st	02:38 am	Sagittarius
23rd	08:17 am	Capricorn
25th	10:15 am	Aquarius
27th	09:56 am	Pisces

March 2006

1st	09:19 am	Aries
3rd	10:23 am	Taurus
5th	02:38 pm	Gemini
7th	10:38 pm	Cancer
10th	09:43 am	Leo
12th	10:24 pm	Virgo
15th	11:13 am	Libra
17th	11:00 pm	Scorpio
20th	08:44 am	Sagittarius
22nd	03:37 pm	Capricorn
24th	07:22 pm	Aquarius
26th	08:33 pm	Pisces
28th	08:31 pm	Aries
30th	09:01 pm	Taurus

April 2006

1st	11:50 pm	Gemini
4th	06:15 am	Cancer
6th	04:26 pm	Leo
9th	04:59 am	Virgo
11th	05:47 pm	Libra
14th	05:09 am	Scorpio
16th	02:20 pm	Sagittarius
18th	09:14 pm	Capricorn
21st	01:56 am	Aquarius
23rd	04:44 am	Pisces
25th	06:12 am	Aries
27th	07:27 am	Taurus
29th	09:58 am	Gemini

May 2006

1st	03:18 pm	Cancer
4th	12:18 am	Leo
6th	12:21 pm	Virgo
9th	01:11 am	Libra
11th	12:25 pm	Scorpio
13th	08:57 pm	Sagittarius
16th	02:59 am	Capricorn
18th	07:20 am	Aquarius
20th	10:40 am	Pisces
22nd	01:24 pm	Aries
24th	04:01 pm	Taurus
26th	07:20 pm	Gemini
29th	12:34 am	Cancer
31st	08:52 am	Leo

June 2006

2nd	08:18 pm	Virgo
5th	09:09 am	Libra
7th	08:42 pm	Scorpio
10th	05:06 am	Sagittarius
12th	10:20 am	Capricorn
14th	01:33 pm	Aquarius
16th	04:06 pm	Pisces
18th	06:54 pm	Aries
20th	10:23 pm	Taurus
23rd	02:50 am	Gemini
25th	08:48 am	Cancer
27th	05:09 pm	Leo
30th	04:15 am	Virgo

July 2006

2nd	05:06 pm	Libra
5th	05:14 am	Scorpio
7th	02:14 pm	Sagittarius
9th	07:25 pm	Capricorn
11th	09:47 pm	Aquarius
13th	11:00 pm	Pisces
16th	12:39 am	Aries
18th	03:45 am	Taurus
20th	08:39 am	Gemini
22nd	03:28 pm	Cancer
25th	12:25 am	Leo
27th	11:37 am	Virgo
30th	12:28 am	Libra

August 2006

1st	01:08 pm	Scorpio
3rd	11:14 pm	Sagittarius
6th	05:20 am	Capricorn
8th	07:48 am	Aquarius
10th	08:11 am	Pisces
12th	08:22 am	Aries
14th	10:00 am	Taurus
16th	02:08 pm	Gemini
18th	09:04 pm	Cancer
21st	06:34 am	Leo
23rd	06:08 pm	Virgo
26th	07:02 am	Libra
28th	07:57 pm	Scorpio
31st	07:00 am	Sagittarius

September 2006

2nd	02:35 pm	Capricorn
4th	06:15 pm	Aquarius
6th	06:57 pm	Pisces
8th	06:24 pm	Aries
10th	06:30 pm	Taurus
12th	09:00 pm	Gemini
15th	02:54 am	Cancer
17th	12:16 pm	Leo
20th	12:07 am	Virgo
22nd	01:07 pm	Libra
25th	01:55 am	Scorpio
27th	01:17 pm	Sagittarius
29th	10:02 pm	Capricorn

October 2006

2nd	03:25 am	Aquarius
4th	05:33 am	Pisces
6th	05:33 am	Aries
8th	05:05 am	Taurus
10th	06:07 am	Gemini
12th	10:22 am	Cancer
14th	06:39 pm	Leo
17th	06:16 am	Virgo
19th	07:20 pm	Libra
22nd	07:55 am	Scorpio
24th	06:54 pm	Sagittarius
27th	03:48 am	Capricorn
29th	10:17 am	Aquarius
31st	02:11 pm	Pisces

November 2006

2nd	03:47 pm	Aries
4th	04:05 pm	Taurus
6th	04:47 pm	Gemini
8th	07:46 pm	Cancer
11th	02:35 am	Leo
13th	01:19 pm	Virgo
16th	02:15 am	Libra
18th	02:47 pm	Scorpio
21st	01:16 am	Sagittarius
23rd	09:26 am	Capricorn
25th	03:41 pm	Aquarius
27th	08:21 pm	Pisces
29th	11:30 pm	Aries

December 2006

2nd	01:27 am	Taurus
4th	03:06 am	Gemini
6th	06:01 am	Cancer
8th	11:52 am	Leo
10th	09:32 pm	Virgo
13th	10:01 am	Libra
15th	10:43 pm	Scorpio
18th	09:11 am	Sagittarius
20th	04:39 pm	Capricorn
22nd	09:49 pm	Aquarius
25th	01:44 am	Pisces
27th	05:04 am	Aries
29th	08:09 am	Taurus
31st	11:17 am	Gemini

January 2007

2nd	03:14 pm	Cancer
4th	09:15 pm	Leo
7th	06:19 am	Virgo
9th	06:16 pm	Libra
12th	07:08 am	Scorpio
14th	06:12 pm	Sagittarius
17th	01:50 am	Capricorn
19th	06:16 am	Aquarius
21st	08:49 am	Pisces
23rd	10:53 am	Aries
25th	01:29 pm	Taurus
27th	05:10 pm	Gemini
29th	10:17 pm	Cancer

February 2007

1st	05:15 am	Leo
3rd	02:34 pm	Virgo
6th	02:16 am	Libra
8th	03:10 pm	Scorpio
11th	03:02 am	Sagittarius
13th	11:43 am	Capricorn
15th	04:35 pm	Aquarius
17th	06:31 pm	Pisces
19th	07:06 pm	Aries
21st	08:04 pm	Taurus
23rd	10:42 pm	Gemini
26th	03:48 am	Cancer
28th	11:30 am	Leo

March 2007

2nd	09:32 pm	Virgo
5th	09:26 am	Libra
7th	10:17 pm	Scorpio
10th	10:38 am	Sagittarius
12th	08:35 pm	Capricorn
15th	02:52 am	Aquarius
17th	05:31 am	Pisces
19th	05:42 am	Aries
21st	05:16 am	Taurus
23rd	06:07 am	Gemini
25th	09:49 am	Cancer
27th	05:05 pm	Leo
30th	03:27 am	Virgo

April 2007

1st	03:44 pm	Libra
4th	04:36 am	Scorpio
6th	04:57 pm	Sagittarius
9th	03:37 am	Capricorn
11th	11:24 am	Aquarius
13th	03:39 pm	Pisces
15th	04:47 pm	Aries
17th	04:11 pm	Taurus
19th	03:51 pm	Gemini
21st	05:51 pm	Cancer
23rd	11:38 pm	Leo
26th	09:24 am	Virgo
28th	09:45 pm	Libra

May 2007

1st	10:42 am	Scorpio
3rd	10:48 pm	Sagittarius
6th	09:22 am	Capricorn
8th	05:48 pm	Aquarius
10th	11:32 pm	Pisces
13th	02:19 am	Aries
15th	02:49 am	Taurus
17th	02:34 am	Gemini
19th	03:38 am	Cancer
21st	07:57 am	Leo
23rd	04:27 pm	Virgo
26th	04:17 am	Libra
28th	05:12 pm	Scorpio
31st	05:07 am	Sagittarius

June 2007

2nd	03:10 pm	Capricorn
4th	11:16 pm	Aquarius
7th	05:25 am	Pisces
9th	09:27 am	Aries
11th	11:30 am	Taurus
13th	12:24 pm	Gemini
15th	01:46 pm	Cancer
17th	05:25 pm	Leo
20th	12:46 am	Virgo
22nd	11:44 am	Libra
25th	12:27 am	Scorpio
27th	12:24 pm	Sagittarius
29th	10:05 pm	Capricorn

July 2007

2nd	05:24 am	Aquarius
4th	10:53 am	Pisces
6th	02:57 pm	Aries
8th	05:54 pm	Taurus
10th	08:10 pm	Gemini
12th	10:40 pm	Cancer
15th	02:44 am	Leo
17th	09:40 am	Virgo
19th	07:54 pm	Libra
22nd	08:19 am	Scorpio
24th	08:30 pm	Sagittarius
27th	06:22 am	Capricorn
29th	01:14 pm	Aquarius
31st	05:41 pm	Pisces

August 2007

2nd	08:43 pm	Aries
4th	11:16 pm	Taurus
7th	02:02 am	Gemini
9th	05:37 am	Cancer
11th	10:42 am	Leo
13th	06:03 pm	Virgo
16th	04:04 am	Libra
18th	04:14 pm	Scorpio
21st	04:45 am	Sagittarius
23rd	03:20 pm	Capricorn
25th	10:36 pm	Aquarius
28th	02:35 am	Pisces
30th	04:25 am	Aries

September 2007

1st	05:36 am	Taurus
3rd	07:30 am	Gemini
5th	11:08 am	Cancer
7th	05:00 pm	Leo
10th	01:10 am	Virgo
12th	11:32 am	Libra
14th	11:37 pm	Scorpio
17th	12:21 pm	Sagittarius
19th	11:52 pm	Capricorn
22nd	08:19 am	Aquarius
24th	12:56 pm	Pisces
26th	02:23 pm	Aries
28th	02:17 pm	Taurus
30th	02:34 pm	Gemini

October 2007

2nd	04:57 pm	Cancer
4th	10:28 pm	Leo
7th	07:04 am	Virgo
9th	05:58 pm	Libra
12th	06:14 am	Scorpio
14th	06:59 pm	Sagittarius
17th	07:04 am	Capricorn
19th	04:52 pm	Aquarius
21st	11:03 pm	Pisces
24th	01:25 am	Aries
26th	01:07 am	Taurus
28th	12:12 am	Gemini
30th	12:50 am	Cancer

November 2007

1st	04:49 am	Leo
3rd	12:45 pm	Virgo
5th	11:48 pm	Libra
8th	12:19 pm	Scorpio
11th	12:59 am	Sagittarius
13th	01:01 pm	Capricorn
15th	11:30 pm	Aquarius
18th	07:15 am	Pisces
20th	11:25 am	Aries
22nd	12:19 pm	Taurus
24th	11:30 am	Gemini
26th	11:07 am	Cancer
28th	01:24 pm	Leo
30th	07:45 pm	Virgo

December 2007

3rd	06:02 am	Libra
5th	06:31 pm	Scorpio
8th	07:12 am	Sagittarius
10th	06:51 pm	Capricorn
13th	05:02 am	Aquarius
15th	01:16 pm	Pisces
17th	06:53 pm	Aries
19th	09:39 pm	Taurus
21st	10:15 pm	Gemini
23rd	10:19 pm	Cancer
25th	11:53 pm	Leo
28th	04:45 am	Virgo
30th	01:38 pm	Libra

January 2008

2nd	01:33 am	Scorpio
4th	02:14 pm	Sagittarius
7th	01:44 am	Capricorn
9th	11:14 am	Aquarius
11th	06:45 pm	Pisces
14th	12:24 am	Aries
16th	04:13 am	Taurus
18th	06:30 am	Gemini
20th	08:05 am	Cancer
22nd	10:21 am	Leo
24th	02:49 pm	Virgo
26th	10:36 pm	Libra
29th	09:36 am	Scorpio
31st	10:09 pm	Sagittarius

February 2008

3rd	09:53 am	Capricorn
5th	07:10 pm	Aquarius
8th	01:47 am	Pisces
10th	06:18 am	Aries
12th	09:34 am	Taurus
14th	12:20 pm	Gemini
16th	03:12 pm	Cancer
18th	06:52 pm	Leo
21st	12:07 am	Virgo
23rd	07:45 am	Libra
25th	06:06 pm	Scorpio
28th	06:23 am	Sagittarius

March 2008

1st	06:34 pm	Capricorn
4th	04:25 am	Aquarius
6th	10:53 am	Pisces
8th	02:24 pm	Aries
10th	04:14 pm	Taurus
12th	05:55 pm	Gemini
14th	08:38 pm	Cancer
17th	01:04 am	Leo
19th	07:26 am	Virgo
21st	03:46 pm	Libra
24th	02:07 am	Scorpio
26th	02:11 pm	Sagittarius
29th	02:44 am	Capricorn
31st	01:35 pm	Aquarius

April 2008

2nd	08:56 pm	Pisces
5th	12:28 am	Aries
7th	01:20 am	Taurus
9th	01:27 am	Gemini
11th	02:44 am	Cancer
13th	06:29 am	Leo
15th	01:07 pm	Virgo
17th	10:11 pm	Libra
20th	09:01 am	Scorpio
22nd	09:08 pm	Sagittarius
25th	09:47 am	Capricorn
27th	09:28 pm	Aquarius
30th	06:11 am	Pisces

May 2008

2nd	10:52 am	Aries
4th	11:59 am	Taurus
6th	11:18 am	Gemini
8th	11:02 am	Cancer
10th	01:11 pm	Leo
12th	06:49 pm	Virgo
15th	03:47 am	Libra
17th	03:00 pm	Scorpio
20th	03:19 am	Sagittarius
22nd	03:56 pm	Capricorn
25th	03:52 am	Aquarius
27th	01:39 pm	Pisces
29th	07:53 pm	Aries
31st	10:19 pm	Taurus

June 2008

2nd	10:06 pm	Gemini
4th	09:16 pm	Cancer
6th	10:01 pm	Leo
9th	02:02 am	Virgo
11th	09:56 am	Libra
13th	08:53 pm	Scorpio
16th	09:20 am	Sagittarius
18th	09:52 pm	Capricorn
21st	09:34 am	Aquarius
23rd	07:33 pm	Pisces
26th	02:50 am	Aries
28th	06:51 am	Taurus
30th	08:04 am	Gemini

July 2008

2nd	07:53 am	Cancer
4th	08:16 am	Leo
6th	11:04 am	Virgo
8th	05:32 pm	Libra
11th	03:35 am	Scorpio
13th	03:50 pm	Sagittarius
16th	04:21 am	Capricorn
18th	03:41 pm	Aquarius
21st	01:08 am	Pisces
23rd	08:23 am	Aries
25th	01:15 pm	Taurus
27th	03:56 pm	Gemini
29th	05:12 pm	Cancer
31st	06:22 pm	Leo

August 2008

2nd	09:00 pm	Virgo
5th	02:28 am	Libra
7th	11:27 am	Scorpio
9th	11:11 pm	Sagittarius
12th	11:42 am	Capricorn
14th	10:57 pm	Aquarius
17th	07:47 am	Pisces
19th	02:10 pm	Aries
21st	06:38 pm	Taurus
23rd	09:49 pm	Gemini
26th	12:19 am	Cancer
28th	02:51 am	Leo
30th	06:19 am	Virgo

September 2008

1st	11:45 am	Libra
3rd	08:02 pm	Scorpio
6th	07:11 am	Sagittarius
8th	07:45 pm	Capricorn
11th	07:20 am	Aquarius
13th	04:05 pm	Pisces
15th	09:40 pm	Aries
18th	12:57 am	Taurus
20th	03:17 am	Gemini
22nd	05:49 am	Cancer
24th	09:14 am	Leo
26th	01:53 pm	Virgo
28th	08:06 pm	Libra

October 2008

1st	04:27 am	Scorpio
3rd	03:15 pm	Sagittarius
6th	03:49 am	Capricorn
8th	04:03 pm	Aquarius
11th	01:32 am	Pisces
13th	07:08 am	Aries
15th	09:32 am	Taurus
17th	10:26 am	Gemini
19th	11:41 am	Cancer
21st	02:36 pm	Leo
23rd	07:40 pm	Virgo
26th	02:48 am	Libra
28th	11:48 am	Scorpio
30th	10:42 pm	Sagittarius

November 2008

2nd	11:14 am	Capricorn
5th	12:02 am	Aquarius
7th	10:44 am	Pisces
9th	05:27 pm	Aries
11th	08:06 pm	Taurus
13th	08:12 pm	Gemini
15th	07:53 pm	Cancer
17th	09:08 pm	Leo
20th	01:13 am	Virgo
22nd	08:20 am	Libra
24th	05:55 pm	Scorpio
27th	05:14 am	Sagittarius
29th	05:48 pm	Capricorn

December 2008

2nd	06:45 am	Aquarius
4th	06:24 pm	Pisces
7th	02:45 am	Aries
9th	06:53 am	Taurus
11th	07:34 am	Gemini
13th	06:40 am	Cancer
15th	06:23 am	Leo
17th	08:36 am	Virgo
19th	02:23 pm	Libra
21st	11:37 pm	Scorpio
24th	11:13 am	Sagittarius
26th	11:57 pm	Capricorn
29th	12:43 pm	Aquarius

January 2009

1st	12:28 am	Pisces
3rd	09:50 am	Aries
5th	03:46 pm	Taurus
7th	06:12 pm	Gemini
9th	06:14 pm	Cancer
11th	05:41 pm	Leo
13th	06:33 pm	Virgo
15th	10:31 pm	Libra
18th	06:21 am	Scorpio
20th	05:31 pm	Sagittarius
23rd	06:19 am	Capricorn
25th	06:57 pm	Aquarius
28th	06:13 am	Pisces
30th	03:25 pm	Aries

February 2009

1st	10:09 pm	Taurus
4th	02:15 am	Gemini
6th	04:06 am	Cancer
8th	04:44 am	Leo
10th	05:39 am	Virgo
12th	08:33 am	Libra
14th	02:51 pm	Scorpio
17th	12:54 am	Sagittarius
19th	01:26 pm	Capricorn
22nd	02:07 am	Aquarius
24th	01:00 pm	Pisces
26th	09:24 pm	Aries

March 2009

1st	03:34 am	Taurus
3rd	08:00 am	Gemini
5th	11:08 am	Cancer
7th	01:25 pm	Leo
9th	03:35 pm	Virgo
11th	06:46 pm	Libra
14th	12:23 am	Scorpio
16th	09:22 am	Sagittarius
18th	09:19 pm	Capricorn
21st	10:07 am	Aquarius
23rd	09:09 pm	Pisces
26th	05:03 am	Aries
28th	10:10 am	Taurus
30th	01:36 pm	Gemini

April 2009

1st	04:31 pm	Cancer
3rd	07:33 pm	Leo
5th	11:02 pm	Virgo
8th	03:23 am	Libra
10th	09:24 am	Scorpio
12th	06:01 pm	Sagittarius
15th	05:28 am	Capricorn
17th	06:20 pm	Aquarius
20th	05:56 am	Pisces
22nd	02:09 pm	Aries
24th	06:47 pm	Taurus
26th	09:03 pm	Gemini
28th	10:39 pm	Cancer

May 2009

1st	12:56 am	Leo
3rd	04:37 am	Virgo
5th	09:52 am	Libra
7th	04:48 pm	Scorpio
10th	01:50 am	Sagittarius
12th	01:10 pm	Capricorn
15th	02:02 am	Aquarius
17th	02:17 pm	Pisces
19th	11:31 pm	Aries
22nd	04:41 am	Taurus
24th	06:34 am	Gemini
26th	06:58 am	Cancer
28th	07:45 am	Leo
30th	10:18 am	Virgo

June 2009

1st	03:17 pm	Libra
3rd	10:44 pm	Scorpio
6th	08:24 am	Sagittarius
8th	08:00 pm	Capricorn
11th	08:53 am	Aquarius
13th	09:33 pm	Pisces
16th	07:52 am	Aries
18th	02:21 pm	Taurus
20th	05:01 pm	Gemini
22nd	05:12 pm	Cancer
24th	04:51 pm	Leo
26th	05:47 pm	Virgo
28th	09:25 pm	Libra

July 2009

1st	04:19 am	Scorpio
3rd	02:11 pm	Sagittarius
6th	02:08 am	Capricorn
8th	03:04 pm	Aquarius
11th	03:44 am	Pisces
13th	02:40 pm	Aries
15th	10:30 pm	Taurus
18th	02:42 am	Gemini
20th	03:52 am	Cancer
22nd	03:28 am	Leo
24th	03:23 am	Virgo
26th	05:26 am	Libra
28th	10:56 am	Scorpio
30th	08:11 pm	Sagittarius

August 2009

2nd	08:09 am	Capricorn
4th	09:08 pm	Aquarius
7th	09:35 am	Pisces
9th	08:24 pm	Aries
12th	04:50 am	Taurus
14th	10:26 am	Gemini
16th	01:14 pm	Cancer
18th	01:57 pm	Leo
20th	02:01 pm	Virgo
22nd	03:12 pm	Libra
24th	07:17 pm	Scorpio
27th	03:17 am	Sagittarius
29th	02:45 pm	Capricorn

September 2009

1st	03:43 am	Aquarius
3rd	03:59 pm	Pisces
6th	02:15 am	Aries
8th	10:18 am	Taurus
10th	04:17 pm	Gemini
12th	08:20 pm	Cancer
14th	10:40 pm	Leo
16th	11:57 pm	Virgo
19th	01:27 am	Libra
21st	04:53 am	Scorpio
23rd	11:43 am	Sagittarius
25th	10:19 pm	Capricorn
28th	11:07 am	Aquarius
30th	11:26 pm	Pisces

October 2009

3rd	09:21 am	Aries
5th	04:34 pm	Taurus
7th	09:47 pm	Gemini
10th	01:48 am	Cancer
12th	05:03 am	Leo
14th	07:46 am	Virgo
16th	10:30 am	Libra
18th	02:23 pm	Scorpio
20th	08:50 pm	Sagittarius
23rd	06:40 am	Capricorn
25th	07:08 pm	Aquarius
28th	07:46 am	Pisces
30th	05:57 pm	Aries

November 2009

2nd	12:45 am	Taurus
4th	04:53 am	Gemini
6th	07:43 am	Cancer
8th	10:23 am	Leo
10th	01:31 pm	Virgo
12th	05:23 pm	Libra
14th	10:25 pm	Scorpio
17th	05:22 am	Sagittarius
19th	03:01 pm	Capricorn
22nd	03:11 am	Aquarius
24th	04:08 pm	Pisces
27th	03:11 am	Aries
29th	10:35 am	Taurus

December 2009

1st	02:24 pm	Gemini
3rd	04:01 pm	Cancer
5th	05:07 pm	Leo
7th	07:06 pm	Virgo
9th	10:48 pm	Libra
12th	04:32 am	Scorpio
14th	12:26 pm	Sagittarius
16th	10:32 pm	Capricorn
19th	10:39 am	Aquarius
21st	11:43 pm	Pisces
24th	11:40 am	Aries
26th	08:27 pm	Taurus
29th	01:14 am	Gemini
31st	02:46 am	Cancer

January 2010

2nd	02:42 am	Leo
4th	02:53 am	Virgo
6th	04:59 am	Libra
8th	10:01 am	Scorpio
10th	06:11 pm	Sagittarius
13th	04:54 am	Capricorn
15th	05:17 pm	Aquarius
18th	06:18 am	Pisces
20th	06:37 pm	Aries
23rd	04:40 am	Taurus
25th	11:12 am	Gemini
27th	02:02 pm	Cancer
29th	02:11 pm	Leo
31st	01:24 pm	Virgo

February 2010

2nd	01:42 pm	Libra
4th	04:56 pm	Scorpio
7th	12:04 am	Sagittarius
9th	10:44 am	Capricorn
11th	11:24 pm	Aquarius
14th	12:23 pm	Pisces
17th	12:31 am	Aries
19th	10:56 am	Taurus
21st	06:48 pm	Gemini
23rd	11:29 pm	Cancer
26th	01:09 am	Leo
28th	12:53 am	Virgo

March 2010

2nd	12:32 am	Libra
4th	02:12 am	Scorpio
6th	07:36 am	Sagittarius
8th	05:14 pm	Capricorn
11th	05:43 am	Aquarius
13th	06:44 pm	Pisces
16th	06:32 am	Aries
18th	04:30 pm	Taurus
21st	12:29 am	Gemini
23rd	06:16 am	Cancer
25th	09:39 am	Leo
27th	10:58 am	Virgo
29th	11:22 am	Libra
31st	12:41 pm	Scorpio

April 2010

2nd	04:53 pm	Sagittarius
5th	01:07 am	Capricorn
7th	12:51 pm	Aquarius
10th	01:48 am	Pisces
12th	01:32 pm	Aries
14th	10:55 pm	Taurus
17th	06:08 am	Gemini
19th	11:39 am	Cancer
21st	03:42 pm	Leo
23rd	06:25 pm	Virgo
25th	08:17 pm	Libra
27th	10:29 pm	Scorpio
30th	02:36 am	Sagittarius

May 2010

2nd	10:00 am	Capricorn
4th	08:52 pm	Aquarius
7th	09:34 am	Pisces
9th	09:30 pm	Aries
12th	06:49 am	Taurus
14th	01:18 pm	Gemini
16th	05:46 pm	Cancer
18th	09:07 pm	Leo
20th	11:59 pm	Virgo
23rd	02:50 am	Libra
25th	06:18 am	Scorpio
27th	11:16 am	Sagittarius
29th	06:45 pm	Capricorn

June 2010

1st	05:08 am	Aquarius
3rd	05:34 pm	Pisces
6th	05:50 am	Aries
8th	03:41 pm	Taurus
10th	10:11 pm	Gemini
13th	01:51 am	Cancer
15th	03:55 am	Leo
17th	05:41 am	Virgo
19th	08:14 am	Libra
21st	12:14 pm	Scorpio
23rd	06:11 pm	Sagittarius
26th	02:22 am	Capricorn
28th	12:52 pm	Aquarius

July 2010

1st	01:10 am	Pisces
3rd	01:45 pm	Aries
6th	12:30 am	Taurus
8th	07:51 am	Gemini
10th	11:39 am	Cancer
12th	12:54 pm	Leo
14th	01:15 pm	Virgo
16th	02:25 pm	Libra
18th	05:42 pm	Scorpio
20th	11:49 pm	Sagittarius
23rd	08:39 am	Capricorn
25th	07:39 pm	Aquarius
28th	08:00 am	Pisces
30th	08:42 pm	Aries

August 2010

2nd	08:14 am	Taurus
4th	04:55 pm	Gemini
6th	09:51 pm	Cancer
8th	11:24 pm	Leo
10th	11:01 pm	Virgo
12th	10:43 pm	Libra
15th	12:27 am	Scorpio
17th	05:34 am	Sagittarius
19th	02:18 pm	Capricorn
22nd	01:38 am	Aquarius
24th	02:11 pm	Pisces
27th	02:50 am	Aries
29th	02:36 pm	Taurus

September 2010

1st	12:20 am	Gemini
3rd	06:51 am	Cancer
5th	09:46 am	Leo
7th	09:53 am	Virgo
9th	09:01 am	Libra
11th	09:22 am	Scorpio
13th	12:52 pm	Sagittarius
15th	08:30 pm	Capricorn
18th	07:35 am	Aquarius
20th	08:15 pm	Pisces
23rd	08:48 am	Aries
25th	08:17 pm	Taurus
28th	06:11 am	Gemini
30th	01:46 pm	Cancer

October 2010

2nd	06:21 pm	Leo
4th	08:00 pm	Virgo
6th	07:52 pm	Libra
8th	07:52 pm	Scorpio
10th	10:09 pm	Sagittarius
13th	04:17 am	Capricorn
15th	02:24 pm	Aquarius
18th	02:52 am	Pisces
20th	03:24 pm	Aries
23rd	02:30 am	Taurus
25th	11:48 am	Gemini
27th	07:15 pm	Cancer
30th	12:39 am	Leo

November 2010

1st	03:52 am	Virgo
3rd	05:19 am	Libra
5th	06:16 am	Scorpio
7th	08:28 am	Sagittarius
9th	01:37 pm	Capricorn
11th	10:32 pm	Aquarius
14th	10:25 am	Pisces
16th	10:59 pm	Aries
19th	10:05 am	Taurus
21st	06:46 pm	Gemini
24th	01:15 am	Cancer
26th	06:02 am	Leo
28th	09:34 am	Virgo
30th	12:16 pm	Libra

December 2010

2nd	02:44 pm	Scorpio
4th	06:00 pm	Sagittarius
6th	11:16 pm	Capricorn
9th	07:31 am	Aquarius
11th	06:41 pm	Pisces
14th	07:15 am	Aries
16th	06:49 pm	Taurus
19th	03:38 am	Gemini
21st	09:23 am	Cancer
23rd	12:51 pm	Leo
25th	03:14 pm	Virgo
27th	05:38 pm	Libra
29th	08:50 pm	Scorpio

January 2011

1st	01:22 am	Sagittarius
3rd	07:39 am	Capricorn
5th	04:08 pm	Aquarius
8th	02:57 am	Pisces
10th	03:24 pm	Aries
13th	03:37 am	Taurus
15th	01:23 pm	Gemini
17th	07:29 pm	Cancer
19th	10:16 pm	Leo
21st	11:11 pm	Virgo
23rd	11:59 pm	Libra
26th	02:16 am	Scorpio
28th	06:55 am	Sagittarius
30th	02:05 pm	Capricorn

February 2011

1st	11:22 pm	Aquarius
4th	10:24 am	Pisces
6th	10:46 pm	Aries
9th	11:23 am	Taurus
11th	10:21 pm	Gemini
14th	05:49 am	Cancer
16th	09:15 am	Leo
18th	09:39 am	Virgo
20th	09:01 am	Libra
22nd	09:29 am	Scorpio
24th	12:46 pm	Sagittarius
26th	07:32 pm	Capricorn

March 2011

1st	05:15 am	Aquarius
3rd	04:47 pm	Pisces
6th	05:14 am	Aries
8th	05:53 pm	Taurus
11th	05:32 am	Gemini
13th	02:30 pm	Cancer
15th	07:34 pm	Leo
17th	08:54 pm	Virgo
19th	08:04 pm	Libra
21st	07:17 pm	Scorpio
23rd	08:46 pm	Sagittarius
26th	01:58 am	Capricorn
28th	11:00 am	Aquarius
30th	10:39 pm	Pisces

April 2011

2nd	11:16 am	Aries
4th	11:46 pm	Taurus
7th	11:22 am	Gemini
9th	09:02 pm	Cancer
12th	03:38 am	Leo
14th	06:41 am	Virgo
16th	06:59 am	Libra
18th	06:20 am	Scorpio
20th	06:50 am	Sagittarius
22nd	10:25 am	Capricorn
24th	05:59 pm	Aquarius
27th	04:58 am	Pisces
29th	05:34 pm	Aries

May 2011

2nd	05:59 am	Taurus
4th	05:10 pm	Gemini
7th	02:32 am	Cancer
9th	09:36 am	Leo
11th	01:59 pm	Virgo
13th	03:57 pm	Libra
15th	04:32 pm	Scorpio
17th	05:23 pm	Sagittarius
19th	08:16 pm	Capricorn
22nd	02:32 am	Aquarius
24th	12:24 pm	Pisces
27th	12:37 am	Aries
29th	01:02 pm	Taurus
31st	11:57 pm	Gemini

June 2011

3rd	08:37 am	Cancer
5th	03:04 pm	Leo
7th	07:34 pm	Virgo
9th	10:31 pm	Libra
12th	12:34 am	Scorpio
14th	02:39 am	Sagittarius
16th	05:59 am	Capricorn
18th	11:48 am	Aquarius
20th	08:46 pm	Pisces
23rd	08:24 am	Aries
25th	08:53 pm	Taurus
28th	07:57 am	Gemini
30th	04:13 pm	Cancer

July 2011

2nd	09:43 pm	Leo
5th	01:16 am	Virgo
7th	03:54 am	Libra
9th	06:32 am	Scorpio
11th	09:47 am	Sagittarius
13th	02:14 pm	Capricorn
15th	08:31 pm	Aquarius
18th	05:13 am	Pisces
20th	04:26 pm	Aries
23rd	04:59 am	Taurus
25th	04:35 pm	Gemini
28th	01:12 am	Cancer
30th	06:16 am	Leo

August 2011

1st	08:42 am	Virgo
3rd	10:05 am	Libra
5th	11:58 am	Scorpio
7th	03:21 pm	Sagittarius
9th	08:38 pm	Capricorn
12th	03:48 am	Aquarius
14th	12:55 pm	Pisces
17th	12:02 am	Aries
19th	12:37 pm	Taurus
22nd	12:54 am	Gemini
24th	10:31 am	Cancer
26th	04:09 pm	Leo
28th	06:14 pm	Virgo
30th	06:26 pm	Libra

September 2011

1st	06:49 pm	Scorpio
3rd	09:04 pm	Sagittarius
6th	02:04 am	Capricorn
8th	09:43 am	Aquarius
10th	07:27 pm	Pisces
13th	06:50 am	Aries
15th	07:25 pm	Taurus
18th	08:07 am	Gemini
20th	06:54 pm	Cancer
23rd	01:56 am	Leo
25th	04:50 am	Virgo
27th	04:51 am	Libra
29th	04:06 am	Scorpio

October 2011

1st	04:42 am	Sagittarius
3rd	08:16 am	Capricorn
5th	03:19 pm	Aquarius
8th	01:14 am	Pisces
10th	12:58 pm	Aries
13th	01:36 am	Taurus
15th	02:16 pm	Gemini
18th	01:38 am	Cancer
20th	10:06 am	Leo
22nd	02:41 pm	Virgo
24th	03:50 pm	Libra
26th	03:09 pm	Scorpio
28th	02:46 pm	Sagittarius
30th	04:39 pm	Capricorn

November 2011

1st	10:08 pm	Aquarius
4th	07:18 am	Pisces
6th	07:03 pm	Aries
9th	07:46 am	Taurus
11th	08:11 pm	Gemini
14th	07:19 am	Cancer
16th	04:18 pm	Leo
18th	10:19 pm	Virgo
21st	01:17 am	Libra
23rd	01:59 am	Scorpio
25th	01:58 am	Sagittarius
27th	03:05 am	Capricorn
29th	07:02 am	Aquarius

December 2011

1st	02:46 pm	Pisces
4th	01:52 am	Aries
6th	02:35 pm	Taurus
9th	02:53 am	Gemini
11th	01:26 pm	Cancer
13th	09:49 pm	Leo
16th	03:59 am	Virgo
18th	08:07 am	Libra
20th	10:33 am	Scorpio
22nd	12:03 pm	Sagittarius
24th	01:48 pm	Capricorn
26th	05:15 pm	Aquarius
28th	11:46 pm	Pisces
31st	09:49 am	Aries

January 2012

2nd	10:17 pm	Taurus
5th	10:45 am	Gemini
7th	09:06 pm	Cancer
10th	04:36 am	Leo
12th	09:45 am	Virgo
14th	01:29 pm	Libra
16th	04:34 pm	Scorpio
18th	07:29 pm	Sagittarius
20th	10:41 pm	Capricorn
23rd	02:54 am	Aquarius
25th	09:12 am	Pisces
27th	06:28 pm	Aries
30th	06:29 am	Taurus

February 2012

1st	07:15 pm	Gemini
4th	06:04 am	Cancer
6th	01:24 pm	Leo
8th	05:33 pm	Virgo
10th	07:55 pm	Libra
12th	10:02 pm	Scorpio
15th	12:57 am	Sagittarius
17th	05:04 am	Capricorn
19th	10:29 am	Aquarius
21st	05:32 pm	Pisces
24th	02:48 am	Aries
26th	02:30 pm	Taurus
29th	03:27 am	Gemini

March 2012

2nd	03:09 pm	Cancer
4th	11:18 pm	Leo
7th	03:27 am	Virgo
9th	04:51 am	Libra
11th	05:25 am	Scorpio
13th	06:54 am	Sagittarius
15th	10:24 am	Capricorn
17th	04:12 pm	Aquarius
20th	12:06 am	Pisces
22nd	09:58 am	Aries
24th	09:44 pm	Taurus
27th	10:44 am	Gemini
29th	11:08 pm	Cancer

April 2012

1st	08:36 am	Leo
3rd	01:54 pm	Virgo
5th	03:33 pm	Libra
7th	03:18 pm	Scorpio
9th	03:13 pm	Sagittarius
11th	05:02 pm	Capricorn
13th	09:48 pm	Aquarius
16th	05:38 am	Pisces
18th	03:59 pm	Aries
21st	04:06 am	Taurus
23rd	05:06 pm	Gemini
26th	05:43 am	Cancer
28th	04:11 pm	Leo
30th	11:03 pm	Virgo

May 2012

3rd	02:04 am	Libra
5th	02:20 am	Scorpio
7th	01:40 am	Sagittarius
9th	02:01 am	Capricorn
11th	05:03 am	Aquarius
13th	11:42 am	Pisces
15th	09:46 pm	Aries
18th	10:04 am	Taurus
20th	11:06 pm	Gemini
23rd	11:32 am	Cancer
25th	10:12 pm	Leo
28th	06:07 am	Virgo
30th	10:46 am	Libra

June 2012

1st	12:32 pm	Scorpio
3rd	12:33 pm	Sagittarius
5th	12:31 pm	Capricorn
7th	02:17 pm	Aquarius
9th	07:22 pm	Pisces
12th	04:22 am	Aries
14th	04:22 pm	Taurus
17th	05:25 am	Gemini
19th	05:34 pm	Cancer
22nd	03:48 am	Leo
24th	11:43 am	Virgo
26th	05:16 pm	Libra
28th	08:33 pm	Scorpio
30th	10:04 pm	Sagittarius

July 2012

2nd	10:52 pm	Capricorn
5th	12:26 am	Aquarius
7th	04:30 am	Pisces
9th	12:14 pm	Aries
11th	11:31 pm	Taurus
14th	12:27 pm	Gemini
17th	12:32 am	Cancer
19th	10:14 am	Leo
21st	05:25 pm	Virgo
23rd	10:39 pm	Libra
26th	02:30 am	Scorpio
28th	05:18 am	Sagittarius
30th	07:30 am	Capricorn

August 2012

1st	09:56 am	Aquarius
3rd	01:59 pm	Pisces
5th	08:59 pm	Aries
8th	07:29 am	Taurus
10th	08:11 pm	Gemini
13th	08:28 am	Cancer
15th	06:05 pm	Leo
18th	12:34 am	Virgo
20th	04:46 am	Libra
22nd	07:54 am	Scorpio
24th	10:51 am	Sagittarius
26th	01:59 pm	Capricorn
28th	05:39 pm	Aquarius
30th	10:32 pm	Pisces

September 2012

2nd	05:38 am	Aries
4th	03:42 pm	Taurus
7th	04:10 am	Gemini
9th	04:50 pm	Cancer
12th	03:01 am	Leo
14th	09:31 am	Virgo
16th	12:56 pm	Libra
18th	02:46 pm	Scorpio
20th	04:35 pm	Sagittarius
22nd	07:21 pm	Capricorn
24th	11:33 pm	Aquarius
27th	05:24 am	Pisces
29th	01:15 pm	Aries

October 2012

1st	11:27 pm	Taurus
4th	11:47 am	Gemini
7th	12:46 am	Cancer
9th	11:56 am	Leo
11th	07:24 pm	Virgo
13th	11:02 pm	Libra
16th	12:07 am	Scorpio
18th	12:26 am	Sagittarius
20th	01:42 am	Capricorn
22nd	05:03 am	Aquarius
24th	11:01 am	Pisces
26th	07:32 pm	Aries
29th	06:16 am	Taurus
31st	06:41 pm	Gemini

November 2012

3rd	07:44 am	Cancer
5th	07:40 pm	Leo
8th	04:35 am	Virgo
10th	09:36 am	Libra
12th	11:11 am	Scorpio
14th	10:53 am	Sagittarius
16th	10:36 am	Capricorn
18th	12:11 pm	Aquarius
20th	04:56 pm	Pisces
23rd	01:12 am	Aries
25th	12:19 pm	Taurus
28th	12:59 am	Gemini
30th	01:55 pm	Cancer

December 2012

3rd	01:58 am	Leo
5th	11:52 am	Virgo
7th	06:36 pm	Libra
9th	09:51 pm	Scorpio
11th	10:22 pm	Sagittarius
13th	09:43 pm	Capricorn
15th	09:53 pm	Aquarius
18th	12:49 am	Pisces
20th	07:44 am	Aries
22nd	06:26 pm	Taurus
25th	07:14 am	Gemini
27th	08:07 pm	Cancer
30th	07:46 am	Leo

January 2013

1st	05:35 pm	Virgo
4th	01:11 am	Libra
6th	06:10 am	Scorpio
8th	08:29 am	Sagittarius
10th	08:55 am	Capricorn
12th	09:02 am	Aquarius
14th	10:50 am	Pisces
16th	04:08 pm	Aries
19th	01:37 am	Taurus
21st	02:05 pm	Gemini
24th	03:01 am	Cancer
26th	02:21 pm	Leo
28th	11:28 pm	Virgo
31st	06:36 am	Libra

February 2013

2nd	12:02 pm	Scorpio
4th	03:46 pm	Sagittarius
6th	05:56 pm	Capricorn
8th	07:17 pm	Aquarius
10th	09:20 pm	Pisces
13th	01:52 am	Aries
15th	10:08 am	Taurus
17th	09:51 pm	Gemini
20th	10:45 am	Cancer
22nd	10:13 pm	Leo
25th	06:53 am	Virgo
27th	01:02 pm	Libra

March 2013

1st	05:34 pm	Scorpio
3rd	09:11 pm	Sagittarius
6th	12:14 am	Capricorn
8th	03:02 am	Aquarius
10th	06:19 am	Pisces
12th	11:18 am	Aries
14th	07:09 pm	Taurus
17th	06:10 am	Gemini
19th	06:56 pm	Cancer
22nd	06:50 am	Leo
24th	03:50 pm	Virgo
26th	09:32 pm	Libra
29th	12:54 am	Scorpio
31st	03:14 am	Sagittarius

April 2013

2nd	05:36 am	Capricorn
4th	08:42 am	Aquarius
6th	01:01 pm	Pisces
8th	07:03 pm	Aries
11th	03:22 am	Taurus
13th	02:13 pm	Gemini
16th	02:50 am	Cancer
18th	03:14 pm	Leo
21st	01:09 am	Virgo
23rd	07:25 am	Libra
25th	10:26 am	Scorpio
27th	11:32 am	Sagittarius
29th	12:22 pm	Capricorn

May 2013

1st	02:20 pm	Aquarius
3rd	06:26 pm	Pisces
6th	01:04 am	Aries
8th	10:10 am	Taurus
10th	09:22 pm	Gemini
13th	09:57 am	Cancer
15th	10:38 pm	Leo
18th	09:33 am	Virgo
20th	05:08 pm	Libra
22nd	08:56 pm	Scorpio
24th	09:50 pm	Sagittarius
26th	09:29 pm	Capricorn
28th	09:49 pm	Aquarius
31st	12:31 am	Pisces

June 2013

2nd	06:34 am	Aries
4th	03:54 pm	Taurus
7th	03:33 am	Gemini
9th	04:16 pm	Cancer
12th	04:58 am	Leo
14th	04:26 pm	Virgo
17th	01:19 am	Libra
19th	06:39 am	Scorpio
21st	08:31 am	Sagittarius
23rd	08:09 am	Capricorn
25th	07:27 am	Aquarius
27th	08:33 am	Pisces
29th	01:07 pm	Aries

July 2013

1st	09:43 pm	Taurus
4th	09:22 am	Gemini
6th	10:14 pm	Cancer
9th	10:49 am	Leo
11th	10:12 pm	Virgo
14th	07:41 am	Libra
16th	02:25 pm	Scorpio
18th	05:55 pm	Sagittarius
20th	06:39 pm	Capricorn
22nd	06:07 pm	Aquarius
24th	06:23 pm	Pisces
26th	09:30 pm	Aries
29th	04:43 am	Taurus
31st	03:42 pm	Gemini

August 2013

3rd	04:30 am	Cancer
5th	04:58 pm	Leo
8th	03:57 am	Virgo
10th	01:08 pm	Libra
12th	08:18 pm	Scorpio
15th	01:05 am	Sagittarius
17th	03:26 am	Capricorn
19th	04:07 am	Aquarius
21st	04:44 am	Pisces
23rd	07:13 am	Aries
25th	01:14 pm	Taurus
27th	11:08 pm	Gemini
30th	11:33 am	Cancer

September 2013

2nd	12:01 am	Leo
4th	10:44 am	Virgo
6th	07:13 pm	Libra
9th	01:45 am	Scorpio
11th	06:36 am	Sagittarius
13th	09:56 am	Capricorn
15th	12:06 pm	Aquarius
17th	01:59 pm	Pisces
19th	04:58 pm	Aries
21st	10:34 pm	Taurus
24th	07:35 am	Gemini
26th	07:25 pm	Cancer
29th	07:58 am	Leo

October 2013

1st	06:52 pm	Virgo
4th	03:00 am	Libra
6th	08:33 am	Scorpio
8th	12:22 pm	Sagittarius
10th	03:18 pm	Capricorn
12th	06:00 pm	Aquarius
14th	09:06 pm	Pisces
17th	01:18 am	Aries
19th	07:27 am	Taurus
21st	04:15 pm	Gemini
24th	03:36 am	Cancer
26th	04:12 pm	Leo
29th	03:45 am	Virgo
31st	12:22 pm	Libra

November 2013

2nd	05:36 pm	Scorpio
4th	08:15 pm	Sagittarius
6th	09:44 pm	Capricorn
8th	11:30 pm	Aquarius
11th	02:37 am	Pisces
13th	07:40 am	Aries
15th	02:50 pm	Taurus
18th	12:07 am	Gemini
20th	11:24 am	Cancer
22nd	11:57 pm	Leo
25th	12:11 pm	Virgo
27th	10:00 pm	Libra
30th	04:03 am	Scorpio

December 2013

2nd	06:32 am	Sagittarius
4th	06:50 am	Capricorn
6th	06:54 am	Aquarius
8th	08:35 am	Pisces
10th	01:06 pm	Aries
12th	08:41 pm	Taurus
15th	06:41 am	Gemini
17th	06:17 pm	Cancer
20th	06:48 am	Leo
22nd	07:19 pm	Virgo
25th	06:18 am	Libra
27th	01:58 pm	Scorpio
29th	05:38 pm	Sagittarius
31st	06:02 pm	Capricorn

January 2014

2nd	05:04 pm	Aquarius
4th	04:59 pm	Pisces
6th	07:46 pm	Aries
9th	02:24 am	Taurus
11th	12:26 pm	Gemini
14th	12:25 am	Cancer
16th	01:01 pm	Leo
19th	01:24 am	Virgo
21st	12:44 pm	Libra
23rd	09:44 pm	Scorpio
26th	03:13 am	Sagittarius
28th	05:05 am	Capricorn
30th	04:34 am	Aquarius

February 2014

1st	03:45 am	Pisces
3rd	04:55 am	Aries
5th	09:47 am	Taurus
7th	06:44 pm	Gemini
10th	06:33 am	Cancer
12th	07:16 pm	Leo
15th	07:26 am	Virgo
17th	06:23 pm	Libra
20th	03:33 am	Scorpio
22nd	10:12 am	Sagittarius
24th	01:51 pm	Capricorn
26th	02:56 pm	Aquarius
28th	02:53 pm	Pisces

March 2014

2nd	03:40 pm	Aries
4th	07:13 pm	Taurus
7th	02:38 am	Gemini
9th	01:34 pm	Cancer
12th	02:09 am	Leo
14th	02:18 pm	Virgo
17th	12:46 am	Libra
19th	09:14 am	Scorpio
21st	03:40 pm	Sagittarius
23rd	08:04 pm	Capricorn
25th	10:39 pm	Aquarius
28th	12:11 am	Pisces
30th	01:54 am	Aries

April 2014

1st	05:21 am	Taurus
3rd	11:48 am	Gemini
5th	09:40 pm	Cancer
8th	09:51 am	Leo
10th	10:08 pm	Virgo
13th	08:34 am	Libra
15th	04:21 pm	Scorpio
17th	09:44 pm	Sagittarius
20th	01:28 am	Capricorn
22nd	04:19 am	Aquarius
24th	06:56 am	Pisces
26th	10:01 am	Aries
28th	02:24 pm	Taurus
30th	08:56 pm	Gemini

May 2014

3rd	06:14 am	Cancer
5th	05:56 pm	Leo
8th	06:25 am	Virgo
10th	05:20 pm	Libra
13th	01:08 am	Scorpio
15th	05:44 am	Sagittarius
17th	08:12 am	Capricorn
19th	09:58 am	Aquarius
21st	12:19 pm	Pisces
23rd	04:02 pm	Aries
25th	09:28 pm	Taurus
28th	04:48 am	Gemini
30th	02:14 pm	Cancer

June 2014

2nd	01:44 am	Leo
4th	02:20 pm	Virgo
7th	02:02 am	Libra
9th	10:39 am	Scorpio
11th	03:24 pm	Sagittarius
13th	05:05 pm	Capricorn
15th	05:28 pm	Aquarius
17th	06:26 pm	Pisces
19th	09:26 pm	Aries
22nd	03:04 am	Taurus
24th	11:06 am	Gemini
26th	09:06 pm	Cancer
29th	08:43 am	Leo

July 2014

1st	09:24 pm	Virgo
4th	09:44 am	Libra
6th	07:34 pm	Scorpio
9th	01:25 am	Sagittarius
11th	03:25 am	Capricorn
13th	03:07 am	Aquarius
15th	02:41 am	Pisces
17th	04:07 am	Aries
19th	08:43 am	Taurus
21st	04:37 pm	Gemini
24th	03:00 am	Cancer
26th	02:55 pm	Leo
29th	03:37 am	Virgo
31st	04:10 pm	Libra

August 2014

3rd	02:57 am	Scorpio
5th	10:19 am	Sagittarius
7th	01:39 pm	Capricorn
9th	01:53 pm	Aquarius
11th	12:56 pm	Pisces
13th	01:01 pm	Aries
15th	03:58 pm	Taurus
17th	10:42 pm	Gemini
20th	08:45 am	Cancer
22nd	08:50 pm	Leo
25th	09:33 am	Virgo
27th	09:55 pm	Libra
30th	08:53 am	Scorpio

September 2014

1st	05:17 pm	Sagittarius
3rd	10:15 pm	Capricorn
5th	11:59 pm	Aquarius
7th	11:47 pm	Pisces
9th	11:34 pm	Aries
12th	01:17 am	Taurus
14th	06:27 am	Gemini
16th	03:25 pm	Cancer
19th	03:11 am	Leo
21st	03:54 pm	Virgo
24th	04:00 am	Libra
26th	02:30 pm	Scorpio
28th	10:51 pm	Sagittarius

October 2014

1st	04:41 am	Capricorn
3rd	08:01 am	Aquarius
5th	09:25 am	Pisces
7th	10:07 am	Aries
9th	11:45 am	Taurus
11th	03:52 pm	Gemini
13th	11:31 pm	Cancer
16th	10:30 am	Leo
18th	11:08 pm	Virgo
21st	11:12 am	Libra
23rd	09:10 pm	Scorpio
26th	04:41 am	Sagittarius
28th	10:04 am	Capricorn
30th	01:53 pm	Aquarius

November 2014

1st	04:37 pm	Pisces
3rd	06:54 pm	Aries
5th	09:34 pm	Taurus
8th	01:45 am	Gemini
10th	08:39 am	Cancer
12th	06:45 pm	Leo
15th	07:09 am	Virgo
17th	07:30 pm	Libra
20th	05:32 am	Scorpio
22nd	12:20 pm	Sagittarius
24th	04:32 pm	Capricorn
26th	07:23 pm	Aquarius
28th	10:04 pm	Pisces

December 2014

1st	01:14 am	Aries
3rd	05:15 am	Taurus
5th	10:29 am	Gemini
7th	05:35 pm	Cancer
10th	03:15 am	Leo
12th	03:19 pm	Virgo
15th	04:05 am	Libra
17th	02:52 pm	Scorpio
19th	09:56 pm	Sagittarius
22nd	01:26 am	Capricorn
24th	02:53 am	Aquarius
26th	04:07 am	Pisces
28th	06:36 am	Aries
30th	10:57 am	Taurus

January 2015		
1st	05:09 pm	Gemini
4th	01:08 am	Cancer
6th	11:03 am	Leo
8th	10:58 pm	Virgo
11th	11:57 am	Libra
13th	11:45 pm	Scorpio
16th	08:01 am	Sagittarius
18th	12:05 pm	Capricorn
20th	01:00 pm	Aquarius
22nd	12:48 pm	Pisces
24th	01:32 pm	Aries
26th	04:38 pm	Taurus
28th	10:37 pm	Gemini
31st	07:09 am	Cancer

February 2015		
2nd	05:41 pm	Leo
5th	05:46 am	Virgo
7th	06:44 pm	Libra
10th	07:06 am	Scorpio
12th	04:47 pm	Sagittarius
14th	10:25 pm	Capricorn
17th	12:14 am	Aquarius
18th	11:48 pm	Pisces
20th	11:14 pm	Aries
23rd	12:29 am	Taurus
25th	04:54 am	Gemini
27th	12:50 pm	Cancer

March 2015		
1st	11:35 pm	Leo
4th	11:58 am	Virgo
7th	12:53 am	Libra
9th	01:10 pm	Scorpio
11th	11:31 pm	Sagittarius
14th	06:40 am	Capricorn
16th	10:14 am	Aquarius
18th	10:58 am	Pisces
20th	10:29 am	Aries
22nd	10:41 am	Taurus
24th	01:23 pm	Gemini
26th	07:46 pm	Cancer
29th	05:48 am	Leo
31st	06:13 pm	Virgo

April 2015		
3rd	07:08 am	Libra
5th	07:05 pm	Scorpio
8th	05:09 am	Sagittarius
10th	12:47 pm	Capricorn
12th	05:44 pm	Aquarius
14th	08:12 pm	Pisces
16th	09:00 pm	Aries
18th	09:32 pm	Taurus
20th	11:28 pm	Gemini
23rd	04:26 am	Cancer
25th	01:13 pm	Leo
28th	01:08 am	Virgo
30th	02:04 pm	Libra

May 2015		
3rd	01:48 am	Scorpio
5th	11:13 am	Sagittarius
7th	06:17 pm	Capricorn
9th	11:23 pm	Aquarius
12th	02:54 am	Pisces
14th	05:14 am	Aries
16th	07:03 am	Taurus
18th	09:28 am	Gemini
20th	01:56 pm	Cancer
22nd	09:43 pm	Leo
25th	08:52 am	Virgo
27th	09:43 pm	Libra
30th	09:34 am	Scorpio

June 2015		
1st	06:40 pm	Sagittarius
4th	12:51 am	Capricorn
6th	05:02 am	Aquarius
8th	08:17 am	Pisces
10th	11:14 am	Aries
12th	02:17 pm	Taurus
14th	05:51 pm	Gemini
16th	10:51 pm	Cancer
19th	06:23 am	Leo
21st	04:59 pm	Virgo
24th	05:41 am	Libra
26th	05:57 pm	Scorpio
29th	03:22 am	Sagittarius

July 2015		
1st	09:12 am	Capricorn
3rd	12:21 pm	Aquarius
5th	02:24 pm	Pisces
7th	04:38 pm	Aries
9th	07:50 pm	Taurus
12th	12:17 am	Gemini
14th	06:15 am	Cancer
16th	02:16 pm	Leo
19th	12:47 am	Virgo
21st	01:23 pm	Libra
24th	02:08 am	Scorpio
26th	12:25 pm	Sagittarius
28th	06:48 pm	Capricorn
30th	09:41 pm	Aquarius

August 2015		
1st	10:37 pm	Pisces
3rd	11:25 pm	Aries
6th	01:30 am	Taurus
8th	05:40 am	Gemini
10th	12:09 pm	Cancer
12th	08:53 pm	Leo
15th	07:46 am	Virgo
17th	08:23 pm	Libra
20th	09:25 am	Scorpio
22nd	08:42 pm	Sagittarius
25th	04:22 am	Capricorn
27th	08:04 am	Aquarius
29th	08:52 am	Pisces
31st	08:34 am	Aries

September 2015		
2nd	09:02 am	Taurus
4th	11:48 am	Gemini
6th	05:40 pm	Cancer
9th	02:36 am	Leo
11th	01:56 pm	Virgo
14th	02:42 am	Libra
16th	03:43 pm	Scorpio
19th	03:32 am	Sagittarius
21st	12:33 pm	Capricorn
23rd	05:52 pm	Aquarius
25th	07:44 pm	Pisces
27th	07:29 pm	Aries
29th	06:58 pm	Taurus

October 2015		
1st	08:04 pm	Gemini
4th	12:22 am	Cancer
6th	08:31 am	Leo
8th	07:51 pm	Virgo
11th	08:46 am	Libra
13th	09:39 pm	Scorpio
16th	09:19 am	Sagittarius
18th	06:53 pm	Capricorn
21st	01:38 am	Aquarius
23rd	05:18 am	Pisces
25th	06:22 am	Aries
27th	06:08 am	Taurus
29th	06:25 am	Gemini
31st	09:10 am	Cancer

November 2015		
2nd	03:48 pm	Leo
5th	02:23 am	Virgo
7th	03:15 pm	Libra
10th	04:03 am	Scorpio
12th	03:15 pm	Sagittarius
15th	12:22 am	Capricorn
17th	07:25 am	Aquarius
19th	12:22 pm	Pisces
21st	03:13 pm	Aries
23rd	04:27 pm	Taurus
25th	05:16 pm	Gemini
27th	07:27 pm	Cancer
30th	12:48 am	Leo

December 2015		
2nd	10:10 am	Virgo
4th	10:34 pm	Libra
7th	11:26 am	Scorpio
9th	10:26 pm	Sagittarius
12th	06:47 am	Capricorn
14th	12:59 pm	Aquarius
16th	05:45 pm	Pisces
18th	09:27 pm	Aries
21st	12:13 am	Taurus
23rd	02:32 am	Gemini
25th	05:27 am	Cancer
27th	10:32 am	Leo
29th	06:59 pm	Virgo

January 2016

1st	06:41 am	Libra
3rd	07:37 pm	Scorpio
6th	06:57 am	Sagittarius
8th	03:08 pm	Capricorn
10th	08:23 pm	Aquarius
12th	11:54 pm	Pisces
15th	02:49 am	Aries
17th	05:49 am	Taurus
19th	09:13 am	Gemini
21st	01:29 pm	Cancer
23rd	07:21 pm	Leo
26th	03:46 am	Virgo
28th	03:00 pm	Libra
31st	03:51 am	Scorpio

February 2016

2nd	03:50 pm	Sagittarius
5th	12:45 am	Capricorn
7th	06:00 am	Aquarius
9th	08:32 am	Pisces
11th	09:55 am	Aries
13th	11:36 am	Taurus
15th	02:35 pm	Gemini
17th	07:24 pm	Cancer
20th	02:18 am	Leo
22nd	11:25 am	Virgo
24th	10:42 pm	Libra
27th	11:27 am	Scorpio
29th	11:57 pm	Sagittarius

March 2016

3rd	10:02 am	Capricorn
5th	04:23 pm	Aquarius
7th	07:09 pm	Pisces
9th	07:41 pm	Aries
11th	07:44 pm	Taurus
13th	09:04 pm	Gemini
16th	12:57 am	Cancer
18th	07:55 am	Leo
20th	05:40 pm	Virgo
23rd	05:24 am	Libra
25th	06:10 pm	Scorpio
28th	06:47 am	Sagittarius
30th	05:45 pm	Capricorn

April 2016

2nd	01:38 am	Aquarius
4th	05:46 am	Pisces
6th	06:46 am	Aries
8th	06:11 am	Taurus
10th	05:59 am	Gemini
12th	08:07 am	Cancer
14th	01:54 pm	Leo
16th	11:23 pm	Virgo
19th	11:24 am	Libra
22nd	12:18 am	Scorpio
24th	12:47 pm	Sagittarius
26th	11:55 pm	Capricorn
29th	08:47 am	Aquarius

May 2016

1st	02:34 pm	Pisces
3rd	05:05 pm	Aries
5th	05:11 pm	Taurus
7th	04:35 pm	Gemini
9th	05:24 pm	Cancer
11th	09:33 pm	Leo
14th	05:52 am	Virgo
16th	05:33 pm	Libra
19th	06:30 am	Scorpio
21st	06:49 pm	Sagittarius
24th	05:34 am	Capricorn
26th	02:27 pm	Aquarius
28th	09:07 pm	Pisces
31st	01:10 am	Aries

June 2016

2nd	02:47 am	Taurus
4th	03:02 am	Gemini
6th	03:42 am	Cancer
8th	06:48 am	Leo
10th	01:46 pm	Virgo
13th	12:34 am	Libra
15th	01:19 pm	Scorpio
18th	01:35 am	Sagittarius
20th	11:55 am	Capricorn
22nd	08:09 pm	Aquarius
25th	02:31 am	Pisces
27th	07:08 am	Aries
29th	10:04 am	Taurus

July 2016

1st	11:45 am	Gemini
3rd	01:21 pm	Cancer
5th	04:29 pm	Leo
7th	10:42 pm	Virgo
10th	08:33 am	Libra
12th	08:53 pm	Scorpio
15th	09:15 am	Sagittarius
17th	07:33 pm	Capricorn
20th	03:11 am	Aquarius
22nd	08:36 am	Pisces
24th	12:33 pm	Aries
26th	03:38 pm	Taurus
28th	06:17 pm	Gemini
30th	09:09 pm	Cancer

August 2016

2nd	01:12 am	Leo
4th	07:34 am	Virgo
6th	04:57 pm	Libra
9th	04:52 am	Scorpio
11th	05:25 pm	Sagittarius
14th	04:12 am	Capricorn
16th	11:53 am	Aquarius
18th	04:35 pm	Pisces
20th	07:19 pm	Aries
22nd	09:20 pm	Taurus
24th	11:40 pm	Gemini
27th	03:07 am	Cancer
29th	08:12 am	Leo
31st	03:23 pm	Virgo

September 2016

3rd	12:56 am	Libra
5th	12:39 pm	Scorpio
8th	01:20 am	Sagittarius
10th	12:55 pm	Capricorn
12th	09:29 pm	Aquarius
15th	02:24 am	Pisces
17th	04:23 am	Aries
19th	04:59 am	Taurus
21st	05:54 am	Gemini
23rd	08:34 am	Cancer
25th	01:49 pm	Leo
27th	09:43 pm	Virgo
30th	07:53 am	Libra

October 2016

2nd	07:43 pm	Scorpio
5th	08:27 am	Sagittarius
7th	08:40 pm	Capricorn
10th	06:34 am	Aquarius
12th	12:44 pm	Pisces
14th	03:09 pm	Aries
16th	03:05 pm	Taurus
18th	02:30 pm	Gemini
20th	03:29 pm	Cancer
22nd	07:35 pm	Leo
25th	03:17 am	Virgo
27th	01:51 pm	Libra
30th	02:01 am	Scorpio

November 2016

1st	02:44 pm	Sagittarius
4th	03:06 am	Capricorn
6th	01:56 pm	Aquarius
8th	09:46 pm	Pisces
11th	01:45 am	Aries
13th	02:24 am	Taurus
15th	01:24 am	Gemini
17th	12:58 am	Cancer
19th	03:15 am	Leo
21st	09:35 am	Virgo
23rd	07:43 pm	Libra
26th	08:02 am	Scorpio
28th	08:46 pm	Sagittarius

December 2016

1st	08:53 am	Capricorn
3rd	07:45 pm	Aquarius
6th	04:32 am	Pisces
8th	10:16 am	Aries
10th	12:41 pm	Taurus
12th	12:42 pm	Gemini
14th	12:09 pm	Cancer
16th	01:15 pm	Leo
18th	05:52 pm	Virgo
21st	02:40 am	Libra
23rd	02:33 pm	Scorpio
26th	03:19 am	Sagittarius
28th	03:13 pm	Capricorn
31st	01:29 am	Aquarius

January 2017

2nd	09:58 am	Pisces
4th	04:20 pm	Aries
6th	08:19 pm	Taurus
8th	10:07 pm	Gemini
10th	10:49 pm	Cancer
13th	12:08 am	Leo
15th	03:53 am	Virgo
17th	11:17 am	Libra
19th	10:10 pm	Scorpio
22nd	10:46 am	Sagittarius
24th	10:44 pm	Capricorn
27th	08:37 am	Aquarius
29th	04:11 pm	Pisces
31st	09:47 pm	Aries

February 2017

3rd	01:51 am	Taurus
5th	04:45 am	Gemini
7th	07:03 am	Cancer
9th	09:42 am	Leo
11th	01:52 pm	Virgo
13th	08:43 pm	Libra
16th	06:41 am	Scorpio
18th	06:53 pm	Sagittarius
21st	07:08 am	Capricorn
23rd	05:18 pm	Aquarius
26th	12:25 am	Pisces
28th	04:52 am	Aries

March 2017

2nd	07:43 am	Taurus
4th	10:06 am	Gemini
6th	12:55 pm	Cancer
8th	04:46 pm	Leo
10th	10:08 pm	Virgo
13th	05:29 am	Libra
15th	03:11 pm	Scorpio
18th	03:00 am	Sagittarius
20th	03:32 pm	Capricorn
23rd	02:29 am	Aquarius
25th	10:07 am	Pisces
27th	02:11 pm	Aries
29th	03:48 pm	Taurus
31st	04:41 pm	Gemini

April 2017

2nd	06:28 pm	Cancer
4th	10:14 pm	Leo
7th	04:20 am	Virgo
9th	12:35 pm	Libra
11th	10:42 pm	Scorpio
14th	10:27 am	Sagittarius
16th	11:05 pm	Capricorn
19th	10:52 am	Aquarius
21st	07:43 pm	Pisces
24th	12:33 am	Aries
26th	01:57 am	Taurus
28th	01:40 am	Gemini
30th	01:49 am	Cancer

May 2017

2nd	04:13 am	Leo
4th	09:47 am	Virgo
6th	06:21 pm	Libra
9th	05:01 am	Scorpio
11th	05:00 pm	Sagittarius
14th	05:38 am	Capricorn
16th	05:50 pm	Aquarius
19th	03:53 am	Pisces
21st	10:11 am	Aries
23rd	12:33 pm	Taurus
25th	12:16 pm	Gemini
27th	11:25 am	Cancer
29th	12:13 pm	Leo
31st	04:16 pm	Virgo

June 2017

3rd	12:04 am	Libra
5th	10:47 am	Scorpio
7th	11:00 pm	Sagittarius
10th	11:37 am	Capricorn
12th	11:45 pm	Aquarius
15th	10:18 am	Pisces
17th	05:55 pm	Aries
19th	09:54 pm	Taurus
21st	10:45 pm	Gemini
23rd	10:07 pm	Cancer
25th	10:07 pm	Leo
28th	12:42 am	Virgo
30th	07:03 am	Libra

July 2017

2nd	05:00 pm	Scorpio
5th	05:09 am	Sagittarius
7th	05:45 pm	Capricorn
10th	05:35 am	Aquarius
12th	03:52 pm	Pisces
14th	11:53 pm	Aries
17th	05:05 am	Taurus
19th	07:32 am	Gemini
21st	08:10 am	Cancer
23rd	08:34 am	Leo
25th	10:33 am	Virgo
27th	03:38 pm	Libra
30th	12:24 am	Scorpio

August 2017

1st	12:02 pm	Sagittarius
4th	12:37 am	Capricorn
6th	12:16 pm	Aquarius
8th	09:56 pm	Pisces
11th	05:23 am	Aries
13th	10:40 am	Taurus
15th	02:07 pm	Gemini
17th	04:14 pm	Cancer
19th	05:55 pm	Leo
21st	08:26 pm	Virgo
24th	01:05 am	Libra
26th	08:53 am	Scorpio
28th	07:48 pm	Sagittarius
31st	08:19 am	Capricorn

September 2017

2nd	08:07 pm	Aquarius
5th	05:29 am	Pisces
7th	12:02 pm	Aries
9th	04:23 pm	Taurus
11th	07:30 pm	Gemini
13th	10:13 pm	Cancer
16th	01:09 am	Leo
18th	04:53 am	Virgo
20th	10:07 am	Libra
22nd	05:41 pm	Scorpio
25th	04:01 am	Sagittarius
27th	04:25 pm	Capricorn
30th	04:41 am	Aquarius

October 2017

2nd	02:27 pm	Pisces
4th	08:40 pm	Aries
6th	11:57 pm	Taurus
9th	01:45 am	Gemini
11th	03:39 am	Cancer
13th	06:42 am	Leo
15th	11:19 am	Virgo
17th	05:36 pm	Libra
20th	01:41 am	Scorpio
22nd	11:57 am	Sagittarius
25th	12:13 am	Capricorn
27th	12:59 pm	Aquarius
29th	11:47 pm	Pisces

November 2017

1st	06:43 am	Aries
3rd	09:47 am	Taurus
5th	10:27 am	Gemini
7th	10:45 am	Cancer
9th	12:30 pm	Leo
11th	04:42 pm	Virgo
13th	11:27 pm	Libra
16th	08:19 am	Scorpio
18th	07:00 pm	Sagittarius
21st	07:15 am	Capricorn
23rd	08:15 pm	Aquarius
26th	08:05 am	Pisces
28th	04:31 pm	Aries
30th	08:39 pm	Taurus

December 2017

2nd	09:22 pm	Gemini
4th	08:37 pm	Cancer
6th	08:38 pm	Leo
8th	11:09 pm	Virgo
11th	05:02 am	Libra
13th	01:59 pm	Scorpio
16th	01:08 am	Sagittarius
18th	01:34 pm	Capricorn
21st	02:30 am	Aquarius
23rd	02:42 pm	Pisces
26th	12:27 am	Aries
28th	06:24 am	Taurus
30th	08:31 am	Gemini

January 2018

1st	08:11 am	Cancer
3rd	07:23 am	Leo
5th	08:13 am	Virgo
7th	12:15 pm	Libra
9th	08:06 pm	Scorpio
12th	07:05 am	Sagittarius
14th	07:43 pm	Capricorn
17th	08:33 am	Aquarius
19th	08:27 pm	Pisces
22nd	06:28 am	Aries
24th	01:40 pm	Taurus
26th	05:40 pm	Gemini
28th	06:58 pm	Cancer
30th	06:53 pm	Leo

February 2018

1st	07:14 pm	Virgo
3rd	09:48 pm	Libra
6th	03:57 am	Scorpio
8th	01:54 pm	Sagittarius
11th	02:22 am	Capricorn
13th	03:12 pm	Aquarius
16th	02:42 am	Pisces
18th	12:05 pm	Aries
20th	07:12 pm	Taurus
23rd	12:08 am	Gemini
25th	03:07 am	Cancer
27th	04:42 am	Leo

March 2018

1st	05:58 am	Virgo
3rd	08:21 am	Libra
5th	01:24 pm	Scorpio
7th	10:03 pm	Sagittarius
10th	09:53 am	Capricorn
12th	10:45 pm	Aquarius
15th	10:13 am	Pisces
17th	06:58 pm	Aries
20th	01:07 am	Taurus
22nd	05:30 am	Gemini
24th	08:53 am	Cancer
26th	11:45 am	Leo
28th	02:31 pm	Virgo
30th	05:53 pm	Libra

April 2018

1st	10:58 pm	Scorpio
4th	06:56 am	Sagittarius
6th	06:02 pm	Capricorn
9th	06:51 am	Aquarius
11th	06:41 pm	Pisces
14th	03:26 am	Aries
16th	08:52 am	Taurus
18th	12:03 pm	Gemini
20th	02:27 pm	Cancer
22nd	05:10 pm	Leo
24th	08:41 pm	Virgo
27th	01:13 am	Libra
29th	07:12 am	Scorpio

May 2018

1st	03:20 pm	Sagittarius
4th	02:07 am	Capricorn
6th	02:49 pm	Aquarius
9th	03:11 am	Pisces
11th	12:41 pm	Aries
13th	06:16 pm	Taurus
15th	08:44 pm	Gemini
17th	09:48 pm	Cancer
19th	11:11 pm	Leo
22nd	02:03 am	Virgo
24th	06:52 am	Libra
26th	01:40 pm	Scorpio
28th	10:30 pm	Sagittarius
31st	09:27 am	Capricorn

June 2018

2nd	10:07 pm	Aquarius
5th	10:54 am	Pisces
7th	09:26 pm	Aries
10th	04:04 am	Taurus
12th	06:53 am	Gemini
14th	07:20 am	Cancer
16th	07:21 am	Leo
18th	08:41 am	Virgo
20th	12:30 pm	Libra
22nd	07:11 pm	Scorpio
25th	04:30 am	Sagittarius
27th	03:53 pm	Capricorn
30th	04:37 am	Aquarius

July 2018

2nd	05:32 pm	Pisces
5th	04:50 am	Aries
7th	12:51 pm	Taurus
9th	04:59 pm	Gemini
11th	05:59 pm	Cancer
13th	05:32 pm	Leo
15th	05:31 pm	Virgo
17th	07:43 pm	Libra
20th	01:14 am	Scorpio
22nd	10:13 am	Sagittarius
24th	09:49 pm	Capricorn
27th	10:41 am	Aquarius
29th	11:28 pm	Pisces

August 2018

1st	10:55 am	Aries
3rd	07:52 pm	Taurus
6th	01:32 am	Gemini
8th	04:01 am	Cancer
10th	04:18 am	Leo
12th	04:00 am	Virgo
14th	04:58 am	Libra
16th	08:55 am	Scorpio
18th	04:46 pm	Sagittarius
21st	04:01 am	Capricorn
23rd	04:56 pm	Aquarius
26th	05:33 am	Pisces
28th	04:36 pm	Aries
31st	01:31 am	Taurus

September 2018

2nd	08:02 am	Gemini
4th	12:04 pm	Cancer
6th	01:55 pm	Leo
8th	02:30 pm	Virgo
10th	03:20 pm	Libra
12th	06:16 pm	Scorpio
15th	12:46 am	Sagittarius
17th	11:08 am	Capricorn
19th	11:52 pm	Aquarius
22nd	12:28 pm	Pisces
24th	11:04 pm	Aries
27th	07:16 am	Taurus
29th	01:27 pm	Gemini

October 2018

1st	06:01 pm	Cancer
3rd	09:13 pm	Leo
5th	11:20 pm	Virgo
8th	01:11 am	Libra
10th	04:10 am	Scorpio
12th	09:54 am	Sagittarius
14th	07:17 pm	Capricorn
17th	07:36 am	Aquarius
19th	08:21 pm	Pisces
22nd	06:59 am	Aries
24th	02:34 pm	Taurus
26th	07:41 pm	Gemini
28th	11:28 pm	Cancer
31st	02:43 am	Leo

November 2018

2nd	05:48 am	Virgo
4th	09:02 am	Libra
6th	01:03 pm	Scorpio
8th	07:00 pm	Sagittarius
11th	03:55 am	Capricorn
13th	03:46 pm	Aquarius
16th	04:42 am	Pisces
18th	03:56 pm	Aries
20th	11:43 pm	Taurus
23rd	04:11 am	Gemini
25th	06:38 am	Cancer
27th	08:36 am	Leo
29th	11:08 am	Virgo

December 2018

1st	02:49 pm	Libra
3rd	07:55 pm	Scorpio
6th	02:49 am	Sagittarius
8th	12:02 pm	Capricorn
10th	11:40 pm	Aquarius
13th	12:40 pm	Pisces
16th	12:45 am	Aries
18th	09:38 am	Taurus
20th	02:35 pm	Gemini
22nd	04:29 pm	Cancer
24th	04:59 pm	Leo
26th	05:50 pm	Virgo
28th	08:24 pm	Libra
31st	01:24 am	Scorpio

January 2019

2nd	08:59 am	Sagittarius
4th	06:55 pm	Capricorn
7th	06:47 am	Aquarius
9th	07:44 pm	Pisces
12th	08:18 am	Aries
14th	06:32 pm	Taurus
17th	01:01 am	Gemini
19th	03:44 am	Cancer
21st	03:55 am	Leo
23rd	03:23 am	Virgo
25th	04:03 am	Libra
27th	07:31 am	Scorpio
29th	02:33 pm	Sagittarius

February 2019

1st	12:48 am	Capricorn
3rd	01:04 pm	Aquarius
6th	02:03 am	Pisces
8th	02:35 pm	Aries
11th	01:29 am	Taurus
13th	09:33 am	Gemini
15th	02:03 pm	Cancer
17th	03:22 pm	Leo
19th	02:48 pm	Virgo
21st	02:18 pm	Libra
23rd	03:57 pm	Scorpio
25th	09:20 pm	Sagittarius
28th	06:49 am	Capricorn

March 2019

2nd	07:07 pm	Aquarius
5th	08:11 am	Pisces
7th	08:28 pm	Aries
10th	07:10 am	Taurus
12th	03:49 pm	Gemini
14th	09:50 pm	Cancer
17th	12:57 am	Leo
19th	01:42 am	Virgo
21st	01:29 am	Libra
23rd	02:17 am	Scorpio
25th	06:07 am	Sagittarius
27th	02:08 pm	Capricorn
30th	01:46 am	Aquarius

April 2019

1st	02:49 pm	Pisces
4th	02:57 am	Aries
6th	01:07 pm	Taurus
8th	09:16 pm	Gemini
11th	03:32 am	Cancer
13th	07:51 am	Leo
15th	10:14 am	Virgo
17th	11:23 am	Libra
19th	12:41 pm	Scorpio
21st	04:00 pm	Sagittarius
23rd	10:51 pm	Capricorn
26th	09:28 am	Aquarius
28th	10:12 pm	Pisces

May 2019

1st	10:25 am	Aries
3rd	08:19 pm	Taurus
6th	03:41 am	Gemini
8th	09:07 am	Cancer
10th	01:14 pm	Leo
12th	04:22 pm	Virgo
14th	06:51 pm	Libra
16th	09:26 pm	Scorpio
19th	01:22 am	Sagittarius
21st	07:57 am	Capricorn
23rd	05:50 pm	Aquarius
26th	06:08 am	Pisces
28th	06:32 pm	Aries
31st	04:44 am	Taurus

June 2019

2nd	11:48 am	Gemini
4th	04:18 pm	Cancer
6th	07:16 pm	Leo
8th	09:46 pm	Virgo
11th	12:30 am	Libra
13th	04:03 am	Scorpio
15th	09:04 am	Sagittarius
17th	04:14 pm	Capricorn
20th	02:01 am	Aquarius
22nd	02:02 pm	Pisces
25th	02:38 am	Aries
27th	01:32 pm	Taurus
29th	09:10 pm	Gemini

July 2019

2nd	01:24 am	Cancer
4th	03:20 am	Leo
6th	04:26 am	Virgo
8th	06:08 am	Libra
10th	09:29 am	Scorpio
12th	03:06 pm	Sagittarius
14th	11:05 pm	Capricorn
17th	09:19 am	Aquarius
19th	09:20 pm	Pisces
22nd	10:03 am	Aries
24th	09:43 pm	Taurus
27th	06:30 am	Gemini
29th	11:31 am	Cancer
31st	01:19 pm	Leo

August 2019

2nd	01:21 pm	Virgo
4th	01:30 pm	Libra
6th	03:32 pm	Scorpio
8th	08:35 pm	Sagittarius
11th	04:51 am	Capricorn
13th	03:36 pm	Aquarius
16th	03:50 am	Pisces
18th	04:33 pm	Aries
21st	04:38 am	Taurus
23rd	02:35 pm	Gemini
25th	09:06 pm	Cancer
27th	11:54 pm	Leo
29th	11:58 pm	Virgo
31st	11:09 pm	Libra

September 2019

2nd	11:35 pm	Scorpio
5th	03:09 am	Sagittarius
7th	10:38 am	Capricorn
9th	09:24 pm	Aquarius
12th	09:52 am	Pisces
14th	10:33 pm	Aries
17th	10:32 am	Taurus
19th	08:58 pm	Gemini
22nd	04:51 am	Cancer
24th	09:20 am	Leo
26th	10:37 am	Virgo
28th	10:04 am	Libra
30th	09:42 am	Scorpio

October 2019

2nd	11:45 am	Sagittarius
4th	05:44 pm	Capricorn
7th	03:43 am	Aquarius
9th	04:06 pm	Pisces
12th	04:46 am	Aries
14th	04:24 pm	Taurus
17th	02:31 am	Gemini
19th	10:43 am	Cancer
21st	04:29 pm	Leo
23rd	07:30 pm	Virgo
25th	08:20 pm	Libra
27th	08:30 pm	Scorpio
29th	09:59 pm	Sagittarius

November 2019

1st	02:39 am	Capricorn
3rd	11:20 am	Aquarius
5th	11:09 pm	Pisces
8th	11:49 am	Aries
10th	11:19 pm	Taurus
13th	08:46 am	Gemini
15th	04:16 pm	Cancer
17th	09:58 pm	Leo
20th	01:55 am	Virgo
22nd	04:20 am	Libra
24th	05:59 am	Scorpio
26th	08:12 am	Sagittarius
28th	12:33 pm	Capricorn
30th	08:14 pm	Aquarius

December 2019

3rd	07:11 am	Pisces
5th	07:45 pm	Aries
8th	07:30 am	Taurus
10th	04:48 pm	Gemini
12th	11:24 pm	Cancer
15th	03:57 am	Leo
17th	07:17 am	Virgo
19th	10:05 am	Libra
21st	12:58 pm	Scorpio
23rd	04:35 pm	Sagittarius
25th	09:46 pm	Capricorn
28th	05:21 am	Aquarius
30th	03:42 pm	Pisces

January 2020

2nd	04:01 am	Aries
4th	04:16 pm	Taurus
7th	02:12 am	Gemini
9th	08:44 am	Cancer
11th	12:17 pm	Leo
13th	02:07 pm	Virgo
15th	03:44 pm	Libra
17th	06:21 pm	Scorpio
19th	10:42 pm	Sagittarius
22nd	05:01 am	Capricorn
24th	01:21 pm	Aquarius
26th	11:44 pm	Pisces
29th	11:51 am	Aries

February 2020

1st	12:28 am	Taurus
3rd	11:30 am	Gemini
5th	07:04 pm	Cancer
7th	10:45 pm	Leo
9th	11:39 pm	Virgo
11th	11:38 pm	Libra
14th	12:38 am	Scorpio
16th	04:07 am	Sagittarius
18th	10:37 am	Capricorn
20th	07:42 pm	Aquarius
23rd	06:38 am	Pisces
25th	06:48 pm	Aries
28th	07:30 am	Taurus

March 2020

1st	07:21 pm	Gemini
4th	04:26 am	Cancer
6th	09:28 am	Leo
8th	10:48 am	Virgo
10th	10:04 am	Libra
12th	09:29 am	Scorpio
14th	11:10 am	Sagittarius
16th	04:26 pm	Capricorn
19th	01:17 am	Aquarius
21st	12:34 pm	Pisces
24th	12:59 am	Aries
26th	01:37 pm	Taurus
29th	01:39 am	Gemini
31st	11:44 am	Cancer

April 2020

2nd	06:27 pm	Leo
4th	09:19 pm	Virgo
6th	09:17 pm	Libra
8th	08:17 pm	Scorpio
10th	08:36 pm	Sagittarius
13th	12:06 am	Capricorn
15th	07:38 am	Aquarius
17th	06:30 pm	Pisces
20th	07:01 am	Aries
22nd	07:37 pm	Taurus
25th	07:21 am	Gemini
27th	05:28 pm	Cancer
30th	01:07 am	Leo

May 2020

2nd	05:36 am	Virgo
4th	07:10 am	Libra
6th	07:05 am	Scorpio
8th	07:16 am	Sagittarius
10th	09:39 am	Capricorn
12th	03:39 pm	Aquarius
15th	01:25 am	Pisces
17th	01:36 pm	Aries
20th	02:11 am	Taurus
22nd	01:36 pm	Gemini
24th	11:09 pm	Cancer
27th	06:34 am	Leo
29th	11:41 am	Virgo
31st	02:38 pm	Libra

June 2020

2nd	04:06 pm	Scorpio
4th	05:18 pm	Sagittarius
6th	07:45 pm	Capricorn
9th	12:55 am	Aquarius
11th	09:32 am	Pisces
13th	09:04 pm	Aries
16th	09:36 am	Taurus
18th	09:01 pm	Gemini
21st	06:02 am	Cancer
23rd	12:34 pm	Leo
25th	05:05 pm	Virgo
27th	08:17 pm	Libra
29th	10:48 pm	Scorpio

July 2020

2nd	01:22 am	Sagittarius
4th	04:49 am	Capricorn
6th	10:09 am	Aquarius
8th	06:13 pm	Pisces
11th	05:07 am	Aries
13th	05:35 pm	Taurus
16th	05:20 am	Gemini
18th	02:25 pm	Cancer
20th	08:17 pm	Leo
22nd	11:41 pm	Virgo
25th	01:54 am	Libra
27th	04:13 am	Scorpio
29th	07:25 am	Sagittarius
31st	11:59 am	Capricorn

August 2020

2nd	06:12 pm	Aquarius
5th	02:28 am	Pisces
7th	01:05 pm	Aries
10th	01:29 am	Taurus
12th	01:47 pm	Gemini
14th	11:36 pm	Cancer
17th	05:39 am	Leo
19th	08:21 am	Virgo
21st	09:16 am	Libra
23rd	10:17 am	Scorpio
25th	12:50 pm	Sagittarius
27th	05:37 pm	Capricorn
30th	12:38 am	Aquarius

September 2020

1st	09:35 am	Pisces
3rd	08:23 pm	Aries
6th	08:44 am	Taurus
8th	09:28 pm	Gemini
11th	08:23 am	Cancer
13th	03:33 pm	Leo
15th	06:38 pm	Virgo
17th	06:56 pm	Libra
19th	06:33 pm	Scorpio
21st	07:32 pm	Sagittarius
23rd	11:17 pm	Capricorn
26th	06:09 am	Aquarius
28th	03:34 pm	Pisces

October 2020

1st	02:48 am	Aries
3rd	03:13 pm	Taurus
6th	04:03 am	Gemini
8th	03:46 pm	Cancer
11th	12:25 am	Leo
13th	04:56 am	Virgo
15th	05:54 am	Libra
17th	05:06 am	Scorpio
19th	04:43 am	Sagittarius
21st	06:44 am	Capricorn
23rd	12:17 pm	Aquarius
25th	09:19 pm	Pisces
28th	08:45 am	Aries
30th	09:20 pm	Taurus

November 2020

2nd	10:00 am	Gemini
4th	09:46 pm	Cancer
7th	07:19 am	Leo
9th	01:30 pm	Virgo
11th	04:10 pm	Libra
13th	04:19 pm	Scorpio
15th	03:47 pm	Sagittarius
17th	04:35 pm	Capricorn
19th	08:25 pm	Aquarius
22nd	04:06 am	Pisces
24th	03:05 pm	Aries
27th	03:44 am	Taurus
29th	04:17 pm	Gemini

December 2020

2nd	03:34 am	Cancer
4th	12:53 pm	Leo
6th	07:47 pm	Virgo
9th	12:02 am	Libra
11th	01:59 am	Scorpio
13th	02:40 am	Sagittarius
15th	03:35 am	Capricorn
17th	06:28 am	Aquarius
19th	12:40 pm	Pisces
21st	10:33 pm	Aries
24th	10:56 am	Taurus
26th	11:33 pm	Gemini
29th	10:29 am	Cancer
31st	06:59 pm	Leo

January 2021		
3rd	01:13 am	Virgo
5th	05:43 am	Libra
7th	08:54 am	Scorpio
9th	11:16 am	Sagittarius
11th	01:30 pm	Capricorn
13th	04:45 pm	Aquarius
15th	10:18 pm	Pisces
18th	07:08 am	Aries
20th	06:57 pm	Taurus
23rd	07:44 am	Gemini
25th	06:52 pm	Cancer
28th	02:55 am	Leo
30th	08:03 am	Virgo

February 2021		
1st	11:26 am	Libra
3rd	02:15 pm	Scorpio
5th	05:17 pm	Sagittarius
7th	08:52 pm	Capricorn
10th	01:21 am	Aquarius
12th	07:24 am	Pisces
14th	03:55 pm	Aries
17th	03:12 am	Taurus
19th	04:04 pm	Gemini
22nd	03:53 am	Cancer
24th	12:23 pm	Leo
26th	05:08 pm	Virgo
28th	07:18 pm	Libra

March 2021		
2nd	08:39 pm	Scorpio
4th	10:43 pm	Sagittarius
7th	02:21 am	Capricorn
9th	07:42 am	Aquarius
11th	02:45 pm	Pisces
13th	11:45 pm	Aries
16th	10:57 am	Taurus
18th	11:48 pm	Gemini
21st	12:18 pm	Cancer
23rd	09:57 pm	Leo
26th	03:26 am	Virgo
28th	05:23 am	Libra
30th	05:34 am	Scorpio

April 2021		
1st	05:59 am	Sagittarius
3rd	08:14 am	Capricorn
5th	01:04 pm	Aquarius
7th	08:31 pm	Pisces
10th	06:12 am	Aries
12th	05:44 pm	Taurus
15th	06:36 am	Gemini
17th	07:26 pm	Cancer
20th	06:11 am	Leo
22nd	01:09 pm	Virgo
24th	04:07 pm	Libra
26th	04:19 pm	Scorpio
28th	03:43 pm	Sagittarius
30th	04:17 pm	Capricorn

May 2021		
2nd	07:32 pm	Aquarius
5th	02:09 am	Pisces
7th	11:53 am	Aries
9th	11:47 pm	Taurus
12th	12:44 pm	Gemini
15th	01:31 am	Cancer
17th	12:45 pm	Leo
19th	09:00 pm	Virgo
22nd	01:36 am	Libra
24th	03:01 am	Scorpio
26th	02:40 am	Sagittarius
28th	02:24 am	Capricorn
30th	04:05 am	Aquarius

June 2021		
1st	09:08 am	Pisces
3rd	05:59 pm	Aries
6th	05:47 am	Taurus
8th	06:48 pm	Gemini
11th	07:23 am	Cancer
13th	06:23 pm	Leo
16th	03:03 am	Virgo
18th	08:54 am	Libra
20th	11:59 am	Scorpio
22nd	12:56 pm	Sagittarius
24th	01:05 pm	Capricorn
26th	02:09 pm	Aquarius
28th	05:51 pm	Pisces

July 2021		
1st	01:22 am	Aries
3rd	12:28 pm	Taurus
6th	01:24 am	Gemini
8th	01:52 pm	Cancer
11th	12:21 am	Leo
13th	08:31 am	Virgo
15th	02:32 pm	Libra
17th	06:39 pm	Scorpio
19th	09:08 pm	Sagittarius
21st	10:37 pm	Capricorn
24th	12:13 am	Aquarius
26th	03:30 am	Pisces
28th	09:58 am	Aries
30th	08:09 pm	Taurus

August 2021		
2nd	08:47 am	Gemini
4th	09:18 pm	Cancer
7th	07:32 am	Leo
9th	02:56 pm	Virgo
11th	08:08 pm	Libra
14th	12:02 am	Scorpio
16th	03:12 am	Sagittarius
18th	05:59 am	Capricorn
20th	08:49 am	Aquarius
22nd	12:43 pm	Pisces
24th	06:57 pm	Aries
27th	04:27 am	Taurus
29th	04:42 pm	Gemini

September 2021		
1st	05:26 am	Cancer
3rd	03:59 pm	Leo
5th	11:06 pm	Virgo
8th	03:21 am	Libra
10th	06:05 am	Scorpio
12th	08:35 am	Sagittarius
14th	11:35 am	Capricorn
16th	03:24 pm	Aquarius
18th	08:23 pm	Pisces
21st	03:13 am	Aries
23rd	12:39 pm	Taurus
26th	12:37 am	Gemini
28th	01:35 pm	Cancer

October 2021		
1st	12:54 am	Leo
3rd	08:38 am	Virgo
5th	12:42 pm	Libra
7th	02:23 pm	Scorpio
9th	03:25 pm	Sagittarius
11th	05:16 pm	Capricorn
13th	08:48 pm	Aquarius
16th	02:22 am	Pisces
18th	10:05 am	Aries
20th	08:00 pm	Taurus
23rd	07:58 am	Gemini
25th	09:01 pm	Cancer
28th	09:08 am	Leo
30th	06:10 pm	Virgo

November 2021		
1st	11:12 pm	Libra
4th	12:53 am	Scorpio
6th	12:53 am	Sagittarius
8th	01:04 am	Capricorn
10th	03:04 am	Aquarius
12th	07:54 am	Pisces
14th	03:49 pm	Aries
17th	02:18 am	Taurus
19th	02:33 pm	Gemini
22nd	03:34 am	Cancer
24th	03:59 pm	Leo
27th	02:12 am	Virgo
29th	08:55 am	Libra

December 2021		
1st	11:56 am	Scorpio
3rd	12:13 pm	Sagittarius
5th	11:31 am	Capricorn
7th	11:49 am	Aquarius
9th	02:54 pm	Pisces
11th	09:47 pm	Aries
14th	08:11 am	Taurus
16th	08:43 pm	Gemini
19th	09:42 am	Cancer
21st	09:54 pm	Leo
24th	08:25 am	Virgo
26th	04:25 pm	Libra
28th	09:17 pm	Scorpio
30th	11:09 pm	Sagittarius

January 2022

1st	11:03 pm	Capricorn
3rd	10:44 pm	Aquarius
6th	12:17 am	Pisces
8th	05:27 am	Aries
10th	02:48 pm	Taurus
13th	03:09 am	Gemini
15th	04:11 pm	Cancer
18th	04:04 am	Leo
20th	02:03 pm	Virgo
22nd	10:03 pm	Libra
25th	03:58 am	Scorpio
27th	07:35 am	Sagittarius
29th	09:10 am	Capricorn
31st	09:43 am	Aquarius

February 2022

2nd	11:00 am	Pisces
4th	02:57 pm	Aries
6th	10:53 pm	Taurus
9th	10:27 am	Gemini
11th	11:27 pm	Cancer
14th	11:18 am	Leo
16th	08:43 pm	Virgo
19th	03:52 am	Libra
21st	09:20 am	Scorpio
23rd	01:30 pm	Sagittarius
25th	04:28 pm	Capricorn
27th	06:36 pm	Aquarius

March 2022

1st	08:54 pm	Pisces
4th	12:53 am	Aries
6th	08:00 am	Taurus
8th	06:40 pm	Gemini
11th	07:25 am	Cancer
13th	07:32 pm	Leo
16th	04:59 am	Virgo
18th	11:27 am	Libra
20th	03:45 pm	Scorpio
22nd	07:00 pm	Sagittarius
24th	09:55 pm	Capricorn
27th	12:56 am	Aquarius
29th	04:32 am	Pisces
31st	09:31 am	Aries

April 2022

2nd	04:51 pm	Taurus
5th	03:05 am	Gemini
7th	03:31 pm	Cancer
10th	04:00 am	Leo
12th	02:08 pm	Virgo
14th	08:46 pm	Libra
17th	12:23 am	Scorpio
19th	02:17 am	Sagittarius
21st	03:53 am	Capricorn
23rd	06:18 am	Aquarius
25th	10:15 am	Pisces
27th	04:10 pm	Aries
30th	12:20 am	Taurus

May 2022

2nd	10:47 am	Gemini
4th	11:06 pm	Cancer
7th	11:50 am	Leo
9th	10:54 pm	Virgo
12th	06:35 am	Libra
14th	10:34 am	Scorpio
16th	11:51 am	Sagittarius
18th	12:03 pm	Capricorn
20th	12:53 pm	Aquarius
22nd	03:50 pm	Pisces
24th	09:40 pm	Aries
27th	06:23 am	Taurus
29th	05:23 pm	Gemini

June 2022

1st	05:50 am	Cancer
3rd	06:39 pm	Leo
6th	06:22 am	Virgo
8th	03:23 pm	Libra
10th	08:42 pm	Scorpio
12th	10:32 pm	Sagittarius
14th	10:15 pm	Capricorn
16th	09:45 pm	Aquarius
18th	11:02 pm	Pisces
21st	03:38 am	Aries
23rd	11:58 am	Taurus
25th	11:14 pm	Gemini
28th	11:54 am	Cancer

July 2022

1st	12:40 am	Leo
3rd	12:32 pm	Virgo
5th	10:25 pm	Libra
8th	05:16 am	Scorpio
10th	08:35 am	Sagittarius
12th	09:02 am	Capricorn
14th	08:14 am	Aquarius
16th	08:19 am	Pisces
18th	11:18 am	Aries
20th	06:23 pm	Taurus
23rd	05:11 am	Gemini
25th	05:54 pm	Cancer
28th	06:37 am	Leo
30th	06:11 pm	Virgo

August 2022

2nd	04:06 am	Libra
4th	11:47 am	Scorpio
6th	04:39 pm	Sagittarius
8th	06:39 pm	Capricorn
10th	06:46 pm	Aquarius
12th	06:45 pm	Pisces
14th	08:43 pm	Aries
17th	02:23 am	Taurus
19th	12:07 pm	Gemini
22nd	12:30 am	Cancer
24th	01:10 pm	Leo
27th	12:25 am	Virgo
29th	09:45 am	Libra
31st	05:12 pm	Scorpio

September 2022

2nd	10:40 pm	Sagittarius
5th	02:03 am	Capricorn
7th	03:42 am	Aquarius
9th	04:43 am	Pisces
11th	06:48 am	Aries
13th	11:40 am	Taurus
15th	08:17 pm	Gemini
18th	08:00 am	Cancer
20th	08:38 pm	Leo
23rd	07:54 am	Virgo
25th	04:43 pm	Libra
27th	11:15 pm	Scorpio
30th	04:04 am	Sagittarius

October 2022

2nd	07:38 am	Capricorn
4th	10:21 am	Aquarius
6th	12:48 pm	Pisces
8th	03:57 pm	Aries
10th	09:04 pm	Taurus
13th	05:09 am	Gemini
15th	04:11 pm	Cancer
18th	04:45 am	Leo
20th	04:26 pm	Virgo
23rd	01:25 am	Libra
25th	07:19 am	Scorpio
27th	10:55 am	Sagittarius
29th	01:22 pm	Capricorn
31st	03:43 pm	Aquarius

November 2022

2nd	06:47 pm	Pisces
4th	11:08 pm	Aries
7th	05:15 am	Taurus
9th	01:38 pm	Gemini
12th	12:23 am	Cancer
14th	12:48 pm	Leo
17th	01:04 am	Virgo
19th	10:58 am	Libra
21st	05:17 pm	Scorpio
23rd	08:16 pm	Sagittarius
25th	09:19 pm	Capricorn
27th	10:08 pm	Aquarius
30th	12:16 am	Pisces

December 2022

2nd	04:42 am	Aries
4th	11:39 am	Taurus
6th	08:49 pm	Gemini
9th	07:49 am	Cancer
11th	08:09 pm	Leo
14th	08:46 am	Virgo
16th	07:50 pm	Libra
19th	03:31 am	Scorpio
21st	07:13 am	Sagittarius
23rd	07:50 am	Capricorn
25th	07:14 am	Aquarius
27th	07:34 am	Pisces
29th	10:37 am	Aries
31st	05:09 pm	Taurus

January 2023

3rd	02:45 am	Gemini
5th	02:15 pm	Cancer
8th	02:41 am	Leo
10th	03:16 pm	Virgo
13th	02:57 am	Libra
15th	12:09 pm	Scorpio
17th	05:34 pm	Sagittarius
19th	07:12 pm	Capricorn
21st	06:29 pm	Aquarius
23rd	05:36 pm	Pisces
25th	06:49 pm	Aries
27th	11:43 pm	Taurus
30th	08:35 am	Gemini

February 2023

1st	08:12 pm	Cancer
4th	08:49 am	Leo
6th	09:15 pm	Virgo
9th	08:47 am	Libra
11th	06:35 pm	Scorpio
14th	01:32 am	Sagittarius
16th	05:00 am	Capricorn
18th	05:35 am	Aquarius
20th	04:57 am	Pisces
22nd	05:14 am	Aries
24th	08:30 am	Taurus
26th	03:48 pm	Gemini

March 2023

1st	02:41 am	Cancer
3rd	03:16 pm	Leo
6th	03:39 am	Virgo
8th	02:45 pm	Libra
11th	12:06 am	Scorpio
13th	07:21 am	Sagittarius
15th	12:06 pm	Capricorn
17th	02:26 pm	Aquarius
19th	03:13 pm	Pisces
21st	04:02 pm	Aries
23rd	06:43 pm	Taurus
26th	12:42 am	Gemini
28th	10:23 am	Cancer
30th	10:32 pm	Leo

April 2023

2nd	10:58 am	Virgo
4th	09:52 pm	Libra
7th	06:30 am	Scorpio
9th	12:57 pm	Sagittarius
11th	05:34 pm	Capricorn
13th	08:43 pm	Aquarius
15th	10:57 pm	Pisces
18th	01:10 am	Aries
20th	04:30 am	Taurus
22nd	10:12 am	Gemini
24th	06:59 pm	Cancer
27th	06:30 am	Leo
29th	07:00 pm	Virgo

May 2023

2nd	06:10 am	Libra
4th	02:33 pm	Scorpio
6th	08:05 pm	Sagittarius
8th	11:34 pm	Capricorn
11th	02:06 am	Aquarius
13th	04:40 am	Pisces
15th	07:56 am	Aries
17th	12:28 pm	Taurus
19th	06:48 pm	Gemini
22nd	03:29 am	Cancer
24th	02:35 pm	Leo
27th	03:06 am	Virgo
29th	02:51 pm	Libra
31st	11:46 pm	Scorpio

June 2023

3rd	05:04 am	Sagittarius
5th	07:32 am	Capricorn
7th	08:42 am	Aquarius
9th	10:15 am	Pisces
11th	01:21 pm	Aries
13th	06:32 pm	Taurus
16th	01:46 am	Gemini
18th	10:58 am	Cancer
20th	10:05 pm	Leo
23rd	10:36 am	Virgo
25th	10:58 pm	Libra
28th	08:56 am	Scorpio
30th	03:00 pm	Sagittarius

July 2023

2nd	05:21 pm	Capricorn
4th	05:31 pm	Aquarius
6th	05:33 pm	Pisces
8th	07:20 pm	Aries
10th	11:56 pm	Taurus
13th	07:27 am	Gemini
15th	05:14 pm	Cancer
18th	04:40 am	Leo
20th	05:13 pm	Virgo
23rd	05:55 am	Libra
25th	04:56 pm	Scorpio
28th	12:25 am	Sagittarius
30th	03:45 am	Capricorn

August 2023

1st	03:58 am	Aquarius
3rd	03:06 am	Pisces
5th	03:20 am	Aries
7th	06:25 am	Taurus
9th	01:06 pm	Gemini
11th	10:53 pm	Cancer
14th	10:37 am	Leo
16th	11:15 pm	Virgo
19th	11:54 am	Libra
21st	11:23 pm	Scorpio
24th	08:08 am	Sagittarius
26th	01:06 pm	Capricorn
28th	02:32 pm	Aquarius
30th	01:57 pm	Pisces

September 2023

1st	01:25 pm	Aries
3rd	03:00 pm	Taurus
5th	08:07 pm	Gemini
8th	05:00 am	Cancer
10th	04:37 pm	Leo
13th	05:19 am	Virgo
15th	05:45 pm	Libra
18th	04:59 am	Scorpio
20th	02:07 pm	Sagittarius
22nd	08:21 pm	Capricorn
24th	11:30 pm	Aquarius
27th	12:19 am	Pisces
29th	12:18 am	Aries

October 2023

1st	01:19 am	Taurus
3rd	05:04 am	Gemini
5th	12:32 pm	Cancer
7th	11:25 pm	Leo
10th	12:02 pm	Virgo
13th	12:23 am	Libra
15th	11:05 am	Scorpio
17th	07:37 pm	Sagittarius
20th	01:55 am	Capricorn
22nd	06:07 am	Aquarius
24th	08:34 am	Pisces
26th	10:02 am	Aries
28th	11:45 am	Taurus
30th	03:08 pm	Gemini

November 2023

1st	09:31 pm	Cancer
4th	07:22 am	Leo
6th	07:40 pm	Virgo
9th	08:09 am	Libra
11th	06:40 pm	Scorpio
14th	02:24 am	Sagittarius
16th	07:42 am	Capricorn
18th	11:28 am	Aquarius
20th	02:30 pm	Pisces
22nd	05:20 pm	Aries
24th	08:29 pm	Taurus
27th	12:41 am	Gemini
29th	06:54 am	Cancer

December 2023

1st	04:01 pm	Leo
4th	03:51 am	Virgo
6th	04:35 pm	Libra
9th	03:35 am	Scorpio
11th	11:12 am	Sagittarius
13th	03:32 pm	Capricorn
15th	05:57 pm	Aquarius
17th	07:59 pm	Pisces
19th	10:47 pm	Aries
22nd	02:51 am	Taurus
24th	08:15 am	Gemini
26th	03:16 pm	Cancer
29th	12:24 am	Leo
31st	11:54 am	Virgo

January 2024

3rd	12:47 am	Libra
5th	12:40 pm	Scorpio
7th	09:09 pm	Sagittarius
10th	01:34 am	Capricorn
12th	03:02 am	Aquarius
14th	03:30 am	Pisces
16th	04:49 am	Aries
18th	08:13 am	Taurus
20th	01:59 pm	Gemini
22nd	09:52 pm	Cancer
25th	07:37 am	Leo
27th	07:12 pm	Virgo
30th	08:05 am	Libra

February 2024

1st	08:38 pm	Scorpio
4th	06:29 am	Sagittarius
6th	12:09 pm	Capricorn
8th	02:00 pm	Aquarius
10th	01:43 pm	Pisces
12th	01:26 pm	Aries
14th	03:03 pm	Taurus
16th	07:40 pm	Gemini
19th	03:25 am	Cancer
21st	01:41 pm	Leo
24th	01:38 am	Virgo
26th	02:30 pm	Libra
29th	03:10 am	Scorpio

March 2024

2nd	01:57 pm	Sagittarius
4th	09:16 pm	Capricorn
7th	12:39 am	Aquarius
9th	01:04 am	Pisces
11th	12:20 am	Aries
13th	12:29 am	Taurus
15th	03:16 am	Gemini
17th	09:41 am	Cancer
19th	07:33 pm	Leo
22nd	07:42 am	Virgo
24th	08:38 pm	Libra
27th	09:03 am	Scorpio
29th	07:52 pm	Sagittarius

April 2024

1st	04:06 am	Capricorn
3rd	09:08 am	Aquarius
5th	11:13 am	Pisces
7th	11:25 am	Aries
9th	11:24 am	Taurus
11th	12:59 pm	Gemini
13th	05:46 pm	Cancer
16th	02:25 am	Leo
18th	02:11 pm	Virgo
21st	03:09 am	Libra
23rd	03:20 pm	Scorpio
26th	01:38 am	Sagittarius
28th	09:38 am	Capricorn
30th	03:20 pm	Aquarius

May 2024

2nd	06:52 pm	Pisces
4th	08:41 pm	Aries
6th	09:43 pm	Taurus
8th	11:21 pm	Gemini
11th	03:14 am	Cancer
13th	10:37 am	Leo
15th	09:33 pm	Virgo
18th	10:23 am	Libra
20th	10:35 pm	Scorpio
23rd	08:25 am	Sagittarius
25th	03:36 pm	Capricorn
27th	08:45 pm	Aquarius
30th	12:33 am	Pisces

June 2024

1st	03:29 am	Aries
3rd	05:56 am	Taurus
5th	08:37 am	Gemini
7th	12:42 pm	Cancer
9th	07:29 pm	Leo
12th	05:39 am	Virgo
14th	06:13 pm	Libra
17th	06:39 am	Scorpio
19th	04:32 pm	Sagittarius
21st	11:09 pm	Capricorn
24th	03:15 am	Aquarius
26th	06:08 am	Pisces
28th	08:53 am	Aries
30th	12:01 pm	Taurus

July 2024

2nd	03:51 pm	Gemini
4th	08:52 pm	Cancer
7th	03:56 am	Leo
9th	01:48 pm	Virgo
12th	02:07 am	Libra
14th	02:53 pm	Scorpio
17th	01:25 am	Sagittarius
19th	08:14 am	Capricorn
21st	11:44 am	Aquarius
23rd	01:24 pm	Pisces
25th	02:53 pm	Aries
27th	05:23 pm	Taurus
29th	09:28 pm	Gemini

August 2024

1st	03:20 am	Cancer
3rd	11:10 am	Leo
5th	09:17 pm	Virgo
8th	09:32 am	Libra
10th	10:34 pm	Scorpio
13th	10:01 am	Sagittarius
15th	05:52 pm	Capricorn
17th	09:45 pm	Aquarius
19th	10:52 pm	Pisces
21st	11:02 pm	Aries
24th	12:01 am	Taurus
26th	03:05 am	Gemini
28th	08:48 am	Cancer
30th	05:10 pm	Leo

September 2024

2nd	03:49 am	Virgo
4th	04:12 pm	Libra
7th	05:19 am	Scorpio
9th	05:26 pm	Sagittarius
12th	02:38 am	Capricorn
14th	07:54 am	Aquarius
16th	09:40 am	Pisces
18th	09:25 am	Aries
20th	09:03 am	Taurus
22nd	10:25 am	Gemini
24th	02:51 pm	Cancer
26th	10:48 pm	Leo
29th	09:42 am	Virgo

October 2024

1st	10:20 pm	Libra
4th	11:23 am	Scorpio
6th	11:35 pm	Sagittarius
9th	09:39 am	Capricorn
11th	04:32 pm	Aquarius
13th	07:56 pm	Pisces
15th	08:35 pm	Aries
17th	08:00 pm	Taurus
19th	08:08 pm	Gemini
21st	10:50 pm	Cancer
24th	05:25 am	Leo
26th	03:48 pm	Virgo
29th	04:30 am	Libra
31st	05:30 pm	Scorpio

November 2024

3rd	05:20 am	Sagittarius
5th	03:18 pm	Capricorn
7th	10:58 pm	Aquarius
10th	04:01 am	Pisces
12th	06:26 am	Aries
14th	07:00 am	Taurus
16th	07:09 am	Gemini
18th	08:51 am	Cancer
20th	01:52 pm	Leo
22nd	11:02 pm	Virgo
25th	11:20 am	Libra
28th	12:21 am	Scorpio
30th	11:54 am	Sagittarius

December 2024

2nd	09:10 pm	Capricorn
5th	04:22 am	Aquarius
7th	09:50 am	Pisces
9th	01:38 pm	Aries
11th	03:56 pm	Taurus
13th	05:22 pm	Gemini
15th	07:22 pm	Cancer
17th	11:40 pm	Leo
20th	07:38 am	Virgo
22nd	07:08 pm	Libra
25th	08:07 am	Scorpio
27th	07:47 pm	Sagittarius
30th	04:38 am	Capricorn

January 2025

1st	10:50 am	Aquarius
3rd	03:22 pm	Pisces
5th	07:02 pm	Aries
7th	10:12 pm	Taurus
10th	01:07 am	Gemini
12th	04:25 am	Cancer
14th	09:13 am	Leo
16th	04:46 pm	Virgo
19th	03:34 am	Libra
21st	04:21 pm	Scorpio
24th	04:29 am	Sagittarius
26th	01:43 pm	Capricorn
28th	07:32 pm	Aquarius
30th	10:53 pm	Pisces

February 2025

2nd	01:11 am	Aries
4th	03:34 am	Taurus
6th	06:44 am	Gemini
8th	11:05 am	Cancer
10th	05:01 pm	Leo
13th	01:08 am	Virgo
15th	11:46 am	Libra
18th	12:19 am	Scorpio
20th	12:55 pm	Sagittarius
22nd	11:09 pm	Capricorn
25th	05:40 am	Aquarius
27th	08:47 am	Pisces

March 2025

1st	09:53 am	Aries
3rd	10:37 am	Taurus
5th	12:30 pm	Gemini
7th	04:29 pm	Cancer
9th	11:00 pm	Leo
12th	07:56 am	Virgo
14th	07:00 pm	Libra
17th	07:31 am	Scorpio
19th	08:18 pm	Sagittarius
22nd	07:29 am	Capricorn
24th	03:25 pm	Aquarius
26th	07:32 pm	Pisces
28th	08:37 pm	Aries
30th	08:16 pm	Taurus

April 2025

1st	08:26 pm	Gemini
3rd	10:51 pm	Cancer
6th	04:35 am	Leo
8th	01:41 pm	Virgo
11th	01:12 am	Libra
13th	01:55 pm	Scorpio
16th	02:38 am	Sagittarius
18th	02:13 pm	Capricorn
20th	11:22 pm	Aquarius
23rd	05:07 am	Pisces
25th	07:25 am	Aries
27th	07:17 am	Taurus
29th	06:35 am	Gemini

May 2025

1st	07:23 am	Cancer
3rd	11:30 am	Leo
5th	07:40 pm	Virgo
8th	07:07 am	Libra
10th	07:59 pm	Scorpio
13th	08:35 am	Sagittarius
15th	07:58 pm	Capricorn
18th	05:30 am	Aquarius
20th	12:29 pm	Pisces
22nd	04:26 pm	Aries
24th	05:39 pm	Taurus
26th	05:22 pm	Gemini
28th	05:33 pm	Cancer
30th	08:17 pm	Leo

June 2025

2nd	03:01 am	Virgo
4th	01:39 pm	Libra
7th	02:23 am	Scorpio
9th	02:56 pm	Sagittarius
12th	01:55 am	Capricorn
14th	11:01 am	Aquarius
16th	06:09 pm	Pisces
18th	11:09 pm	Aries
21st	01:53 am	Taurus
23rd	02:58 am	Gemini
25th	03:45 am	Cancer
27th	06:06 am	Leo
29th	11:44 am	Virgo

July 2025

1st	09:17 pm	Libra
4th	09:34 am	Scorpio
6th	10:07 pm	Sagittarius
9th	08:55 am	Capricorn
11th	05:22 pm	Aquarius
13th	11:45 pm	Pisces
16th	04:33 am	Aries
18th	07:59 am	Taurus
20th	10:22 am	Gemini
22nd	12:27 pm	Cancer
24th	03:29 pm	Leo
26th	08:56 pm	Virgo
29th	05:44 am	Libra
31st	05:26 pm	Scorpio

August 2025

3rd	06:01 am	Sagittarius
5th	05:05 pm	Capricorn
8th	01:19 am	Aquarius
10th	06:51 am	Pisces
12th	10:34 am	Aries
14th	01:23 pm	Taurus
16th	04:01 pm	Gemini
18th	07:06 pm	Cancer
20th	11:17 pm	Leo
23rd	05:25 am	Virgo
25th	02:09 pm	Libra
28th	01:28 am	Scorpio
30th	02:05 pm	Sagittarius

September 2025

2nd	01:45 am	Capricorn
4th	10:33 am	Aquarius
6th	03:55 pm	Pisces
8th	06:38 pm	Aries
10th	08:04 pm	Taurus
12th	09:39 pm	Gemini
15th	12:31 am	Cancer
17th	05:21 am	Leo
19th	12:24 pm	Virgo
21st	09:41 pm	Libra
24th	09:01 am	Scorpio
26th	09:38 pm	Sagittarius
29th	09:56 am	Capricorn

October 2025

1st	07:52 pm	Aquarius
4th	02:08 am	Pisces
6th	04:49 am	Aries
8th	05:13 am	Taurus
10th	05:13 am	Gemini
12th	06:38 am	Cancer
14th	10:48 am	Leo
16th	06:06 pm	Virgo
19th	04:02 am	Libra
21st	03:43 pm	Scorpio
24th	04:20 am	Sagittarius
26th	04:54 pm	Capricorn
29th	03:56 am	Aquarius
31st	11:47 am	Pisces

November 2025

2nd	03:40 pm	Aries
4th	04:16 pm	Taurus
6th	03:21 pm	Gemini
8th	03:07 pm	Cancer
10th	05:34 pm	Leo
12th	11:52 pm	Virgo
15th	09:44 am	Libra
17th	09:45 pm	Scorpio
20th	10:27 am	Sagittarius
22nd	10:53 pm	Capricorn
25th	10:16 am	Aquarius
27th	07:24 pm	Pisces
30th	01:08 am	Aries

December 2025

2nd	03:13 am	Taurus
4th	02:49 am	Gemini
6th	01:55 am	Cancer
8th	02:49 am	Leo
10th	07:21 am	Virgo
12th	04:05 pm	Libra
15th	03:52 am	Scorpio
17th	04:39 pm	Sagittarius
20th	04:53 am	Capricorn
22nd	03:52 pm	Aquarius
25th	01:09 am	Pisces
27th	08:02 am	Aries
29th	11:58 am	Taurus

VENUS CHARTS

1925		1926		1927		1928		1929	
15 Jan	Cp	6 Apr	Pi	9 Jan	Aq	4 Jan	Sa	7 Jan	Pi
8 Feb	Aq	7 May	Ar	2 Feb	Pi	29 Jan	Cp	3 Feb	Ar
4 Mar	Pi	3 Jun	Ta	27 Feb	Ar	23 Feb	Aq	8 Mar	Ta
28 Mar	Ar	29 Jun	Ge	23 Mar	Ta	18 Mar	Pi	20 Apr	Ar
21 Apr	Ta	24 Jul	Ca	17 Apr	Ge	12 Apr	Ar	3 Jun	Ta
16 May	Ge	18 Aug	Le	12 May	Ca	6 May	Ta	8 Jul	Ge
9 Jun	Ca	12 Sep	Vi	8 Jun	Le	30 May	Ge	5 Aug	Ca
4 Jul	Le	6 Oct	Li	8 Jul	Vi	24 Jun	Ca	31 Aug	Le
28 Jul	Vi	30 Oct	Sc	10 Nov	Li	18 Jul	Le	26 Sep	Vi
22 Aug	Li	23 Nov	Sa	9 Dec	Sc	12 Aug	Vi	20 Oct	Li
16 Sep	Sc	17 Dec	Cp			5 Sep	Li	13 Nov	Sc
12 Oct	Sa					29 Sep	Sc	7 Dec	Sa
7 Nov	Cp					24 Oct	Sa	31 Dec	Cp
6 Dec	Aq					17 Nov	Cp		
						12 Dec	Aq		

1930		1931		1932		1933		1934	
24 Jan	Aq	4 Jan	Sa	19 Jan	Pi	14 Jan	Cp	6 Apr	Pi
17 Feb	Pi	7 Feb	Cp	13 Feb	Ar	7 Feb	Aq	6 May	Ar
13 Mar	Ar	6 Mar	Aq	9 Mar	Ta	3 Mar	Pi	2 Jun	Ta
6 Apr	Ta	1 Apr	Pi	5 Apr	Ge	28 Mar	Ar	28 Jun	Ge
1 May	Ge	26 Apr	Ar	6 May	Ca	21 Apr	Ta	24 Jul	Ca
25 May	Ca	21 May	Ta	13 Jul	Ge	15 May	Ge	18 Aug	Le
19 Jun	Le	15 Jun	Ge	29 Jul	Ca	9 Jun	Ca	11 Sep	Vi
15 Jul	Vi	10 Jul	Ca	9 Sep	Le	3 Jul	Le	5 Oct	Li
10 Aug	Li	3 Aug	Le	7 Oct	Vi	28 Jul	Vi	29 Oct	Sc
7 Sep	Sc	27 Aug	Vi	2 Nov	Li	22 Aug	Li	22 Nov	Sa
12 Oct	Sa	21 Sep	Li	27 Nov	Sc	16 Sep	Sc	16 Dec	Cp
22 Nov	Sc	15 Oct	Sc	21 Dec	Sa	11 Oct	Sa		
		8 Nov	Sa			7 Nov	Cp		
		2 Dec	Cp			6 Dec	Aq		
		26 Dec	Aq						

1935		1936		1937		1938		1939	
9 Jan	Aq	4 Jan	Sa	6 Jan	Pi	23 Jan	Aq	5 Jan	Sa
2 Feb	Pi	29 Jan	Cp	2 Feb	Ar	16 Feb	Pi	6 Feb	Cp
26 Feb	Ar	22 Feb	Aq	10 Mar	Ta	12 Mar	Ar	6 Mar	Aq
22 Mar	Ta	18 Mar	Pi	14 Apr	Ar	6 Apr	Ta	31 Mar	Pi
16 Apr	Ge	11 Apr	Ar	4 Jun	Ta	30 Apr	Ge	26 Apr	Ar
12 May	Ca	5 May	Ta	8 Jul	Ge	25 May	Ca	21 May	Ta
8 Jun	Le	30 May	Ge	5 Aug	Ca	19 Jun	Le	14 Jun	Ge
8 Jul	Vi	23 Jun	Ca	31 Aug	Le	14 Jul	Vi	9 Jul	Ca
10 Nov	Li	18 Jul	Le	25 Sep	Vi	10 Aug	Li	3 Aug	Le
9 Dec	Sc	11 Aug	Vi	20 Oct	Li	7 Sep	Sc	27 Aug	Vi
		4 Sep	Li	13 Nov	Sc	14 Oct	Sa	20 Sep	Li
		29 Sep	Sc	7 Dec	Sa	16 Nov	Sc	14 Oct	Sc
		23 Oct	Sa	31 Dec	Cp			7 Nov	Sa
		17 Nov	Cp					1 Dec	Cp
		12 Dec	Aq					25 Dec	Aq

1940		1941		1942		1943		1944	
19 Jan	Pi	14 Jan	Cp	7 Apr	Pi	8 Jan	Aq	3 Jan	Sa
12 Feb	Ar	7 Feb	Aq	6 May	Ar	1 Feb	Pi	28 Jan	Cp
9 Mar	Ta	3 Mar	Pi	2 Jun	Ta	26 Feb	Ar	22 Feb	Aq
5 Apr	Ge	27 Mar	Ar	28 Jun	Ge	22 Mar	Ta	17 Mar	Pi
7 May	Ca	20 Apr	Ta	23 Jul	Ca	16 Apr	Ge	11 Apr	Ar
6 Jul	Ge	15 May	Ge	17 Aug	Le	11 May	Ca	5 May	Ta
1 Aug	Ca	8 Jun	Ca	11 Sep	Vi	8 Jun	Le	29 May	Ge
9 Sep	Le	3 Jul	Le	5 Oct	Li	8 Jul	Vi	23 Jun	Ca
7 Oct	Vi	27 Jul	Vi	29 Oct	Sc	10 Nov	Li	17 Jul	Le
2 Nov	Li	21 Aug	Li	22 Nov	Sa	8 Dec	Sc	11 Aug	Vi
27 Nov	Sc	15 Sep	Sc	16 Dec	Cp			4 Sep	Li
21 Dec	Sa	11 Oct	Sa					28 Sep	Sc
		6 Nov	Cp					23 Oct	Sa
		6 Dec	Aq					16 Nov	Cp
								11 Dec	Aq

1945	
6 Jan	Pi
2 Feb	Ar
11 Mar	Ta
8 Apr	Ar
5 Jun	Ta
8 Jul	Ge
4 Aug	Ca
31 Aug	Le
25 Sep	Vi
19 Oct	Li
12 Nov	Sc
6 Dec	Sa
30 Dec	Cp

1946	
23 Jan	Aq
16 Feb	Pi
12 Mar	Ar
5 Apr	Ta
29 Apr	Ge
24 May	Ca
18 Jun	Le
14 Jul	Vi
9 Aug	Li
7 Sep	Sc
16 Oct	Sa
8 Nov	Sc

1947	
6 Jan	Sa
6 Feb	Cp
5 Mar	Aq
31 Mar	Pi
25 Apr	Ar
20 May	Ta
14 Jun	Ge
9 Jul	Ca
2 Aug	Le
26 Aug	Vi
20 Sep	Li
14 Oct	Sc
7 Nov	Sa
1 Dec	Cp
25 Dec	Aq

1948	
18 Jan	Pi
12 Feb	Ar
8 Mar	Ta
5 Apr	Ge
7 May	Ca
29 Jun	Ge
3 Aug	Ca
9 Sep	Le
7 Oct	Vi
1 Nov	Li
26 Nov	Sc
20 Dec	Sa

1949	
13 Jan	Cp
6 Feb	Aq
2 Mar	Pi
26 Mar	Ar
20 Apr	Ta
14 May	Ge
7 Jun	Ca
2 Jul	Le
27 Jul	Vi
21 Aug	Li
15 Sep	Sc
10 Oct	Sa
6 Nov	Cp
6 Dec	Aq

1950	
7 Apr	Pi
6 May	Ar
2 Jun	Ta
27 Jun	Ge
23 Jul	Ca
17 Aug	Le
10 Sep	Vi
4 Oct	Li
28 Oct	Sc
21 Nov	Sa
15 Dec	Cp

1951	
8 Jan	Aq
1 Feb	Pi
25 Feb	Ar
21 Mar	Ta
15 Apr	Ge
11 May	Ca
7 Jun	Le
8 Jul	Vi
10 Nov	Li
8 Dec	Sc

1952	
3 Jan	Sa
28 Jan	Cp
21 Feb	Aq
17 Mar	Pi
10 Apr	Ar
4 May	Ta
29 May	Ge
22 Jun	Ca
17 Jul	Le
10 Aug	Vi
3 Sep	Li
28 Sep	Sc
22 Oct	Sa
16 Nov	Cp
11 Dec	Aq

1953	
5 Jan	Pi
2 Feb	Ar
15 Mar	Ta
31 Mar	Ar
5 Jun	Ta
7 Jul	Ge
4 Aug	Ca
30 Aug	Le
24 Sep	Vi
19 Oct	Li
12 Nov	Sc
6 Dec	Sa
30 Dec	Cp

1954	
22 Jan	Aq
15 Feb	Pi
11 Mar	Ar
4 Apr	Ta
29 Apr	Ge
24 May	Ca
18 Jun	Le
13 Jul	Vi
9 Aug	Li
7 Sep	Sc
24 Oct	Sa
27 Oct	Sc

1955	
6 Jan	Sa
6 Feb	Cp
5 Mar	Aq
30 Mar	Pi
25 Apr	Ar
20 May	Ta
13 Jun	Ge
8 Jul	Ca
1 Aug	Le
26 Aug	Vi
19 Sep	Li
13 Oct	Sc
6 Nov	Sa
30 Nov	Cp
24 Dec	Aq

1956	
18 Jan	Pi
11 Feb	Ar
8 Mar	Ta
4 Apr	Ge
8 May	Ca
24 Jun	Ge
4 Aug	Ca
8 Sep	Le
6 Oct	Vi
1 Nov	Li
26 Nov	Sc
20 Dec	Sa

1957	
13 Jan	Cp
6 Feb	Aq
2 Mar	Pi
26 Mar	Ar
19 Apr	Ta
13 May	Ge
7 Jun	Ca
1 Jul	Le
26 Jul	Vi
20 Aug	Li
14 Sep	Sc
10 Oct	Sa
6 Nov	Cp
7 Dec	Aq

1958	
7 Apr	Pi
5 May	Ar
1 Jun	Ta
27 Jun	Ge
22 Jul	Ca
16 Aug	Le
10 Sep	Vi
4 Oct	Li
28 Oct	Sc
21 Nov	Sa
14 Dec	Cp

1959	
7 Jan	Aq
31 Jan	Pi
24 Feb	Ar
21 Mar	Ta
15 Apr	Ge
11 May	Ca
7 Jun	Le
9 Jul	Vi
20 Sep	Le
25 Sep	Vi
10 Nov	Li
8 Dec	Sc

1960	
2 Jan	Sa
27 Jan	Cp
21 Feb	Aq
16 Mar	Pi
9 Apr	Ar
4 May	Ta
28 May	Ge
22 Jun	Ca
16 Jul	Le
9 Aug	Vi
3 Sep	Li
27 Sep	Sc
22 Oct	Sa
15 Nov	Cp
10 Dec	Aq

1961	
5 Jan	Pi
2 Feb	Ar
6 Jun	Ta
7 Jul	Ge
4 Aug	Ca
30 Aug	Le
24 Sep	Vi
18 Oct	Li
11 Nov	Sc
5 Dec	Sa
29 Dec	Cp

1962	
22 Jan	Aq
15 Feb	Pi
11 Mar	Ar
4 Apr	Ta
28 Apr	Ge
23 May	Ca
17 Jun	Le
13 Jul	Vi
9 Aug	Li
7 Sep	Sc

1963	
7 Jan	Sa
6 Feb	Cp
4 Mar	Aq
30 Mar	Pi
24 Apr	Ar
19 May	Ta
13 Jun	Ge
7 Jul	Ca
1 Aug	Le
25 Aug	Vi
18 Sep	Li
12 Oct	Sc
6 Nov	Sa
30 Nov	Cp
24 Dec	Aq

1964	
17 Jan	Pi
11 Feb	Ar
8 Mar	Ta
4 Apr	Ge
9 May	Ca
18 Jun	Ge
5 Aug	Ca
8 Sep	Le
6 Oct	Vi
31 Oct	Li
25 Nov	Sc
19 Dec	Sa

1965	
12 Jan	Cp
5 Feb	Aq
1 Mar	Pi
25 Mar	Ar
19 Apr	Ta
13 May	Ge
6 Jun	Ca
1 Jul	Le
26 Jul	Vi
20 Aug	Li
14 Sep	Sc
10 Oct	Sa
6 Nov	Cp
7 Dec	Aq

1966	
7 Feb	Cp
25 Feb	Aq
7 Apr	Pi
5 May	Ar
1 Jun	Ta
26 Jun	Ge
22 Jul	Ca
16 Aug	Le
9 Sep	Vi
3 Oct	Li
27 Oct	Sc
20 Nov	Sa
14 Dec	Cp

1967	
7 Jan	Aq
31 Jan	Pi
24 Feb	Ar
20 Mar	Ta
14 Apr	Ge
10 May	Ca
7 Jun	Le
9 Jul	Vi
9 Sep	Le
2 Oct	Vi
10 Nov	Li
7 Dec	Sc

1968	
2 Jan	Sa
27 Jan	Cp
20 Feb	Aq
16 Mar	Pi
9 Apr	Ar
3 May	Ta
28 May	Ge
21 Jun	Ca
16 Jul	Le
9 Aug	Vi
2 Sep	Li
27 Sep	Sc
21 Oct	Sa
15 Nov	Cp
10 Dec	Aq

1969	
5 Jan	Pi
2 Feb	Ar
6 Jun	Ta
7 Jul	Ge
3 Aug	Ca
29 Aug	Le
23 Sep	Vi
18 Oct	Li
11 Nov	Sc
5 Dec	Sa
28 Dec	Cp

1970	
21 Jan	Aq
14 Feb	Pi
10 Mar	Ar
3 Apr	Ta
28 Apr	Ge
23 May	Ca
17 Jun	Le
13 Jul	Vi
8 Aug	Li
7 Sep	Sc

1971	
7 Jan	Sa
6 Feb	Cp
4 Mar	Aq
30 Mar	Pi
24 Apr	Ar
19 May	Ta
12 Jun	Ge
7 Jul	Ca
31 Jul	Le
25 Aug	Vi
18 Sep	Li
12 Oct	Sc
5 Nov	Sa
29 Nov	Cp
23 Dec	Aq

1972	
17 Jan	Pi
10 Feb	Ar
7 Mar	Ta
4 Apr	Ge
11 May	Ca
12 Jun	Ge
6 Aug	Ca
8 Sep	Le
5 Oct	Vi
31 Oct	Li
25 Nov	Sc
19 Dec	Sa

1973	
12 Jan	Cp
5 Feb	Aq
1 Mar	Pi
25 Mar	Ar
18 Apr	Ta
12 May	Ge
6 Jun	Ca
30 Jun	Le
25 Jul	Vi
19 Aug	Li
13 Sep	Sc
9 Oct	Sa
6 Nov	Cp
8 Dec	Aq

1974	
30 Jan	Cp
1 Mar	Aq
7 Apr	Pi
5 May	Ar
31 May	Ta
26 Jun	Ge
21 Jul	Ca
15 Aug	Le
8 Sep	Vi
3 Oct	Li
27 Oct	Sc
19 Nov	Sa
13 Dec	Cp

1975	
6 Jan	Aq
30 Jan	Pi
23 Feb	Ar
20 Mar	Ta
14 Apr	Ge
10 May	Ca
6 Jun	Le
9 Jul	Vi
3 Sep	Le
4 Oct	Vi
10 Nov	Li
7 Dec	Sc

1976	
2 Jan	Sa
26 Jan	Cp
20 Feb	Aq
15 Mar	Pi
8 Apr	Ar
3 May	Ta
27 May	Ge
21 Jun	Ca
15 Jul	Le
8 Aug	Vi
2 Sep	Li
26 Sep	Sc
21 Oct	Sa
14 Nov	Cp
10 Dec	Aq

1977	
5 Jan	Pi
2 Feb	Ar
6 Jun	Ta
7 Jul	Ge
3 Aug	Ca
29 Aug	Le
23 Sep	Vi
17 Oct	Li
10 Nov	Sc
4 Dec	Sa
28 Dec	Cp

1978	
21 Jan	Aq
14 Feb	Pi
10 Mar	Ar
3 Apr	Ta
27 Apr	Ge
22 May	Ca
16 Jun	Le
12 Jul	Vi
8 Aug	Li
7 Sep	Sc

1979	
7 Jan	Sa
5 Feb	Cp
4 Mar	Aq
29 Mar	Pi
23 Apr	Ar
18 May	Ta
12 Jun	Ge
6 Jul	Ca
31 Jul	Le
24 Aug	Vi
17 Sep	Li
11 Oct	Sc
4 Nov	Sa
29 Nov	Cp
23 Dec	Aq

1980	
16 Jan	Pi
10 Feb	Ar
7 Mar	Ta
4 Apr	Ge
13 May	Ca
5 Jun	Ge
7 Aug	Ca
8 Sep	Le
5 Oct	Vi
30 Oct	Li
24 Nov	Sc
18 Dec	Sa

1981	
11 Jan	Cp
4 Feb	Aq
28 Feb	Pi
24 Mar	Ar
18 Apr	Ta
12 May	Ge
5 Jun	Ca
30 Jun	Le
25 Jul	Vi
19 Aug	Li
13 Sep	Sc
9 Oct	Sa
6 Nov	Cp
9 Dec	Aq

1982	
23 Jan	Cp
2 Mar	Aq
7 Apr	Pi
5 May	Ar
31 May	Ta
26 Jun	Ge
21 Jul	Ca
14 Aug	Le
8 Sep	Vi
2 Oct	Li
26 Oct	Sc
19 Nov	Sa
13 Dec	Cp

1983	
6 Jan	Aq
30 Jan	Pi
23 Feb	Ar
19 Mar	Ta
13 Apr	Ge
9 May	Ca
6 Jun	Le
10 Jul	Vi
27 Aug	Le
6 Oct	Vi
9 Nov	Li
7 Dec	Sc

1984	
1 Jan	Sa
26 Jan	Cp
19 Feb	Aq
15 Mar	Pi
8 Apr	Ar
2 May	Ta
27 May	Ge
20 Jun	Ca
14 Jul	Le
8 Aug	Vi
1 Sep	Li
26 Sep	Sc
20 Oct	Sa
14 Nov	Cp
9 Dec	Aq

1985

Date	Sign
4 Jan	Pi
2 Feb	Ar
6 Jun	Ta
6 Jul	Ge
2 Aug	Ca
28 Aug	Le
22 Sep	Vi
17 Oct	Li
10 Nov	Sc
4 Dec	Sa
27 Dec	Cp

1986

Date	Sign
20 Jan	Aq
13 Feb	Pi
9 Mar	Ar
2 Apr	Ta
27 Apr	Ge
22 May	Ca
16 Jun	Le
12 Jul	Vi
8 Aug	Li
7 Sep	Sc

1987

Date	Sign
7 Jan	Sa
5 Feb	Cp
3 Mar	Aq
29 Mar	Pi
23 Apr	Ar
17 May	Ta
11 Jun	Ge
6 Jul	Ca
30 Jul	Le
24 Aug	Vi
17 Sep	Li
11 Oct	Sc
4 Nov	Sa
28 Nov	Cp
22 Dec	Aq

1988

Date	Sign
16 Jan	Pi
10 Feb	Ar
6 Mar	Ta
4 Apr	Ge
18 May	Ca
27 May	Ge
7 Aug	Ca
7 Sep	Le
5 Oct	Vi
30 Oct	Li
24 Nov	Sc
18 Dec	Sa

1989

Date	Sign
11 Jan	Cp
4 Feb	Aq
28 Feb	Pi
24 Mar	Ar
17 Apr	Ta
11 May	Ge
5 Jun	Ca
29 Jun	Le
24 Jul	Vi
18 Aug	Li
13 Sep	Sc
9 Oct	Sa
5 Nov	Cp
10 Dec	Aq

1990

Date	Sign
17 Jan	Cp
4 Mar	Aq
6 Apr	Pi
4 May	Ar
30 May	Ta
25 Jun	Ge
20 Jul	Ca
14 Aug	Le
7 Sep	Vi
2 Oct	Li
26 Oct	Sc
18 Nov	Sa
12 Dec	Cp

1991

Date	Sign
5 Jan	Aq
29 Jan	Pi
22 Feb	Ar
19 Mar	Ta
13 Apr	Ge
9 May	Ca
6 Jun	Le
11 Jul	Vi
22 Aug	Le
7 Oct	Vi
9 Nov	Li
6 Dec	Sc

1992

Date	Sign
1 Jan	Sa
25 Jan	Cp
19 Feb	Aq
14 Mar	Pi
7 Apr	Ar
2 May	Ta
26 May	Ge
19 Jun	Ca
14 Jul	Le
7 Aug	Vi
1 Sep	Li
25 Sep	Sc
20 Oct	Sa
14 Nov	Cp
9 Dec	Aq

1993

Date	Sign
4 Jan	Pi
3 Feb	Ar
6 Jun	Ta
6 Jul	Ge
2 Aug	Ca
28 Aug	Le
22 Sep	Vi
16 Oct	Li
9 Nov	Sc
3 Dec	Sa
27 Dec	Cp

1994

Date	Sign
20 Jan	Aq
13 Feb	Pi
9 Mar	Ar
2 Apr	Ta
26 Apr	Ge
21 May	Ca
15 Jun	Le
11 Jul	Vi
8 Aug	Li
8 Sep	Sc

1995

Date	Sign
8 Jan	Sa
5 Feb	Cp
3 Mar	Aq
28 Mar	Pi
22 Apr	Ar
17 May	Ta
11 Jun	Ge
5 Jul	Ca
30 Jul	Le
23 Aug	Vi
16 Sep	Li
10 Oct	Sc
3 Nov	Sa
28 Nov	Cp
22 Dec	Aq

1996

Date	Sign
15 Jan	Pi
9 Feb	Ar
6 Mar	Ta
4 Apr	Ge
7 Aug	Ca
7 Sep	Le
4 Oct	Vi
30 Oct	Li
23 Nov	Sc
17 Dec	Sa

1997

Date	Sign
10 Jan	Cp
3 Feb	Aq
27 Feb	Pi
23 Mar	Ar
16 Apr	Ta
11 May	Ge
4 Jun	Ca
29 Jun	Le
24 Jul	Vi
18 Aug	Li
12 Sep	Sc
8 Oct	Sa
5 Nov	Cp
12 Dec	Aq

1998

Date	Sign
10 Jan	Cp
5 Mar	Aq
6 Apr	Pi
4 May	Ar
30 May	Ta
25 Jun	Ge
20 Jul	Ca
13 Aug	Le
7 Sep	Vi
1 Oct	Li
25 Oct	Sc
18 Nov	Sa
12 Dec	Cp

1999

Date	Sign
5 Jan	Aq
29 Jan	Pi
22 Feb	Ar
18 Mar	Ta
13 Apr	Ge
9 May	Ca
6 Jun	Le
13 Jul	Vi
16 Aug	Le
8 Oct	Vi
9 Nov	Li
6 Dec	Sc
31 Dec	Sa

2000

Date	Sign
25 Jan	Cp
18 Feb	Aq
13 Mar	Pi
7 Apr	Ar
1 May	Ta
26 May	Ge
19 Jun	Ca
13 Jul	Le
7 Aug	Vi
31 Aug	Li
25 Sep	Sc
19 Oct	Sa
13 Nov	Cp
8 Dec	Aq

2001

Date	Sign
4 Jan	Pi
3 Feb	Ar
6 Jun	Ta
6 Jul	Ge
2 Aug	Ca
27 Aug	Le
21 Sep	Vi
15 Oct	Li
9 Nov	Sc
2 Dec	Sa
26 Dec	Cp

2002

Date	Sign
19 Jan	Aq
12 Feb	Pi
8 Mar	Ar
1 Apr	Ta
26 Apr	Ge
21 May	Ca
15 Jun	Le
11 Jul	Vi
7 Aug	Li
8 Sep	Sc

2003

Date	Sign
8 Jan	Sa
5 Feb	Cp
3 Mar	Aq
28 Mar	Pi
22 Apr	Ar
16 May	Ta
10 Jun	Ge
5 Jul	Ca
29 Jul	Le
22 Aug	Vi
16 Sep	Li
10 Oct	Sc
3 Nov	Sa
27 Nov	Cp
21 Dec	Aq

2004

Date	Sign
15 Jan	Pi
9 Feb	Ar
6 Mar	Ta
4 Apr	Ge
7 Aug	Ca
7 Sep	Le
4 Oct	Vi
29 Oct	Li
23 Nov	Sc
17 Dec	Sa

2005

Date	Sign
10 Jan	Cp
3 Feb	Aq
27 Feb	Pi
23 Mar	Ar
16 Apr	Ta
10 May	Ge
4 Jun	Ca
28 Jun	Le
23 Jul	Vi
17 Aug	Li
12 Sep	Sc
8 Oct	Sa
5 Nov	Cp
16 Dec	Aq

2006

Date	Sign
2 Jan	Cp
5 Mar	Aq
6 Apr	Pi
3 May	Ar
30 May	Ta
24 Jun	Ge
19 Jul	Ca
13 Aug	Le
6 Sep	Vi
30 Sep	Li
24 Oct	Sc
17 Nov	Sa
11 Dec	Cp

2007

Date	Sign
4 Jan	Aq
28 Jan	Pi
21 Feb	Ar
18 Mar	Ta
12 Apr	Ge
8 May	Ca
6 Jun	Le
15 Jul	Vi
9 Aug	Le
8 Oct	Vi
9 Nov	Li
6 Dec	Sc
31 Dec	Sa

2008

Date	Sign
24 Jan	Cp
18 Feb	Aq
13 Mar	Pi
6 Apr	Ar
1 May	Ta
25 May	Ge
18 Jun	Ca
13 Jul	Le
6 Aug	Vi
31 Aug	Li
24 Sep	Sc
19 Oct	Sa
13 Nov	Cp
8 Dec	Aq

2009

Date	Sign
4 Jan	Pi
3 Feb	Ar
12 Apr	Pi
24 Apr	Ar
6 Jun	Ta
5 Jul	Ge
1 Aug	Ca
27 Aug	Le
21 Sep	Vi
15 Oct	Li
8 Nov	Sc
2 Dec	Sa
26 Dec	Cp

2010

Date	Sign
19 Jan	Aq
12 Feb	Pi
8 Mar	Ar
1 Apr	Ta
25 Apr	Ge
20 May	Ca
14 Jun	Le
10 Jul	Vi
7 Aug	Li
9 Sep	Sc
8 Nov	Li
30 Nov	Sc

2011

Date	Sign
8 Jan	Sa
4 Feb	Cp
2 Mar	Aq
27 Mar	Pi
21 Apr	Ar
16 May	Ta
10 Jun	Ge
4 Jul	Ca
29 Jul	Le
22 Aug	Vi
15 Sep	Li
9 Oct	Sc
2 Nov	Sa
27 Nov	Cp
21 Dec	Aq

2012

Date	Sign
14 Jan	Pi
8 Feb	Ar
5 Mar	Ta
4 Apr	Ge
8 Aug	Ca
7 Sep	Le
3 Oct	Vi
29 Oct	Li
22 Nov	Sc
16 Dec	Sa

2013

Date	Sign
9 Jan	Cp
2 Feb	Aq
26 Feb	Pi
22 Mar	Ar
15 Apr	Ta
10 May	Ge
3 Jun	Ca
28 Jun	Le
23 Jul	Vi
17 Aug	Li
11 Sep	Sc
8 Oct	Sa
5 Nov	Cp

2014

Date	Sign
6 Mar	Aq
6 Apr	Pi
3 May	Ar
29 May	Ta
24 Jun	Ge
19 Jul	Ca
12 Aug	Le
6 Sep	Vi
30 Sep	Li
24 Oct	Sc
17 Nov	Sa
11 Dec	Cp

2015

Date	Sign
4 Jan	Aq
28 Jan	Pi
21 Feb	Ar
17 Mar	Ta
12 Apr	Ge
8 May	Ca
6 Jun	Le
19 Jul	Vi
1 Aug	Le
9 Oct	Vi
9 Nov	Li
5 Dec	Sc
30 Dec	Sa

2016

Date	Sign
24 Jan	Cp
17 Feb	Aq
12 Mar	Pi
6 Apr	Ar
30 Apr	Ta
24 May	Ge
18 Jun	Ca
12 Jul	Le
6 Aug	Vi
30 Aug	Li
24 Sep	Sc
18 Oct	Sa
12 Nov	Cp
8 Dec	Aq

2017

Date	Sign
3 Jan	Pi
4 Feb	Ar
3 Apr	Pi
29 Apr	Ar
6 Jun	Ta
5 Jul	Ge
1 Aug	Ca
26 Aug	Le
20 Sep	Vi
14 Oct	Li
7 Nov	Sc
1 Dec	Sa
25 Dec	Cp

2018

Date	Sign
18 Jan	Aq
11 Feb	Pi
7 Mar	Ar
31 Mar	Ta
25 Apr	Ge
20 May	Ca
14 Jun	Le
10 Jul	Vi
7 Aug	Li
9 Sep	Sc
1 Nov	Li
3 Dec	Sc

2019

Date	Sign
7 Jan	Sa
4 Feb	Cp
2 Mar	Aq
27 Mar	Pi
21 Apr	Ar
15 May	Ta
9 Jun	Ge
4 Jul	Ca
28 Jul	Le
21 Aug	Vi
15 Sep	Li
9 Oct	Sc
2 Nov	Sa
26 Nov	Cp
20 Dec	Aq

2020

Date	Sign
14 Jan	Pi
8 Feb	Ar
5 Mar	Ta
4 Apr	Ge
8 Aug	Ca
6 Sep	Le
3 Oct	Vi
28 Oct	Li
22 Nov	Sc
16 Dec	Sa

2021

Date	Sign
9 Jan	Cp
2 Feb	Aq
26 Feb	Pi
22 Mar	Ar
15 Apr	Ta
9 May	Ge
3 Jun	Ca
27 Jun	Le
22 Jul	Vi
16 Aug	Li
11 Sep	Sc
7 Oct	Sa
5 Nov	Cp

2022

Date	Sign
6 Mar	Aq
6 Apr	Pi
3 May	Ar
29 May	Ta
23 Jun	Ge
18 Jul	Ca
12 Aug	Le
5 Sep	Vi
29 Sep	Li
23 Oct	Sc
16 Nov	Sa
10 Dec	Cp

2023

Date	Sign
3 Jan	Aq
27 Jan	Pi
20 Feb	Ar
17 Mar	Ta
11 Apr	Ge
8 May	Ca
6 Jun	Le
9 Oct	Vi
8 Nov	Li
5 Dec	Sc
30 Dec	Sa

2024

Date	Sign
23 Jan	Cp
17 Feb	Aq
12 Mar	Pi
5 Apr	Ar
29 Apr	Ta
24 May	Ge
17 Jun	Ca
12 Jul	Le
5 Aug	Vi
30 Aug	Li
23 Sep	Sc
18 Oct	Sa
12 Nov	Cp
7 Dec	Aq

2025

Date	Sign
3 Jan	Pi
4 Feb	Ar
27 Mar	Pi
1 May	Ar
6 Jun	Ta
5 Jul	Ge
31 Jul	Ca
26 Aug	Le
20 Sep	Vi
14 Oct	Li
7 Nov	Sc
1 Dec	Sa
25 Dec	Cp

MARS CHARTS

1925		**1926**		**1927**		**1928**		**1929**	
5 Feb	Ta	9 Feb	Cp	22 Feb	Ge	19 Jan	Cp	11 Mar	Ca
24 Mar	Ge	23 Mar	Aq	17 Apr	Ca	28 Feb	Aq	13 May	Le
10 May	Ca	4 May	Pi	6 Jun	Le	8 Apr	Pi	4 Jul	Vi
26 Jun	Le	15 Jun	Ar	25 Jul	Vi	17 May	Ar	22 Aug	Li
13 Aug	Vi	1 Aug	Ta	11 Sep	Li	26 Jun	Ta	7 Oct	Sc
29 Sep	Li			26 Oct	Sc	9 Aug	Ge	19 Nov	Sa
14 Nov	Sc			8 Dec	Sa	3 Oct	Ca	29 Dec	Cp
28 Dec	Sa					20 Dec	Ge		

1930		**1931**		**1932**		**1933**		**1934**	
7 Feb	Aq	17 Feb	Ca	18 Jan	Aq	7 Jul	Li	4 Feb	Pi
17 Mar	Pi	30 Mar	Le	25 Feb	Pi	26 Aug	Sc	14 Mar	Ar
25 Apr	Ar	11 Jun	Vi	3 Apr	Ar	9 Oct	Sa	23 Apr	Ta
3 Jun	Ta	2 Aug	Li	12 May	Ta	19 Nov	Cp	3 Jun	Ge
15 Jul	Ge	17 Sep	Sc	22 Jun	Ge	28 Dec	Aq	16 Jul	Ca
28 Aug	Ca	31 Oct	Sa	5 Aug	Ca			31 Aug	Le
21 Oct	Le	10 Dec	Cp	21 Sep	Le			18 Oct	Vi
				14 Nov	Vi			11 Dec	Li

1935		**1936**		**1937**		**1938**		**1939**	
30 Jul	Sc	15 Jan	Pi	6 Jan	Sc	31 Jan	Ar	29 Jan	Sa
17 Sep	Sa	22 Feb	Ar	13 Mar	Sa	12 Mar	Ta	21 Mar	Cp
29 Oct	Cp	2 Apr	Ta	15 May	Sc	24 Apr	Ge	25 May	Aq
7 Dec	Aq	13 May	Ge	9 Aug	Sa	7 Jun	Ca	22 Jul	Cp
		26 Jun	Ca	30 Sep	Cp	23 Jul	Le	24 Sep	Aq
		10 Aug	Le	12 Nov	Aq	8 Sep	Vi	20 Nov	Pi
		27 Sep	Vi	22 Dec	Pi	25 Oct	Li		
		15 Nov	Li			12 Dec	Sc		

1940		**1941**		**1942**		**1943**		**1944**	
4 Jan	Ar	5 Jan	Sa	12 Jan	Ta	27 Jan	Cp	28 Mar	Ca
17 Feb	Ta	18 Feb	Cp	7 Mar	Ge	9 Mar	Aq	23 May	Le
2 Apr	Ge	2 Apr	Aq	26 Apr	Ca	17 Apr	Pi	12 Jul	Vi
18 May	Ca	16 May	Pi	14 Jun	Le	27 May	Ar	29 Aug	Li
3 Jul	Le	2 Jul	Ar	1 Aug	Vi	8 Jul	Ta	14 Oct	Sc
20 Aug	Vi			17 Sep	Li	24 Aug	Ge	26 Nov	Sa
6 Oct	Li			2 Nov	Sc				
21 Nov	Sc			16 Dec	Sa				

1945		1946		1947		1948		1949	
6 Jan	Cp	23 Apr	Le	25 Jan	Aq	12 Feb	Le	5 Jan	Aq
14 Feb	Aq	20 Jun	Vi	5 Mar	Pi	19 May	Vi	12 Feb	Pi
25 Mar	Pi	10 Aug	Li	12 Apr	Ar	17 Jul	Li	22 Mar	Ar
3 May	Ar	25 Sep	Sc	21 May	Ta	4 Sep	Sc	30 Apr	Ta
11 Jun	Ta	7 Nov	Sa	1 Jul	Ge	17 Oct	Sa	10 Jun	Ge
23 Jul	Ge	17 Dec	Cp	14 Aug	Ca	27 Nov	Cp	23 Jul	Ca
8 Sep	Ca			1 Oct	Le			7 Sep	Le
12 Nov	Le			1 Dec	Vi			27 Oct	Vi
27 Dec	Ca							26 Dec	Li

1950		1951		1952		1953		1954	
28 Mar	Vi	23 Jan	Pi	20 Jan	Sc	8 Feb	Ar	10 Feb	Sa
12 Jun	Li	2 Mar	Ar	28 Aug	Sa	20 Mar	Ta	13 Apr	Cp
11 Aug	Sc	10 Apr	Ta	12 Oct	Cp	1 May	Ge	3 Jul	Sa
26 Sep	Sa	22 May	Ge	22 Nov	Aq	14 Jun	Ca	25 Aug	Cp
6 Nov	Cp	4 Jul	Ca	31 Dec	Pi	30 Jul	Le	22 Oct	Aq
15 Dec	Aq	18 Aug	Le			15 Sep	Vi	4 Dec	Pi
		5 Oct	Vi			2 Nov	Li		
		24 Nov	Li			20 Dec	Sc		

1955		1956		1957		1958		1959	
15 Jan	Ar	14 Jan	Sa	29 Jan	Ta	4 Feb	Cp	11 Feb	Ge
26 Feb	Ta	29 Feb	Cp	18 Mar	Ge	17 Mar	Aq	10 Apr	Ca
11 Apr	Ge	15 Apr	Aq	5 May	Ca	27 Apr	Pi	1 Jun	Le
26 May	Ca	3 Jun	Pi	22 Jun	Le	7 Jun	Ar	20 Jul	Vi
11 Jul	Le	6 Dec	Ar	8 Aug	Vi	21 Jul	Ta	6 Sep	Li
27 Aug	Vi			24 Sep	Li	21 Sep	Ge	21 Oct	Sc
13 Oct	Li			9 Nov	Sc	29 Oct	Ta	4 Dec	Sa
29 Nov	Sc			23 Dec	Sa				

1960		1961		1962		1963		1964	
14 Jan	Cp	5 Feb	Ge	2 Feb	Aq	3 Jun	Vi	13 Jan	Aq
23 Feb	Aq	7 Feb	Ca	12 Mar	Pi	27 Jul	Li	20 Feb	Pi
2 Apr	Pi	6 May	Le	20 Apr	Ar	12 Sep	Sc	29 Mar	Ar
11 May	Ar	29 Jun	Vi	29 May	Ta	26 Oct	Sa	8 May	Ta
20 Jun	Ta	17 Aug	Li	9 Jul	Ge	5 Dec	Cp	17 Jun	Ge
2 Aug	Ge	2 Oct	Sc	22 Aug	Ca			31 Jul	Ca
21 Sep	Ca	14 Nov	Sa	12 Oct	Le			15 Sep	Le
		25 Dec	Cp					6 Nov	Vi

1965		**1966**		**1967**		**1968**		**1969**	
29 Jun	Li	30 Jan	Pi	13 Feb	Sc	9 Jan	Pi	25 Feb	Sa
21 Aug	Sc	10 Mar	Ar	31 Mar	Li	17 Feb	Ar	21 Sep	Cp
4 Oct	Sa	18 Apr	Ta	20 Jul	Sc	28 Mar	Ta	5 Nov	Aq
14 Nov	Cp	29 May	Ge	10 Sep	Sa	9 May	Ge	16 Dec	Pi
23 Dec	Aq	11 Jul	Ca	23 Oct	Cp	21 Jun	Ca		
		26 Aug	Le	2 Dec	Aq	6 Aug	Le		
		13 Oct	Vi			22 Sep	Vi		
		4 Dec	Li			9 Nov	Li		
						30 Dec	Sc		

1970		**1971**		**1972**		**1973**		**1974**	
25 Jan	Ar	23 Jan	Sa	11 Feb	Ta	12 Feb	Cp	27 Feb	Ge
7 Mar	Ta	12 Mar	Cp	27 Mar	Ge	27 Mar	Aq	20 Apr	Ca
19 Apr	Ge	4 May	Aq	13 May	Ca	8 May	Pi	9 Jun	Le
2 Jun	Ca	7 Nov	Pi	29 Jun	Le	21 Jun	Ar	28 Jul	Vi
18 Jul	Le	27 Dec	Ar	15 Aug	Vi	13 Aug	Ta	13 Sep	Li
3 Sep	Vi			1 Oct	Li	30 Oct	Ar	28 Oct	Sc
20 Oct	Li			16 Nov	Sc	24 Dec	Ta	11 Dec	Sa
7 Dec	Sc			31 Dec	Sa				

1975		**1976**		**1977**		**1978**		**1979**	
22 Jan	Cp	19 Mar	Ca	1 Jan	Cp	26 Jan	Ca	21 Jan	Aq
3 Mar	Aq	16 May	Le	9 Feb	Aq	11 Apr	Le	28 Feb	Pi
12 Apr	Pi	7 Jul	Vi	20 Mar	Pi	14 Jun	Vi	7 Apr	Ar
21 May	Ar	24 Aug	Li	28 Apr	Ar	4 Aug	Li	16 May	Ta
1 Jul	Ta	9 Oct	Sc	6 Jun	Ta	20 Sep	Sc	26 Jun	Ge
15 Aug	Ge	21 Nov	Sa	18 Jul	Ge	2 Nov	Sa	9 Aug	Ca
17 Oct	Ca			1 Sep	Ca	13 Dec	Cp	25 Sep	Le
26 Nov	Ge			27 Oct	Le			20 Nov	Vi

1980		**1981**		**1982**		**1983**		**1984**	
12 Mar	Le	7 Feb	Pi	3 Aug	Sc	18 Jan	Pi	11 Jan	Sc
4 May	Vi	17 Mar	Ar	20 Sep	Sa	25 Feb	Ar	18 Aug	Sa
11 Jul	Li	25 Apr	Ta	1 Nov	Cp	6 Apr	Ta	5 Oct	Cp
29 Aug	Sc	5 Jun	Ge	10 Dec	Aq	17 May	Ge	16 Nov	Aq
12 Oct	Sa	18 Jul	Ca			29 Jun	Ca	25 Dec	Pi
22 Nov	Cp	2 Sep	Le			14 Aug	Le		
31 Dec	Aq	21 Oct	Vi			30 Sep	Vi		
		16 Dec	Li			18 Nov	Li		

1985		1986		1987		1988		1989	
3 Feb	Ar	2 Feb	Sa	9 Jan	Ar	9 Jan	Sa	19 Jan	Ta
15 Mar	Ta	28 Mar	Cp	21 Feb	Ta	22 Feb	Cp	11 Mar	Ge
26 Apr	Ge	9 Oct	Aq	6 Apr	Ge	7 Apr	Aq	29 Apr	Ca
9 Jun	Ca	26 Nov	Pi	21 May	Ca	22 May	Pi	17 Jun	Le
25 Jul	Le			7 Jul	Le	14 Jul	Ar	4 Aug	Vi
10 Sep	Vi			23 Aug	Vi	24 Oct	Pi	20 Sep	Li
28 Oct	Li			9 Oct	Li	2 Nov	Ar	4 Nov	Sc
15 Dec	Sc			24 Nov	Sc			18 Dec	Sa

1990		1991		1992		1993		1994	
30 Jan	Cp	21 Jan	Ge	9 Jan	Cp	28 Apr	Le	28 Jan	Aq
12 Mar	Aq	3 Apr	Ca	18 Feb	Aq	23 Jun	Vi	7 Mar	Pi
21 Apr	Pi	27 May	Le	28 Mar	Pi	12 Aug	Li	15 Apr	Ar
31 May	Ar	16 Jul	Vi	6 May	Ar	27 Sep	Sc	24 May	Ta
13 Jul	Ta	1 Sep	Li	15 Jun	Ta	9 Nov	Sa	4 Jul	Ge
31 Aug	Ge	17 Oct	Sc	27 Jul	Ge	20 Dec	Cp	17 Aug	Ca
14 Dec	Ta	29 Nov	Sa	12 Sep	Ca			5 Oct	Le
								12 Dec	Vi

1995		1996		1997		1998		1999	
23 Jan	Le	8 Jan	Aq	3 Jan	Li	25 Jan	Pi	27 Jan	Sc
26 May	Vi	15 Feb	Pi	9 Mar	Vi	5 Mar	Ar	6 May	Li
21 Jul	Li	25 Mar	Ar	19 Jun	Li	13 Apr	Ta	5 Jul	Sc
7 Sep	Sc	3 May	Ta	14 Aug	Sc	24 May	Ge	3 Sep	Sa
21 Oct	Sa	13 Jun	Ge	29 Sep	Sa	6 Jul	Ca	17 Oct	Cp
1 Dec	Cp	26 Jul	Ca	9 Nov	Cp	21 Aug	Le	26 Nov	Aq
		10 Sep	Le	18 Dec	Aq	8 Oct	Vi		
		30 Oct	Vi			27 Nov	Li		

2000		2001		2002		2003		2004	
4 Jan	Pi	15 Feb	Sa	19 Jan	Ar	17 Jan	Sa	3 Feb	Ta
12 Feb	Ar	9 Sep	Cp	2 Mar	Ta	5 Mar	Cp	21 Mar	Ge
23 Mar	Ta	28 Oct	Aq	14 Apr	Ge	22 Apr	Aq	7 May	Ca
4 May	Ge	9 Dec	Pi	28 May	Ca	17 Jun	Pi	24 Jun	Le
17 Jun	Ca			14 Jul	Le	17 Dec	Ar	10 Aug	Vi
1 Aug	Le			30 Aug	Vi			26 Sep	Li
17 Sep	Vi			16 Oct	Li			11 Nov	Sc
4 Nov	Li			2 Dec	Sc			26 Dec	Sa
24 Dec	Sc								

2005		2006		2007		2008		2009	
7 Feb	Cp	18 Feb	Ge	17 Jan	Cp	1 Jan	Ge	5 Feb	Aq
21 Mar	Aq	14 Apr	Ca	26 Feb	Aq	4 Mar	Ca	15 Mar	Pi
1 May	Pi	4 Jun	Le	6 Apr	Pi	10 May	Le	23 Apr	Ar
12 Jun	Ar	23 Jul	Vi	16 May	Ar	2 Jul	Vi	1 Jun	Ta
28 Jul	Ta	8 Sep	Li	25 Jun	Ta	19 Aug	Li	12 Jul	Ge
		24 Oct	Sc	7 Aug	Ge	4 Oct	Sc	26 Aug	Ca
		6 Dec	Sa	29 Sep	Ca	16 Nov	Sa	17 Oct	Le
						27 Dec	Cp		

2010		2011		2012		2013		2014	
7 Jun	Vi	16 Jan	Aq	4 Jul	Li	2 Feb	Pi	26 Jul	Sc
30 Jul	Li	23 Feb	Pi	24 Aug	Sc	12 Mar	Ar	14 Sep	Sa
15 Sep	Sc	2 Apr	Ar	7 Oct	Sa	20 Apr	Ta	26 Oct	Cp
28 Oct	Sa	11 May	Ta	17 Nov	Cp	31 May	Ge	5 Dec	Aq
8 Dec	Cp	21 Jun	Ge	26 Dec	Aq	14 Jul	Ca		
		3 Aug	Ca			28 Aug	Le		
		19 Sep	Le			15 Oct	Vi		
		11 Nov	Vi			8 Dec	Li		

2015		2016		2017		2018		2019	
12 Jan	Pi	4 Jan	Sc	28 Jan	Ar	27 Jan	Sa	1 Jan	Ar
20 Feb	Ar	6 Mar	Sa	10 Mar	Ta	18 Mar	Cp	14 Feb	Ta
1 Apr	Ta	28 May	Sc	21 Apr	Ge	16 May	Aq	31 Mar	Ge
12 May	Ge	3 Aug	Sa	5 Jun	Ca	13 Aug	Cp	16 May	Ca
25 Jun	Ca	27 Sep	Cp	21 Jul	Le	11 Sep	Aq	2 Jul	Le
9 Aug	Le	9 Nov	Aq	5 Sep	Vi	16 Nov	Pi	18 Aug	Vi
25 Sep	Vi	19 Dec	Pi	23 Oct	Li			4 Oct	Li
13 Nov	Li			9 Dec	Sc			19 Nov	Sc

2020		2021		2022		2023		2024		2025	
3 Jan	Sa	7 Jan	Ta	25 Jan	Cp	25 Mar	Ca	5 Jan	Cp	6 Jan	Ca
16 Feb	Cp	4 Mar	Ge	6 Mar	Aq	21 May	Le	13 Feb	Aq	18 Apr	Le
31 Mar	Aq	23 Apr	Ca	15 Apr	Pi	10 Jul	Vi	23 Mar	Pi	17 Jun	Vi
13 May	Pi	12 Jun	Le	25 May	Ar	28 Aug	Li	1 May	Ar	7 Aug	Li
28 Jun	Ar	30 Jul	Vi	5 Jul	Ta	12 Oct	Sc	9 Jun	Ta	22 Sep	Sc
		15 Sep	Li	20 Aug	Ge	24 Nov	Sa	21 Jul	Ge	5 Nov	Sa
		31 Oct	Sc					5 Sep	Ca	15 Dec	Cp
		13 Dec	Sa					4 Nov	Le